HUMAN MEMORY

HUMAN MEMORY
EXPLORATION AND APPLICATION

KARL HABERLANDT

Trinity College

ALLYN AND BACON

Boston   London   Toronto   Sydney   Tokyo   Singapore

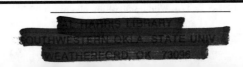

Senior Editor: Carolyn O. Merrill
Editorial Assistant: Amy Goldmacher
Director of Field Marketing: Joyce Nilsen
Editorial-Production Administrator: Annette Joseph
Editorial-Production Coordinator: Susan Freese
Editorial-Production Service and Electronic Composition: TKM Productions
Graphic Artists: Asterisk Group and Monotype Composition
Composition Buyer: Linda Cox
Manufacturing Buyer: Megan Cochran
Cover Administrator: Jenny Hart
Cover Designer: Brian Gogolin

Copyright © 1999 by Allyn & Bacon
A Viacom Company
160 Gould Street
Needham Heights, MA 02494

Internet: www.abacon.com

Library of Congress Cataloging-in-Publication Data

Haberlandt, Karl
    Human memory : exploration and application / Karl Haberlandt.
        p.   cm.
    Includes bibliographical references (p.   ) and index.
    ISBN 0-205-18992-X (pbk.)
    1. Memory.   I. Title.
  BF371.H28   1998
  153.1'2—dc21   97-16954
                                                                            CIP

Printed in the United States of America
10   9   8   7   6   5   4   3   2   1   03   02   01   00   99   98

To Susan Haberlandt

Brief Contents

CHAPTER 1   INTRODUCTION   1

CHAPTER 2   THE PIONEERS OF MEMORY RESEARCH
             FROM EBBINGHAUS TO LASHLEY   17

CHAPTER 3   MEMORY AND BRAIN   41

CHAPTER 4   MEMORY FOR FACTS   69

CHAPTER 5   MEMORY FOR SKILLS   103

CHAPTER 6   WORKING MEMORY   127

CHAPTER 7   MODELS OF MEMORY   157

CHAPTER 8   MEMORY FROM INFANCY TO OLD AGE:
             DEVELOPMENTAL CHANGES   189

CHAPTER 9   AUTOBIOGRAPHICAL AND
             EMOTIONAL MEMORIES   219

CHAPTER 10   MEMORY IMPAIRMENTS   249

CHAPTER 11   ISSUES IN MEMORY RESEARCH   275

CHAPTER 12   MEMORY IN EVERYDAY LIFE   303

CONTENTS

PREFACE   xv

CHAPTER 1 INTRODUCTION   1

Thinking about Memory   2
   Metaphors of Memory   2
   Attributes of Memory   3

Investigating Memory   4
   Paradigms of Memory Research   5
   Explaining Memory Phenomena   9

Memory in the Context of Cognition   12
   Attention   12
   Pattern Recognition   13
   Problem Solving   14

Preview   15

**CHAPTER 2 THE PIONEERS OF MEMORY RESEARCH
                 FROM EBBINGHAUS TO LASHLEY   17**

Experimental Study of Memory   17
   Hermann Ebbinghaus (1850–1909)   18
   Alfred Binet (1857–1911)   24
   Richard Semon (1859–1918)   26
   Sir Frederic Bartlett (1886–1969)   27

Neuropsychological and Psychodynamic Views of Memory   30
   Theodule Ribot (1839–1916)   31
   Sigmund Freud (1856–1939)   33

Learning and Memory in Animals   35
   Paradigms of Animal Learning   36
   The Search for the Engram   38

Conclusion   38

CHAPTER 3 MEMORY AND BRAIN   41

Research Methods in Neuroscience   43
   Imaging Methods   43
   Event-Related Potentials   47
   Monitoring Activity at the Cellular Level   49
   Case and Population Studies   50

Plasticity in the Brain   52
   Neurons   52
   Neurotransmitters and the Formation of Memories   53

Are There Memory-Enhancing Drugs?   *54*
Plasticity of Neural Structures   *55*

Where Are Memories Located?   58
Act I: From Extreme Localization to No Function at All   *59*
Act II: Localization Theory Becomes Respectable   *59*
Act III: From Equipotentiality to Memory Cells   *60*
Act IV: Networks of Local Specialists   *60*

The Hippocampus   62
Consolidation of Memories   *62*
Space Cells in the Hippocampus   *63*
Is Spatial Learning Based on Long-Term Potentiation?   *64*
Does the Hippocampus Support All Memories?   *64*

Frontal Lobes   65
Maintaining Information in Working Memory   *65*
Executive Function   *66*
Long-Term Memory Encoding and Retrieval   *67*

Conclusion   68

CHAPTER 4   MEMORY FOR FACTS   69

Episodic Memory   70
Acquiring Facts   *71*
Theories of Forgetting   *78*
Retrieval   *82*

Semantic Memory   90
Representation of Concepts   *90*
Propositions and Causal Relations   *95*
Schemas   *97*
Perspectives from Neuropsychology   *99*

Conclusion   101

CHAPTER 5   MEMORY FOR SKILLS   103

Implicit Memory   103
Priming   *104*
Implicit Learning   *111*

Learning and Remembering Cognitive Skills   115
Sample of Skills   *115*
Representation of Skills   *117*
Skill Acquisition   *117*
Supermemory: Memory as a Skill   *120*

Conclusion   125

Endnotes   126

CHAPTER 6   WORKING MEMORY   127

The Two-Store Model of Memory and Its Critics   127
  Differences between Short-Term Memory and Long-Term Memory   128
  Waugh and Norman's (1965) Two-Store Model   132
  Atkinson and Shiffrin's (1968) Model   132
  Critics of the Two-Store Model   134

Activity in Working Memory   135
  Problem Solving   135
  Storage versus Computation   136
  Language Comprehension   136
  Search in Working Memory: The Sternberg Paradigm   138
  Tracking Mental Work On-Line   139

The Multiple-Components Model of Working Memory   142
  Phonological Loop   144
  Visuospatial Sketchpad   147
  Semantic Information in Working Memory   148
  Central Executive   149

Conclusion   154

CHAPTER 7   MODELS OF MEMORY   157

The SAM Model   159
  Assumptions of the SAM Model   160
  Retrieval in List Learning   163
  Application of SAM to Important Memory Experiments   165
  Evaluation of the SAM Model   166

Neural Network Models   166
  Distributed Memories   167
  Retrieval from Neural Networks   169
  Learning in Neural Networks   173
  Applications of Neural Networks   174
  Evaluation of the Neural Network Approach   177

Anderson's ACT Framework   178
  The Architecture of ACT   179
  Memory and Rational Analysis   182
  Research Applications of ACT   183
  Evaluation of ACT   186

Conclusion   187

Endnotes   188

CHAPTER 8   MEMORY FROM INFANCY TO OLD AGE:
            DEVELOPMENTAL CHANGES   189

Memory Development during Childhood   190
  Event Memory in Preverbal Infants   191

Memory for Skills   *194*
Memory for Facts   *197*
Working Memory   *202*

Memory Changes during Older Adulthood   204
Memory for Facts   *206*
Memory for Skills   *210*
Working Memory   *212*

Conclusion   216

CHAPTER 9   AUTOBIOGRAPHICAL AND EMOTIONAL MEMORIES   219

Autobiographical Memory   220
Studying Autobiographical Memory   *221*
Organization of Autobiographical Memory   *224*
Autobiographical Memory Viewed as Narrative   *226*
Impairment of Autobiographical Memory   *229*

Remembering Emotional Events   230
Research on the Repression Hypothesis   *230*
Are Flashbulb Memories Special?   *231*
Memories of Witnesses and Victims of Crime   *232*
Laboratory Studies of Emotion and Memory   *233*
Emotion, Memory, and the Brain   *235*

The Memory Wars   238
The Issues   *239*
Clinical Views of Early Childhood Memories   *240*
Remembering Pain and Abuse   *241*
Suggestibility of Memory and Implanting False Memories   *243*
Can Science Distinguish between True and False Memories?   *244*
Where Do We Stand? The American Psychological Association Seeks a Response   *245*

Conclusion   246

CHAPTER 10   MEMORY IMPAIRMENTS   249

The Amnesic Disorders   251
Case Studies   *251*
Performance Patterns in Amnesia   *254*
Explaining Amnesia   *257*

Impairment of Specialized Memory Functions   261
Semantic Memory Deficits   *262*
Neuropsychology of Working Memory Functions   *264*

Alzheimer's Disease   266
Deficits in Memory for Facts   *267*
Working Memory   *270*

Deficits in Memory for Skills   *272*
Alzheimer's Disease: A Retrospective   *273*

Conclusion   274

CHAPTER 11   ISSUES IN MEMORY RESEARCH   275

How Many Memories?   275
Multiple Memory Systems: Two Taxonomies of Memory   *277*
Justifying Systems of Memory   *280*
A Single-Memory System with Different Processes   *286*
Memory Systems Gain Acceptance   *291*

Memory: What Are the Important Questions?   293
Neisser's Call to Arms   *293*
Banaji and Crowder Declare Everyday Memory Bankrupt   *294*
Rebuttals to Banaji and Crowder   *296*
The Correspondence Metaphor of Memory   *299*

Conclusion   301

CHAPTER 12   MEMORY IN EVERYDAY LIFE   303

Remembering and Forgetting in Everyday Life   304
Mnemonic Techniques   *304*
Skilled Memory   *306*
Verbatim Memory versus Giving Plausible Answers   *309*

Education   310
Practicing Skills   *310*
Remembering Skills for the Long Haul   *312*
Study Skills in Reading   *314*
Is There Transfer of Training?   *316*

Memory and the Law   317
Memory Distortions   *318*
Problems in Eyewitness Testimony   *319*
Improving Eyewitness Testimony   *323*

Coping with Memory Impairments   325
Internal and External Memory Aids   *326*
Capitalizing on Spared Functions   *328*
Prospective Memory Training   *330*

Conclusion   332

REFERENCES   335

INDEX   363

This is an exciting time for the study of human memory. New research methods are being introduced, discoveries are being reported, and fierce debates are being waged in research laboratories as well as in the public arena. Memory research has been in ferment as a result of converging advances in traditional experimental psychology, in the neurosciences, in neuropsychology, and in research on memory applications.

This book was written to provide an overview of the multifaceted psychological study of memory. The book is intended as a text for undergraduate courses in Human Memory and as a source on human memory research in related courses, including Learning and Memory, Memory and Cognition, and Memory and Amnesia. This book is also aimed at the broader audience of graduate students, researchers, and professionals in psychology and education seeking an overview of research on memory. It introduces the principal issues of research on human memory, describes important research paradigms, and identifies connections across different traditions of memory research.

Human Memory: Exploration and Application is predicated on the notion that an understanding of human memory requires familiarity with memory issues as seen from a variety of perspectives, including the psychobiological, developmental, neuropsychological, and applied perspectives as well as the traditional cognitive perspective. However, no overview of the field, including the one presented here, can be exhaustive or definitive. Rather, the strategy in this text is to treat memory research as a study in progress, to identify constituent content areas of the field with their theoretical developments and methodologies, and to emphasize recent advances within the context of continuing themes.

Thanks to the increasing collaboration between researchers in different disciplines, great strides have been made toward the goal of gaining a better understanding of human memory. *Human Memory: Exploration and Application* is informed by the developments during the last two decades in the major constituent disciplines—the neurosciences, cognitive psychology, neuropsychology—and in research on the uses of memory in the real world.

Neuroscience

Believing that memory is best studied at the level of abstract functions such as encoding, storage, and retrieval of information, most classical memory researchers and information-processing theorists have turned a deaf ear to the calls for investigations of the hardware of memory, its biological bases. Today, researchers readily acknowledge that memory is constrained by the biological properties of neural tissue, and, as a result, memory research is experiencing significant changes, as is the rest of cognitive science. The field has become more exciting. Even old issues have acquired new lustre: How are memories stored in the brain? Is it possible to localize specific memories in the brain? and What are the processes of growth and decay in neural circuits that affect the formation and retrieval of memories?

Cognitive Psychology

The mainstream of memory research promoted by cognitive psychologists has not stood still during the last two decades. Cognitive research has had its own momentum and has continued to blossom, in part due to cross-fertilization from other specialties. Significant contributions include theoretical innovations in implicit memory, memory for skills, and memory retrieval and its relation to encoding processes. Cognitive psychologists have broadened their horizons by extending memory research from the domain of list and item learning to such new domains as skill learning, language comprehension, and problem solving. Computer-based recording techniques, brain imaging, and electrophysiological methods complement traditional performance measures and have greatly increased the scope of memory research.

Neuropsychology

Beginning with Ribot's (1887) review of case studies of patients with memory impairments, there have been sporadic contacts between mainstream memory researchers and practitioners seeking to understand and eventually treat memory dysfunction. However, it was not until Milner's work in the 1960s on an epileptic patient, H. M., that neuropsychology, the study of individuals with brain damage, began to have a lasting impact on the field. Following lesions of his temporal lobes intended to treat his epilepsy, H. M. suffered unforeseen and grave side effects. He could neither remember recent events nor commit new experiences to memory, yet he retained childhood memories and could repeat information for the short term. This case of discontinuity between short-term and long-term memory, along with several findings from research laboratories, prompted memory researchers to adopt the distinction between two stores of memory: the short-term store and the long-term store (Atkinson & Shiffrin, 1968). The case of H. M. and other patients legitimized neuropsychology in the eyes of memory researchers, thus opening a rich source of data and conceptualizations for the rest of the field (Schacter & Tulving, 1994b).

Applications

People use their memories quite successfully, regardless of the labors of memory researchers. We remember appointments and chores, recall technical terms, and retain skills from algebra to understanding a foreign language. Of course, people are never satisfied with their memories, and so mnemonic devices have been invented as a spur to our memories. One of these is the method of loci (*loci* is the Latin word for *places*). Using this method, the learner imagines that different items to be memorized are located in various physical places. The person recalls the items by mentally visiting the locations, thus retrieving the stored items. Research on the uses of memory in everyday life includes studies on classroom learning, eyewitness testimony, and prospective memory—the remembering of tasks to be executed in the future.

Plan for the Text

Human Memory: Exploration and Application includes 12 chapters whose content is guided by the developments just sketched. Following a review of basic issues and the introduction of the attributes of memory in the first chapter, the second chapter traces classical research from the pioneers in the nineteenth century to Lashley's search for the engram in the brain. The third chapter discusses the biological bases of memory in the nervous system. With these foundations in place, the next set of chapters present principal types of memory: memory for facts (Chapter 4), which refers to information we can become aware of; memory for skills (Chapter 5), which includes knowledge of cognitive skills we are usually unaware of; and working memory (Chapter 6), which involves relatively short-lived information that is needed for executing a variety of mental processes, from memory search to comprehension.

Chapter 7 is devoted to comprehensive theoretical models of memory advanced by cognitive psychologists and neural network theorists. Developmental changes in memory from infancy to old age are considered in Chapter 8. Chapter 9 treats autobiographical memories, including the relation between affect and memory. Chapter 10 examines memory impairments and underscores the implications of such cases for basic research. Chapter 11 focuses on theoretical issues, including the debate between advocates of a unitary memory and those who favor multiple memory systems. The applications of memory in everyday life are inherently as fascinating as they are theoretically interesting. Chapter 12 discusses memory applications and the way in which they illuminate theoretical concerns.

Each chapter develops selected issues in depth, illustrating research paradigms in a manner accessible to undergraduates who have taken a prior course in cognition. This background will enable readers to appreciate the argumentative nature of memory research as well as its complexities. The insights readers gain from working through theories, data, and applications will be well worth the effort. Interest is piqued by frequent references to applications, ranging from skill acquisition to memory management in accident victims, and to the debates that invigorate the discipline. Disagreements exist over many issues, such as the following: Does exceptional memory depend on an innate talent, or can anyone become a memory expert? Is remembering based on a single memory system or on several independent systems? and Can memories from early childhood be fully recovered, or are they subject to suggestions and distortions? The search for answers to these questions is fascinating and animates much of the current research in memory.

ACKNOWLEDGMENTS

I gratefully acknowledge the support from many people who helped me complete this project: Elizabeth Adorno, Peter Avery, Christine Bradley, Pat Bunker, Lynn Crawford, Kris Matney, Sarah Raskin, Jane Shea, Sonya Worthy, and Dawn Zorgdrager assisted in different stages of manuscript preparation. I also thank the following individuals, who reviewed this book and offered useful suggestions: Paul C. Amrhein, University of New Mexico; Richard B. Anderson, Bowling Green State University; Jill Booker, University of Indianapolis; Lisa Coates-Shrider, McMurry University; Ira S. Fischler, University of Florida–Gainesville; Thomas J. Gerstenberger, State University of New York–Potsdam; Robert W. Newby, Tarleton State University; Michael W. O'Boyle, Iowa State University; William A. Overman, University of North Carolina, Wilmington; Patrick S. Williams, University of Houston–Downtown; and John Wixted, University of California–San Diego.

The staff at Allyn and Bacon—including Carolyn Merrill, Amy Goldmacher, Annette Joseph, and Susan Freese—coordinated development, review, and production of the book. Lynda Griffiths guided the manuscript through all phases of production with characteristic care and good cheer. My colleagues at Trinity College, including the members of the Department of Psychology and the Faculty Research Committee 1995–96, created a productive environment that enabled me to think and write. Finally, I owe thanks to my family, especially to my wife Susan, for inspiring and supporting my research and writing efforts throughout the years.

HUMAN MEMORY

CHAPTER 1

INTRODUCTION

Everything we know involves memory, whether it is our proficiency in understanding language, our facility in exercising a multitude of mental or motor skills, or our ability to recognize the objects and events that surround us. If it were not for memory, there would be no systematic thought, no awareness of the past, and no planning for the future. Thanks to recent research advances in cognitive psychology and neuroscience, scientists have gained a fuller understanding of the power and fragility of memory. This book presents an overview of the diverse research efforts by psychologists devoted to understanding human memory.

Research on memory begins, as does research on any subject, with a series of questions. Scientists want to know how memories are acquired, maintained, and retrieved. They want to know what causes forgetting and whether forgetting means losing the information or failing to find it in the recesses of the mind. If memories are permanent yet become unavailable, it would be useful to determine if and how the information can be recovered. At the root of these issues lies the age-old practical concern with memory improvement: How can I improve my memory? People want to know what are the most effective strategies for remembering a set of facts, whether it is a shopping list, material for a test, or names of new colleagues. They want to know how best to learn a skill, whether it is speaking a second language, solving mathematical prob-

lems, or playing a musical instrument. Investigations of memory are equally driven by our curiosity about the patterns of remembering and forgetting in everyday life. We wonder why we cannot recall events from our early childhood, why memories of catastrophes such as the Oklahoma City bombing in 1995 stand out, and why we are unable to remember where we left our car keys.

It is easy to formulate questions about memory. It is quite another matter to find the answers to those questions, because memory, unlike physical objects, is not tangible and directly manipulable. Memory is an abstraction; it describes the property of organisms to acquire and retain information. Psychologists have begun to uncover the secrets of memory through a combination of experimental research and conceptual analysis. This book presents a comprehensive overview of memory research, covering advances on memory for facts, memory for skills, working memory, and memory impairments within the framework of cognitive psychology augmented by psychobiological and applied perspectives. The focus is on human memory at the behavioral level, although reference is made to animal and computer models when they help to illuminate human memory. However interesting, other lines of inquiry—such as research on animal cognition (Mackintosh, 1994), the molecular mechanisms of memory (Abel et al., 1995), and the social forces that influence expressions of memory (Schacter, 1995)—are beyond the scope of this volume.

THINKING ABOUT MEMORY

Metaphors of Memory

Scientists often use metaphors in seeking to understand phenomena in an abstract domain, whether it is the nature of light, the genetic code, or the acquisition and use of memories (Gentner & Grudin, 1985; Koriat & Goldsmith, 1996; Roediger, 1980). Although metaphors by themselves do not explain the phenomena, they can help to clarify the phenomena by transforming them into the context of a familiar domain. The wave analogy popular in physics offers a good illustration. Waves of water are visible and easily manipulated. When a still body of water is disturbed by objects thrown in different locations, waves emanate from these locations. The waves interfere with or magnify each other, depending on the location and the timing of the disturbance. It turns out that the dynamics of waves of water have given physicists a better grasp of the otherwise abstract properties of sound, light, and the movements of atoms.

Psychologists and philosophers before them used metaphors in thinking about memory. They have described memory in terms of analogies as diverse as the wax tablet, the sieve, the library, the workbench, the network, the storehouse, and the computer. These analogies capture different properties of memory, but they also exhibit a fundamental commonality. Consider the different aspects: The wax tablet reflects the notion of traces left by experience; the sieve captures the idea of forgetting; the library expresses the organization among memories; the workbench suggests that memory is an active processor; and the network captures the idea that memories are interconnected, much as concepts in a dictionary are defined by way of other concepts.

However different the analogies may be, they share the common assumption of memory as a kind of space. The spatial conceptualization of memory is reflected as well in the language we use to refer to memory and mind. Consider the following expressions: We *search* our memories for information that has been *lost;* we *bring back* a memory from the *deep recesses* of our minds; we keep an idea on the *back burner;* we forget ideas that are *out of sight;* we allow *room* for new ideas that must *sink in;* and, when successful, we *find* the solution to a problem (Roediger, 1980).

The notion of memory as a storehouse has been the most enduring analogy of memory. It has provided the framework for a large body of experimental research on memory and survives in the computer metaphor of memory (Chapter 11; Koriat & Goldsmith, 1996). According to the storehouse metaphor, items are received, stored, and discharged, much as physical items are handled in a physical store. The computer metaphor retains the attributes of a storehouse but adds more detail by including various storage devices and by describing memory mechanisms such as coding, rehearsal, and transformation. The computer accepts discrete units of input, transforms the information, and produces discrete units of output. The terms *encoding, storage,* and *retrieval,* introduced first in the context of computer-based information processing, are now widely used both in memory research and in everyday language.

Encoding refers to acquiring information and forming a memory record. *Storage* refers to maintaining the record over a time interval. *Retrieval* means accessing and using the information. Successful remembering depends on a proper functioning of each of these three stages. Failing to encode information means no record is formed, leaving nothing to store or to retrieve; a breakdown in storage or retrieval causes a failure in recall. Viewing memory in terms of encoding, storage, and retrieval has provided researchers with a useful framework to generate research questions, whether they address the effect of encoding strategies on retention (Chapter 4), the changes of retrieval strategies in normal aging (Chapter 8), or the role of encoding deficits in memory impairments (Chapter 10).

Thinking of memory in terms of a space implies entities located there. The entities are units of information typically referred to as *memory traces, memory records,* or, in general, *memory representations.* Memory representations are assumed to be manipulable; they can be consolidated, searched, and accessed. Even though representations serve as a convenience, they raise fundamental issues, including the following: What is the nature of memory representations? Are there different representations for different types of memories, such as remembering a beautiful sunset versus remembering that Albany is the capital of New York? and What is the relation of these representations to those assumed to underlie implicit memories and cognitive skills, whether it is problem solving or piano playing?

Attributes of Memory

Memory involves the acquisition of information, the creation of memory representations, and the retrieval of the information. Introspectively, the life of a memory representation begins with the events a person is aware of in the immediate present, the here and now. These experiences, as well as those that have occurred during the past few moments, require no recollection. William James (1890) referred to such experiences as *primary memory.* He contrasted primary memory with *secondary memory,* our awareness of a previous "state of mind after it has already once dropped from consciousness" (James, 1892, p. 287).

James's contemporary and the founder of experimental memory research, Hermann Ebbinghaus (1885), defined memory in terms of three different ways of retrieving information. First, we can recollect past experiences and facts *intentionally.* This will bring back to consciousness temporarily unavailable past sensations, feelings, and images, even if only partially. In the second case, mental content is brought back to consciousness *unintentionally* because an associated event reminds us of the original event. As an adult, the French writer Marcel Proust, for example, was reminded of his childhood when his mother served him tea and cookies one Sunday afternoon. Memories of his childhood home, his room, his family, and their afternoon tea parties streamed back into his consciousness with great force and vividness (Proust, 1988).

Intentional and unintentional memories accord with James's conception of memory as a conscious experience. Today, such memories are variously referred to as *explicit memory* or *declarative memory* to indicate that their content can be declared, whether it is a fact memorized in a memory test (e.g., the digits 8 2 4 1 9 3), an item of general knowledge (e.g., George Washington was the first president of the United States), or an autobiographical recollection (e.g., your first day at college). Declarative memory differs from another kind of memory known as *nondeclarative,* or *procedural, memory.* The latter involves the knowledge of skills that are typically difficult to verbalize (e.g., riding a bike, tying a shoelace, or speaking your native language).

In contrast to James, Ebbinghaus's (1885) third kind of information retrieval allowed that memory can become manifest *without* becoming conscious. According to Ebbinghaus, recollections may "give proof of their existence through their lasting effect, even when they do not reenter consciousness." Ebbinghaus used a learning paradigm, the savings method, to detect the effects of memory concealed from consciousness. He learned a set of materials on two occasions separated by an interval of varying duration. He found that relearning the same material typically was quicker than learning it the first time and he attributed the savings to the effects of such implicit memory (Chapter 2).

Ebbinghaus recognized that learning and memory are intimately related. Learning presupposes memory, specifically the retention of prior learning episodes. The two terms are often used as a single concept; indeed, *Learning and Memory* serves as a popular book title (e.g., Anderson, 1995a; Crowder, 1976; Houston, 1991; Norman, 1982; Schwartz & Reisberg, 1991; Thompson, 1989). However, the two terms do have distinct meanings. *Learning* refers to relatively permanent changes in performance as a result of experience, whereas *memory* refers to the record of those experiences (Anderson, 1995a). Learning is observed experimentally in a variety of situations, from conditioning experiments to investigations of implicit memory. In all of these cases, repeated exposure to a stimulus facilitates the processing of the stimulus, often without the person's awareness.

James and Ebbinghaus emphasized the reproductive aspects of memory—that is, its capacity to reinstate parts of an original perception or experience. In their view, the contributions of the learner to recollection was of little interest, if any. It was Bartlett (1932), another pioneer of memory research, who recognized the importance of reconstructive processes in remembering (Chapter 2). He considered remembering as recreating past events and experiences, based in part on the external event itself and in part on the person's knowledge of the world, also known as *semantic memory*.

Neisser (1967) articulated the notion of reconstruction when he noted that "one does not recall objects or responses simply because traces of them exist in the mind, but after an elaborate process of *re*construction" (Neisser's emphasis, p. 285). Neisser likened the reconstruction of memories to the work of a paleontologist who rebuilds a "fully fleshed-out skincovered dinosaur" using only bone fragments and the knowledge of dinosaur anatomy. The reconstructive view of memory accommodates the influence of diverse sources on recollection in addition to a person's semantic knowledge. Expectations, desires, and information acquired subsequent to an experience can have an impact on retrieval and often produce distortions of memory. Such distortions are the subject of research on memory illusions and on the reliability of eyewitness testimony and patient accounts of abuse (Chapters 9 and 12).

Memories are multifaceted; they are reproductive and reconstructive, intentional and unintentional, and explicit and implicit. They also differ in duration (from very short to very long) and in scope (from the general to the most specific). The heterogeneity of memory is not surprising in light of the many uses of memory in everyday life. We use memory to recall events and experiences as well as facts of all kinds, melodies, jokes, conversations, and the pronunciation of words, however irregular they may be. We use memory to navigate city streets, perform numerical calculations, and recognize such varied stimuli as smells, wildflowers, and faces in the crowd. We can train memory for use in specialized contexts, as well, whether it is to remember hundreds of lines of dialogue of a play, to employ strategies in the game of chess, or to play a difficult piece on the piano.

The diversity of the forms of memory requires an arsenal of methods equipped to tap the different expressions of remembering. Different paradigms assess memory for lists, autobiographical memory, semantic memory, implicit memory, prospective memory, and memory for skills. Observational techniques differ for infants, college students, and older adults, as well as patients with amnesia. A sample of these paradigms will be sketched in the next section, and more details will be presented in the remainder of the book.

INVESTIGATING MEMORY

The goal of memory research is to understand human memory in its complexity and to arrive at generalizations about remembering. A *generalization* means that performance observed in one context can be replicated in the same context as well as in other contexts. The goal of specific studies is to examine under which conditions a generalization applies and what its limits are. These stipulations do not preclude research with individual participants; rather, as explained in different chapters of this book, discoveries made in individuals are of interest to the extent that they stimulate hypotheses about memory in general (Chapters 3, 9, and 11).

Here are some examples of generalizations about memory (Anderson, 1995a; Kihlstrom, 1996):

— *The forgetting curve*. The rate of forgetting is most rapid immediately after learning and diminishes after longer intervals (Chapter 2; Ebbinghaus, 1885; Wixted & Ebbesen, 1991).
— *The power law of practice*. Performance on a specific task improves as a function of continued practice on the task, but the benefits of each successive practice episode become smaller and smaller (Chapters 4, 5, and 7; Newell & Rosenbloom, 1981).
— *The encoding specificity principle*. Retention increases to the degree that the environment during testing is similar to the learning environment (Chapters 4, 8, and 10; Tulving & Thomson, 1973).

Scientists arrive at generalizations such as these through research governed by the interplay between theoretical questions and empirical data, which is characteristic of science. The data on human memory have been acquired using a great variety of research paradigms. Without these methods, research on human memory would not be possible. The methods have contributed as much to the advances in memory research over the past century as the questions we ask about memory.

Paradigms of Memory Research

The methods used to investigate memory are diverse; they vary in terms of the stimuli and events committed to memory, the factors thought to influence retention, the measures of performance, and the contexts of observation, including real-world contexts. The methods include techniques to assess memory for facts, memory for skills, implicit memory, as well as manifestations of memory at the level of neural structures, both large and small. We begin the review of paradigms by introducing two major experimental techniques for assessing memory for facts, or declarative memory: the free-recall and the recognition tasks. Both of these tasks typically include a study phase followed at various intervals by a test phase. During the study phase, the subjects memorize a set of items; during the test phase, they attempt to remember the items.

Free Recall

The free-recall task resembles memorizing items on a shopping list. Assume your shopping list included the following items: *broccoli, milk, bologna, soap, matches, peanuts, bread, squash,* and *hamburger.* Assume further that you misplaced the list. Trying to recall the list without regard to order represents *free recall.* In the free-recall paradigm, the experimenter instructs the person to memorize a set of items, usually a list of words, and to recall them in any order. In immediate free recall, typically the most recent items and the initial items of the list are recalled best, whereas items in the center are poorly recalled (see Figure 1.1). This serial position effect is one of the most replicable findings and has generated a considerable amount of theoretical work during the past century (Chapters 2 and 4).

Recognition

During the study phase of the recognition paradigm, the experimenter presents a list of items to the subject, as illustrated by the miniature list in

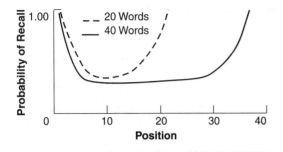

FIGURE 1.1   Recall level as a function of the serial position in a list in free recall. The serial position effect is independent of list length, as illustrated by the primacy and recency effects for lists of 20 and 40 words.

Figure 1.2A. (Typically, 10 or more items are presented.) In the test phase, retention is assessed by presenting a test list consisting of a subset of studied items (i.e., the "old" items; italicized in Figure 1.2A and a subset of items not studied (i.e., the "new" items), also known as the *distractor items*. During testing, new and old items are randomly mixed and the subject decides whether each test item is new or old. Stimuli and responses may be classified in terms of

FIGURE 1.2   A recognition trial. *(A)* Study phase and testing. *(B)* Categories of responses in recognition testing.

Study List
Cattle, Form, Tribute, Style, Hint

Test List
Tribute, Cotton, Attic,*Style,* Madness, *Form, Hint,* Star, Elbow,*Cattle*

(A) *Note:* Old items are italicized for illustration only.

		Stimulus	
		Old	*New*
Response	*Old*	Hit	False alarm
	New	Miss	Correct rejection

(B)

old and *new*, yielding the four response categories shown in Figure 1.2B.

Comparisons of the level of retention in recall and recognition tests typically reveal a recognition advantage. The recognition advantage has stimulated numerous theoretical models and efforts to demonstrate its limits, including the attempt to find the contrary effect, an advantage of recall relative to recognition performance (Chapters 4, 11, and 12).

The recognition task is a favorite research paradigm among experimenters. It lends itself readily for quantification in terms of the choice of the stimulus materials, the number of items, the similarity among items, the retention interval, and the schedule of rewards and penalties for hits and false alarms, respectively. Stimulus materials have included individual words, numbers, sentences, passages, and visual scenes. In addition to the response types in Figure 1.2B, a widely used performance measure in recognition tests is the speed of responding. The reaction time has proven to be a sensitive measure of retrieval speed and of the assumed strength of association between memory representations.

The recall and recognition paradigms assess a kind of declarative memory known as *episodic memory*. This term refers to a person's memory of specific episodes known by their time and place of acquisition. In episodic memory experiments, items are learned during a designated acquisition period, called the *study phase*. In assessing *semantic memory*, a person's knowledge of the world, there is no explicit study phase because the focus is on knowledge the person acquired outside the research laboratory—in other words, the person's preexperimental knowledge. Consequently, semantic memory experiments typically include only a test phase, as illustrated in the following sentence verification task.

Sentence Verification Task
Decide quickly whether each of the following statements is true or false:

(1.1) A canary is a bird.

(1.2) A shark has fins.

(1.3) A canary is an animal.

(1.4) Coca-Cola is blue.

People are usually correct in their judgments; however, the speed of making the response differs. It turns out that it takes longer to verify the statement *A canary is an animal* than *A canary is a bird*. This category size effect is consistent with the view of memory as a space where a greater distance must be bridged between *canary* and *animal* than between *canary* and *bird* (Chapter 4).

We turn next to two research paradigms that assess procedural memory: the priming paradigm and the skill-learning paradigm. As in Ebbinghaus's savings method, in these tasks retention is evaluated in terms of performance rather than in terms of explicit recollections. In measuring priming and skilled performance, volunteers are repeatedly exposed to a set of stimuli while they perform a specific task, whether it involves identifying a stimulus, completing a word fragment, or executing a motor or cognitive skill.

Priming

Priming tasks involve an inspection phase and a testing phase. During the inspection phase, the subject reads a sequence of stimuli—for example, a list including the word *motel*. In word-stem completion testing, word stems from previously seen stimuli (e.g., MOT – –) and from new stimuli (WAG – –) are presented one at a time and the person is asked to name the word that the fragment reminds him or her of. There is an advantage in identifying word fragments of old stimuli; this effect is known as the *priming effect*. Typically, people are unaware of the effect, much as they are of their knowledge of the rules of language, for example.

Performance in the word-stem completion task can be compared with performance in a cued-recall test, an explicit memory test. Here, the person reads the same stimulus list as in the priming condition during the inspection phase, except with instructions to memorize the items. In testing, cues such as MOT – – and WAG – – are presented as prompts to recall the entire word explicitly. People tend to have little difficulty in retrieving old words in response to the cues; however, amnesic patients are not able to do so.

Remarkably, however, amnesic patients exhibit evidence of implicit memory in the word-stem completion task. Their performance in completing word fragments previously shown is almost as good as that of nonamnesic individuals.

The finding that implicit memory is spared in amnesics means that they can acquire new information. This result has had important theoretical and practical implications. It encouraged the hypothesis that explicit and implicit memory may be based on different memory systems rather than a single system (Chapter 11; Warrington & Weiskrantz, 1982), and it gave neuropsychologists a tool for training patients to acquire new knowledge, even if only on a modest scale (Chapters 10 and 12).

Measuring Practice Effects

Researchers assess memory for skills by measuring changes in the speed that it takes people to perform a task, whether it is reading, problem solving, or retrieving information from memory. Kolers (1975) exposed people to a novel task: He asked them to read passages that were printed in a mirror-inverted font and recorded the reading times as people read 160 pages in sessions distributed over a two-month period. Readers found the first few pages of inverted text very difficult to decode, taking up to 22 times as long as for normal text. Over the two-month training period, the readers improved considerably, achieving a rate of 1.3 times the reading time for normal text.

Figure 1.3 shows the improvement in reading time averaged across eight readers. The figure uses the logarithmic scale for both variables, the number of pages and the reading time. Logarithms compress the distance between larger numbers and tend to yield straight-line functions of the practice/performance relationship. Researchers typically express the relation between practice and performance in terms of logarithms because logarithmic functions are mathematically simpler than other types of functions. The linear function in Figure 1.3 reflects the power law of practice: There is a continued improvement in reading performance, but the benefits get smaller as a function of added practice. This generalization has been documented for numerous other procedural or nondeclarative skills from cigar rolling to playing card games (Chapters 4, 5, 7, and 12).

PET Imaging

The effects of learning and practice depend on neural structures of different levels of complexity ranging from groups of neurons to entire brain regions. Although dependencies between

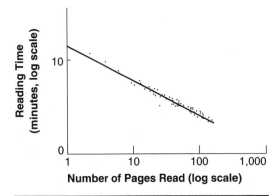

FIGURE 1.3 Effect of practice on performance. Reading times diminish as readers continue to learn reading text printed in a mirror-inverted font. The figure shows the log-log transformation of reading times and the number of pages read.

memory and brain were assumed for a long time, systematic research on documenting these relations occurred only in the last few decades. The impetus for the new developments were due to the dramatic progress in developing neuroimaging and electrophysiological methods. Neuroimaging methods combine brain-scanning techniques and computer technology to measure the brain's transient activity as a person engages in a mental task, such as memory retrieval (Posner & Raichle, 1994). The neuroimaging methods are based on the fact that brain tissue at work consumes more blood than when at rest. One of the neuroimaging methods is the positron emission tomography (PET) scan, where a nontoxic radioactive substance is injected into the bloodstream. The PET scan detects changes in blood-flow patterns via a battery of detectors surrounding the person's head.

PET imaging has been used by memory researchers to track the brain's activity as a person encodes or retrieves information from memory. Consider a study by Martin and colleagues that illustrates the use of PET imaging in memory research (Martin, Haxby, Lalonde, Wiggs, & Ungerleider, 1995; Martin, Wiggs, Ungerleider, & Haxby, 1996). The study assessed changes of cerebral blood flow as people performed a semantic memory task. They were shown pictures of familiar objects drawn in black and white (e.g., a pencil, a hammer, and a saw) and asked on separate trials to name the color of the object or the activity for which the object was used. Martin and colleagues made the interesting discovery that retrieving color information (e.g., yellow) and retrieving actions (e.g., writing) led to activation of different regions of the brain's left hemisphere, as shown in Figure 1.4. This result is interesting because it suggests that information about the same concept may be distributed in different regions of the brain. PET imaging and other neuroimaging methods have found increasing use in memory research—for instance, to detect changes in brain activity as volunteers

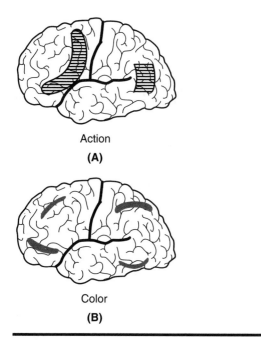

Action

(A)

Color

(B)

FIGURE 1.4 PET imaging reveals changes in regional cerebral blood flow as people retrieve the actions *(A)* and the color *(B)* associated with target words (e.g., *pencil*) (Martin et al., 1995).

execute different memory tasks (Chapter 11), to track different short-term memory processes (Chapter 6), and to reveal differences between factual and false memories (Chapter 9).

PET imaging has great promise as a tool for investigations of memory but it is not without problems (Posner & Raichle, 1994; Roland, Kawashima, Gulyas, & O'Sullivan, 1995). One of these is the comparative slowness of PET images relative to the fast-paced mental processes. It typically takes up to several minutes to record a PET image, whereas recognition and retrieval processes take no more than a few seconds, at most. Another problem is that the spatial resolution is no less than 5 millimeters, thus showing the activity of tens of thousands of neurons rather than isolating the activity of a smaller set of cells. Scientists address these and other problems by

using several research tools jointly, including PET imaging, electrophysiological methods, and behavioral methods (Chapter 3).

Explaining Memory Phenomena

Using the paradigms just introduced, among others, researchers have made a large body of discoveries about memory. Figure 1.5 lists a sample of these results. The list could easily be expanded, as new findings are being made at an increasing rate, thus attesting to the vitality of the discipline. No researcher is content by just adding another finding to the literature. Rather, researchers seek to understand an effect and to identify the conditions under which it occurs. To achieve these ends, memory models of varying scope have been proposed. Some models address specific memory effects, such as the category size effect in semantic memory introduced

FIGURE 1.5 A partial list of memory phenomena investigated by researchers.

Recency effect in free recall (2, 6)
Distinctiveness effect in recall (4, 9)
Mapping of brain regions through neuroimaging
  (3, 5, 6, 11)
Effects of organization on retention (4, 12)
Forgetting function (2, 4, 9)
Memory and face cells in the brain (3)
Encoding specificity principle (4, 8, 10)
Brain wave patterns and recall (3)
Power law of practice (4, 5, 7)
Levels of processing (4, 6, 8)
Fan effect (4, 7, 8)
Retrieval practice (4, 12)
Spreading activation (4, 7)
Implanting false memories (9, 12)
Childhood amnesia (8, 9)
Priming effects (5, 10, 11)
Exceptional memories (5)
Trade-off between storage and computation (6)
Retention of autobiographical memories (9)

Note: Numbers in parentheses indicate the chapter(s) in which the effect is reviewed.

earlier (Chapter 4), the serial position effect (Chapter 4), and the recoding effect in memorizing digits (Chapter 6). Other memory models are global; they organize a body of data within a broad framework. Some global models address list-learning phenomena (Atkinson & Shiffrin, 1968; Raaijmakers & Shiffrin, 1981), others include both memory for facts and skills (Anderson, 1993), and still others represent memory in terms of neural networks (McClelland & Rumelhart, 1981; McClelland, Rumelhart, & Hinton, 1986). Even though global models may appear abstract and removed from reality, they represent, according to some of their authors, the best prospect of extending research from the laboratory to the real world (Anderson, Reder, & Lebiere, 1996). Memory models will be reviewed in several chapters, including Chapters 6, 7, and 11. For the moment, we will consider two memory models: one inspired by the serial computer and the other by neural processes in the brain. The first model is Atkinson and Shiffrin's (1968) two-store model, and the second model is McClelland and Rumelhart's (1981) word recognition model.

A Two-Store Model of Memory

Among the earliest and most influential memory models was the two-store model of memory introduced by Atkinson and Shiffrin (1968). This model organized the knowledge on memory available in the late 1960s in functional terms, without reference to neural or brain processes. The components of the model, shown in Figure 1.6, were conceived as successive phases of the life of a memory representation. Sensory memory reflects the trace of a stimulus immediately after perceiving it, much like the echo of a sound. The sensory trace is assumed to last as long as it takes to recognize the stimulus, typically no longer than a few hundred milliseconds.

Short-term memory, reminiscent of William James's *primary memory,* refers to representations of information currently in active use, such

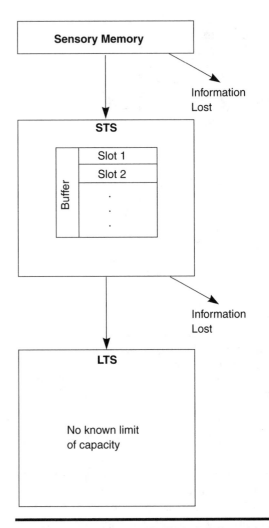

FIGURE 1.6 Atkinson and Shiffrin's (1968) model of memory was influenced by the computer metaphor. The model includes a sensory memory and two stores: the short-term store (STS) and the long-term store (LTS).

as that which occurs when a person tries to remember a phone number. Unless rehearsed, this information is forgotten after a few seconds. The rehearsal process momentarily maintains the information and transfers it to the next stage, *long-term memory* (James's *secondary memory*). The more rehearsals an item receives, the greater its strength in long-term memory and the more likely that it will be recalled on a recall test. Long-term memory has no known limits; it includes all the information we have acquired, whether it is as recent as a list of words learned in a memory experiment a few minutes ago or as distant as a person's recollection of her high school graduation.

The Atkinson and Shiffrin (1968) model was able to explain a large body of list-learning data, including various rehearsal phenomena and the serial position curve (Figure 1.1). Even though the model was subsequently challenged by alternative approaches (Chapter 6), it has had an enduring influence on subsequent conceptualizations of memory. The multistore distinction and other attributes of the model survive as part of other memory models, including Anderson's (1990) ACT and Raaijmakers and Shiffrin's (1981) SAM models (reviewed in Chapter 7), the multicomponent model of working memory (Chapter 6), and the models of Pashler and Carrier (1996) and Potter (1993), among others.

Neural Networks

One of the most remarkable achievements of the human memory system is its ability to recognize a multitude of stimuli with great speed and accuracy and without apparent effort. What kind of memory mechanism would account for this ability? To simplify matters, consider the problem of word recognition. One strategy of recognizing words involves a sequential search. On encountering a word, whether written or spoken, the memory system searches all word representations in long-term memory serially, recognizing the word when a representation is found to match the features of the stimulus. Even assuming a high-speed comparison, a sequential search for every word encountered in a discourse would take very long. Consequently, many theorists favor a parallel process of word recognition in which evidence about different interpretations of a stimulus is collected simultaneously.

Neural network models have been developed to simulate word recognition and other cognitive functions in terms of parallel processes. Deriving in equal measure from neuroscience and computer science, such models handle the acquisition and retrieval of information via simulations of neural networks in living organisms. The models consist of many small neuronlike processors that integrate the inputs they receive from neighboring processors through multiple links.

In McClelland and Rumelhart's (1981) model of word recognition, each processor, known as a *node,* is dedicated to fulfill a specific job—for example, to recognize a letter feature, a letter, or a word. Even though each node fulfills only one task, the network gains its power by links that connect all of the units. Taken as a whole, the network examines the stimulus and develops various hypotheses that differ in confidence about the identity of the stimulus.

Figure 1.7 displays an illustrative network of units and links to represent processing of the words *the boy.* The network in Figure 1.7 is a subnetwork of a much larger network whose repertoire includes all words, letters, and features known by the system. McClelland and Rumelhart's (1981) system, for example, has a lexicon of 1,200 words, 26 letters, and 16 letter features. By saying the network *knows* a stimulus, it is implied that the system has a representation of the features of the stimulus and the relations among them. The representation for the letter *Y,* for example, would consist of the fact that two oblique lines are joined at the bottom and are supported by a vertical line.

When a string of letters, such as *B O Y,* is presented, all corresponding features in the network are assumed to be activated in parallel. Activation passes in turn from the features to the superordinate units in the network, the word units. In the case of this example, words beginning with *B* and *BO* would be activated (e.g., *BOB, BOG,* and *BOY*). The network is assumed to evaluate the competing hypotheses and to select the interpre-

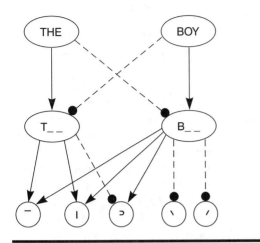

FIGURE 1.7 Portion of a neural network to illustrate letter and word recognition. The network is a subnetwork of a larger network, including all the words, letters, and features represented in the simulation. The illustration involves processing the words *the boy* presented in capital letters. Solid lines indicate stimulus patterns that are consistent with existing network knowledge (e.g., *B* is consistent with the word *BOY*), whereas broken lines indicate inconsistencies (e.g., *T* is inconsistent with *BOY*).

tation that fits the evidence presented by the stimulus best.

McClelland and Rumelhart's recognition model is one of many neural network models to simulate processes executed by real neural networks in the brain, whether it is learning associations, constructing memories, or retrieving information. Neural networks produce a response when the stimulus is degraded or when the network itself is damaged—for instance, when the links that connect the processors are disabled. In either case, the response of the network is similar to the intended response. Because of their capability to yield partially correct responses, neural networks have been used to simulate memory impairments (Chapter 11; e.g., Farah & McClelland, 1991).

Neural network models reflect the close connection between memory and the rest of cogni-

tion, including pattern recognition, learning, and language comprehension. Isolating memory from other cognitive functions is a matter of convenience for researchers and authors. Even though books on memory are, by definition, about memory, in the living human there are no well-defined borders between memory, on the one hand, and the rest of the mental functions, on the other. All the cognitive functions cannot be covered here, but it is instructive to mention a few of them, nevertheless. I have chosen to sketch three functions to illustrate the role of memory within the context of cognition: attention, pattern recognition, and problem solving.

MEMORY IN THE CONTEXT OF COGNITION

Memory plays a fundamental role in cognition; it is involved whenever a representation acquired in the past is used to execute a task or when experiences are encoded and memory records are formed. Pattern recognition, the use of language, learning concepts and categories, decision making, and problem solving would be impossible without memory. Although the demands on memory come from many directions, its capabilities are not unlimited. The system may not be able to encode as much information within a given unit of time as needed, nor might it be able to recollect as much information as necessary in the execution of a task. The efficient use of the limited resources is achieved by focusing them on the task at hand, the process known as *attention*.

Attention

The close relation between attention and memory was recognized by William James (1890), who identified primary memory, the information we can attend to at any given time, as "a pulse of consciousness." James knew that primary memory was limited, permitting no "plurality of ideas." James's concept of a limited primary memory has survived in the notion of a memory processor of limited capacity, the short-term store (Chapter 6; Atkinson & Shiffrin, 1968; Miller, 1956; Waugh & Norman, 1965). The capacity limit of short-term memory has been conceptualized both in terms of storage capacity and processing capacity (e.g., Navon, 1984). The two types of capacity are fundamental to understanding retention in many situations; we will return to them in several chapters, especially when it comes to the operations of working memory—the memory system that, according to Shiffrin (1993), "encompasses virtually everything" in cognition (Chapters 4, 6, and 8).

Storage capacity refers to the number of items one can attend to within a very short span of time, whether it is a phone number, the content of a sentence, or the result of an interim calculation in adding large numbers. Storage capacity is typically measured by the digit span test, in which a person must remember as many digits as possible. *Processing capacity* refers to the resources the system can bring to bear on a task within a unit of time. Navon (1984) characterized these resources "as any internal input essential for processing" (p. 217). The amount of available resources determines performance on a task in terms of speed and accuracy. If the task is novel, it commands much attention, a large amount of resources. After extended practice, however, fewer resources are required and performance becomes less prone to error, faster, and less susceptible to interference. In other words, it becomes automatic.

Processing capacity can be assessed by observing a person executing two tasks concurrently, whether it is in everyday life or in the laboratory. A skilled driver, for example, can drive while carrying on a conversation. An experienced computer programmer can remember the structure of the program and write code at the same time. A chess master can play against several opponents in the same session. In the laboratory, researchers use the dual-task technique to assess the availability of resources. In this paradigm, the person is executing two concurrent tasks. For instance, the person is remembering digits, such as 7 3 5 8 2 6, and performing a concurrent operation on a subset of the digits, such as adding the last two digits (2 6) or stating whether they are greater than a target (e.g., 40; Chapter 6). The expectation is that the two tasks compete for resources and, depending on the person's expertise, performance on one or both of the tasks deteriorates.

Pattern Recognition

Environmental stimuli, regardless of modality, are not recognized instantaneously. Rather, their identification takes time, even though it may involve only a fraction of a second. Until the recognition process is completed, a sensory trace of the stimulus is assumed to persist in a raw and unidentified format. This stimulus trace has been referred to as *sensory memory;* it is captured in Atkinson and Shiffrin's model of memory by the component entitled *"Sensory Memory"* in Figure 1.6. Sensory traces in the register are thought to last from about 1 to 4 seconds, depending on the modality. Visual information (e.g., of letters or words) is retained up to about 1 second (Sperling, 1960; for a review, see Massaro & Loftus, 1996), an interval presumably sufficient to complete identification of the stimuli.

Recognition would be impossible without assuming representations of the target stimuli in long-term memory, whether they are templates, feature analyzers, or the neuronlike processors illustrated in Figure 1.7. The recognition process presumably transforms the stimulus input into a format that permits access to the representations and compares the stimulus with several likely representations. In turn, the comparison is assumed to produce the candidate that fits the stimulus best, as illustrated in Figure 1.7. Even though this illustration of letter and word recognition is highly simplified, it demonstrates the function of memory in identifying stimuli of varying complexity. The stimuli may be as simple as pure tones or as complex as the configuration of symptoms of a disease. In each case, memory is necessary in order to interpret the stimulus.

Problem Solving

Memory is indispensable for problem solving. People solve problems continuously, whether checking errors in a spreadsheet or devising a strategy to maximize sales. Memory psychologists study problem solving using such standard tasks as card games, numerical problems, and puzzles that involve physical moves of pieces into certain locations and under certain constraints (Chapters 5, 6, and 7).

Consider the role of memory in numerical problem solving, such as in adding two-digit numbers (e.g., $23 + 17$). The problem solver has to marshal a large amount of knowledge to arrive at the apparently simple solution of 40. The person must know such basic facts as the sums of $1 + 1 = 2$, $1 + 2 = 3$, $1 + 3 = 4$, and so on, and basic addition rules, including the following:

1. Perform the addition by columns.
2. Begin by adding the digits in the right column.
3. Add all of the digits of a column.
4. If the sum is less than 10, write it out.
5. If the sum is 10 or greater, write out the right number and set a carry.
6. If there is a carry, add the carried value to the sum of the digits in the next column.

Knowing the facts and rules of addition, however, is not sufficient for adequate performance. One must be able to retrieve the knowledge from memory and apply it correctly. As a problem solver applies the rules, she must remember the intermediate results, remember which interim goal she is trying to achieve, and identify the rule applicable to the current state of the problem.

In the case of our problem $23 + 17$, the person would arrange the numbers as follows:

$$\begin{array}{r} 23 \\ + \ 17 \\ \hline \end{array}$$

and begin performing the addition in the right column. She would add 7 and 3 and, assuming she remembers the result, obtain the sum of 10. Using rules 4 and 5 above, she would write out the 0, carry the tens value of 1, and focus on the left column. Using rule 3, she would add 2 and 1 and the carry value of 1 to get 4. She would enter this number to the left of the 0. Next, she would check whether there are any columns left and, noting that none are left, she would conclude the calculation.

This calculation appears easy, yet many things could go wrong, including an erroneous retrieval of facts or an erroneous sequencing of the rules. Clearly, even in a problem as simple as adding two numbers, many steps could misfire. In more complex problems (e.g., $423 + 956 = ?$, $1312 - 989 = ?$, or $178 \times 109 = ?$), more rules are necessary, more intermediate results must be remembered, and more things can go wrong. The function of memory in numerical problem solving, then, is to retrieve basic numerical facts, to remember and to apply the rules, and to maintain the intermediate results.

According to memory theorists, different types of memory contribute to numerical problem solving and to problem solving in general. Basic numerical facts are assumed to be stored in fact memory, or declarative memory (Chapter 4). Memory of rules is assumed to be represented in memory for skills, or procedural memory (Chapter 5). Intermediate results are assumed to be maintained in a working memory, which is the processor that both operates on and stores information (Chapter 6).

As the mind's system in charge of acquiring, retaining, and retrieving information, memory is central to cognition. No cognitive function is feasible without the support of memory, whether it is learning, pattern recognition, problem solving, perception, reasoning, or comprehension. In turn, each of these functions exerts an impact on memory. Executing mental tasks changes memory representation and makes the system more adaptive to environmental demands (Anderson, 1990; Craik & Lockhart, 1972; Crowder, 1993). Having set the stage for memory research and placed the field within the study of cognition, we are ready to review the state of the field.

PREVIEW

The treatment of memory in this book reflects the wide range of approaches to memory both in terms of substance and exposition. The book seeks to provide an overview of the principal research areas without getting lost in them, to describe important experimental paradigms, to introduce applications of memory research, and to present the major debates in the field within their historical contexts.

The goal of presenting a broad panorama of memory research necessarily entails a trade-off in that many issues cannot be developed to the extent possible in specialized volumes such as *Brain and Memory* (McGaugh, Weinberger, & Lynch, 1995), *Memory and Brain* (Squire, 1987), *Visuo-Spatial Working Memory* (Logie, 1995), *Prospective Memory* (Brandimonte, Einstein, & McDaniel, 1996), and *Memory for Proper Names* (Cohen, 1993). Much more could be added, for example, on metamemory, motor memory, hemispheric specialization, and other topics than is possible under the constraints of a general overview. The choices made in this book reflect my background and interest in cognitive psychology; they do not imply a ranking of topics in terms of significance.

Advances in memory research result from the development of theories and of experimental paradigms. Researchers pose questions on specific memory phenomena, develop hypotheses, and design experiments to address the issues. The experiment provides the best available avenue of subjecting a phenomenon to systematic scrutiny. It allows experimenters to manipulate the factors thought to influence an effect, to control confounding variables, and to arrive at the generalizations about memory that we all seek. Experimental paradigms treated in detail in the following chapters include the savings method, the retrieval practice paradigm, the levels-of-processing manipulation, several neuroscience methods, and methods of assessing autobiographical memories and retention in preverbal infants, among others. The emphasis on the experimental approach does not preclude reference to such methods as case studies and field studies. Research on memory impairment and memory applications often begins with observations using these methods (Chapters 3, 8, 9, and 12).

Memory research is a field enlivened by debates of differing scope. Theorists debate everything from the reasons for a particular experimental outcome to the architecture of memory and the relevance of memory research to everyday issues. Among the most widely debated topics is the issue of a single memory system versus several independent memory systems, and, if the latter is the case, what those systems are. This issue has implications for topics covered throughout this book, including procedural memory (Chapters 5 and 7), semantic memory (Chapters 4 and 10), episodic memory (Chapter 4), autobiographical memory (Chapters 4 and 9), and working memory (Chapter 6). In addition to discussing the global architecture of memory, theorists debate issues within specific domains. Thus, they debate the causes of forgetting facts (Chapter 4), the causes of memory changes in childhood and in aging (Chapter 8), the issue of childhood amnesia (Chapter 8), the effect of emotions on retention (Chapter 9), and whether memory traces in the brain are localized or distributed (Chapter 3). Finally, psychologists debate the relevance of memory research to the real world and to what extent results discovered in the laboratory have a bearing on real-world applications (Chapters 11 and 12).

No topic has been more controversial among psychologists than the notion of recovered memories—the idea that traumatic experiences, once suppressed, can be recovered. The nature and volume of this argument go beyond the issues that are usually debated by researchers and reviewed in standard treatments of memory (Anderson, 1995a; Baddeley, 1990; Bjork & Bjork, 1996). However, whether memory researchers approve or not, the public at large looks to them for a position on this issue. Recently, memory researchers have responded to the call, as indicated by the growing scholarly literature devoted to the recovered memory versus false memory controversy (e.g., Ceci, 1995; Conway, 1997; Erdelyi, 1996; Loftus, 1993; Pezdek & Banks, 1996; Schacter, 1995). This controversy (treated in Chapter 9) demonstrates the significance of basic memory research for the community as a whole.

These and other issues provide the motivating force for the research reviewed in this text. Even though many issues remain unresolved, not all the issues in memory research have been intractable. On the contrary, lawful generalizations such as the law of practice and the encoding specificity principle, have been widely documented and, as will be pointed out repeatedly, there are many applications of memory research in the real world (Chapters 2, 4, 5, 7, 11, and 12). One of the important findings relevant to improving retention is that learners themselves exercise control over acquiring a body of knowledge. The key ingredient for successful remembering requires that learners allow sufficient time for practice, distribute the learning sessions over time, and study a set of materials repeatedly within different contexts.

CHAPTER 2

THE PIONEERS OF
MEMORY RESEARCH
FROM EBBINGHAUS TO LASHLEY

Memory fascinated scholars well before psychology came into existence as an empirical discipline. Plato likened memory to a wax tablet; Aristotle formulated his theory of memory associations, which was later taken up and developed by Hume and Herbart; and Descartes and Kant, among others, thought of simple and complex ideas as the units of thought and memory. None of them, however, had the means of investigating memory empirically. It was the introduction of empirical methods that distinguished the psychological approach to memory from prior approaches.

This chapter reviews early psychological research on memory; it discusses the work of experimenters such as Ebbinghaus, Binet, and Bartlett; it reviews Semon's theory of memory stages as well as Ribot's work on amnesia and Freud's psychodynamic account of memory; it describes the animal learning research of Pavlov and Thorndike; and it concludes with a discussion of Lashley's studies on the search for the memory trace in the brain. As a group, these scientists represent the same specialties of memory research that exist today—the experimental, neuropsychological, and neuroscience approaches. The early researchers may have lacked the imaging methods and the computer technology available today but their writings reveal deep insights about memory, the formation of memory traces, their endurance over time, and their retrieval.

The pioneers we shall discuss differed widely in their approaches to memory. Ebbinghaus and Binet were experimenters seeking to understand the functional relations between learning and remembering. Bartlett's experiments were motivated by his curiosity about the influence of cultural attitudes and conventions on remembering. Semon viewed memory as a natural property of neural tissue. Ribot described memory and memory impairments in phenomenological terms, citing numerous clinical case studies. Seeking to understand mental illness, Freud developed a psychodynamic theory that incorporated important assumptions about memory. The animal learning theorists felt that learning and memory are best studied in simpler organisms and that any insights gained on animal memory would ultimately illuminate issues of human memory.

EXPERIMENTAL STUDY OF MEMORY

The experimental study of memory was pioneered by Ebbinghaus and Binet toward the end of the nineteenth century. Between them, these experimenters investigated list memory, sentence memory, and text memory; these topics continue to occupy memory researchers today.

Ebbinghaus and Binet sought to determine the parameters that influence retention and forgetting, including the amount of information memorized, the time between study episodes, and, most importantly, the interval between study and testing. They believed that memory was grounded in the brain, but they did not pursue the possibilities inherent in this assumption. Similarly, neither Ebbinghaus nor Binet developed their rudimentary theoretical views, in part because there was no sufficient body of data to inspire and support the theories. Indeed, Rubin and Wenzel (1996), two contemporary memory researchers, claimed, much as Ebbinghaus did, that theory development is inefficient and premature in the absence of documented regularities of memory phenomena.

Hermann Ebbinghaus (1850–1909)

Hermann Ebbinghaus's experimental work on memory was inspired by his admiration for the lawfulness of psychophysical functions resulting from the empirical studies of Fechner on the relation between the physical properties of stimuli and psychological sensations. He began his studies on nonsense syllables at the University of Berlin as part for an advanced degree in philosophy and described the results of his research in a concise volume titled *Über das Gedächtnis (On Memory)* in 1885. The book was an instant success, notably in the United States where recently founded universities sought to attract top talent from Europe. Indeed, Cornell University made a generous offer to Ebbinghaus, affording him great opportunities to develop an experimental psychology laboratory and the then generous salary of $3,000 to $4,000. Ebbinghaus was tempted to accept the invitation but he finally declined for personal reasons. (It was another psychologist famous at the turn of the twentieth century, Titchener, who accepted the position.)

Ebbinghaus on Memory

Ebbinghaus (1905) defined *memory* as the faculty of the mind to bring back past experiences into consciousness. He viewed reproduction and memory as analogous to work and energy, respectively. Work is an actual observable act, whereas memory is the potential to execute the act even if the act does not occur (1905, p. 635). Ebbinghaus agreed with the associationist tenets of his day that memory rests on the association between experiences. For instance, if experiences *A* and *B* occurred together in the past, when given *A* at some future point, *B* is reproduced. Ebbinghaus acknowledged that the triggering stimulus need not be identical to *A*—for example, a child will use the label *dog* for other medium-sized four-legged animals such as cats. Ebbinghaus speculated that associations are based on excitatory processes in the cortex (1905, p. 641).

Ebbinghaus's strength lay in his empirical approach and his inventiveness as an experimenter. No one prior to Ebbinghaus had ever undertaken the systematic and controlled experimental study of memory that he launched. In order to appreciate this accomplishment, one must remember that in his day, there were no psychology laboratories, no subject pools, no statistical tests, and no sets of stimulus materials. Ebbinghaus improvised any and all of these aspects of research. He used himself as a subject. He was among the first psychologists to analyze data statistically, except he had to develop the statistical tests himself! He even invented his own stimulus materials by introducing the nonsense syllable intended to minimize the influence of meaningful associations. The nonsense syllables had the form consonant-vowel-consonant (e.g., *zeb, baf, lub*).

Ebbinghaus introduced other methodological innovations: He invented a criterion for learning, using one or two recitations of a specific list without error as the criterion. He thought of different ways of achieving experimental control in his research. He sought to keep learning and testing conditions constant and would conduct no experiments when there were disruptions of his daily routine. Of course, Ebbinghaus was concerned that he was the only subject and was cautious about generalizing results to other people. Whenever possible, he would replicate an experiment across different research periods separated by four years.

The Savings Method and the Forgetting Curve

Ebbinghaus's forgetting curve is among the most frequently cited research findings in psychology. He determined the forgetting curve through the savings method. He learned the same list of syllables at two different times separated by differing time intervals. Next, he measured the time required for each learning and expressed the savings in terms of the ratio *OL–NL/OL*, where *OL* is original learning and *NL* is new learning. Ebbinghaus used seven retention intervals: 19 minutes, 1 hour, 8.8 hours, 24 hours, 48 hours, 6 days, and 31 days. On each trial, he learned eight lists of 13 syllables each. Ebbinghaus required 952 seconds, on average, to learn the lists the first time. After 19 minutes, he took 452 seconds to relearn a list. This yields saving of $(952 – 452)/952 = 57.7\%$ for the 19-minute retention interval. The forgetting curve in Figure 2.1 consists of the savings measures for each of the seven retention intervals.

The savings measure is a sensitive measure of retention; it detects learning even when explicit recall or recognition measures yield zero retention (Nelson, 1985; Slamecka, 1985). In a recall test, the person reproduces the items memorized during the study phase. Retention is usually measured by the probability of items recalled correctly. The savings measure, however, is based on the time it takes a person to relearn some information. The savings method continued to be

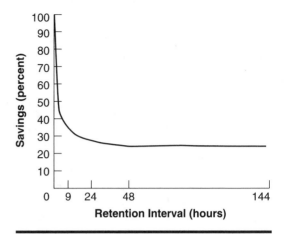

FIGURE 2.1   Ebbinghaus's (1905) forgetting curve. Forgetting is expressed in terms of savings on relearning relative to original learning.

popular for years after Ebbinghaus introduced it. A good illustration of its use is Burtt's research with memory for stanzas from the classical Greek, described in Figure 2.2.

Additional Highlights of Ebbinghaus's Research

Ebbinghaus's wide-ranging interest in human memory led him to study many other memory phenomena. The following list includes some highlights:

— Ebbinghaus (1885) investigated what is now known as the *digit span* and what he later called immediate memory (Ebbinghaus, 1905). He determined that the number of syllables remembered after one reading without error is seven (p. 64). *Immediate memory* refers to the reproduction of associations immediately after learning them.

— Ebbinghaus studied *list-length effects* by measuring the number of trials needed to achieve a criterion of one error-free recitation. He found that only one repetition was required for a list of seven syllables, the digit span. Increasing the list

FIGURE 2.2   It's Greek to me! This dramatic case of savings was observed by Burtt (1941).

Burtt (1941) read daily a passage from Sophocles' *Oedipus Tyrannus* in the original Greek to a boy beginning shortly after his first birthday. Each section consisted of approximately 240 syllables of verse. Each of 12 selections was repeated about 90 times over a span of three years. The boy relearned some of the old passages when he was 8, 14, and 18 years old, respectively. He also was given new control passages to recite. Burtt found that at ages 8 and 14, the boy required significantly fewer trials to learn selections that had been read to him years ago than the new selections. At age 18, the advantage of prior learning was gone; either the trace of the earlier learning was no longer accessible or, after so much learning, the student had simply become so proficient at reciting Sophocles that it made no difference whether the selection was new or old. The interesting point is that at ages 8 and 14, savings was observed for what were initially nonsense materials.

length beyond seven produced a rapid rise in the number of repetitions required. Thus, for a list of two dozen items, as many as 45 repetitions were needed. Thereafter, the function flattens somewhat, so that relatively fewer repetitions are required for the same increments in list length, suggesting that after this point, proportionally less learning time is required for each added item (Slamecka, 1985).

Discussing list-length effects, Ebbinghaus (1905) anticipated the concept of *chunking* (Miller, 1956; Simon, 1974). He recognized that the degree of effort is similar for the learning of lists of equal length that consisted of such different materials as letters, syllables, or words. In every case, the learner seeks to facilitate memorization by forming groups of individual items. Half a century later, Miller (1956) introduced the notion of *7 ± 2 chunks* to indicate the capacity of immediate memory. Seven nonsense syllables was, of course, the limit of immediate memory that Ebbinghaus had established.

— Ebbinghaus invented the nonsense syllable. For reasons of experimental control, however, he did research on *meaningful materials,* as well. He determined that the advantage of meaning over nonsense materials was huge: Ebbinghaus required 10 times longer to learn a list of 80 nonsense syllables than an equally long poem by Byron. He attributed the advantages of the poem to the same reasons researchers cite today: semantics, syntax, and rhyme inherent in language.

— Ebbinghaus found that *distributed practice* is better for retention than massed practice. He cited Jost's law: Given two associations of equal strength but of different ages, a repetition will benefit the older association more than the younger one (Jost, 1897). The issue of distributed practice became a major concern for memory researchers (Chapter 4).

— Ebbinghaus (1905) distinguished between *two types of reproduction*—one type requires the intervention of consciousness; the other, known as spontaneous recollection, can be triggered unconsciously (p. 687). Both types of reproduction are based on associations, even when we are not aware of them. Here is an example Ebbinghaus gave: If you see a wine glass, you may think about its uses, its fragility, its price, or that it was blown by a glassblower. Ebbinghaus himself happened to think of the latter, simply because he once saw a pair of eyeglasses that had been manufactured by a glassblower. The thought of the eyeglasses was an intermediate association that made Ebbinghaus think of the manufacturing of the drinking glass.

— His two psychology textbooks (Ebbinghaus, 1905, 1913) include a review of memory research done since 1885. The review encompasses topics that continue to be investigated over a century later. Among them are the acquisition of habits, now known as *procedural skills*. In the two textbooks, Ebbinghaus reviewed other topics, as well, several of which are once again the focus of research, including individual differences, memory development, the role of memory in eyewitness testimony, memory illusions, and educational implications of memory research.

Ebbinghaus: A Retrospective and an Evaluation

Ebbinghaus remains the most frequently cited memory researcher to this day. In 1985, the community of memory researchers celebrated the centenary of Ebbinghaus's (1885) memory book in various conferences, books, and a special issue of the *Journal of Experimental Psychology: Learning, Memory, and Cognition.* The views of Ebbinghaus's contribution differed according to the reviewers' own research interests. Those interested in list learning, such as Norman Slamecka, praised his work, whereas investigators of memory for meaningful materials, such as Walter Kintsch, criticized him.

Kintsch faulted Ebbinghaus for his "austere associationism" and for inspiring trends that were "pernicious" (Kintsch, 1985, p. 461). Kintsch explained, "What a terrible struggle our field has had just to overcome the nonsense syllable! Decades to discover the 'meaningfulness' of nonsense syllables, and decades more to finally turn away from the seductions of this chimera. Instead of the simplification that Ebbinghaus had hoped for, the nonsense syllable, for generations of researchers, merely screened the central problems of memory from inspection with the methods that Ebbinghaus had bequeathed us" (p. 461). In Kintsch's view, Ebbinghaus's restriction to investigating only the functional relations between learning and retention was the gravest problem. Rather than seeking to illuminate the mental processes that underlie memory, Ebbinghaus limited himself to measure the effects of patterns of practice on recall (see also Bartlett, 1932, pp. 4–7). Although he did investigate memory for meaningful mate-

rials, he failed to distinguish between memory representations of nonsense syllables and meaningful materials (Bartlett, 1932; Eysenck, 1986).

Reviewers such as Murdock (1985), Nelson (1985), and Slamecka (1985), who have continued Ebbinghaus's work on list learning, however, view him very favorably. Slamecka (1985) described Ebbinghaus's lasting influence on psychology as follows: "In this day of fast fads and hot topics, where yesterday's model is made obsolete by today's latest entry . . . Ebbinghaus' contribution, by contrast, stands like a rock of granite" (p. 433). Slamecka believes that Ebbinghaus would have welcomed the changes in the past 100 years—that is, the use of meaningful materials (including words, sentences, and prose) and further development in the accuracy of the chronometric method. Wertheimer (1986) wrote in a similar vein when he said that "it is a testament to his genius, his originality, and his thoroughness that his structure of the known facts of rote memory still stands today, largely unchanged; he invented most of the methods, and discovered most of the phenomena" (p. 35).

For all of his erudition, there were important topics in the area of memory investigated in Ebbinghaus's day that he chose not to treat in depth, if at all, such as the following:

— Although Ebbinghaus firmly believed that memory was grounded in the brain, he did not seek to investigate those relations. In his book on memory, Ebbinghaus (1885) was reserved on implementing the physiological approach to memory, making only rare references to what he called "physiological" hypotheses. For example, in the context of trace theory, he referred to the potential role of ganglion cells (p. 87), and in the context of remote associations, Ebbinghaus noted that those associations will be more fully understood within a physiological framework.

— Focusing on memory in normal individuals, Ebbinghaus neither reviewed nor examined the memory impairments described by his contemporaries, Ribot (1839–1916) and Korsakoff (1853–1900). Broca's and Wernicke's discoveries on language aphasia are mentioned in Ebbinghaus's (1913, p. 728) chapter on language, but they are not linked to memory. Ebbinghaus cited Ribot's works on the psychology of personality but not his study on the diseases of memory. Ebbinghaus's choice to emphasize memory in normal individuals established a tradition in memory research that has been adhered to by mainstream researchers of memory to this day. On the one hand, there are good reasons for this separation. Science proceeds through specialization, and memory research is no exception, as each domain of memory research has its own questions, methodologies, and complexities. On the other hand, memory researchers have paid a price for the separation by overlooking opportunities and synergies (Squire, 1987; Schacter & Tulving, 1994a).

— Ebbinghaus failed to work on what are today the most interesting issues of memory: the mental processes that support memory (Anderson, 1985; Bartlett, 1932; Kintsch, 1985). He did not develop the notion of association and of memory itself beyond the proposals of associationist philosophers. Like the philosophers before him, Ebbinghaus viewed associations as unidimensional entities, as items linked by mere contiguity. However, the concept of association is more complex than Ebbinghaus had foreseen. The study of semantic memory led to the discovery that associations are hierarchically structured; for example, instances of a category are linked via subset associations to their superordinate terms (*A canary is a bird*; see Chapter 4).

It is likely that Ebbinghaus was aware that there are different expressions of memory, perhaps even of different memory systems. Introducing the topic of memory in the first chapter of his volume, he distinguished between intentional reproduction, unwitting recall, and mnemonic aftereffects. Today, we would call the former explicit memory and the two latter implicit memory. *Explicit memory* refers to the conscious recall of information; *implicit memory* refers to the role of memory in the processing of items presented repeatedly. Although Ebbinghaus made these distinctions, he treated memory as unitary: In his research, he used the same type of stimulus materials, typically nonsense syllables, and he largely used the same method, the savings method.

— Ebbinghaus focused on what he considered as memory in its pure form without much concern for applications. His contemporaries and successors, however, wanted to understand memory in its uses (Bartlett, 1932; Binet & Henri, 1894). Binet and Henri emphasized the retention of textual materials by schoolchildren. Bartlett expressly studied the role of affect and attitudes in learning and memory. He did so because real-life memories are subject to emotions and the latter are therefore part and parcel of memory itself.

These limitations notwithstanding, it was Ebbinghaus who launched the psychology of memory as a fundamental research discipline. It was he who posed the important questions, invented the methods, and established the high standards of experimental control that have served memory researchers for over a century.

Associationism: Ebbinghaus's Legacy

Ebbinghaus and his followers—including Hull, Irwin, McGeoch, Martin, Osgood, Postman, and Underwood—all adhered to the associationist tradition. McGeoch (1942), who was an influential theorist in the associationistic tradition, defined *stimulus-response associations* as follows: "Two or more psychological events (are) associated when, as a function of prior experience, one elicits or stands for the other" (p. 25). Therefore, it was not surprising that he favored the paired-associate method as the learning paradigm. During the study phase, the learner was presented with a stimulus term, *A*, and a response term, *B*. During testing, the learner was prompted with *A* and asked to respond with *B*. It was presumably the *A-B* association that supported the memory of the *B* response. Stimulus materials were drawn from a wide variety of sources, and the nonsense syllables continued to be popular. Figure 2.3 provides an example.

Remaining faithful to Ebbinghaus, memory researchers emphasized the functional relations governing retention, not mental structures and processes. Researchers examined the relation between time and retention, and they graphed forgetting curves for all kinds of materials; their main interest was to document the course of forgetting and to understand its causes. To some extent, they also studied acquisition and, like animal learning researchers, they believed that the strength of the stimulus-response connection grew gradually as a function of the number of pairings.

Forgetting was understood as interference between memory traces of shared associations—for example, between *A-B* and *A-C* pairs learned in succession. Interference causes either unlearning or blocking of associations. Two types of interference were distinguished: retroactive and proactive interference. *Retroactive interference* refers to the interfering effects of later traces on traces laid down earlier, whereas *proactive interference* refers to the effects of earlier traces on later traces (Chapter 4).

FIGURE 2.3 Paired associates formed from nonsense syllables.

xej-fon
tel-cum
cij-dul
hod-bof
bip-qes

Association theory has undergone change since McGeoch's days; his basic view still stands, however: Two events are associated when, as a function of prior experience, one comes to elicit the other. What has changed is the definition of the events that participate in an association—that is, the interpretation of the concept *association* itself and the view of prior experience. For the early associationists, events were relatively simple stimuli and responses, such as nonsense syllables. During the 1960s, events came to be seen as complex configurations of component stimuli. It was acknowledged that (1) stimuli do not exist in isolation but are part of a context that includes other list items and the experimental environment and (2) each presumably simple stimulus may be considered as a compound of elemental features. A typical nonsense syllable—for example, *xcl*—has visual, phonetic, semantic, and other features. The *visual features* of *xcl* refer simply to the pattern of printed lines formed by *x*, *c*, and *l*. Because of its *phonetic features*, you can pronounce *xcl* producing a sound similar to *excl.* This sound may remind you of the word *excel,* thus illustrating a *semantic feature* of *xcl*. The syllable also includes s*erial order information*—namely, *x* in position 1, *c* in position 2, and *l* in position 3.

Traditionally, associations were simply regarded as a link between two events without further specification of the link. However, research by linguists, computer scientists, and cognitive psychologists with meaningful stimuli, including words and sentences, led to a specification of different types of associations defined by propositional relations. The latter refer to the functional role of concepts as they are governed by the predicate—usually the verb—of a sentence. Sentences typically include an actor and an object, with other roles being optional. For example, the sentence *Caesar attacked the Gauls* includes *Caesar* as agent and *the Gauls* as object. Each of these roles may be considered as an association that expresses a propositional relation (Anderson & Bower, 1973; Kintsch & van Dijk, 1978; Chapter 4).

Given all these changes, associationism remains alive. It survives in a number of information-processing models and in the connectionist approach (Chapter 7). The semantic representations of concepts and their relations are part of many cognitive theories. Connectionist theories are based on connections—associations—between very simple processing elements. It is the pattern of many such associations that constitutes knowledge, according to the connectionist approach. The retrieval models of memory that emerged in the 1980s are associationist, as well (Chapter 4).

Alfred Binet (1857–1911)

Born in Nice, France, Alfred Binet went to medical school, as did other pioneers of psychology, including Fechner, Freud, Helmholtz, Pavlov, and Wundt. Binet is best known for the development of the Binet-Simon scales of intelligence. At the turn of the century, he was asked by the French Minister of Education to help improve the training of children who were mentally retarded. The public remembers Binet for his work on intelligence tests, but his interests extended beyond intelligence measurements and included the experimental study of memory.

Binet and Victor Henri published research on prose memory (Henri & Binet, 1894; Thieman & Brewer, 1978). Their interest in memory was first and foremost motivated by an interest in teaching and learning in the school system. The first sentence of their paper reflects their interest in memory applications; they wrote as follows: "Verbal memory is of special interest to educators because, for better or worse, it is the principal foundation of instruction and includes all forms of language, spoken or written" (1894, p. 1).

Highlights of Binet's Research

Because Binet was interested in classroom learning, he used materials similar to those used in the classroom: words, sentences, and passages. Experimenters, typically the students' teachers, read several lists of these items to the children. Retention was tested through a free-recall test at two intervals—immediately after each list or passage and after all lists (or passages) had been presented. Subjects recalled the information in writing. The retention interval between immediate and delayed recall was five to six minutes. After the completion of the experiment, the subjects were asked to report their impressions and describe their recall strategies.

Several important discoveries were made by Binet and subsequently confirmed by others. He observed the list-length effect, the serial position effect for word lists, and the importance effect in sentence and passage recall. As for list-length effects, children aged 7 to 13 years recalled 4.6 words of 7 words; adults recalled 5.7 of 7 words. As list length increased from 5 to 9 words, the absolute level of recall increased from 4.3 to 5.6, but not in proportion with list length. Delayed recall reduced the number of words retained in memory to about half of the words recalled immediately.

Binet and Henri observed the serial position effect that was to occupy memory researchers for the next century (see Figure 1.1). The *serial position effect* refers to the finding that, independent of list length, first and final words of a list tend to be better recalled than intermediate words. Binet and Henri's account for the serial position effect is very similar to that advanced by information-processing psychologists 70 years later (e.g., Glanzer & Cunitz 1966). They explained the effect as follows: "The first word has the advantage of novelty and attracts attention, while subsequent words appear boring. The final word, however, has an advantage too because it remains in memory like an echo without being obscured by the sound of any following words"

(p. 13). Information-processing theorists attributed the primacy effect to increased rehearsal and therefore better transfer to long-term memory, and the recency effect to the most recent items still remaining in short-term memory (Chapter 6).

Binet and Henri were not content with a quantitative analysis. They also examined the types of errors made by learners. Among other findings, they discovered that errors in immediate recall tended to be based on acoustic confusions (e.g., *mystique* instead of *mutisme*), whereas delayed recall errors tended to be semantic confusions (*voiture* instead of *carosse*, or *fourmi* instead of *insect*). This result anticipated findings in the 1960s of acoustic confusions in short-term memory and semantic confusions in long-term memory (Kintsch & Buschke, 1969).

Using the expression *awakening of memories* (French *mode d'éveil des souvenirs*), Binet and Henri (1894) were intrigued with the retrieval of memories, more so than Ebbinghaus was. They suggested three means of achieving retrieval of a target word (p. 22):

1. The word persists through an internal voice.
2. The word is recalled because it is analogous to another word on the list.
3. The word is recalled because it is contiguous with another word on the list.

Retrieval of words may sometimes also occur when one has only a very vague idea of what the words were. Binet and Henri were fully aware that learners were not passive listeners but active problem solvers as they tried to retain the lists of words. Students did everything they could to facilitate retrieval; one successful way of doing this was to construct an image or a story to link the isolated words.

Binet and Henri's Research on Prose Memory

In their experiments on prose memory, Binet and Henri presented sentences and passages to 500 schoolchildren in Paris. Passages of different length were read to the children. The students were asked to listen to the stories for the purpose of having to recall them. Binet and Henri wrote wistfully that the experiment took only half an hour for the students but that the researchers' "own much longer work began only then; . . . reviewing the recall protocols, counting the errors" and doing the analyses. Anyone who has done work on text memory will appreciate this sentiment (see Bovair & Kieras, 1985, for a modern approach to the analysis of protocols from prose memory experiments).

The findings of Binet and Henri on prose memory anticipate discoveries made decades later. Binet found that the number of words retained from passages was greater than that retained from lists of isolated words (see Ebbinghaus, 1885). Binet attributed the better text memory to the closer association among the ideas in the passage, as compared to the jumble of unrelated meanings of lists of words. Today, theorists say that the representation of a passage is coherent, whereas individual words have their own disconnected representation and are therefore more difficult to store and to retrieve.

Binet and Henri also discovered the importance effect: Phrases essential to the meaning of a passage were better recalled than the remaining phrases. They provided a good definition of importance of idea units in sentences. An *important phrase* is a segment that cannot be omitted; otherwise, the passage would lose its meaning. *Less important idea units* merely embellish the text and can easily be left out without loss of meaning. The important phrases are the segments that are best recalled, both in immediate recall and three weeks later.

Speculations about the relation between encoding and retaining important text segments were voiced by Binet and Henri. They suggested that the better recall of important text units reflects the greater attention that listeners devote to them as they hear the passage. Attention is not uniform but rises and falls, depending on the information in the text. This hypothesis has surfaced 70 years later but still awaits experimental testing (e.g., Carpenter & Just, 1989).

Binet and Henri discovered the primacy of memory for meaning over memory for wording that was replicated by contemporary researchers: Listeners tended to recall passages in terms of their meaning rather than their choice of words. Listeners used synonyms for many of the words and phrases, and, as the retention interval increased, so did the use of synonyms. Interestingly, the synonyms were frequently less complex words than presented in the original. Anticipating Bartlett's (1932) results on constructive recall, Binet and Henri (1894) found that the students assimilated the passage text and its expressions to their own background and that they simplified the passages not only lexically but also syntactically.

Research on memory for meaningful materials was introduced by Binet and Henri. Except for Bartlett's (1932) work, this line of research was not resumed until the 1970s, with Anderson and Bower's (1973) sentence-recognition studies, Kintsch's research on text recall (Kintsch et al., 1975), and Mandler and Johnson's (1977) work on story structure and recall. Research on memory for meaningful information has since become an equal partner with research on list learning.

Richard Semon (1859–1918)

Although not as well known as Ebbinghaus and Binet, Richard Semon made important conceptual contributions to the psychology of memory. He emphasized the retrieval of memories within his three-stage framework of encoding, storage, and retrieval processes. Semon (1921) called his book *The Mneme* for the Greek goddess of memory. Her name survives in the term *mnemonic techniques*, which are strategies to memorize information. Semon examined memory from an interdisciplinary point of view, considering biological, linguistic, as well as applied factors (Schacter, 1996). He viewed memory as a property of the organism or, to use his terms, an "irritable organic substance."

Semon's Three Memory Stages: Engraphy, Engram, and Ecphory

Semon coined the term *engraphy* for the processes of laying down (encoding) of impressions. The term *engram* refers to the storage of the memory trace in the brain. *Ecphory* refers to revival or retrieval of the trace from memory. Lashley used the term *engram* in his important article "In Search of the Engram" (Lashley, 1950). Semon's theory of ecphory, although overlooked at the time, turned out to be important half a century later, when Tulving (e.g, Tulving & Psotka, 1971) revived interest in retrieval processes. Semon held that the engram, the memory trace, was merely a potential memory. For the trace to become a full-fledged memory, it was necessary to "awaken" it. He believed that environmental events, now known as *cues*, were capable of triggering the engram into consciousness.

In his chapter called "Ecphory of the Engram: The Two Principal Mnemic Laws," Semon anticipated the encoding specificity principle formulated by Tulving (1974). Semon defined *ecphory of an engram* as the transformation of the "engram from a latent to a manifest state" (1921, p. 138). He fully understood that the reactivation of the engram into a manifest state was a result of the repeated occurrence of the environmental conditions that existed during encoding. In his words, "The ecphoric factor . . . consists of the partial or entire repetition of that energetic condition which formerly acted engraphically" (p. 138).

Semon, however prescient, was not an experimenter; it remained for Tulving and his colleagues to provide the experimental support for Semon's ecphoric hypothesis. The evidence that Semon did provide in support of the ecphoric principle was anecdotal; it was an illustration of state-dependent memory. Citing Ribot, Semon described the case of an alcoholic, who, having formed a memory in an intoxicated state, could recall it only when in that state, but not when he was sober. An engram will become independent of its encoding context only when it is deeply fixed and frequently retrieved in a variety of contexts (see Chapter 4). It was the achievement of Tulving and his colleagues to undergird the encoding specificity principle experimentally. In many studies, these researchers demonstrated that the extent to which a memory is activated depends on the reinstatement of the conditions that prevailed when they were formed.

Sir Frederic Bartlett (1886–1969)

Beginning with Ebbinghaus, the association theorists were interested in reproductive and verbatim memory and in retention of individual items. Sir Frederic Bartlett (1932) viewed memory and the role of the learner very differently. According to Bartlett's constructive approach, the learner does not reproduce information but reconstructs it in remembering, by drawing both on the target information and on background knowledge. In story recall, listeners assimilate the content of the story to their prior knowledge and reconstruct the content when asked to tell the story. Bartlett's approach was well ahead of his time; because of the gap between his constructive approach and the association approach, his influence on memory research remained limited until the 1970s, when researchers sought an alternative to list learning and the interference paradigm (Bransford & Johnson, 1973; Loftus & Palmer, 1974; Neisser, 1967; Thieman & Brewer, 1978).

Most of Bartlett's life was spent at Cambridge University. He started to work in 1914 at the newly founded Cambridge Psychological Laboratory, and became its director in 1922 and its first professor of experimental psychology in 1931. He established the Applied Psychology Unit of the Medical Research Council and the Department of Experimental Psychology at Cambridge University—two institutions that later became the home of such distinguished psychologists as Baddeley, Broadbent, Morton, and Zangwill. Bartlett retired in 1952 but remained professionally active close to his death.

Bartlett's approach to memory differed from Ebbinghaus's, both in substance and in style. Bartlett was unabashed about his interest in theory and in mental processes. Rather than confining himself to nonsense syllables as stimulus materials and a single subject, Bartlett used a wide range of stimuli, including drawings, poems, and stories. He also had a diverse set of experiment participants, from British college students to Swazi tribesmen. Rather than banishing the influence of attitudes, moods, and temperament, Bartlett sought to keep them fully alive in his research because they form a part of real life. He viewed remembering as part of a person's interaction with the world; therefore, perception, imaging, and social processes must be part of the study of memory. Nevertheless, Bartlett, like Ebbinghaus, was firmly committed to the experiment as the vehicle to advance knowledge of memory and its processes. However, unlike Ebbinghaus, he described his results qualitatively, avoiding quantitative description and analysis.

Remembering Stories

Bartlett introduced the method of repeated reproductions to assess remembering. He selected stories of unfamiliar structure and content (e.g., a story about a war among ghosts) in order to study the effects of attitudes on memory. Volunteers listened to the stories, with the first reproduction occurring after 15 minutes followed by additional reproductions after intervals of increasing length up to 10 years.

Bartlett found that listeners recalled the stories as more coherent and plausible than they actually were. For example, references to the mystical and supernatural were resolved and adapted to conventional story norms. Subjects shortened the stories by omitting details and used more familiar expressions than the original; they constructed a scenario using elements from the original passage as well as from other sources. As the retention interval increased, so did the tendency to construct rather than to reproduce the passage.

Bartlett found that the constructive tendency he observed in story recall was at work as well in remembering visual patterns. He was therefore persuaded that construction rather than veridical recall was a fundamental property of human remembering.

Remembering Visual Information

Bartlett used the method of picture writing, among others, to study visual memory. Picture writing involved studying visual symbols together with their verbal labels and redrawing the picture in response to the label. Bartlett likened the process of picture writing to the acquisition of a symbolic writing system. He used 80 visual symbols with corresponding labels from an ethnography book. The set of symbols included direct representations of objects (e.g., an ear, a house, or a person) and abstract renditions of objects or concepts (e.g., an inn, people, and mischief) (see Figure 2.4). Symbols were drawn one per card along with the associated word. In train-ing, subjects received the deck of all cards at once; in testing, people were given the words and asked to redraw the sign.

Subjects memorized the symbols by first sorting the cards into groups such as items belonging to a man, belonging to a house, or having some other common reference. Not surprisingly, subjects acquired the direct symbols more quickly than the abstract symbols. In testing, subjects recalled best those signs that they had classified according to some principle during training. They tended to omit signs not grouped with others during the learning period. Grouping signs helped retention in many instances, but it also led to confusions, so that subjects would mix features of symbols placed into the same group. Subjects tended to simplify drawings that were familiar to them. For example, they omitted the brows from the eye. On the other hand, there were also elaborations, specifically of odd and novel detail. Redrawings were almost never veridical; rather, the constructive nature of memory was evident in almost every reproduction.

Bartlett's Theory of Memory: Construction and the Schema

Based on his findings, Bartlett rejected the notion of veridical memory traces assumed by Ebbinghaus and his followers. Whether recalling stories or pictures, subjects tended to make the stimuli more conventional and to adapt them to familiar information. People's reproductions reflect the active and constructive nature of the human mind. What accounts for the constructive

For Ear   For House   For People   For Mischief

FIGURE 2.4   Types of stimuli used by Bartlett (1932) in his picture writing study.

nature of memory and where do people's creative solutions come from? The short answer is: They come from the person's experience and knowledge.

Bartlett's view of knowledge structures was influenced by a theory developed by the English physiologist Sir Henry Head, whose research dealt with motor functions and memory for postures and motor movements. Head assumed that motor responses are grouped in terms of schemas. Bartlett used Head's term *schema* to understand the results from his own memory experiments. In Bartlett's language, a schema is an organized pattern generated by past responses and experiences of the individual. Bartlett illustrated the schema notion with reference to skilled motor movements from tennis and cricket. A particular stroke depends on the combination of perceiving the current state of the game with those perceptions and motor responses that preceded it. As a result of experience, the athlete has many such response patterns or schemas; they are not static—rather, they are adaptable and creative and fit for each new situation.

Contemporary researchers define a *schema* as a configuration of prototypical knowledge a person has of familiar objects and events (see Chapter 4; Rumelhart & Ortony, 1977). For example, people have knowledge of a typical room—it has four walls, a door, a floor, a ceiling, and windows—or a typical birthday party—there are guests singing "Happy Birthday," presents, and a birthday cake. Schemas are flexible and can handle diverse instances of the general pattern. For example, rooms differ in sizes, in functions, in spatial layout, and in the furniture they contain. Birthday parties differ in the age of the celebrant, the location, the number of guests, and the types of presents.

According to Bartlett, a sensory stimulus activates a schema, the organism's accumulated knowledge of the stimulus. The organism interprets the stimulus in light of the schema but the

schema may also be altered by the stimulus. The processing of a stimulus is every time a constructive act; there is no passive re-excitation of lifeless traces (Bartlett, 1932, p. 213). Not only is the schema constructive but it also includes feelings and attitudes. This is reflected in Bartlett's finding that recollection of a story often began with the person's recall of the emotional tone of the passage as exciting or adventurous. Only then were the main events of the story adapted to the person's knowledge recalled.

Evaluation of Bartlett's Contribution

Bartlett's influence was at first muted; he published his work during the ascendancy of behaviorism from the 1930s to 1950s and behaviorists were not well disposed toward such unobservable entities and processes as schemas and construction. As the tide turned toward cognitive processes in the 1960s and 1970s, Bartlett was rediscovered and became very influential in memory research. Neisser's (1967) seminal text *Cognitive Psychology* credited Bartlett's emphasis on construction in seeing, hearing, and remembering as the principal influence on the nascent field of cognitive psychology.

Bartlett's legacy is to have advanced theoretical understanding of memory. His contribution was (1) to emphasize the learner's creative processes in learning and remembering and (2) to view memory in its relation to such other cognitive functions as perception, thinking, and attitude formation. He inspired many studies on the role of schemas in learning and comprehension. Bransford and Johnson (1973), for example, had people read stories that were worded ambiguously and had no title. Thus, in one passage, vague references were made to materials that had to be put into a pile and to an unspecified procedure that had to be repeated over and over again. The story was incomprehensible without a schema to organize the jumbled activities. When subjects were given the title of the story before reading it—Washing Clothes—they recalled more than double the amount of control subjects who had not seen the title. The schema notion was very influential in memory research, whether it was verbal, visual, or motor memory, but it eventually faded because of its own success: The schema notion had become so flexible as to handle every experimental result (Chapter 4; Hintzman, 1993).

As for Bartlett's empirical work, there were researchers such as Bransford and Johnson (1972) who demonstrated constructive effects in memory. However, there were also dissenters, including some of Bartlett's own students in England. In revisiting Bartlett's book *Remembering* on the occasion of delivering the Sir Frederic Bartlett lecture in 1971, Zangwill (1972), for example, argued that far from being constructive, recall was abstractive in the sense of omitting details. Using passages with familiar story content, these researchers found that recall was very accurate. Errors were not due to creative and adaptive distortions but to omissions. This result led Zangwill to the formulation of abstractive recall rather than constructive recall of stories.

Concerning visual memory, Zangwill (1937) demonstrated that, contrary to Bartlett's theory, people tended to remember visual stimuli relatively well, even after a two-week interval. In a visual-recognition study, Zangwill presented drawings of faces to participants, asking them to return to the laboratory after 1, 2, 4, 6, 10, and 18 days in order to redraw the stimuli. At the end of the study, a recognition test was given in which the original target was presented along with people's reproductions and several distractors. The question of interest was whether people would choose the original target or their own recent reproductions of the target. The subjects selected the original target at a rate of almost two to one, thus suggesting that the trace of the original stimulus remained intact even though the reproductions reflected a continuous change during the retention interval (see also Chapter 4; Estes, 1997).

No pioneer can be expected to advance a field on all of its fronts. Bartlett chose to emphasize certain aspects of memory while disregarding others, much like Ebbinghaus. Bartlett, for example, disregarded the relation between memory and the brain. Zangwill (1972) found this omission particularly puzzling because Bartlett was a student of Sir Henry Head's, a physiologist, and was aware of physiological and neuropsychological research, including Head's own research on amnesia. The neuropsychological study of memory remained for Bartlett's successors in England, including Baddeley, Conway, Gathercole, Hitch, Logie, Shallice, Warrington, and Wilson. There were other commonalities between Bartlett and Ebbinghaus, as well. Both regarded memory as a unitary entity (they did not propose multiple memories) and both chose to investigate long-term memory (the retention of information over relatively long intervals). The systematic study of short-term memory still lay in the future. In such studies, researchers investigate subjects' retention in the first few seconds that follow learning. Finally, Bartlett's work on the attitudinal and cultural influences on memory is being discovered by memory researchers (Wyer & Srull, 1989). For Bartlett, these influences were central to gaining a full understanding of memory.

NEUROPSYCHOLOGICAL AND PSYCHODYNAMIC VIEWS OF MEMORY

The turn of the century witnessed a flourishing of advances in the field of memory, not only in experimental and conceptual work but also in clinical and neuropsychological work. Some researchers, such as Ribot and Korsakoff, were expressly concerned with memory; others worked on issues of memory in the context of other pursuits. Anatomists Paul Broca (1824–1880) and Carl Wernicke (1848–1904) worked with patients who had suffered lesions to the left frontal lobes and whose comprehension or speech were impaired as a result. These discoveries encouraged the view that language memories were located in the left hemisphere. Neurologist John Hughlings-Jackson (1835–1911) assumed that cognitive functions resulted from the integrated operation of various brain regions and that more complex functions, such as language, require the involvement of more brain regions. Sigmund Freud developed his psychodynamic theory and in the process laid the foundations on understanding the relation between emotion and memory (Chapter 9).

Here, we consider two of these investigators for review: Ribot and Freud. Research on memory impairments is important for practical and theoretical reasons. It holds the potential of finding treatments to ameliorate the impairment and it may illuminate memory functions in intact individuals.

Theodule Ribot (1839–1916)

Although Theodule Ribot is known for his work on memory impairment (*les maladies de la memoire*), he addressed general aspects of memory, as well. He distinguished the three stages of memory—acquisition, conservation, and reproduction—that are now known as encoding, storage, and retrieval (see also Ebbinghaus, 1905; Semon, 1908). Unlike other researchers who assumed a unitary memory, Ribot distinguished between two major types of memory: organic memory and psychological memory. Among *organic memories,* he included skilled motor movements, as used in manufacturing, games of skill, and bodily exercises (1887, p. 15). We would call these *memory for skills* (or procedural memories). According to Ribot, skill acquisition is, at first, fragile and unorganized. With extended practice, however, skills become firmer, whatever the domain. Ribot held that it is through practice that a skill becomes an organic memory; that is, we exercise the skill without

awareness (p. 63). This view, too, has found an echo among modern memory researchers (e.g., Anderson, 1983a).

Psychological memory is acquired through practice, as is organic memory, except for the fact that people are conscious of psychological memories. According to Ribot (1887), there are any number of recollections in a person's consciousness—images of other people, animals, cities, and facts of all kinds. A person forms a series of these experiences according to the laws of association (p. 42). The most complex, but also the least stable, form of psychological memory is the act of *recollection* (retrieval). Recollections vary in the ease in which they occur; some are easy, others are made with hesitation, and still others are of a dreamlike quality. Ribot made the observation that recollections contract the length of the original experience. For example, a two-hour trip to a castle the previous year was contracted in his recollection to several minutes. In general, recent events occupy a proportionally longer time segment of consciousness than distant events of equal duration.

Ribot made an important and frequently overlooked point about the adaptive nature of forgetting when he wrote that forgetfulness is one of the conditions of memory. He continued, "Without the total obliteration of an immense number of states of consciousness, and the momentary repression of many more, recollection would be impossible. Forgetfulness, except in certain cases, is not a disease of memory, but a condition of health and life" (1887, p. 61). He saw forgetting as an adaptive process that saves us from being overwhelmed by the multitude of past experiences, most of which are unimportant (see also Schacter, 1996).

Memory Systems à la Ribot: Memory Dissociations in Amnesia and Expertise
In addition to the two major types of memory, Ribot postulated "varieties of memory," now called *memory systems* (Schacter & Tulving,

1994a, 1994b). Much like modern psychologists, Ribot used dissociations in performance as support for the different systems. As examples of dissociations, Ribot cited cases of partial amnesia and of domain-specific expertise. A dissociation is observed in partial amnesia patients who lose one set of memories yet retain others. For example, the patients may lose their recollections of words but other memories will remain intact. Other patients may lose their memory for music but retain everything else. As for domain-specific expertise, memories develop differently in different individuals. When a person develops his or her skills and sense modalities to different degrees, the corresponding brain centers are modulated differently, and ultimately different memory systems are induced (pp. 140–141). Contemporary research has documented the facility of experts for a specific domain, such as chess or music, but not for other domains (see Ericsson et al., 1993). Although no one knows for sure, different types of expertise are likely to implicate different brain regions (Posner & Raichle, 1994, p. 238).

Ribot (1887) advocated the idea of local memory centers interacting with one another, believing that the brain is "made up of a certain number of totally differentiated organs, each having a special function to perform, while remaining in the most intimate relations with its fellows" (p. 141). Although one can find language in Ribot's book that suggests a localist bias (pp. 141–142), Ribot was a forerunner of neural network theorists who advocated distributed memories (Chapter 7). Ribot used the same justification for distributed memories advanced today when he noted that an association—for example, for a particular motor act—may become part of many other complexes. "We see that [a] single modification may enter into different combinations, and produce different results" (p. 27). He likened the distributed property of memory to that of letters: Each letter retains its own identity, yet it becomes part of millions of words in many languages. In other words, although the basic number of memory units may be small, the same units are reused and contribute to many different memories.

Rejecting the notion that memory is a passive storehouse of facts, Ribot favored the model of a "contingent of clerks," each charged with a particular function. When one of the clerks ceases to work, others may take up the slack without disturbing the system. Ribot's theory of multiple memories was based on his work on memory impairment. He was fully aware that experimental psychologists did not accept varieties of memory; rather, they favored a single memory system. The two different approaches to memory survive to this day—for example, in the multiple memory approach of Schacter (1996) and the unitary approach of Roediger (1993).

Diseases of Memory

Because cases of memory impairment are rarely clear-cut, Ribot found it difficult to arrive at a taxonomy of the amnesias (see Baddeley, 1990). When Ribot chose to distinguish between temporary amnesia, periodical amnesia, and progressive amnesia, he did so primarily for the convenience of describing the conditions than for any medical or theoretical reasons.

Temporary amnesia occurs and ends suddenly, lasting anywhere from a few minutes to several years. Epileptic seizures tend to be accompanied by brief blackouts during which the patient loses awareness of events, however dramatic. Ribot recounts the case of an epileptic shoemaker who stabbed his father-in-law on his wedding day but had no recollection of these events. Ribot cited other longer-lasting cases of amnesia from the medical literature of his day, including the case of a 24-year-old married woman who became sick and apparently lost her memory and her ability to speak. After two months, the woman "recovered from her torpor," but she had lost almost all of her previous knowledge. "Everything seemed new to her, and she did not recognize a single individual—not even her nearest relatives. . . . In a short time . . . her memory was found to be retentive with respect to everything she saw or heard subsequently to her disorder" (Ribot, 1887, pp. 85–87). The patient also reacquired some of her previous knowledge, including her language ability. She committed initially a few semantic errors, such as substituting the word *juice* for *tea,* or using opposites, such as *white* when she intended to say *black.* Partly as a result of rehabilitation training, she also learned to read again and practice music, as she had before her sickness.

Ribot also described cases of *periodic amnesia,* such as the case of a woman who exhibited two distinct personalities without knowledge of each other, and of *progressive amnesia,* where the disintegration of memory is slow but irreversible. The symptomatology he gave of progressive amnesia sounds much like Alzheimer's disease, whose discovery by the physician Alois Alzheimer was still a quarter of a century away. Reviewing several cases of progressive amnesia as well as of head trauma, Ribot observed that amnesia follows a certain course such that memories acquired last are the first to degenerate. This generalization was later confirmed by other researchers and came to be known as *Ribot's law.* According to Ribot's law, the fate of memories mirrors the "fact in organic life that structures last formed are the first to degenerate" (1887, p. 127, see also Fuster, 1995).

Among memory disorders, Ribot included a variety of other phenomena, two of which are widely investigated today: agnosias and hypermnesia. *Agnosias* are memory impairments that are strictly circumscribed—the inability to recognize certain symbols. The failure to understand the meaning of once familiar words or objects is an example. *Hypermnesia* refers to enhanced memory where "functions that were apparantyl obliterated are revived and vague recollections attain extraordinary intensity" (1887, p. 174). Ribot included hypermnesia

among disorders because he viewed them as an anomaly. The current definition of hypermnesia differs; hypermnesia is an increase in retention performance as a function of repeated test opportunities without feedback (see Erdelyi & Kleinbard, 1978).

Except for the fact that Ribot published no empirical research, his theoretical outlook has a contemporary flavor: He used the three-stage memory framework of encoding, storage, and retrieval; assumed distributed memories; and advocated multiple memory systems, the latter encouraged by his neuropsychological perspective. Each of these are themes found in current treatments of memory (Fuster, 1995; Schacter, 1996; Schacter & Tulving, 1994b).

Sigmund Freud (1856–1939)

Although Sigmund Freud conducted no memory research himself, he is a pioneer of thought on memory; he developed a framework of memory that was to become very influential and inspired numerous empirical studies. Freud developed his views of memory in the course of his work on psychosomatic illness. He sought to get a better understanding of the patients' retention, forgetting, and recovery of mostly painful emotional states. He attributed psychosomatic symptoms to the continued life of memories that, although not accessible to consciousness, were converted into somatic actions.

The Origin of Freud's Views on Memory

Freud and his colleague, Josef Breuer, developed a conversion theory in the course of treating hysteric patients (Erdelyi, 1985). Freud believed that these patients have memories so painful that they banish them from consciousness. Unfortunately for the patient, banishing the memory does not extinguish it; rather, it survives in a different form and becomes manifest as a bodily symptom, whether it is a paralysis, a tick, or a phobia. The term *conversion hysteria* reflects a reminiscence or recovery of a memory in converted and unconscious form.

The case of Anna O. was among the first to lead Breuer and Freud (1955) in the direction of their psychoanalytic theory. Anna O. exhibited a wide range of symptoms that became unbearable and rendered her dysfunctional when she took care of her dying father. The gravest symptoms were that she had an extremely strong aversion to drinking water and that she suffered from a paralysis of her limbs. There were such additional symptoms as hallucinations of threatening animals and skeletons, fear of sounds, retrograde amnesia, and pathological loss of appetite. Breuer tried various approaches in treating these symptoms—suggesting the symptoms away under hypnosis, distracting Anna from her problems by talking about anything that came to mind, and simply listening to her apparently aimless talk. Breuer made the important discovery that there was some relief in Anna's symptoms when she could be made to talk about topics indirectly related to them. For example, once she complained that she had seen a dog drinking water from a glass, which was a horrible sight to her, as she hated both water and dogs. Anna voiced her disgust at length about the dog drinking water; surprisingly, her fear of water vanished on the spot. She suddenly asked for a drink of water and was never afraid of it again. Breuer succeeded in eliminating other symptoms in a similar "talking cure." He adopted the term *catharsis* for this treatment, a word of Greek origin meaning purging of tension that produces mental relief.

Working with additional patients, Freud discovered that success through catharsis was very difficult. He believed that catharsis worked when he managed to have the patient lift the painful memory to his or her consciousness. Breuer and Freud formulated the view that the painful memory was transformed from thoughts into acts, or, in contemporary terms, the memory was recoded from a mental to a somatic representation (Erdelyi, 1985). It was the goal of psychoanalysis to uncover the original source memory and thereby release the pathological energy associated with the unconscious memory. Implicit in Freud's view of memory is that memories are permanent; they do not decay and they are not lost.

Freud's Influence on the Psychology of Memory

Freud's views have had a strong and continuing influence on memory research. His work has inspired researchers to work on hypermnesia (Erdelyi, 1985, 1996), infantile amnesia (Nelson, 1993a), the effects of hypnosis on memory (Erdelyi, 1996), and the free-association method (Fuster, 1995, p. 213). However, his repression hypothesis has had the most far-reaching and long-lasting impact of all.

The repression hypothesis has been influential in several arenas, in psychoanalysis itself, in the debate on recovered versus false memories, and in the research laboratory. Consider the following:

— Psychoanalysis rests on the theory of repressed memories of painful and embarrassing events. The memories nevertheless survive in different form and may lead to maladaptive behaviors. It is the goal of psychoanalysis to uncover the repressed memories as the root cause of the illness.

— In the 1980s and 1990s, a fierce public debate on repressed memories of sexual abuse arose. One side argues that recovery of such repressed memories is possible; this may lead to legal action against the alleged abusers, often decades after the event took place. The critics argue that researchers have no means of assessing the veracity of the recovered information and that many memories are a result of suggestion and thus are false (Chapter 9; Loftus, 1993).

— The repression hypothesis has generated much empirical work and spawned many experiments (Kleinsmith & Kaplan, 1964; Levinger & Clark, 1961; Meltzer, 1930; see review by Zeller, 1950). *Repression* means that episodes associated with negative emotions are so painful that they are pushed into the unconsciousness; they are forgotten. Adapted to an experimental paradigm, such as a recall test, the repression hypothesis would predict that information charged with a negative affect should be remembered less well than neutral information. In some studies, subjects were required to commit items (e.g., odors, sounds, or words) to memory, and were tested for recall or recognition. In other studies, negative experiences were induced, such as having the subjects fail on a certain task. In all of these studies, recall for the negatively charged information was compared to neutral or positive control experiences. The evidence on the repression hypothesis was mixed, with some studies lending support and others calling it into question but on the whole, the repression hypothesis was not supported. The overall evidence was that retention was better for neutral items at short retention intervals in apparent support of the repression hypothesis but better for negative items at longer intervals, thus contradicting the hypothesis (Bradley & Baddeley, 1990).

In any case, the equivocal nature of the empirical results is moot as far as the debate on recovered versus false memories is concerned. For ethical reasons, experimenters cannot duplicate in the laboratory the severity of the emotional experiences suffered by victims of abuse.

▬ The repression hypothesis has been theoretically fruitful and spawned both related and alternative notions of forgetting. Theoretically, repression could result from the lowering of the activity of a target trace, a process known as *inhibition*. Experimental support for the inhibition hypothesis has been reported both in behavioral studies (Chapter 4; Anderson, Bjork et al., 1994) and brain-imaging studies (Schacter, 1996, p. 235). Janet's (1904) dissociation hypothesis is an alternative theory to account for the forgetting of affective information. The dissociation view holds that memory consists of several systems and that negative information is not integrated across different cognitive systems. As a result, the painful memories may no longer be accessible to consciousness but may nevertheless influence performance implicitly (Schacter, 1996).

Freud published no experimental work on memory. Nevertheless, his views had a great impact on research in traditional laboratories. His view provided an alternative to the sparse associationism of the verbal learning tradition laboring in Ebbinghaus's name and his prolific writings provided a rich source for formulating hypotheses on the function of memory (see Chapter 9).

LEARNING AND MEMORY IN ANIMALS

Pioneers such as Pavlov and Thorndike investigated learning in animals because of the similarity in basic functions in all organisms; organisms take in food, they dispose of waste, they respond to stimuli, they move about, and they reproduce. Because of these behavioral similarities, early researchers believed that the basic laws of learning in different species were similar, too. Thorndike expressed this philosophy when he wrote in 1911 that all organisms are "systems of connections subject to change by the law of exercise and effect, and they differ only in the particular connections formed as well as in the efficiency of the connections" (p. 280). Conditioning provided many of the key concepts for interpreting human memory phenomena during the behaviorist period. In particular, interference theory, the major theory of forgetting at the time, drew on concepts from the conditioning paradigm. In this section, we consider the two principal animal learning paradigms—classical and instrumental conditioning—and an application of the animal model to the debate between localist and distributional views of memory.

Paradigms of Animal Learning

Classical Conditioning
Ivan P. Pavlov (1849–1936), a physiologist by training, devoted his life to the study of conditioning. Using dogs as subjects in his research, he investigated the nerves supporting the heart and the stomach. He also became interested in digestive physiology and, in the course of this research, found that secretions in the stomach and pancreas, as well as salivation in the mouth, were involved in digestion. Pavlov observed that dogs salivated before they received food, much like you salivate when you smell food.

When we give meat to a dog, the dog salivates while eating the meat. This is a natural reflex occurring without prior conditioning. Hence, Pavlov chose the term *unconditioned stimulus* (US) for the meat and *unconditioned response* (UR) for the flow of saliva triggered by the meat. Incidental events associated with the meat do not at first produce salivation. However, if the event, say the sounding of a bell, occurs each time the dog is fed, the bell soon comes to elicit salivation. An association is established between the bell and the food; and as a result, the dog salivates when the bell rings. Pavlov called incidental stimuli (e.g., the bell) *conditioned stimuli* (CS); the responses elicited by the conditioned stimuli were called *conditioned responses* (CR).

The arrangement of CS and US in Pavlov's conditioning trials is shown in panel A of Figure 2.5. The panel shows time lines for the CS and the US, respectively. The CS starts well *before* the US; both are turned off at the same time. Panel B shows the cumulative amount of saliva on one of the first conditioning trials; it is a response to the US. In Panel C, however, the CS elicits saliva prior to the presentation of the US. This response is anticipatory; it is therefore a conditioned response. Conditioning is essen-

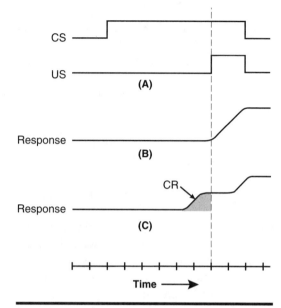

FIGURE 2.5   Classical conditioning in dogs. *(A)* shows temporal pattern of CS and US presentations. *(B)* and *(C)* show cumulative amount of salivation on trials early and late in training, respectively. The shaded region in *(C)* indicates the CR.

tially an adaptive phenomenon; the CR prepares the organism for the US. Thus, the saliva helps to dissolve the food.

Pavlov found that at least 10 trials are required to produce conditioned salivation in dogs. To acquire other responses by classical conditioning, for example—the conditioned eyelid response—may take as many as 100 trials. When it comes to learning events that signal danger, however, fewer trials are sufficient.

Instrumental Conditioning
Psychologists have devised many situations for instrumental learning; the standard is the Skinner box in which hungry rats press a bar or hungry pigeons peck a key for reinforcement. There are also mazes, shuttle-boxes, discrimination chambers, and other types of equipment. In addition to diverse experimental apparatus, different

types of reinforcers are available, positive as well as negative. In all cases, however, the reinforcement, the US, is contingent on the organism's behavior. In each case, instrumental responses become more frequent when they repeatedly produce a reinforcement. This observation led Edward L. Thorndike (1874–1949) to formulate the Law of Effect; which states that the probability of a response increases if it is repeatedly followed by reinforcement.

The experimenter motivates the animal (e.g., restricts access to food) and then shapes the animal's response through successive approximations. Initially during shaping, the animal is reinforced for a wide range of behaviors, including the target response. As the target response becomes more frequent, only the behaviors similar to the target response are reinforced. Finally, only the target response itself is reinforced. You should note that there are constraints on such learning; not every response can be learned by every organism. Bar pressing is relatively easy for rats and dogs, for example, but not for cats. Pulling on a string, however, is easy for cats but not for rats and dogs.

Basic Learning Phenomena: Acquisition, Extinction, and Spontaneous Recovery

Whether classical or instrumental, conditioning usually begins with strengthening the response through repeated reinforcements. This phase is known as the *acquisition phase;* the probability and the amplitude of the response increase. When the schedule is changed so that no reinforcement is given when the organism makes a response, the probability of the response diminishes. In Pavlov's experiment, for example, after the acquisition phase, the experimenter would present the bell-CS without feeding the dog. Initially, the CS would still elicit the CR, but after several trials, it no longer would. This phase of associative learning is called *extinction*. Figure 2.6 shows response patterns in the acquisition and extinction phases of a typical learning exper-

iment. If a rest period intervenes between two phases of extinction training, during which the animal is removed from the experimental apparatus, the CR is made again, an apparent case of spontaneous recovery. As the extinction schedule continues, the CR continues to diminish further, as shown on the right of Figure 2.6.

A discriminative training schedule involves the presentation of two distinct CSs to the organism during acquisition: the CS+, which is reinforced, and the CS–, which is not. The stimuli to be discriminated may be of different modalities (e.g., a light versus a tone) or they may be different stimuli of the same modality (e.g., tones of different pitch or lights of different color). After a period of initial confusion, where the organism tends to respond to both CSs, it will learn eventually to discriminate between them by exhibiting a response to the CS+, but not the CS–.

The learning phenomena that Pavlov and Thorndike had discovered in animal conditioning were adapted by human memory researchers to investigations of forgetting in the paired-associate paradigm. For example, the original learning of associations was viewed as analogous to

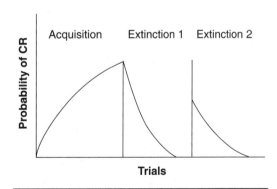

FIGURE 2.6 Acquisition, extinction, and spontaneous recovery of conditioned responses. The abscissa represents trials during acquisition and two extinction schedules separated by a rest period; the ordinate indicates the probability of a CR.

acquisition, and forgetting came to be seen as an analog of extinction. The title of a classical paper on human memory by Briggs (1954), "Acquisition, Extinction, and Recovery Functions in Retroactive Inhibition," illustrates the influence of the animal learning approach.

The Search for the Engram

Animal models were particularly useful to address issues where experimental research on humans was not possible. One of these was the debate between localist and distributional memory theorists. Localist theorists believed in well-defined localization of memory functions in circumscribed regions of the brain. Their views were encouraged by case studies by Broca and Wernicke on language aphasias that suggested localization of language functions in specific sites of the left hemisphere. Distributional theorists thought that memories are distributed over several locations in the brain—indeed, the whole brain. Biopsychologist Karl Lashley (1890–1958) used an innovative research paradigm involving animals to address the localization issue. Using Semon's term *engram* for memory trace, he embarked on the search for the engram (e.g., Lashley, 1950).

Lashley combined the instrumental learning paradigm with the technique of lesioning the brain in order to identify brain sites implicated in memory. In the typical study, animals were trained to make an instrumental response; for example, rats learned to traverse a maze to receive a food reward. When the instrumental escape response was firmly established, the brain was lesioned at diverse locations. After a recovery period, the animals were returned to the maze and required to execute the response. Lashley's results were very surprising to the research community; he could not find the engram (Squire, 1987). He found that rats' performance was affected by the *amount* of the lesion but, surprisingly, it made little difference *where* the lesion

was made (see Chapter 3, Where Are Memories Located?).

CONCLUSION

The localization debate provided but one instance of using animal models in an effort to illuminate issues of human memory. Others include research on consolidation and amnesia (Chapter 3). The animal learning model also provided a conceptual framework for human memory research. To be sure, traditions in animal and human memory research differed to some extent. The basic emphases were different; animal learning researchers focused on the acquisition of responses, whereas human learning researchers emphasized the retention of responses over time. Nevertheless, animal learning theorists and human memory researchers shared the behaviorist approach. Both were interested in the functional relations between stimuli and responses, not in the mental apparatus that mediates between observable events. Both groups of researchers were also associationists, considering themselves stimulus-response psychologists.

The stimulus-response framework remained dominant in human memory research until it was superseded in the 1960s by the information-processing approach. This approach was fueled by the computer metaphor (Feigenbaum, 1963; Newell & Simon, 1972; Quillian, 1968) and best exemplified by Atkinson and Shiffrin's (1968) model of memory (Chapters 1 and 6). The computer provided the impetus for the idea that humans process information in terms of discrete stages, and learning and memory were considered as a kind of computation. Researchers adopted the view that the physical differences between information-processing operations in humans and machines mattered less than the functional similarities of those operations. In part, due to this attitude, little, if any, notice was taken of important advances in biopsychological research and in learning research, whether it involved humans or animals.

The interest in the neural correlates of memory, however, did not become extinct, surfacing again in recent decades. As described in Chapter 3, neuroimaging and electrophysiological techniques, the discovery of neural plasticity, and a better understanding of the functions of different brain regions have strengthened the hand of those scientists who sought to document the relation between brain and memory that eluded Lashley and his generation (Chapter 3). These advances in neuroscience—together with developments in neuropsychology, applied research, and cognitive psychology—have shaped the ecumenical approach to memory characteristic of the field at the beginning of its second century.

CHAPTER 3

MEMORY
AND BRAIN

The anatomy of the brain, identified by Aristotle as the seat of memory, is easy to describe; it is far more difficult to establish the links between brain and memory that scientists have assumed for so long. The brain includes three major divisions, each coming in pairs: the hindbrain, the forebrain, and, at the border between them, the limbic system (see Figure 3.1). The hindbrain includes important brain stem structures and the cerebellum. The brain stem is phylogenetically the most ancient part of the brain. It houses a diffuse system of neurons that modulate fundamental functions of the body, including its heart rate, temperature, and general arousal level. The cerebellum, located posterior to the brain stem, is an important center for the control of motor movement. The thalamus abuts the brain stem; it is the principal relay station and processing center of sensory information on its way from the sensory organs to the cerebral cortex.

The forebrain represents the anterior part of the brain. It consists of the left and right hemispheres that communicate with one another and with subcortical structures via major pathways. The surface of the forebrain is occupied by the cerebral cortex, or simply the cortex. To maximize the area within the limited space of the skull, the cortex is molded in elevations and groves, the gyri and the sulci. Larger sulci form the boundaries between the four cortical lobes—the frontal, temporal, parietal, and occipital lobes. The frontal lobes are thought to be in-

volved in the encoding and retrieval of memories, and in working memory. The other lobes process sensory and motor information and fulfill mental functions ranging from pattern recognition and language comprehension to long-term memory.

The limbic system includes the hippocampus, the amygdala, and the basal ganglia. Each of these structures makes distinctive contributions to memory and other cognitive functions. The hippocampus is critical for the formation of memory of facts, the amygdala is implicated in emotional memories, and the basal ganglia subserve motor memory as well as other sensory and motor functions.

At the cellular level, the brain contains as many as 10^{12} neurons supported by blood vessels and glia cells. The blood vessels carry critical nutrients—including oxygen, glucose, and various neurochemicals—consumed by the brain as it does its job. Any disruption of the brain's blood supply, however brief, has very serious consequences for the affected brain structures. The glia cells serve as housekeeper of the brain; they are the source of important neurochemical agents required for the growth or the removal of neural tissue—for example, following a neurological disease, an accident, or a stroke.

Two factors were instrumental in advancing research on brain and memory: the increasing collaboration among scientists from different disciplines and the development of innovative

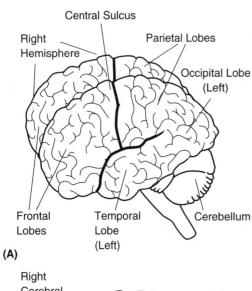

Central Sulcus

Right
Hemisphere

Parietal Lobes

Occipital Lobe
(Left)

Frontal
Lobes

Temporal
Lobe
(Left)

Cerebellum

(A)

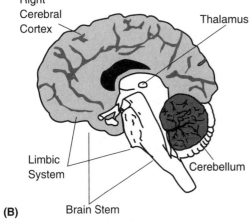

Right
Cerebral
Cortex

Thalamus

Limbic
System

Cerebellum

(B)   Brain Stem

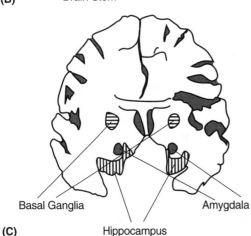

Basal Ganglia

Amygdala

(C)   Hippocampus

methods of observing the brain in action. Today, brain and memory research is an interdisciplinary effort driven by several specialties, including cognitive psychology, neuropsychology, physiology, endocrinology, chemistry, and even genetics. Cognitive psychologists furnish the performance measures of memory in humans and animals. Neuropsychologists study memory impairments in patients and seek to make inferences on the functions of intact memory. Physiologists, endocrinologists, and chemists investigate processes at the cellular level that undergird learning and memory (Bear, Connors, & Paradiso, 1996). Geneticists contribute experimental manipulations that permit a relatively precise isolation of structures implicated in memory with minimal effect on neighboring structures (Stevens, 1996).

Advances in electronics, in computing power, and in imaging technology have given neuroscientists the tools to monitor the time course and the location of neural processes in the brain. These tools—neuroimaging, electrophysiological techniques, and single-cell recordings —are capable of tracking the subtle changes in energy level as different units of the brain communicate. The new technologies, together with the traditional animal and case studies, give scientists an investigatory power not available in the past. Interdisciplinary synergies and methodological advances have fostered theoretical models that capture the discoveries made at all levels of neural structure, from the synaptic level (Kandel, 1991) to the level of global networks

---

FIGURE 3.1   Perspectives of the human brain.
(A) The side view shows the right hemisphere and left hemisphere (in foreground), four lobes, and the cerebellum partially occluded by the cortex.
(B) The sagittal section shows the cerebral cortex surrounding the limbic system, the brain stem, and the cerebellum. *(C)* The coronal section shows the hippocampus (vertical shading), the basal ganglia (horizontal shading), and the amygdala (dark region).

(J. A. Anderson, 1995). With these innovations, there is great ferment in neuroscience, especially in research on the neural bases of memory.

Although no single chapter can review all of the discoveries, we can at least gain a sense of the field as it seeks to uncover the relations between brain and memory. We begin the review with the research methods that have been the catalyst of the great leap in knowledge in this area. Then, we discuss the plasticity of neural structures, the attribute that makes learning and memory possible. Next, we look at the localization debate on whether memories are localized in specific brain sites, a debate that has not gone away in two centuries. Finally, in the two concluding sections, we examine the role of the hippocampus and the frontal lobes, two brain structures that have attracted the attention of neuroscientists.

RESEARCH METHODS IN NEUROSCIENCE

In the past, considerable advances in neuroscience were achieved through animal studies, anatomical studies, clinical case studies, and population studies. In animal studies, experimenters manipulate certain variables, lesion specific neural structures, observe behaviors, and use the results to extrapolate to memory functions in the human. Anatomical studies use staining techniques to trace neural structures and pathways. In case studies, inferences about function and localization are based on correlations between structural injuries and cognitive impairments. In population studies, the performance of people grouped according to certain criteria such as age is compared. Each of these methods is still in use today; however, each has been greatly augmented by the new research methods developed in the past decade and a half.

The new methods probe in areas where no investigation was previously possible; they afford a view on neural activity as it unfolds in real time within seconds and milliseconds of external events. These methods depend on the fact that neural tissue expends physical energy as it fulfills its functions, whether it is detecting stimuli, acquiring facts, retrieving information, or executing a skill. The energy exchange by the neurons manifests itself in characteristic changes of metabolic activity, blood flow patterns, and electrophysiological responses. These manifestations of neural work can be made visible through a variety of techniques, including scans of cerebral blood flow (PET scans), functional magnetic resonance images (fMRIs), event related potentials (ERPs), and single-cell recordings. The new techniques have potential measurement and interpretational problems, as do other methods, but they already have become indispensable in the study of memory and cognitive processes at the neural level (Posner & Raichle, 1994).

Imaging Methods

Brain-imaging methods developed from computed tomography, the CT scan, which combines radiography and computer analysis. When a CT scan is performed, the person's head is placed in a tire-shaped ring containing an x-ray emitter and a detector on opposite sides of the head. X-rays are projected through several planes of the brain; the radiation passing the brain is recorded, the ring is rotated by a few degrees and the procedure is repeated. By recording x-rays of several different planes, the computer constructs a three-dimensional image of specific brain structures. CT scans are useful to analyze static brain structures but they cannot detect brain processes as they occur in real time. The PET and functional MRI procedures permit researchers to investigate brain and mental operations on line.

Positron Emission Tomography
Positron emission tomography, the PET scan, detects changes in blood flow in particular brain regions. Cerebral blood flow is measured by in-

jecting the patient with a nontoxic, slightly radioactive substance, such as glucose or oxygen-15, and then monitoring the progress of the substance as it is absorbed by the blood and transported to the brain. As a specific brain region processes information and executes commands, its metabolic requirements increase relative to a resting condition. The radioactive substances in the blood are picked up by the PET scan and photographed.

Researchers' goal in using the PET scan is to correlate changes in blood-flow patterns in the brain with a specific target activity. However, because the brain executes many other activities in parallel with the targeted activity, researchers make two scans of blood-flow patterns in the brain. The first scan, the load scan, is taken when the person executes a specific mental task—for example, memorizing a list of words, distinguishing between old and new stimuli in a recognition test, or looking at a visual pattern. The second scan, the baseline scan, is taken when the person is at rest or looks at a blank stimulus screen. Finally, the image of the baseline scan is subtracted from the image of the load scan to yield the difference image. The images resulting from each of these steps are illustrated in Figure 3.2A.

Roland, Kawashima, Gulyas, and O'Sullivan (1995) used PET imaging to identify brain sites implicated in visual learning and memory. The study involved a resting condition, a learning condition during which participants studied colored geometrical patterns, and a recognition test. The recognition test involved the presentation of the same patterns people had studied during learning mixed with a set of new patterns. During the learning phase, the researchers found increased PET activity in primary and secondary visual areas, in the anterior hippocampus, and in the prefrontal cortex. In recognition testing, the same areas were activated. This study illustrates the use of imaging in research, but it poses the interpretational problem of whether the meta-bolic activity resulted from perceiving or remembering the stimuli. This is because the stimuli were available to participants for visual inspection during learning and testing.

Memory functions and perceptual operations were separated in a subsequent study in Roland's laboratory (Roland et al., 1995). Subjects memorized the positions of visual targets located on a screen. The targets differed in size, and subjects were instructed to point to them in the order of their size. During the memory phase, the targets were *not* shown on the screen, and subjects had to point to the location they previously occupied. During this phase, PET activity was most pronounced in the visual association areas in the occipital gyri and in parts of the parietal lobes. Roland and colleagues interpreted these activations as reflecting long-term storage and wrote that the subjects "must have kept an internal representation of the target positions in their minds" (p. 786).

Using PET imaging, researchers have begun to identify different brain regions subserving memory and related cognitive functions (Posner & Raichle, 1994; Ungerleider, 1995). Figure 3.2B indicates a sample of brain areas implicated in such memory tasks as recognizing faces, matching faces to a sample, and remembering spatial locations for the short term.

As research by Martin, Haxby, Lalonde, Wiggs, and Ungerleider (1995) illustrates, PET scans enable scientists to get a highly differentiated view of brain regions implicated in memory. Martin and colleagues demonstrated the involvement of different brain regions in the representations of different aspects of the *same* concept. These researchers presented line drawings of common objects (e.g., a pencil) to volunteers and asked them to report either the typical color (yellow) or action (write) of those objects. When subjects recalled the objects' colors, the ventral region in the temporal cortex became active, but when they reported the actions associated with the objects, the middle temporal gyrus

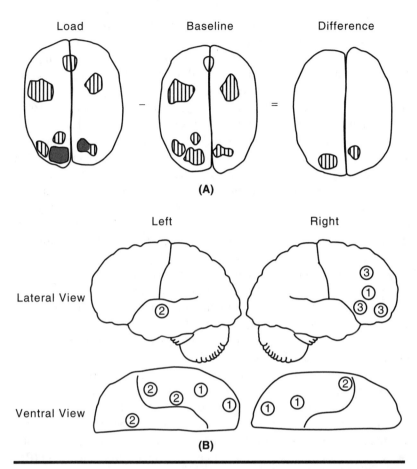

FIGURE 3.2   PET scanning. *(A)* The subtraction paradigm. The image on the left results from a scan when the person looks at a visual pattern (Load condition). The center image is generated when the person looks at a blank stimulus screen (Baseline condition). On the right is the difference between scans obtained in the load and baseline conditions (Posner & Raichle, 1994). *(B)* Selected brain sites of PET activity are shown in different memory tasks (adapted from Ungerleider, 1995). *Top Row:* Lateral views of the two hemispheres. *Bottom Row:* Ventral views of the two hemispheres. Numbers indicate task: (1) face and location matching to sample, (2) face identity, (3) spatial working memory.

became active, a region implicated in the perception of motion (Chapter 1).

However good the localization achieved with PET imaging may be, the temporal resolution of this technique is limited (Ungerleider, 1995). The recording time of PET images extends over minutes, whereas the cognitive phenomena

(e.g., visual recognition) often take less than a second. It is for this reason that cognitive neuroscientists usually employ additional recording techniques to assess both the localization and the time course of mental activities. Better temporal resolution is achieved by magnetic resonance imaging and recording event-related potentials.

Functional MRI

Functional magnetic resonance imaging (fMRI) monitors changes in blood flow of brain regions, as does PET imaging. The technique is based on the properties of oxygen atoms in a magnetic field. The oxygen atoms inside and around blood vessels in the brain change according to the degree of blood flow in the vessel: When a brain region works hard, more blood and, as result, more oxygen are imported. This leads to a transitory surplus of oxygen in the blood vessel that is picked up by fMRI (Raichle, 1994). The fMRI technology has several advantages: It has no known health risks; no external agents are injected into the blood stream; and the spatial precision is better than for PET imaging. However, because fMRI requires magnets stronger than those available at most hospitals, it is not as widely used as PET scans (Posner & Raichle, 1994).

A study by Karni and colleagues (1995) illustrates the use of fMRI in tracking the learning of motor skills at the neural level. Using fMRI patterns, the researchers were able to document a shift of brain structures as a person acquired the type of sequential finger movement used in typing and piano playing. Subjects participated in four weeks of training to execute finger movements with one hand (e.g., tapping the sequence of little finger, index finger, ring finger, middle finger) as fast as possible without looking at the hand.

The area activated by learning the tapping sequence was a region in the primary motor cortex. Initially, the area activated became smaller in successive learning sessions. However, as the training continued for up to four weeks, the fMRI images revealed that a larger area of the motor cortex was engaged. Karni and colleagues believe that these changes in the size of the area indicate distinct phases of skill acquisition (Chapter 5). During the initial phase, learners presumably acquire a response set relevant to the task, whereas in the later phase, the long-term representation of the skill is formed (Karni et al., 1995).

Functional magnetic resonance imaging has also been used to monitor encoding processes and visual memory processes. Using fMRI in an encoding study, Demb and colleagues (1995) find increased activity in the frontal lobes when learners seek to memorize items by connecting them with previous knowledge. Using the fMRI technology in a visual memory task, researchers have uncovered an interesting contrast between prefrontal neurons and neurons in the primary visual areas in the occipital cortex. As the retention interval between stimulus presentation and testing increased, fMRI activity in the visual area diminished while it was sustained in the prefrontal region, thus indicating the involvement of the latter in working memory tasks (see review by Ungerleider, 1995).

Neuroimaging methods allow researchers to investigate dynamic processes as they occur in real time; thus, they present an opportunity of uncovering a range of memory effects that are otherwise not detectable, whether they involve different stages in motor learning (Karni et al., 1995), the distinction between perceptual and memory processes in recognition learning (Roland et al., 1995), or the representation of distinct stimulus attributes in different brain regions (Martin et al., 1995). In subsequent chapters, we will see that neuroimaging methods are widely used throughout memory research, including in research on semantic memory (Chapter 4), explicit and implicit memory (Chapter 5), working memory (Chapter 6), as well as in research on memory illusions (Chapters 9 and 12).

Although the neuroimaging methods have become quite popular, caution must be exercised in interpreting the data acquired. Among the problems is the fact that PET and fMRI signals tend to be slower than many fast-paced mental processes. Another problem is that scans from individual trials tend to be noisy, making it necessary to average images across trials and across different subjects. The latter is potentially problematic because of individual differences in brain sizes and topographies (Churchland & Sejnowski, 1992; Ungerleider, 1995). In response to these and other challenges, scientists tend to combine the neuroimaging tools with other methods in order to achieve converging evidence on the memory effects under investigation.

Event-Related Potentials

Neurons continuously generate electrical impulses as their level of activity changes in the course of transmitting information. The signal of single neurons is weak, but in concert, millions of neurons generate brain waves known as the electroencephalogram (EEG) recorded at the surface of the skull. EEGs are measured by placing electrodes on multiple sites distributed over the skull. An event-related potential (ERP) is a pattern of brain-wave activity time-locked to an external event. ERPs are obtained by averaging EEG patterns recorded over as many as 100 trials (e.g., Kutas & Hillyard, 1980). As a result of averaging, random signals in the EEG are excluded and characteristic peaks and valleys of electrical activity in response to the stimulus emerge.

The peaks are either negative or positive at certain latencies after stimulus onset (e.g, P300, N400), as illustrated in Figure 3.3A. The P300,

found in humans as well as monkeys, is a positive ERP wave with a latency of 300 milliseconds elicited by surprising events. The N400 wave is a negative ERP wave observed in re-

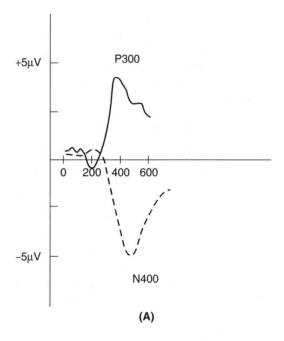

(A)

FIGURE 3.3 Event-related potentials. *(A)* Characteristic voltage peaks of ERPs reflect different polarities (positive or negative) and different latencies (e.g., 300 or 400 milliseconds) after stimulus onset. The P300 wave typically is elicited by surprising auditory stimuli, whereas N400 is frequently observed when the person processes a semantically anomalous sentence. *(B)* Event-related potentials are averaged according to the performance on a subsequent recall test. Solid lines represent ERPs to words that were later recalled, whereas broken lines indicate ERPs to words not recalled (Paller, 1990).

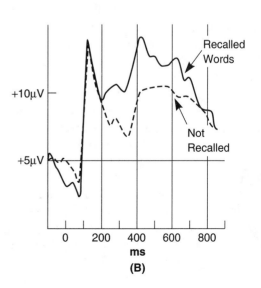

(B)

sponse to certain linguistic stimuli—for example, reading the word *socks* in the semantically anomalous sentence *He spread the warm bread with socks* elicits a N400 wave. The amplitude of N400 is also used as an indicator of the extent of visual and auditory priming, a facilitation in identifying a previously presented stimulus.

Event-related potentials have found wide application in recording the time course of cognitive processes in attention, learning, and memory. Consider three memory effects revealed by ERP patterns: the subsequent memory effect, the old/new effect in recognition testing, and the detection of concealed memories.

The subsequent memory effect was established by recording ERP patterns during the learning phase of recall studies and by analyzing the patterns separately for words subsequently recalled versus words not recalled. It turned out that ERPs during encoding were more positive for words recalled compared to words not recalled (see Figure 3.3B). It appears that learners invest more effort and exercise the brain harder for the words they eventually retained. However, the cognitive mechanisms supporting that effort have not yet been identified (Rugg, 1995).

The old/new effect refers to differences in ERP patterns for old and new items in the continuous recognition paradigm. In this task, new and old words are continuously presented and the subject indicates for each whether it was presented for the first or second time. ERPs revealed differences in processing of old and new items in that old items tended to produce more positive ERPs than new items. Interestingly, the old/new differences were observed even when the subjects were not required to make overt *yes* or *no* responses (Paller, 1990). Participants read words under different encoding conditions. Testing involved item identification; no recognition was required. However, identification was made more difficult by presenting the items too quickly for perfect identification. Although

there was no overt recognition judgment, ERP patterns revealed the same processing differences of old and new items found in the overt recognition tests.

Because of certain complexities in the data, the significance of the old/new effect remains unclear. The pattern of the differences varies for different experimental conditions, for different intervals following the stimulus, for ERP recordings from the two hemispheres, for words differing in familiarity, and for different subject groups (Rugg, 1995). Some researchers attribute the old/new effect to different components of the recognition process, others link it to implicit memory phenomena, and still others speculate that the ERP patterns for old words represent a physiological correlate of the conscious experience of recognizing the words (Paller, Kutas, & McIsaac, 1995).

Because the ERP patterns reflect automatic brain activity not under the control of the person, researchers have begun exploring the use of ERPs as a tool to detect concealed memories, as another "lie detector" so to speak. Bashore and Rapp (1993) showed that people have difficulty concealing the fact that they were familiar with specific target information. The Bashore and Rapp study included three phases: a training phase, a testing phase, and a concealment phase. During the training phase, subjects committed a list of words to memory—which they did easily enough, as indicated by their success in the testing phase. In testing, the subjects were shown old and new words and they had to press a key when they recognized one of the memorized words. In the concealment phase, the learners were shown another list of words that included some of the previously learned ones. However, this time, they were to conceal their knowledge of the memorized items. In other words, they were *not* to press the key when a target word appeared. Subjects succeeded in this overt task. However, their ERP patterns exhibited a P300 wave; whenever a target word was shown, the P300 gave their knowledge away! Because subjects sought to conceal their knowledge, as one does when one feels guilty, this methodology is known as the *Guilty Knowledge Test.*

Convergence of Evidence

The imaging and electrophysiological methods share the goal of monitoring the time course and pinpointing the location of cognitive processes. One would expect, therefore, to be able to tap the same mechanism using both methods in parallel studies. Two studies by Posner and Raichle (1994) illustrate this two-pronged approach. In their first study, the two scientists used the ERP technique to find brain locations implicated in a word association task. They recorded ERP patterns as subjects were making an association to a given word. They found three successive waves of increased ERP activity in the left lateral frontal cortex, the left posterior cortex, and the right insular cortex. As expected, the PET activity recorded from the same brain regions in a companion experiment mirrored the ERP activity recorded in the first study.

The parallel results from the imaging and electrophysiological methods observed in Posner and Raichle's research represent an instance of the convergence of evidence that researchers are looking for when they measure mental processes. Convergence of evidence means that similar results are observed for the same task when different measures of mental activity are recorded. In Posner and Raichle's (1994) research, the two methods complement one another nicely. ERPs offer temporal resolution on the order of milliseconds; however, their spatial resolution is not very good. PET scans offer better spatial resolution, but the temporal resolution leaves much to be desired. Used in tandem, the two methods can pinpoint both the location and the temporal pattern of brain activity. Nevertheless, it is still quite possible that there are important neural processes not detectable by either of these methods. For example, ERP cannot detect

neural activity that is not projected to the scalp or masked by other electrical activity.

Event-related potentials and neuroimaging methods have moved us far along in our understanding of neural processes underlying memory; however, these methods are not designed to identify individual neurons implicated in a memory process, whether it is encoding, maintaining, or retrieving information. The next section shows how researchers have made some forays into this microscopic realm within the context of animal research.

Monitoring Activity at the Cellular Level

Activity at the cellular level is recorded by inserting microelectrodes into specific brain regions of animals (e.g., the inferotemporal cortex, the frontal lobes, or the hippocampus). Consider Fuster and Jervey's (1981) study with macaque monkeys as an illustration. The scientists took extracellular measurements of the discharge of individual neurons in the inferotemporal cortex as the monkeys tried to maintain information over an interval of up to half a minute in the delayed matching-to-sample task.

On each trial of this task, the researchers presented a succession of three displays of translucent buttons. During the initial display, one of the buttons, the target button, was illuminated in a certain color (e.g., red). As the monkey pressed a button, the color was turned off and the monkey faced a set of grey buttons (see Figure 6.5). After a delay of 30 seconds, the buttons were illuminated with different colors, including the target color red. The monkey had to press the same-colored button that was shown in the first display in order to receive a squirt of fruit juice as a reward. After months of training, monkeys achieved a high level of accuracy at this task, making almost no mistakes.

Fuster and Jervey found that certain inferotemporal neurons exhibited two characteristic effects: color sensitivity and temporal specificity. The neurons were responsive only to specific colors (e.g., red or green). "Red" neurons responded when the target button was red, whereas "green" neurons responded when the button was green. The neurons increased their activity only during the 30-second delay between the sample and the test stimulus when the buttons were grey. As soon as the test stimulus occurred and the response was made, the cell's activity returned to its previous baseline. According to Fuster (1995), the cell's activity reflects the activity of working memory, a process to maintain the stimulus representation across the delay (Chapter 6). Fuster further notes that the color specificity of the neurons is less remarkable than the fact that the neurons respond "if, and only if," the stimulus needs to be remembered for the short term.

The involvement of specific inferotemporal cells of the monkey in face recognition was documented in single-unit studies by Desimone and Ungerleider (1989) and Rolls, Baylis, Hasselmo, and Nalwa (1989). The research identified cells that were differentially sensitive to different faces as well as their orientation in the viewing plane. Single-cell recording has been used in species other than mammals, as well. Thus, we owe important discoveries on neuronal plasticity in mollusks to the single-unit recording technique. As the mollusks underwent behavioral habituation, sensitization, and conditioning training, there were concomitant patterns of discharge at the neuronal level (see Plasticity of Neural Structures later in this chapter).

Case and Population Studies

In traditional memory research, differences among people were considered as a distraction, at best. Any such differences were erased by the use of average measures of performance. Researchers began to change their view of individual differences when they discovered that case studies and population studies could serve as an important source of data on memory, especially when used in conjunction with other approaches. Differences came to be viewed as a natural experiment on the cognitive architecture and on memory rather than an error of observation.

Neurological case studies were made possible after autopsies became acceptable to the public in the nineteenth century. Two neurologists, Paul Broca (1824–1880) and Carl Wernicke (1848–1904), correlated results of autopsies with specific cognitive deficits. The two scientists found lesions in specific regions of the left hemisphere of patients who had speech impairments. Based on a large body of subsequent data, researchers attributed specific language skills of production and comprehension to Broca's and Wernicke's areas in the left hemisphere (but see Ojeman, 1991). Using the same rationale, specific memory deficits were correlated with brain structures in case studies. Memory loss in patients with Korsakoff's syndrome was correlated with damage and atrophy in the hippocampus and adjacent structures. More recently, the dysexecutive syndrome, a pattern of disabilities in the control of working memory, has been linked with damage to the frontal lobes. The loss for very specific memories (e.g., faces or certain semantic categories) was correlated with an impairment to circumscribed neural structures (e.g., the temporal lobe and the basal ganglia) (Hillis & Caramazza, 1991).

The most widely cited case study in the memory literature is Milner's (1963) patient H. M. When he was 27 years old, H. M. underwent bilateral sectioning of the temporal lobes, including the hippocampus, in order to ameliorate the effects of severe epileptic seizures. There was an unforeseen side effect of this procedure: Although he could still retrieve memories from his childhood and youth and maintain information for a very brief period of time, H. M. was no longer capable of new learning. His life literally stood still sometime in 1953, the year of his surgery. Years later, H. M. still gave his age as 27; he had not learned his new address, yet he knew the old one perfectly well. He would reread newspapers without noticing that he had read them before, and he did not retain the names of nurses and doctors who cared for him for many years (Hilts, 1995).

Beginning with Milner's report on H. M., the hippocampus became a focus for investigators seeking to uncover the brain processes subserving memory. Also, information-processing theorists used the disability exhibited by H. M. for new learning in support of the two-store model of memory (Atkinson & Shiffrin, 1968).

Case studies typically involve one individual or a contrast between two individual patients (e.g., Hillis & Caramazza, 1991). In population studies, researchers group individuals in terms of certain population criteria and observe the groups' performance on different measures of memory. Population criteria typically include different age groups, patient groups, and professional groups; memory measures include scores on psychometric tests, retention achieved in experiments, or the incidence of memory disabilities.

Consider as an illustration a study on the incidence of Alzheimer's disease as a function of the educational level of 600 senior citizens. At the beginning of the four-year study, all of the individuals were over 60 years old and none was demented (Stern et al., 1994). Within a period of 4 years, about 1 in 6 of the individuals exhibited some symptoms of dementia. The population analysis indicated that individuals affected with dementia tended to be less well educated than those not demented. On average, the former group had only 7.1 years of formal education, whereas the latter group had 10.1 years of education.

Stern and colleagues, fully aware that recording such a difference does not explain it, proceeded to examine a number of reasons to account for their results, including the following:

- A lower level of education causes Alzheimer's.
- There is a test bias in that less educated people are less savvy in taking the tests and thus they fail on items that indicate Alzheimer's disease.
- The greater incidence of Alzheimer's among less educated individuals is stroke related.

The researchers ruled out each of these hypotheses on the basis of careful statistical analyses and suggested a fourth possibility—namely, that education supplies "a reserve that allows an individual to cope longer before Alzheimer's is clinically expressed. This reserve could be an acquired set of skills . . . or could be the result of increased synaptic density in neocortical association cortex acquired on the basis of stimulation" (1994, p. 1009). Whatever the explanation for the finding of Stern's team, their study illustrates the approach of population studies, the kind of data such studies yield, and the inherent interpretational problems.

Because population studies yield correlational data, they cannot isolate the causes of any group differences observed. As for clinical populations, there is the additional problem posed by averaging performance across cases that tend to be unique. Case studies necessarily involve individuals who exhibit unusual performance patterns. Furthermore, in case studies, performance deficits are attributed to damage in a specific brain area. However, it is possible that the damage is not strictly localized and that it extends, unknown to the researcher, to other brain areas, thus making it difficult to trace the cause of the memory deficit. Finally, theorists debate whether it is warranted to draw inferences from processing in a damaged brain to processing in the intact brain (Sejnowski & Churchland, 1989). In spite of these caveats, case and population studies have gained an important place in the neuroscience of memory; they represent, together with other methodologies, an important source of data; and they have added a perspective to memory research otherwise not available.

In general, the greatest promise for illuminating the putative links between brain and memory lies in combining two or more of these research methods. It is now common, for example, to combine classical verbal memory methods with neuroimaging, as in Roland's research (1995), with electrophysiological measurements, as in Rugg's (1995) research, or with both of these methods, as in Posner and Raichle's (1994) studies. Researchers have combined the neuropsychological and experimental approaches by inducing reversible impairments in human participants via drugs that temporarily block memory functions (Polster, 1993). Where tests with humans are not possible for ethical reasons, researchers have used animal models to assess hypotheses. Assuming a correspondence between brain structures in humans and animals, scientists have lesioned neural structures in animals in an effort to infer specific memory functions of the structure under investigation, whether it is the amygdala, the hippocampus, the thalamus, or the frontal cortex.

PLASTICITY IN THE BRAIN

The capacity to learn is a property of the neural systems of all species from mollusks to homo sapiens. It has long been assumed that learning at the neural level is based on associative processes at the synapse, the junction between two neurons. It was Hebb who formulated the learning rule that when two neurons are jointly activated, the associative link between them is strengthened (Hebb, 1949). Hebb imagined a biological growth process at the synapse that increases the efficiency of transmitting signals, but at the time, neuroscience was not equipped to evaluate his hypothesis. After half a century of investigation, a consensus has emerged among neuroscientists that neurons form networks capable of learning and that learning depends on synaptic changes

(Hawkins & Bower, 1989). This section reviews the structure of neurons, communication between neurons, and changes in neural processes that are observed in such learning situations as habituation, conditioning, and long-term potentiation.

Neurons

A neuron is enclosed by a membrane, which includes the cell body (the soma) and projections (axons and dendrites), as shown in Figure 3.4. The soma contains the nucleus and tissue that supports the operation of the cell. The axon is a long extension, similar to a tube, that conducts electrical impulses to the terminal buttons. The terminal buttons send chemically coded information to neighboring neurons across the synapse. On the other side of the synapse, information is received by the cell body and via the dendrites. The dendrites are treelike projections usually shorter than the axons. Neurons communicate with each other, as well as with sensory organs, muscles, and other organs. Sensory neurons are located in sensory receptors. They transduce the physical energy from environmental stimuli into neural activity.

A synapse is the junction between two neurons; here, the membranes of two neurons come into close vicinity, thus facilitating the transmission of neurochemical agents, the neurotransmitters. The structure and function of most human synapses is fairly similar. Most pass information in a one-way manner; usually one neuron sends information and another receives it. The membrane of the sending neuron is called the *presynaptic membrane;* it is opposite the receiving neuron, which is called the *postsynaptic membrane.*

Neurons are communication stations; signals travel within neurons along axons and between neurons across the synapses. Neural transmission is different from electrical messages in a wire; it is based on both electrophysiological and

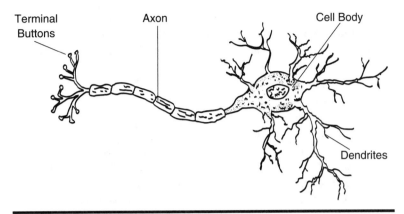

FIGURE 3.4 A neuron includes the cell body and two types of projections: the axons and the dendrites. Terminal buttons are shown at the end of the axon.

neurochemical processes. At the synapses, neural transmission is achieved through neurotransmitters. Neurotransmitters are released from the presynaptic membrane across the synapse to the postsynaptic membrane; they change the permeability of the membrane and trigger a series of neurochemical processes in the postsynaptic membrane (e.g., Abel et al., 1995). The receiving neuron integrates the synaptic inputs, whether excitatory or inhibitory, in a variety of ways. In the simplest case, it aggregates the inputs to arrive at their algebraic sum, as shown in expression (3.1).

(3.1) Net stimulation = Sum of all postsynaptic inputs

When the net stimulation is stronger than a certain threshold, the neuron produces (or fires) an output in the form of action potentials. As the intensity of the stimulation increases, so does the neuron's firing. When excitatory and inhibitory postsynaptic potentials cancel each other out, there is no action potential. In short, the neuron is a biological computer that processes inputs and decides how to dispose of it, whether to forget it or to transmit further (see Kalat, 1995, p. 64).

The insights on neural transmission at the cellular level have given rise to computer-based simulation models of neural networks. These models are abstractions of the neurophysiological processes; they are not intended to capture all of the biological processing details. Their value lies in their ability to mimic a variety of memory phenomena of living organisms, including encoding and retrieval and the distributed representation of information (Chapter 7).

Neurotransmitters and the Formation of Memories

Synaptic activity throughout the brain is modulated by several neurotransmitter systems based in the brain stem. Scientists have no direct evidence on the effect of neurotransmitters on memory, but they infer their role from animal studies and from examining the level of neurotransmitters in patients afflicted with memory impairments. Rats and mice are trained in a variety of paradigms—including mazes, avoidance tasks, and delayed response tasks—and are treated with specific neurotransmitters and their antagonists. Based on these studies, neuroscientists have identified several neurotransmitters implicated in memory, including acetylcholine, epinephrine, dopamine, norepinephrine, serotonin, and gamma-aminobutyric acid (GABA).

Acetylcholine (ACh) originates in neurons known as cholinergic nuclei in the brain stem. The function of ACh depends on the location of the synapse that it serves. In synapses in the brain, ACh is involved in learning and memory; it is thought to speed synaptic transmission of rapidly changing information (e.g., about auditory and visual stimulation and motor movements). The effects of ACh became widely known when researchers discovered that the brains of Alzheimer's patients produce little acetylcholine and that the decline in memory performance in older individuals is correlated with reduced ACh levels. In animal learning studies, performance was enhanced or inhibited by using acetylcholine and its antagonists, respectively. In a study with human volunteers, neurochemical agents (e.g., scopolamine) that shorten the effects of ACh at the synapse have been shown to reduce memory performance, as well. In fact, the volunteers exhibited deficits similar to those of senile people (Kalat, 1995).

Epinephrine, dopamine, serotonin, and other agents are thought to act jointly on the amygdala, a structure involved in the regulation of emotions and memory formation (Chapter 9; Fuster, 1995; McGaugh, 1995). Epinephrine has been shown to enhance memory in rats when administered in small doses immediately after training. McGaugh (1995) attributed this effect to the possibility that the transmitter produced emotional arousal, which, in turn, facilitated the consolidation of memory traces.

Gamma-aminobutyric acid and glutamate are amino acids found throughout the brain; the first is inhibitory, the latter is excitatory. Glutamate, an almost universal transmitter from the simplest species to humans, plays an important role in long-term potentiation (LTP) in the hippocampus. Long-term potentiation involves an increase in synaptic responsiveness to stimuli as a result of training (see Hippocampus later in this chapter). In the hippocampus, there are special glutamate receptors,

one of which is the NMDA receptor (N-methyl-D-asparate), thought to be critical in learning at the molecular level (Bear, Connors, & Paradiso, 1996; Fuster, 1995; Kandel, 1991).

Are There Memory-Enhancing Drugs?

The hope of a memory drug predates the research efforts of neuroscientists into the neural and chemical basis of memory. The hope was fueled by expectations of the benefits of such a drug for people of all ages, from students cramming for exams to senior citizens, especially those suffering from Alzheimer's disease. It is no wonder, then, that psychologists took up the cause and explored the effects of various agents on learning and memory. Karl Lashley reported some success as early as 1917 with caffeine and strychnine, showing that both improved the rate of learning in rats, presumably via the process of memory consolidation (Lashley, 1917).

The claims in favor of caffeine and strychnine were soon forgotten, but the discovery of neurotransmitters encouraged a hunt for other memory-enhancing drugs. Promising candidates included agents interacting with the cholinergic system, the system that controls the metabolism of acetylcholine. One of these drugs is physostigmine, once heralded as a potential memory enhancer for Alzheimer's patients (Bartus, 1990). Physostigmine strengthens the effects of acetylcholine in synaptic transmission by suppressing the enzyme that decomposes acetylcholine. However, physostigmine and other drugs have been of limited use because their effectiveness dissipates rapidly and because of undesirable side effects.

Bartus (1990) reviewed the effects of nootropics (from the Greek *influencing the mind*) which, although not related to neurotransmitters, presumably strengthen memory consolidation, as well. Nootropics have been administered in experimental animals at certain time intervals after training—for example, in rat avoidance learning and in rabbit classical conditioning (Woodruff-Pak & Li, 1994, used nefiracetam [DM-9384]), with the result that experimental animals exhibited better retention than animals who received certain control chemicals.

In the 1990s, the media, including the Internet, have been abuzz with news of memory enhancers, whether natural substances such as the extract of the ginkgo tree or "smart" drugs with such names as *ampakines, aricept, cognex,* and *UCB-6215.* Even geneticists have contributed candidate processes, including the so-called CREB switch, a molecule that presumably programs a cell to store information for the short term or the long term (Hall, 1998).

Thus far, however, no agent has been found to serve as an unqualified memory enhancer, as the problems of such drugs outweigh their promises. The drugs have been tested either in animals or in patient populations, but not in the general public. Their effects have been small and short lasting, and they have undesirable side effects from dizziness to diarrhea, not to mention potential long-term health problems. There may even be unintended mnemonic side effects of using memory drugs: When you use a memory enhancer to study for a test and a mosquito begins to torment you, your retention for the whine of the insect might be enhanced more effectively than that for the information you meant to memorize (Hall, 1998). Another issue is that the effects of drugs on memory may be indirect and result from an enhancement of attention or arousal thought to facilitate memory consolidation. These drugs include peptide cholecystokinin, opiod peptides, vasopressin, and the glucocorticoids (McGaugh, 1995). No doubt, in the future, we will hear more about memory drugs as neuropharmacologists and geneticists continue the advances on structural changes in the nerve cell and at the synapse, the junction between nerve cells (Chapter 10; Weingartner et al., 1996).

In concluding this section, you should note that neuropharmacological agents have the potential to work both ways—to improve memory formation and to inhibit it. Among the latter are scolopamine, lorazepam, diazepam, midazolam, the glucocorticoids, and others (e.g., Polster, 1993). The glucocorticoids, released by the adrenal gland, activate the body's resources in response to imminent danger. In order to meet the danger and cope with stress, the glucocorticoids accelerate the organism's heart rate, increase the blood pressure, prime the effector system, and briefly sharpen attention and perception (Chapter 9). The glucocorticoids thus trigger an adaptive mechanism that benefits the organism in the short run, but they have negative consequences if released over a sustained period. It is thought that an overproduction of glucocorticoids contributes to atrophy in the hippocampus and reduces the ability to learn and remember in the long run (Sapolsky, 1994).

Plasticity of Neural Structures

Beginning with Hebb's (1949) first speculations on neural plasticity, scientists have accumulated evidence of the malleability of neural structures and processes (Rosenzweig, 1979). Changes due to learning are evident at many levels in the brain—in the size and number of synapses, in the structure of individual synapses, in increases and decreases of neurotransmitter substance, and in the responsiveness of hippocampal cells to stimulation, among others.

Changes in the Size of Neural Structure

An increase in the number and the size of synapses in rats as a result of experience was found by Turner and Greenough (1985). The two scientists reared one group of rats in a stimulating environment (a cage with many toys and objects, a sort of "rat heaven") and another group in a boring environment. After training, the brains of the experimental animals were better developed than those of control animals. There were more capillaries and the surface area of their brains were larger.

The brain growth in the pampered rats was not due to hormonal factors that may have stimulated neural tissue indiscriminately. Rather, the training effects were specific to the hemisphere exposed to the environment. This laterality was established in rats that had one eye occluded by a mask, thus leaving only one eye open to explore the environment. The increased neuronal branching occurred only in the hemisphere that received information from the open eye, but not in the other hemisphere (Swain et al., 1995).

Nottebohm (1985) observed both increases and decreases in neural structure as a function of the degree of use. Investigating the song of the male canary, he found that two nuclei (HVc and RA) in the canary's brain doubled in size as they were used during the singing season in fall and winter, and that they decreased in size during the birds' silent season in the summer. Nottebohm believes that these nuclei support memory and other functions related to song. Although the type of neuronal changes that Nottebohm has documented in the canary have not been shown in primates, he believes that his discovery is nevertheless important. It is an example of the correlation between neural change and performance for which neuroscientists have been searching.

Changes at the Synapse

In addition to growing new synapses, training also improves transmission of existing synapses. Such improvement can occur through one of several mechanisms involving the presynaptic membrane, the postsynaptic membrane, or both. In the presynaptic membrane, any of the following could increase: the number of sites that release neurotransmitters, the probability of releasing the neurotransmitter substance, and the rate of synthesizing or taking up the transmitter. At the postsynaptic membrane, the number of receptors could increase and the membrane properties could change so that the postsynaptic

potential is propagated more effectively. Unfortunately, synaptic transmission can also diminish in pathological conditions, such as in severe cases of Alzheimer's disease (Selkoe, 1991).

Improvements of synaptic transmission have been examined in such basic learning situations as habituation, sensitization, classical conditioning, and long-term potentiation. In the following list, I sketch each of these learning paradigms:

— *Habituation* refers to a decrease in the response of an organism to the repeated presentation of a stimulus, such as when one gets used to a loud noise. Habituation is mediated by the central nervous system, unlike sensory adaptation, which is a peripheral effect at the sensory organs. *Sensitization* involves an increase in the response to a neutral stimulus if it was preceded by a painful and potentially noxious stimulus. People tend to get jumpy after hearing a gun shot, for example.

— *Classical conditioning* involves forming an association between a neutral stimulus (the conditioned stimulus, e.g., a bell) and a stimulus (the unconditioned stimulus, e.g., food) that reflexively elicits a response (the unconditioned response, e.g., salivation). When the CS and the US are repeatedly paired, the CS comes to elicit the conditioned response (e.g., conditioned salivation) (Chapter 2).

— *Long-term potentiation* is observed at hippocampal synapses in mammals. It refers to a response enhancement after rapid stimulation that may last up to several weeks.

Learning in the Sea Hare Aplysia

A relatively simple mollusk, *Aplysia Californica*, the sea hare, lives in the Pacific Ocean off the California coast. *Aplysia* looks somewhat like a hare with fins. It has gills and a head with eyes and small feelerlike tentacles. Toward the back, it has a tail and a spout, the siphon, for water intake and output. The siphon contracts reflexively when touched; the contraction is equivalent to withdrawal reflexes in vertebrae, except that the neural circuitry is much simpler in *Aplysia.*

Aplysia has several simple circuits, including the two circuits shown in Figure 3.5. On the left, there is a monosynaptic circuit involving two neurons: (1) the sensory neuron receiving inputs from the siphon and (2) the motor neuron sending signals to the gill. The other circuit includes (1) the sensory neuron of the tail, (2) an interneuron, and (3) the motor neuron controlling the gill.

Habituation and Sensitization.   Kandel and colleagues (e.g., Castellucci & Kandel, 1976) studied habituation and sensitization in *Aplysia* by correlating its behavior and the rate of neurotransmitter release in the synapses. When initially touched, *Aplysia* vigorously retracted its siphon. After repeated touching, however, *Aplysia* habituated, making a smaller withdrawal reflex. At the synaptic level, there was a concomitant reduction in the release of neurotransmitters. Sensitization in *Aplysia* was produced by

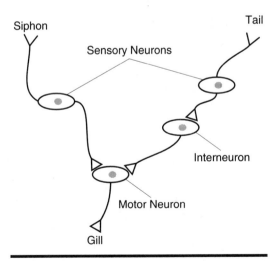

FIGURE 3.5   Schematic drawing of neural circuits in *Aplysia.* The circuit connecting the siphon and the gill is monosynaptic, including a synapse between a sensory neuron and the motor neuron. The tail circuit includes a sensory neuron, an interneuron, and the motor neuron. There are two synapses in this circuit.

applying strong pressure to its head or tail, followed by repeated touching of the siphon. This procedure resulted in an increase of both the withdrawal reflex and neurotransmitter activity.

Classical Conditioning.   To demonstrate conditioning in *Aplysia,* Kandel and colleagues applied a gentle touch (the CS) to the siphon and an electrical shock (the US) to the tail. At the beginning of training, the touch produced no consistent siphon response. After several paired presentations of the two stimuli, there was a vigorous conditioned siphon withdrawal in response to the touch.

Aplysia is smart enough to discriminate between a CS paired with the US (the CS+) and a CS that has never been paired with the US (the CS–). The CS+ involved touching the mantle consistently in one location followed by presentation of the US. The CS– involved touching *Aplysia* in a different location without shock. After about 10 trials, *Aplysia* withdrew its siphon in response to the CS+, but did not respond to the CS–.

Conditioning was evident at the cellular level, as well; the US activated the motor neuron, thus eliciting the unconditioned withdrawal. The US also caused an increase in the release of neurotransmitter substance from the sensory neurons. In discrimination learning, the CS+ produced an increase in neurotransmitter substance at the sensory neuron, but the CS– did not. Random presentation of the CS and US had no neural effect. The important factor that produces learning, therefore, is the fact that the CS is a reliable predictor of the US.

Conditioning in the neural structures of *Aplysia* is readily transparent due to the relative simplicity of mollusks. Scientists have uncovered parallels between conditioning at the behavioral and neural levels in mammals, as well. Researchers found that conditioning in rabbits, for example, is based on the joint activation of neurons, just as in *Aplysia.* In the rabbit, the relevant neurons are in the cerebellum and the hippocampus (Canli & Donegan, 1995; Schmajuk & DiCarlo, 1992). The rabbit research was particularly interesting in that the various conditioning phenomena—including acquisition, extinction, and spontaneous recovery—can often be detected neurally well before there is any observable change at the behavioral level.

Long-Term Potentiation and Long-Term Depression

Long-term potentiation has been observed at specific synapses in the hippocampus of rats, rabbits, and other mammals. It is induced by observing the animals in three experimental phases, as illustrated in Figure 3.6. During the first phase, a baseline of responding at the postsynaptic membrane is established by stimulating the synapse with brief individual pulses presented over several seconds. In the second phase, a rapid volley of impulses is fired at the synapse for up to five seconds at a rate of 100 impulses per second. In the third phase, the individual slow test impulses from the first phase are administered again. Bliss and Lomo (1973) and subsequent researchers observed an increase in the postsynaptic response relative to the baseline; this enhancement is referred to as *long-term potentiation (LTP)*. It is long term because it may persist up to several weeks after the high-frequency stimulation is applied (Bliss & Lomo, 1973; Racine & de Jonge, 1988).

If the same synapse is stimulated repeatedly but infrequently (e.g., at a rate of 1 pulse per second for 60 seconds), the strength of the synapse is reduced and long-term depression (LTD) is observed. Long-term depression is the reverse of long-term potentiation; both of these effects are based on neurochemical processes involving the NMDA receptors at the synaptic membranes.

Long-term potentiation has been detected throughout the central nervous system but occurs primarily in the hippocampus, a region implicated in learning and memory. Researchers have been tempted to view long-term potentiation as support for Hebb's (1949) theory of syn-

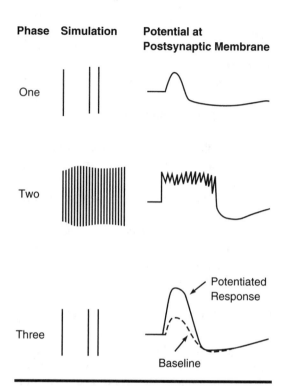

FIGURE 3.6   Three phases of inducing long-term potentiation. During the first phase, a baseline potential in response to brief individual pulses is established. In the second phase, a volley of pulses is presented. In the third phase, potentiation is observed: A slow pulse rate produces a potential increased relative to the baseline potential (broken line). The interval between the first and second phase may extend up to several weeks and still produce the response enhancement known as long-term potentiation.

aptic change. The relation between enhancement at the synaptic level, however, and learning at the behavioral level is controversial, with some researchers claiming that they have found conclusive leads (Tsien, Huerta, & Tonegawa, 1996), while others remain unconvinced (Shors & Matzel, 1997).

WHERE ARE MEMORIES LOCATED?

Few issues in the history of memory research have been as widely debated as the question:

Where are memories located in the brain? What appears to be a simple question at first glance turns out to be very difficult to answer. The debate has swung back and forth between the localist and distributional views of memory. The localist view holds that memories are located in specific sites in the brain, whereas the distributionist position believes that memories are distributed across the brain. Over the course of two centuries, the evidence has favored one view or the other, with opinions shifting between the two poles. This section traces the debate between the positions in four acts, beginning with the extreme localist position propagated by the phrenologists. We will see that, although the actors and the level of analysis have changed, the basic argument between localists and distributionists has remained the same.

Act I: From Extreme Localization to No Function at All

Philosophers from Aristotle to Descartes speculated about the localization of memory, one assigning it to the brain, the other believing that memory could not be localized any more than the ephemeral soul. Empirical investigations were rare until the invention of the microscope and the subsequent anatomical studies of the body and brain. At the beginning of the nineteenth century, knowledge of anatomy had sufficiently advanced to include the following discoveries about the brain:

- There are two nearly symmetrical cortical hemispheres.
- The neocortex consists of lobes separated by indentations, the gyri and sulci.
- Cortical tissue consists of cells.
- Fibers connect the sensory organs and specific brain regions.

The anatomical studies by themselves, of course, did not reveal the functions of any of these structures. However, anatomists made inferences on the functions of brain regions by studying corre-

lations between injuries to those regions and loss of function. Anatomist Franz Gall (1758–1828), for example, had a patient who lost his speech as a result of a fencing wound below the eye into the frontal lobe. Gall therefore concluded that the frontal lobe was the site for the use of language.

Encouraged as much by anatomical discoveries and clinical observations as by the flight of fantasy, Gall and his disciples, the phrenologists, assigned diverse functions to specific parts of the brain. The phrenologists undertook no empirical studies of the brain. Rather, they postulated on the basis of casual observations that bumps of the skull reflected particular traits. For example, a bump immediately over the ear was taken as a sign of destructiveness, a bump above that meant secretiveness, and a bump still higher indicated cautiousness. Gall was led to such speculations by encounters with individuals whom he judged to have certain traits. He assumed that memory was located in brain regions posterior to the eyes, because he had met several individuals who had protruding eyes and prodigious mnemonic faculties.

Gall's enterprise never became part of mainstream medicine or psychology. Phrenology was criticized widely and easily discredited by simple empirical demonstrations. Pierre Flourens (1794–1867) extirpated sections of the brains of pigeons and noted the recovery of memory and other functions, unless one removed most of the birds' brains. He therefore concluded that there was no localization of function. Going further still, he argued that most brain regions are not assigned and, true to Descartes' spirit to whom he had dedicated his work, Flourens questioned whether the brain exercised any function at all.

Act II: Localization Theory Becomes Respectable

The pendulum swung back from Flourens's agnosticism toward localization theory with Paul Broca's (1824–1880) observation of severe speech defects in patients with lesions in a small area in the left temporal lobe that later came to be known as Broca's area. Broca thought that this area was the center of speech production because the patients exhibited no loss of comprehension. He and his students embarked on systematic neuropsychological investigations of patients with a specific loss of motor or mental function, and correlated the impairment with anatomical studies. The search was on for brain areas that subserved specific mental functions; the goal was a functional map of the brain. Here are some of the assumptions made at the turn of the nineteenth century in the wake of Broca's work:

- Language comprehension was located in Wernicke's area in the left hemisphere.
- Sensory perception was located in the posterior part of the central fissure.
- Motor movements were controlled by the anterior part of the central fissure.

The mapping of motor centers in the brain was accomplished by Gustav Frisch and Eduard Hitzig in the 1870s. They introduced a powerful new investigatory tool: electrical stimulation of specific brain sites. The two scientists applied weak electrical currents to regions of the neocortex of dogs and elicited movements from different body parts from head to toes. Frisch and Hitzig produced the maps of the sensorimotor cortices known as *motor homunculus* that are now found in elementary neuroscience and psychology textbooks.

Act III: From Equipotentiality to Memory Cells

Armed with the precise mapping of the sensorimotor cortex, it appeared to be merely a question of time until the remaining cortex was mapped and localization theory was established once and for all. Thanks to Lashley's work on equipotentiality, however, that was not to be. As described in Chapter 2, Lashley's equipotentiality results supported the distributional hypothesis. Lashley trained rats on a maze task and re-

moved a certain percentage of brain tissue either before training or before testing. As expected, rats with lesioned brains performed less well than intact rats; however, contradicting the localist expectation, the localization of the lesions mattered little. Whether they were made frontally, laterally, or occipitally had little effect on learning and retention. The determining factor was the amount of tissue lesioned.

The localist position was to gain renewed strength from animal studies that limited the generality of Lashley's results, and especially from Penfield's neurosurgical stimulation studies. Wilder Penfield, a Canadian neurosurgeon, sought to lessen the impact of epileptic seizures by removing small portions of the temporal lobe. During the course of his career, Penfield accumulated an observational base of 1,200 cases, half of whom underwent surgery. Because the brain has no pain receptors, the operation was conducted on the conscious patient under local anesthesia. In an effort not to lesion brain tissue essential for memory and other functions, Penfield applied electrical stimuli to various points on the surface of the cortex, probing the putative functions. Penfield elicited memory recollections in about 8% of his patients. One patient, for example, reported the image of being at a railroad station in a town in Kentucky with the wind blowing outside. Others reported childhood recollections, hearing musical tunes or the voices of relatives. Penfield thought that he had located memory cells for specific experiences. But his speculations turned out to be a dead end (Kalat, 1995). Over 90% of his patients reported no recollections. The few patients who did have recollections recalled different events when stimulated at the same site, and, in any case, there was no verification of the memories that the patients reported.

Act IV: Networks of Local Specialists

Where do we stand on the localist and distributionist positions two centuries after the first anatomical investigations of the brain? The consensus of scientists is that both positions are right to some extent; networks of different brain regions are involved in memory, thus agreeing with the distributional view; however, each of the regions makes a unique contribution, thus agreeing with the localist position. In other words, both positions are accommodated within a model that includes networks and local specialists. Raichle (1994) used the orchestra analogy to express this view: "Just as specific members of a large orchestra perform together in a precise fashion to produce a symphony, a group of localized brain areas performing elementary operations work together to exhibit an observable human behavior" (p. 58).

Research is advancing on several fronts to flesh out the model of networks and specialists. Scientists are looking for nuclei subserving specific memory functions as well as for networks that subsume the nuclei. The latter has proven difficult because nuclei may be multiply connected and thus contribute to different networks. Parallel to the anatomical and neurophysiological research has been the development of simulation models of neural networks (Chapter 7). Evidence for the notion of networks of local specialists comes from single-cell studies and brain-imaging studies (e.g., Martin et al., 1995). Here, we consider research on visual memory cells in monkeys as an illustration of the network-specialist model.

Memory and Face Cells
in the Inferotemporal Cortex

In seminal work, Fuster and Jervey (1981) discovered that the inferotemporal cortex of the monkey includes single nuclei that maintain short-term visual information. The scientists made this discovery recording single-cell activity in monkeys as they worked on the delayed matching-to-sample task. In this task, the monkeys tried to remember the color of target buttons for a period of 30 seconds (see Research Methods in Neuroscience earlier in this chapter). During the interval, only neurons responsive to the target color were activated. Because of its multiple manifestations of visual memory, the speculative proposal has surfaced that the inferotemporal cortex serves as a convergence node for categorical visual memory (Fuster, 1995). Presumably, memories for specific categories—including faces, fruits, and tools—are coordinated by the inferotemporal lobes.

In support of this speculation, scientists have discovered neurons in the inferotemporal cortex of the monkey that respond to faces of other monkeys and of humans but not to other stimuli. The researchers recorded from various single cells in the inferotemporal region in awake monkeys and observed high-frequency responses when facial stimuli were presented (Desimone & Ungerleider, 1989). When a set of faces was first shown, different inferotemporal cells responded to the faces at a similar level of activity. After repeated exposures, however, a specialization became apparent, with cells responding differentially to different faces (Rolls et al., 1989). Fuster (1995) believes that the inferotemporal cells form a link in a long-term memory network capable of learning. The network is assumed to include both perceptual association areas and motor areas. Damage to the inferotemporal cells and other components of their networks may result in a disability of recognizing familiar faces, a condition known as *prosopagnosia* (see Chapter 10).

The research on face cells in the inferotemporal lobe illustrates the success of neuroscientists in identifying cortical centers involved in a specific memory function. Scientists conjecture that the centers do not act independently but in concert with other brain regions; that is, the regions constitute networks. The configuration of the networks and how they function as a whole, however, is still elusive.

One proposal is Damasio's (1990) theory of convergence zones. A *convergence zone* is an area in the brain where neural information of different aspects of remembered events converges. This idea reflects the multimodal nature of the stimuli we encounter. A familiar face, for example, has a name and a visual appearance, and it tends to convey an emotional expression. A convergence zone acts much like an indexing system that contains for each concept pointers to different locations in the brain. Anatomically, cortical areas from different modalities provide input to a convergence zone; the zone, in turn, keeps representations subsumed under a given memory activated. The convergence zones confer coherence on different sensory aspects of a memory.

In sum, the localist versus distributionist debate has reached an equilibrium. Both the distributionist and localist views remain viable—the former because structures distributed throughout the brain may support a memory function and the latter because there is evidence that different brain structures fulfill specific memory functions. Two such structures, the hippocampus and the frontal lobes, are discussed in the two remaining sections of the chapter (for other regions, see reviews by Markowitsch, 1995, and Squire, 1993).

THE HIPPOCAMPUS

No other brain structure has attracted as much attention by neuroscientists in the last two decades as the hippocampus. Researchers have identified the hippocampus as the prime organ implicated in the encoding of declarative memories, in memory consolidation, and in spatial learning. *Declarative memories* are memories that one can verbalize, such as the names of the U.S. presidents, a list of paired associates, or one's social security number.

Based on case studies of amnesia and on animal studies, the hippocampus is viewed as instrumental in the consolidation of memories following learning. The hippocampus is thought to

coordinate memories and confer unity on them, possibly through the process of long-term potentiation. Studies on spatial learning suggest that the hippocampus is the mind's geographer, as it monitors locations in space and the relations between them (e.g., McClelland, McNaughton, & O'Reilly, 1995; Schacter & Tulving, 1994b).

The hippocampus (Latin for *sea horse*) derives its name from its sea-horse shape. It is located at the interior edge of each hemisphere adjacent to the temporal lobes (see Figure 3.1C). Figure 3.7, a schematic of the hippocampus in the rat, shows the principal structures of the hippocampal formation: the CA1 and CA3 regions, the dentate gyrus, and the enthorhinal cortex (CA for *cornu ammonis*, Latin for *Ammon's Horn*). Small as it may seem, the hippocampus and such adjacent structures as the amygdala occupy a major junction for projections from the association regions in the temporal, frontal, and parietal lobes.

Consolidation of Memories

The notion that memories are initially transitory and later become consolidated is at least a cen-

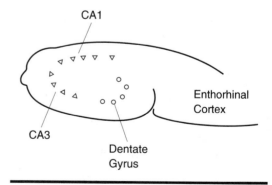

FIGURE 3.7 The rat hippocampus includes the dentate gyrus, the enthorhinal cortex, and the CA1 and CA3 regions, including the pyramidal cells (represented as triangles).

tury old (Mueller & Pilzecker, 1900). The experiences of amnesic patients such as H. M. were certainly consistent with the consolidation hypothesis. Following temporal lobe resection and lesioning of his hippocampus, H. M. could retain new facts only for up to one minute but he did remember events from the very distant past. Old consolidated memories were not perturbed by the trauma—only young and fragile memories were.

There are numerous studies where amnesia was induced in rats, cats, and monkeys by lesioning the hippocampus. Squire and colleagues (1993) reviewed a study on memory consolidation over a 16-week span in monkeys. The animals received paired-associate training in which each learning episode involved an association of 1 of 20 different objects with food reward. Learning episodes occurred at different intervals, ranging from 2 to 16 weeks before bilateral surgery of the hippocampus. Retention varied as the function of the interval between surgery and test: When the monkeys learned the association only 2 weeks before surgery, memory was poor; when 12 weeks elapsed between learning and surgery, retention was far better. The researchers describe this retention function as evidence for a gradual process of consolidation in memory. They attribute the consolidation to the hippocampus and note that "as time passes after learning, the contribution of the hippocampal formation gradually diminishes and a more permanent memory system develops, presumably in the neocortex, which is independent of the hippocampal formation" (p. 404).

To date, it is not fully clear what mechanisms are at work to produce consolidation at various intervals following initial learning. Research is under way to determine the contribution of long-term potentiation in the hippocampus, of other brain structures (e.g., Shadmehr & Holcomb, 1997), and of the neurotransmitters, as well as the interaction among these factors. Further, the function of consolidation is not fully understood.

It is possible that consolidation serves to reorganize the information after learning or that irrelevant stimulus aspects are dropped and abstract representations developed (Churchland & Sejnowski, 1992).

Space Cells in the Hippocampus

The contribution of the hippocampal formation to spatial learning and memory has been documented in studies involving rats and monkeys, among several other species. Olton, Collison, and Werz (1977) found that rats whose hippocampus was lesioned could not learn to navigate a radial maze. This is a maze that consists of alleys radiating from a central goal box, much like spokes of a wheel. Mishkin and Appenzeller (1987) reported that monkeys with hippocampus lesions could not remember the location of hidden food (e.g., a red cup in the right corner of yard), whereas lesions of amygdala, another structure in the brain stem, did not impair location memory at all. O'Keefe and Dostoyevsky (1971) discovered place cells in the hippocampus of rats. Recording from the brains of rats exploring the radial maze, these researchers found that specific pyramidal cells are sensitive to unique locations in space; specific cells responded maximally when the rat was approaching a particular location. When the rat moved to another location, other cells became active.

Place cells in the hippocampus correspond to specific locations in the environment, say in the kitchen, but the hippocampal map is not congruent with the spatial layout of the environment. A location near the right wall of the kitchen may have its place cell in the center of the cognitive map, and a location in the left wall may have its place cell on the right edge of the mental map. Animals learn spatial layouts within minutes, whether it is in natural or experimental situations, as, for example, in the water maze. In the water maze, the animal, usually a rat or mouse, must locate a block hidden in a small basin of muddy water. Finding the block enables the rat to sit and rest rather than having to swim around.

Is Spatial Learning Based on Long-Term Potentiation?

The first clue supporting the hypothesis of a link between spatial learning and long-term potentiation came from a study using the drug AP5, a LTP suppressant in the hippocampus. The researchers wanted to find out whether the drug would block the acquisition of overt spatial learning in the water-maze paradigm. Sure enough, animals treated with AP5 had great difficulty in learning the maze, whereas control animals learned the maze easily (Churchland & Sejnowski, 1992). Although these results supported the correlation between spatial learning and LTP, it was not certain that the effects of AP5 were restricted to the hippocampus; the drug could have disrupted other regions of the rats' brains and thus interfered with maze learning. A more conclusive study would use a mechanism to interfere with LTP at specific sites in the hippocampus and demonstrate adverse effects on spatial learning as a result (Stevens, 1996).

This is precisely what a team of scientists at Massachusetts Institute of Technology (MIT) succeeded in doing. The researchers were able to link LTP and spatial learning by using an innovative genetic tool. Tsien, Huerta, and Tonegawa (1996) interfered genetically with NMDA processing and LTP in the CA1 region of the hippocampus in mice, the region implicated in spatial learning. The researchers genetically changed the gene that controlled the function of the NMDA receptors in the CA1 region without affecting other functions. Thus, the scientists designed mice that did not have the receptor implicated in LTP but that were in all other respects normal. Unlike untreated control mice, the genetically altered mice were not able to learn the water maze and to form spatial memories. It appears that long-term potentiation is, as sus-

pected, instrumental in the formation of new memories in the hippocampus. In an editorial in the journal *Cell,* Stevens (1996) described the research of the MIT team as a start, not as an end. Stevens interpreted the results as supporting the hitherto elusive link between synaptic plasticity, spatial memory, and hippocampal nerve cell activity.

Does the Hippocampus Support All Memories?

The hippocampus clearly has its hand in diverse learning and memory functions, including memory consolidation, the formation of declarative memories, and spatial learning. Some researchers even speculate that there is a causal link between hippocampus size and memory capacity. As support for this claim, they cite correlations between memory decrements and a reduction in the size of the hippocampus due to aging (Golomb et al., 1994 ; but see Sullivan, Marsh, & Pfefferbaum, 1995) and emotional distress (Sapolsky, 1994). Does the body of these data mean that the hippocampus promotes the learning and remembering of everything? The answer is no. One can learn certain skills without the hippocampus.

Milner and other researchers had already demonstrated that H. M. was able to remember a variety of skills, although his hippocampus was lesioned. He acquired mirror drawing skills, which is quite difficult; one must draw shapes by looking in a mirror rather than at the sheet one uses to draw on. H. M. and other amnesic patients were shown to improve their visual recognition of stimuli, whether objects or words, after prior exposure. This facilitation is known as *priming*. Amnesic patients acquire conditioned responses in classical and instrumental conditioning situations, as well. Motor learning, priming, and conditioning have in common that the patient cannot verbalize what he or she has learned, nor does the patient remember that the episode of mirror drawing, for example, ever took place. Because one cannot declare them, such memories are known as *nondeclarative memories* (Chapter 5).

In sum, the hippocampus is a key structure in the acquisition of declarative memories, but it does not figure in learning of nondeclarative skills. The hippocampus does not serve as the storage site of the declarative memories. Rather, it is instrumental in the transfer of information from a fragile to a more permanent state; it is "the teacher of the cortex" (Churchland & Sejnowski, 1992, p. 297).

FRONTAL LOBES

Occupying the anterior section of the cortex, the frontal lobes extend from behind the forehead to the central sulcus (see Figure 3.1). The frontal cortex is phylogenetically young; its relative size increases substantially as one goes up the ladder of species from the lower mammals to homo sapiens. The frontal cortex includes three principal regions: the primary motor cortex, the premotor cortex, and the prefrontal cortex. It is the latter that this section focuses on.

Unlike other cortical regions, the prefrontal cortex does not communicate directly with any of the sensory systems. Rather, the prefrontal region enters into circuits with different sensory projection areas and such brain structures as the hippocampus, the amygdala, the thalamus, the temporal region, and dopamine-related nuclei in the brain stem. Forming part of so many different loops undoubtedly explains the many functions served by the prefrontal cortex (Fuster, 1995; Shimamura, 1995).

Injuries to the frontal cortex produce an inconsistent pattern of effects. On the one hand, there are few impairments of new learning, as measured by standardized tests; patients can still learn and remember paired associates, word lists, and line drawings. This is in contrast with hippocampus-impaired patients who lose the capacity for long-term learning. On the other hand, frontal lobe patients exhibit a wide variety of mental dysfunctions, deficits in planning and decision making, loss of initiative and creativity, change of personality, and impairment of memory processes.

Evidence from different sources indicates that the frontal and prefrontal regions contribute to several important memory functions: maintenance of information in working memory, executive functions in working memory, and encoding and retrieval of facts from long-term memory. Working memory includes information available for a short time, typically less than a minute. Unless they are rehearsed, items in working memory rapidly decay and are replaced by other content. According to Baddeley and Hitch's (1974) influential model, working memory includes components to process information in terms of phonological, visual, and spatial codes (Baddeley & Hitch, 1974, 1994; Chapter 6), and a central executive system assumed to control those processes.

Maintaining Information in Working Memory

One of the sources on the role of the frontal lobes in maintaining information is the delayed response paradigm combined with neuroimaging or single-cell recordings. In the delayed response paradigm, a stimulus is presented and a certain response is elicited; then the stimulus is turned off, a delay is introduced, and a test occurs to see whether the subject remembers the response (e.g., Fuster & Jervey, 1981). The stimulus may be the color or the location of a response key, a face, or a sequence of letters. During the interval, brain activity is recorded through PET or fMRI scanning or single-cell measurements (see Chapter 6).

Friedman and Goldman-Rakic (1994) recorded blood-flow activity from rhesus monkeys trained to remember the location of stimuli on the screen for a brief interval. During the interval, PET activity increased in the principal sulcus region of the prefrontal cortex (in addition to regions of the inferior parietal cortex). The greater the accuracy of the monkeys in remembering the stimuli, the greater was the brain activity. In a parallel study, using magnetic resonance imaging, researchers found increased activity in corresponding neural circuits in human volunteers who executed a task similar to that of the monkeys (McCarthy, Blamire, Rothman, Gruetter, & Shulman, 1993). The researchers attributed the increased activity in the midfrontal gyrus in both species to the maintenance of spatial information in working memory (see also Chapter 6).

The frontal lobes are activated in nonspatial working memory tasks, as well. Cohen and colleagues (1994) tracked frontal lobe activity as human learners monitored letter sequences on a screen. The task was to press a key when a target letter was repeated, for example—as in MXM as compared to MXB. Different regions of the prefrontal cortex became active as the learners worked on the letter tracking task. When the task was made more difficult by increasing the number of intervening letters, a larger area of the prefrontal cortex was recruited to maintain the increased load of information.

The contribution of the frontal lobes in maintaining information has been revealed in lesion studies that used permanent as well as reversible lesions. Goldman-Rakic (1994a) lesioned the principal sulcus in monkeys through surgery and found that the monkeys had difficulties maintaining spatial memories in the delayed response task. The monkey was rewarded for looking at a target on a computer screen. From time to time, flashes appeared in other locations of the monitor; in some cases, the monkey was required to change its gaze toward these flashes and then return its gaze to the original location that either was still illuminated or not. Lesioned monkeys had no problem gazing at the target as long as the

light remained illuminated, but once the light was turned off, they did not remember its previous location.

Fuster (1995) achieved reversible lesioning by cooling down the activity of the frontal lobes. He applied a thermoelectric cooler directly over the exposed lobes to reduce the temperature to 20 degrees Celsius. Cooling the prefrontal area significantly reduced performance in the delayed matching task, whereas cooling the parietal region had no negative effect on this task.

Executive Function

Influential models of cognition assume that attention and memory operations occur under the aegis of an executive system variously known as the supervisory activating system (Norman & Shallice, 1986), the executive attention network (Posner & Raichle, 1994), or the central executive (Baddeley & Hitch, 1974, 1994). The executive is believed to control memory and cognitive processes in encoding, retrieval, problem solving, and decision making, among others.

That the frontal lobes fulfill executive functions has long been suspected on the basis of neuropsychological case studies. Frontal lobes patients suffer from a disability that Baddeley (e.g., 1996) called *dysexecutive syndrome;* this condition involves reduced control of behavior and difficulty in coordinating actions to meet a specific goal. Neuropsychologists use the Wisconsin Card Sorting Task, among others, to diagnose impairments of executive functions. In this task, patients are asked to sort a deck of cards on successive trials under different sorting criteria, including shape, number, and color. The patients are not explicitly told the sorting criterion in a given series; they simply receive feedback from the experimenter for each response. The patients must remember the changing feedback patterns and infer the rule the experimenter is using. Patients with prefrontal lesions readily learn the first sorting criterion in a series, but they cannot shift to another criterion. Therefore, the patients are said to be susceptible to proactive interference, the inhibiting effects of prior learning on new learning (Shimamura, 1995).

Executive control is required in tasks where subjects must suppress habitual responses. The frontal structure implicated in such suppression is the angulate cingulate gyrus. This region becomes active in people working on the Stroop test (Pardo, Pardo, Janer, & Raichle, 1990), a task that involves suppression of familiar responses. In the Stroop task, the person is shown the names of colors printed in colors different from the name (e.g., the word *red* is printed in green) and the person must name the color of the word *(green)*. This task is difficult because of people's tendency to read the word rather than naming the color. When the angulate cingulate gyrus is lesioned as a result of an accident or disease, patients have great difficulty with the Stroop test, owing to their difficulty in inhibiting the tendency of reading the familiar words (Posner & Raichle, 1994).

Distinguishing frontal lobe and hippocampus functions, Moscovitch (1994) described the frontal lobes as *working-with-memory structures*. According to his model, the frontal lobes organize information sent as input to the hippocampus. The frontal lobes also receive output from the hippocampus and impose temporal order on the items. Using this information, certain frontal lobe structures presumably "guide further mnemonic searches, direct thought, or plan future action. In short, the frontal lobes are necessary for converting remembering from a stupid reflexive act triggered by clue to an intelligent, reflective, goal-directed activity under voluntary control" (pp. 278–279).

Moscovitch supported his speculation by noting that frontal memory deficits lead to impaired judgment of the frequency of occurrence of events, poor retention of the temporal order of events, difficulties with the delayed response task, and remembering the order of pointing to locations, even if the order is generated by the patients themselves. By contrast, hippocampus lesions result in impairment of storage and retention of information. According to this view, the hippocampus provides the raw information and the prefrontal structures refine the information.

Long-Term Memory Encoding and Retrieval

Scientists disagree on the role of the prefrontal lobes in long-term memory functions. Reviewing a body of research, Squire (1987) concluded that the prefrontal cortex fulfills working memory functions, but that it is "not involved in general long-term retentive capacity" (p. 238). Others, however, believe that the prefrontal cortex contributes to encoding and retrieval of long-term memories (Buckner, 1996; Nyberg, Cabeza, & Tulving, 1996; Posner & Raichle, 1994; Schacter et al., 1996). Posner and Raichle (1994), for example, reported that volunteers exhibit an increase in prefrontal lobe activity, especially on the left side, when researchers asked them to think (retrieve) sad thoughts.

Nyberg and colleagues (1996) proposed the hemispheric encoding retrieval asymmetry (HERA) hypothesis of long-term memory retrieval. According to the HERA model, the left prefrontal cortex is implicated in retrieving information from semantic memory, whereas the right prefrontal cortex contributes to the retrieval of episodic information. Semantic memory involves one's knowledge of facts about the world; by contrast, episodic memory involves remembering personally experienced events, including the facts memorized in a memory experiment (Chapters 1 and 4). Recollection of episodic memories is improved when learners invoke their semantic memory in a condition called the *deep encoding condition*. Thus, when one tries to remember a list of words (e.g., *ladder, cup*) and one thinks of associated verbs (e.g., *climb, drink*), recollection is better than in a shallow encoding condition where the nouns are simply repeated.

Nyberg and colleagues (1996) recorded PET activity from subjects memorizing words under the deep and shallow encoding conditions. They found the *left* prefrontal lobes engaged in the deep encoding condition but not in the shallow condition. To assess brain activity in episodic memory, the researchers conducted neuroimaging scans as participants worked on a recognition test in which they discriminated items repeated from prior trials from new items. In this task, brain activity was greater in the *right* prefrontal lobes on the old trials than in the control condition, where the items were new. These data suggest the involvement of the prefrontal cortex in long-term memory retrieval and support the notion of hemispheric asymmetry. However, they do not reveal the mechanisms that produce the retrieval asymmetry (Buckner, 1996).

Taken together, these studies testify to the contribution of the prefrontal cortex to working memory, long-term memory, and executive control operations. Given the growth of knowledge on the frontal lobes, it is difficult to believe that not too long ago they were judged dispensable enough to be removed in the notorious lobotomy procedure. Today, no authority questions the critical place of the frontal lobes in cognitive functions, including memory.

CONCLUSION

As we begin the twenty-first century, research on the biological basis of memory is one of the most active of all subfields of memory research. The much vaunted Decade of the Brain announced in the late 1980s promises to extend and to accelerate. The reasons are easy to see. We now have the opportunity afforded by innovative methodologies to examine the microstructure of the brain and study the interactions among different brain structures. Further, there is the combination of cognitive and neuroscience tools in addressing important issues, including the issue of independent memory systems (to be taken up in Chapter 11). As well, there are the computer simulation models of brain processes, including the neural network models discussed in Chapter 7 and the research questions that they raise. And, finally, there is the great practical need of understanding brain processes in aging, sick, and injured individuals.

The renewed attention paid to brain processes in memory represents a return to the questions asked by Ribot, Korsakoff, Lashley, and Hebb. Certainly, the research has gone far beyond what these pioneers imagined—indeed, beyond the traditional disciplines of psychology, physiology, and anatomy; it is from researchers in neurochemistry and neurogenetics that we can expect new insights on brain and memory (Stevens, 1996; Tsien, Huerta, & Tonegawa, 1996). It is, however, likely that such fundamental questions as Are memories located or distributed? What are the mechanisms of synaptic plasticity? and Are there different memory systems and, if so, what are the corresponding neural structures? will remain the same (Squire, 1987); they just will be asked at different levels of inquiry.

CHAPTER 4

MEMORY
FOR FACTS

In everyday conversation, the word *memory* means memory for facts and the word *forgetting* refers to forgetting of facts. The battle of Gettysburg, the square root of 36, a colleague's telephone number, the meaning of the word *sextant*, and one's computer password are all facts one remembers. People remember thousands of facts; no upper limit is known. Facts include knowledge about the physical and social world; about symbol systems, including a speaker's linguistic knowledge; as well as recollections from one's personal life, from one's bar mitzvah to the most recent vacation and the last weekend.

Research on memory began with investigations of memory for facts. These were facts psychologists selected and constructed for the purpose of researching memory in controlled experiments. Most of the facts were expressly designed to be meaningless. The nonsense syllable is the prime example. Meaningful materials, sentences, passages, and pictures were also used but to a smaller extent and generally not until later (Bartlett, 1932).

Memory experiments consist of designated study episodes that usually take place under laboratory conditions where subjects are given lists of items to memorize. Each list is designated by a marker, such as the ordinal number of the list or the title of a passage. In testing, the marker is used as a cue for the learner to recall the information committed to memory during the study episode. The study-test paradigm has been the dominant research tool of memory researchers for much of the first century of memory research.

Tulving (1972, 1983) subsumed information presented to learners in experiments under the term *episodic memory* to indicate that subjects remember the specific episode, the context, in which the information was acquired. He was fully aware, however, that episodic memory is much larger than what memory researchers were investigating. Specifically, he noted that episodic memory stores information about any "temporally dated episodes and events, and temporal-spatial relations among them" (1983, p. 21), including a person's autobiographical memories. We shall consider autobiographical memory in Chapter 8. This chapter focuses on episodic memory and semantic memory as studied in the laboratory.

Tulving (1972) used the term *semantic memory* to denote facts that people know without recalling the specific temporal-spatial context in which the information was acquired. *Is a canary a bird? Is Coca-Cola a beverage?* and *What is the product of 3 × 4?* We remember the answer to these questions, but, as a rule, we do not remember the context in which we learned the facts. Words occur in so many different contexts that it would be counterproductive to remember the contexts; indeed, no purpose would be served by doing so. Semantic memory is "timeless knowledge of the world that a person shares with others" (Tulving, 1983, p. v). Perhaps because of its vastness and complexity, memory research-ers initially shied away from semantic memory. In the 1970s, however, research on semantic memory took off because of two developments: (1) the introduction of hierarchical models of computer memory (Quillian, 1968) and (2) for-mulations of the representation of word mean-ings (e.g., Kintsch, 1972; Quillian, 1968).

Tulving's distinction between episodic and semantic memory has been controversial for at least a couple of reasons. He postulated different memory systems to support semantic and epi-sodic information, a distinction many psycholo-gists resisted (Chapter 11). Nor was it clear that episodic and semantic memory could be sepa-rated at all, since research shows that people re-member episodic information in terms of seman-tic memory. For the present, we keep clear of these controversies and focus on the distinction between episodic and semantic memory for de-scriptive purposes.

To be sure, episodic and semantic memory share commonalities. Both can be acquired in relatively short order, both can be articulated or declared, and both have a truth value. In each of these respects, memory for facts is distinct from memory for skills. One has to practice at a skill for a long time but one can learn in one trial that 6 is the square root of 36 or that the syllable *mev* is the last item on a study list. A person can put each of these facts into words. It is for this reason that memory for facts is also known as declara-tive memory, unlike procedural memory where procedures are difficult to articulate if at all.

Facts have truth values; consider each of the following statements:

Albany is the capital of New York.

Four is the square root of thirty-six.

Mev is the last item on the study list.

In principle, one can decide for each of the facts whether it is true or false. Skills, on the other hand, have no truth value (Tulving, 1983).

EPISODIC MEMORY

In episodic memory experiments, the experi-menter presents a list of items to the subject with the instruction to remember the list. Classical ex-perimental paradigms include paired-associate learning, serial and free recall, and recognition tests. In paired-associate learning, volunteers are presented with lists of pairs consisting of a stim-ulus and response term—for example, *mev-tox, 483-wheel*, and *la lumiere-light*. During the study phase, the person studies the list of pairs; in testing, the stimulus term is presented as a cue to recall the response term. In recall tasks, the per-son is given a list of items (see example 4.1) fol-lowed by a prompt to recall the items, usually in any order. Subjects tend to remember the first and the final items of the lists best, thus produc-ing the U-shaped serial position curve bordered by primacy and recency effects.

In the recognition paradigm, a list of items, the old items, is presented for study (Chapter 1). In testing, old items are mixed with new items not presented during study, and the subject has to indicate whether an item was a member of the study list. Recognition measures include such accuracy measures as hits, false alarms, the d' measure, as well as recognition latencies. A *hit response* refers to correct recognition of an old study item, whereas a *false alarm* refers to false recognition of a new study item (see Figure 1.2). The *d' measure* combines hits and false-alarm rates into one index that controls for partici-pants' guessing rates (Swets, Tanner, & Birdsall, 1961).

(4.1) Light, roof, shirt, clog, mare, court, slot, hand, dirt, latch

Episodic memory experiments test participants' memories for such unfamiliar information as nonsense syllables, foreign language vocabu-lary, visual scenes, and faces. Frequently, the items in memory experiments are quite familiar to learners, as, for example, the words in list

(4.1). What the learner commits to memory in these cases is the particular configuration of the items—their membership in the list.

Learners pick up more information about events than the typical memory experiment detects. In addition to memorizing the items themselves, people also learn about attributes of the items, such as their occurrence frequency and distribution. These aspects, however, have typically been subsumed under implicit memories because learners are often not aware of them, let alone of having acquired them. Episodic memory research investigates explicit aspects of retention, the acquisition of facts, their forgetting, and their recovery from memory. Borrowing from the computer metaphor, the acquisition stage is referred to as *encoding,* the period between study and testing is known as the *storage stage,* and the recovery of memories is referred to as *retrieval* (Chapter 1).

Acquiring Facts

Everyone knows that memory is based on practice. Students, teachers, and researchers know that practice is necessary for retention; the issue is to determine how the amount and the kind of practice affect retention. There is great latitude in the amount and the kind of practice that promote retention. Given a time limit, should learners memorize materials in one block or distribute the learning episodes, and, if so, how? And what strategies are optimal for recall, rehearsing items, thinking about them, visualizing them, or some other activity? In the following two sections, we will seek answers to these questions.

Amount and Spacing of Practice

The saying *Practice makes perfect* captures the relation between amount of practice and retention well (Dempster, 1996). Keeping other factors constant, the more frequently one memorizes an item, the stronger the memory trace. The

effects of the number of repetitions on retention have been widely demonstrated in animal and human learning by Ebbinghaus, Thorndike, Pavlov, Hull, and Hebb, among others. Ebbinghaus (1885) documented the relation of practice and performance using the savings method. On separate occasions, Ebbinghaus learned lists of 16 nonsense syllables and relearned them the next day. He varied the number of times he studied the lists, 8, 16, 32, and 64 times, among others. As a control condition, Ebbinghaus learned a list from scratch with 0 prior repetitions; this took him 1,270 seconds. Relearning the lists the second time, for 8, 16, 32, or 64 times, produced savings of 103, 192, 407, and 816 seconds, respectively.

The results of Ebbinghaus's experiment are plotted in Figure 4.1 on a log-log scale. A logarithmic scale compresses the distance between larger numbers. For example, using a base of 2, the logarithms for 8, 16, 32, and 64 trials are 3, 4, 5, and 6, respectively. Using logarithms to express the relation between practice and perfor-

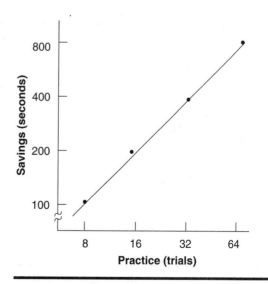

FIGURE 4.1 An increase in practice increases the amount of savings when a list is relearned (Ebbinghaus, 1885).

mance produces the straight-line functions graphed in Figures 4.1 and 4.2B.

The Power Law of Practice. Researchers express the regular relation between practice and retention in terms of the power law of practice (e.g., Anderson, 1981, 1995a; Newell & Rosenbloom, 1981; Rubin & Wenzel, 1996; Chapter 1). John Anderson and colleagues replicated the power law of practice in numerous studies using different paradigms, stimulus materials, and measures of learning. Pirolli and Anderson (1985), for example, showed in a sentence-recognition experiment that performance on a relatively small set of sentences continued to improve during a training period spanning 25 days. During the study phase, subjects memorized 16

simple sentences such as *The minister shot the hippie* and *The debutante hated the teacher.* In testing, subjects were shown old and new sentences; they had to make recognition judgments.

In Figure 4.2A, recognition latencies are plotted as a function of the number of days of practice. The curve is negatively accelerated; performance improves continuously, with the rate of improvement diminishing as practice continues. A function such as the one graphed in Figure 4.2A is known as a *power function,* where the dependent variable is expressed as a power of the independent variable. Expression (4.2) is the power function that Pirolli and Anderson fit to their data.

(4.2) $T = 1.40\, P^{-.24}$

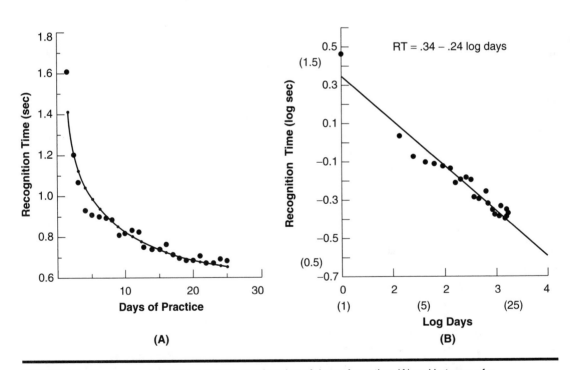

FIGURE 4.2   Recognition latencies graphed as a function of days of practice *(A)* and in terms of a log-log plot *(B)*. The data have been transformed into natural logarithms, *e* = 2.718. The y-axis includes negative values because logarithms smaller than 1 have negative values. The original values representing latencies and days are provided in parentheses (Pirolli & Anderson, 1985).

In expression (4.2), T indicates recognition latencies and P indicates the amount of practice in terms of the number of days. Expressing both variables, performance and practice, in terms of logarithms yields the equivalent linear function in Figure 4.2B.

The Pirolli and Anderson (1985) data reflect the relation of performance and practice that has been observed in a wide range of studies, whether they assessed memory for facts or for skills (Chapters 1, 5, and 7). Theorists have proposed a variety of learning mechanisms to account for the power function of practice, but a resolution among the competing proposals must await future research (e.g., Anderson, 1995a; Anderson & Schooler, 1991; Newell & Rosenbloom, 1981; Rubin & Wenzel, 1996).

Spacing Effects. It is a truism that memory depends on study time: The longer the study time, the better is retention. Study time, however, could be distributed in different ways. Suppose a learner has 60 minutes to learn some material. Should he or she devote an uninterrupted block of 60 minutes to studying the material or distribute the time, and, if so, how? Are two sessions of 30 minutes as effective as four sessions of 15 minutes? According to the total time hypothesis, distribution does not matter and retention should be a function of the total amount of study time. Bugelski (1962) found support for this hypothesis in a paired-associate experiment using nonsense syllables. Presentation time of pairs was varied from 6 to 19 seconds. It took subjects 10.2 trials to learn the list when they had 6 seconds per item; it took them only 3.3 trials when they had 19 seconds. The total study times for two conditions, however, were just about equal: 61.2 and 62.2 seconds, respectively. The total time hypothesis did hold for simple paired associates. It is, however, contradicted by spacing effects widely found for more complex stimulus materials.

Spacing of practice has been a major research issue since Ebbinghaus (1885) first discovered the lag effect—that retention is better when repeated presentations of an item are separated by other items. The lag effect has since been replicated in a wide range of tasks and for different stimulus materials, where tasks included paired-associate learning, free recall, and recognition testing, and stimuli included words, sentences, pictures, and faces. Spacing effects are not only frequent, they are also large and robust. Memorizing information in two distributed sessions often produces twice as much recall as memorizing it in one massed session of equal length. Dempster (1996) notes an important advantage of distributed practice in educational settings: Distribution not only increases the *amount* of material recalled but it also affects the *kind* of information recalled. For example, when students read science passages in distributed sessions, not only did their recall increase but their understanding of the scientific principles explained in the text also increased.

Although spacing effects are ubiquitous, the relationship between spacing and performance is not a simple one. McGeoch (1942) was already aware of the complexity among distributional factors affecting performance and concluded distribution of practice is a function of an "intricate context of conditions" (p. 123). Various intervals characterizing the distribution of practice and the time of testing affect retention, including the interval between learning sessions, the interval between presentations within a session, and the retention interval between training and testing. As for the intersession interval, the optimal rest interval depends on the type of task. In every case, an interval is better than none; the length of the intersession interval, however, should not be so long as to produce forgetting. Concerning the interpresentation interval, Madigan (1969) demonstrated that retention improves in a free-recall task when the interval between repeated presentations of the same word is increased (but see

Toppino & Gracen, 1985, who found no lag effect in free recall). Madigan presented lists of 48 different words in 72 presentations and used the following lags between repetitions: 0, 2, 4, 8, 20, and 48 intervening items. Figure 4.3 shows Madigan's results.

Unfortunately, the relation between spacing and retention is more complex than Figure 4.3 would suggest. A study by Glenberg (1976) found that the effects of distributed practice depend both on the lag between repeated trials and on the retention interval. He examined recall as a function of the retention interval (short vs. long) and the lag between repetitions (0, 1, 4, 8, 20, and 40 intervening items). He used a continuous paired-associate task (e.g., Atkinson & Shiffrin, 1968), illustrated in Figure 4.4.

Glenberg found an interaction between inter-item interval and the retention interval. At the short retention interval, repetition was more effective when the target items were separated by a few items in the learning list. On the other hand, at the long retention interval, repetition was more effective when the target items were separated by many items. In short, recall was best when the testing lag matched the study lag; that is, recall was best either when both lags were

FIGURE 4.4 Continuous paired-associate task (Glenberg, 1976). The lag between repetitions (lag = 1) is illustrated by the interval between items marked (1) and (2). The retention interval extends across eight pairs from (2) to (3).

. . .

door-seat (1)
lamp-trap
door-seat (2)
ring-move
leaf-term
ring-?
late-deep

. . .

. . .

. . .

. . . .

door-? (3)

. . .

---

short or when both lags were long. One can rationalize this interaction as follows: At short retention intervals, the trace of the two close repetitions is still effective; after long retention intervals, however, the trace of two close repetitions has effectively become one trace and is therefore not as effective as when the target item is separated by many intervening items.

The effect of spaced practice is apparent after retention intervals of up to eight years (Bahrick & Phelps, 1987). Students learned a vocabulary of 50 English-Spanish word pairs in learning sessions separated by 0, 1, or 30 days. Everyone was tested immediately after learning and then eight years later. Immediate retention did not differ in the three conditions. After eight years, however, retention in the 30-day group was 2.5 times that of the massed condition. The lesson is: If one wants to remember for the long term, distributed practice beats massed practice.

Helpful as distribution of practice is, it is not clear what mechanisms account for it. Several hypotheses have been advanced, including the encoding variability hypothesis, the attentional

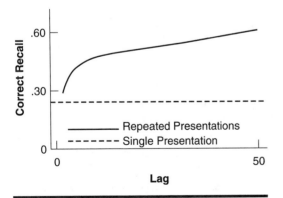

FIGURE 4.3 Probability of correct recall as a function of lag as expressed by the number of intervening items (Madigan, 1969).

effect hypothesis, and the consolidation hypothesis:

— *Encoding variability.* During the interval between repetitions, the context of the target information changes and the information is associated with diverse contexts. This yields more retrieval paths than a single presentation would (Estes, 1955).

— *Attentional effects.* Massed presentations habituate learners to the information; they do not register all aspects of the information, failing to encode it fully. On the other hand, when there is an interval, certain stimulus aspects appear novel, attracting more attention, and are processed more deeply by the learner.

— *Consolidation.* The consolidation view suggests that a memory trace is not fully formed during encoding but reorganized subsequently (Shadmehr & Holcomb, 1997). Neuroscientists assume that such reorganization is based on a "strengthening of synaptic connections," which requires new protein synthesis and other molecular processes (Abel et al., 1995). Until these processes have run their course, the memory trace is presumably fragile and subject to interference (Chapters 3 and 5).

These mechanisms are not mutually exclusive; each of them could contribute to the learning advantage resulting from distributed practice. Practically it makes little difference which factor accounts for the advantage as distributed practice improves retention in any case.

Kind of Practice: Levels of Processing

Craik and Lockhart (1972) issued a programmatic challenge to the then dominant two-store model of memory (Atkinson & Shiffrin, 1968). Whereas Atkinson and Shiffrin believed that memories are copied to the long-term store simply by being maintained in the short-term store, Craik and Lockhart (1972) argued that information undergoes a series of analyses, including perceptual analysis, pattern recognition, and semantic elaboration. The two authors described their framework as the *depth of processing* approach "where greater 'depth' implies a greater degree of semantic or cognitive analysis" (p. 675). By emphasizing encoding processes, Craik and Lockhart changed researchers' views of memory. Memory was no longer an autonomous cognitive system but a by-product of encoding processes. The greater the contribution of meaning to these processes, the stronger the memory trace. Craik and Lockhart's paper provided the framework for the levels of processing approach and became the harbinger of influential studies on the type of processing that enhances memory. We will review three of these studies.

Semantic Processing Produces Better Retention than Perceptual Processing.

Hyde and Jenkins (1973) presented the same set of stimulus materials to three groups of volunteers. Nobody was asked to memorize the words. Rather, each group worked under a different orienting task. One group was asked to rate the words for their pleasantness, the second group was asked to detect the phonemes /e/ and /g/ in words that were read to them, and the third group decided whether the word fit into a specific sentence frame. After the volunteers completed the orienting phase, a surprise recall test was given. The results revealed a clear influence of the kind of processing during encoding. Subjects who had ranked words in terms of pleasantness recalled the most words, whereas the two other groups recalled about one-third less. Judging words for their pleasantness calls on learners to think of the context in which the words are used. Doing so engages learners' semantic knowledge and provides a richer set of associations.

In other experiments, memory researchers established that the depth-of-processing effect occurred whether or not participants had the intention to learn the materials. In either case, retention was a function of the kind of encoding the learner devotes to the material. When the person attends to relatively superficial perceptual features of the stimulus, the memory trace tends to be transient, but when he or she elaborates the stimulus and links it with semantic background knowledge, the trace is stronger and more durable.

Complexity of Semantic Processing Influences Retention. Craik and Tulving (1975) presented sentence frames followed by target words and had subjects judge whether the target word would complete the sentence. Sentences included simple sentences, such as *He dropped the _____*, and complex sentences, such as *The old man hobbled across the room and picked up the valuable _____*. Target words (e.g., *watch*) were twice as memorable for complex than for simple sentences. Semantic processing was necessary in both sentence types; the latter, however, engaged deeper processing, involving more associations, and thus produced better recall.

The Generation Effect: Items Generated by Learners Are Remembered Better. Slamecka and Graf found the generation effect in a study involving a read condition and a generate condition (Slamecka & Graf, 1978). In both conditions, certain volunteers inspected items printed on index cards. In the generate condition, a card included a context word and the first letter of a related word (e.g., *rapid-f*). In the read condition, both words were printed (e.g., *rapid-fast*). There were five relations among the two words: association *(lamp-light)*, category *(ruby-diamond)*, opposite *(long-short)*, synonym *(sea-ocean)*, and rhyme *(save-cave)*. In the read condition, people simply read both words on the card and proceeded to the next card. In the generate condition, subjects were told the relation for a set of cards and asked to generate the target word. Following

the orientation phase, there was an immediate recognition test. Recognition probability was substantially better for people who generated the targets than for readers, regardless of the relation between context word and target.

Can the generate effect help instruction? Professors believe that students learn better when they generate answers themselves. The experimental evidence, however, is equivocal. Carrol and Nelson (1993) failed to replicate the generate effect using general information questions as stimuli—for example, *What is the capital of Finland?* Healy and Sinclair (1996), however, obtained a generate effect when they taught students multiplication in a generate condition. In the read condition, the problems and solutions were read by subjects, in the generate condition, only the problem was given and the subjects had to generate the solution. According to Healy's view, the generate condition encouraged learners to use the multiplication procedure, whereas the read condition did not. Therefore, the better memory resulted from executing and practicing the multiplication skill (Chapter 5).

Evaluating the Levels-of-Processing Framework. The levels-of-processing approach was very successful in promoting research on the effect of encoding conditions on memory and in providing a framework for a host of previous discoveries. The latter include the effects of mnemonic devices such as the method of loci, the beneficial effects of organization on recall (Chapter 12; Bower, Clark, Lesgold, & Winzenz, 1969; Miller, 1956), and the improved recall when learners make up a story or form a vivid image involving the target items (Bower, 1970). In each of these cases, the more elaborate the learner's processing, the better the retention.

Levels-of-processing theorists have accounted for these results by assuming that deeper semantic processing leads to more meaningful and more durable memory traces. Critics have argued, however, that depth is a vague, and, indeed circular notion because it cannot be measured independently of the presumed memory benefits (Nelson, 1977). To be sure, there have been numerous efforts to explain the depth concept more fully. According to one view, deeper processing means to associate the target information with familiar background knowledge, whether it involves easily remembered locations, numbers, or stories. Another interpretation is that thinking of elaborations and generating responses create retrieval paths and therefore provide additional opportunities to recover the target memories (Anderson & Reder; 1979). Mäntylä (1986) suggested that generating responses makes them more distinctive to the learner and thus more memorable.

The beneficial effect of distinctiveness on retention was demonstrated long ago by von Restorff (1933). She embedded deviant items among homogeneous items and found superior recall for the distinctive targets (see also Graesser, Gordon, & Sawyer, 1979). Consider the following list: *ford, chevy, mazda, pineapple, toyota, cadillac, chrysler.* The oddball stimulus, *pineapple,* stands out and attracts attention and therefore has an encoding advantage. The extra encoding operations accorded to an oddball stimulus have even been detected at the level of brain processes: Researchers have found that deviant stimuli elicit characteristic event-related brain potentials and cerebral blood-flow patterns (Fabiani & Donchin, 1995; Schacter, 1996).

Semantic elaboration affords more distinctions than does phonological encoding. Consider the word *cat* in phonological terms—for example, its phonemes /c/, /a/, and /t/, and the rhymes you can form with it: *hat, bat, mat.* There are relatively few dimensions by which one can characterize *cat* in phonological terms. It is far easier to come up with semantic links to *cat:* cat and dog, my friend's cat, Siamese cat, different types of domestic cats, the cat species, cats in literature, and so on. The point is that semantic coding is richer and allows creation of a more differentiated memory trace (Baddeley, 1990).

Distinctiveness need not be defined in semantic terms; items may be distinctive because of their physical features or because of their unique position in the list of learned items. Glenberg (1987) suggests that the recency effect in free recall results from the fact that recent items are temporally more distinctive than other list items. Baddeley (1990) notes that learners can enhance the distinctiveness of items by encoding them in terms of a motor response. When learners perform a motor act on an object, such as turning a screw, they remember the object better than when they are read an instruction of how to perform the action (Glenberg, 1997).

The familiarity account, the retrieval path hypothesis, and the distinctiveness hypothesis offer theoretical interpretations of levels of processing in encoding. They do not provide the assessment of processing levels independent from performance that Nelson (1977) called for. Kapur and colleagues (1994) believe that imaging measures of learners' brain activity as they work in different orienting tasks provides that independent assessment. These authors recorded cerebral blood-flow changes as subjects engaged in a shallow orienting task and a deeper semantic task. In the shallow task, volunteers checked target words for the presence of the letter *a.* In the semantic task, they decided whether a target word described a living or nonliving entity. As expected, recognition performance was superior following the semantic task than the letter-checking task. Importantly, the researchers found that when subjects performed the semantic task, there was increased regional blood flow in the left inferior prefrontal cortex. The implication is not that this region is *the* seat of episodic memories. Rather, the researchers speculate that the left inferior prefrontal structures form part of an episodic memory network and that activity in this region produces a more accessible memory trace. These measures of brain activity validate the abstract formulations of processing levels and are consistent with performance measures at the same time.

Transfer-Appropriate Processing

The data attributed to levels of processing permit an alternative interpretation known as the *transfer-appropriate processing hypothesis*. According to this hypothesis, a retention test is a kind of transfer test, and, as in other transfer tests, it is the similarity between encoding and retrieval that determines retention rather than encoding processes alone (Morris, Bransford, & Franks, 1977; Roediger & Guynn, 1996). As an illustration, consider the effects of phonetic encoding on retention in light of the two theories: The levels-of-processing theory says that phonetic encoding produces poor recall because phonetic traces are shallow. The transfer-appropriate processing theory says that in the standard levels-of-processing paradigm phonetic encoding produces poor retention because different processes are used in encoding and testing: phonetic processing in encoding versus semantic processing in testing. However, one can increase retention for the phonetic encoding condition simply by using a phonetic prompt in testing. Doing so would increase the similarity between learning and testing conditions, thus yielding better transfer and retention.

Morris and colleagues (1977) demonstrated support of the transfer-appropriate processing view in an experiment in which they manipulated the similarity between encoding and retrieval conditions using a 2 × 2 design. There were two encoding tasks: a semantic encoding task and a phonetic encoding task. In both tasks, people were given sentences with one word missing followed by a target word. In the semantic encoding task, sentences were of the form *The _____ had a silver engine.* Each sentence was followed by a target word that was semantically consistent or inconsistent with the sentence (e.g., *train* vs. *eagle*). The subjects' task was to judge the word's consistency with the sentence. In the phonetic encoding task, sentences were of the form _____ *rhymes with legal.* Target words either formed rhymes with the sentence frame or not (e.g., *eagle* vs. *peach*). In this condition, the subjects' task was to judge whether the target words rhymed with the sentence. As is customary in the levels-of-processing paradigm, subjects were told in neither condition that a subsequent memory test would be given. All they had to do was to make the semantic or phonetic judgments about the target words.

In testing, half of the volunteers received the standard recognition test in which their retention was tested for the target words presented in the study phase. As expected, in this condition, performance was better for the semantic encoding condition than for the rhyming condition. The other half of the subjects were given a recognition test where the test items were rhymes of the items they had seen during study. For example, subjects who heard *eagle* during study were prompted with *regal* during testing. In this condition, subjects who had encoded the target words in terms of rhymes performed better than subjects who had received the standard encoding instructions, just as the transfer-appropriate processing theory predicted. The point of these results is that it is the degree of transfer between encoding and testing conditions that determines memory rather than the encoding task by itself.

Theories of Forgetting

Once a memory trace is encoded, we can explore its fate during the retention interval. The story of memories after study is simply told: Many of the memories are forgotten. Immediately after learning, the rate of forgetting is relatively rapid. Subsequently, the rate of forgetting levels off, with almost no forgetting at longer retention intervals (see Figure 2.1). Because the forgetting curve is best described by a power function, the relation between forgetting and the retention interval has been called the *Power Law of Forgetting* (Anderson, 1995a; Wixted & Ebbesen, 1991, 1997). The power function captures the course of forgetting of all kinds of materials, in different species, and across different individuals (for the exception of autobiographical memories, see Rubin & Wenzel, 1996).

The reasons for forgetting are less clear. Except for Thorndike (1911), early memory researchers attributed forgetting to interference between associations. Thorndike thought that memory associations decay as a result of disuse, much like muscles weaken when one does not exercise. The disuse notion was challenged for empirical and conceptual reasons. The empirical challenge came from studies demonstrating that recall sometimes improves during the retention interval. Brown (1923) demonstrated that people remembered more facts on a second of two recall tests, even after a lengthy retention interval and without additional learning opportunity, an effect known as *hypermnesia* (Chapter 2; Erdelyi & Kleinbard, 1978).

The conceptual challenge to disuse theory was raised by McGeoch (1942) when he wrote,

> *Forgetting could not be accounted for by disuse, if disuse means only passage of time, for time, in and of itself, is not a determining condition of events in nature. It is a conceptual framework in which activities go their ways and in terms of which events are plotted. In time, iron may rust and men grow old, but the rusting and the aging are understood in terms of the chemical and other events which occur in time, not in terms of time itself. (McGeoch, 1942, p. 455)*

Classical Interference Theory

McGeoch distinguished between retroactive interference and proactive interference. The former refers to the inhibiting effects of later learning on earlier learning, whereas the latter refers to the competition of earlier learning with subsequent learning.

Retroactive Interference. *Retroactive interference* means that new information disrupts retention of some prior information. Memory researchers introduced the A-B, A-C paradigm to study retroactive interference. In original learning, experimental subjects receive paired-associate training trials on a list of stimulus items denoted A, paired with a list of responses denoted B. Then, after an interval, experimental subjects receive training with the original list of stimuli paired with a new list of responses, denoted C, whereas control subjects rest. Interference is reflected by the result on the subsequent A-B test list. Recall is poorer for the experimental group than the control group.

Experimental Group: A-B, A-C, A-B
Control Group: A-B, Rest, A-B

Table 4.1 contains sample lists of paired associates for the experimental and control groups of the A-B, A-C design used to study retroactive interference. Note that the experimental group

TABLE 4.1 A-B, A-C Design for the Study of Retroactive Interference

Experimental Group		
Original Learning A-B List	Interpolated Learning A-C List	Test A-B List
xej-fon	xej-sec	xej-fon
tel-cum	tel-qih	tel-cum
cij-dul	cij-pac	cij-dul
hod-bof	hod-jek	hod-bof
bip-qes	bip-loj	bip-qus
Control Group		
Original Learning A-B List	Rest Rest	Test A-B List
xej-fon		xej-fon
tel-cum		tel-cum
cij-dul		cij-dul
hod-bof		hod-bof
bip-qes		bip-qes

sees the same stimulus terms in the A-B and A-C phases of training. What differs is the response term. Thus, the first stimulus term, *xej*, must be memorized together with *fon* during original learning and then with *sec* during interpolated learning. In testing, *fon* is the correct response. In the control group, *xej-fon* is the only combination learned and tested. This group rests while the experimental group learns the A-C list in the interpolated learning phase. In final A-B testing, the control group typically performs better than the experimental group.

Proactive Interference. *Proactive interference* refers to the interfering effects of prior learning on later learning. It is as if the prior learning competes with the capacity available for later learning. Researchers assess proactive interference in the following paradigm:

Experimental Group: A-C, A-B, A-B
Control Group: Rest A-B, A-B

In one study of proactive interference by Greenberg and Underwood (see Underwood, 1983), subjects learned four lists of 10 adjective pairs on four successive days. Two days later, they had to recall each list. Underwood found proactive interference: Recall decreased substantially with the number of prior lists (see also Anderson, 1983b).

The Unlearning Hypothesis. One influential theory of forgetting, the *unlearning hypothesis,* attributed the deficit of the experimental group versus the control group in the retroactive interference design to unlearning, or extinction, of the original A-B associations during interpolated A-C learning (Melton & Irwin, 1940). When the subject responded with *fon* to *xej* in interpolated learning, the *xej-fon* association was extinguished in terms of the conditioning paradigm (see Chapter 2).

The unlearning hypothesis entails a prediction that experimenters can easily test. The argument runs as follows: If paired-associate learning obeys the principles of conditioning and if the A-B associations are extinguished during interpolated A-C learning, then one would expect spontaneous recovery of A-B associations during the interval following the A-C phase. Briggs (1954) tested this prediction in a modified free-recall test. At various intervals after A-C learning, the learners were given the A-terms and asked to respond with whatever term, B or C or something else, they thought of first.

Figure 4.5 is a schematic of Briggs's results. Figure 4.5A shows the learning curve for A-B responses in Briggs's (1954) study. Figure 4.5B shows the increase of A-C responses with the concomitant unlearning of A-B responses during A-C learning, as predicted by the unlearning hypothesis. And Figure 4.5C shows, again as predicted, that C responses decrease as the B responses spontaneously recover, at least in relative terms, during the interval following A-C learning. Although these data support the unlearning hypothesis, it ultimately lost support, if for no other reason than the nebulous nature of the concept of spontaneous recovery (see Crowder, 1976). Recovery was assumed to occur spontaneously as a function of the passage of time, much like autonomous decay in decay theory. However, if McGeoch's criticism that "time, in and of itself, is not a determining condition of events in nature" holds against decay, it must hold against for spontaneous recovery, as well.

In the 1960s, classical interference theory was dominant and able to account for a broad array of experimental results. Subsequently, challenges to the theory were raised and it lost supporters with the rise of such alternative models as the information-processing framework and Tulving's retrieval theory. One of the challenges was the finding that interference depends on the type of stimulus material. Whereas interference is observed with nonsense syllables and individual words, there is very little interference when

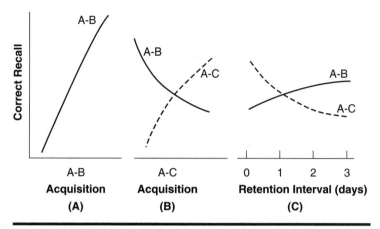

FIGURE 4.5   Learning, unlearning, and recovery in paired-associate training. *(A)* Learning of A-B responses in the first stage of Briggs's (1954) study. *(B)* Learning of A-C responses and concurrent unlearning of A-B responses during A-C learning. *(C)* Decrease in C responses as B responses spontaneously recover during the interval following A-C learning.

meaningful passages are used. Furthermore, according to interference theory, there have to be multiple learning phases of prior, original, and interpolated learning to produce forgetting. Yet forgetting occurs, even when subjects have to learn single lists or even only single items. In these cases, one must identify sources of extra-experimental interference arising from outside the laboratory. These, however, were difficult to specify.

As for decay theory, consider a reinterpretation in terms of interference at the neural level. McGeoch (1942) advocated interference as the cause of forgetting because he believed that traces could not decay as a function of the passage of time alone. He could not have foreseen the advances in the neurosciences that have given researchers a better understanding of the molecular events at the synaptic level as associations are formed. It is now known that associations at the synaptic level undergo changes as a function of time that can strengthen and weaken associations (Abel et al., 1995). In light of such discoveries, decay may be interpreted as inter-ference among neurochemical processes during the retention interval.

Interference as Resource Diffusion

The concept of interference among associations has survived in different guises in episodic memory models, even after the demise of classical-interference theory. According to Watkins's (1979) cue-overload principle, the strength of a recall prompt diminishes as the number of items that are associated with the cue increases. According to another interpretation, interference may be viewed as diffusion of a limited resource. Consider a memory model that assumes memory representations, activation levels of representations, and links between the representations. Assume the representations and links illustrated in Figure 4.6. The figure includes three nodes for the representations, A, B, and C, where A corresponds to the stimulus, B and C correspond to responses, and A-B, and A-C represent associations. Resource diffusion models assume a finite amount of activation shared among associations such A-B and A-C. If one strengthens one of

FIGURE 4.6 Stimulus A is associated with two responses, B and C, thus diffusing the total amount of activation available to each.

these associations, the other is weakened, and the more associations exist, the less activation is available for each of them (see Fan Effect in Chapter 7).

Reprise on Interference Theory

We have reviewed research on interference conducted in the laboratory. However, note that early researchers were interested in interference because of its role in everyday life, especially in the classroom and in the courtroom. Eyewitness testimony and ways of changing it were a prime example of interference that the pioneers of memory research had in mind. Binet reported as early as 1900 that children's recall of a scene could be distorted by leading questions (Binet, 1900). Binet's study inaugurated the suggestion design where subjects were exposed to some new information after observing an event. The new information changed the person's recollection of the original event; we will return to these issues in Chapter 12 (Loftus, Feldman, & Dashiell, 1995).

Although interference occurs in everyday life and has been demonstrated in the laboratory, including at the molecular level, there is more to forgetting and remembering than interference. Even if a trace survives interference from other traces during the retention interval, this does not mean that it will be recovered. In the next section, we will see that facts apparently lost can be recovered, provided that effective retrieval cues are used. In general, retention depends to a much larger degree on the interplay between processes learners engage in during study and testing than the major theories of forgetting acknowledged.

Retrieval

Retrieval occurs every time we recognize a familiar stimulus, whether it is a sound, word, or face. *Retrieval* literally means recovering information from memory. In episodic memory experiments, retrieval is explicitly triggered by prompting the learner with a retrieval cue to recollect facts memorized in the learning phase. This section will show that retrieval of information depends on the relation between encoding and retrieval contexts. In general, retrieval is improved when there are retrieval cues to reinstate the environment, both internal and external, that existed when the information was memorized in the first place.

It was Endel Tulving who advanced retrieval theory in the 1970s as an alternative to classical interference theory (Tulving, 1974). Recalling Semon's emphasis on retrieval of traces (Chapter 2), Tulving asserted that a memory trace, however intact it may be, remains dormant unless elicited by the appropriate stimulus. He and his colleagues demonstrated the role of retrieval cues in numerous paradigms, three of which will be reviewed: (1) the retrieval of previously unavailable information, (2) the role of the number of cues to recover information, and (3) the recall superiority over recognition.

Role of Retrieval Cues

Use of Category Cues to Recover Unavailable Information. Tulving and Psotka (1971) illustrated the role of retrieval cues by construing a condition in which previously unavailable information was recovered. The researchers had subjects memorize lists of categorized words, including cities, car models, colors, and fruits. Recall testing was accomplished in two stages.

First, the volunteers tried to recall the words without seeing the category names; then, category names were presented as cues. Recall increased from 40 to 70%. The cues had brought to light information that appeared to have been forgotten.

Number of Cues to Access a Memory Trace. It is well known that recognition testing produces better retention performance than recall testing. Tulving attributed this recognition superiority to retrieval effects. In the recognition paradigm, learners see a list of items both during study and testing; in the recall paradigm, they see the list only during learning. In recall testing, learners receive only a general recall prompt; no information of the items themselves is provided. Tulving argued that a recognition test mimics the encoding environment better than a recall test does. If at least some item cues were given to learners during testing, their retention should improve.

Tulving and Watkins (1973) evaluated this hypothesis in a design that sought to keep the memory trace constant while varying the number of cues available in different retrieval conditions. They had volunteers learn 28 five-letter words. Retention was tested by presenting a varying set of letters of the target words to different subject groups. The sets varied from zero letters to all five letters. For example, for the word *grape,* different subject groups would be given the following cues: -, *g-, gr-, gra-, grap-,* or *grape.* The probability of recalling a word increased from 0.25 to 0.85 as the number of cues was increased from zero to five. The zero condition is equivalent to the conventional free-recall paradigm, and the five-letter condition corresponds to the recognition test. Since the target items and the encoding operations were identical in the different conditions, the memory traces must have been identical and the increase in recall from the zero-letter condition to the full-word condition must have come from the increase of the number of retrieval cues in testing (for an alternative view on recognition superiority, see Anderson & Bower, 1972).

The Tulving and Watkins study produced the superiority of recognition typically found. Is it possible to reverse the typical result? In other words, are there conditions under which recall produces better retention than recognition? The answer to this question is yes. All one needs to do is to increase the similarity of encoding and retrieval in recall and decrease it in the recognition test. Tulving and Thomson (1973) implemented this idea in an experiment involving multiple phases.

Recall Superiority. In the first phase of their study, Tulving and Thomson (1973) had subjects memorize words presented in pairs such as *ground-cold,* where *cold* was the to-be-remembered target and *ground* was a weak associate (as opposed to a strong associate such as *hot*). In the second phase, subjects were given a list of the strong associates of the target words (e.g., *hot*). Subjects were asked to write any word next to these items that they could think of. For example, a subject might write in response to *hot* the following words: *cold, winter, Arctic, Florida,* and so on. Then, using the list of words that they had written down, subjects were asked to identify among the written words all those words that they had seen in the first phase of the experiment, (e.g., *cold*). This, of course, was the recognition test. Recall was tested by giving the volunteers the associates of target words they had seen during the first phase (e.g., *ground*). Their task was to recall the target (e.g., *cold*). In this experiment, retention was better in recall than in recognition because the experimenters had succeeded in constructing a recall test that preserved the encoding environment better than the recognition test did. At the time, this finding created a great furor among memory researchers because the superiority of recognition over recall had never been challenged.

The Relation of Encoding and Retrieval Environments

William James already knew that what is now called the *encoding context* makes a difference in remembering materials. His advice was to memorize information in several different contexts so as to link the items to many "hooks" in the mind. In his study of the advantages of distributed over massed practice, Madigan (1969) came to a similar conclusion (Estes, 1955).

Clearly, the relation between encoding and retrieval was intuitively understood, but that insight had little influence on memory research until Tulving elevated retrieval to the celebrated place it now enjoys and formulated the *encoding specificity principle.* The principle states that retrieval is successful to the extent that the retrieval cues match the cues the learner used during the study phase. Experimental demonstrations of the encoding specificity principle are straightforward: The experimenter covaries encoding and retrieval conditions in a 2 × 2 factorial design. Two encoding conditions, A and B, and two retrieval conditions, a and b, are used. The encoding specificity principle predicts superior performance in cells Aa and Bb where encoding and retrieval conditions match and poorer performance in cells Ab and Ba where they do not match, as illustrated in Figure 4.7. This design has been realized in several experimental contexts, varying verbal materials, physical environments, as well as mental states and moods of the learners. In every case, retention was better when the retrieval condition matched the encoding condition.

Verbal Materials.   Using the 2 × 2 design in Figure 4.7 and paired associates as stimulus materials, Fisher and Craik (1977) covaried encoding and retrieval conditions. They used rhyme-based pairs such as *hat-cat* and semantically based pairs such as *dog-cat*. Half of the subjects learned the *hat-cat* pairs; the other half learned the *dog-cat* pairs. In testing, both groups were divided into two subgroups for tests with the rhyme and the semantic associate, respectively. Fisher and Craik found that recall of the targets (e.g., *cat*) was best when the testing and retrieval cues were the same (see Figure 4.8A).

Environmental Conditions.   Godden and Baddeley (1975) varied environmental conditions during study and testing. They trained deep-sea divers to memorize a list of words in two training environments: either on land or in an underwater tank. In testing, the divers were exposed to the same or the alternate context. Recall was best when the divers were tested in the same rather than in the alternate environment (see Figure 4.8B).

Mental and Mood States of Learners.   In studies of state-dependent memory, volunteers were in one of two pharmacological states during learning: intoxicated or sober. For testing, the subjects were either in the same state or shifted to the other state. Retrieval was better when the volunteers were in the same state during learning and testing. Figure 4.8C shows the number of words recalled under the four conditions in a study on state-dependent memory by Eich, Weingartner, Stillman, and Gillin (1975). The encoding specificity principle applies to learning and remembering under different mood states: Recall is better when mood states in learning and testing match than when they do not (Figure 4.8D).

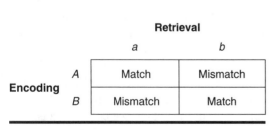

FIGURE 4.7   2 x 2 factorial design to covary encoding and retrieval conditions.

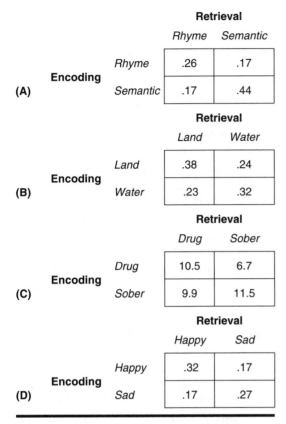

		Retrieval	
		Rhyme	Semantic
Encoding	Rhyme	.26	.17
(A)	Semantic	.17	.44

		Retrieval	
		Land	Water
Encoding	Land	.38	.24
(B)	Water	.23	.32

		Retrieval	
		Drug	Sober
Encoding	Drug	10.5	6.7
(C)	Sober	9.9	11.5

		Retrieval	
		Happy	Sad
Encoding	Happy	.32	.17
(D)	Sad	.17	.27

FIGURE 4.8 The encoding/retrieval paradigm as realized in four experimental contexts. *(A)* Verbal conditions (Fischer & Craik, 1977). *(B)* Physical conditions (Godden & Baddeley, 1975). *(C)* State-dependent memory (Eich, Weingartner, Stillman, & Gillin, 1975). *(D)* Mood-dependent memory (Eich & Metcalfe, 1989).

In sum, the principal results on the role of retrieval and its relation to encoding are the following:

— Information thought forgotten can be recovered when retrieval cues are provided that reinstate the encoding environment.

— Recognition typically is better than recall because it provides more cues from the study context than recall does. However, if one construes a recall task so that it provides the cues necessary for successful retrieval, recall can be made to be superior to recognition.

— The encoding specificity principle captures the results from diverse experimental paradigms: Retention is best when the retrieval cues match the cues the learner used during study in order to encode the information.

This body of research makes a strong case for retrieval theory and for the congruity of encoding and retrieval conditions as the learner recovers information from memory. Retrieval theory has changed memory research during the past quarter century. The theory led to a reinterpretation of the benefits of mnemonic devices and memory training in terms of retrieval structures. In both cases, learners generate a retrieval device during encoding; at testing, they use the retrieval structure to access the set of memorized facts. Retrieval and structures to support retrieval became an integral part of every major memory model (e.g., Raaijmakers & Shiffrin, 1981). Retrieval theory has yielded tangible dividends as well for applied cognitive psychologists who used the encoding specificity principle to enhance recall in applied contexts, such as in eyewitness recall (see Chapter 12).

Retrieval Practice and Inhibition
The research focus on retrieval led to the discovery of important cognitive dynamics of retrieval. Researchers discovered that learners can practice retrieval and thereby improve retention much as they practice other skills. On the other hand, retrieval may also produce forgetting. Practicing retrieval of some instances of the members of a category to be memorized may inhibit recall of the other members of that category that did not have the benefit of practice.

Retrieval Practice. Ordinarily, tests are thought of as means of assessing what students have learned. Educators, however, know that tests can advance learning, as well. Numerous studies have shown that taking preliminary tests, even without feedback, improves students' performance on the final test (Dempster, 1996; Erdelyi & Kleinbard, 1978). Critics have argued that the repeated tests provided learners with additional opportunities to encode the material and thus improve retention. An experiment by Carrier and Pashler (1992) ruled out this possibility by equating the encoding opportunities in a retrieval practice and a control condition.

Carrier and Pashler (1992) used a paired-associate task mimicking a vocabulary learning situation. Stimulus materials included nonsense syllables paired with numbers and pairs of words in a dialect of the Inuit language and their English counterparts. The experiment included a study phase, a retrieval practice phase, and a testing phase. During study, all paired associates were presented one at a time on a computer screen. During retrieval practice, some of the pairs were presented in terms of pure study trials and the others in terms of test trial/study trials, as indicated in Figure 4.9. In both conditions, subjects were asked to say aloud the appropriate response term as soon as the stimulus term appeared on the screen. For pure study trials, this simply meant that subjects were reading the response terms. In test trial/study trials, the response term was not shown at first and the

learner had to retrieve it; hence the term *retrieval practice*. After a five-second interval, the response was shown on the computer screen.

During testing, subjects' retention was assessed by presenting only the stimulus terms. Retrieval practice produced better retention, even after an interval of 24 hours. Effects were moderate; learners gained anywhere from 8 to 15% over the pure study trials. Nevertheless, retrieval practice has implications for educational practice—for example, for learning vocabulary, as in the Carrier and Pashler study and for the learning of terminologies in general.

Retrieval practice can be made even more effective by implementing the expanded rehearsal technique introduced by Landauer and Bjork (1978). Using a paired-associate paradigm, these two investigators asked learners to memorize the first names of fictitious persons paired with their last names. The researchers used two schedules of spacing repetitions of trials: an expanding schedule and a contracting schedule. In the expanding rehearsal schedule, the lags between repetitions of the study pairs increased in three steps from 1 to 10 intervening trials. In the contracting schedule, the lags decreased (10, 4, 1 intervening trials). Landauer and Bjork found superior recall in the expanding condition, suggesting that longer intervals between rehearsals boosted an item's memory strength just prior to the point of forgetting. Bjork (1988) described the expanded rehearsal procedure as a way of shaping the memory trace to become resistant to forgetting. He equated the benefits of the procedure with those of mnemonic devices that are intended to enhance the retention of factual information (see also Banaji & Crowder, 1989; Chapters 5, 11, and 12).

Remembering Can Cause Forgetting! The title for this section is not an exaggeration: Research on output interference established decades ago that remembering of some target information can cause forgetting of competing in-

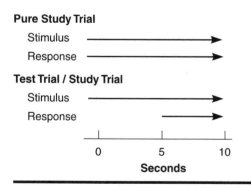

Pure Study Trial

Stimulus

Response

Test Trial / Study Trial

Stimulus

Response

0   5   10

Seconds

FIGURE 4.9 Types of trials during retrieval practice (Carrier & Pashler, 1992).

formation (Tulving & Arbuckle, 1963; Anderson & Neely, 1996, p. 270). Similar interference effects were observed by Brown (1968) in a semantic memory study. Brown investigated people's recall of the 50 U.S. states in two conditions. In one condition, volunteers were simply told to recall any state they could think of, whereas in the other condition, volunteers received help from the experimenter; they were given the names of 25 states and the opportunity to study them for 10 minutes in the expectation that the hint would afford subjects new access routes to the remaining states and thus increase recall of those states. Brown, however, found the opposite result: People who received the extra study opportunity recalled fewer states than people given no hint at all. In episodic memory research, this effect is known as the *part-list cueing effect:* Providing learners with cues for a subset of the target list reduces the recall probability of the remaining items (Raaijmakers, 1993; Tulving & Hastie, 1972). Results such as these demonstrate that remembering may, indeed, cause forgetting.

What is the forgetting due to? According to M. Anderson and colleagues, it is due to active inhibition produced during the retrieval of target items. Anderson supported his hypothesis in several studies using the retrieval practice paradigm consisting of three phases: learning, retrieval practice, and testing. We shall review two of Anderson's studies here.

Demonstrating Inhibition. During the learning phase of their first experiment, Anderson, Bjork, and Bjork (1994) had subjects study eight categories of six exemplars each (e.g., *fruit-orange, fruit-tomato, tool-pliers*), as shown in the left column of Table 4.2. In the retrieval practice phase, items were classified as follows:

1. During retrieval practice, half of the studied categories were shown (e.g., *fruit or _____*); the subjects had to supply the rest of the stem.

TABLE 4.2 Retrieval Practice Design Used in Anderson, Bjork, and Bjork's (1994) Study

Learning Phase	Retrieval Practice	Testing
	Retrieval Practice (target category)	
Fruit-orange	Fruit or_____	Fruit
Fruit-nectarine	Fruit ne_____	
Fruit-pineapple	Fruit pi_____	
	Unpracticed (target category)	
Fruit-banana		
Fruit-grape		Fruit
Fruit-lemon		
	Unpracticed (other category)	
Insects-fly		Insects
Insects-mosquito		
Insects-grasshopper		

2. Not shown during retrieval practice were (a) the other half of the items of the *fruit* category (labeled Unpracticed [target category] in Table 4.2) and (b) exemplars of the baseline category (labeled Unpracticed [other category]; e.g., insects).

In testing, subjects were given the names of all categories they had seen during study and asked to recall as many instances for each of the categories as possible.

The experimenters were interested in the effect of retrieval practice on the retention of the unpracticed members of the target category (e.g., unpracticed fruits) relative to the not practiced baseline category (e.g., insects). Recall was best for practiced exemplars of the target category (73.6%), intermediate for exemplars from the baseline category (48.5%), and poorest for unpracticed exemplars of the target category (37.5%).

Retrieval inhibition is reflected by the *lower recall* of instances of the same category that were not practiced than items of the other unpracticed category, the baseline category. Whereas retrieval practice improved the recall of practiced items, it *reduced* the recall of unpracticed items of the target category compared to the baseline category. The retrieval practice effect is not surprising; the depressed recall of unpracticed items of the same category, however, is. According to Anderson and colleagues (1994), the retrieval-induced forgetting effect results from active inhibition. If it were not for such inhibition, the recall level of the two unpracticed categories (e.g., unpracticed fruits and insects) would be equivalent.

Demonstrating the Spread of Inhibition across Categories. In a second research project, Anderson and Spellman (1995) studied the inhibition processes further. Specifically, they explored the hypothesis that inhibition spreads to items that are semantically related to the target category, even if they are members of a different category. The researchers used the retrieval practice paradigm and had learners go through the same three phases described before. In the learning phase, category-exemplar pairs were presented for study (e.g., *red-blood, red-tomato, food-strawberry*). Note the two former pairs were considered members of a category defined by the color red. During retrieval practice, only half of the category-exemplar pairs (e.g., *red-blood*) were practiced, while the other half was not practiced. By definition, members of the unpracticed category (e.g., *food*) were not presented during retrieval practice. In testing, the goal was to recall as many items of each category as possible.

In order to evaluate the idea that inhibition spreads to related items of other categories, Anderson and Spellman (1995) introduced a new manipulation. They introduced a semantically related condition and an unrelated condition and varied the relatedness between the unpracticed and the practiced categories. In the related condition, illustrated in Table 4.3A, there were implicit links between the practiced cate-

TABLE 4.3   Recall as a Function of Category Relatedness and Retrieval Practice (Anderson et al., 1995, Experiment 1)

	A. Related Condition		
	Learning Phase	*Retrieval Practice*	*Testing*
Practiced items	RED-BLOOD	RED-BL____	try to recall (74)
Unpracticed items	RED-TOMATO	unpracticed	all items of (22)
Unpracticed	FOOD-STRAWBERRY	unpracticed	categories (22)
	B. Unrelated Condition		
	Learning Phase	*Retrieval Practice*	*Testing*
Practiced items	TOOL-PLIERS	TOOL-PL____	try to recall (69)
Unpracticed items	TOOL-DRILL	unpracticed	all items of (24)
Unpracticed category	FOOD-STRAWBERRY	unpracticed	categories (38)

gory (e.g., red items) and items of the unpracticed category (e.g., *strawberry*). In the unrelated condition, illustrated in Table 4.3B, the practiced category (e.g., *tools*) was not related to the unpracticed category (e.g., *strawberry*).

The spreading inhibition hypothesis predicts the following scenario for the related condition. Due to spreading inhibition, retrieval practice on items of the type *red-bl____* would depress recall not only of same category items (e.g., *red-tomato)* but also of unpracticed items in the unpracticed related category (e.g., *food-strawberry*). In other words, inhibition should spread to other items related to *red*, even if they belong to another category. Anderson and Spellman referred to such inhibition as *cross-category inhibition*.

In the unrelated condition, there were no implicit links between practiced items (e.g., the *tool* category) and the unpracticed category (e.g., *food-strawberry*). Consequently, inhibition would remain confined to the practiced category and its items, and recall of the pair *food-strawberry* would not be inhibited. The results confirmed the spreading inhibition account. Recall of critical pairs, such as *food-strawberry,* was 22% in the related condition versus 38% in the unrelated condition (see percentages listed in parentheses in Table 4.3).

The research on retrieval practice and inhibition has both theoretical and practical implications. The retrieval practice effects and cross-category interference suggest that interference is based in part on inhibition. Inhibition counters activation but, much like activation, it spreads to related items in a category. As for inhibiting recollections, the inhibition concept is similar to the dissociation concept advanced by clinical psychologists. In this context, *dissociation* refers to the temporary block of memories that are emotionally painful. These memories are not obliterated; rather, the emotional trauma has rendered them inaccessible to consciousness. Schacter argues further that inhibition is a basic process in the brain designed to reduce the impact of a multitude of feelings, thoughts, and external stimuli. In fact, brain-imaging studies have demonstrated that brain activity may be reduced in certain regions when subjects seek to retrieve specific target information (Schacter, 1996, p. 235).

Retrieval inhibition also has implications for such applications as eyewitness testimony. Following a crime or an accident, witnesses are typically questioned about the events they have observed. Such questioning constitutes a kind of retrieval practice. Responding to the questions may strengthen the information that has been queried and inhibit traces of events that were not queried. Shaw, Bjork, and Handal (1995) demonstrated just such an effect in a simulated eyewitness experiment. The moral of their experiment is this: Interviewers must ensure that the interview is complete and not based on a subset of the events the person has witnessed. Asking the person about a subset of the events witnessed is equivalent to an incomplete retrieval task, one in which retrieval blocking tends to occur.

Our review of episodic memory from the encoding to the retrieval stage was based on the simplifying assumption that episodic and semantic memory are separate. Episodic and semantic memory are, however, interdependent. Much of our semantic knowledge resulted from encoding it first in the context of some episode, however fleeting—for example, when we first learn the meaning of an unfamiliar word. Episodic memory, in turn, depends on semantic memory. When people memorize paired associates, word lists, and sentences, they encode the information in terms of their linguistic and world knowledge. Retention of episodic memories is improved when learners succeed in assimilating the target information to their knowledge of the world. In semantic memory research, the focus is on such preexperimental knowledge. Semantic memory research addresses the representation and retrieval of semantic knowledge rather than its acquisition.

SEMANTIC MEMORY

Semantic memory comprises the vast knowledge people have of the meaning of words, of the properties and structure of objects, and of typical events in everyday life and the relations among them. People can express this knowledge if needed, but as a rule, they do not know how they acquired it. This section discusses such entities of semantic memory as concepts, causal relations, and schemas. None of these constructs was invented by psychologists. They were advanced by philosophers from Aristotle's time to the present. The innovation of psychologists was to formulate structural assumptions and processing models subject to experimental testing.

Representation of Concepts

Concepts are the fundamental units of thought. They organize the multitude of objects in the environment and reduce them to a smaller number; if there were no concepts, one would have to refer to all individual instances one by one. Concepts embody knowledge about objects that is not immediately apparent but can easily be inferred. Concepts and their representation in the mind have been the subject of philosophical thought and psychological research. Here, we will review three psychological models of the representation of concepts: semantic networks, prototype models, and exemplar models.

Semantic Networks

Semantic network models entered psychology by way of computer science. Collins and Quillian (1969) developed a semantic network model in order to achieve efficient retrieval of information from computer memory. In the 1960s, computer memories were very limited and storage was expensive. Collins and Quillian conceived of a network of concepts—for example, of animals and plants—taking advantage of the fact that concepts are related to one another in numerous ways.

The two theorists represented class or subset membership in terms of a hierarchical network. The network included property relations describing the features of the classes and instances. The network in Figure 4.10 depicts a set of animals in a three-level hierarchy, including the category *animal*, two classes (e.g., *bird, fish*), and several subclasses (e.g., *canary, salmon*).

Each concept forms a configuration of links pointing to other concepts. This configuration captures the meaning of the concept. Concepts are represented economically without redundancies; *canary*, for example, does not contain general information about breathing and flying that could be inferred from superordinate categories. Exceptions such as *ostrich,* however, have special tags to indicate that the superordinate property does not apply.

Processing Assumptions about Fact Retrieval from Semantic Networks. Fact retrieval was assumed to occur through spreading activation. When a person reads and encodes a statement, the corresponding concepts become active and the activation spreads along the links in the semantic network. When you read the assertion *A canary is a bird,* activation is assumed to spread from *canary* and *bird* along the network links. When the two sources of activation intersect, the statement is found to be true and verified.

Collins and Quillian (1969) tested their structural and processing assumptions using a sentence verification paradigm in which people were asked to verify statements of the form *A subject is a predicate.* Their hypothesis was that verification would take longer the larger the category, or the more distant the subject and predicate nodes are in the network. According to this category size effect, *A canary is a bird* would be verified faster than *A canary is an animal.*

Collins and Quillian's data shown in Figure 4.11 reflect the category size effect implied by their network model. However, as pointed out by Rips, Shoben, and Smith (1973), the Collins and

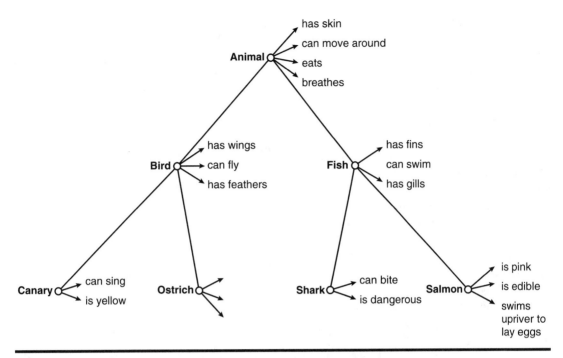

FIGURE 4.10   Illustration of Collins and Quillian's (1969) semantic network. The network shows the memory structure for a three-level hierarchy. The top level, *animal,* is designated as 0; the classes represent level 1; and the subclasses represent level 2 of the hierarchy.

Quillian model failed to account for two critical results, among others. First, because the model was strictly taxonomic, the predictions did not always mirror people's familiarity with concepts. Statements like *A dog is an animal* are verified faster than *A dog is a mammal,* though the order should be reversed according to the category size prediction. Second, statements that should take the same time to verify do not; the statements *A robin is a bird* and *A chicken is a bird* have the same relation to their superordinate term *bird* but they differ in their typicality. Most people consider a robin a more typical bird than a chicken (see Table 4.5, later). As a result, people verify the first statement faster than the second. Collins and Quillian's original model made no provision for such typicality effects. The prototype model considered in the next section sought to account for typicality.

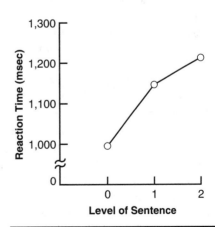

FIGURE 4.11   Category size effect in Collins and Quillian's (1969) sentence verification experiment. The abscissa represents the level in the network hierarchy and the ordinate indicates the reaction time in milliseconds.

Prototype Models

The network model represents the meaning of a concept through its associations with neighboring concepts and properties. In contrast, in prototype models, the meaning of a concept is defined in terms of its similarity to a prototype; there are no hierarchical relations. A *prototype* is an idealized and abstract representation that captures an average of the members of the category (Smith & Medin, 1981; Posner, 1969). It does not include attributes of individual exemplars. For example, the prototype of *bird* includes the average size and color of all birds encountered but no information on individual bird species. The bird prototype also captures correlational information people possess about birds, such as the fact that small birds typically sing.

Let us illustrate a prototype using the example of two fictitious gangs: the Big Wheels and the Centurions (McClelland, Rumelhart, & Hinton, 1986). Each gang has eight members with certain characteristics, including age, years of education, and months spent in jail. Averaging across the members of each gang yields the prototype for the gang. For example, the prototypical Big Wheel is 33.5 years old with 10.88 years of education. If we meet a new gang member, Ron, who is age 37 and has had 11 years of education, we would judge him to be a member of the Big Wheels (see Table 4.4).

In prototype theory, and, as we shall see, in exemplar theory, the meaning of a concept is computed by assessing its similarity relative to a model. Although similarity is a fundamental notion, it is difficult to pin down, and many similarity metrics exist (see Goldstone, 1996). Here, we consider Malt and Smith's (1984) proposal of expressing similarity. These authors measured similarity empirically by the overlap between the features of the concepts. Subjects were asked to report typical features of concepts—for example, *bird, robin, penguin,* and others. The experimenters then subtracted the number of dissimilar features from the number

TABLE 4.4 Two Fictitious Gangs Illustrate Prototype Concept

Name	Age	Years of Education	Months in Jail
Big Wheels			
George	32	10	13
Paul	42	8	0
Neil	39	11	24
Greg	25	12	0
Jeff	27	9	7
Salvador	36	14	2
Dick	36	12	8
Hassan	31	11	0
Mean	33.5	10.88	6.75
Centurions			
Miguel	24	9	28
Brad	19	8	9
Rajandra	21	12	0
John	28	12	34
Colin	25	8	14
Peter	18	7	20
Seth	21	9	3
Mike	26	11	0
Mean	22.75	9.5	13.5

of overlapping features to get a similarity score as follows:

Similarity = number of common features
– number of unique features

This is illustrated in Table 4.5. The experimenters simply asked subjects to list the properties they could think of. Frequently mentioned properties are indicated by a + sign. Features never mentioned by subjects are indicated by a – sign.

Table 4.5 shows the similarity of each of the concepts with the prototype bird. *Robin, bluebird,* and *swallow* are similar to *bird,* whereas *chicken, flamingo,* and *penguin* are dissimilar. Sentence verification and categorization experiments have shown that decision times correlate with these empirical similarity measures. In the categorization paradigm, the subject sees the name of a category—for example, *bird*—and then a concept that either belongs to the category

TABLE 4.5 Similarity between Instances and the Prototype Bird

Properties	Robin	Bluebird	Swallow	Starling	Vulture
Flies	+	+	+	+	+
Sings	+	+	+	+	−
Lays eggs	+	+	+	−	−
Is small	+	+	+	+	−
Nests in trees	+	+	+	+	+
Eats insects	+	+	+	+	−
Similarity to bird	6 − 0 = 6	6 − 0 = 6	6 − 0 = 6	5 − 1 = 4	2 − 4 = −2

Properties	Sandpiper	Chicken	Flamingo	Penguin	Bird
Flies	+	−	−	−	+
Sings	+	−	−	−	+
Lays eggs	+	+	−	+	+
Is small	+	−	−	−	+
Nests in trees	−	−	−	−	+
Eats insects	+	−	−	−	+
Similarity to bird	5 − 1 = 4	1 − 5 = −4	0 − 6 = −6	1 − 5 = −4	

or not, such as *robin* or *shark*. Decision times are faster for typical instances of concepts (e.g., *robin)* than for atypical ones (e.g., *chicken*).

The properties in Table 4.5 are listed in order of their typicality. Malt and Smith found that more typical properties tend to be mentioned first and verified fastest by subjects. People will mention that a bird flies before they mention that a bird nests in trees. Incidentally, children tend to acquire typical properties before less typical ones (Smith, 1988).

Discussion of prototypes thus far has been restricted to natural concepts—namely, animals. People represent and process concepts of humanmade objects like *furniture* and *clothing* in a similar manner. They can easily judge such concepts in terms of category membership and typicality. For example, *shirt* and *slacks* are considered typical instances of clothing, whereas *watch* and *belt* are less typical. Note that subjects produced *watch* and *belt* as instances of clothing, though you may disagree with this classification. A belt is worn like other clothing, but it doesn't have buttons and keep you warm, which are two typical properties of clothing. Thus, the proto-

type view naturally allows for flexible and imprecise definitions—those that the philosopher Zadeh called *fuzzy concepts.*

Prototype analysis also lends itself to composite concepts (e.g., *red juicy fruit*), to abstract concepts including numbers, and to social concepts. Try to think of the typical odd number. If you came up with 3, you were right; 15, however, is an atypical odd number. When subjects had to verify sentences like *Is X an odd number?* they responded faster for typical than atypical numbers. Social concepts represent a person's stereotypical knowledge. For example, people's memory includes stereotypes about groups of people, including jocks, nerds, yuppies, lawyers, senior citizens, WASPs, and so on.

Exemplar Models

Exemplar models assume that people represent concepts in terms of the exemplars they remember rather than in terms of an idealized average (Medin & Shaffer, 1978; Barsalou, 1992; Vokey & Brooks, 1992). When a person encounters a new instance, he or she compares it with exemplars in memory and chooses the best-fitting exemplar to name the new instance. For example, a person might classify an edible yellow object with a short brown stem and shaped like a lightbulb as a fruit because it reminds him or her of an apple, which he or she knows to be a fruit. Consider another example: A person can infer the fact that large birds do not tend to sing but small birds do, from retrieving exemplars of large and small birds and their attributes; a robin sings, a cardinal sings, a canary sings—they are all small birds. Contrarily, large birds—such as geese, swans, and pelicans—are not known to sing. When a person encounters an unknown small bird, he or she is likely to infer that it sings, because of its similarity to remembered exemplars of singing birds.

The match between a test instance and a remembered exemplar is based on the similarity between the test instance and a remembered exemplar relative to the similarity between the test instance and other exemplars. Similarity is defined on the basis of features; in the case of birds, these include the size of the bird and the fact that some birds sing. Prototype and exemplar theory agree that a new instance is compared with a memory representation. What differs is the memory representation that is used for the comparison; in prototype theory, it is the prototype, whereas in exemplar theory, it is an exemplar, which may differ from one comparison to the next.

Although exemplar theory has some theoretical difficulties—for example, in explaining how a category was formed in the first place (Medin & Ross, 1992)—it readily accounts for the major semantic memory effects. Consider the following:

— Typicality effects are handled by the assumption that typical instances of a category are more likely to be stored as exemplars than untypical instances. When a new test instance is presented, the typical exemplars are more likely to be retrieved as standard representations. As a result,

identification latency is quicker for these exemplars.

— Posner (1969) found that people learned abstract prototypes from seeing a set of related stimuli that did not include the prototype itself (Chapter 5). Exemplar theory accounts for this effect by assuming that the prototype has a greater similarity with frequently presented exemplars than with rare exemplars.

— Exemplar theory explains people's abilities to learn ill-defined categories—for example, of artifacts whose exemplars have no apparent similarity. Consider the diverse exemplars of the category *game;* it includes such different instances as chess, bridge, and tennis. On the other hand, it is quite difficult to determine the prototypical game (Wittgenstein, 1953).

Issues on Representation of Concepts

The network model, in its original form, no longer has empirical support, but the prototype and exemplar models can readily account for such empirical effects as the category size, the typicality, and the abstraction effects. Brooks, Norman, and Allen (1991) have proposed a *hybrid of memory* that includes information on both prototypes and exemplars (see also Knowlton & Squire, 1996; Chapter 5). In a medical diagnosis task, Brooks and colleagues used photographic slides of common dermatological problems as learning materials. They found that residents in family medicine exhibited memory for both prototypes and exemplars, thus indicating that both models may be right to some extent.

Even as theorists may come to an agreement on prototype and exemplar models of semantic memory, the typical paradigm of semantic memory research has come under criticism. Researchers have used the judgment paradigm, including sentence verification and similarity ratings, as their principal tool to illuminate structures and processes of semantic memory. Reaction time has been the dependent variable of choice. Reaction time, however, affords only a single time measure of the verification process. According to Kounious (1996), verification is not a monolithic process; rather, it is a gradual process involving several stages such as stimulus encoding, retrieval of relevant semantic information, and computing the relations expressed in the test sentence. According to Kounious, reaction time is too crude a measure to illuminate these subprocesses. Kounious calls for research that examines the full temporal profile of processing, including brain processes, in the judgment paradigm rather than just reporting a single time point when the subject completed a judgment.

Propositions and Causal Relations

Semantic memory includes people's knowledge of concepts as well as their knowledge of events and of typical event sequences. Cognitive scientists have proposed several memory structures to represent such knowledge, including propositions, causal relations, and schemas. Consider, for instance, the proposition, an abstract representation of the meaning of a sentence. It was a sentence recognition study by Sachs (1967) that documented the role of sentence meaning as listeners remember brief passages. She demonstrated that we remember the gist of sentences rather than such surface details as the voice, syntactic structure, and the choice of words (Sachs, 1967; Zwaan, 1994). Sachs had volunteers listen to a passage that included sentences such as expression (4.7).

(4.7) He sent a letter about it to Galileo, the great Italian scientist.

When Sachs changed the target sentence in a subsequent recognition test to the passive voice, people were less likely to notice the change than when she introduced semantic changes, by asserting, for example, that it was Galileo who sent the letter. What listeners remember, then, is the semantic content of a sentence—that is, they remember the action, the actor, and the object of the sentence. Theorists chose to represent this type of information in terms of propositions (Anderson & Bower, 1973; Kintsch & van Dijk, 1978).

Propositions are formally represented as an ordered list of concepts (see expression [4.8]) governed by a predicate.

(4.8) (Predicate: x, Agent: y, Object: z, . . .).

Typically, the predicate is a verb. Each verb specifies a set of semantic roles expected by the verb. There is always an agent, whereas such other roles as object, recipient, and instrument are optional. Consider the following list of statements and their corresponding propositions:

(4.9a) Six is the square root of sixteen.

(4.9b) (Predicate: *is-square-root-of;* Subject: *six;* Predicate: *sixteen*)

(4.10a) The study list contained item *mev.*

(4.10b) (predicate: *contain;* subject: *study-list;* predicate: *item mev*)

(4.11a) A canary is a bird.

(4.11b) (Predicate: *is-a;* Subject: *canary;* Predicate: *bird*)

(4.12a) The bandit stole the passport.

(4.12b) (Predicate: *steal;* Agent: *bandit;* Object: *passport*)

(4.13a) John grew the plants with fertilizer.

(4.13b) (Predicate: *grow;* Agent: *John;* Object: *plant;* Instrument: *fertilizer*)

Adopting a standard order of predicate and arguments, psychologists use a short form to represent propositions. For example, the latter two propositions are represented in forms (4.12c) and (4.13c), respectively.

(4.12c) *(steal, bandit, passport)*

(4.13c) *(grow, John, plant, fertilizer)*

Propositional theory has been validated in several experimental paradigms. Ratcliff and McKoon (1978) conducted an item-recognition study and demonstrated that facts are remembered in terms of propositions. The experiment consisted of several alternating study and testing phases. During the study phase, subjects memorized sentences such as (4.14) displayed on a computer screen. Sentence (4.14) contains the two propositions shown in expression (4.14a).

(4.14)   The bandit who stole the passport faked the signature.

(4.14a)   *(steal, bandit, passport)*

(fake, bandit, signature)

During testing, a list of words was presented on the screen one word at a time for a speeded recognition test. Subjects had to decide as quickly as possible whether or not the word had appeared in one of the sentences just read. Ratcliff and McKoon found that subjects responded more quickly to targets that were preceded (primed) by a concept from the *same* proposition (e.g., *bandit, passport*) than a concept from a different proposition (e.g., *signature, passport*). In other words, the subjects established closer links between two concepts that belonged to the same rather than to different propositions.

The propositional representation is readily extended to entire texts, as illustrated in Figure 4.12 for a miniature text containing two sentences. The repeated arguments—for example, *Babylonian* and *garden*, in Figure 4.12—reflect the referential coherence of the passage. In text-recall studies, researchers have established that (1) passage recall improves in proportion with textual coherence, as indicated by the number of repeated arguments, and (2) recall of a sentence in a passage improves in proportion with the number of references made to the sentence in the subsequent text. It certainly is not coincidental that the sentences frequently referred to are those judged to be more important for both theoretical

FIGURE 4.12   A miniature passage to illustrate propositional representations of texts (e.g., Kintsch & van Dijk, 1978)

1 (build, Babylonian, garden)
2 (beautiful, garden)
3 (location: on, garden, hill)
4 (plant, Babylonian, flower)
5 (lovely, flower)
6 (construct, Babylonian, fountain)
7 (design, Babylonian, pavilion)
8 (has, queen, pleasure)

Text: The Babylonians built a beautiful garden on a hill. They planted lovely flowers, constructed fountains, and designed a pavilion for the queen's pleasure.

Note: Location in proposition 3 serves as a predicate.

and empirical reasons (Kintsch & van Dijk, 1978).

Useful as propositions are, they do not reveal our full knowledge of the underlying causal relations among actions. Schank's (1973) conceptual dependency theory does just that. Consider sentence (4.13a) *John grew the plants with fertilizer.* This statement embodies much more information known to listeners than the proposition *(grow, John, plant, fertilizer)* reveals. Growing plants means that the plants' sizes change from small to large as a result of many actions John took: He dug small holes in the ground, he planted the plants, he watered them, he removed weeds, and he applied fertilizer. Each of these actions involves supporting activities, and these, in turn, depend on specific prior events. This type of knowledge is not captured by the minimal representation afforded by propositions. In order to express people's knowledge of such rich scenarios, more complex mental representations than propositions have been proposed, including the causal chain (Schank, 1973; van den Broek, 1990) and several types of schemas (Bartlett,

FIGURE 4.13 Sample text for illustrating causal structure (van den Broek, 1990).

1. There once was a boy named Peter,
2. who wanted to buy a bike.
3. He called a bike store to ask for prices.
4. He counted his money.
5. The money was not enough for a bike.
6. He put his piggy bank back on the top shelf of his closet
7. and covered it with clothes.
8. Peter wanted to get some money
9. so he asked his mother for some.
10. His mother said, "No, you should earn your own."
11. Peter decided to get a paper route.
12. He called the newspaper agency
13. and asked about a route.
14. The secretary told him to come in.
15. Peter talked to the manager
16. and got his job.
17. He worked very hard on his job
18. and earned a lot of tips.
19. Pretty soon he had earned $200.
20. He went to a bike store
21. and bought a beautiful bike.
22. He was the happiest kid in town.

1932; Rumelhart & Ortony, 1977; Schank & Abelson, 1977).

Causal chains are best illustrated with an example. Consider the story about a boy named Peter in Figure 4.13. The sentences of the story differ in the extent to which they lead to subsequent events. Sentence 2 states Peter's goal of trying to get a bike, and thus motivates the entire story; it is linked to many other sentences, including sentences 3, 4, 8, and so on. Sentences 6 and 7, however, are not related. Sentence 2 forms part of the causal chain of the story, whereas sentences 6 and 7 are isolated dead-ends. According to the causal chain hypothesis, sentences 2, 3, 4, and 8 should be remembered better because of the causal links between them. Van den Broek (1990) evaluated this prediction by analyzing readers' recall of stories such as

the Peter story. He found that, as predicted, the better-connected sentences had a better chance of being recalled. The causal chain between the sentences serves as a mental glue that facilitates retention, whether in the laboratory or in everyday memory (Chapter 12).

Passages such as the Peter story tend to reflect a prototypical sequence of events consisting of a goal, one or more attempts of achieving the goal, and an outcome. Such a sequence has been referred to as the *episode schema*, or the *story schema* (Mandler & Johnson, 1977). Thus, after introducing the protagonist, Peter, in sentence 1, the second sentence states Peter's overall goal. Sentences 3 and 4 describe one attempt of achieving the goal (counting his savings), and sentence 5 relates an outcome (his savings were not sufficient). The goal-attempt-outcome schema recurs between sentences 8 and 19, even though the events themselves are different from the first episode of the story. The story schema is one example of a class of memory representations reviewed next, the schemas.

Schemas

Winning a lottery, getting married, receiving a job offer, going to a restaurant, attending a lecture class, and going to a dentist are all events. We are familiar with these scenarios; we know what to expect and how to act. At a dentist's office, the patient takes a seat in the dentist's chair, opens his or her mouth for the dental examination, and the dentist conducts the examination, using dental tools, a mirror, and lights. The patient would be very surprised if the dentist were to bring a menu and asked the patient what he or she wanted to eat. People's expectations are based on experience, whether personal or through reading and watching TV. According to psychologists, people's expectations are represented in memory in terms of such structures as schemas and scripts (Bartlett, 1932; Rumelhart & Ortony, 1977).

A *schema* is a configuration of general knowledge about objects and events. A typical office, for example, contains a desk, a lamp, a telephone, and filing cabinets. Other information is peripheral—for example, the number of windows, the color of the telephone, the number of chairs, and the size of the filing cabinets. The schema provides a framework for expressing features, without detailing the unique features of a specific office, for example. A schema usually includes subschemas; each of the objects in the office may be viewed as a schema, from desks to computers, and in turn each of these include subschemas.

Schemas vary in their abstractness. A computer program, for example, may include a *loop;* at the most abstract level, *loop* refers to some repeated operation. At a less abstract level, one would specify the function of the loop—for example, adding numbers. Schemas are flexible. Certain aspects may be missing; for example, the typical theater has a stage, seats, and a curtain, but there are theaters without stages, seats, or curtains.

The schema notion is related to the term *prototype;* the former, however, is more flexible. It contains variables to represent attributes describing an object without specifying actual values. A prototype provides those values. The prototype of a Big Wheel in Table 4.4, for example, is 33.5 years old with 10.88 years of education. The schema for Big Wheels includes age and years of education as variables but no values.

A *script* is a schema describing a typical sequence of events, such as attending a lecture, going shopping, and going to a restaurant. The restaurant script represents the knowledge we have of eating in a restaurant. Figure 4.14 illustrates one type of restaurant script: the coffee shop. There are props, roles, and four scenes: entering, ordering, eating, and exiting. Scripts, like schemas, are generic; they describe typical events and allow for some variability (e.g., restaurants

FIGURE 4.14   The restaurant script.

Title: RESTAURANT
Track: Coffee Shop
Props: Tables   Roles: Customer
         Menu   Waiter
         Food   Cashier
         Check   Owner

Scene 1:   Entering
Customer enters the restaurant
Customer looks for a table
Customer goes to a table and sits down

Scene 2:   Ordering
Waiter brings the menu
Customer studies the menu
Customer signals to the waiter
Waiter takes the order

Scene 3:   Eating
Waiter brings the meal
Customer eats the meal

Scene 4:   Exiting
Waiter writes the check
Customer takes the check to cashier and pays
Customer leaves the restaurant

differ, from coffee shops to five-star establishments).

Implied Script Concepts

Based on script memory, listeners and readers are able to infer actions not explicitly stated in a text or conversation. For instance, we have no difficulty understanding text (4.15a):

(**4.15a**)   John went to a restaurant.

He ordered chicken.

He left a large tip.

Reading the first sentence of expression (4.15a) presumably activates the restaurant script, with its underlying knowledge. Thus, the reader's understanding may look something like the passage in expression (4.15b):

(4.15b)   John went to a restaurant.

He sat down.

He looked at the menu.

He ordered chicken.

He ate the chicken.

He left a large tip.

He paid the check.

He left the restaurant.

The statements in italics are easily inferred; in recall and recognition experiments, subjects mistakenly believe that they actually read such implied statements (e.g., Bower, Black, & Turner, 1979; Graesser, Gordon, & Sawyer, 1979). This recall pattern extends Bartlett's (1932) research on constructive memory. Bartlett had students read *The War of the Ghosts,* a story that was unfamiliar to them, and found that people reconstructed the story content according to their own knowledge and expectations (Chapter 2). The fact that people's expectations may override and even distort story content and observed events has been replicated in numerous studies (Chapter 12; Dooling & Christiaansen, 1977; Loftus et al., 1995; Reyna & Titcomb, 1997; Schacter, 1995). Of course, learners' inferences and elaborations also improve retention, especially if they are relevant to the target information (Bradshaw & Anderson, 1982).

Evaluation of the Schema Notion

Researchers agree that the schema concept has been useful to account for a wide variety of memory data, from reconstructive recall of stories, the recall patterns of prototypical stories, to memory of visual scenes. Both memory distortions and correct recall have been attributed to the schema. Herein, however, lies a problem for schema theory; schemas are so flexible that they can account for almost any data. When learners adapt a passage according to their preconceptions, they do so on the basis of a schema. When they mistakenly believe their inferences were

part of the story, the schema notion accounts for it. When a person cannot understand a passage, schema theory can explain that, too. Critics have asked with some justification whether the schema concept is too broad to permit empirical testing (Hintzman, 1993). As a result, theorists who once advocated the schema notion have turned toward alternative formalisms, such as neural networks (Rumelhart & Todd, 1993).

Perspectives from Neuropsychology

Healthy individuals have a uniformly effective memory. They remember facts about the world as well as facts from their personal lives. People with brain damage, however, often have fragmentary or "broken" memories (Baddeley, Wilson, & Watts, 1995; Campbell & Conway, 1995; Schacter, 1996; Vargha-Khadem, 1997). They may not remember that they have been in a traffic accident but they remember events from their college days; they may recollect the meaning of such complex terms as *supplication* (making a serious request for help) or *arbiter* (a person seeking to find a solution), but not that of common words such as *geese* or *needle* (Patterson & Hodges, 1995). They may recognize human-made objects but not animals and plants (Hillis & Caramazza, 1991). Unfortunate as these cases are, they represent an opportunity for neuroscientists to gain a fuller understanding of brain structures and processes in supporting episodic and semantic memory. Particularly informative are cases where semantic and episodic memory are selectively impaired. In some patients, semantic memory has remained intact while episodic memory is impaired; in others, the reverse pattern is observed. These patients exhibit semantic dementia while episodic memory is intact.

Based on such dissociations between episodic and semantic memory, theorists have conjectured that not only are the two kinds of memory functionally different but they also constitute separable memory systems supported by different brain systems (Schacter & Tulving, 1994a). Schacter and Tulving (1994a) have speculated that semantic memory processes are largely based in centers in the medial-temporal lobe, whereas episodic memory processes depend on certain prefrontal-cortical areas. Of course, common brain structures are implicated in the two systems, as well.

The case of patient H. M. presents a classic dissociation between episodic and semantic memory. As described in Chapter 3, H. M. lost his memory for personal events as a result of neurosurgery, but his semantic memory was largely spared. Many similar cases have been documented in the past few decades (Baddeley, Wilson, & Watts, 1995; Campbell & Conway, 1995). Schacter (1996), for example, described the case of Gene, who sustained damage to the frontal lobe and the temporal lobes, including the left hippocampus, as a result of a motorcycle accident. Gene lost all episodic memories, yet his semantic memory remained intact. Schacter found that "asking Gene about his personal past is an almost unnerving experience.... No amount of prompting or cueing helps Gene recall specific past events, whether happy or sad, at school or at work, or including family or friends" (p. 149). Yet Gene still has knowledge of the world, and he knows the meaning of words, including the technical terms he used in his manufacturing job.

The dissociation between episodic and semantic memory is perhaps even more striking in patients whose episodic memories were impaired from childhood on, but who nevertheless acquired semantic knowledge well enough to attend mainstream schools. Vargha-Khadem and colleagues (1997) described such a dissociation in three patients who suffered brain injuries during early childhood. The injuries involved the hippocampus, sparing the surrounding regions of the cortex. The three children exhibited epi-

sodic memory deficits serious enough to require almost continuous supervision, even by the time they were young adults. They failed to learn their way to familiar places, to remember appointments and events, and to recount the day's activities, whether at home or at school. On the other hand, the patients were not mentally retarded. Rather, they attended regular schools and learned to become proficient in speech, reading, and writing, much as other students of the same age (for more details, see Vargha-Khadem et al., 1997).

Semantic dementia occurs in individuals who suffered impairments to the anterolateral areas of temporal neocortex as a result of Alzheimer's disease and encephalitis or of head injuries (Patterson & Hodges, 1995). Consider patient P. P., a 69-year-old woman. She was unable to answer such questions as "Is a cat an animal?" She would repeat the question and respond, "I wish I could remember what an animal was." The woman retained her ability to form sentences, but word meanings tended to be erased. P. P. retained memory for recent episodes but she had difficulty describing the events, in part because she could not remember the appropriate terms for individuals and objects. For example, she remembered visiting her granddaughter recently, but she could no longer use the term *granddaughter;* she referred to her granddaughter as "the little girl."

In clinical assessments of semantic memory, patients like P. P. do poorly on a range of semantic memory tasks, such as assigning colors to familiar objects. When given a choice between a orange carrot and a blue carrot, such patients will respond at chance. Unfortunately, semantic dementia tends to worsen as time progresses. This was true for patient P. P. When Patterson and Hodges (1995) first met her, she was able to distinguish between animals and humanmade objects, and she was still better than chance in distinguishing land from water animals, but she could not distinguish native from foreign animals. Subsequently, she lost the more abstract distinctions, as well.

Considered together, cases such as Gene's and P. P.'s represent a double dissociation: In different patients, different brain systems are impaired (hippocampus vs. medial-temporal lobe), resulting in reverse pattern of memory dysfunction (episodic impaired and semantic intact vs. semantic impaired and episodic intact). The interpretation of double dissociations is controversial. Some theorists view double dissociations as evidence for independent and separable brain systems (e.g., Schacter & Tulving, 1994a, 1994b), whereas others demur, either for reasons of methodology or parsimony (Neely, 1989; Roediger, 1993; Chapter 11).

Going beyond the difference between episodic and semantic memory, some neuroscientists have proposed distinctions within semantic memory. Hypotheses about divisions in semantic memory stem from neuropsychological case studies and investigations using neurophysiological measures such as ERPs and the PET scan. Citing different ERP patterns as support, Kounious (1996) suggested that the left hemisphere is primarily a repository of abstract semantic memory, whereas concrete information is presumably represented in both hemispheres. Martin and colleagues (1996) concluded on the basis of PET imaging studies that "the brain regions active during object identification are dependent, in part, on the intrinsic properties of the objects presented" (p. 649). They speculated that semantic knowledge of objects is represented in terms of networks distributed over several brain regions, including the ventral temporal lobe. Based on highly selective agnosias—for example, when patients lose their memory for a specific semantic category such as humanmade objects—some authors have raised the possibility

of category-specific semantic memories (Hillis & Caramazza, 1991). These interpretations, however, remain controversial because the data either come from studies with very new methods or they represent case studies with very few observations. In any case, the larger issue of separate memory systems is still being debated. In particular, it remains an open issue just how many systems there can be (Chapter 11). Nevertheless, neuropsychological and imaging approaches have invigorated semantic memory research once thought to be dormant (Kintsch, 1980).

CONCLUSION

The experimental study of memory for facts, also known as declarative memory, constitutes the core of classical memory research. The writings of Ebbinghaus (1885), McGeoch (1942), Crowder (1976), and Tulving (1983), and a handbook on memory (Bjork & Bjork, 1996) were almost exclusively devoted to memory for facts. There are good reasons for this emphasis; declarative memory is tied to each person's linguistic and world knowledge and it contains the record of the episodes that person has experienced in his or her life.

Because of its centrality, memory for facts will be revisited in each of the remaining chapters of this book. Among other things, we will see that autobiographical memories represent a special set of facts linked to the self of the learner, that memory for facts is influenced by emotions (Chapter 9), that it changes systematically as a function of development (Chapter 8), that it does not imply accurate memory (rather, it is subject to suggestion and distortion) (Chapters 10 and 12), and that it can make important contributions to people's memory for skills (Chapter 5).

CHAPTER 5

MEMORY
FOR SKILLS

Memory for skills differs from memory for facts. If you know the facts, you can report them with ease. It is easy to name the capital of California, the square root of 49, or a synonym for *automobile*. Skills are different; although you may know how to execute a skill, it is far more difficult to describe how you do so. Try to explain how you tie your shoelaces, how you recognize a familiar face, how you add two-digit numbers, or how you utter words and sentences.

Memory for skills manifests itself implicitly in improved performance after prior exposure. Seeing a stimulus once facilitates recognizing it on the second encounter, and completing a task once speeds the process the next time around. These cases of implicit memory are known as *priming effects;* they are reviewed in the first section of this chapter. The section also reviews implicit learning, as reflected in people's knowledge of rules, stimulus patterns, and event sequences. However complex, people retain memory for this type of information, and they often do so without intention or awareness.

The second section of the chapter considers learning and remembering of cognitive skills from mathematical problem solving to medical expertise. All of us are experts in solving mundane problems—indeed, so much so that we do not need to think about everyday routines as problems. People view those tasks as problems that are executed infrequently, whether it is balancing the checkbook, installing a new piece of equipment, or remembering 20 restaurant orders. Having an excellent memory is a skill, too! In its final section, the chapter introduces individuals who exhibit exceptional memories and explores whether a special talent is necessary for supermemory or whether anyone can become a memory expert.

IMPLICIT MEMORY

Visualize the following scenario: A young woman appears to be lost as she walks aimlessly through a neighborhood. Finally, the police pick the woman up. The woman has no recollection of who she is, nor does she have any identification on her (Matlin, 1994). Fortunately, the police officers are ingenious; they have the woman dial phone numbers—any numbers. As it turns out, one of the numbers the woman dials is her mother's. However, the woman has no awareness of having done so and what the number represents. This story illustrates implicit memory: A person is able to marshal knowledge without awareness. Explicit memory, on the other hand, involves the conscious and deliberate recollection of knowledge, events, and experiences.

The contrast between implicit and explicit memory was documented at the turn of the century by Swiss psychologist Edouard Claparede (1873–1940). Claparede described the case of a 47-year-old amnesic patient. The woman's knowledge of subjects such as arithmetic and geography she had learned in her childhood were relatively unimpaired. However, she did not recognize her doctors or nurses, whom she had seen almost every day for five years. Claparede conducted the following experiment to demonstrate that the patient could retain experiences, even if unconsciously: He gently pricked the woman's hand with a needle hidden between his fingers. The woman forgot the light pain quickly. However, when Claparede again reached out for her hand sometime later, she pulled it back in a reflex fashion, not knowing why. In Tulving's (1989) terms, the woman knew but didn't remember. The woman had no conscious recollection of the physician but she knew that shaking his hand might result in a pin prick.

This case illustrates a dissociation between implicit memory and explicit memory: The two memory assessments produce divergent results. There is no evidence of explicit memory of individuals the patient had encountered, but her action revealed implicit knowledge of prior experiences. Physicians have been familiar with such dissociations; it has been up to psychologists, however, to investigate implicit memory and compare it with explicit memory in controlled laboratory experiments. Most of these studies have focused on priming, the enhancement in perception and performance that results from prior experience with the task.

Priming

A seminal study by Warrington and Weiskrantz (1968) provided the impetus for research on priming. These researchers found that a change in the manner of assessing the memory of amnesic patients changed their memory performance substantially. In each of two experimental conditions, a recall and a naming condition, the patients were shown the same list of words—for example, *evidence, window,* and *telephone.* In the recall condition, the patients did poorly, as one would expect. In the naming condition, the

beginning syllable of the target words were shown and patients had to complete the words—for example, *evi-----.* Surprisingly, in this condition, the patients did no worse than normal subjects, indicating that their memories had registered some information, however surreptitiously. Warrington and Weiskrantz (1982) suggested that performance in the priming condition improved as a result of an automatic facilitatory effect in the neural structures implicated in perception and recognition, and that these structures remained intact in the patients.

Priming effects have been demonstrated in nonimpaired populations, as well. Reading researchers know that context facilitates the identification of words in reading. People recognize words primed by prior context more quickly than control words. For example, the word *avalanche* is identified more easily when readers first read the phrase *The skiers were buried alive by the sudden....* Whereas early investigators considered such priming effects as transient perceptual phenomena, Jacoby (1983) advanced the view that priming may be long lasting and thus be an expression of memory.

Jacoby (1983) compared priming and explicit memory as a function of different encoding conditions. His priming study included a study phase and a testing phase. In the study phase, there were three encoding conditions: the no-context condition, the context condition, and the generate condition. The conditions differed in terms of the stimulus that preceded the target word, such as *cold.* In the no-context condition, the person would see a row of *xxxx* followed by *cold.* In the context condition, the prime would be *hot,* followed by the target *cold.* In the generate condition, the prime was *hot* and the subject was asked to think of the antonym of *hot* and thus to generate the target on his or her own.

The test phase included one of two tests: a perceptual identification test for testing implicit memory and a recognition memory test for testing explicit memory. In the identification test, a target word was flashed on the screen and subjects had to read it as quickly as possible. In the recognition test, the same set of words was used, except they were typed on a sheet of paper, with old and new words mixed. The subjects had to mark those words they had either seen or generated in the study phase (see Figure 5.1). Jacoby found a dissociation between implicit and explicit memory measures: Identification was best in the no-context condition and worst in the generate condition. The recognition results exhibited the reverse pattern; performance was best in the generate condition and worst in the no-context condition (Roediger, 1990; Schacter, Chiu, & Ochsner, 1993).

Priming effects have been reported in traditional laboratory tasks such as word completion, lexical decision, and picture identification, as well as in many other situations, including reading comprehension, problem solving, and judgment and attitude formation. Priming in cognition is so general that the term *implicit social cognition* has been coined (Greenwald & Banaji, 1995). Let us review the priming effects in con-

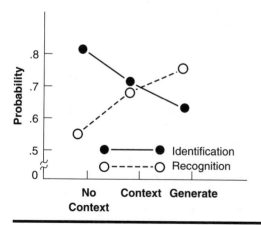

FIGURE 5.1 Dissociation between explicit and implicit memory (Jacoby, 1983). Recognition performance is enhanced by semantic elaboration, whereas priming is enhanced by the physical similarity of the stimuli between study and testing.

ventional cognitive paradigms and a couple of related effects from research on social cognition. Afterward, we shall consider attributes of priming.

Priming Effects in Cognitive Psychology and Social Psychology

Cognitive Paradigms. Consider priming effects in several cognitive paradigms:

— In the *word completion task,* participants initially inspect a series of words during an inspection phase without being asked to memorize them. During a testing phase, people receive word stems, such as *riv,* or word fragments, such as *e_e__an_,* and are asked to report the first word that comes to mind. Typically, words presented during the inspection phase are more likely to be completed than control words that the subjects did not see.

— In the *lexical decision task,* a string of letters is shown—for example, *grobse, type, slame,* and *hang*—and the person has to decide whether the string represents an English word. When an item has been repeated, there is a speedup in the decision latencies. A similar repetition advantage has been observed in normal reading where repeated words tend to be read faster. In both situations, the repetition advantage is greater for rare words (e.g., *thermoluminescence)* than for more familiar words (e.g., *door*) (Just & Carpenter, 1980; Haberlandt & Graesser, 1985).

— In *picture priming studies,* viewers see drawings of objects and name the objects as quickly as possible. Naming latencies are reduced for objects shown repeatedly (e.g., Biederman & Cooper, 1991). Facilitation also occurs when subjects look at picture segments that they have to identify or when they have to decide whether a drawing represents a real or imaginary object. Every time, repetition speeds up the response time and increases accuracy (Schacter et al., 1993).

— In *problem solving,* people sometimes take credit for solutions produced by someone else; this mistaken belief is known as *unconscious plagiarism* or *cryptomnesia.* Marsh and Bower (1993) demonstrated cryptomnesia using a computer game called Boggle. The computer, which served as the playing partner, presented a series of 4 × 4 matrices of 16 letters. Each player would then alternate to generate words from letters in the matrix. For example, from the matrix

S T E Y

C A O S

G L I N

A N L D

the following words can be generated: *act, again, call, dial, gate, lion, note,* and *yes.* From time to time, the experimenter interrupted the game and asked the subjects to recall words they had generated themselves. It turned out that people frequently recalled words produced by the computer, claiming with high confidence that the words were their own creations.

Implicit Social Cognition. Effects related to priming occur when people make judgments of objects and of individuals. We tend to view objects and individuals more favorably the more frequently we have been exposed to them. Consider the frequency of exposure effect and the false-fame effect.

The Frequency of Exposure Effect. Social psychologist R. B. Zajonc (1980) found that frequency of exposure is a powerful determinant of the appeal of various initially unfamiliar stimuli, whether they are Turkish words, photographs of unknown individuals, object drawings, or Japanese pictograms. For example, researchers exposed sets of Japanese pictograms at different frequencies to subjects not familiar with Japanese. Afterward, the subjects rated the pictograms for their appeal. The researchers found

that people tended to like frequent pictograms better than infrequent ones, although the subjects were not aware of the difference in frequency (Zajonc, 1980). Advertisers have put this effect to practical use in the service of merchandise from soap to cars and on behalf of political candidates in election campaigns.

Repetition does not always produce the effects intended by advertisers. For example, a study by Bekerian and Baddeley (1980) illustrated the failure to remember radio advertisements. The advertisements were aired by the British Broadcasting Corporation to announce a change in its wavelength. Interviews with listeners revealed practically no retention of these announcements, even though the listeners were estimated to have heard them more than 1,000 times. On the other hand, even if advertisements are not effective immediately, they may influence customers sometime later. Frequent exposure to racial and gender stereotypes, for example, may lead to unwanted attitudes, an issue investigated by social psychologists (Greenwald & Banaji, 1995; Wilson & Brekke, 1994).

The False-Fame Effect. Jacoby and colleagues (1989) presented a list of names to subjects, asking them to rate how famous the individuals were. The list included nonfamous names and names that were relatively famous at the time of the study. The latter included the athlete Roger Bannister, the entertainer Minnie Pearl, and the author Christopher Wren. Nonfamous names were picked from the telephone book, such as Sebastian Weisdorf, Valerie Marsh, and Adrian Marr. Immediately after reading the list, nobody rated the nonfamous people as famous. After a 24-hour delay, however, subjects tended to judge the nonfamous people mistakenly as famous. They did so on the basis of having been exposed to the names; the names were more familiar, but the specific context, whether the person was famous, was not remembered. Remembering a name while forgetting the context in which it was encountered can be a problem in eyewitness testimony. Witnesses may mistakenly identify a person as a perpetrator simply because they heard the name or saw the picture during prior questioning, not because they saw the person commit the crime (Reisberg & Schwartz, 1991).

Priming reflects the effects of prior experience on performance, however unintended and automatic. Priming effects have been established in a wide range of situations, from word identification, word fragment completion, and decision tasks to problem solving and judging the attractiveness of objects and the fame of people. Priming is robust and replicable and it provides memory researchers with an important tool of assessing memory in addition to such explicit memory tests as recall and recognition. Theorists agree that priming reveals a kind of knowledge different from explicit knowledge. Tulving (1989) used the terms *remembering* and *knowing* to describe these two types of knowledge. *Remembering* refers to one's knowledge of an event and the circumstance during which an event occurred. *Knowing* refers to the familiarity one has with a stimulus even if it is not remembered explicitly (Rajaram, 1993; Tulving, 1989, 1993; Chapter 11).

Attributes of Priming Effects

Priming is similar to explicit memory in some respects; it differs in others, however. The two are similar in that the number of stimulus exposures increases the strength of the memory trace in both, and lengthening the retention interval diminishes trace strength both in priming and in explicit memory. It is because of the differences between priming and explicit memory that priming has received so much attention from researchers. As noted, priming is spared in amnesic patients, whereas explicit recollection is impaired. Stimulus modality exerts a greater influence on priming than on explicit memory.

And, finally, researchers have identified different brain structures implicated in priming and explicit memory.

Modality Effects. Modality effects are the norm in priming situations: When there are changes in the stimulus modality (e.g., from a visual to an auditory presentation) between study and testing, priming effects are reduced. Explicit memory, on the other hand, is far less subject to changes in modality, if at all. Most researchers agree that it is the meaning, not the surface form, of items that people elaborate and remember (e.g., Sachs, 1967; Jarvella, 1979). Modality effects have been demonstrated in different priming tasks both across and within modalities (Schacter et al., 1993). In word fragment completion, priming is reduced when subjects first listen to a list of target words and are subsequently tested with visual word fragments. Priming is reduced when the font of the stimuli is changed between study and testing. In word identification, too, priming is diminished with a change in modality. Srivinas (1993) reported modality effects in pictorial tasks using outline drawings of objects and photographs. When the studied target stimuli were physically changed, priming was reduced; this occurred even when the only attribute that was changed was the viewing angle of the objects. Although priming is optimal when the stimulus conditions in study and testing are highly similar, some cross-modality priming does occur. Here, the person is presented with a stimulus in one modality and tested with a cue in another modality.

Forgetting. The course of forgetting in an explicit memory task (e.g., in recall) is measured by having subjects commit a list of items to memory and asking them to recall the list at various intervals after learning. The forgetting function in priming is measured by administering priming tests at various intervals following original study. The degree of facilitation of target stimuli is compared to performance on control stimuli not presented during the study phase. In a typical experiment, six retention intervals ranging from a few minutes to 16 months were used. During the study phase, students copied about 100 words and judged each word for its familiarity. Subjects were told to be prepared for an unspecified memory test. In testing, fragments from studied words and new words were presented. Figure 5.2 shows the priming effect as a function of the retention interval. The data show the superiority in the proportion of words completed among the studied words compared to new words. The priming advantage declined as a function of retention interval; it remained significant, however, even for the longest interval (Sloman et al., 1988).

Sloman and colleagues also investigated whether priming is subject to interference. Testing retroactive interference in one of their experiments, they had subjects inspect a list of words and then presented one of two interpolated activities: a verbal-recall task or a video game (a nonverbal task). Then the word fragment completion test followed. Test results did not differ as a function of interpolated activity, indicating that priming was not subject to retro-

active interference. The absence of interference effects in the implicit memory tasks is in contrast with the widely documented interference effects in explicit memory tasks. Indeed, for a long time, interference was thought to be the most important source of forgetting in memory (Chapter 4).

Priming Effects in Amnesia. The discovery by Warrington and Weiskrantz (1968) that amnesic patients profit from prior experience propelled priming to its prominence in memory research. After all, *amnesia* means the loss of mnemonic faculty. Warrington and Weiskrantz found that patients were able to use word fragment cues to identify the previously shown items. Patients also showed evidence of savings when the study and test phases were repeated.

Subsequent research revealed that amnesic patients exhibit priming in a variety of priming paradigms (Shimamura, 1986). Among other effects, research has established that the magnitude of the priming effect depends on the specific instructions given to the patient. When the patient is told to use fragments as cues to improve recall, the effect is smaller than when the task is construed as a game of naming any words that come to mind. There is disagreement among researchers whether amnesia patients exhibit priming for nonwords such as *defnodel*. This question is of interest because priming for such novel items would indicate that the patients' memory systems are sensitive to new experiences, however implicit. This would contrast with the inability of amnesic patients to acquire new information explicitly. The duration of priming effects in amnesia is also under debate. Some studies suggest that priming effects in amnesia are relatively short-lived, lasting no longer than two hours (Graf, Squire, & Mandler, 1984). On the other hand, a case study by Tulving, Hayman, and MacDonald (1991) indicates priming effects lasting for as long as a year. The study involved a patient, known as K. C., who had vir-

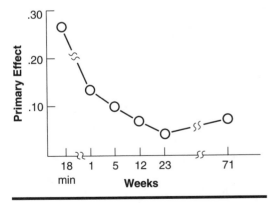

FIGURE 5.2 Forgetting function in a priming task. The priming effect as a function of retention interval.

tually no episodic memory (Chapter 12). K. C. exhibited perceptual priming effects but failed to recognize the same stimuli in explicit memory tests, nor did he have any recollection of having participated in the many stages of the study.

Priming effects have been observed in different patient groups across a range of tasks. Priming has been established among brain-injured accident victims such as K. C., Korsakoff patients, stroke victims, and individuals undergoing electroconvulsive shock therapy. Tasks include word completion, judging preference, category reminding, reading, spelling, and visual object priming. Whereas priming is observed in diverse patient groups and tasks, it is not found in all the possible patient-task combinations. For example, Alzheimer's patients exhibit priming in lexical decision and word identification tasks, but not in the word-stem completion task. Researchers have correlated such patterns of priming with brain sites impaired in the patients in an effort to find out whether these brain regions support priming (Schacter et al., 1993). Of course, there are also more direct methods of studying the neural correlates of priming and explicit memory.

Neuroscience Perspectives. Early investigators gained their knowledge on the relation of brain structures and memory from case studies of accident victims and of patients who underwent neurosurgery or who suffered from specific neural diseases. Early studies with amnesia patients uncovered impairments to the limbic system and the hippocampal region; it was therefore assumed that these regions were responsible for the degradation of explicit memory but not involved in priming. The search for brain structures involved in priming and explicit memory has intensified with the introduction of brain-imaging methods, sophisticated behavioral designs, and electrophysiological measurements. Consider studies representative of each of these methods. Although the studies provide no clear-cut mappings of memory functions and brain structures, they have given rise to interesting speculations.

PET Research. Squire (1994) describes an experiment using positron emission tomography (PET) imaging in an explicit condition and in a priming condition. During the study phase of both conditions, words were presented in uppercase letters *(MOTEL)*. In recall testing, word stems (e.g., *MOT*) were used as prompts to recall the target items. In the priming test, people were shown the word stems and asked to name any words that came to mind. The patterns of cerebral blood flow differed substantially as the subjects executed these different tasks. In the recall condition, PET activity was elevated in frontal brain regions, including the hippocampus. In the priming condition, however, PET activity was reduced in the right extrastriate cortex. This reduction was relative to the control condition, in which subjects completed words they had not seen during the study phase. Not surprisingly, people were faster to complete primed test words than nonprimed control words. Squire speculated that the reduced blood flow reflects perceptual fluency at the neural level: When a word (e.g., *MOTEL*) is presented for the second time, less neural effort is necessary (see also Schacter, 1996; Ungerleider, 1995).

Behavioral Methods. Behavioral evidence on the relation of priming and brain structures comes from a study that used the divided visual-field paradigm (Marsolek, Kosslyn, & Squire, 1992). This paradigm takes advantage of the architecture of the visual field where information in the left visual field is projected to the right brain hemisphere and information in the right visual field is projected to the left brain hemisphere. The experimenters found that priming depended on an interaction between the physical form of the test stimuli, including their type font and the hemisphere processing the information. When the stimuli had the same type font during study and testing, priming was more pronounced when word stems were processed by the right hemisphere than the left hemisphere. When fonts differed, the right-hemisphere advantage was eliminated. Similarly, there was no hemispheric difference in the recall condition where subjects were given the word stems as cues to recall the words.

These results suggest that priming and recall engage the two brain hemispheres to different degrees: The right hemisphere has an edge when it comes to word-stem completion priming. This presumably occurs because of form-specific processors located primarily in the right hemisphere. Squire (1994) speculated that recently perceived words are stored in distributed networks "and that one component of this network in the right hemisphere is dominant in supporting priming and that a different component in the left hemisphere is dominant in supporting cued recall" (p. 217).

Electrophysiological Measures. Paller and Kutas (1992) measured event-related potential (ERP) patterns in implicit and explicit memory conditions. The implicit memory condition involved a priming test in a word identification task; the explicit test included recall and recognition testing. There were two orienting tasks during the study phase of both conditions: an imagery task where subjects were asked to give a size estimate of the stimulus and an orthography task where they were asked to count the letters of the word. Priming was observed in both imagery and orthography conditions. Recall and recognition performance were better in the imagery than in the orthography condition, as one would expect from the levels-of-processing effect. Of particular interest were the differences in ERP patterns in the priming and recollection tasks. Brain potentials elicited in the two tasks were different in terms of amplitude, latency, and location: For the explicit tasks, ERPs had their peaks at laten-

cies of 500 to 800 milliseconds, whereas for the priming tasks, EPRs peaked between 400 and 500 milliseconds. In the explicit tasks, brain potentials were most prominent at the left, anterior locations; in priming, they were prominent at posterior locations.

Issues in Priming

When a research phenomenon is new, scientists are excited; they draw clear distinctions to characterize the phenomenon, they are not overly concerned with confounds, and they have clear-cut theories to account for the results. Once knowledge accumulates, however, potential confounds become a concern, distinctions become blurred, and alternative accounts for the findings compete. The priming literature is a case in point. Investigators are concerned about confounds and see more similarities among previously distinct aspects of priming, and theories become more complex.

Consider a potential confound in priming research—namely, the possibility that priming is contaminated by explicit memory. Priming has been attributed to automatic facilitation in the perceptual representation system, a rudimentary memory system assumed to operate separately from explicit memory and to emerge early in development (Schacter, 1996; Tulving & Schacter, 1990). Priming, however, could also occur when subjects remember the stimuli explicitly and use that memory to facilitate processing when they encounter the stimuli again in testing. Nonimpaired subjects at least could be expected to do so. Priming researchers reject this possibility for two reasons. First, if there was an influence of explicit memory, variables that affect the latter should also have an effect on priming. However, the levels-of-processing effect only affects explicit memory; it does not enhance priming. Second, the contamination view could not explain priming in amnesic patients; these patients do not have recourse to explicit memory.

Next, consider a distinction that has become blurred. Because of modality effects, priming was initially viewed as akin to perceptual processes, whereas explicit memory was linked with semantic knowledge. However, as cross-modal priming was discovered, theorists came to entertain the hypothesis of semantic priming. In cross-modal priming tests, stimuli in one modality are facilitated although they were first studied in another modality. Cross-modal priming suggests that the study episode activated not only the perceptual system but also the abstract meaning of the stimulus. When the stimulus was presented in another modality and facilitated, the facilitation must have been due to residual activation in the semantic structures. Such semantic priming has, in fact, been accepted by researchers; however, the researchers nevertheless maintain that priming is primarily perceptual because semantic priming is of lesser magnitude (Schacter, 1994.)

Finally, consider a theoretical issue that arises from the dissociations between priming and explicit memory. Stimulus modality affects performance in priming situations, but not in declarative memory tasks. On the other hand, level of processing is important in declarative memory, but not in priming. Priming is generally not subject to interference, but declarative memory is. The acquisition of explicit memories depends on the hippocampal region, whereas priming does not. As a result, priming remains intact in patients who have suffered injuries to the hippocampus, yet their explicit memory is impaired. Clearly, priming and declarative memory are different. Nobody disputes that difference; theorists differ, however, in explaining these differences. Are they due to different systems, as Schacter (1992, 1994, 1996) believes or to different processes within a unitary memory system, as Roediger (1990) believes? For now, I shall leave this question open. We'll return to it in Chapter 11.

Implicit Learning

Priming involves implicit memory for specific individual stimuli, whether it is a visual figure, a printed word, or a spoken word. However, people also exhibit implicit memory for patterns of stimuli, probabilities of events, covariation of events, and temporal sequences (Seger, 1994). This section reviews implicit learning in several experimental paradigms, including the acquisition of artificial grammars, abstractions, correlated events, and sequential patterns. Although each situation involves complex knowledge, people acquire that knowledge readily, and they do so without intention and awareness. Indeed, the performance of amnesic patients in these learning situations is similar to that of unimpaired individuals (Seger, 1994).

Learning Rules: Artificial Grammars

The following 12 letter strings belong to two different categories, A and B. See if you can identify for each string the correct category.

1. PVPXVPS
2. TSXS
3. PTTTVPVS
4. PVTVV
5. TSSXXVSS
6. TTVV
7. PTTTTVPS
8. PVV
9. PTTPS
10. TXXTTVPS
11. TSXXTTVV
12. PVXPVXPX

Strings 1, 2, 7, 8, 9, and 11 belong to category A and the remaining strings belong to category B. Each of the category A strings was generated according to a rule of an artificial grammar (Reber, 1967, 1993; Seger, 1994). Artificial grammars generate lawful strings of letters equivalent to sentences in a natural language.

Reber used a state grammar with *n* states and any number of transitions between them. Figure 5.4 illustrates one such grammar, where circles indicate states and arrows reflect transitions. The vocabulary of the grammar consists of the letters *P, S, T, V,* and *X*. The sequence of legal letter strings is dictated by the transitions provided in the grammar. Any string is legal that follows the sequence of states and transitions in Figure 5.4. For instance, *PVV* (string 8) is a simple string based on the transitions between states 1, 3, 5, and 6. Slightly more complex is string *PTVV*. This string uses the recursive transition shown at state 3. According to the grammar, there is no limit on the number of recursions allowed, so any string of the form *PT...TVV* (e.g., *PTTTVV, PTTTTTTVV,* etc.) is legal. A more complex string is based transitions between 1, 2, 4, 3, 5, 4, 6 (e.g., *TSXXTVPS*). Illegal strings violate the sequence of transitions or the permissible vocabulary. Strings 3, 4, 5, 6, 10, and 12, for example, are not legal according to the grammar in Figure 5.3.

Researchers have used a variety of tasks to assess learners' knowledge of stimuli generated by such artificial grammars: learning, discrimination, recognition, and transfer. Subjects typically cannot explicate the rules used to generate the stimulus materials. Nevertheless, learners acquire grammatical strings more quickly than ungrammatical strings; they readily discriminate between string types; in recognition tests, they respond more quickly to grammatical strings; and they transfer their knowledge of learned strings to new sets of strings constructed similarly. Finally, amnesic patients perform relatively well in the artificial grammar learning task, as they do in other implicit learning tasks.

Transfer. Reber (1969) conducted a transfer experiment involving two successive phases of grammar learning. In the study phase, learners acquired a string discrimination based on a specific grammar, such as that in Figure 5.3. During the testing phase, one aspect of the learning task was changed: either the syntax of the grammar or the vocabulary. In the changed-syntax condition, Reber changed the grammatical rules between study and testing but kept the letters the same. In the same-syntax condition, Reber changed the set of letters but kept the syntax the same. Both types of change produced a decrement in testing; the decrement was, however, greater in the changed-syntax condition than in the same-syntax condition, suggesting that the learners had acquired and transferred knowledge of the rules.

Artificial Grammar Learning in Amnesic Patients. Acquiring an artificial grammar is one of the skills that is spared in amnesic patients. Comparing performance of amnesic patients and control subjects in an explicit recognition test and an implicit classification task, Knowlton, Ramus, and Squire (1992) found a dissociation—the telltale sign that amnesic patients retain implicit information but not explicit information. Both groups of subjects were shown a list of grammatical strings, one at a time, that they had to recall in an immediate test. Both groups succeeded equally well at this task. In classification testing, the subjects were shown

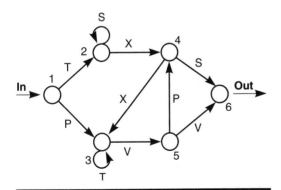

FIGURE 5.3 Miniature grammar to simulate syntactic rules; circles indicate states and arrows reflect transitions (Reber, 1993).

new grammatical strings and new ungrammatical strings. They were asked to classify the strings in terms of the rule they had previously learned. Patients and nonpatients performed about equally well at this task. However, patients fared more poorly in the recognition task. Although the advantage of the control subjects was relatively small, results like these contribute to a debate on what sort of knowledge learners acquire in artificial grammar learning. Do they acquire abstract rules implicitly or do they memorize specific exemplars that are accessible to explicit memory?

What Do Learners Learn?   Key issues in artificial grammar learning are what sort of knowledge learners acquire in the grammar learning task and whether that knowledge is, in fact, implicit. Researchers have given three different answers to the first question: learners acquire abstract rules, individual exemplars, and chunks of letters.

The *rule-learning hypothesis* has been based on the finding in the transfer paradigm that performance is better in the same-syntax condition than in the changed-syntax condition. According to Reber, this result could not have been based on individual exemplars because all exemplars change between the two experimental phases. Reber assumes that learners' knowledge of rules is not accessible to consciousness. Rather, it is implicit in the same way as their knowledge of the rules of language (Reber, 1989). Since knowledge of rules is implicit, this hypothesis assumes naturally that amnesic patients can learn the grammar in the absence of declarative memory.

According to the second hypothesis, people remember *individual exemplars,* and the memory of such exemplars is explicit (Vokey & Brooks, 1992). The exemplar hypothesis fully accepts the transfer effects, accounting for them by the assumption that learners compare test strings to learned strings in terms of their structural similarity. For example, the test string *BDCCCB* is analogous to the study string *MTVVVM.* Forming an analogy is an abstraction much like rule learning; however, this process occurs during *testing,* not during study (see Redington & Chater, 1996). Opinions differ on whether memory for exemplars is explicit or implicit. Retention of exemplars would appear to be prima facie evidence of explicit memory. Knowlton and Squire (1996), however, have proposed that people can acquire both abstract rules and exemplars and that both types are independent of declarative memory.

The third hypothesis of artificial grammar learning holds that subjects acquire neither rules nor exemplars; rather, subjects come to learn which *chunks or letter combinations* of two or three letters are legal (Redington & Chater, 1996; Servan-Schreiber & Anderson, 1990). According to the grammar in Figure 5.3, the following chunks would be legal: *PV, TXX, XVV, TVV, XS,* and *PTT.* As a result of training, stimuli composed of grammatical chunks, such as *TXXVPXVV ((TXX) (VP) (XVV)),* would be judged grammatical; otherwise, subjects judge the strings as ungrammatical. For example, the letter combinations *TPT, SX,* and *PP,* and strings including them, would be ungrammatical. To date, there has been no crucial experiment to distinguish between these three views, and the debate continues (Redington & Chater, 1996). This issue is important. It addresses the fundamental nature of human categorization. A similar debate has been waged in research on concept formation and categorization (Estes, 1994).

Learning Abstract Ideas

Our ability to form abstractions is important for reasons of cognitive economy. If it were not for this ability, we would have to use a new term for the same object under different circumstances and taking on different forms. Imagine using a different term for a pizza when it is whole or half-eaten, or using a different term for the same item viewed under different perceptual conditions, whether it is a change in the viewing angle, the distance, or the illumination (see Chapter 4). People learn to abstract the prototype underlying similar stimuli, disregarding relatively fleeting perceptual particulars. An important study of prototype abstraction was carried out by Posner (1969), who used dot patterns such as those in Figure 5.4. The first three patterns shown were based on the prototype pattern on the far right, which was not shown during study.

In testing, all of the patterns were shown along with new patterns, and subjects were asked to judge whether they had seen the test patterns. The subjects judged the old patterns correctly as old, but tended to false-alarm to the prototypes even though they had not been displayed during study. As subjects judged the patterns, they came up with idiosyncratic descriptions and labels. However, as is common in implicit learning, they were not able to verbalize the correct mapping between patterns. Amnesic patients have been shown to acquire such pattern abstractions almost as well as nonimpaired individuals do (Knowlton & Squire, 1992).

Learning Correlations between Events
People develop reasonably good intuitions about the co-occurrence of events, whether they are health related, economic, or meteorological; for example, a sore throat often precedes a cold; lower interest rates tend to make homes more affordable; and heat and humidity are often precur-

sors to thunderstorms. To be sure, there are no guarantees that the relation always holds. Covariation learning, as illustrated by these instances, readily lends itself to laboratory study. The following sample study demonstrates that people learn weather forecasting in a miniature world of only two conditions—rain or shine—each correlated with probabilistic cues.

People participating in the study were shown sets of cards on a computer screen where each card exhibited one of four shapes: triangles, circles, diamonds, or squares. The card patterns were correlated with the two weather outcomes, rain and shine, on a probabilistic basis. For example, a pair of cards, one exhibiting triangles and the other showing squares, was associated with sunshine about 80% of the time. Subjects inspected the cards, made their weather prediction, and were given immediate feedback. After only 50 trials, subjects achieved a correct response level of 70%. Importantly, amnesic patients did as well on this task as nonpatient controls (Squire, 1995). However, on an explicit memory test assessing subjects' retention of the layout of the screen, the control subjects did far better than the patients.

Learning Event Sequences
In the sequence-learning paradigm, subjects respond to sequences of letters or lights displayed in certain locations on a computer screen (Lewicki, 1986). They learn to make a specific response for each individual stimulus in the se-

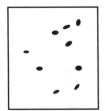 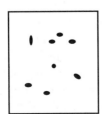 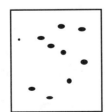 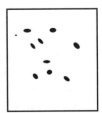

FIGURE 5.4 Patterns used by Posner (1969) to document the genesis of abstraction.

quence, but at first they are not aware of the sequential pattern of the stimuli. Learning is detected when subjects come to respond to previously presented patterns more accurately and rapidly than to new patterns. Amnesic patients are capable of learning and retaining this skill. Frequently, the speedup in responses occurs before learners become aware of the stimulus sequences. Even brain-wave patterns reveal subjects' different states of knowledge, as a study by Eimer, Goschke, Schlaghecken, and Stuermer (1996) demonstrates. These researchers recorded ERP patterns as subjects made specific responses to the letters *A, B, C,* and *D* presented in successive patterns on a screen. The standard sequence was *CDBABDCBDA;* it was constantly repeated, with each letter occurring in a particular screen location. Control sequences included letters that occurred in unpredictable screen locations.

Reaction times were faster and error rates lower for standard stimuli than for unpredictable control stimuli. This was true for subjects who became aware of the sequence (explicit subjects) as well as those who did not (implicit subjects.) The ERP patterns exhibited the typical effects for unpredictable stimuli: There was an increased N200 amplitude when subjects were processing the control stimuli. The N200 is a ERP wave with a negative amplitude peaking around 200 milliseconds after a target event. It is indicative of the brain's reaction to a surprising event (Chapter 3). The ERP difference between standard and control stimuli increased as the experiment progressed; the difference was greater for explicit subjects than for implicit subjects. Interestingly, the occurrence of the N200 pattern was anticipated by the speedup of reaction times to the standard stimuli.

Each of the implicit learning situations—grammar learning, abstraction, and acquiring the correlation between events and the sequence of events—reflects an aspect of our environment. In order to survive, animals have had to evolve so

as to be sensitive to such patterned events and to remember them. Learning in each of these situations is robust; the skill is acquired without explicit intent and retained over time. According to Reber (1993), implicit learning is phylogenetically prior and therefore more resistant to injury than explicit memory. As a result, implicit memory persists better in impaired populations than conscious learning. The latter is a "superstructure" that is relatively complex and more easily disrupted.

LEARNING AND REMEMBERING COGNITIVE SKILLS

Problem solving is the cognitive skill par excellence. We solve problems all the time, frequently without even thinking of them as problems: getting up in the morning, driving to work, finding one's way to the cafeteria, choosing a particular program on TV, and so on. We are familiar with each of these situations, remember what to do, and solve the problem effortlessly. Problems in arithmetic, computer programming, chess playing, and medical diagnosis are less familiar, if at all, and require much thought and effort. As we shall see, people can train to become experts in these and other domains. Although experts usually cannot report how they execute their craft, they do so accurately and seem to retain the skill practically forever. In this section, we consider a sample of cognitive skills, discuss the acquisition of skills, and conclude with the fascinating story of individuals who exhibit extraordinary memories; memory has become their skill.

Sample of Skills

Problem Solving
When a person solves a problem, he or she seeks to achieve a goal within a set of constraints. A problem has an initial state and a goal state, which is achieved by taking certain steps via a

series of intervening states. When you think of problems, you are likely to think of the math problems from your middle school and high school days—algebra, arithmetic, and geometry. Here are a couple of such problems:

— A high school basketball team has won 40% of its first 15 games. Beginning with the 16th game, how many games in a row does the team have to win in order to have a 55% winning record?

— The supply department at IBM has to make sure that scientists get computers. On a particular day, there are 11 computers and 8 scientists requesting computers. Each scientist randomly chooses his or her computer but do so in alphabetical order. What is the probability that the first three scientists will get the lowest, second lowest, and third lowest serial number?

Computer Programming. Computer programming is related to mathematical problem solving in that programmers typically work on well-defined problems. Did you ever watch an expert programmer writing a program? Her fingers fly across the keyboard, she composes and tests code, and debugs procedures, all with apparent ease. When you interrupt her and ask what she was just doing, chances are that she cannot tell you.

Of course, there are many other types of problems than math and programming problems. Researchers in cognitive science have adopted a number of standard problems for their research studies. Popular among such problems are navigation problems and the Tower of Hanoi problem.

— Rome is one of the most challenging cities in which to drive. There are no clearly defined blocks; instead, narrow and winding one-way streets and alleys lead through a maze of neighborhoods. They often make sharp turns and stop at a flight of steps without outlet for motor vehicles. Yet, local taxi drivers have no difficulty in getting bewildered passengers from one end of town to the other with great ease. The geographical knowledge of the drivers, in addition to their driving skill, are a marvel to everyone observing them practice their art.

— The Tower of Hanoi puzzle involves moving a pyramidal stack of disks from one peg to another (see Figure 6.2). Certain constraints apply—among them are that only one disk may be moved at a time, smaller disks must always be on top of larger disks, and the player must use pegs to place the disks rather than the surrounding table space.

Cognitive skills extend beyond problem solving to include most of a person's activities from the use of language to artistic expression. Consider but two illustrations of such skills: language comprehension and musical performance.

Language Comprehension. We comprehend our native language in all of its subtleties and use its regularities and exceptions with ease and usually without awareness. Native speakers of English have no difficulty understanding the different meanings of sentences (5.1a) and (5.1b).

(5.1a) John thinks he won.

(5.1b) He thinks John won.

In sentence (5.1a), *John* and *he* may refer to the same individual (John) but *he* and *John* must be different individuals in sentence (5.1b). Speakers know this distinction, although it is unlikely that they have ever been taught any rules to do so, and it takes linguists considerable effort to explicate such rules (e.g., Lasnik, 1990).

Musical Performance. Perhaps no other skill elicits as much admiration as musical performance, whether it is instrumental or vocal. Just think of Yoyo Ma performing on the cello or of John Lennon singing "Imagine." It is no secret that these artists have had to spend countless hours of daily practice to develop and maintain their skills. However, it is far less clear what memory structures support the skill.

It is the performance of expert musicians, computer programmers, mathematicians, and others that beckons psychologists with questions on the representation, acquisition, and retention of skills. What is the best way to teach and to practice them? How does a person maintain a skill? Can anyone acquire the skill or does the individual have to have a special talent? First, however, we shall consider the representation of cognitive skills within Anderson's ACT framework (Anderson, 1993).

Representation of Skills

According to the ACT theory, cognitive skills form part of procedural memory (see also Chapter 7). Procedural memory differs from declarative memory in terms of its basic units; these units are pattern-recognition routines, technically known as *production rules*.

Production rules capture the cognitive and motor components that underlie a skill. Each production rule may be thought of as a little demon trained to perform a specific action. Usually the demon rests; when certain conditions are met, however, it awakens and fulfills its designated action. Production rules specify a set of actions given certain conditions. The general format of production rules is given in expression (5.2).

(**5.2**) IF these are the conditions,
THEN execute these actions.

Expression (5.3) is a production rule to illustrate the recognition of a geometrical shape, a polygon. The rule is general in that it can be used for any figure with any number of sides. The words *figure* and *sides* are printed in capital letters to indicate that they represent variables.

(**5.3**) IF a FIGURE is two dimensional
and the SIDES are all equal

and the number of SIDES is less than eight
THEN classify the FIGURE as a polygon.

In order to solve a problem within a domain (e.g., in geometry), the problem solver requires a whole battery of production rules. The set of rules for geometry includes rules to identify different shapes as well as rules for geometric postulates, such as the side-side-side postulate and the side-angle-side postulate (Anderson, 1983a). Production rules in arithmetic include rules for each of the basic operations of addition, subtraction, multiplication, and so on. Each of these operations consists of subskills formalized in terms of production rules. The addition of multidigit numbers, for example, proceeds in terms of columns going from right to left. There are rules to arrange the numbers to be added, to add single digits, and to recognize and record carries. Every skill is based on production rules, even if they are not optimal and contain bugs (Van Lehn, 1990).

The representation of skills undergoes an important change as a result of practice. According to Anderson's theory, initially information about skills tends to be based on whatever facts the beginning student can marshall about the skill. That information is captured in terms of propositions. As a result of training, the declarative information is compiled into productions, much as a computer program is compiled.[1]

Scientists conduct research on the acquisition of skills for practical reasons; everyone wants to know how to learn a skill in the most efficient way possible. Science still has to go some distance in order to answer this question and it is clear that the answer will not be a simple one.

Skill Acquisition

Researchers characterize skill acquisition in terms of three successive stages: the cognitive stage, the associative stage, and the autonomous stage (Anderson, 1993; Fitts, 1964; Van Lehn, 1996). During the *cognitive stage,* a teacher explains to students the rules underlying the skill. In the case of adding multiple-digit numbers, for example, the teacher shows the students sample problems and explains that, first, the digits in the right-most column must be added, and then, the procedure is repeated, moving left column by column. The student is assumed to create a declarative representation of this knowledge, including a set of textbook examples. In the *associative stage,* the student practices the rules by doing many addition problems. During this stage, the student begins using addition rules almost without being aware of doing so. In the *autonomous stage,* declarative knowledge is assumed to be transformed into procedures—the production rules. The rules are used automatically and their application is well coordinated. As a result, addition problems are solved faster and with fewer errors.

How should a person best learn a skill, whether it is an addition problem, the Tower of Hanoi puzzle, or a physics problem? Here are three recommendations from researchers:

— Continue to practice a skill, even after you think you have mastered it.
— Distribute practice sessions over time rather than trying to learn too much too fast.
— Generate solutions on your own rather than

ask the teacher right away for the correct answer.

Continued Practice

Can a person afford to stop practicing after learning a skill? Far from it; as a result of continued practice, declarative knowledge continues to be transformed into procedural knowledge. The former requires slow retrieval of propositional representations, whereas the latter is based on fast retrieval of productions. Slow mental calculations are replaced by memory retrieval of routines. With additional practice, productions become more efficient; they are pruned or combined for more effective application. The individual becomes faster in solving the problems and makes fewer errors as the knowledge is transformed into production rules specific to the target domain. The improvement in performance as a function of practice is described by the power law of practice (see Figure 5.5), a generalization that applies to perceptual, cognitive, and motor skills, as well as to the acquisition of facts (Chapters 1, 4, and 7).

Distributed Practice

This text makes repeated reference to the advantages of distributed practice compared to massed practice (Chapters 1, 2, 4, and 12). Here, I present a neuroimaging study involving

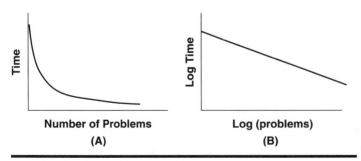

FIGURE 5.5   The power law of practice. The speedup of performance as a function of continued practice graphed in terms of the number of problems *(A)* and in terms of a log-log plot *(B).*

the acquisition of a motor skill that illustrates the advantages of "taking time out" to let the skill solidify. Two scientists at Johns Hopkins University, Reza Shadmehr and Henry Holcomb (1997), used neuroimaging methods to track brain processes as one group of volunteers was learning a very complex motor tracking task. The scientists found that initially in training, the right prefrontal cortex was highly activated. After a rest period of six hours, the volunteers had retained the complex skill surprisingly well. This time, the PET analysis revealed increased brain activity in a set of other brain regions, the premotor area among them. Another group of learners who were allowed no rest, but had to learn a second motor task immediately following the first task, did not remember the first task very well.

Shadmehr and Holcomb reasoned that the memory representation of the skill, presumably a set of procedural rules, is initially fragile but becomes more stable and more resistant to interference during the rest period. Remarkably, it appears that the brain engages different regions to support the skill during its various stages of acquisition. The practical lesson of this study is that when you acquire a new skill, it is not sufficient to practice, but you have to allow time for the brain to consolidate the knowledge of the skill.

Self-Generation

Research has shown that when a teacher encourages students to generate their own explanations, they learn problem solving more effectively, whatever the domain, whether it is mechanics, physics, or computer programming (Healy & Bourne, 1995). When left on their own, students tend to solve the problems by referring back to similar examples and by providing their own explanations of the problems. Protocols taken from problem solvers indicate that the more successful students tend to generate such self-explanations and inferences, whereas the poorer students simply read or paraphrase the textbook problem. Self-explanations even help when you learn to use a videocassette recorder! Self-explanations have proven particularly helpful during the initial stages of problem solving in a domain. Unfortunately, coming up with self-explanations is not always easy for students; the adage "No pain, no gain" says it all (Van Lehn, 1996).

Finally, consider a perhaps unexpected by-product of practicing a skill: One would think that more practice on a given skill would produce better transfer of the skill to other skills. Although this is true to some extent, transfer is limited by the degree of shared knowledge procedures between tasks (Chapter 12). Typically, once practice has established a skill firmly, there is less transfer and the skill has become specific. According to Anderson (1993), this is a sign that the knowledge is no longer declarative; rather, it has become procedural and automatic. Thus, in order to reinforce knowledge of a skill, it is necessary to practice that specific skill.

Adding numbers, recognizing geometric figures, and solving puzzles is simple compared to the problems encountered in such knowledge-rich fields as physics, engineering, and medicine. Acquiring expertise in these domains necessitates years of continued practice and training. Cognitive scientists have examined skilled memory in physics and medicine by comparing the manner in which novices and experts solve problems. Experts tend to focus on fundamental principles of a problem, whereas novices tend to consider superficial aspects of the problem. Medical experts have a more richly developed vocabulary of the physiological function of organs and of disease dimensions, as the following section illustrates.

Medical Expertise

Research on medical expertise attracted both physicians and cognitive scientists who joined in the effort of developing computer-based expert systems to assist physicians in diagnostic work.

The key issue was to find out what sort of knowledge experts were able to bring to bear on a diagnosis. Scientists quickly came to realize that asking the experts about making diagnoses was not sufficient to understand the processes by which they arrived at a diagnosis. The paradigm of choice became simply to watch experts and novices at work as they examined charts and formulated hypotheses about the underlying disease. A study by Feltovich, Johnson, Moller, and Swanson (1984) is representative of this methodology.

Feltovich and colleagues presented charts of four fictitious pediatric cardiology patients to two groups: fourth-year medical students who had received six weeks of clinical practice and training in pediatric cardiology, and cardiologists who had been in the field at least 20 years. The four cases were based on medical records of actual patients seen at the University of Minnesota Hospital. The researchers constructed the cases so that they included symptoms to suggest alternative diseases that initially appeared equally plausible. Each participant studied the four cases and reported aloud his or her thoughts when reading the file. At certain points, subjects were asked to give their hunches about the disease.

Subjects' protocols and diagnoses indicated that the experts tended to consider a disease in the context of related diseases. For the experts, a set of related diseases presumably constitutes a category in memory. The experts evaluated the symptoms relative to the entire set of plausible diseases, whereas the medical students did not consider alternatives. The students committed factual errors in combining symptoms with inappropriate diseases, and they interpreted the symptoms either in an overly general or an overly restrictive manner.

According to Feltovich and colleagues, medical students' familiarity with cases is limited to just one prototypical disease within a category: the textbook case. As physicians gain experience, more cases and more models of diseases are added to their long-term memories. The disease models include the underlying physiology of the disease—the principle underlying the disease, features of the disease, and its clinical presentation.

The experts' memories not only include knowledge of more diseases but they allow the experts to evaluate hypotheses about different diseases in parallel. Patel, Arocha, and Kaufman (1994) found that experts were able to produce accurate hypotheses early during the diagnostic process. According to a model authored by Ericsson and Kintsch (1995), the experts are able to do so because by exercising their profession they have developed a highly accessible retrieval structure in long-term memory that supports the rapid recruitment of the accurate diagnosis.

In the next section, we shall see that memory itself may be considered a skill; we shall discuss memorists who have become famous for their mnemonic prowess, and we will see how ordinary people have become memory experts. Indeed, each of us is a memory expert in those skills that we continuously exercise in the course of our daily lives. These skills include the language skills of encoding and producing utterances, our knowledge of words and their meaning, as well as our knowledge of the physical and social environment.

Supermemory: Memory as a Skill

Every generation of psychologists has known its memory experts. There was S., who remembered everything and forgot nothing (Luria, 1976); there was V. P., whose recall on standard lab tasks was many times that of control subjects (Hunt & Love, 1972); and there was Sol Finkelstein, a calculating expert who was hired in the 1932 presidential elections by the broadcasting stations to calculate election results. Neisser (1982a) sought to take a memory census and documented several cases of supermemory.

Here, I describe three cases: the musician Toscanini, the mathematician Aitken, and the memorist Rajan, whose story will be described in greater detail.[2]

Arturo Toscanini

Arturo Toscanini (1867–1957) is known for his great musical accomplishments. Just how much those achievements depended on his spectacular memory is less well known. Neisser (1982a) cites a report given by the violinist Augusto Rossi about Toscanini's prodigious memory: "It was in St. Louis, just before the start of the concert, that the second bassoonist, Umberto Ventura, came to Toscanini. He was in great agitation. He had just discovered that the key for the lowest note on his instrument was broken: he couldn't use it. What was to be done? Toscanini, shading his eyes, thought for a moment and then said, 'It is alright—that note does not occur in tonight's concert.'" In a similar feat, in New York, Toscanini managed to reproduce from memory the score of a piece of music that was not available and that he hadn't played in several decades. Toscanini was believed to have been able to remember every note of every instrument of 350 symphonies and operas!

A. C. Aitken

Professor A. C. Aitken (1895–1967) was a mathematics professor at the University of Edinburgh with a stupendous ability as a mental calculator. When Professor Aitken was 66 years old, psychologist Ian Hunter studied his achievements (Hunter, 1977). Among other problems, Hunter asked Aitken to express the fraction 4/47 in terms of decimals; Aitken paused for a few seconds and then produced the answer of .0851063829787234042553191914 at a rate of one digit every 0.75 second. Another problem was the square root of 851 that Professor Aitken solved in 15 seconds as 29.17190429.

Hunter (1977) attributed Aitken's achievements to his huge repertoire of mathematical facts and computational algorithms. He spent his entire life, at least from age 13, building up his mathematical vocabulary until he eventually reached a point where he was able to "recognize and to think of quite large numbers as distinctive, unitary items: this is comparable to the ability of literate people to deal with a word as a unit rather than as an unwieldy collection of letters or sounds" (p. 36). According to Hunter, extensive and continuous practice was the key factor in Aitken's calculational ability. As a result of practice, Aitken developed both knowledge structures in long-term memory and his short-term memory capacity; the latter was necessary to allow him to remember and process the intermediate results of his calculations.

Rajan

At age 30, Rajan came to Charles Thompson's psychology lab at Kansas University in 1987 already well established as a memorist (Thompson, Cowan, & Frieman, 1993). His achievements included gaining entry into the *Guinness Book of World Records* by recalling the first 31,811 digits of pi. *Pi,* the ratio of the circumference of a circle relative to its diameter, is, along with *e*, the most frequently used constant of mathematics. Because of its wide use, tables containing the decimal digits of pi have been published. These are the tables that Rajan and other memorists memorize as a benchmark of memory. The printed tables include pages of 5,000 digits. Each page lists 50 rows of digits with 100 digits per row. Each row is arranged in terms of 10-digit strings with 10 strings per row. For example, the first three 10-digit strings of the printed pi table are printed in expression (5.4).

(5.4) 1415926535 8979323846 2643583279...

When Rajan arrived at the Kansas University lab, his goal was to study his own memory. After convincing themselves that an unusual individual had chanced into their lab, Thompson and colleagues undertook a five-year research project on Rajan's memory. Here, we will focus on Rajan's memory representation of the digits of pi and on the manner in which he used this representation to achieve his record-breaking mnemonic feats.

Unlike other memorists, Rajan did not use visual imagery or photographic memory. The researchers established this in a recall study where Rajan and control subjects were given number matrices ranging from 5×5 to 20×20 rows and columns, respectively. Needless to say, the controls were not able to memorize the larger matrices, whereas Rajan retained all of these matrices with ease. If Rajan had used visual imagery to retrieve digits from mental matrices, the time to recall rows and columns should have been very similar. However, this was not the case; recall by rows was much faster than recall by columns (8 seconds vs. 60 seconds). That Rajan's visual imagery was in no way special was confirmed by the finding that his recall for spatial locations was actually poorer than that of control subjects. Taken together, these results suggest that Rajan used some other means of encoding and retrieving information.

How did Rajan retrieve information from a much larger set of numbers? Thompson and colleagues used the first 10,000 decimal digits of pi as their test stimuli. These were the digits that Rajan had learned particularly well. The researchers had Rajan participate in a memory search task by prompting him on each trial to produce the digit in a specific target position in the pi table. For example, Rajan might see the number 8,347 on the screen, indicating that he was to recall the digit of pi in the 8,347th position. According to Rajan's verbal description, his memory was organized in terms of the table from which he memorized the digits. He retrieved a target digit by locating the correct row and then counting across the row to find the target digit. Sure enough, the observed retrieval times supported Rajan's self-assessment: Memory search times increased as a function of location in a row but not with the location of the row.

Rows in the source table included 100 digits in 10 strings of 10 each. Thompson and colleagues obtained evidence that Rajan treated the printed 10-digit strings as a chunk. The researchers hypothesized as follows: If printed 10-digit strings are chunks, Rajan should be able to find a target sequence of digits more quickly when it corresponded to a string as printed in the source table. On the other hand, a string of 10 digits copied *across* two columns should take longer to retrieve. Thompson and colleagues came up with a clever task to test this hypothesis. Rajan was given 5 digits from the pi table as a prompt and asked to reproduce the 5 subsequent digits. There were two types of prompts: the complete-string prompt and the spanning-string prompt. The complete-string prompt was completed by the remaining 5 digits of a printed 10-digit string; for the spanning-string prompt, the next 5 digits appeared across the space. The two types of prompts are illustrated here:

Source strings 8979323846 2643583279...

Complete   89793

Spanning   23846

As predicted, Rajan's response times were much faster for complete strings than for spanning strings (8 seconds vs. 81 seconds)! Clearly, Rajan treated the 10-digit strings as chunks. According to Thompson, these chunks had the properties of lexical items, much as the mathematician Aitken treated large numbers as word units.

However impressive Rajan's memory for numbers is, it did not extend to other domains. Rajan's letter span, although above normal, was nowhere near his digit span, and in everyday life situations, he was not much different from you or me: He, too, tended to forget where he had placed his keys. Does Rajan have talent? Thompson and colleagues think he does, at least for memorizing numbers (see also Hunt & Love, 1972).

In the next section, we will discuss an alternative account of supermemory. According to the alternative theory, memory is a trainable skill like any other, and whoever is sufficiently motivated can become a memorist. We shall discuss research conducted with chess masters who had a specialized memory for chess and with people who were willing to become memorists. The idea underlying memory training is to increase memory performance by making more efficient use of working memory resources. The working memory is assumed to maintain information for a brief period of time in an active state so as to facilitate rapid access and retrieval.

Memory Improves with Practice

The storage and processing capacity of working memory is limited; fortunately, however, there are strategies to use these resources to their fullest extent. This section describes how working memory can be stretched by practice that creates retrieval structures in long-term memory. We study such memory skills in two different domains: in the digit span and in chess. In both cases, the working memory load depends on the manner in which the information is chunked or packaged. *Chunking* is a process that expands the capacity of working memory (Miller, 1956) by accessing and retrieving more information from long-term memory (see Chase & Ericsson, 1981).

Digit Span. In the digit span test, increasingly longer lists of digits are presented to a subject for immediate recall. First, the person is given three digits, then four, and so on, until he or she can no longer recall the entire sequence correctly. The average digit span is seven. Chase and Ericsson (1981) developed an effective mnemonic technique to increase the digit span dramatically. They trained a college student to expand his digit span over a 40-week period and recorded experimental protocols as the student recalled the test digits.

Their subject, S. F., was an undergraduate of average intelligence (SAT = 990) at Carnegie-Mellon University. His digit span of eight was also average when the study began. Over a two-year time period, S. F. participated in the experiment for about 250 sessions, being paid each time. During the course of those sessions, his digit span increased tenfold!

During the first four training sessions, S. F.'s performance and protocol showed no difference from other subjects. On the fifth day, however, S. F. began using a new coding scheme and his recall exceeded his previous day's recall by four standard deviations. Being a runner, he coded some of the digits as running times. S. F. was a member of the cross-country team and several other running clubs. He also participated regularly in races, where his best events were the three-mile, five-mile, and marathon. His best times in these events were 14:39, 25:40, and 2:39:36, respectively. Over subsequent training sessions, S. F. continued to use the running-time coding scheme and refined it over the two-year period. For example, given the sequence 4 1 3 1 7 7 8 4 0 6 0 3 4 9 4 8 7 0 9 4 6 2, he coded the last four digits by saying, "I ran it in nine forty six point . . . two." He had 11 categories of running times, ranging from a short distance of half-mile to marathon length. Thus, he memorized the 946.2 as running time for a distance of two miles. Beginning with the shortest distance, S. F. used these categories to code the digits for each session. At recall, he used the different race categories as a retrieval system.

Ericcson and Polson (1988) documented the effective use of a personalized retrieval system in a waiter, J. C., who was able to remember as many as 20 orders without writing them down. Having worked for several years as a waiter, J. C. developed a scheme of encoding orders in terms of such categories as entree (e.g., filet mignon and barbecue), temperature (e.g., well done), and starches (e.g., fries and rice). Using the initial letters of these and other types of food, he formed words and phrases that were memorable to him. He used food categories, letters, and words as retrieval cues when reporting the orders to the kitchen staff. Interestingly, J. C.'s memory for materials other than restaurant orders (e.g., a list of animal names) was no better than average.

The point of the studies with S. F. and J. C. is this: A person can strengthen his or her retention by mapping the to-be-remembered information in terms of something that is familiar and sensible to the person. This is the principle that the inventors of mnemonic techniques have successfully used since antiquity. It makes no difference what the content is—whether it is computer programming, typing, arithmetic, interpreting x-rays, reading architectural plans, or employing strategies in games such as chess—all that is required is that the learner devote extensive practice to it.

Both memory experts, S. F. and J. C., had practiced their memorization skills. When presented with a list of digits or orders from a menu, they could repeat it. Experts in other domains also exhibit superior recall of information specific to their area of expertise. Consider next Chase and Simon's study on memory for chess.

Memory for Chess.   Chase and Simon (1973) have shown that chess masters have excellent memory for chess positions on a chessboard, even though their memory capacity for digits is no greater than that of novices. With extended chess training, players learn to chunk chess positions and are able to fit more into working memory. This is analogous to learning a retrieval structure in Chase and Ericsson's research (1981). The expert's advantage includes his or her richer knowledge structure in long-term memory, and a better retrieval system for pulling that information into working memory.

Chase and Simon (1973) presented chessboards to three people: a master player, an intermediate player, and a beginner. The subjects inspected the chess positions for five seconds and re-created the positions from memory. There were two conditions in the experiment: a chess and a control condition. In the chess condition, real chess games copied from chess books were presented to the subjects. In the control condition, randomized games with an equal number of pieces as in the chess condition were shown. Naturally, the chessmaster recalled more chess positions in the chess condition than the other players. Surprisingly, however, the master did no better in the randomized control condition. The master's better retention of the chess positions was not due to any differences in working memory. Rather, his knowledge of chess made the difference.

In order to appreciate that difference, consider the following statistics. The master player was one of the top 25 players in the country at the time of the study; he had played or studied chess for an estimated 25,000 hours. The intermediate player was ranked at the 85th percentile of players by the Chess Federation; his estimated playing time was 3,000 hours of chess. The beginner had played no more than 100 hours. To give you an idea just how much time the master spent on chess, imagine that you work at chess for 40 hours of each week of the year, thus totaling 2,080 hours per year. You would have to work at chess full time for about 12 years to approximate the time this chessmaster spent on it. Of course, as a result of such extended training, you would learn anywhere from 10,000 to 100,000 different chess configurations. This number is comparable to the number of words in a reader's vocabulary. In other words, masters have learned to "speak" chess. For them, a chunk is like a word that points to knowledge in long-term memory, a recognizable pattern. Thus, expertise involves the use of pattern recognition rather than rote rehearsal of unrelated information.

Theory of Memory Skill

Common to the cases we have reviewed—whether it was the digit span recall, a waiter's recall, or recall in chess—is the notion that practice promotes a more efficient use of long-term memory. According to memory skill theory, practice changes long-term processes in three critical ways. First, the learner stores the information to be remembered rapidly in long-term memory. This is possible because the person learns to encode information in terms of preexisting semantic memory structures meaningful to him or her. These can be running times, acronyms, chess rules, or some other scheme. In each case, the learner endows the information with meaning, which, in turn, integrates the to-be-remembered information with existing memories.

Second, the learner develops an effective retrieval structure that is accessible through retrieval cues. For these cues to become effective, they must be linked with the target information during encoding and storage. A familiar example of a retrieval structure is the method of loci. People use this technique by mentally placing items in specific locations—for example, the rooms of a house or different sites on a university campus. In testing, learners retrieve the information by first accessing the imagined locations and then the target information associated with a location.

The final tenet of memory skill theory is that, as result of practice, both encoding and retrieval operations of long-term memory become faster, so that long-term memory comes to resemble working memory (Chase & Ericsson, 1981; Ericsson & Kintsch, 1995; Richman, Staszewski, & Simon, 1995). A fundamental feature of working memory is that information is readily accessible for use (Chapter 6). Availability of information is, of course, necessary for the mental calculations of a Professor Aitken or the lightning moves made by a chessmaster.

Expert memory in a domain is in some respects similar to expertise in other domains; in other respects, it is different. Skilled memory is similar because it can be achieved through deliberate and extended practice, as we have seen. On the other hand, skilled memory differs from other skills: The memorist's skill consists of remembering facts; his or her skill is the ability to report memorized information. Perceptual and problem-solving skills, by contrast, are usually implicit and not reportable.

CONCLUSION

As wide as the range of skills is that was reviewed in this chapter, the universe of human skills extends well beyond that sample. Even writing novels becomes faster with practice. Consider the case of science-fiction writer Isaac Asimov, who wrote close to 500 novels in his lifetime (Ohlsson, 1992). Asimov completed the first set of 100 novels in about 20 years, but the final set in only 3 years and 6 months! Georges Simenon, the writer who created the police detective Maigret and who sold 550 million copies of his books, wrote close to 400 novels in addition to hundreds of short stories and autobiographical novels. At the height of his career, Simenon wrote as many as 80 pages a day, a novel a week, and 38 novels a year. According to an anecdote, film producer Alfred Hitchcock once telephoned Simenon and was told that the writer could not come to the phone because he had just started another novel. "That's no problem," Hitchcock is reported to have replied, "I'll wait" (*Le Nouvel Observateur,* April 25, 1996).

Memory for all of these skills, whether they involve cognitive or motor performance, is reflected in the improvement of performance as a function of exercising the skill. The solution to math problems becomes easier, writing becomes faster, and medical diagnosis more accurate. After extended practice, the skill has become automatic and, as a result, it is more difficult to report how one executes the skill; it has turned into tacit knowledge.

Skills tend to be spared to some extent when factual memory is impaired; amnesic patients exhibit priming effects in perception and performance, and they continue to be able to learn rules and acquire knowledge of stimulus sequences and patterns. They can speak and write reasonably well, and even the patient H. M. was able to solve the Tower of Hanoi problem. Research has shown that patients tend to retain the skill of tracking targets, playing billiards and golf, solving jigsaw puzzles, and reading mirror-reversed texts, among others. Because of its resistance to injury, several theorists assume that, in terms of an evolutionary perspective, memory for skills represents a fundamental memory system upon which other systems build (Fuster, 1995; Reber, 1993; Schacter, 1996; Squire, 1987). However

far from being separate, memory for facts and memory for skills are interdependent, in that many skills are acquired via a cognitive stage, and knowledge of facts is necessary to execute the skills.

ENDNOTES

1. According to Anderson (1990), procedural skills become less reportable as a result of practice. Karmiloff-Smith (1992), however, suggests the opposite: Through practice, the learner becomes better at explaining the skill and describing it.
2. Do not think that memorists have perfect minds. Luria (1976) described the memorist S. Whereas S. had a prodigious memory, all of his impressions remained isolated and he was overwhelmed by the sensory aspects of the memories. Frequently, S. could make no sense out of all the information that he remembered and that he could not forget.

CHAPTER 6

WORKING
MEMORY

Suppose you participate in a memory experiment and the experimenter reads syllables such as *xjm* one at a time to you. You are asked to recall the syllable after 20 seconds. What do you think your chances are of recalling the syllable: 100%, 80%, or 50%? Taking the Ebbinghaus forgetting curve as a guide, your chances of recalling the syllable are very good; according to the forgetting curve, people remember about 50% after one hour and 25% after seven days (see Figure 2.1).

You can well imagine the surprise of researchers when they conducted this test and found very poor retention after intervals of less than a minute. A British psychologist, Brown (1958), and two American researchers, Peterson and Peterson (1959), found that people remember only 20% after an interval of only 18 seconds! Because learners tend to rehearse information during the retention interval, these experimenters used a rehearsal preventing technique called the *distractor paradigm.*

Using the distractor paradigm, Peterson and Peterson (1959) presented a three-lettered trigram (e.g., *sba*) followed by a number (e.g., 396), and instructed the subject to count backwards by threes until the prompt was presented to recall the trigram. The Petersons used retention intervals from 3 to 18 seconds—hardly very long. The probability of correct recall dropped very precipitously; it was 80% after 3 seconds, 20% after 12 seconds, and 10% after 18 seconds. To be sure, the Brown-Peterson distractor task used different methods from the familiar long-term memory experiment, but the difference in results was too large to be attributed to details of procedure alone.

The reaction among researchers to the discovery of rapid forgetting in the distractor paradigm was profound. Coming at a time when researchers had grown tired of the associationist view of memory, the short-term forgetting data contributed to a fundamental change in attitude toward memory. Researchers began to speculate about different memory traces, different stores, even an entirely different architecture of memory—something that would have been unthinkable when memory research was informed by the principles of associationism and behaviorism. Memory research had moved to a new plane energized by the debate between the promoters of the new look and those who maintained the unity of memory. The former invented a new framework and looked for and found an increasing number of data to support it.

THE TWO-STORE MODEL OF MEMORY AND ITS CRITICS

The new framework was the two-store model of memory. It fit naturally with the information-processing approach that was emerging from the communication and human factors research during World War II. Communications researchers were interested in the transmission of signals by radar and telephone operators. The psychological laws governing signal transmission in communication channels were well understood and some of these were extended to human communication (e.g., Broadbent, 1958). An important characteristic of communication channels is their capacity limit; only a certain amount of information can be passed in a unit of time, whether it is a second, a minute, or an hour. Miller (1956) was one of the researchers to investigate the limited channel capacity of humans. Miller found that people could retain no more than an average of seven items from a single exposure, whether the items were digits, letters, words, or entire phrases. It was in this context that Miller advanced the notion of the short-term memory as a limited-capacity buffer (see Capacity on this page).

The other major impetus for the two-store model came from the increasing acceptance of the computer as a model for information processes (Miller, Galanter, & Pribram, 1960). The computer could not have been more welcome to researchers looking for a theoretical home to replace associationism (Chapter 2). Like memory, the computer accepts information, stores it, and produces a symbolic output (Chapter 1). As the computer metaphor gained ground among psychologists, rule-based systems and symbol-processing approaches became the focus of study, and interest diminished in associations of elemental units and in the laws of learning.

At this time, psychologists rediscovered distinctions on memory made by William James (1890) and Sigmund Freud (Freud, 1964/1933). James distinguished between memories people are aware of and those they are not (Waugh & Norman, 1965). He used the term *primary memory* for the former and the term *secondary memory* for the latter. Freud partitioned memory into different sections, depending on the accessibility of the information. Likening memory to an iceberg, Freud thought that consciousness was analogous to the tip of the iceberg visible at the surface. The preconscious and unconscious were analogous to the far larger portion of the iceberg that is submerged. The preconscious is just below the surface and can be readily reawakened, whereas the unconscious is completely hidden (Erdelyi, 1985; Freud, 1964/1933). Thus, not only did data support the idea of two memory stores but also history offered prominent precedents for the new view.

Differences between Short-Term Memory and Long-Term Memory

Proponents of the two-store view collected data in different paradigms in support of the new approach. They discovered a number of attributes distinguishing between the stores, including differences in capacity, memory codes, the speed of access, and the nature of interference. In addition, it was shown that the two stores made different contributions to performance in the free-recall task. Two-store theorists also marshaled a clinical case, the case of H. M., as evidence for the two-store memory model.

Capacity

Miller (1956) used the digit span test to assess a person's capacity to remember information from one presentation. The digit span test was originally introduced as part of intelligence tests by Binet at the turn of the century. Increasingly larger sets of digits are read to the person with the instruction to repeat the digits (e.g., 5 4 3, 8 2 1 4, 3 9 7 2 5, 5 2 8 4 9 3) until the person can no longer do so. Miller found that whatever stimulus materials experimenters used—binary digits, decimal digits, letters of the alphabet, or English words—subjects were able to repeat no more than 7 ± 2 items from immediate memory. Miller called these items *chunks* to indicate that they, in turn, may contain additional items (e.g., acronyms such as IBM or USA contain three words). Unlike immediate memory, long-term memory has no such limit. Ebbinghaus found that he could remember lists of 40—indeed, 100—nonsense syllables over long periods of time, given that he had memorized them well enough.

Evidence for Two Stores from the Free-Recall Paradigm

The Brown-Peterson distractor task established the principal attribute of the short-term store—namely, that information decays rapidly, unless it is rehearsed. A by-product of the rehearsal is transfer of the information to the long-term store. The more rehearsals accorded an item, the better its long-term retention.

The free-recall paradigm provided an excellent opportunity to assess the beneficial effects of rehearsal and of the two-store notion. In free-recall studies, the person is read a list of words and asked to recall them in any order. When asked to recall the list immediately, the subject usually recalls the most recent and the very first items best. This recall pattern is captured in the characteristic U-shaped serial position function exhibiting the primacy and recency effects (see Chapter 1).

According to an influential theory (Glanzer & Cunitz, 1966), learners maintain the most recent items through rehearsal in a short-term store. When hearing the recall prompt, a subject simply "dumps" the content of this rehearsal buffer right away. These are the items that are most accessible; this assumption was confirmed by recording the order in which subjects reported the words (Rundus, 1971; Waugh, 1970).

Recall of the first items of a list is superior because these items receive more rehearsals than the rest of the list and are therefore transferred more successfully to long-term memory. Recall of the intermediate items is relatively poor because they benefit neither from the rehearsals nor from being in short-term memory (see also Chapter 2; Henri & Binet, 1894).

Glanzer and Cunitz evaluated the two-store model experimentally using a dissociation technique in the free-recall paradigm. The experimenters used two variables that affected short-term memory and long-term memory differently: retention interval and rate of presentation. Consider the retention interval first. In one condition, the recall prompt was given immediately after learning the list; in the other condition, the prompt occurred after a delay of 30 seconds. During the delay, subjects executed some arithmetic problems in order to prevent rehearsal. The level of recall was independent of the interval for early list positions but not for recent items. After the 30-second interval, recall of recent items dropped significantly, as Figure 6.1A shows. This result confirms the hypothesis of two-store theorists that the delay would wipe the recent items from the rehearsal buffer, but leave early and intermediate items alone.

Consider next the rate of presentation. Two rates were used: a fast and a slow rate. Figure 6.1B shows that the slow rate benefited the early items but not the recent items. According to the two-store view, the improvement of early list items is due to the opportunity for additional rehearsals. Recent items, however, were not expected to receive a boost because they were in the rehearsal buffer anyhow.

In both of Glanzer and Cunitz's conditions, the predictions of the two-store model were upheld. The pattern of results was particularly persuasive because the two experimental variables produced a cross-over effect, or a double dissociation: Delay affected the recency section of the serial position curve, but not the primacy section, whereas presentation rate affected the primacy sections, but not the recency section.

Interference in Short-Term Memory and Long-Term Memory

Theorists disagreed on the nature of forgetting in the two stores. Broadbent (1958) and Brown (1958) attributed the rapid forgetting in the distractor paradigm to trace decay, to distinguish it from interference, which was thought to be re-

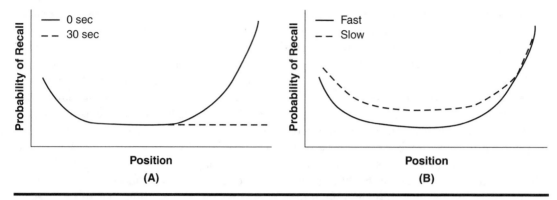

FIGURE 6.1   Evaluating the two-store notion in the free-recall task. *(A)* Delaying the recall prompt by 30 seconds reduces recall of recent items but has no effect on early and intermediate items of the list. *(B)* Manipulating the rate of presentation affects the primacy effect but not the recency effect.

sponsible for forgetting in long-term memory (Chapter 4). The decay hypothesis became less tenable after Keppel and Underwood (1962) demonstrated that interference was a cause of short-term forgetting. These researchers showed that proactive interference contributed to the rapid loss of information in the distractor task. *Proactive interference* refers to the interfering effects of prior learning on later learning. This is in contrast with retroactive interference, where recent information disrupts memory for information acquired in prior learning episodes (Chapter 4).

Keppel and Underwood (1962) analyzed Peterson and Peterson's data for each trial separately rather than averaging them across trials, as is customary in memory research. The two investigators found that on the first trial, there was no forgetting during the 18-second interval. On subsequent trials, as proactive interference built up, there was more forgetting. Their results, averaged across trials, reflected the steep loss of information over 18 seconds that the Petersons had found.

Agreeing with Keppel and Underwood's analysis, Kintsch (1970) proposed nevertheless that the nature of interference was different in the two stores. In the long-term store, it is the simi-

larity of materials that produces interference. Interference occurs among items of the same kind—letters versus letters, and numbers versus numbers—but not between different materials. In short-term memory, however, it is not the similarity between materials that produces interference. Rather, any work interferes with retention, whether it is counting backward, as in the distractor paradigm, hearing more items, as in free recall, or doing long division. The more difficult the task and the harder the work, the greater is the forgetting in short-term memory. Kintsch's position reflects the view that short-term memory fulfills both storage and work functions and that these compete with one another (Baddeley & Hitch, 1974; Posner & Rossman, 1965).

Coding in Short-Term Memory and Long-Term Memory

Because rehearsal is the process people use to maintain information for the short term, theorists made the plausible assumption that information in short-term memory was represented in terms of an acoustic code. Evidence to bolster this hypothesis came from several experiments, two of which we consider here. An experiment by Conrad (1964) used the letter confusion paradigm. Conrad compared letter recall confusions from two conditions: a listening condition and a recall condition. In the listening condition, listeners had to recall items; in the recall condition, people read the letters and recalled them. Under both tests, errors were based on the acoustic confusability between letters rather than on their visual similarity (e.g., *V* and *B,* and *S* and *F* were confused rather than *F* and *E,* and *B* and *R*).

In the other experiment, learners memorized five-word lists from each of four types: acoustically similar words (e.g., *mad, map, man*), dissimilar control words (e.g., *pen, day, rig*), semantically similar words (e.g., *huge, big, great*), and semantically dissimilar words (e.g., *bun, day, few*). As predicted by the acoustic-code hypothesis, short-term recall was poorer for acoustic items than for semantic items, compared to their respective control words (Baddeley, 1976). Reviewing studies such as these for short-term memory and long-term memory, Baddeley (1976) summarized the view in the early 1970s that short-term retention was a function of acoustic similarity, whereas long-term retention was a function of semantic similarity (but see Shulman, 1972).

A Neuropsychological Case Study

Hardly any case study has had as great an impact on memory research as Milner's (1966) work with a patient known as H. M. He was an epileptic patient, who, at age 27, underwent hippocampal surgery in order to contain the seizures he suffered. The surgery was successful in reducing the patient's seizures, but it also had a very deleterious effect on his memory. H. M. was no longer able to learn any new information, no matter how frequently he was exposed to it. Based on this deficit, Milner postulated two memory stores: the short-term store and the long-term store. Milner concluded that H. M.'s memory deficit did not affect long-term memory, because he correctly remembered information from the period prior to his operation. Neither was his short-term memory affected, because he could be made to retain information by constantly rehearsing it, at least for a limited time span. Milner attributed H. M.'s amnesia to a faulty transfer mechanism from the short-term store to the long-term store, and proposed that the hippocampus was implicated in that transfer (Chapter 3).

The differences between the two stores reported in the first decade of research on short-term memory are listed in Table 6.1. Different codes, different capacities, different rates of forgetting and of retrieval—all pointed to two distinct memory stores. It was not that everyone was persuaded by these data. According to critics (Melton, 1963), nothing was gained by assuming the existence of a separate working memory

TABLE 6.1   Different Attributes of Short-Term Memory (STM) and Long-Term Memory (LTM) Widely Accepted in Early 1970s

	STM	LTM
Maintenance of information	Rehearsal	Organization
Format of information	Primarily acoustic	Primarily semantic
Capacity	7 ± 2 chunks	No known limit
Forgetting	Work interference	Interference by similarity
Duration of information	Up to one minute	Up to years
Retrieval	Probably automatic	Search process
Retrieval time	Fast	Slow

store, nor was it necessary to postulate discrete stores for two aspects of the same trace. The same pattern of data could be accounted for by a unitary mechanism—for example, by modifications to classical memory trace theory (Wickelgren, 1973)—or by assuming that the two stores merely represent different perspectives on the same phenomena (Crowder, 1982a, 1989, 1993). Nevertheless, the mainstream of memory researchers adopted the two-store framework. Reviewing the state of knowledge at the time, Baddeley (1976) concluded that it "is not easy to see how the complex phenomena [reviewed] could be explained in terms of a unitary system" (p. 120).

Waugh and Norman's (1965) Two-Store Model

Waugh and Norman (1965) were among the first researchers to introduce a formal two-store model of memory. Their model sought to account for data from different paradigms, including the free-recall paradigm, the distractor task, and the probe digit task. The model included two stores, primary memory and secondary memory differing in their state of awareness and their capacity, among other factors. Adopting James's (1890) distinction, Waugh and Norman reserved primary memory for information of which people are aware, whereas secondary memory represented the information of which people are not aware. Primary memory had, of course, a smaller capacity processor than secondary memory. It was through rehearsal that information was maintained in primary memory and transferred to secondary memory. The two stores, however, had one common attribute: the cause of forgetting in both was attributed to interference.

Waugh and Norman assessed the interference mechanism in a new paradigm—the probe digit task. This task was designed to minimize rehearsal. The experimenters presented a list of 16 single digits in succession (e.g., 3 5 2 1 7 5 4 8

5 9 0 4 1 3 7 2). The final digit in each list, the probe digit (e.g., 2), had occurred exactly once before in positions 3 through 14. On the second occurrence of the probe digit, signaled by a tone (indicated by underline), the subject was to name the successor digit on the first presentation of the probe digit (e.g., 1). Recall accuracy dropped continuously and approached 0% after 12 interfering digits.

Waugh and Norman varied the rate of presentation of digits per second (either one or four per second). They found that recall was a function of the number of intervening digits, not of the rate of presentation. It is for this reason that they attributed short-term forgetting to interference rather than decay. Waugh and Norman developed a mathematical model for estimating the joint contribution of primary memory and secondary memory to performance in various tasks, obtaining an excellent fit for the data, including the serial position curve in the free-recall task. Waugh and Norman's model was very influential and inspired other models (Chapter 7); the most prominent of these was Atkinson and Shiffrin's (1968) model.

Atkinson and Shiffrin's (1968) Model

Atkinson and Shiffrin's (1968) model of memory was the culmination of a decade's work on the sensory register, on the short-term store, and on its relation to long-term memory (Chapter 1). The model summarized the structural assumptions put forth by Sperling's (1960) research on the sensory trace of visual information, known as the *icon;* Peterson and Peterson's (1959) research on the short-term store; Waugh and Norman's (1965) theory of the transfer of information from short-term to long-term memory; and traditional long-term memory work. The model is captured by the boxes in Figure 1.6. The boxes represent the sensory memory, the short-term store, and the long-term store. Atkinson and Shiffrin (1968) listed the visual icon investigated by Sperling (1960) as the primary example of information in sensory memory. The information is sensory because it has not yet been recognized. It is also fragile and susceptible to disruption from other sensory stimuli. Once the information is recognized, the person can verbalize and rehearse it in the short-term store. The short-term store includes a rehearsal buffer that serves as the transfer device of information to long-term memory.

In addition to these structural assumptions, Atkinson and Shiffrin (1968) proposed control processes in short-term memory to describe the subject's mental activities. Introducing such mental operations as attentive, strategic, and search processes was an important step. It broke with the views of the stimulus-response approach; the learner was no longer viewed as a passive receiver of information but an active participant of remembering. The subject's mental activities became an important focus of research. Atkinson and Shiffrin and their students were most interested in rehearsal—the process that resulted in the transfer of information from the short-term to the long-term store.

Rehearsal Processes

Rehearsal occurs whenever one silently repeats information in order to remember it, such as telephone numbers, names, and appointments. Even children know that rehearsing information helps them remember it (Chapter 8). Experiencing rehearsal and quantifying it are quite different matters, however. How could a researcher assess a subject's rehearsal? Rundus (1971) thought of a way of making rehearsal observable; he introduced the overt rehearsal technique in the free-recall paradigm. Rundus's subjects saw a list of words, projected on a screen one word at a time for five seconds. He asked his subjects to say each word they thought of aloud as the words were presented. He recorded the subjects' utterances on a tape recorder. Every five seconds, the projector would emit a click that was recorded on

the tape. At the end of the list of words, a recall prompt was given and subjects recalled the words in any order. Rundus therefore had two related sets of data: the usual recall probabilities of words and the rehearsal protocol. The latter was divided into rehearsal sets of five seconds' duration corresponding to the exposure duration of each word. Rehearsal sets are illustrated in Table 6.2.

Rundus correlated the rehearsal frequency and recall probability of the words in the list, and he was able to observe two important relationships that earlier researchers had suspected but not recorded. First, the recall probability of words was positively correlated with their frequency of rehearsal. The more a word was rehearsed by a subject, the more likely it was recalled. This included the initial words in the list, those words that contributed to the primacy effect. Second, Rundus found that items in the last rehearsal set were the ones recalled first. These are the most recent items of the list, accounting for the recency effect.

With research such as that by Glanzer and Cunitz (1966), Waugh and Norman (1965), Atkinson and Shiffrin (1968), and Rundus (1971), the two-store framework of memory had achieved its high point. Subsequent researchers discovered important problems for this approach. All along, some critics argued that it was not efficient to assume two, three, or even more different memory traces. However,

TABLE 6.2 Rehearsal Sets Observed in a Free Recall Experiment (adapted from Rundus, 1971)

Item	Words Rehearsed
1. Cattle	*cattle, cattle, cattle, cattle*
2. Tribute	*tribute, cattle, tribute, cattle*
3. Hint	*hint, tribute, cattle, cattle*
4. Golf	*golf, hint, tribute*
. . .	
20. Maiden	*maiden, . . .*

experimental evidence calling into question the rehearsal and the buffer notion was more damaging. The two-store model had become popular because of two successes: The model successfully predicted the positive correlation between frequency of rehearsal and recall, and it could handle the recency effect. Consider two sets of results that cast doubt on these two achievements.

Critics of the Two-Store Model

Glanzer and Cunitz (1966) had observed that the recency effect was wiped out when recall was delayed by 30 seconds. They attributed this to loss of the information from the short-term store. Eight years later, however, two researchers demonstrated that the recency effect does survive a delay. Bjork and Whitten (1974) had subjects learn a word list in a free-recall experiment (see also Thapar & Greene, 1993). Their recall experiment differed in one respect from the usual procedure: After each item, the person was given a number and had to count backward for a 12-second interval. Then, after the last item of the list, there followed the 30-second interval of mental arithmetic that Glanzer and Cunitz had used. Unlike Glanzer and Cunitz, however, Bjork and Whitten observed a recency effect. According to the two-store theory, the 30-second interval of backward counting should have resulted in a loss of the most recent items from the short-term store, but it did not. Bjork and Whitten (1974) invoked a visual metaphor to account for the recency effect, whether it occurred immediately following learning or after a delay. When looking along a row of telephone poles, the poles close to the viewer are more distinct than distant poles. In analogous fashion, recent words in a list of items are more discriminable, and hence more memorable than intermediate items (for a formal model of this analogy, see Glenberg, 1987).

The repetition view of association was soon challenged by a wide range of studies showing little or no effect of mere repetition on memorability. In Chapter 5, I mentioned the remarkable results by Bekerian and Baddeley (1980) on the failure of saturation advertising. The British Broadcasting Corporation (BBC) intended to change some wavelengths for its broadcasts and announced the new wavelengths for several weeks 10 times per hour. Even casual BBC listeners must have heard the information at least 1,000 times. Bekerian and Baddeley found that people simply did not remember what had been presented to them so many times. They concluded that mere repetition does not ensure good retention.

Challenges to the rehearsal theory and therefore to the two-store theory of memory were raised by advocates of the levels-of-processing perspective reviewed in Chapter 4. Studies by Craik and his colleagues demonstrated that rehearsal, as such, was not as important as had been believed; what mattered most was the type of processing that the target word would receive. Craik and Tulving (1975), for example, demonstrated the effect of levels of processing on retention (Chapter 4). In one of their experiments, the investigators presented nouns one at a time to their subjects (e.g., *horse, potato,* and *orange).* For each noun, the person had to answer a question. There were three types of questions intended to manipulate the degree to which the person had to think about the noun. The first type of question called for a superficial and easy analysis of the physical shape of the word. The second type of question required the person to make a judgment on the way the word sounded. Presumably, this required somewhat more thought and processing than judging word shape. Still more processing was required by the third type of question, which required semantic analysis of the target word. As predicted by Craik and Tulving, memory strength and performance were a function of the depth of processing elicited by the question; that is, recall was best for words that received a semantic analysis during encoding and worst for words that were superficially analyzed. Craik and Tulving concluded that it is not the mere number of repeated rehearsals (maintenance rehearsal) that determines memory strength, but the degree of elaboration (elaborative rehearsal) that the item receives.

Elaborative rehearsal works because it creates associations between the to-be-remembered information and the person's knowledge in long-term memory. As a result of these associations, there are added access routes to the information in memory. This insight forms the basis of mnemonic techniques where the learner forms links between a set of target materials and familiar information, whether it is a series of locations, a series of digits, or a set of facts that is subjectively memorable (Chapter 12).

Reviewing the two-store model of memory, Kintsch (1977) concluded that it began with two types of memory stores (short-term store and long-term store) and ended with two types of processes (maintenance and elaborative rehearsal). He continued that "many psychologists today are no longer satisfied with the box metaphor that underlies the earlier models of short-term memory. Instead, a more dynamic conception of the memory system is evolving, with an emphasis on differential processes rather than on separate boxes for the short-term store and long-term store" (p. 225). Indeed, after 1977, the term *short-term store* has been largely replaced by the term *working memory*. The working memory is the cognitive processor where mental operations such as rehearsal, elaboration, search, comparison, recoding, and others are assumed to take place. The remainder of this chapter is devoted to the working memory and its processes.

ACTIVITY IN WORKING MEMORY

This section reviews a sample of the mental activities supported by working memory, problem solving, comprehension, arithmetic computation, and memory search. We will begin the review with problem solving. It was in this context that the term *working memory* was first used (Miller, Galanter, & Pribram, 1960). In problem solving, people develop a set of goals that they must remember in order to solve the problem. In discourse comprehension, listeners keep track of topics as they execute a variety of other interpretive processes. Research involving memorization and arithmetic computation illustrates the competition between these operations. In the memory search task, an increase in workload increases the processing time. In each of these cases, competing operations in working memory involve a trade-off: As computational demands increase, performance decreases, whether it is measured in terms of accuracy or speed.

Problem Solving

According to Greeno (1973), working memory contains the plan used to solve the problem; the problem solver represents the structure of the problem (its initial, intermediate, and goal states), much like a list of words in a recall experiment. Transformations and intermediary results are also held in working memory for easy access. Difficulties in problem solving arise when the plan does not fit into working memory, either because it is too complex or because working memory is limited or impaired. A common problem used by cognitive psychologists is the Tower of Hanoi puzzle. It involves the movement of a set of disks from one location to another, such as from peg 1 to peg 3 in Figure 6.2. The problem is difficult because of specific constraints. There are only three pegs, only one disk may be moved at a time, and smaller disks must always be placed on larger disks.

Given three disks, A, B, and C, as in Figure 6.2, the problem may be solved by satisfying three goals: (1) moving the set of disks A and B (AB) from peg 1 to peg 2; (2) moving C to peg 3; and moving AB from peg 2 to peg 3. The first goal requires that disk A be moved individually

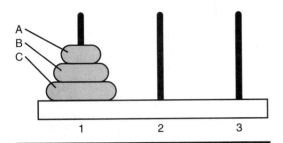

FIGURE 6.2 The Tower of Hanoi puzzle. Disks must be moved from peg 1 to peg 3 under specific constraints explained in the text.

to peg 3. It cannot be placed on peg 2 because that is the destination for the larger B disk, which must be at the bottom. Disk B, however, can be moved to peg 2, once disk A is on peg 3. Then disk A is moved to peg 2. Thus, the first goal has been fulfilled in three moves. Now the second goal can be attacked and so on. The problem solver must keep each goal, the sequence of sub-goals, and the moves to be made in working memory. As the number of disks is increased, the number of subgoals and moves also increases, thus pushing the load of working memory to its limit and beyond. According to Simon (1975), this is the principal difficulty of the Tower of Hanoi problem.

Research in problem solving convinced theorists that working memory is a computational processor in addition to being a store. The next section shows that the storage and computational functions compete if the load resulting from either function is too great.

Storage versus Computation

Posner and Rossman (1965) demonstrated in a dual-task experiment that the workload in working memory competes with the storage capacity in a direct way (Baddeley & Hitch, 1974; Anderson, Reder, & Lebiere, 1996). Subjects tried to memorize a set of digits as well as perform different numerical transformations on the digits. In four different condi-

tions, subjects heard 8 digits on each trial, such as 8 3 4 4 2 5 9 1. In each of the conditions, one of four types of transformations was performed on the final two digits: recording, addition, backward counting, and classification, respectively. Subjects in the recording condition wrote down the last two digits that were presented (e.g., 9 1). Subjects in the addition task had to add two adjacent digits and report the result (e.g., 10). In the backward counting condition, subjects counted backwards by threes from the last two numbers of each trial (e.g., 91 88 85, etc.). Subjects in the classification task had to identify each pair of digits as *high* (50 and above) or *low* (below 50). In this case, 91 would be classified as high. After reporting the results of the transformation, subjects had to recall the first three digits of the series—namely, 8 3 4. Posner and Rossman's study involved four retention intervals: 5, 10, 20, and 30 seconds. The results are presented in Figure 6.3. The figure shows that the more difficult the transformation, the more errors in recall were made. This response pattern reflects a trade-off between transformation and storage; the more work the subject expends on the transformation task, the less capacity remains for storage.

Language Comprehension

Working memory plays a key role in sentence comprehension, as it does in problem solving. We could not understand a full sentence if we did not remember words from its initial phrases. Consider the word *it* in the last clause of sentence (6.1):

(6.1) A familiar example used to illustrate the function of working memory is the storage of a telephone number between the time when it is looked up in a phone directory and the time when it is dialed.

The pronoun *it* refers to *telephone number*. About 16 words intervened between the referent

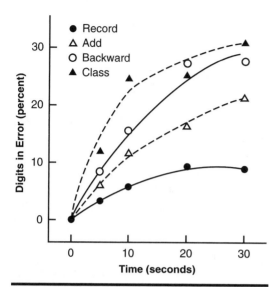

FIGURE 6.3 Correct recall of digits as a function of the difficulty of numerical transformation (Posner & Rossman, 1965)

lated words (i.e., the final words of the sentences) while comprehending sets of sentences. This is a kind of stress test of the memory span. When comprehending a sentence such as (6.1), the reader decodes the words, accesses their meanings, processes the sentence structure, and keeps long-distance dependencies in mind; the span test requires that the subject maintain an extraneous load. Consider the following list of two sentences:

(**6.2**) When at last his eyes opened, there was no gleam of triumph, no shade of anger.

(**6.3**) The taxi turned up Michigan Avenue where they had a clear view of the lake.

After reading these two sentences, the subject was to recall the words *anger* and *lake*. If the subject is able to do so, three sentences are presented and three final words must be recalled, and so on, up to seven sentences. The reading span is the largest number of words recalled.

Daneman and Carpenter (1980) reasoned that remembering referents, such as the telephone number in sentence (6.1), should be easy for a person with a high reading span. They tested their hypothesis in a reading experiment. The experiment consisted of two phases. In the first phase, using test sentences like (6.2) and (6.3), the reading span was measured for each of the subjects. In the second phase, the subjects read passages and later tried to identify specific referents in each passage. Daneman and Carpenter found that subjects' ability to identify the correct referent increased with their reading span: The greater the reading span, the better people's success in remembering the correct referents. Daneman and Carpenter's (1980) research proved to be very influential. First, it provided a measure to assess the joint storage and processing function of working memory in comprehension. Second, it demonstrated the relation between individual differences in comprehension and working memory capacity. Subsequent research established that Daneman and

and its pronoun. In order to understand the pronoun, the referent must be active in the reader's working memory, either through continued activation or by reinstating the activation. The reader must recognize the word *it,* search working memory for a referent, and relate the components *telephone* and *number,* realizing they represent one concept. In addition to remembering referents, the reader accesses the meaning of the words in semantic memory, analyzes the structure of the sentence, and integrates it with prior sentences. All of these activities, subsumed under the term *comprehension,* tax the storage capacity of working memory.

Daneman developed the reading span test, which is a span measure expanding on the familiar digit span test (see Daneman & Carpenter, 1980; Just & Carpenter, 1992). This span test evaluates *both* processing and storage capabilities. The subject reads a list of unrelated sentences aloud and recalls the final word of each sentence. The reader must store several unre-

Carpenter's span measure was a better predictor of language comprehension than such measures as the digit span, which assessed only the "raw" storage of working memory (Daneman & Merikle, 1996).

Search in Working Memory: The Sternberg Paradigm

One of the most widely investigated operations in working memory is search; searching involves looking for a target among a set of items. For example, when you search for a specific book on the shelf, you have a memory record of the book and you compare a row of books, one book after another, against the record. You find the book when one of the books on the shelf matches your mental record of the book. In general, in a search, a person forms a representation of the target and compares the target to the items in a search set. Sternberg (1966) introduced the scanning task in order to investigate search in working memory. Subjects were first shown a memory set ranging from one to six digits, well below the digit span, and then a single-target digit. They had to decide whether the target digit was a member of the memory set. Assume the memory set consists of the digits 4, 9, 0, and 2, and the target digit is 9. In this case, the correct response is yes. If the target is a 3, the correct response is no.

Sternberg recorded reaction times as a function of the size of the memory set. He found that reaction times increased linearly with the number of digits in the memory set. Sternberg reasoned that the person represents the memory set in working memory, encodes the test digit, and searches the memory set for a match. The search could be either parallel or serial. In a *parallel* search, the target digit is compared simultaneously to each of the digits in the memory set; in a *serial* search, it is compared sequentially. The two search models predict different reaction time functions. According to a simple parallel

model, reaction times would not increase with the size of the memory set; the function is flat. The serial model assumes that each comparison takes a discrete amount of time, however short, and therefore each added digit increases the reaction time.

Sternberg distinguished between two types of serial searches: a self-terminating and an exhaustive search. Trials with a negative outcome necessarily involve an exhaustive search, as each item of the set must be scanned. Thus, the number of comparisons between target and memory set items should be equal to the size of the memory set.

In the case of *yes* responses, a self-terminating search appears more plausible; on average, fewer comparisons are required for a self-terminating search than for an exhaustive search. Given that *no* responses must be based on an exhaustive search, whereas *yes* responses could result from a self-terminating search, the slope of *yes* times should be less than that of *no* times. These functions are plotted in Figure 6.4A. If *yes* responses were based on an exhaustive search, the slopes of reaction times for *yes* and *no* responses should be the same. The slope represents the mean increase in search time with each added digit in the memory set; the lower the slope, the greater the scanning rate and the efficiency of working memory.

Sternberg found parallel functions for *no* and *yes* responses (Figure 6.4B). He interpreted this result in support of his hypothesis of a serial and exhaustive search. Subsequent research, however, revealed that Sternberg's results—as well as additional memory scanning data—are better accounted for in terms of a limited resources parallel search model (e.g., McElree & Dosher, 1993). According to this view, working memory capacity is limited and, as the workload increases, the time it takes to execute a task increases, as well. Thus, adding digits to the memory set taxes the capacity and slows down processing.

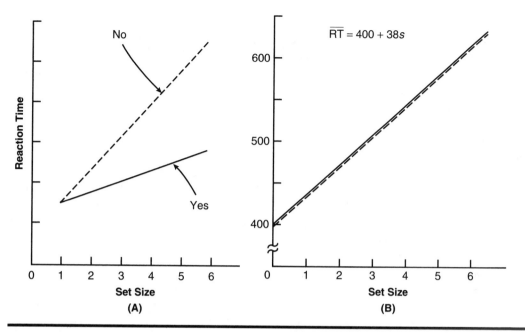

FIGURE 6.4 Sternberg's item-recognition task. *(A)* Reaction time functions for *yes* and *no* responses assuming a self-terminating search for *yes* responses. *(B)* Reaction time functions actually observed by Sternberg suggest an exhaustive search for both *yes* and *no* responses.

Tracking Mental Work On-Line

Working memory is the workhorse of the mind. Experiments as well as everyday applications show the results of mental work, such as numbers added, problems solved, skills practiced, and conversations carried out. The challenge for the researcher is to track a mental operation as it unfolds on-line. The term *on-line* refers to the process as it extends over several seconds. During this period, an individual's mental load usually changes. Frequently, these changes are reflected by overt activity; for example, readers move their larynx in silent speech when grappling with difficult passages; individuals' pupils dilate as they commit digits to memory, and people fixate their eyes on critical aspects of the stimulus when problem solving. There are changes in the electrophysiological activity of the brain, and, of course, subjects can tell an experimenter what they are thinking about and pro-

vide a record of their thoughts—a think-aloud protocol. Although no single measure is perfect, the use of several measures allows researchers to track the activities of working memory and provide a window into the mind. I will describe two neurophysiological methods—single-cell recording and PET imaging—used to assess mental operations on-line.

Single-Cell Activity

Hebb (1949) was among the first theorists to speculate that immediate memory involves increased activity in neurons. He proposed the idea of reverberatory circuits; these are neuron loops activated by electrical activity over a short period of time. Hebb's proposal inspired a search for reverberatory circuits in the brain; however, these were difficult to isolate until reliable single-cell recordings could be made (Chapter 3).

Using monkeys in a visual discrimination task, Fuster and Jervey (1981) found increased electrical activity in specific neurons implicated in visual processing. Fuster and Jervey implanted monkeys with electrodes that recorded activity in single nuclei in the inferior temporal cortex. The researchers used the delayed matching-to-sample paradigm, a widely used task in research on animal memory (see Figure 6.5).

On each experimental trial, a monkey was shown a sample color projected to a button; the colored light was turned off when the monkey pressed the button. After a delay of up to 32 seconds, four buttons were simultaneously illuminated, one of them identical with the sample. If the monkey pressed the button matching the sample, it received fruit juice as a reinforcement. The investigators found that, after extended training on the task, specific neurons exhibited increased spike activity when the sample was lit. These results are shown in Figure 6.6.

The neuron activity increased only during the delay and only when the sample was red, as indicated in the bottom panel of Figure 6.6. As soon as the match was made at the end of the delay, the

neuron's activity returned to its baseline level. Fuster and Jervey interpreted the increased activity as a reflection of mental work necessary to retain the information of the sample stimulus, a kind of rehearsal. Goldman-Rakic (1990) viewed the transitory activation as an expression of the kind of work that gives working memory its name.

Activity Revealed by PET Scan

Posner, Petersen, Fox, and Raichle (1988) used another technique to measure mental activity in human subjects: the PET scan (see Chapter 3). The PET scan detects changes in the flow of blood in cerebral regions. Posner and his colleagues compared PET activity during rest, and during one of two mental tasks, reading or listening. Any increase in PET activity relative to rest was attributed to mental work. In Posner's reading task, a subject read a list of nouns; during the rest period, he fixated on a dot on a screen. Posner found that during reading periods, but not during rest, blood flow increased in specific regions of the occipital lobe, one of the visual processing areas. When the same nouns were pre-

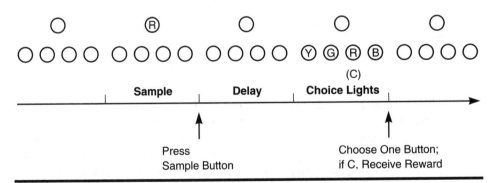

FIGURE 6.5 Delayed matching-to-sample task. Each panel includes five lights: a sample and four choice lights. The sample indicates the target to be remembered (for this trial, a red light). The center panel represents the delay when the lights are turned off. After the delay, the monkey faces a choice of four lights (from Fuster, 1995).

Note: C = correct response; B = blue; G = green; R = red; Y = yellow

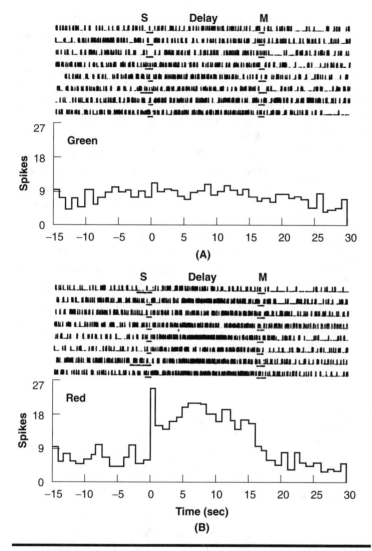

FIGURE 6.6 During the delay in the matching-to-sample task, cell activity increases only for red but not for green sample (from Fuster & Jervey, 1981). Spike activity recorded on individual trials is shown in the samples at the top of each panel. The histograms show the average spike activity across trials.

sented to subjects on audiotape, there was increased activity in the auditory regions, but not in the visual regions. Like the single-cell recordings, these results reflect the transitory activity associated with cognitive processes. They also show that the activity is localized to neural structures specific to the modality of the task, reading or listening.

THE MULTIPLE-COMPONENTS MODEL OF WORKING MEMORY

In the original dual-store models of memory (Waugh & Norman, 1965; Atkinson & Shiffrin, 1968), short-term memory was considered as a unitary system. The function of the short-term store was to maintain information temporarily and transfer it to long-term memory. The discovery of a variety of functions and types of information supported by working memory gave rise to the alternative view that working memory consists of multiple components rather than forming a single store. Baddeley and Hitch (1974) introduced the multiple-components model because the unitary view had difficulty in handling the growing body of data on short-term memory. After successive refinements during the past two decades, the Baddeley model has become the dominant model of working memory (Becker, 1994; Jonides, 1995; Logie, 1996; Potter, 1993; Richardson, 1996; Smith & Jonides, 1997; for an alternative view, see Nairne, 1996).

Baddeley's (1992a, 1992b) working memory model includes three components, each fulfilling specific functions: (1) the phonological loop to process phonological information, (2) the visuospatial sketchpad to process visual and spatial information, and (3) the central executive to supervise and coordinate the other two components.

In addition to Baddeley's original three components, researchers have identified information in working memory from other sources, including procedural knowledge and semantic-abstract information (e.g., Anderson, 1983a; Potter, 1993). These sources of information in working memory and the central executive are shown in Figure 6.7. The empty circle indicates potential other sources that have not been as widely investigated, such as tactile and motor memory.

Evidence for the multiple-components view

of working memory comes from different lines of research, including case studies, dissociations observed in dual-task studies (Logie, 1996; Logie, Gilhooly, & Wynn, 1994), and neuroimaging research that suggested the involvement of different brain regions for different working memory tasks (Jonides, 1995; Smith & Jonides, 1997).

Applying the dissociation logic to the principal components of working memory, theorists have recently introduced subsystems within the phonological loop and the visuospatial sketchpad (Jonides, 1995; Logie et al., 1994; Smith & Jonides, 1997; Wilson, O'Scalaidhe, & Goldman-Rakic, 1993). According to these formulations, the phonological loop includes a separate phonological store and a separate rehearsal mechanism, whereas the visuospatial sketchpad includes a processor for visual information and a separate processor for spatial information.

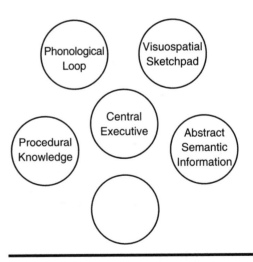

FIGURE 6.7   Multiple-components model of working memory includes the visuospatial sketchpad, the phonological loop, buffers for procedural knowledge and for abstract semantic information, and the central executive.

Case Study.   Warrington and Shallice (1969) described the case of K. F., a victim of a motorcycle accident, who suffered injury to the left parieto-occipital region and exhibited severe limitations of his verbal short-term memory. He exhibited no recency effect in free-recall learning and could not remember more than two digits—a very low level compared to H. M. and other amnesic patients. Remarkably, however, K. F. was able to acquire new information for the long term. Advocates of the view that information enters long-term memory via rehearsal in short-term memory (e.g., Atkinson & Shiffrin, 1968; Waugh & Norman, 1965) had no easy answers for this finding. Either K. F. was able to transfer the information to long-term memory by way of an alternate route, thus bypassing short-term memory, or there were components in short-term memory other than the verbal rehearsal buffer that were still intact. Indeed, K. F.'s digit span increased when the target items were presented visually rather than acoustically. This retention pattern suggests that K. F. had recourse to a visual short-term memory processor to memorize the information.

Experimental Dissociation.   Using the dual-task technique (Chapter 1), researchers were able to demonstrate a number of dissociations between the three components of Baddeley's model. In the dual-task design, the experimenter presents learners with two tasks to be executed concurrently. If performance suffers, the assumption is supported that the two tasks engage the same working memory component; if performance on the tasks remains intact, it is assumed that they depend on different components. An experiment by Brooks (1968) was among the first of numerous studies using concurrent tasks to demonstrate such experimental dissociations.

Brooks (1968) used a 2 × 2 factorial design in which he covaried task (visual vs. verbal) and mode of response (visual vs. verbal). The visual task involved visual imagery and either a verbal response or a visual response. Subjects were asked to visualize a block letter, for example, an $\mathbb{F}$, trace the letter mentally, and indicate whether the letter has an outside or inside corner. (For example, the corner at the upper left of the *F* is considered as an outside corner, whereas the corners of the horizontal bar in the middle are considered inside corners.) As people scanned the letter image with their mental eyes, they made a verbal or a visual response to indicate their choice. The verbal response consisted of saying *yes* or *no*, whereas the visual response involved pointing to *y*s or *n*s printed in irregular patterns on a sheet. Any interference between visualization and the concurrent visual response would indicate that both tasks engaged the same processing system, presumably the visuospatial sketchpad.

Brooks's (1968) verbal task involved memorizing sentences such as *A bird in the hand is worth two in the bush*. Participants were asked to think of the sentence word by word and indicate for each whether it was a noun. Subjects made either verbal responses or visual responses as in the letter tracing task. Brooks found a dissociation between these two tasks, suggesting two separate components of working memory: The visual response was faster in the verbal task, whereas the verbal response was quicker in the visual task. When task and response type were the same, presumably the same processor was engaged, thus producing interference. When task and response type were from different modalities, different components were taxed and no interference occurred. Brooks's results supported the distinction between the phonological component and the visuospatial sketchpad in Figure 6.7.

Neuroimaging Results.   Jonides (1995) recorded PET images from different brain regions as volunteers were executing tasks thought to engage the phonological buffer and the visuospatial sketchpad. He used two tasks—the two-back task (a phonological task) and the dot-location task (a visuospatial task) to tap the two respective systems. In the two-back task, the person sees a sequence of individual letters (e.g., *M P F P . . .*) presented at a rate of one letter every three seconds (Figure 6.8A). The subject makes a *yes* response whenever a letter is shown that had occurred two positions back; otherwise, *no* is the correct response. In the sequence *M P F P* the correct responses are *no, no, no, yes*. The two-back task is relatively complex; the person has to keep letter triplets continuously in mind, compare the current letter with the one shown two letters back, and update the letter triplets as soon as a new letter appears. In order to separate the load on working memory from encoding processes, Jonides presented the same sequence of letters in a control condition, asking subjects to compare the letters to a letter announced prior to the series, such as *P*. This minimized the memory load, as no updating was required but the same encoding operations occurred as in the memory condition.

The dot-location task involves the presentation of three dots in different locations on the screen for 200 msec (see Figure 6.8B). This pattern is followed by a blank screen for 3 seconds. Then the test follows: An outline circle is presented on a location of the screen and subjects must indicate whether that location was occupied by one of the dots of the previous screen. In a perceptual control condition, the dots remain on the screen until the outline circle is presented.

Neuroimaging revealed that the verbal and visual tasks led to activation in different brain regions. The two-back task produced increased cerebral blood flow in several regions in the *left* hemisphere—namely, in Broca's area, in the frontal lobe, and in the parietal lobe. The spatial task produced increased activation in the *right* hemisphere—namely, in the frontal lobe, the pa-

rietal lobe, and the occipital lobe. Jonides (1995) concluded that the PET data for the two tasks present a "clear dissociation between working memory for phonological and spatial information" (p. 247).

Phonological Loop

Early memory models (Waugh & Norman, 1965; Atkinson & Shiffrin, 1968) considered phonological coding as the signature of a short-term store separate from long-term memory. Initially, the assumption of such phonological coding appeared plausible on the basis of introspective reports: When someone memorizes information—whether it is phone numbers, names of people, or foreign language vocabulary—he or she rehearses it by repeating the information subvocally. Subsequently, the assumption of phonological processing working memory was supported by the discovery of a growing number of empirical effects, including the following:

■ *Phonological suppression.* If you interfere with rehearsal by having a person repeat such simple words as *the,* or *one, two, three,* retention of target materials is suppressed even if the information is presented visually.

■ *Word length.* The span of working memory is related to the length of the words to be memorized. For example, it is easier for people to remember one-syllable words such as *wit* and *mate* than multisyllabic words such as *university* and *opportunity.* The reason is that in a limited period, an individual can rehearse more words if they are short. An interesting difference in the digit span of speakers of different languages is attributed to the length effect. The digit span is inversely related to the time it takes to pronounce digits in a particular language. The span is greater in languages whose digits are spoken quickly (e.g., Chinese). Hoosain and Salili (1988) found a negative correlation between ar-

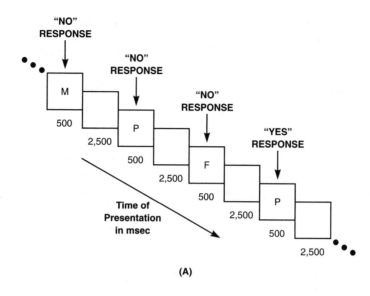

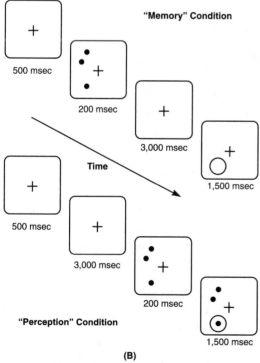

FIGURE 6.8 *(A)* Jonides's two-back task: A sequence of letters is presented. Participants indicate for each letter whether it matches the letter presented two positions back. *(B)* The dot-location task and its perceptual control task. In the memory task, participants had to remember the locations of the dots for three seconds before the probe (an outline circle) appeared. In the perceptual control condition, dots and probe were shown simultaneously (Jonides, 1995).

ticulation length and digit span for three languages: Chinese, English, and Welsh. Their results are shown in Table 6.3.

— *Phonological similarity.* There is greater memory interference for items that sound similar, regardless whether the items are presented acoustically or visually. People often confuse letters that sound alike (e.g., *PGTVCD)*, but do not confuse dissimilar letters (e.g., *RHXKWY*). This indicates that learners use a phonological code in working memory in order to remember strings of letters.

Phonological Store versus Rehearsal Buffer

As evidence on phonological processing in working memory accumulated, the hypothesis was proposed that the phonological loop includes two independent subsystems—a phonological store and a rehearsal buffer—each fulfilling distinct functions. The phonological store holds verbal information and the rehearsal process refreshes the information in the store (Baddeley, 1992a, 1992b; Logie et al., 1994; Smith & Jonides, 1997). Consider a neuroimaging study by Smith and Jonides (1997) in support of the two phonological subsystems. The study suggested that the subsystems implicate different regions in the brain. The experiment involved two conditions: the two-back task in Figure 6.8A and a rehearsal task. As illustrated in Figure 6.8A, the two-back task is a verbal memory task where learners must memorize letters that occurred two positions back. In the rehearsal task, the same

TABLE 6.3 Relation between Articulation Length and Digit Span in Three Languages

Language	Length (in ms)	Mean Digit Span
Chinese	265	9.9
English	321	6.6
Welsh	385	5.8

trial and event sequence as in the two-back task were presented, except that learners had to rehearse the current letter. Thus, for the stimuli in Figure 6.8A, subjects would rehearse letters as follows *M M M, P P P, F F F,* and *P P P.* Neuroimages were recorded in both tasks. As we saw earlier, in the verbal memory condition, there was an increase in activity in the left hemisphere, in Broca's area, and in the posterior parietal lobe. In the rehearsal task, however, only Broca's area was activated, but not the posterior parietal lobe. On the basis of the subtraction logic (see Chapter 3), Smith and Jonides concluded that the phonological store is supported by neural centers in the parietal lobe, whereas the rehearsal buffer is supported by centers in Broca's area.

The Phonological Loop: A Reprise

Theorists' conceptions of memory processes tend to undergo changes as the empirical evidence of the processes grows. This has been true for many topics in memory research, whether it is short-term memory, semantic memory, priming, or the components of working memory, including the phonological loop. A topic tends to be clear-cut when it is first introduced and a relatively small set of data exists. However, when further experiments are done and more data become available, the initial clarity becomes blurred. Thus, the initial clarity of each of the variables implicating the phonological loop, word length, phonological similarity, and phonological suppression, as well as their interactions, has given way to a picture of contradictions. The word length effect was found not to be as general as initially assumed. Indeed, it can be explained in terms of mechanisms other than the phonological loop (Nairne, 1996). Furthermore, learners do not always rehearse when memorizing information, which suggests that rehearsal is not automatic but that it is under the strategic control of the learner (Logie, 1996). Finally, Baddeley and Hitch (1994), who are the authors of the multicomponent model, complained themselves that existing conceptualizations of the phonological loop were insufficient to generate precise predictions.

Of course, none of these problems are severe enough to warrant abandoning the notion of the phonological loop. I mention them only to remind you that conceptualizations of memory processes are rarely final. Rather, the models serve as frameworks to guide the research, to generate questions, and to integrate a body of experimental data in a domain.

Visuospatial Sketchpad

The visuospatial sketchpad represents the second major component of the multiple component model in Figure 6.7. The sketchpad is assumed to include a visual information subsystem to process color and shape, and a spatial subsystem to process spatial information and to plan movements through space (Logie et al., 1994). Evidence supporting the visuospatial sketchpad includes the interference effects from the concurrent task paradigm such as Brooks's (1968) study, single-cell research in monkeys, and neuroimaing. As described earlier, Brooks found interference between visual images of letters and visual responses, but not between visual images and verbal responses. Consider another study that makes the same point as the Brooks study: Baddeley (1992a) described a dual-task study assessing memory for chess patterns in players of varying skill. Volunteers studied chess patterns and concurrently executed one of two secondary tasks: a verbal or a spatial task. When the secondary task was verbal (e.g., subjects uttered an irrelevant sound), there was no interference, but when the second task was visuospatial (e.g., subjects tapped a series of keys according to a specified spatial pattern), retention of the chess positions was reduced for both novices and experts.

Spatial versus Visual Processes

Baddeley (1990) introduced the term *visuospatial sketchpad* to describe the working memory component "responsible for setting up and manipulating of visuospatial images" (p. 97). He made an explicit distinction between visual and spatial images, offering a person's memory for light patches of different brightness as an instance of a visual image, and a person's memory for the changing locations of sources of sound in a dark room as an instance of a spatial image. In agreement with Baddeley, Smith and Jonides (1997) considered visual and spatial information as independent. These two researchers cited the color and shape of objects as examples of visual information and the relation among objects in space as an example of spatial information. Whether the two kinds of information are handled by different working memory systems, and possibly by different brain structures, is an empirical question. Several theorists have adopted the idea of separate subsystems for spatial versus visual information in working memory (Jonides, 1995; Smith & Jonides, 1997; Wilson et al., 1993). They base their view on evidence from behavioral studies (Baddeley, 1992a), neurophysiological studies (Wilson, O'Scalaidhe, & Goldman-Rakic, 1993), and neuroimaging studies (Smith & Jonides, 1997).

Here, we consider evidence from neuroimaging research by Smith and Jonides (1997). Using an imaginative experimental design, Smith and Jonides (1997) succeeded in documenting the involvement of different brain regions in spatial and visual working memory. The two researchers used the same set of stimuli and the same sequence of trial events for two different tasks, with one task assessing spatial working memory and the other assessing visual memory. The target stimuli were two irregular objects located in random locations of the screen, as illustrated in Figure 6.9. The probe stimulus consisted of a single object. In the spatial memory task, the volun-

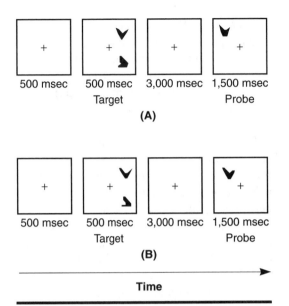

500 msec | 500 msec | 3,000 msec | 1,500 msec
 | Target | | Probe

(A)

500 msec | 500 msec | 3,000 msec | 1,500 msec
 | Target | | Probe

(B)

Time

FIGURE 6.9 Trial events (going from left to right) in the memory condition of the visual memory task and the spatial memory task in the Smith and Jonides (1997) study. *(A)* In the visual memory task, subjects indicate whether the probe stimulus has the *same shape* as the target stimuli. Here, the correct response is *yes*. *(B)* In the spatial task, they indicate whether the probe occurs in the *same location* as one of the target stimuli. Here, the correct response is *no* (adapted from Smith & Jonides, 1997).

teers were asked whether the probe was in the same location as one of the target stimuli. In the visual memory task, subjects were asked to report whether the probe had the same form as one of the target stimuli. The control conditions for the visual and spatial tasks were identical to the memory condition except that the retention interval lasted 250 ms rather than 3,000 ms.

Although the stimuli and the trial sequence were identical in the two tasks, neuroimaging results revealed a clear dissociation. Given the spatial memory instructions, it was the right hemisphere that became active, specifically regions in the prefrontal cortex, the premotor cortex, the occipital cortex, and the parietal cortex. On the

other hand, given the visual memory instructions, two regions in the left hemisphere were activated—namely, the parietal cortex and the inferotemporal cortex.

The Smith and Jonides study, as well as studies using other methodologies, suggest separate visual and spatial subsystems in working memory. To date, however, these investigations have not progressed much beyond demonstrating the existence of these subsystems (Baddeley, 1996a; Baddeley & Hitch, 1994; Nairne, 1996). Future research is necessary to illuminate specific memory processes involving the visuospatial sketchpad, including its storage capacity; its rate of forgetting; its role, if any, in the transfer of visuospatial information to long-term memory; and its rehearsal processes. Hypotheses about the rehearsal of visual and spatial information have been introduced but not yet tested. Thus, Smyth and Schole (1994) have entertained the possibility that rehearsal of spatial information is controlled by the same system that guides eye movements. On the other hand, Smith and Jonides (1997) have linked spatial working memory processing with attentional mechanisms.

Semantic Information in Working Memory

According to early advocates of the two-store view (Conrad, 1964), information in short-term memory was represented phonologically, whereas information in long-term memory was coded semantically. This view was called into question when researchers demonstrated semantic confusion errors in short-term memory in addition to phonological ones (e.g., Dale & Gregory, 1966; Shulman, 1972). For example, Shulman (1972) found in a short-term memory task that synonyms such as *heap-pile* and *grieve-mourn* were more confusable than unrelated words. Nevertheless, neither Baddeley's multicomponent model nor such other memory models as HAM and ACT (Anderson, 1983a;

Anderson & Bower, 1973) included direct representations of semantic information in working memory.

According to the HAM and ACT models, semantic information became automatically part of working memory whenever the information became active. In these models, working memory was defined as the most active part of long-term memory. Potter (1993) wanted to know whether semantic information could be created in working memory rather than be reactivated from long-term memory. She cited two phenomena in support for new semantic working memory structures. Both effects are based on the rapid serial visual presentation (RSVP) technique, a paradigm used in language comprehension research. Words were presented in rapid succession of up to 12 items per second on a screen. When the words were unrelated, viewers could not identify them, let alone remember them. But when the words formed a sentence, viewers identified the words, suggesting that they had created a semantic interpretation of the sentence on the fly and that the semantic structure facilitated the recognition of the words. The structure viewers created clearly was a transient one, as they did not remember the words beyond an interval of a few seconds.

The second finding also involves word identification in the RSVP paradigm. Readers were able to interpret nonwords—actually, misspellings of words—in light of a context sentence. Thus, the nonword *dack*, presented in the context of the sentence *The child fed the dack in the pond,* was correctly interpreted as *duck*. If it had not been for the semantic representation, the reader would not have been able to read *dack* as *duck*. Both of these findings support the notion that working memory computes new semantic structures rather than merely reactivating them from long-term memory.

Given Shiffrin's (1993) view that working memory "encompasses virtually everything that we are concerned with in human cognition"

(p. 193), it is not surprising that working memory should contain semantic codes (see also Martin & Romani, 1994). If Shiffrin is right, working memory should contain all of the codes supported by the cognitive system. Presumably, the empty circles in Figure 6.7 accommodate such additional modalities as taste and olfaction, as well as motor codes.

Central Executive

The central executive presides over the operations of working memory. It is the processor that allocates resources, governs attentional processes (see Chapter 1), and adjusts goal priorities moment by moment (Jonides, 1995). The central executive has much in common with control structures proposed in attention research and neuropsychology. Influential models of attention and the control of performance include the *supervisory activating system (SAS)* (Norman & Shallice, 1986) the *executive attention network* (Posner & Raichle, 1994), and the *attention control* model (Gopher, 1993). Although using different terminologies, all of these theories view attention as a mechanism that controls the scheduling of limited cognitive resources when the person must execute two or more tasks concurrently.

Neuropsychological models of action control were formulated in the context of work with frontal lobe patients who exhibit disabilities in the coordination of actions. According to Kolb and Whishaw (1990), the control over scheduling of activities, however mundane, is under the aegis of *temporal memory*. Executing a plan as simple as making a sandwich involves temporal coordination of sequential stages from locating the ingredients—bread, mustard, and ham—and finding the accessories—knife and sandwich bags—to remembering the steps completed and those that remain to be done.

When Baddeley and Hitch (1974) first introduced the central executive, it was a speculative notion. Although it is still controversial, as we shall see, its advocates list three lines of evidence in its support: behavioral studies using the concurrent task design, neuropsychological case studies with patients who suffered frontal lobe damage, and neuroscientific research implicating specific brain regions and individual cells in attentional control.

Evidence from Behavioral Studies: The Concurrent Task Paradigm

We have seen earlier how researchers use the concurrent task paradigm to identify the putative components of working memory (Baddeley, 1992a; Brooks, 1968). In order to track the central executive, experimenters have volunteers work on a target task thought to tax the central executive and one of several secondary tasks. When a secondary task produces a decrement in the target performance, it is assumed that both tasks engage the central executive. Consider an illustrative study by Logie and colleagues (1994). These investigators used arithmetic problem solving as the target task. Addition problems such as $13 + 18 + 13 + 21 + 13 + 25 = ?$ and $18 + 48 + 22 + 18 + 27 = ?$ were presented to the volunteers via headphones.

Four secondary tasks were paired with the arithmetic task in four different conditions: the random generation task, the irrelevant picture condition, the movement condition, and the phonological suppression condition. In the random generation task, volunteers were instructed to generate items at random from such familiar item sets as the alphabet or a set of 10 digits. Producing random strings required the volunteers to monitor the previous items and to resist the temptation of generating stereotypical sequences (e.g., *ABCD* and *3 4 5 6)*. In the irrelevant picture condition, volunteers viewed line drawings projected on the screen as they solved the arithmetic problems. In the movement condition, they were asked to press a series of four buttons in a sequence given by the experimenter.

Random generation disrupted solving the addition problems the most; the error rate was about 40% in the random generation condition versus 15% in the three other conditions. Logie and colleagues attributed the deficit in the random generation group to the similarity between the random generation and arithmetic tasks; both tasks presumably involve the planning and control functions attributed to the central executive.

The pattern of interference observed by Logie's team could have occurred for a different reason. Suppose the random generation task was more difficult than the other three secondary tasks. Logie and colleagues dismissed this alternative on the grounds that each of the other tasks has been shown to interfere with modality-specific recall: picture viewing interferes with recall of visual information, phonological suppression interferes with recall of phonological information, and motor movements interfere with recall of a set of target movements.

The random generation task has been shown to interfere with other tasks involving executive control, such as generating instances of a specific category, strategic thought in chess, learning simple contingencies in artificial grammars, and syllogistic reasoning. The reason for the performance decrement of the primary tasks is the same: arithmetic, chess, and reasoning engage the central executive, as does random generation (Baddeley, 1996a).

The concurrent task design is not just another laboratory exercise; it captures processing in any activity that involves concurrent mental operations. Writing is a good example; writing can be viewed as a collection of multiple processes intended to achieve the goal of expressing thoughts on paper. Consider Black's (1982) apt account of the conflicting tasks with which a writer must cope:

> *A writer caught in the act [of writing] looks much more like a very busy switchboard operator trying to juggle a number of demands on her attention and constraints on what she can do:*

- *She has two important calls on hold. (Don't forget that idea.)*
- *Four lights just started flashing. (They demand immediate attention or they'll be forgotten.)*
- *A party of five wants to be hooked together. (They need to be connected somehow.)*
- *A party of two thinks they have been incorrectly connected? (Where did they go?) (p. 52)*

Playing basketball, driving a car, going on a trip, or simply leaving the house every morning for work—each of these activities makes concurrent demands on the central executive. Does this scenario sound familiar? It is 8 o'clock in the morning. You are running late to meet your friend for a ride for school. You try to collect everything needed for the day—books, notes, paper, and a computer. You want to leave the house in good order, so you are busy turning off the appliances, locking the doors, and taking the garbage out. Just at that moment, the phone rings and you learn that your friend's car has broken down and you will have to take the bus! Under these circumstances, it is all too easy to do something unintended, such as locking yourself out or forgetting an important item, whether wallet, appointment book, or keys. These conflicting demands overextend the central executive and cause *slips of action,* as Norman (1988) called them in analogy with the term *slips of the tongue*.

Neuropsychological Evidence: The Dysexecutive Syndrome

Numerous case studies have established links between impairments of executive control and the frontal lobes (Chapter 3). The frontal lobes occupy one-third of the human cortex, more than in any other animal. Individuals who suffer injury to the frontal lobes exhibit reduced control of behavior and have difficulty in coordinating their actions to meet a specific goal. These symptoms are known under the term *frontal lobe syndrome* or *dysexecutive syndrome* (Baddeley, 1996a).

Eslinger and Damasio (1985) described a case of executive dysfunction in patient E. V. R., an accountant who developed a tumor in the frontal lobes. Surgical lesions in the frontal cortex, intended to remove the tumor, produced a disabling side effect. The patient could no longer make any decisions; he would take hours in choosing a restaurant, and, once there, he could not decide where to sit or what to order. Similarly, he could not purchase any items without examining alternative brand names and prices in the greatest detail. Although his IQ remained in the 97th percentile, E. V. R.'s disability was so severe that he could not hold any job at all.

Neuropsychologists use a variety of tasks to assess performance deficits of the dysexecutive syndrome. Each of the tasks involves the kind of planning authored by the central executive (see also Chapter 10). Consider the following:

- In the Wisconsin Card Sorting Task, patients are asked to sort a deck of cards according to such criteria as color, shape, or number. The task in itself is not very difficult; however, from time to time, the experimenter shifts the criterion without giving continuous feedback.

- In the verbal fluency task, the person is asked to generate as many words from a specific category as he or she can (e.g., fruits beginning with the letter *P*) (Benton & Hamsher, 1983).

- Motor sequencing requires the patient to mimic a sequence of hand movements demonstrated by the experimenter—for example, touching the right shoulder or the left ear, or reaching out toward a target.

- In the Stroop task, the person is given a list of color names printed in conflicting colors and is asked to name the color the word is printed in. For example, the word *red* is printed in green letters. Naming the color is difficult because of the tendency of reading the word.

Frontal lobe patients exhibit two major problems in tasks such as these: perseveration and distraction. *Perseveration* means the patient continues to pursue the initial goal of a sequence of different goals. In the Wisconsin Card Sorting Task, for example, patients tend to use the first sorting criterion after the experimenter has switched it. Some patients do so, even though they know declaratively that there is a new goal (Cohen & O'Reilly, 1996). Goldman-Rakic (1994b) attributes perseverance in schizophrenic patients to a defect in the frontal lobes. *Distraction* occurs when no goal exists to guide the patient's action; the patient may become distracted by any stimulus coming from the environment. When someone puts a glass on the table, the patient will try to drink from it; when someone places scissors in front of her, she will try to cut (see Baddeley, 1990).

Executive disorders depend on the specific structure that is injured. Injury to the dorsolateral frontal areas (regions located at the top and side of the frontal lobes) may result in impaired performance in delayed response tasks (Allport, 1993), whereas injury to the inferior and orbital frontal cortex may occasion an inability to suppress well-learned or otherwise dominant response tendencies (Fuster, 1995). Injury to the prefrontal region often results in impaired judgment of frequency of occurrence, poor retention of temporal order, difficulties with the delayed response task, and remembering the order of pointing to locations even if the order is generated by the patients themselves (Moscovitch, 1994). By contrast, patients who suffered lesions to the hippocampus cannot retain the target event itself (Chapter 3).

Occasionally, people not afflicted by brain injury have the experience of losing control over thoughts and behavior. They experience unbidden thoughts, frequently of a depressive nature, against their will. Baddeley (1993a) attributes this phenomenon to a transient loss of executive control over focal awareness. In order to reinstate control and banish unwanted thoughts, the person can try such simple tasks

as saying *the* at random intervals or generate random letter strings. Doing so ties up the central executive and eliminates the intruding thoughts.

Thinking about irrelevant aspects of a task usually impedes performance. This experience, although sporadic in young people, is more common among older people. The person finds it difficult to suppress irrelevant information, and, as a result, there is a performance decrement in the target task (Shimamura, 1995). In Hasher and Zacks's (1988) formulation, the presence of irrelevant information reflects a failure of inhibitory selection mechanisms (Chapter 8).

Evidence from Neuroimaging Research
Neuroimaging techniques have been used in an effort to track executive processes. Scientists have detected increased activity in the frontal lobes when volunteers are engaged in executive processes—for instance, when they prepare to perform a task or when an ongoing task makes the greatest scheduling demands. Roland (1985) reported that when subjects prepared to fulfill a set of instructions, PET activity increased in the superior prefrontal area. Once the task was underway, the activity returned to its base level. Posner and Raichle (1994) observed that the anterior cingulate gyrus became active when participants had to generate a new word or note the presence of a unique target among a set of targets. The same gyrus lit up when the volunteers sought to resist interference in the Stroop interference task (Pardo et al., 1990). Petrides and colleagues (1993) have shown activation in the frontal cortex when subjects were required to maintain information about the temporal order of verbal stimuli. Based on neuroimaging results such as these, Posner and Raichle (1994) proposed an *executive attention network* centered in the anterior cingulate gyrus of the frontal lobe. This network detects an object, brings it into conscious awareness, and absorbs attention in a way that resists interference by other signals.

Can the Central Executive Be Trained for Greater Efficiency?

The answer to this question depends on one's view of the central executive and on the task used to engage it. Consider random generation; here, the person must generate strings of items that have no similarity to items generated previously. Random generation is thus at the opposite end of achieving automaticity through practice (Baddeley, 1996a). It is, however, still open to empirical tests whether random generation does, in fact, become more difficult with practice. Fortunately, random generation is not a skill one needs in everyday life!

Gopher (1993) approached training the central executive from the perspective of skill training (Chapter 5). He selected an interesting concurrent task situation for training: the video game Space Fortress. Space Fortress is an arcade game that involves coordination of several activities such as moving the player's spaceship on the screen, firing missiles, and destroying an enemy spaceship. Both spaceships rotate, track, and fire at one another. Different obstacles, mines, and space debris pop up and must be dealt with to avoid injury and loss of one's spaceship. Learners were initially overwhelmed and experienced panic, but they eventually mastered the task by learning one component after another (e.g., fortress control, mine control, targeting missiles, etc.).

If you think Space Fortress is just another arcade game, consider what Gopher did next: He trained an experimental group of student pilots in the Israeli air force on the Space Fortress game, whereas a control group received no such training. Gopher found that the game-trained pilots achieved better scores in training flights with actual airplanes. Even "a year and a half later, the actual percentage of graduates in the experimental group was twice as high as in the control group" (p. 317).

Training of executive skills is important for frontal lobe patients. Although cognitive deficits caused by organic lesions cannot be removed, the effort to ameliorate them has yielded positive results for some patients, such as in prospective memory training. *Prospective memory* refers to the retention of goals to be executed at some future time, whether it is taking one's medication every 12 hours or paying bills at the end of the month. Raskin and Sohlberg (1996) have successfully used a simple regimen to train two patients to remember to execute chores at some future point (Chapter 12).

Evaluating the Theory of the Central Executive

Baddeley's theory of the central executive postulates a specific processor that coordinates mental processes implicated in diverse actions from problem solving to motor movements. The notion of the central executive has been challenged on empirical and conceptual grounds. As for empirical issues, it is not clear that performance attributed to the central executive is, in fact, explained by it. The empirical data, the goal-directedness, and the impairments found in patients can be simulated by memory models that do not include a central executive. Rather, goal-directedness emerges dynamically from the interaction of molecular processes, whether they are productions in a production system such as ACT or a neural network (Chapter 7). Working within the ACT framework, Kimberg and Farah (1993) simulated intact and impaired performance on four different tasks, including the Stroop test and the Wisconsin Card Sorting Task. Diminished performance in each of these has been observed in patients with frontal lobe damage and attributed to dysfunction of the central executive (e.g., Baddeley, 1990, 1996a).

Kimberg and Farah's simulation assumed a production system architecture, including a working memory but no central executive. The working memory contained elements linked via associations of varying strength. Kimberg and Farah succeeded in simulating performance deficits on the four tasks simply by reducing the association strengths between working memory elements by 50% or 80% from their normal levels. This reduction eliminated those aspects of performance that advocates of the central executive have attributed to planning and scheduling. Kimberg and Farah offered the alternative hypothesis that the frontal lobes maintain associations among the working memory elements and that damage to the frontal lobes interferes with these associations.

The central executive poses conceptual issues, as well. To begin, there is the question: What is common to such different tasks as the Tower of Hanoi, the Wisconsin Card Sorting Task, and the Stroop test to justify a unitary executive processor? Is executive control an abstract skill independent of the task a person acquires or is it specific to the domain, as is memory for skills from chess to medical diagnosis (Chapter 5)? Allport (1993) has argued that the heterogeneity of these and other tasks make the central executive highly implausible. Defending the central executive, Jonides (1995) sees commonalities across the tasks controlled by working memory. According to Jonides, the critical commonality of all of the tasks is that several subtasks must be executed simultaneously and goals must be tracked.

Even if theorists were to agree that executive control is common across different skills, it is not clear just what "executive control" means. The assumption of a central executive amounts to postulating a homunculus in the mind—a little person that makes all the important decisions, as Baddeley (1996a) said. What is it that scientists gain by creating the homunculus? Baddeley (1996a) sees the homunculus as a friend, not a foe. His research strategy is to attribute functions to the homunculus and examine them one by one until the homunculus can eventually be declared superfluous. What researchers have gained in the process is a set of well-documented working memory functions. Thus, the central executive

has a heuristic value for documenting cognitive control functions and for the discovery of mechanisms that support those functions.

CONCLUSION

Working memory is one of the most popular research areas in cognitive psychology, in part because more and more functions have been attributed to it. Conceived originally as a short-term store of phonologically coded information, other codes (visual, spatial, semantic, and conceptual) and other functions (problem solving, comprehension, and computation) have been added to working memory. Four decades after it was introduced, working memory seems to comprise everything; it is no longer easy to identify operations that are *not* included among its functions. To what extent does *working memory* still serve as a descriptive term? Has it come to represent all of cognition, as Shiffrin (1993) believes? Even if the latter were the case, research on working memory offers a different perspective on cognitive processes because the temporal resolution is much finer than in investigations of long-term memory (Crowder, 1993). This perspective illuminates previously unexamined topics, including the competition between mental operations and the time course of those operations as they occur in terms of seconds and milliseconds.

Increasing the scope of working memory has not diminished the number of research issues. On the contrary, there are many problems that will continue to occupy researchers. Theorists differ on the relation between working memory and long-term memory (Richardson, 1996). According to early theorists, short-term memory and long-term memory were independent (Miller, Galanter, & Pribram, 1960), whereas later theories viewed them either as interdependent (Atkinson & Shiffrin, 1968) or as subsumptive with working memory as the active subset of long-term memory (Anderson, 1976).

Scientists are debating whether working memory represents an all-purpose resource or a system consisting of domain-specific resources. Kyllonen and Christal (1990) and Cantor and Engle (1993) have taken the former view, whereas Carpenter and colleagues (1995) support the latter. Combining both of these positions, Ericsson and Kintsch (1995) have proposed two types of working memory: long-term working memory as a domain-specific processor and short-term working memory as a general processor for familiar as well as unfamiliar information.

There are disagreements on the best strategy of doing research on working memory. Some psychologists take the view that working memory is best studied in terms of memory per se, without involving the rest of cognition (Nairne, 1996), whereas others see cognition and working memory as interdependent (Shiffrin, 1993). The relation among the functions of working memory continues to elicit controversy, as well. Some question the view that short-term memory involves working memory (Klapp, Marshburn, & Lester, 1983; La Pointe & Engle, 1990). According to these investigators, remembering digits in the digit span task is independent of the mental operations assumed to occur in working memory. Indeed, it is well known that simple span measures are not related to such complex processes as reading comprehension (Daneman & Carpenter, 1980). On the other hand, evidence reviewed in this chapter (Posner & Rossman, 1965) suggests a trade-off between the storage and computational functions of working memory: Storage capacity declines when people perform difficult computations and it increases when the computations are easy.

CHAPTER 7

MODELS
OF MEMORY

The introduction of memory models in the 1960s and 1970s was the result of several converging events: an ever larger and more diverse body of data in need of organization; the dissatisfaction with an associationism that looked at stimuli and responses but not the mind; and the emergence of the computer as a metaphor for cognitive processes. By this time, empirical research had become voluminous with hundreds of papers published on the serial position effect alone. Short-term memory scanning introduced by Sternberg (1966) generated considerable attention, and scientists began to explore new territory, including primary memory (Waugh & Norman, 1965), semantic memory (Collins & Quillian, 1969), and sentence memory (Sachs, 1967). Not only did memory research become broader in scope but it also became qualitatively different from the associationist era. Thanks to the impetus from linguistics (Chomsky, 1957, 1965), memory psychologists began to look at retention patterns of sentences and stories; and thanks to the computer as a research tool, new performance measures were introduced, among them more accurate measures of recognition performance, response latencies, and functions capturing trade-offs between response speed and accuracy.

It was during this exciting period that the first memory models made their debut. Two types of models were introduced: those that account for an individual effect and those more general models that cover a broad range of data. Examples of the former include models on forgetting in paired-associate learning (Atkinson & Crothers, 1964), on the effects of organization in recall and recognition (Kintsch, 1977), and on the semantic relation between concepts (Collins & Quillian, 1969). The list of models for specific effects could easily be continued; none of them was meant to be general.

The general models took advantage of the computer metaphor that gave rise to the human information-processing framework. This framework was global; it included successive stages encompassing everything from the reception of information at the sensory organs to its storage in long-term memory. Atkinson and Shiffrin's (1968) memory model is an example of this approach (Chapters 1 and 6). There were many others at the time (Norman, 1970) and more models were to follow. Some of these are tabulated in Table 7.1.

Why bother with memory models at all? Why not just perform experiments and record the observations? (Churchland & Sejnowski, 1992, p. 5). The answer is that models of memory serve the same purpose that models serve in other sciences, whether it is genetics, physics, or vision research (Hintzman, 1991). Consider the following reasons for using models of memory:

— Models serve to organize a wealth of data into a systematic framework. The framework

TABLE 7.1   Selected Memory Models

Author(s)	Model
Feigenbaum (1963)	EPAM
Waugh & Norman (1965)	Two-store model
Atkinson & Shiffrin (1968)	Two-store model
Craik & Lockhart (1972)	Levels of processing
Anderson & Bower (1973)	HAM (human associative memory)
Baddeley & Hitch (1974, 1994)	Multicomponent model of working memory
Raaijmakers & Shiffrin (1981)	SAM (search of associative memory)
Murdock (1982)	TODAM (theory of distributed associative memory)
Eich (1982)	CHARM (composite holographic associative recognition memory)
Hintzman (1984)	Minverva II
Grossberg (1987)	ART
Ratcliff & McKoon (1988)	Retrieval theory of priming
J. R. Anderson (1983a, 1993)	ACT (adaptive character of thought)
J. R. Anderson (1990)	Rational theory of memory
McClelland & Rumelhart (1986)	PDP (parallel distributed processing)
McClelland, McNaughton, & O'Reilly (1995)	PDP model of hippocampus and neocortex
Richman, Staszewski, & Simon (1995)	EPAM IV

suggests relations between the data and explanations for the findings. For example, Waugh and Norman's (1956) two-store model, introduced in Chapter 6, explained the forgetting curve in the distractor task and the recency effect in free recall, among other findings, within a common framework (see also Atkinson & Shiffrin, 1968). In the distractor task, rapid forgetting is observed immediately after as few as three items are presented. In free recall, there is rapid forgetting of items in inverse proportion of recency. Forgetting in both cases was attributed to the capacity limits of short-term memory: When new items enter the store, they replace prior items and deprive them of the opportunity of being rehearsed and recalled.

━ Constructing a model encourages theorists to formulate explicit predictions, thus providing an opportunity for evaluating and, if necessary, rejecting the model. For example, in Chapter 4, I reported that it takes longer to verify statements such as *A canary is an animal* than *A canary is a bird*. Theorists accounted for this category size

effect in terms of the semantic network model in Figure 4.10. The model assumes that the verification time of a sentence reflects (1) the distance between concepts (e.g., *canary-bird, canary-animal*) in the network and (2) a spreading activation process between network nodes. Hence, the greater distance between concepts should result in longer verification times. However, the category size effect was not as general as initially thought. For example, the statement *A dog is an animal* was verified faster than *A dog is a mammal,* thus contradicting the strictly hierarchical relation specified by the semantic network model. A modification of the model was necessary to accommodate this and other exceptions to the hierarchy. In the end, the model was superseded by models that did a better job of predicting semantic memory data, including prototype models, exemplar models, and similarity models (Chapter 4).

━ Models have practical implications; they represent a stepping stone from which to bridge the divide between research laboratories and the real world. According to Anderson, Reder, and Lebiere (1996), models "offer the only real hope of transferring results from the laboratory to the real world where phenomena are not packaged into neat laboratory categories" (p. 255). Toward the end of the present chapter, an application based on John Anderson's ACT model will be used as an illustration for the potential of models in addressing real-world problems. The illustration involves tutoring Pittsburgh city high school students in geometry.

Given the motivation for developing memory models, it must be acknowledged that the modeling approach is not without problems. One problem is that some models, especially those that involve computer simulations, include components that typically are not published and therefore not open to inspection and criticism from the scientific community. Other problems are that models may incorporate assumptions that are not based on empirical data (Roediger, 1993; Underwood, 1972), and that the models may be so flexible that they account for any type of results, even those that do not occur in the experiments the models seek to simulate (Hintzman, 1993; Massaro, 1988). In spite of these caveats, memory models are useful tools of memory research and deserve our attention because they provide a unified perspective for examining a body of data.

Space limitations do not permit sketching more than a few models from Table 7.1. Having introduced Atkinson and Shiffrin's (1968) model and Baddeley and Hitch's (1974, 1994) multicomponent model in Chapter 6, I have selected three influential models for review in this chapter, each representing a different approach to memory: the SAM model (Raaijmakers & Shiffrin, 1981), the PDP model (McClelland, Rumelhart, & Hinton, 1986), and the ACT model (Anderson, 1976, 1993). SAM is a mathematical model that focuses on list learning in such traditional laboratory paradigms as recog-

nition and recall. The PDP model is a neural network model inspired by the analogy of neurons and neural circuits in the brain. The ACT framework is a production system theory encompassing both memory for facts and memory for skills.

THE SAM MODEL

The SAM model is a mathematical model of memory. In mathematical models, equations are derived from a theory and explicit predictions are generated. These are tested against a body of data from one or more paradigms. The SAM model is representative of such other broad-based approaches as Hintzman's (1984) Minerva model, Metcalfe's (1991) CHARM model, Murdock's (1982) convolution theory, and Ratcliff and McKoon's (1988) theory of priming. These models seek to account for results from many list-learning paradigms. In list learning, people memorize lists of words such as those in Figure 7.1; typically, their retention is tested in a recognition or recall test (Chapters 1 and 4). Although there are important differences between the various memory models, they share two assumptions rooted in empirical findings:

1. Target items are viewed in relation to the memory representations of all other items learned. For example, the items in Figure 7.1 are related to each other, to items not presented in the list, and to the experimental context in which the person learns the list. Presumably, the learner establishes some link between *cattle* and *answer, cattle* and *radio, cattle* and *form,* and so on.

2. To-be-learned materials are associated with context during learning and retrieval. This assumption reflects the encoding specificity effect—the discovery that retention depends on the commonality of contextual cues during encoding and retrieval (Chapter 4).

FIGURE 7.1   A recognition trial: Study phase and testing.

Study List

Cattle	Form
Tribute	Style
Hint	Answer
Golf	Pudding
Maiden	Radio

Test list

Tribute	*Pudding*
Cotton	Attic
Sea	*Answer*
Radio	*Style*
Facility	Madness
Star	*Hint*
Golf	Opinion
Cattle	*Form*
Policeman	Elbow
Pencil	*Maiden*

Note: Old items are italicized only for purposes of illustration. Participants do not receive such visual aids!

In the next section, I review specific assumptions of Raaijmakers and Shiffrin's SAM model, many of which build on prior theoretical efforts, including signal-detection theory (Swets, Tanner, & Birdsall, 1961). Then I introduce SAM's retrieval structure, examine how retrieval works in recognition and recall, and interpret some classical list-learning results in light of the model.

Assumptions of the SAM Model

Words such as those in Figure 7.1 are assumed to have a certain memory strength or familiarity value. When a word is presented during the study phase, a learner is assumed to think about it and rehearse it, which increases the word's memory strength. Because distractors are not presented during the study phase, there is no change in their memory strength.

In recognition testing, a person bases his or her decision about whether an item is old or new on the familiarity of the item. If the item is familiar in the sense of having recently been seen, the person will say *old;* otherwise, he or she will say *new*. It is assumed that the individual adopts an implicit criterion of familiarity on which he or she bases the *old/new* decision. If the familiarity value of the stimulus is greater than the criterion, the person judges it as *old;* otherwise, the person says *new*.

The recognition paradigm and the memory strength theory were adapted from signal-detection theory (Swets et al., 1961). Signal-detection theory, in turn, developed in the context of detection tasks, where people are asked to decide whether a signal occurred in a particular situation—for example, a blip on a radar screen, a heart murmur in a patient, or a tone against a background of noise in a psychophysics experiment. In each of these tasks, it is assumed that the event has a certain signal strength and if that strength exceeds the observer's criterion, the stimulus is detected.

Let me illustrate the use of the recognition criterion and the notion of memory strength for a subset of the items from Figure 7.1. Figure 7.2 lists six such words: four old words *(cattle, answer, radio, and form)* and two distractors *(madness* and *pencil)* and their illustrative memory strengths.

Assume the person's response criterion was $c = 0.40$ on a hypothetical familiarity scale

FIGURE 7.2   Illustrative strength values of four old items and two distractors.

Cattle	0.60
Answer	0.39
Radio	0.94
Form	0.40
Madness	0.185
Pencil	0.41

ranging from 0.0 to 1.0. If the familiarity of a word is greater than 0.40, the response will be *old;* if it is less than 0.40, the response will be *new.* Given this criterion, the words *cattle, radio, form,* and *pencil* would be judged as old. In this case, the response *pencil* would be considered as a false alarm, and *answer* as a miss (Chapter 1).

We assume that the memory representation of each item incorporates information about three cues: (1) the context in which the item was learned, (2) other items in the list, and (3) the item itself, such as its name. In simplified terms, a representation will be retrieved to the extent that it is prompted by any of these three cues, either singly or in combination: (1) the context cues, (2) the associative cues, and (3) the item cues.

Memory Strength

We begin our examination of memory strength by inquiring where the strength values in Figure 7.2 come from. The short answer is that the memory strength depends on the three cues I have just named. The item cues and associative cues depend on the number of rehearsals an item receives during encoding. Items rehearsed frequently have greater item strength than those rehearsed less often. Distractor items are not rehearsed and therefore not strengthened. However, because the distractors tend to be common English words, they have a certain preexperimental familiarity value known as *distractor strength.*

The strength of the item cue expresses the degree of association between the item and its memory representation. It reflects the similarity between the item and its representation. The item is the physical manifestation of a word on a page or computer screen, or the sound of the word if the experiment involves auditory stimuli. The representation refers to the stored record of the word in memory; it is assumed to be abstract. The strength of item cues and associative

cues varies. It may range from very high, as expressed by coefficients close to 1.0, to very low, as expressed by coefficients close to 0.0. Note that these values are arbitrary; they are selected simply for computational ease.

A list of items does not exist in isolation; it occurs in a particular context, and, as many studies have demonstrated, the study context has a large effect on memory strength (Chapter 4). Context cues include the trial number, the list number, and retrieval cues, as well as more general attributes such as the date, time of day, and location where the experiment took place.

The subject retrieves an item's memory record by using a prompt given by the experimenter, such as "Please recall the items on the third list you studied today." This prompt is a context cue assumed to enter working memory. Activation passes from the cue in working memory to associated information in long-term memory. Retrieval is based on a retrieval structure that reflects the factors that jointly govern the memory strength of items and retention performance: context cues, associative cues, and item cues. In the next section, I use numerical examples to illustrate how the cues bring about the retrieval of memory traces.

Retrieval Structure

The retrieval structure of the SAM model reflects the three factors affecting retention identified by memory researchers:

1. In list learning, learners remember information about each individual item, such as its sound, its spelling, and its meaning.
2. As subjects rehearse the list, they establish associative relations among the items of the list.
3. Context also supports retrieval; the encoding specificity effect illustrates the influence of context on retention.

Expression (7.1) summarizes these three retrieval sources:

(7.1) Retrieval = function (item information, associative relations, context)

Figure 7.3 captures the three information sources of the retrieval structure. There is a representation of each memorized item in the structure called *image* by Raaijmakers and Shiffrin (1981). In Figure 7.3, individual images are represented as double circles with arcs pointing back to each circle. The arcs reflect the rehearsal of each item; for example, the person might say *cattle, cattle, cattle*. Arcs connecting double circles represent the associative relations the learner forms among list items during rehearsal—for example, between *answer* and *radio*. The experimental context and its links with representations are represented on the right of the figure. The circles on the left of the figure represent the probe cues; they are widely connected to the list items. For simplicity, only a subset of the contextual connections are shown. Figure 7.3 helps us to visualize the information

sources supporting retrieval according to the SAM model; it does not generate quantitative predictions of the contributions of each type of information to retrieval. Raaijmakers and Shiffrin (1981) proposed a way of calculating the retrieval strength of each probe cue.

Consider the illustration in Table 7.2. The table has two dimensions: probe cues on the left and representations at the top. There are four columns, one for each representation. Note that the entries in the table are arbitrary and are used here only for purposes of illustration. They are intended to reflect the information sources for each probe cue. The first row indicates the context strength of each representation. This value reflects the degree of activation of the specific representation by the experimental context. The six remaining rows indicate item strengths and associative strengths. Values printed in the diagonal and in bold represent the item information. These are the links of each probe cue to its own representation. The other values in rows 2 through 7 represent the associative strength of a probe cue with *other* list items. In general, item information has greater strength than associative relations.

Some cues are similar to the representations of other cues. For example, relative to other associations in the table, the association between *cattle* and *radio* in row 2 and column 3

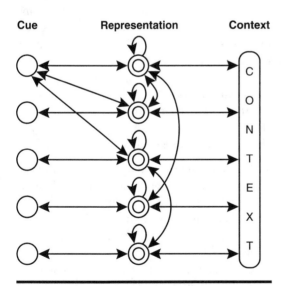

Cue   **Representation**   **Context**

FIGURE 7.3   Three sources of information contribute to retrieval in the SAM model: Individual representations are drawn as double circles, the probe cues are drawn as circles on the left, and the context is shown on the right.

TABLE 7.2   Retrieval Structure of Associative Associations

	Memory Representation			
	Cattle	*Answer*	*Radio*	*Form*
Context	.5	.3	.8	.4
Cattle	**.3**	.3	.4	.1
Answer	.3	**.4**	.1	.1
Radio	.4	.2	**.7**	.3
Form	.1	.1	.2	**.4**
Madness	.1	.05	.1	.1
Pencil	.2	.1	.3	.1

is relatively close, as indicated by an illustrative association strength of 0.40. This value suggests that *cattle* and *radio* were rehearsed together more frequently as the subject was memorizing the list than, say, *answer* and *radio*.

Generally, the distractor items have a lower similarity to the list items than the latter have among themselves. As mentioned earlier, the strength values depend on the number of rehearsals and on the depth of processing of the items during the study phase of the experiment; on the familiarity the person had with the items prior to the experiment; and on the similarity between the context cues during study and during testing.

Our next goal is to calculate the memory strength of each probe cue. Table 7.2 contains the information required. All we need to do is to aggregate the appropriate strength values of each cue. Raaijmakers and Shiffrin (1981) did so in two steps.

1. Combine the context with associative or item information for each representation. (We multiply the context strength by the item or associative strength.) The cells of Table 7.3 represent the products calculated on the basis of the illustrative values in Table 7.2. Consider *radio*. From Table 7.2, row 4 and column 3, we see that the item strength of *radio* is 0.7. The entry in row 1 and column 3 indicates that the strength of the context and *radio* is 0.8. Multiplying these two values, we get a trace strength of 0.56 to the

probe cue. This value is shown in row 4, column 3 of Table 7.3.

2. Add the products for each probe cue to get the aggregate memory strength of each cue. Illustrating this step for *radio*, we add the entries in row 4, .20 + .06 + .56 + .12, to obtain a memory strength of .94. This value is listed in the far right column of Table 7.3. This column represents the familiarity values we have worked with in Figure 7.2 and explains from where the values in that figure come.

The point of this illustration is that an item's activation in response to a cue depends on the joint contribution of the experimental context, of other items in the study list, and on the strength of the item itself. In other words, in SAM, the memory strength for each probe set is global; it is a function of the memory strength of an individual representation as well as of the strengths of all other representations.

Retrieval in List Learning

Using the retrieval structure introduced earlier, this section describes retrieval in recognition and recall situations. The two tasks differ in the manner of identifying the target item in long-term memory. For recognition, a direct familiarity check of the target item compared to other items in long-term memory takes place. For recall, a search is necessary for each individual item.

TABLE 7.3 Strengths to Probe Set

	Cattle	Answer	Radio	Form	Memory Strength
Context	.5	.3	.8	.4	
Context × cattle	.15	.09	.32	.04	.60
Context × answer	.15	.12	.08	.04	.39
Context × radio	.20	.06	.56	.12	.94
Context × form	.05	.03	.16	.16	.40
Context × madness	.05	.015	.08	.04	.185
Context × pencil	.10	.03	.24	.04	.41

Recognition

The familiarity check in recognition tests is fast and automatic. It is global because the familiarity value of an item is based on the extent to which all items in long-term memory are activated by a retrieval cue, as we saw earlier. The test item and the context form a compound that elicits a representation in memory; its familiarity is compared to a criterion value (e.g., $c = .40$ in Figure 7.2). If the item's familiarity is greater than the criterion, the person responds *old;* otherwise, a *new* response is made.

The abscissa in Figure 7.4[1] represents the net familiarity level, increasing from left to right. Familiarity corresponds to the global strength of a memory representation in response to the probe item; the values in the right-hand column of Table 7.3 serve as an example. The ordinate represents the frequency of items at given levels of familiarity. Presenting a word during the study trial raises its familiarity value, as captured by the distribution on the right of Figure 7.4. The familiarity of the distractors is less because they were not presented and rehearsed; they are shown in the left distribution.

The vertical line in Figure 7.4B represents the criterion. It intersects both the new and old distributions. The old distribution has a relatively large region to the right of the criterion; this area represents the probability of making an old response, given that the stimulus is old, a hit (Chapter 1). The area of the old distribution located on the left of the criterion represents the probability of miss responses (vertical shading). Note that the probabilities of hit and miss responses total 1.0.

The distribution of distractor items is also intersected by the criterion. In our example, the area to the right of the criterion is relatively small (horizontal shading). It represents the probability of making an *old* response to a new stimulus, a false alarm. The larger area of the new distribution to the left of the criterion represents the probability of a correct rejection. In Figure 7.4B, the criterion is shown in a fixed location. This is true for any given trial. Across trials, however, the response criterion may vary depending on the payoff the subject receives for making hit and false-alarm responses (Chapter 1).

Retrieval in Recall

For recall, the person must search the retrieval structure. The search process is more complex than the familiarity check in recognition; it involves checking and selecting a starter word followed by selecting additional words. All along, the person determines whether selected words fit the correct context. The subject uses a context cue as the starting point—for example, the name of the experimenter and the trial number, say, *John's third list*. The context cue triggers several search cycles in memory until a word is re-

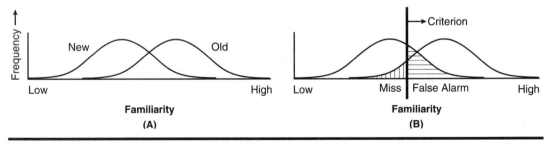

FIGURE 7.4   Strength theory of recognition memory. *(A)* Old items have been shifted to the right on the familiarity dimension. *(B)* The implicit decision criterion adopted by the subject. Because the criterion intersects the old and new distribution, the person makes some false alarms to new items and misses some old items.

called—for example, *radio* (see Figure 7.1). Usually, the most active word in the retrieval structure is recovered first (but see Wixted, Ghadisha, & Vera, 1997). Then another search process starts, based on the context cue and the word just recalled, such as *John's third list-radio*. This process is repeated several times. As a result, the following list might be produced: *radio, form, style, pencil.* For each of the words, at least one search cycle is required. In immediate free recall, the items with the greatest activation levels tend to be the most recent items on the list and they are recalled first. If the activation levels are relatively low, no item can be retrieved and the search is stopped after a certain number of failed attempts.

Application of SAM to Important Memory Experiments

I introduced the SAM model with the claim that it could account for a large set of results. Let me show you next how the framework handles the effect of several important variables on retention, presentation time, retention interval, and so on. Because of space limitations, we cannot cover such other applications of SAM as paired-associate learning, spacing effects, interference phenomena, priming effects, cued recall, sentence learning, semantic memory, discourse memory, and implicit memory.

Presentation Time
An increase in presentation time improves both recall and recognition performance, because the strength of both associative cues and item cues increases, whereas the distractor familiarity remains unchanged. Thus, the associative strength increases for rows 2 through 5, but not for the distractors in rows 6 and 7 of Table 7.2.

Retention Interval
We all know that we retain less when more time has elapsed since study. According to SAM, this occurs because the context cues have changed more as the retention interval increases. New and different contexts emerge during the interval, thus reducing the similarity with the item cues.

Serial Position Effects in Free Recall
Retention in immediate free recall is especially good for items early and late in the list. The curve exhibits primacy and recency effects. The recency effect occurs because the recent items are the most active ones and are therefore recovered first, unless an arithmetic task or some other task intervenes. The primacy items, on the other hand, receive relatively more rehearsals and therefore exhibit greater item strength than items in the middle of the list. (This account is similar to that given by Atkinson and Shiffrin's [1968] two-store model of memory.)

Encoding Specificity
In the retrieval framework, the encoding specificity effect is explained naturally through the context cues in Tables 7.2 and 7.3. Any changes in the context between study and test lower the product of context and item cues in Table 7.3, the level of familiarity, and thus reduce retention performance.

A memory model usually does not make news when it accounts for familiar and intuitive phenomena. However, when a model predicts counterintuitive effects, the research community pays attention. SAM predicts several unexpected effects that have attracted the interest of memory researchers. I name a couple of these effects here, referring you to the original sources for details.

Part-List Cueing Effect
Assume people commit 30 words to memory and, at testing, they are given 15 of those words as cues to aid them in retrieving the remainder of the list. The expectation of most memory theories is that recall should be better than in a group

that did not receive the cues. The cues presumably provide additional retrieval links and thus facilitate recall of the remaining items. However, as mentioned in Chapter 4 in the context of retrieval practice and inhibition, this is not what happens. Recall in the part-list cueing condition is no better than in the no-cueing condition. The SAM model accounts for this paradox in terms of the quality of the cues a learner uses for retrieval: Experimenter-generated cues are inferior to the cues learners generate themselves because the experimenter cues tend to bias the sampling process and may actually interfere with access to the other half of the list (Raaijmakers, 1993, p. 476).

Recall Superiority

The typical finding in comparisons of recognition and recall tests is that recognizing words is easier than recalling words (Chapter 4). This has been attributed to the presence of greater contextual support in recognition than in recall testing. There are, however, instances when words that are not recognized are nevertheless recalled (e.g., Tulving & Thomson, 1973). Because the SAM model incorporates the encoding specificity principle, the level of retention is expected to be a function of the overlap between context cues during study and testing. Accordingly, recall performance would be better than recognition performance whenever the overlap between study cues and testing cues is greater in the recall test than in the recognition test (Gillund & Shiffrin, 1984).

Evaluation of the SAM Model

Raaijmakers and Shiffrin's (1981) SAM model successfully met its original objective of handling a wide range of empirical memory findings, including a number of counterintuitive effects (Raaijmakers, 1993; Wixted et al., 1997). SAM's power was achieved on the basis of relatively simple assumptions. However, according to Roediger (1993), the very power of the SAM model entails a weakness as well—the model has too many assumptions, not all of which are based on observable behavior. For example, in Roediger's view, the SAM model includes assumptions on changes in the associative strength between context cues and memory representations that are mathematical and not empirical. The conceptual power of the SAM model reflects a problem of quantitative models in general: Once the model is sufficiently broad, the danger looms that the model includes too many assumptions to permit empirical testing. Fortunately, researchers have a remedy for this problem, at least in principle: Introduce assumptions only to the extent that they are warranted by aspects of performance or mental processes.

NEURAL NETWORK MODELS

A *neural network model* is a computer simulation of neural networks in the brain. The simulated neural network consists of neurons, as does its counterpart in the brain. Each neuron accepts input either from the environment or from neighboring neurons and produces an output, as determined by an activation function. In organisms, inputs and outputs are measured in terms of physical energy; patterns of light emit energy in the form of waves, so do sound patterns, although at a different range of the wave length continuum. The responses of organisms are forms of mechanical energy expressed in all kinds of bodily actions, from moving the entire body to subtle changes of the vocal cords. In network simulations, such levels of energy are expressed as levels of activation, both excitatory and inhibitory. The activation levels are expressed via convenient, but arbitrary, numerical scales. The typical scale ranges from 1.0 to −1.0.

The neurons in a network are connected through links that carry excitatory and inhibitory information, much like in the nervous system. Networks vary in complexity from two

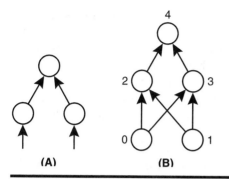

FIGURE 7.5   Neural networks. *(A)* Two-layer network with two input units (bottom) and one output unit. *(B)* Three-layer network includes hidden units in addition to input units and an output unit.

units to thousands of units; they also vary in the number of layers of neurons, their pattern of connectivity, and the flow of information. Figure 7.5 shows two simple types of networks. Figure 7.5A exhibits a two-layer network consisting of two input units and an output unit. Figure 7.5B shows a three-layer network, including input units, an output unit, as well as hidden units.

The role of the units varies. Input units receive stimuli from the environment; output units produce responses. Hidden units are intermediary between input units and output units; they do not communicate with the environment. In general terms, a unit transforms input signals in terms of an activation function and passes them along links to other units. The links between units function like axons in biological nervous systems. The strength of links varies, as reflected in values that are known as *weights*.

Activation levels in the network depend on the characteristics of the input signal (see Retrieval from Neural Nets later in this chapter). The strength of links between neurons, the weights, depends on the network's learning history (see Learning in Neural Networks later in this chapter). In simple models, the output of a

neuron to the environment is based on the input activations, as illustrated in Figure 7.6.

In sum, neural networks consist of:

- Units known as neurons
- Connections between the neurons
- Weights that determine the strength of the connection

The pattern of units and of their connections and the weights represent the knowledge of the network at a particular time. The output of a neural net is based both on the input activation and the pattern of weights of the network. Important properties of neural networks are that they hold distributed memories and that they can learn.

Distributed Memories

In the classical information-processing models, memory was viewed in terms of discrete stores that communicated via well-defined channels. Memory representations were assumed to be localized: one memory cell for one item of information, much as one keeps folders in a file cabinet.

In neural network models, there are no specific locations with unique addresses for memory records. Rather, memories are captured by patterns of activation spread over many neuron-like units and links between them (see Chapter

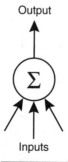

Output

Inputs

FIGURE 7.6   Each unit of a neural network aggregates input activations to produce an output.

1). This is known as a *distributed representation*. Each unit has a level of activation. Units are linked by connections of varying strengths or weights to many other units, as illustrated in Figure 7.7. Because units are multiply connected and because activation readily travels between units, networks are said to be interactive. They are parallel in that activation spreads simultaneously throughout the network.

Distributed representations are best understood when contrasted with localized representations. In localized representations, items of information are stored in discrete and separate units so that each of the units holds a unique item. In Collins and Quillian's semantic net-

work, for example, each node stores only one concept; there is one node for *canary,* another for *robin,* another for *bird,* and so on (Chapter 4). In distributed representations, concepts are presented across different units and each unit contributes to the representation of several items. No single unit represents a concept all by itself.

Example: Jets and Sharks

McClelland (1981) introduced the notion of distributed memories using a data base of individuals belonging to two fictitious gangs, the Jets and Sharks, as illustrated in Figure 7.7. In addition to gang membership, each individual is

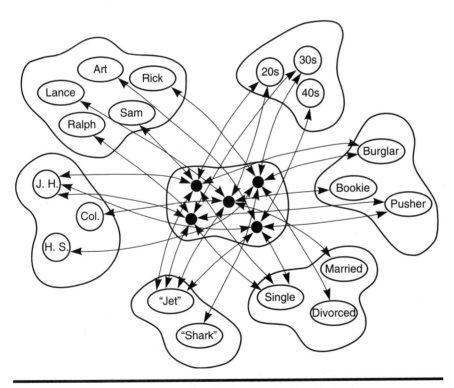

FIGURE 7.7 Units and connections for members of two gangs: the Jets and the Sharks. The network includes seven clusters of units, with person units represented in the center cluster. The center cluster is surrounded by clusters representing various properties. The figure shows excitatory connections between units. The network also includes inhibitory connections, which, to maintain legibility, are omitted here (McClelland, 1981).

classified in terms of five other attributes: name, profession, age, educational status, and marital status.

McClelland introduced a person unit for each gang member; these are shown as filled circles in the center of Figure 7.7. Person units are connected via bidirectional links to each of the properties. Thus, the person unit carrying the name *Art* is connected to Jets, 40s, junior high school, single, and pusher. These connections reflect that Art is a member of the Jet gang, that he is in his forties, and so on. You may consider the person units as analogous to index cards or to the convergence zones mentioned in Chapter 3. According to Damasio's (1990) proposal, a *convergence zone* is a neural region that is connected with multiple neural sites, all of which are implicated in storing information about a stimulus.

The Jets and Sharks network works as a data retrieval system that can be used to answer questions. If any network unit is activated—for example, by a question—the activation spreads along the unit's links to all other connected units.[2] A question about a gang member is initiated by activating the person's name. For example, if we want to learn from the network everything it knows about Art, we enter the name *Art*. According to the network conventions, this results in an activation of the person unit corresponding to Art. From there, the activation spreads to all units connected to Art's person unit, including Jets, junior high school, and so on. The output of these units may be considered as responses to the question about Art.

The network in Figure 7.7 can be used to retrieve information about other gang members or other facts. For example, we could enter the term *Jets* and the network would return all members of the Jet gang. Similarly, the network easily handles searches of combinations of properties. Thus, the probe *Sharks with a college education* will retrieve any Shark who is listed as having attended college.

Retrieval from Neural Networks

Retrieval is the key attribute of natural and humanmade storage systems. Human memory provides a multitude of instances for retrieval both in real-life situations and such laboratory experiments as the paired-associate task. In paired-associate training, pairs of stimulus and response terms are presented together—for example, pairs of nonsense syllables *(XRM-BLC)*, pairs of numbers and words *(324-lamp, 873-screen)*, or pairs of objects and corresponding labels. The person commits both members of each pair to memory and retrieves the response term when presented with the stimulus term in testing (Chapter 4).

Retrieval from neural nets is determined by a rule known as an *activation rule*. The level of activation at each unit depends on the activation arriving from other units and on the links to those units. The activation arriving via a connection is assumed to be the product of the activation and the connection weight between units i and j, Activation$_i$ × Weight$_{ij}$. Given a specific input and a pattern of weights, the activation rule calculates the information retrieved: This is taken as the output or the response of the network vis-à-vis the environment (Figure 7.6). Thus, the response could represent the response term in paired-associate learning or the members of the Jet gang in Figure 7.7.

For a network of two input units, one output unit, two connections, and two weights, as in Figure 7.8B, the input activation at the first unit is multiplied by the first weight and the activation at the second unit is activated by the second weight. The sum of these products represents the output activation of the unit. The summing of input activations to yield an output activation, output$_j$, is captured in expression (7.2).

(**7.2**) Output activation$_j$ = Sum of products (Input activation$_i$ × Weight$_{ij}$)

Both activation and weights may be excitatory or inhibitory, as in real nervous systems. Expression (7.2) is illustrated in the three-unit network in Figure 7.8A. Units 1 and 2 represent the input units, and unit 3 is the output unit. Each of the weights is assumed to have the hypothetical value of 0.5. Assume further that the input activations are −1 and 1, respectively. According to the activation rule in expression (7.2), the output activation of unit 3 is 0 (Figure 7.8C).

Retrieval from larger networks obeys the same principles illustrated for the three-unit network in Figure 7.8A–D. Consider a network of four input units and four output units, as shown in Figure 7.8E. The units are all interconnected, thus yielding 4 × 4 connection weights. Further assume that the network has learned a pair of associates typical in paired-associate learning (e.g., the number *324* as the stimulus term and the word *lamp* as the response term). We represent the input *324* by the arbitrary pattern of activations, 1 −1 −1 1, and the output *lamp* by the pattern −1 −1 1 1. Finally, we assume that the network includes the connection weights shown in matrix (M1), corresponding to the network in Figure 7.8E. Representing networks in terms of matrices facilitates the calculation of output activations according to expression (7.2) and makes generalization to larger networks easier.

The input values of our illustration are represented in the row at the top (labeled "Input *324*") of matrix (M1). Input and output values may correspond to meaningful features of stimuli (e.g., phonemes) and of responses (e.g., articulatory features) (Rumelhart & McClelland, 1987). However, meaningfulness of input and output

(A)

(B)

(C)

(D)

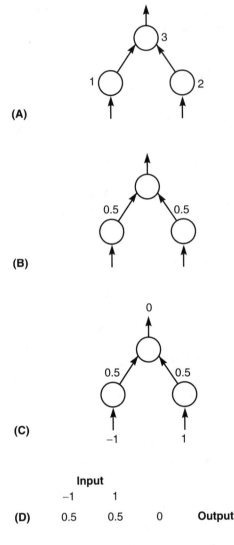

Input			
−1	1		
0.5	0.5	0	**Output**

(E)

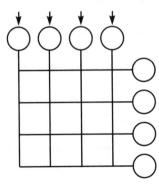

FIGURE 7.8   Activation spreading through neural networks. *(A)* Architecture of a three-unit network. *(B)* Network with connection weights. *(C)* Input and output activations. *(D)* Network in *(C)* shown in matrix form. *(E)* Architecture of a 4 × 4 unit network.

patterns is not necessary. The patterns may be arbitrary, as in the following examples, just as long as different patterns can be discriminated by the network.

For each output unit, we multiply the activation of the connected input units with the corresponding weight and add all of the products according to expression (7.2). For the first output unit, this calculation yields −1, as shown in the following expression:

$$(+1)(-.25) + (-1)(+.25) + (-1)(+.25) + (+1)(-.25) = -1$$

The activations for all four output units are shown in the right-most column (labeled "Output *Lamp*"). The output is to represent the word *lamp*, the response term of the paired associate *324-lamp*.

(M1) Input *324*

+1	−1	−1	+1	Output *Lamp*
−.25	+.25	+.25	−.25	−1
−.25	+.25	+.25	−.25	−1
+.25	−.25	−.25	+.25	+1
+.25	−.25	−.25	+.25	+1

In sum, retrieval of information is accomplished by presenting a connectionist network with a pattern of input activations and then regenerating the output based on the input and the connection weights, according to activation rule (7.2). Retrieval assumes that the association between input and output was previously established. Information about the *324*, for example, is not stored locally in one cell or unit. Rather, it is represented in terms of connection strengths distributed over the entire network. Processing in the network is parallel in that activation spreads simultaneously from the input units to the output units.

Frequently, recognition and perception involve stimuli that are unclear or partially obscured (Chapter 1). Using the *324* example again, one may represent such degraded input by blurring the values of input activation and by using an input pattern such as 1 −1 0 1 rather than 1 −1 −1 1. The connection weights remain the same as in matrix (M1). As you can calculate for yourself, the activation levels for the output units are a little smaller than obtained with the original pattern but they exhibit the same signs. The smaller values illustrate the fact that a person is somewhat less certain about the identity of a blurred pattern than a clear one.

The network we have discussed held just one memory—namely, the association between a number and a word. As claimed earlier, neural nets are designed to hold multiple memories within the same network, as do natural memories. Such distributed memories will be illustrated next.

Illustration of Distributed Representations and Retrieval of Two Patterns from One Network

Consider two input-output associations stored in two different networks: the *324-lamp* pattern in matrix (M1) above and a new pattern to represent the association between *873* and the word *screen* shown in matrix (M2). Note that both input and output patterns are different from the *324-lamp* pattern, as are the weights.

(M2) Input *873*

−1	+1	−1	+1	Output *Screen*
+.25	−.25	+.25	−.25	−1
−.25	+.25	−.25	+.25	+1
−.25	+.25	−.25	+.25	+1
+.25	−.25	+.25	−.25	−1

If we had to represent each of the two (or more) input-output associations in separate networks, long-term memory would have to include an enormous number of different and unrelated networks. Fortunately, networks have the capacity of storing superimposed patterns so that one network accommodates several input-output associations. This is achieved by generating a common set of weights for the different input-output pairs.

We will illustrate the principle of superimposed patterns by using the *324-lamp* and the *873-screen* networks. The idea is to use one network (i.e., one matrix of weights) to accommodate both of these associations. In order to obtain the matrix of weights common to two different patterns, we add the two individual matrices. This is accomplished by adding corresponding cell entries. Adding the corresponding weights for *324-lamp* (M1) and *873-screen* (M2), we obtain matrix (M3).

(M3)

0	0	+.5	−.5
−.5	+.5	0	0
0	0	−.5	+.5
+.5	−.5	0	0

Matrix (M3) contains the information for both the *324* and *873* patterns. We can demonstrate this by presenting the pattern corresponding to the *324* and *873* inputs to the network on successive trials. Using output rule (7.2), we can verify that the composite matrix in (M3) regenerates the appropriate output patterns for the *lamp* and *screen* outputs, respectively. The network with the composite weights exhibits memory for both associations. Note that there is no localized memory of *324-lamp* or *873-screen*. The same set of weights (in matrix 3) handles both kinds of input equally; the matrix illustrates the principle of distributed memories.

Could we continue and add more and more

memories to this network? The answer depends on the size of the network and the types of patterns presented to it. Larger networks have a greater capacity. They can store more patterns than the small networks we have been using. There are, however, limitations to the kinds of patterns that can be represented in the matrix.

Complications

The patterns for *324* and *873* are independent, sharing no common features. When patterns are more similar (e.g., 1 1 1 1 1 1 −1 and 1 1 1 1 1 1), complications arise in discriminating between them unless special provisions are made when the patterns are acquired. Another complication arises when one presents patterns of the kind illustrated in Table 7.4. The pattern represents the exclusive-or problem, a mapping once thought to be unlearnable by neural networks.

The pattern produces an output of 1 when both input values are identical; otherwise, it produces an output of 0. Such mappings are technically known as *XOR-type patterns* (where XOR means "exclusive or"). They occur in contexts where similar responses must be made for different scenarios, such as when the same antibiotic is used for different infections or the same reward is given for different accomplishments. Two-layer networks cannot learn such mappings between input patterns and output patterns (see Figure 7.5A). Hidden units were introduced to handle XOR-type patterns (Figure 7.5B). In addition to a third layer of units, the ac-

TABLE 7.4   The XOR Problem

I1	I2	O
1	1	1
1	0	0
0	0	0
0	0	1

Note: I1 and I2 represent input patterns; O represents the output pattern.

tivation rule had to be altered and a specific learning procedure was required—the generalized delta procedure, also known as *backpropagation learning* (e.g., Bechtel & Abrahamson, 1991).

Learning in Neural Networks

Not only do neural networks handle retrieval easily but learning is a natural feature, as well. Learning involves a change of connection weights in the neural network as a result of presenting successive pairings of input and output patterns. The current weights are changed by a change factor, Change$_{\text{weight}}$, as expressed in expression (7.3).

(7.3) New weight = current weight
$$+ \text{Change}_{\text{weight}}$$

Two learning procedures in neural networks are mentioned here: the Hebb procedure and the delta procedure. The procedures differ in terms of how the change in weights takes place. In the Hebb procedure, joint activation of neurons produces learning; whereas in the delta procedure, error adjustment produces learning. For a fuller treatment of learning in neural networks, consult an excellent introduction to neural networks titled *Connectionism and the Mind* (Bechtel & Abrahamson, 1991). Readers familiar with neural networks will find James Anderson's (1995) *Introduction to Neural Networks* to be an excellent source.

Hebbian Learning
Hebbian learning is based on early speculations by Hebb (1949) that learning and memory depend on neural circuits in the brain. Hebb advanced these thoughts well before discoveries in cognitive neuroscience confirmed his views (Chapter 3). According to Hebb, two neurons become associated when both of them are active at the same time. In terms of neural networks, the strength of the link between two neurons, i

and j, is increased in proportion with their joint activation, as shown in expression (7.4).

(7.4) Change of weight$_{ij}$ = Activation$_i$
$$\times \text{Activation}_j$$

If the activations are weak (e.g., 0.1) for each neuron, the change of weight factor is relatively small—namely, 0.01. When the neurons are highly activated (e.g., 0.5) for each neuron, the increment is larger—namely, 0.25. Thus, in Hebbian learning, the change in connection weights depends only on the joint activity of the two associated neurons. Other factors, such as whether the network produces a correct response, makes no difference.

Delta Learning
In delta learning, the weights of two-layer networks are adjusted according to the agreement between the intended output of the network and the actual output (expression 7.5). If the actual response of the network agrees with the desired response, there is no weight change. Otherwise, weights are changed in proportion with the discrepancy between the actual and desired responses so as to reduce the difference on future trials.

(7.5) Change of weight$_{ij}$ = Activatio n$_i$ × Error$_j$

Intuitively, delta learning makes more sense than Hebbian learning. In delta learning, the network weights are adjusted when the network produces an error; otherwise, they are left unchanged. The delta procedure is very powerful, making it possible to simulate a wide range of empirical learning effects (see Applications of Neural Networks next in this chapter). Importantly, theorists have succeeded to generalize the delta procedure to networks that include hidden units. The generalized delta procedure, also known as backpropagation learning, gives networks the power to learn XOR-type mappings (for more details, see J. A. Anderson, 1995; Bechtel & Abrahamson, 1991).

The delta rule has another advantage sought by scientists. It is applicable in very different research situations in that it expresses the associative strength of pairs of events in both human and animal learning. Working independently from neural network researchers, two learning theorists, Robert Rescorla and Allan Wagner, discovered the delta rule in the context of animal conditioning (Rescorla & Wagner, 1972). They proposed the Rescorla-Wagner rule, a rule that predicts a wide range of phenomena in animal learning and in cognition in general (see Siegel & Allen, 1996). According to the Rescorla-Wagner rule, it is the degree to which a stimulus is unexpected and surprising that it gains strength. By definition, an expected event is known by the organism and produces little, if any, change in the memory trace. What attracts the organism's attention are unexpected events; these events are learned and remembered best.

Applications of Neural Networks

Thanks to different learning procedures, neural networks have the power of learning mappings of input and output patterns, which represent events of virtually any kind. As long as the events can be captured in terms of activation levels, neural networks can learn pairings between them. Many mappings can be handled by Hebbian learning. Delta learning and generalized delta learning, or backpropagation learning, are more powerful because they can acquire confusable patterns and patterns of the XOR-type. If there is a question about the learning procedures, it is not about limits in power but about their psychological reality: They have been criticized for being too powerful and for generating data patterns not obtained in the laboratory (Massaro, 1988). Additional questions have been raised about the neural feasibility of certain learning procedures, including backpropagation learning.

Learning Rules and Exceptions in Language

Delta learning involves corrections of errors as a network acquires arbitrary pairings of patterns, whether these are paired associates in a memory experiment, a set of letters and a set of sounds, or a set of instances and category labels. As learning progresses, network weights are changed to produce the desired output patterns. Because delta learning can detect the average tendency in a set of input patterns, it has been used to mimic a number of important learning and classification effects. We consider one such application: the learning of the past tense of English verbs.

One of the most interesting applications of delta learning has been the simulation of an important form of implicit learning (Chapter 5)—namely, the acquisition of linguistic regularities and exceptions. The acquisition of the past tense of English verbs is a case in point. Research has shown that children acquire both the regular pattern of generating the past tense of English verbs and a large number of irregular verbs. In English, the past tense is usually formed by adding the suffix -ed to the stem of the infinitive, as in walk–walk-ed and climb–climb-ed. Irregular verbs, although they occur quite frequently, have idiosyncratic forms of the past tense, as in run-ran, write-wrote, think-thought, and eat-ate. Children acquire the past tense in three stages in a combination of rote learning and rule learning. First, they learn to use a small number of frequently occurring irregular verbs. As a child encounters more and more regular verbs, he or she learns to form the past tense by adding -ed to the verb's stem. The child learns this rule so well that he or she applies it incorrectly to irregular verbs, as in saying sleeped instead of slept. By adolescence, however, most children master both regular and irregular verbs.

Rumelhart and McClelland (1987) constructed a connectionist network of 460 input units and 460 output units to learn a corpus of about 500 English verbs and their past tenses. They first presented a small corpus of irregular verbs, then a mixture of regular and irregular verbs, and finally the whole set of verbs. The infinitives of verbs and their past tense forms were presented to the network's input and output units respectively. Outputs were produced according to expression (7.2) and errors were adjusted according to the delta rule in expression (7.5). There were 190 learning episodes, each involving the entire training set of verbs. The network not only mimicked the three stages of children's past tense learning successfully but it also simulated some subtle empirical effects. For example, researchers found that children more easily learn those irregular verbs that use the stem for the past tense, as in *hit*. Children also use alternate past tense expressions of a verb during the second stage, such as *go-ed* and *went-ed*. The network produced these patterns as well as some formulations that researchers had not yet tested. One of these was that children would produce double inflection responses for verbs whose stem ends on *p* or *k* so that they will say *dripted* instead of *dripped*.

Models of cognition are judged by the economy of their assumptions, as is the case of models in other domains: The fewer the assumptions and the simpler, so much the better. According to this measure of parsimony, it is a strength of the neural network approach that it can accommodate the learning of regular forms and exceptions within a common framework rather than having to assume different mechanisms. There are other formulations of rules and exceptions that call for different mechanisms for each; for example, the learner acquires a set of rules by one procedure and memorizes exceptions by another (see Pinker & Mehler, 1988). Seidenberg (1992) cites other cases of rules-plus-exceptions in the English language that are readily handled by connectionist networks, such as pronunciation patterns in English. The correspondence between spelling and pronunciation may be considered rulelike for such words as *mint, lint,* and *splint.* Pronouncing each of these words is rulelike, as researchers discovered when they asked people to pronounce pseudowords like *bint.* Subjects typically pronounce this string to rhyme with *lint.* So far, so good; there is, however, the exception—namely, *pint.* Speakers of English acquire exceptions like these easily without giving them a second thought.

Successful learning of the past tense is possible because, using the delta rule, the network detects regularities contained in a set of related patterns. Owing to the rule, the network picks up the prototype among related patterns while noting exceptions if necessary. The delta rule is an excellent vehicle for many other instances of such concept learning. In concept learning, exemplars that are similar are subsumed under a specific category, while other items are sorted with other categories. Concept learning is very flexible and includes the acquisition of the most diverse classes of concepts from highly deterministic ones (Bruner, Goodnow, & Austin, 1956) to such uncertain categories as medical diagnoses (Gluck & Bower, 1988).

Backpropagation Learning

Backpropagation learning or generalized delta learning is useful in situations in which physically different stimuli must be transformed to produce similar responses. In the case of learning the XOR pattern, the trick for the network is to acquire the weights to accomplish the goal of delivering the same response when very different input patterns are presented. This mirrors the accomplishment of organisms: Sometimes it is necessary to respond with similar responses to different situations. For example, teachers award grades of A to different types of performances, whether it is an excellent term paper, a high score on an objective test, or a creative analysis of a set of complex laboratory data.

Reading Text.   NETtalk, one of the most famous neural networks, learns to read aloud. The network accepts English text as input and learns to pronounce the words correctly. The network's architecture includes three layers of units: seven sets of 29 input units corresponding roughly to the English alphabet, 80 hidden units, and 26 output units to capture the speech features of 50 English phonemes. All of these units are widely interconnected, requiring 18,629 weighted links. The creators of NETtalk, Sejnowski and Rosenberg (1986), started their mechanical reader on a set of 1,000 words selected from informal speech of a child. Subsequently, the researchers added a corpus of common words selected from a dictionary. The target output was the correct pronunciation of the text read by a human reader. NETtalk learned to read the sample text after thousands of learning cycles. Of course, this does not mean that NETtalk understands the text. Its accomplishment is to have learned the letter-to-sound correspondence in English, which is no small feat—just observe anyone who is learning English as a second language.

In general, generalized delta learning or backpropagation learning is useful whenever an input must be transformed into an output that includes both regularities and exceptions, including the following:

- Control a simulated car driving on a highway
- Visual quality control items transported at high speed (1,000 per minute) on a conveyor belt—for example, parts of car engines or canned goods
- Interpret x-rays to detect symptoms of diseases

None of these applications make a claim for cognitive validity; they do not seek to simulate human intelligence. Rather, these are engineering applications intended to get the job done efficiently, no matter how. Backpropagation learning has been used, however, to simulate memory effects found in the laboratory, not always successfully, as we shall see next.

Neural Networks and Retroactive Interference.   *Retroactive interference* refers to the decrement in performance when new responses (A-C) must be learned for stimuli that already have been associated with prior responses (A-B). In research with human participants, learning the A-C responses diminishes the strength of the A-B responses, but it certainly does not erase them (Chapter 4). Even after extended A-C training, up to 50% of the A-B responses can be recovered (Barnes & Underwood, 1959).

McCloskey and Cohen (1989) sought to simulate this retroactive interference (RI) effect by using backpropagation learning in a three-layer neural network. Using the sequential training schedule (first A-B, then A-C) as in the RI paradigm, the researchers observed what they described as "catastrophic interference"—indeed, "retrograde amnesia." Even as the first A-C list was presented to the network, the network failed to reproduce *any* correct A-B responses. Correct performance of A-B responses was virtually zero. This differed radically from Barnes and Underwood's (1959) original results showing that their subjects never dropped below a level of 50% correct A-B responses. McCloskey and Cohen next probed their network further by exploring to what extent the catastrophic interference was a result of the particular network architecture (e.g., the number of hidden units) or of the choice of parameters (e.g., the amount of original A-B training, the number of trials on the A-C list, or the manner of representing stimuli and responses). They tried all of these in various combinations and found catastrophic interference in almost every case. According to McCloskey and Cohen, the failure to mimic successive learning is a major problem of connectionist networks because in the real world, much knowledge, such as mathematical knowledge, is acquired in sequential stages.

McCloskey and Cohen (1989) conceded that "it is conceivable that some untried combination of parameter settings, representational formats, and so forth would yield" fitting simulation results (p. 146). Sure enough, two research teams—Chappell and Humphreys (1994) and McClelland, McNaughton, and O'Reilly (1995)—rose to McCloskey and Cohen's challenge and came up with new combinations of networks to deal with catastrophic interference.

Chappell and Humphreys (1994) designed an architecture involving different types of complex neural networks and innovative learning algorithms. Their system of networks was able to handle retroactive interference and a range of other results observed in the laboratory. However, the researchers had to pay a price for this accomplishment. Their model is far more complex than the neural networks that attracted researchers, in part, because of their parsimony in the 1980s.

The approach taken by McClelland and colleagues (1995) was different from that of Chappell and Humphreys in that the former integrated neural network modeling with insights gained by neuroscientists on the role of the hippocampus in learning and retention (Chapter 3). McClelland and colleagues succeeded in simulating the RI effect and avoided catastrophic interference by introducing the "interleaved learning method" in which the new information is "simply added to the training set so that it is interleaved with continued exposure to the full database" (p. 433). The model by McClelland and colleagues (1995) extends well beyond the issue of retroactive interference. It is an attempt to address hippocampal learning effects, including consolidation effects and retrograde amnesia (Chapter 10), differences between implicit and explicit memory (Chapters 5 and 11), as well as semantic memory (Chapter 4).

Evaluation of the Neural Network Approach

Neural networks are enjoying such a popularity in applied disciplines such as engineering, signal analysis, financial analysis, and weather forecasting that some have claimed they will soon be as commonplace as spreadsheets are today. In applications of neural networks, the yardstick of success is simple: Does the application do the job required? In memory research, the yardstick is a different one. Here, researchers ask: Do the neural networks explain the memory effects and do they do so parsimoniously? Let us consider the promises and problems of the neural network approach in memory research and in cognition.

Neural networks are based on a set of relatively simple assumptions. There are primitive processing units, the neurons, that are connected via multiple links. The strength of the connections depends on past experience, the result of which is a set of weights that embodies the knowledge of the network. Events from the environment are registered by the network as patterns of input activation. This activation is passed through the network to produce an output that depends on the current configuration of the weights and pathways in the network.

Given this simple set of assumptions, the connectionist approach has been able to account for a wide array of empirical results in word recognition, categorization, and concept learning. As an added advantage, connectionist networks can learn both regularities and exceptions in a domain, as well as a number of subtle effects that theorists had not known about (e.g., in learning the past tense in English).

One of the appeals of neural networks is that they acquire their knowledge without programmer intervention. This is a bonus in light of the expense researchers have had to invest for expert systems in the symbolic processing framework. It frequently takes years to program an expert system to represent the knowledge that experts possess in a domain.

There are also problems inherent in neural networks. Although they have been used successfully to simulate diverse data in cognition, there have been both failures of prediction and too powerful predictions. Consider the latter point first. Massaro (1988) developed a neural network simulation of speech recognition. He found that the network was able to predict the results typically found in speech recognition experiments. However, the network also predicted many results that have not been and are not likely to be observed in experiments.

There have been failures of prediction, as well. In a study of retroactive interference, one of the best documented instances of forgetting in the laboratory, McCloskey and Cohen (1989) found that the network broke down when it was given successive sets of arithmetic problems. The network suffered total amnesia rather than exhibiting forgetting as human learners do. As we saw, neural network theorists have rescued the network approach vis-à-vis this challenge (Chappell & Humphreys, 1994; McClelland et al., 1995). However, their system had none of the simplicity of the original neural networks. Instead, it included a variety of subnetworks each with different learning algorithms of greater complexity than the connectionist pioneers had first envisioned.

In addition, there are criticisms of specific models, such as the past tense model, and learning algorithms, such as the backpropagation procedure. Pinker (1990) examined the model of past tense learning in a critical light. He argued that the model is based on erroneous empirical assumptions; for example, the model's shift from correct to overgeneralized verb forms between stages is too abrupt and does not agree with the distribution of verbs in children's vocabularies.

The drawback of generalized delta or backpropagation learning is that learning is too slow

and that it is not clear that there are backpropagation pathways in the brain (although some theorists claim that there are). The averaging capability of networks has also come in for criticism—specifically, that new learning is averaged with prior learning and that it is therefore hard to explain that people manage to retain memory for specific exemplars.

Finally, whereas neural networks acquire their knowledge without programmer intervention, the programmer has great latitude in shaping the architecture and processing assumptions of the simulation. The theorist can determine all sorts of attributes of the model—the number of layers of the network; the number of input units, hidden units, and output units; the pattern of connections between units; the initial level of activation of the units; the rate of weight change in learning; the rate of decay of activation; the learning algorithms and parameters; the output function; and so on.

Whatever may be said about the neural network approach, it has become a part of the landscape in memory research and in cognitive science, and will continue to be a significant player in the field. A person needs only to check the World Wide Web in order to get a glimpse of the following the approach enjoys. (At the time of this writing, website www.cnbc.cmu.edu was a good starting point.)

ANDERSON'S ACT FRAMEWORK

The ACT framework is a comprehensive architecture of memory including declarative memory, procedural memory, and working memory. The ACT model differs from prior cognitive models (e.g., the SAM model) by specifying an explicit mechanism for interacting with the environment. That mechanism is furnished by a production system—a system consisting of condition-action rules as captured in expression (7.6) (see Representation of Skills in Chapter 5).

(7.6) IF this is the condition, THEN execute that action.

When the system detects a set of conditions, whether they are environmental or internal, the action specified by a given production rule is triggered. A condition might be, for example, the goal of adding numbers, running into an obstacle while driving on a road, or identifying a given geometric shape.

In the course of the past two decades, Anderson has developed several versions of ACT, including ACT-R (adaptive control of thought-rational). ACT-R combines the production system architecture with Anderson's (1990) rational analysis. According to rational analysis, structures of declarative and procedural memory of the ACT system are analyzed in terms of their fit to environmental demands (Barsalou, 1995). Those structures that meet the demands best are strengthened, whereas those that execute tasks inefficiently are weakened.

The emphasis of all ACT versions has been on modeling the acquisition of problem-solving skills, including those in geometry, physics, and programming computer languages. According to ACT-R, as learners acquire their first skills in each of these domains, they make use of examples and learn by analogy. Examples are encoded in declarative memory. As practice proceeds, the declarative information is converted into units of procedural memory, the production rules. Although less flexible than declarative structures, production rules are more efficient in executing a specific task. With extended practice, use of the production rules becomes automatic and performance becomes smooth and effortless (Chapter 5).

The Architecture of ACT

The term *architecture,* borrowed from computer science, refers to the relative permanent design features of a model of cognition. The ACT ar-

chitecture is similar to that of other models based on production systems, including SOAR (Newell, Rosenbloom, & Laird, 1989) and CAPS (Thibadeau, Just, & Carpenter, 1982). All of these include memory stores for permanent knowledge and processors to control the execution of production rules. ACT's permanent knowledge resides in declarative memory (i.e., the memory for facts) and in procedural memory (i.e., the memory for skills). The accessibility of both types of memory is determined by its memory strength, which, in turn, depends on the history of using that particular memory representation. Units of memory that are currently used are, by definition, the most activated units of the system. They are represented in the working memory, which is the workhorse of the ACT system.

Declarative Memory: Memory for Facts
Facts are represented in ACT's declarative memory in terms of units known as *chunks.* Miller (1956) introduced the term *chunk* to refer to configurations of component stimuli of all kinds (Chapter 6); they may include groups of binary digits recoded in terms of more memorable decimal digits (e.g., 1010001001 as 20-9), letter sequences recoded as letter groups (e.g., LMCIBMLAXVK as LMC IBM LA XVK), as well as random sets of words recoded as a phrase or a sentence.

The chunk is an organizing structure to accommodate as much information as can readily be accessed. The chunk *IBM,* for example, includes three letters each of which represents a word consisting of additional letters. Both everyday experience and experimental research have shown that chunking information aids retention in light of the capacity limits of memory.

Procedural Memory: Memory for Skills

Production Rules. Memory for skills is captured by production rules of the format given in expression (7.6). Here are some informal examples of production rules: stopping at a red light, forming the past tense of regular English verbs, and adding numbers (Chapter 1).

> If you come to a red light,
> Then apply the brakes.

> If the goal is to form the past tense of a regular English verb,
> Then add the ending *-ed* to the stem of the verb.

> If you have added the digits in one column of an addition problem,
> Then focus on the column to the left.

Expression (7.7) is a formal production rule to illustrate the recognition of a geometrical shape (i.e., a polygon) (see Chapter 5).

(7.7) IF a FIGURE is two dimensional
    and the SIDES are all equal
    and the number of SIDES
    is less than eight,
    THEN classify the FIGURE as a polygon.

Expression (7.7) has a list of three conditions and one action. The conditions specify that the geometrical figure must be two-dimensional, it must have less than eight sides, and the sides should be of equal length. If these conditions are met, the figure is recognized as a polygon.

Two of the capitalized words in expression (7.7) are FIGURE and SIDES. These concepts represent variables; the use of such variables makes the production general and applicable to different types of figures. Different shapes (e.g., pentagons, squares, and hexagons) will fit the general category FIGURE, and the number of SIDES will differ from one case to the next.

According to Anderson (e.g., 1983a), every skill is represented as a set of production rules, perhaps including as many as 1,000 rules. Productions are thought to have the right grain size to capture the components underlying a skill.

For instance, arithmetic is based on such operations as addition, subtraction, and multiplication. Each of these, in turn, involves specific component operations—for example, shifting of columns or setting a carry. The latter components are expressed in terms of production rules. The production rules that are used in a particular instance may not be the most efficient ones, especially early in training. Indeed, productions may be incorrect and contain "bugs" (Van Lehn, 1990). It is only through prolonged practice that the production rules are fine-tuned to meet the demands of a specific task.

ACT has a repertoire of several production systems, each dedicated to a familiar skill, whether it is interpreting and generating English sentences (Anderson, 1983a), doing geometry proofs, writing a computer program, or navigating through cities. The ACT system is also equipped to handle problems that it has never encountered before. In order to solve novel problems, the system uses general problem-solving strategies.

General Problem Solving.   Problem solving involves attaining a goal within a set of certain conditions. Typically, the problem solver identifies a gap between the current state and the goal he or she seeks to achieve. To solve the problem, the person uses strategies intended to close the difference between the two states. For example, if Josh's goal is to meet a friend at the movie theater and Josh is at the dorm, he needs to close the gap between dorm and theater. He solves the problem by finding a means of closing the gap. He could walk, take a bus, drive, or ride a bike to get there. Should there be an obstacle to implementing a specific method (e.g., if the bike Josh intended to use is broken), the problem solver sets as a subgoal to remove the obstacle.

Cognitive scientists have formulated a general strategy, called the *means-ends strategy*, to represent the skill of solving such problems. According to this strategy, the problem solver achieves the goal in two steps, which can be expressed as questions:

1. What is the biggest difference between where I am now and where I want to be?
2. What method can I use to reduce the difference?

In the event of an obstacle preventing the implementation of the method, the problem solver can use the same two-step strategy recursively in an attempt to remove the obstacle. The subgoal would be to remove the obstacle in terms of the same two steps used to address the primary goal: (1) identifying the difference between the current state (e.g., broken bike) and the goal state (e.g., functional bike) and (2) finding a method of reducing that difference (e.g., repairing the bike).

Expression (7.8) represents the two steps of the means-ends strategy in terms of a production rule.

(7.8) IF the goal is to close the difference between the current state and the goal by using a method,
THEN identify the method to close the difference and set as subgoal to apply the method.

By breaking down a complex goal into smaller subgoals, the means-end strategy provides an organized approach to solving problems in any domain, including novel problems. Of course, the more subgoals there are, the greater the load on working memory. The Tower of Hanoi problem described in Chapter 6 illustrates this point nicely (see Figure 6.2).

Differences between Declarative Knowledge and Procedural Knowledge

Declarative knowledge and procedural knowledge differ in a number of ways. Declarative knowledge is acquired relatively quickly and is flexible in its use, whereas procedural knowl-edge takes much longer to acquire. Consider assembling a bird feeder for the first time. The bird feeder comes with several pole segments, a feeder consisting of separate food cups and perches, a tray to hold food droppings, a collar to prevent squirrels from stealing the birdseed, and other parts, as well as a set of instructions for assembling the feeder.

The problem solver reads the instructions, which means he or she enters information into declarative knowledge and follows the instructions step by step. This can be done without prior practice, but it takes a long time. Similarly, one can learn to perform other tasks via declarative instruction and by following the steps of instruction, one by one, whether it is to program a videocassette recorder, defrost a freezer, or clean a wound.

Procedural knowledge takes much longer to acquire, but, once practiced, a person can apply it more rapidly than declarative knowledge. Assembling the bird feeder for the third or fifth time is much faster than doing it the first time. Doing it 20, let alone 100 times, reduces the assembly time to a fraction (remember the power law of practice!). Procedural knowledge, however, also has its limitations: The practiced skill is tuned for the specific job and not easily transferred to another task. Practice at assembling bird feeders does not generalize to programming a videocassette recorder or cleaning a wound.

The specificity of skills is based on the directionality inherent in the production rules: IF this is the condition → THEN take this action. Even when the declarative knowledge used by a production rule is entirely symmetrical and would allow processing in both directions, that is not the case with production rules, according to ACT. Consider simple division problems such as $42 \div 7 = ?$ and $42 \div ? = 6$. Both problems are based on the same fact—namely, "42 divided by 7 equals 6." However, training a student on the first type of problem will strengthen the production in expression (7.9) but no other production.

(7.9) IF the goal is to divide 42 by 7,
    THEN write 6.

The directionality of productions has empirical implications: There should be an asymmetry between executing equivalent but directional skills. Teaching students half of the skill by itself does not give them the other half. Learning the vocabulary of a foreign language such as Russian illustrates directionality, as well. If you practice recall of English words in response to the Russian word (e.g., *uliza → street*), you still would have to learn recalling the Russian word when given the English term (e.g., *street → uliza*).

Working Memory: The Processor of ACT
The working memory of ACT fulfills the same functions described in Chapter 6; it processes information and it temporarily stores information—specifically, the information that the system is currently working on. Working memory includes the chunks and productions that are the most activated. The contents of working memory change dynamically as a result of environmental changes, the evolving goal structure, and cycling through the production rules of one of ACT's production systems. Once a production rule is fired, its actions are executed, thus changing the set of conditions for eligible productions. If the conditions of other production rules are satisfied, they will fire and, in turn, create a new set of conditions. Thus, production rules continue to fire and execute actions in successive cycles until a specific goal has been achieved.

Memory and Rational Analysis

According to Anderson's (1990) rational analysis, memory serves the goal of providing information needed at a specific time for a specific purpose. At a given moment, you may need to recall a phone number, remember a name, or use a certain technical term. You search your memory for a trace to meet that need. Rational analysis seeks to capture the gains and costs of the memory search. Turning up irrelevant traces increases the cost of the search because the system must continue to search, whereas finding and retrieving the needed trace represents a gain.

The key factor determining the accessibility of a memory trace is its history of use; the more a trace has been used, the greater its strength and the greater its accessibility. In order to determine historical and current trace use objectively, we would have to monitor a person's use of all facts at every moment. Although that is not possible, we can determine the use of facts in nonhuman retrieval systems. For example, we can objectively determine the use history of a book from a library and quantify the likelihood that a given book is retrieved, given its past use (Anderson & Schooler, 1991).

In the case of human memory, the best estimate of trace strength is provided by the amount of practice a learner devotes to acquiring a target fact or skill. The more a trace has been used in practice, the greater its strength and, hence, its activation will be. This relation has been established both for animal and human learning situations and has been incorporated in classical learning theories (e.g., Hull, 1943).

Trace strength is important for retrieval; in Anderson's ACT-R model, it is the variable that determines the activation of a trace, its availability at retrieval. According to the law of practice (Chapters 1, 4, and 5), trace strength is boosted by the amount of practice; and according to the law of forgetting, trace strength is weakened as a function of the delay between uses of the memory representation.

Finally, as do other memory models, Anderson's ACT-R model incorporates the assumption of resource limits. Specifically, ACT-R assumes a maximum level of the activation of the associations that a given stimulus can support. To simplify matters, it is assumed that given n

associations for a specific stimulus, each association shares equally in the total activation; that is, each association commands $1/n$ of the total activation available.

Research Applications of ACT

The ACT theory incorporates numerous assumptions subject to empirical evaluation. Among the ACT claims that Anderson and his colleagues have assessed are the following assumptions:

- There is an upper limit on activation.
- Access to procedural knowledge is asymmetrical.
- Production rules are valid units of procedural knowledge.
- Goal structures are psychologically real.
- Memory processes are optimized.

This section describes three research projects—the fan effect, learning from examples, and tutoring of LISP learning—to illustrate the ability of the ACT framework to account for the first three of these claims.

The Fan Effect

The fan introduced in Chapter 4 is readily handled by the activation theory of the ACT-R framework. Anderson (1974) demonstrated the effect in the context of a sentence recognition experiment. In the learning phase of the experiment, learners committed a set of sentences illustrated by (7.10) through (7.13) to memory. The sentences had the format *A person is in a location*. The sentences differed in the number of times specific agents and locations were mentioned in a set of sentences (indicated for each sentence in parentheses).

(**7.10**) The sailor is in the bank. (1-1)

(**7.11**) The hippie is in the park. (1-2)

(**7.12**) The doctor is in the church. (2-1)

(**7.13**) The doctor is in the park. (2-2)

These sentences were constructed so that people and locations were combined to varying degrees. The person in sentence (7.10) is named only once in the corpus of sentences; so is the location. By contrast, the person in sentence (7.13) and the location are shared twice.

In the recognition test, Anderson presented old sentences such as (7.10) through (7.13) mixed with distractor sentences (e.g., *The sailor is in the park*). In the distractor sentences, old persons were paired with old locations in new combinations. The subjects had to make a recognition decision for each test sentence. Thus, for any sentence taken from the list (7.10) through (7.13), the correct response would be *old*. Distractor sentences, however, should be judged as *new*.

Assuming that recognition times become slower as the activation of a proposition decreases, Anderson (1995a) predicted latency patterns of sentences from their activation levels. He assumed a maximum strength of 1.0 for both elements of a proposition, person and location. Accordingly, he calculated the strength for each sentence type as follows: For the 1-1 sentence (7.10), the association strength for each person and location was set at the maximum of 1.0, yielding the following activation for sentence (7.10):

$$\text{Strength } (7.10) = 1.0 + 1.0 = 2.0$$

For sentence (7.11), the strength for person was undivided at 1.0, but the location was shared by two facts, giving a value of 0.5. Thus, the activation for sentence (7.11) is as follows:

$$\text{Strength } (7.11) = 1.0 + 0.5 = 1.5$$

Sentence (7.12) also has a strength of 1.5. For sentence (7.13), both persons and locations are shared, giving strength values of 0.5 for each. The activation for sentence (7.13) is as follows:

$$\text{Strength } (7.13) = 0.5 + 0.5 = 1.0$$

In Anderson's experiments, the pattern of recognition latencies corresponded to the predictions: Recognition times were fastest for 1-1-type sentences, intermediate for 1-2-type and 2-1-type sentences, and slowest for 2-2-type sentences. In performance terms, the fan effect demonstrates that the more facts are associated with a concept, the longer it takes to retrieve the concept.

The Use of Skills Is Asymmetrical

In order to assess the prediction that access to procedural knowledge is asymmetrical, Anderson and Fincham (1994) had students learn an easy but novel skill—a simple numerical transformation task. The stimuli had the format *nnWnn*, where each *n* represents a digit, and *W* a letter (e.g., *24m33* and *68n78*). The stimuli were generated by simple rule-based numerical conversions. Each letter reflected the conversion rule for the stimulus. For example, stimulus *24m33* was generated by the *m*-rule, as specified in expression (7.14).

(7.14) *M*-rule

> Increase the first digit by 1
>
> Decrease the second digit by 1
>
> Example: $24 \to 33$
> First digit: $2 + 1 = 3$
> Second digit: $4 - 1 = 3$

The conversion *68n78* was generated according to the *n*-rule: Increase the first digit (e.g., 6) by 1 and leave the second digit (e.g., 8), as is to yield 7 and 8, respectively. Conceptually, these rules are symmetrical: They work equally going from right to left as they do from left to right. According to Anderson and Fincham, the corresponding production (7.15), however, is unidirectional.

(7.15) IF the goal is to use the *M*-rule
>   and the number *NN* has two digits,

THEN increase the first digit by 1
>   and decrease the second digit by 1.

Anderson and Fincham's (1994) study involved four stages: (1) an exposure phase, (2) a memorization phase, (3) a training phase, and (4) a transfer test. In the *exposure phase*, nine stimuli of the general format *nnWnn* were shown to learners without an explanation of the stimulus structure. In the *memorization phase*, learners memorized the nine stimuli. They were prompted by the letter and were asked to supply the digits. For example, given the prompt ___*m*___, the correct response was *24m33*. The third phase was the *training phase* during which learners were told of the underlying rule generating the stimuli. Half the subjects were given a letter and a two-digit number on the left (e.g., *nnW*___) and were told to type the two-digit number on the right. The remaining subjects were given the two-digit number on the right (e.g., ___*Wnn*) and were told to type the two-digit number on the left. The experiment concluded with the transfer phase in which learners received instructions to use the rule in both directions, going from left to right and from right to left.

Accuracy and latencies during training yielded the power function typical for skill acquisition with a continued but diminishing speedup as people solved the problems in successive training sessions. The transfer test revealed the asymmetry predicted by the ACT model: There were fewer errors and latencies were faster for the old direction, the direction that learners had practiced in the training phase. The average number of errors in the transfer trials was about 4% when the old direction was tested, but 8% when the opposite direction was tested. Response latencies were 4.0 seconds for same-direction conversions and 4.5 seconds for opposite conversions.

The point of the Anderson and Fincham study is that procedural knowledge is directional, and hence its access is asymmetrical. It is the directionality that makes the execution of productions efficient (Anderson, 1993). Anderson cited the example of language use in comprehension and production. In both cases, the same language knowledge is involved; however, different productions are required for comprehension and production.

A distinctive feature of the ACT project has been the conscious effort of applying the framework in real-world situations, especially in the teaching of problem-solving skills such as mathematics, computer programming, and physics. Among these are the Pittsburgh Urban Mathematics Project (PUMP), the navigation project, and the LISP tutor, described in the next section.

Tutoring in a Cognitive Skill: Computer Programming

LISP is a flexible and powerful computer language used in computer science research. The language consists of elemental functions that operate on numbers, on symbols (e.g., a, george-washington-bridge), and on lists (e.g., [a b c d], [memory is beautiful]). Using such primitive functions, LISP programs have been written for every purpose imaginable, from question answering to controlling a robot. Although LISP is conceptually easy, LISP learning appears to be chaotic: Students use a trial-and-error approach, often ignore error messages, and repeat previous errors (Anderson, Conrad, & Corbett, 1989).

Anderson and colleagues (1989) created the LISP tutor based on studies of the changing performance patterns of students learning LISP. The researchers developed a cognitive model of the learner in terms of the ACT framework and its production rules. They assumed that students' knowledge of LISP is first expressed in terms of declarative chunks and then converted into units of procedural memory, the production rules. After production rules are initially formed, further learning takes place. Learners change productions that are too general, too spe-

cific, or wrong, and streamline and strengthen those that work correctly.

In extensive research, Anderson and colleagues sought to validate these assumptions. Consider the assumption that the LISP programming skill is represented in terms of production rules. This assumption is important not only for the LISP tutor but also for the ACT framework, in general. Anderson discovered that the learning rate of students revealed a lawful and regular pattern when it was plotted in terms of production rules used to solve the problems rather than in terms of the number of problems solved in succession. The latter is, of course, the conventional measure to estimate learning.

In other words, when the learning unit was the problem number, there was no systematic trend in the data, as illustrated in Figure 7.9. However, when the units of analysis were the productions that are required to solve a problem, the systematic improvement in Figure 7.9 emerged. The contrast between the two func-

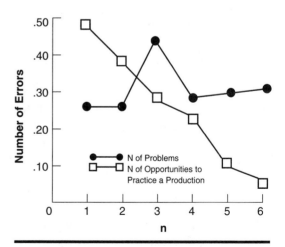

FIGURE 7.9 Mean errors per production as a function of serial position. The circles show performance plotted in terms of the problem number and the squares show performance in terms of the opportunities to practice a given production (Anderson, Conrad, & Corbett, 1989).

tions in Figure 7.9 is significant because it suggests that productions are valid units of procedural memory.

The LISP tutor is based on a model of an idealized learner that embodies 500 production rules (Anderson, 1993, p. 145). The model was derived, in turn, from empirical results reflecting students' learning of LISP functions, their use of examples and error patterns, among other data. The corpus of rules is hidden from the student who works with the tutor via an interface. All the student gets to see is a computer screen partitioned into two sections. One section presents the goal (e.g., writing a given function), and the other screen section provides space for the student to create the solution step by step. As long as the student's efforts are correct, the tutor remains silent; otherwise, it gives feedback that guides the learner toward the solution. Thus, the tutor works incrementally by diagnosing the present state of the learner's knowledge and by presenting problems to move him or her closer to the ideal model.

The LISP tutor was designed in order to assess the assumptions underlying ACT and to evaluate the feasibility of tutors that model the cognitive processes as learners acquire a skill. According to Anderson (1993), the data support the psychological validity of productions and the claims of the ACT theory for procedural skill learning. Since it was first introduced, the LISP tutor has become the prototype for tutors in other subjects, such as geometry and high school algebra.

Evaluation of ACT

Researchers in artificial intelligence seek to develop computer simulations of applications in the real world. Memory researchers want to create models that explain a body of data gathered in the laboratory. The ACT framework seeks to satisfy both of these goals. ACT successfully accounts for a wide range of data, including skill acquisition (Anderson, 1983a), processing in working memory (Anderson, Reder, & Lebiere, 1996; Kimberg & Farah, 1993), problem solving (Lovett & Anderson, 1996), and the effects reviewed in the previous section: the fan effect, the asymmetry effect, and the use of production rules as valid predictors of learning a cognitive skill. Anderson attributes particular importance to the latter result. Learning plotted in terms of the number of problems solved is irregular, but when plotted as a function of the opportunity of practicing the productions, a smooth curve is obtained (Figure 7.9). According to Anderson, production rules have the right grain size to capture human performance, whereas the units in neural nets (see Neural Network Models earlier in this Chapter) are too small and schemas (Chapter 4) are too global to do so.

In spite of the successes of the ACT approach, Anderson (1993) has acknowledged that it requires further development in order to address some vexing problems that remain (Barsalou, 1995). One of these is that models other than ACT can account for some of the data. The fan effect, for example, can be handled by other models that postulate an upper limit of activation and competition between associations.

A second problem is that although there are data to support the validity of production rules, there is no empirical support for any *specific* production rule. It remains for future research to determine whether the improvement in Figure 7.9 depends on the specific rules chosen by researchers or whether an alternative set of rules would yield similar results. Finally, the ACT framework still falls short of one of its own stated goals—the goal of neural plausibility. This means that the memory representations and processes envisioned in ACT would be consistent with current knowledge of neural processes. For example, what are the neural structures that correspond to the three major stores in ACT? How could chunks and production rules be realized in neural terms? And how do fact and skill learning take place in neural terms?

The real-world applications of ACT are of particular interest. The ACT framework has found applications outside the research laboratory for tutoring in geometry, physics, navigation, and computer programming. In collaboration with several Pittsburgh area schools, the ACT group developed the PUMP project (Pittsburgh Urban Mathematics Project). This project uses an ACT-based tutor that creates a cognitive model of the problem-solving processes of individual learners and designs problems tailored for each student. The brain of the tutor is a system of production rules that simulate the math principles as they are understood by an individual student. Via dynamically generated examples, the tutor nudges the student toward learning the principles required in solving the math problems.

During the first decade of the project, over 2,000 students participated in the program. According to the ACT home page on the World Wide Web (http://act.psy.cmu.edu/), these students required one-third of the time to master a subject and increased their test scores by about one standard deviation! However, to date, there are no published empirical evaluations of the ACT-based tutors and other intelligent tutoring systems. Researchers need to document the claims achieved under the tutor and compare it with human tutors, traditional classroom instruction, and a combination of these approaches (Anderson, 1993). Nevertheless, the fact that ACT has found educational applications is a major milestone in its own right. It represents an example for the development of similar intelligent tutors in the future.

CONCLUSION

Memory researchers, like other scientists, use models in order to organize a wealth of data, to generate new research questions, and to make new discoveries. Judging by the popularity of memory models, researchers have been successful in each of these goals. Memory models have evolved from relatively modest beginnings in the early 1960s to the global models of the 1980s and 1990s that encompass large domains of the field. Early models were not intended as "general models of verbal learning or even paired associate learning. Instead they [applied] only to a very specific kind of paired associate experiment" (Kintsch, 1970, p. 61). The research strategy was to investigate a phenomenon in its simplest form first and address larger problems later.

Researchers discovered, however, that memory was too complex to be synthesized piece by piece in the manner of a Lego construction set. As in other domains of cognition, important aspects of the subject are lost when one studies effects isolated from related phenomena and when one overlooks interactions among component structures and processes. Consider, for example, the progress made by investigating the relation between encoding and retrieval (Chapter 4) or by documenting the dissociations between different subsystems in working memory (Chapter 6).

There has been a steady progression in the scope of models introduced in Chapters 6 and 7, beginning with Waugh and Norman's (1965) model and culminating in the PDP and ACT models. The Waugh and Norman model of primary and secondary memory was among the first to include data from several paradigms; such as the free-recall task, the distractor task, and the probe digit task (Chapter 6). The model emphasized the relation between short-term and long-term memory and specified their joint contribution to performance in each of these tasks. Atkinson and Shiffrin (1968) specified structure and processes in each of the memory stores and addressed additional list-learning phenomena. Raaijmakers and Shiffrin's (1981) SAM model is an extension of the Atkinson and Shiffrin model. It incorporates research advances on the interdependence of list items, context cues, and their memory representations, and on the relation between encoding and retrieval as expressed in the encoding specificity principle. The model has been successfully applied to a broad sample of list-learning phenomena from recognition superiority to the partial cueing effect. However, it has not been extended to memory for skills, nor have its authors looked for neural analogs.

The PDP and ACT frameworks are more global than traditional list-learning models. The PDP approach emphasizes the neural foundations of cognition in that its processing assumptions are constrained by our knowledge of the nervous system. The scope of PDP is broad, extending well beyond memory to include related domains such as attention, recognition, and comprehension. The ACT architecture includes a declarative memory, a working memory, and, via its procedural memory, a performance component to handle both list-learning effects and a range of cognitive skills from recognition to problem solving. The ACT research group has expressly sought application of the theory outside of the laboratory while remaining faithful to the psychological validity of its assumptions.

Model builders of all stripes face multiple hurdles—whether it is the data the model can handle, the validity of its parameters, or the constraints on the model. Theorists typically overcome the first of these hurdles by modifying or adding to the components of the model—the parameters, assumptions, and structures. Hebbian learning, for example, is not capable of learning correlated input patterns. This hurdle is overcome by adjusting the manner of weight change in the delta learning procedure. A model may incorporate parameters that have not been tested for their psychological validity (Roediger, 1993). A model may also become too powerful and handle too many data (Massaro, 1988). Alternatively, it may become so complex that it is hard to know which part accounts for its ability to account for the data. Ultimately, these issues will become moot as the success of models will depend on their utility in applications in the real world beyond the research laboratory.

ENDNOTES

1. The account of recognition memory given here is known as the *strength theory* of recognition memory. As noted earlier, it is an adaptation from the theory of signal detection (Swets et al., 1961).

2. In order to simplify matters, my description omits reference to inhibitory processes in the network.

CHAPTER 8

MEMORY FROM INFANCY TO OLD AGE: DEVELOPMENTAL CHANGES

Memory in infancy and childhood improves by leaps and bounds. Babies recognize their parents within the first few weeks, possibly within the first few days, of life. During the first months, infants absorb numerous perceptual, motor, and communication skills. They notice changes made to their rooms; they remember objects that are missing; they recognize the voices of different people; and, of course, they learn all kinds of motor movements from crawling to walking.

At the other end of the age continuum, changes in memory are less dramatic, certainly less so than is commonly believed. Although there is a loss of brain mass in the elderly, people neither lose tens of thousands of brain cells everyday after age 30, as many believe (Loftus, 1980), nor are older people close to being memory impaired. Younger people sometimes tend to overlook their own absentmindedness in favor of the stereotypical grandpa who always seems to tell the same story twice or of the grandma who seems to keep forgetting to take her medicine. The fact is memory does decline in older adulthood, but it clearly is not impaired. On the contrary, many of the most significant achievements are made by people when they are older. Charles Darwin published his seminal work *The Descent of Man* when he was over 60

years old. Grandma Moses turned to painting for the first time in her life at the age of 76, gaining international fame in her eighties. Hans Bethe, the Cornell University physicist and Nobel laureate, continued to be professionally active well into his nineties. The list of celebrities who remained active and blossomed in later life can easily be continued, including British prime minister and wartime leader Winston Churchill, cardiologist William DeBakey, architect Buckminster Fuller, and cognitive scientist Herbert Simon, among others.

This chapter addresses the memory changes at the two ends of the age continuum by reviewing research on memory development during childhood and late adulthood. Each of the two sections of the chapter reviews changes in memory for facts, in memory for skills, and in working memory. As we will see, it is easier to *describe* changes in these domains than to *explain* them. Many explanations have been proposed for memory development in childhood, on the one hand, and in older adulthood, on the other. The changes have been attributed to a variety of factors, including changes in content knowledge, metamemory, and cognitive resources. *Content knowledge* refers to knowledge of the person's social and physical environment; *metamemory* includes one's knowledge of memory and of the use of memory-enhancing strategies; and *cognitive resources* refer to the mental capacities required for information processing, whether they are understood in terms of storage capacity or processing speed. Research has shown that these factors play out differently in childhood and old adulthood.

Consider the differences in language and content knowledge during the two periods. Whereas infants are preverbal and not able to use language, older adults tend to retain their linguistic ability throughout their lives. The knowledge and language differences have consequences for the manner in which infants and older adults form memories. An adult can associate new facts and experiences with previous knowledge; indeed, we know that linking new information with familiar knowledge is one of the most effective ways of acquiring new declarative memories (Chapter 4). Infants cannot use such elaborative encoding; older adults may not routinely use elaboration, but they can be trained to do so. The knowledge and language differences also necessitate different research methods in children and older adults. Verbal memory tests using paired associates, words, sentences, and stories are not possible until the child understands and produces language. Rather, developmental researchers use such performance measures of learning and retention as conditioning, habituation, and reproduction (Bauer, 1996).

To be sure, the *rate* of acquiring linguistic and world knowledge in the early years is remarkable. Children learn new words at a stupendous rate, surpassing the rate of learning at any other age and certainly the rate attainable in the research laboratory (Landauer & Dumais, 1997). They acquire highly complex syntactic principles and rich semantic information largely without formal instruction—an accomplishment that is far more difficult even for college students, let alone the elderly.

Our review, then, will show commonalities as well as differences in memory changes during the early and late years of life. As we shall see, changes in content knowledge and metamemory have been given more prominence in childhood than in late adulthood, whereas changes in cognitive resources have been invoked at both ends of the spectrum.

MEMORY DEVELOPMENT DURING CHILDHOOD

At birth, each child is endowed with a rich repertoire of perceptual, motor, and cognitive skills. The newborn is able to perceive stimuli from different modalities and to react to stimuli with both reflexive and learned responses. However, such neural structures as the prefrontal lobes, the hippocampal region, the visual system, and the corpus callosum, among others, still continue to mature (e.g., Diamond, 1991; Bachevalier, 1992; Kalat, 1995). During the first 18 months after birth, there is a period of rapid growth of synapses and of neural circuits in the prefrontal region. The improved performance on a variety of nonverbal memory tasks, including the delayed response task, during this period has been attributed to the maturation of the prefrontal lobes. The visual system is undergoing rapid growth as well, both in animals (see Chapter 3) and in humans (Hickey & Peduzzi, 1987). Although many structures of the retino-cortical pathway such as the fovea, the lateral geniculate nucleus, and the receptive fields in the visual cortex are in place, they are still not fully developed.

The phenomenon of childhood amnesia—the inability to recall events experienced early in life—has been attributed, in part, to the immaturity of neural structures (Nelson, 1993a; Siegler, 1991). Of course, there are concomitant cognitive factors, as well. Importantly, the child's linguistic competence is still developing and lack of these skills is likely to produce difficulty during encoding. Even if the child does encode certain events, as the encoding specificity principle (Chapter 4) informs us, later retrieval will be difficult, if not impossible, because linguistic and cognitive structures have changed.

However, neither neural nor cognitive changes are so profound that the child cannot remember anything, as suggested by Freud's use of the term *infantile amnesia*. Rather, even preverbal infants are capable of remembering events and facts (Bauer, 1996; Howe & Courage, 1993; Myers, Clifton, & Clarkson, 1987) and children are able to remember significant information, such as the birth of a sibling well into adulthood (Usher & Neisser, 1993; see Chapter 9).

Event Memory in Preverbal Infants

In adults, the clearest evidence of event memory consists of *verbal reports;* an adult can name people involved in an event and describe the actions that occurred. The verbal report serves as a window into the person's memory. Even though there is no such window to tap the memory of preverbal infants, scientists have succeeded in doing so by behavioral methods, including the habituation paradigm, the conjugate conditioning paradigm, and the imitation paradigm. In each of these paradigms, stimuli or events are presented to the infant on repeated occasions. Changes in the infant's reaction to the stimuli are taken as a telltale sign of retention.

Habituation in Infants
Even infants only several days old exhibit the kind of nonassociative learning known as *habituation* (Chapter 3). When one claps one's hands every few seconds, the infant startles reflexively. After the clapping has continued for a couple of minutes, the startle reflex diminishes visibly. Has the infant become too fatigued to respond? That fatigue is not the reason for habit-

uation is easily demonstrated by presenting another stimulus, whether it is a sound or a light flash. The new stimulus produces dishabituation, the recurrence of the startle response, whereas the old stimulus no longer elicits a reaction. The habituation technique rests on the principle that infants are attracted by novel events but lose interest in familiar events.

The habituation paradigm has been widely used to investigate memory in infants, whether it involves memory for the number of objects, for conceptual categories, or for the dimensions of a stimulus. We consider an imaginative study cited by Siegler (1991, p. 176) to illustrate the habituation technique. The study sought to examine recognition memory in 5-month-old infants for the stimulus attributes of objects. The researchers varied the form, orientation, size, and color of the object. For example, during the study phase, they presented a large, black, arrow pointing up, as shown in Figure 8.1A. In recognition testing, the old stimulus was shown together with a new stimulus—for example, one selected from among stimuli (1) through (4) in Figure 8.1B. These stimuli differed from the old one in one or more dimensions, as illustrated in the figure.

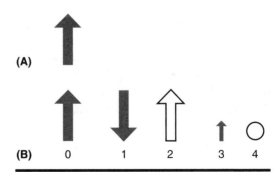

(A)

(B)   0   1   2   3   4

FIGURE 8.1 Habituation paradigm is used to assess retention of stimulus attributes. *(A)* Stimulus presented during inspection period. *(B)* During testing, old stimulus (0) is paired with one of the new stimuli (1–4). (See text for further explanation.)

According to the logic of the habituation paradigm, looking at the new stimulus would indicate that the child retained the memory of the old stimulus. Indeed, in immediate testing, the children chose the new object in all the paired comparisons. After 15 minutes, the children looked at the stimulus of the new color (2) and the new form (4), indicating that they remembered these attributes of the target stimulus but not its direction or size (choices 1 and 3 in Figure 8.1B). After an interval of 24 hours, the children remembered only the form, as revealed by their choice of test stimuli of a different form (e.g., choice 4 in Figure 8.1B).

The habituation paradigm has also been used to demonstrate category learning in infants. In category-learning studies, infants ranging in age between 9 and 24 months are shown a set of instances from a familiar category (e.g., fruits, birds, and furniture) during the inspection phase. In the testing phase, old and new instances of the previously seen category and an item from a previously unseen category are presented (e.g., a car, a horse, or a flower). It turns out that the infants tend to look longer at the member of the new category than at items from the old category, irrespective of the categories themselves. Roberts (1988), for example, had 9-month old infants look at pictures of several birds, all having distinctive shapes and beaks. In the testing phase, the infants were shown pictures of the previous birds, of new birds, and of a horse. They did not look at the birds, whether old or new. The only stimulus that held their interest was the horse, the new category. The choice of the item belonging to the new category suggests that infants do not just recognize specific instances but that they abstract the category.

The Conjugate Reinforcement Paradigm

The conjugate reinforcement paradigm has proven to be a fertile tool for assessing memory in infants of 2 months and older. The paradigm uses instrumental learning as a tool for detecting retention. In instrumental conditioning, the person makes a response in order to gain a reward, whether it is a piece of candy, the opportunity of being exposed to a favorite stimulus, or social approval (Chapter 3). Developmental researchers have adapted this paradigm in different ways in order to investigate memory in infants. In the simplest case, a single response, (e.g., a sucking response) is required to produce the reward, whether it is to look at a visual display or listen to the mother's voice. In discrimination learning, the infant must make different responses in the presence of different stimuli. In one discrimination study, newborns successfully learned to receive a sweet liquid as a reward by turning their heads to one side in response to a buzzer and to the other side in response to a tone (Siqueland & Lipsitt, 1966).

In the conjugate reinforcement paradigm, the infant is placed in a crib with a mobile suspended over the crib. The critical target information is typically displayed on the mobile (e.g., a geometrical pattern, a picture of an animal or a toy, or a particular shape). The experimenter connects the child's ankle via a string to the mobile so that ankle kicking activates the mobile. Here are the details on training and retention testing for 2-month-old infants: A training session usually lasts 15 minutes and consists of three parts: an initial 3-minute baseline period, a 9-minute acquisition period, and a final 3-minute testing period. It is during the acquisition period that the ankle is linked with the mobile, giving the infant control over the mobile movements. When the infant detects the relation between his or her kicking and the mobile movements, the kicking rate typically increases relative to the baseline, thus indicating that the infant has learned the contingency between these events.

During testing, either the same mobile or one that differs in certain attributes is placed over the crib, and the infant's ankle is attached to a hook in order to measure the rate of kicking.

Typically, infants continue to kick in the immediate testing period, thus giving evidence of short-term retention. To demonstrate long-term retention, the infant is taken out of the crib and returned after intervals ranging from 1 minute to over 40 days. According to Rovee-Collier (1997), the conjugate reinforcement paradigm is equivalent to recognition testing in adults with the rate of kicking representing *yes* or *no* responses. When the infants recognize the target on the mobile, they communicate *yes* by kicking at a rate above the baseline. If they do not recognize the stimulus, the kicking rate does not exceed the baseline rate.

The conjugate reinforcement paradigm has enabled researchers to make important discoveries on infant memory, such as the following:

— Recognition improves as infants grow older. The 2-month-old infant remembers stimuli for 3 days, the 3-month-olds do so for 1 week, and the 18-month-olds do so for 13 weeks.

— Infants are susceptible to retroactive interference. For example, when 3-month-old infants are trained with one mobile in session 1, trained with a different mobile in session 2, and tested after a 24-hour delay on the first mobile, they do not remember the original mobile.

— Spacing improves retention, but only up to a limit. For instance, 3-month-old infants exhibit better recognition after an 8-day delay when individual training sessions were separated by 2 days rather than 1 day. However, when the interval between successive training sessions was as long as 4 days, there was no advantage of spacing the training sessions.

— Performance is improved when the infant is given a reminder during the retention interval between study and testing. The infant is returned for a brief period to the crib and watches the mobile set in motion by the experimenter. Such interpolated exposure is assumed to reactivate or prime the original memory record, much as occurs in implicit memory situations with adults.

The conjugate reinforcement paradigm is very versatile and has been used to evaluate the influence of a variety of factors on retention, including the number of studied items, the experimental context, and the child's affect during learning and testing (Rovee-Collier, 1997).

The Imitation Paradigm

In the imitation paradigm retention is evaluated via a reproduction method (Bauer, 1996). The experimenter uses props to model a relatively simple event, such as giving a teddy bear a bath. Following the modeling session, the child is given the props and asked to imitate the experimenter's model. Bauer used both familiar and unfamiliar events as target events. One of the familiar scenes involved putting a teddy bear to bed. This scenario included the following props: a stuffed bear, a doll bed, a small blanket, and a storybook. As she modeled the going-to-bed scene, Bauer narrated the events by saying, "Let's make teddy go night. Put teddy in bed. Cover teddy with the blanket. Read teddy a story."

Target events differed in terms of their familiarity. In addition to familiar events, Bauer used unfamiliar events so as to ensure that children did not merely reproduce routine events but were able to retain novel information. As an unfamiliar event, among others, Bauer selected the building of a gong. Props for the gong scene included a bar, a hooked metal plate, and a mallet to serve as the gong. Target events also differed in terms of the number of modeling steps involved. The simplest events were two-step events, such as "making car go." In this case, the first step involved unfolding a hinged track to form an incline and the second step consisted of releasing the car at the top of the slope and letting it roll down.

Recall testing occurred either immediately or one week after the modeling session. In testing, the props of the target events were placed in front of the child with the instruction to imitate the sequence modeled by the experimenter. "Now you make bear do X, just like I did." Retention was assessed in terms of the correct order of the steps recalled. For a three-step sequence, for example, there was a maximum score of two points—one point for correctly reproducing steps 1 and 2, and another point for reproducing steps 2 and 3.

Using the imitation procedure, researchers found that between ages 1 and 2, immediate reproduction of novel three-step events improves steadily. As they grow older, children retain longer sequences: By 24 months of age, five steps are correctly recalled; by 30 months of age, eight-step sequences are correctly reproduced. In addition, as children grow older, sequences are retained over longer retention intervals. Thus, even 13-month-olds can remember a three-step sequence up to 8 months!

Thanks to the habituation, conjugate reinforcement, and imitation paradigms, researchers have been able to document the capabilities of infant memory. In so doing, they refuted what Bauer (1996) described as the "tenacious and influential assumption that children at this age range simply are unable to remember the events of their lives" (p. 39). These nonverbal analogues of verbal reports demonstrate that (1) children aged 1 and 2 years old are able to retain events for as long as several months and (2) event memory in children is determined by the same factors as in adults, including the number of learning trials, the length of the study period, the context, the availability of reminders, and interference.

Memory for Skills

Every parent knows that infants have a prodigious capacity for the acquisition of cognitive and motor skills. Infants quickly learn to recognize their mothers' faces and voices; they learn to sit up, roll over, grasp moving targets, and walk. In addition, they learn to communicate at a rapid rate, at first nonverbally and then verbally, beginning around their first birthday. In research laboratories, memory for skills in young children is assessed in implicit memory tests and by tracking the acquisition of cognitive and procedural skills. In each of these cases, memory is expressed through improved performance after prior exposure rather than through explicit recall. According to several theorists, such procedural memory is developmentally more primitive, occurring earlier than explicit fact memory (e.g., Fuster, 1995; Nelson, 1993a, 1993b; Reber, 1993; Tulving, 1985).

Implicit Memory

Implicit memory tasks involve the successive presentation of stimuli and the demonstration of facilitated performance on subsequent presentations. Implicit memory in children has been investigated using both verbal and nonverbal materials. Consider an experiment involving pictures in which children aged 4, 5, and 10 years first identified a set of pictures of animals, vehicles, body parts, furniture, and utensils (Hayes & Hennessy, 1996). Following a 48-hour delay, the children were shown fragments of the pictures they had previously seen and fragments of new pictures. If a fragment was not identified correctly, more detail was added until the picture was successfully identified. This incremental exposure yielded an identification threshold for each picture. The researchers found that each age group exhibited the priming effect in that the identification threshold was lower for old than for new fragments. The priming effect did not differ as a result of age. However, in a control condition to assess explicit recognition memory, performance improved from ages 4 to 5 years.

The dissociation between implicit and explicit memory measures as a function of age has implications for general theories of memory. Together with other lines of evidence, the dissociation has been interpreted as support for two kinds of memory systems: explicit and implicit memory (Chapters 5 and 11).

The discussion thus far has shown the great learning capacity in infancy and early childhood. It is during this period that the roots are formed for the acquisition of a wide range of skills, whether they are cognitive, motor, or artistic skills. Some of these skills (e.g., musical skills) require hard and sustained practice; others (e.g., the child's native language) are learned without apparent effort.

Cognitive Skills

Research on the development of cognitive skills owes its existence to Swiss psychologist Jean Piaget (1896–1980). Based on his observations of children and adolescents as they solved a range of problems—including occluded object problems, arithmetic problems, and the balance-scale problem—Piaget proposed a four-stage framework of skill development. From birth to 2 years, during the *sensorimotor period,* children's competencies are largely limited to motor responses. There is evidence of cognitive development, as well, as is illustrated by the developing understanding of the permanence of objects. When an object is removed from view from a 5-month-old, he or she will not look for the object, suggesting that the baby does not understand that the object still exists. By age 2, however, the child will look for the object, because he or she has acquired the understanding of object permanence (see Diamond, 1991, for a neuroscience perspective).

The period from ages 2 to 7 is known as the *preoperational period.* This is a time of explosive skill development, including the development of language, thought, and representational skills, although the child's perspective of the environment is still limited. Children of this age look at their surroundings from their points of view, or, as Piaget termed it, from an *egocentric perspective.* During the *concrete-operational period,* which spans from ages 7 to 11, children

become aware that there are perspectives of the environment other than their own. Children of this age exhibit the ability to categorize objects in terms of size, color, or shape, thus indicating incipient abstract thought. During adolescence, the *formal-operational period* begins; it reflects the children's ability to reason abstractly and formulate hypothetical outcomes of events.

Many refinements and alternatives of Piaget's framework of the development of cognitive skills have been proposed, including the approaches of Elkind (1961), Diamond (1991), Flavell (1971), and Siegler (e.g., 1996). Consider Siegler's (1996) *adaptive strategy choice model (ASCM)* to represent the development of a specific content skill such as arithmetic problem solving. This skill is characterized by a change in strategies the developing child uses to generate answers to simple arithmetic problems.

Ask a 3-year-old how much 2 + 3 is and the child will usually guess the answer. Answers are generally inaccurate up to 4½ years of age. Between ages 4½ and 6, children tend to count using their fingers, an overt strategy. By first grade, children start to use the *min* strategy, counting from the larger addend (e.g., 3, 4, 5). As they progress toward third grade, the children use a retrieval strategy, which involves retrieving the answer from memory and producing a fast and typically accurate response. When asked how they found the answer, the children tend to say, "I just knew it." Figure 8.2 shows the changing use of strategies for children from grades 1, 2, and 3.

Siegler formulated the ASCM to capture the evolution of arithmetic and such other skills as time telling, locomotion, game playing, and decision making. According to Siegler's model, the child acquires strategies that produce answers to the problems. For each strategy, a record is kept of its success history in terms of speed and accuracy. When the problem is encountered again, a strategy is chosen on the basis of its past success or fitness. Alternative

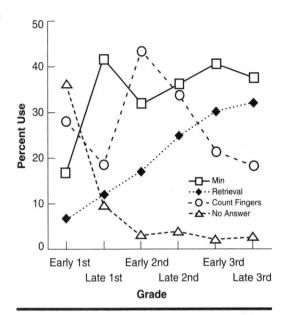

FIGURE 8.2   Change in use of strategies in Swedish first-, second-, and third-graders' addition strategies.

strategies remain available and may be chosen depending on circumstances. Siegler's ASCM reflects the adaptive character of human performance that has become a feature of such other models as John Anderson's ACT model (Chapter 7). Both models assume a parallel between cognitive changes and biological evolution.

The Role of Practice

Motor skills and cognitive skills, including language skills, depend on practice. By age 5, a child is a highly accomplished speaker of his or her native language. Syntax, vocabulary, and semantics have achieved a remarkable level of proficiency—all without explicit instruction. There is no doubt that humans are endowed with a special language instinct that predisposes them to acquire the principles of syntax and semantics as well as a large vocabulary (Pinker, 1994). Nevertheless, cases of language-deprived children demonstrate that linguistic competence is the result of continued practice (Rymer, 1993).

Consider the acquisition of vocabulary, which is usually considered a declarative memory, as a proxy for linguistic knowledge in general.

According to an estimate by Landauer, a 20-year-old undergraduate has command of 100,000 words (Landauer & Dumais, 1997). This is an enormous feat; it means that the person must have acquired words at an average rate of 15 words a day beginning at age 2. During certain periods in early childhood, the rate would probably be still higher, which is a greater rate of learning than has been ever observed in a laboratory. Clearly, language enjoys a privileged status among cognitive skills.

To become competent in such other skills as arithmetic, athletics, and music requires deliberate practice. Deliberate practice is more than merely using the skill; it involves exercising the skill, receiving feedback on performance, and correcting any errors. Expert musicians undergo this kind of rigorous training beginning in early childhood. For instance, Mozart started the violin when he was only 3 years old and thereafter continued to practice daily for 10 hours or more. Research has shown that the most renowned pianists have followed a disciplined schedule of many weekly hours of practice from as early as age 4 (Ericsson, Krampe, & Tesch-Römer, 1993). The effects of such practice accumulate over the years, increasing the advantage of the experts, as shown in Figure 8.3.

From the perspective of Ericsson and colleagues (1993), Figure 8.3 reveals a good news versus bad news contrast common in memory studies. The good news is that, within reasonable limits, every child can aspire to become an expert pianist, baseball player, or mathematician, provided he or she is willing to work at it. The bad news is that a person has to start very early in life to accumulate the requisite hours of practice. We will return to the issue of practice in subsequent sections and see how practice helps experts to maintain a skill well into older adulthood.

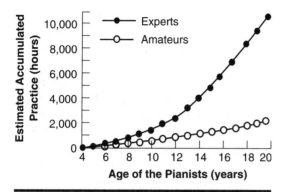

FIGURE 8.3 Accumulated hours of practice estimated on the basis of weekly practice for expert and amateur pianists. The estimates were obtained by extrapolating from the weekly practice periods of the pianists for each year.

Memory for Facts

Memory for facts includes semantic memory, episodic memory, and autobiographical memory. According to Nelson (1993a, 1993b), memory serves as an adaptive system guiding present action and predicting future outcomes, with each kind of memory fulfilling a distinctive ecological function during early development. *Semantic memory* includes generic scriptlike information of frequently recurring events, such as having a snack and going to the baby-sitter's. This knowledge enables the child to make inferences and to predict future events. *Episodic memory* refers to memories of specific events, such as what I had for breakfast this morning, and of novel events, such as the baby-sitter not being home.

Autobiographical memory includes particular episodic memories woven into a person's memory of self. Such memories are personally significant, affording a sense of connectedness with one's past. Nelson illustrates the contrast between episodic and autobiographical memories with the following example: What I had for breakfast this morning is an *episodic memory,* whereas the first professional paper I delivered

at a conference is part of my *autobiographical memory.* Autobiographical memories develop at around age 3, thus marking the end of childhood amnesia, the inability to recall experiences dating from the first few years of life. We will consider autobiographical memories in greater detail in Chapter 9. Next, we will review the development of semantic memory and episodic memory during childhood.

Semantic Memory

Concepts. The increasing vocabulary of a child reflects an increase in the number of concepts the child knows. For each word, the child gains an implicit knowledge of the underlying concept, the function it plays in sentences, and the relation it forms with other concepts, including its possible predicates (Keil, 1989). As an example of such a knowledge base, consider the network representation of a child's dinosaur knowledge generated by two researchers at the University of Pittsburgh, Chi and Koeske (1983). The scientists chose for their investigation a 4½-year-old boy who was an expert on dinosaurs. The boy's parents had exposed him to information on dinosaurs for the preceding two years by reading to him about dinosaurs and by giving him books and models. As is typical of many children of his age, this boy was fascinated by the subject and came to know the names of 40 dinosaurs, their habitats, diets, features, and the relations among different dinosaur species.

To elicit the boy's knowledge, the scientists asked him to tell them the names of all the dinosaurs he knew. He came up with 46 names, including such familiar ones as Brontosaur, Diplodocus, and Triceratops, as well as less familiar names such as Polacanthus, Elasmosaur, and Struthiomimus. He also listed several extinct mammals (e.g., Wooly Rhinoceros) that were pictured in his dinosaur books. To assess the child's knowledge about individual dinosaurs, the experimenters played a clue game with the boy, where they named the properties of a specific dinosaur and the boy guessed the corresponding name.

Using the naming task and the clue game, Chi and Koeske constructed the boy's semantic network, including category links and property links. They estimated the category links by establishing links for dinosaurs that the boy generated in succession in the naming task (e.g., Triceratops and Stegosaur). The researchers identified two clusters of dinosaurs in the boy's

memory: armored dinosaurs and large plant-eating dinosaurs (see Figure 8.4). Not surprisingly, in a recall task in which the experimenters presented him with a list of dinosaurs, the boy grouped the dinosaurs in terms of his semantic network. He tended to separate the names of the armored dinosaurs from those of the plant eaters. Overall, he recalled those dinosaurs best (e.g., Stegosaur) that had many links with others in the network. This effect reflects the common finding—whether in item, sentence, or story re-

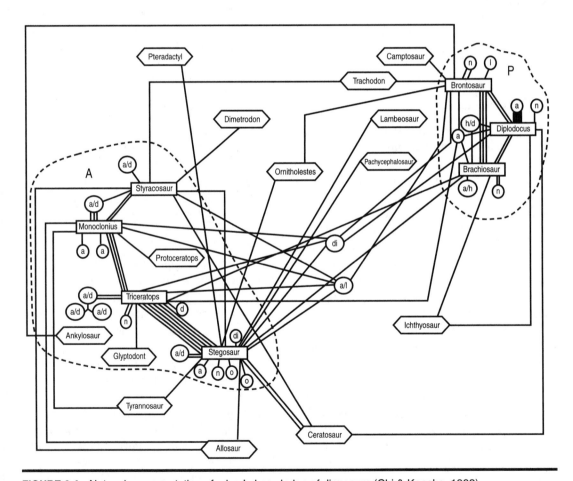

FIGURE 8.4   Network representation of a boy's knowledge of dinosaurs (Chi & Koeske, 1983).
(A = armored; P = giant plant eater; a = appearance; d = defense mechanism; di = diet;
h = habitat; l = locomotion; n = nickname; o = other properties.)

call—that well-connected units are retained best (Kintsch & van Dijk, 1978; Mandler & Johnson, 1977; van den Broek, 1990).

Scripts. Memory for frequently occurring events—such as going to the grocery store, attending a birthday party, or baking cookies—is assumed to be represented in generic knowledge structures referred to as *scripts* (Nelson, 1993b; Schank & Abelson, 1977; Chapter 4). A script includes agents, roles, and props in an abstract framework without specifying details. Thus, the birthday party script includes slots for guests, candles, a birthday cake, and hats, without such details as the name of the guests, the flavor of the cake, or the color of the hats. Based on their knowledge of scripts, children are able to understand events and stories and to predict future actions. Because of their predictive aspect, Nelson (1993a, p. 3) believes that scripts have a greater functional significance than memory for episodes that are "one-time happenings." Beginning at age 3, children can recount routine events as illustrated in Figure 8.5 (Nelson & Gruendel, 1981).

Children learn new schemas such as kindergarten routines very quickly. However, the representations of these routines are abstract. As a result, children have difficulties retelling details of episodes even with extensive prompting from adults (Nelson & Ross, 1980). Children's descriptions of the events are nonspecific and abstract, thus reflecting generic script knowledge in the absence of specific event knowledge (Hudson & Nelson, 1986). Nelson (1993b) considers the underdeveloped state of episodic memory during this period as the principal reason for adults' failure to recall early childhood events (see Clinical Views of Early Childhood Memories in Chapter 9).

Scripts influence children's retention of story events as well as of everyday events. Thus, children tend to believe, as do adults, that a typi-

FIGURE 8.5 A script for baking cookies, from ages 3 to 8 years (Nelson & Gruendel, 1981).

Age 3 Years, 1 Month
Well, you bake them and eat them.

Age 4 Years, 5 Months
My mommy puts chocolate chips inside the cookies. Then ya put 'em in the oven. . . . Then we take them out on the table and eat them.

Age 6 Years, 9 Months
Add three cups of butter. . . . Add three lumps of butter, two cups of sugar, one cup of flour. Mix it up . . . knead it. Get it in a pan, put in the oven. Bake it. . . . Set it up to 30. Take it out and it'll be cookies.

Age 8 Years, 8 Months
First, you need a bowl, a bowl, and you need about two eggs and chocolate chips and an eggbeater. And then you gotta crack the eggs open and put it in a bowl an ya gotta get the chips and mix it together. And put it in a stove for about 5 or 10 minutes, and then you have cookies. Then ya eat them!

cal event was presented in a story when, in fact, it was not (Bower, Black, & Turner, 1979). Children also tend to retain information that is atypical for a given scenario, as Hudson (1988) documented. Hudson distinguished between two kinds of atypical statements: disruptive and irrelevant actions. In the context of grocery shopping, for example, a shopper dropping a carton of eggs represents a *disruptive action,* whereas John tying his shoe illustrates an *irrelevant action.* Using recall to tap memory, Hudson (1988) observed a disruption effect with better recall of disruptive actions than of typical and irrelevant actions. The reason for this disruption effect is that disrupting actions cause subsequent problems that must be dealt with. From story research with adult subjects, it is well known that such statements are particularly well recalled (Davidson, 1994; Mandler & Johnson, 1977; van den Broek, 1990; Chapter 4).

Episodic Memory

Research on the development of episodic memory in childhood has focused on the role of the increase in semantic knowledge, in the use of strategies, and in metamemory in the encoding and retrieval of information. It was Tulving (1983) himself who acknowledged the role of semantic memory in the encoding of episodic memories, which he defined as recollections of "temporally dated" episodes or events. People remember events to the extent that they can elaborate and integrate them in terms of their general world knowledge (Chapter 4). *Metamemory* refers to the person's knowledge of basic memory processes in a given task. Such knowledge includes an understanding of the demands inherent in different tasks, such as recall and recognition, and of the strategies the learner can use to improve performance in these situations. Metamemory research was introduced by Hart (e.g., 1967) in research with adult subjects. However, it flourished in the context of studies of the development of memory in children (Flavell, Friedrichs, & Hoyt, 1970), because developmental memory researchers attributed the age-related memory improvement to an improvement in monitoring and strategic processes as children grow older.

Encoding Processes. Adults remember a list of words best when they can associate the items with prior knowledge, with their semantic memory (Chapter 4). This is no different in children. As the knowledge base of children grows, so do the opportunities for meaningful encoding and improved recall. In agreement with this view, children elaborate more as they get older (Paris & Lindauer, 1976) and they retain information better from domains that they are interested in and familiar with, whether it is dinosaurs, sports, or cars.

Organization. Knowledge helps learners take advantage of the organization provided with the stimulus materials. We know from recall studies involving adults that word lists are better recalled when they include words from a small set of categories than when they come from diverse categories. The beneficial effect of categorization has also been found in children. O'Sullivan (1996) used two 14-word lists; one consisted of 7 animals and 7 parts of the body randomly mixed, whereas the other list included 14 conceptually distinct items (e.g, boat, dandelion, slippers, spoon, wall, corn, hammer, spider, house, etc.). Children from grades 1, 3, and 5 participated in the experiment. At each grade level, recall was better for the categorized list than the inconsistent list.

Are first-graders aware of the advantage bestowed by the organization in the stimulus materials? O'Sullivan sought to find an answer to this question by collecting four metamemory measures: (1) the children's estimates of their own performance, (2) their estimates of the effort required to achieve that level of performance, (3) the reasons given by the children for their recall performance, and (4) the accounts they gave of the strategies they might have used in recall. At each grade level, the children estimated correctly that their recall would be better for categorized than for random lists. However, first-graders were not able to provide any reason for their expectations. Almost all of the third-graders and fifth-graders were aware that the related list was based on two categories and they gave this as the reason for the better recall and for having to spend less effort on the task. Interestingly, however, even the third- and fifth-graders were not able to fully appreciate the advantage of the categorized lists. For reasons not yet understood, the children consistently underestimated their recall level on these lists. The point of these findings, however, is that organization benefits retention, even in children.

Elaboration in Event Recall. Event recall is improved by elaborations, as is the recall of individual items (Paris & Landauer, 1976). Research by Tessler (cited by Nelson, 1993b) indicates that elaboration helps, even if it is provided by the parent rather than by the child. Examining the protocols of mother/child conversations, Nelson (1993b) drew a distinction between pragmatic talk and elaborative talk exhibited by the mothers. In *elaborative talk,* the mother touches on many aspects of an event and describes each fully. *Pragmatic talk,* on the other hand, focuses only on one aspect of an event, such as the name of a fast-food place. Manipulating the manner of conversation, Tessler demonstrated the efficacy of elaborative talk in a study involving mothers and children going on an outing. The mothers and the children visited the Museum of Natural History in New York City. One group of mothers was instructed to chat at length about the exhibits, whereas the other group was told to provide no input beyond answering the child's questions. As expected, children in the elaborative group recalled far more than children under the passive condition.

Use of Strategies in Retrieval.
Encoding and storing of facts alone do not produce retention. The memory trace must be awakened, as Semon (1908) noted, or retrieved, as Tulving (1974) observed. Depending on the context, retrieval of facts is triggered either by a set of cues to remind the person of a certain content or by an explicit prompt from an experimenter. In adults, retrieval is facilitated to the extent that people use a retrieval structure that provides an organizational guide—for example, the use of category names, location, or alphabetical or temporal order. Developmental researchers have sought to discover whether children use such organizational retrieval schemes as well and to what extent the children are aware of how they retrieve information.

Retrieving Familiar Information. Bjorklund and Zeman (1982) observed children from grades 1, 3, and 5 as they tried to recall the names of their current classmates. Recall was consistently high, increasing from 70% in the first grade to 90% in the fifth grade. Children of all grades tended to begin their recall by listing names at random. Sometime during the recall period, the children spontaneously adopted a strategy in that they recalled the names according to a scheme, whether it was by their classmates' sex, race, or seating arrangement. The degree of organization was measured by a clustering score that reflected the joint recall of categorized names relative to randomness. From grades 1 to 5, clustering increased and so did the children's awareness of how they managed to retrieve the names. Asked how they recalled the names, the younger children simply responded, "I just know the kids," whereas older children would say, "Aha! I can remember the names of the kids by where they sit."

Using Retrieval Cues. The power of retrieval cues in activating memory in adults has been widely documented. In a pioneering recall experiment, Tulving and Psotka (1971) asked volunteers to learn lists of categorized words, including cities, car models, colors, and fruits. In recall testing, participants first recalled the words without seeing the category names; then the category names were presented as cues. Thanks to the cues, information became available that was previously not accessible and recall increased from 40 to 70% (see Chapter 4).

As children grow older, they learn to take advantage of retrieval cues, as well. Kobasigawa (1974) recruited children from grades 1, 3, and 6 for a recall experiment involving pictures of familiar objects. The children looked at small pictures of 24 items (e.g., monkey, camel, bear, table, lamp, and couch) drawn from 8 categories (e.g., a zoo with three empty cages and a room). Items from a category were displayed together, with a somewhat larger picture to represent the category. Two recall conditions are of interest: the free-recall condition and the cued-recall condition. In the free-recall condition, children received the standard instruction to recall the items in any order. In the cued condition, they were shown the set of category pictures and were told that, if they wished, they could use the large pictures to try to remember the small ones.

In the free-recall condition, recall increased from 11 items to 13 for grades 1 to 6. In the cued-recall condition, both the proportion of children who spontaneously chose to use the cue cards and the overall recall level increased as a function of age. The number of cue users increased from 33% in grade 1 to 90% in grade 6, and their recall increased from 11.0 to 19.7 items.

Inducing a Retrieval Strategy.   Clearly, the increasing use of retrieval strategies helps improve the children's performance as they grow older, but we do not know how children come to discover the strategies they use. A study by Ackerman (1996) provides a clue by suggesting that even second- and fourth-graders can learn to induce a retrieval strategy on successive recall trials. Ackerman (1996) conducted a recall experiment involving multiple trials with different stimuli on each trial. The stimulus materials were word triplets (e.g., *horse-pig-cow*), where the final word *(cow)* was the target. Three different cue conditions were used in the experiment: a two-cue condition (e.g., *horse-pig*), a one-cue condition *(horse),* and a zero-cue condition. Different stimuli (e.g., *horse-pig-cow; rose-tulip-lily*) were used on successive trials to demonstrate that any improvement between trials was due to the induction of a retrieval strategy.

Ackerman found that children in grades 2 and 4 learned to use retrieval cues effectively, compared to the zero-cue baseline condition. In the baseline condition, there was no improvement for second-graders and only a small improvement for fourth-graders. However, when retrieval cues were presented, there was an improvement in recall between trials, with the improvement increasing as the number of cues increased and as a function of grade (see Figure 8.6).

FIGURE 8.6   Recall as a function of grade and number of cues for trials 1 and 2. When given cues, children learn to induce a retrieval strategy (Ackerman, 1996).

		Trial	
Grade	**Cues**	*1*	*2*
2	0	33	29
	1	36	53
	2	56	75
4	0	44	54
	1	42	61
	2	67	82

Research on the encoding and retrieval of episodic information suggests that improved strategies improve the recall performance of children as they grow older. Whether the memory improvement results from more fully developed metamemory processes is not clear because of the contributions of the rapid growth in content knowledge. In addition, the correlation between which children perform best and which children have the most knowledge of memory is a weak one, at best (Siegler, 1991). It remains, therefore, for future research to identify the contributions of each of the potential factors, strategies, metamemory, and content knowledge.

Working Memory

Working memory is the hub of cognition. It holds information in a highly accessible state for fast-paced cognitive operations of all kinds, whether they involve attention, comprehension, or problem solving. It was the capacity of short-term memory, subsequently known as *working memory,* that has attracted most of the interest of developmental researchers. In the early 1970s, capacity was viewed in terms of a mental computing space assumed to increase continuously as a function of chronological age (Case, 1972).

In more recent formulations, the capacity construct was complemented and replaced with other formulations such as the cognitive speed hypothesis (Kail & Salthouse, 1994) and the inhibition model (Hasher & Zacks, 1988). Although different, both of these proposals share the goal of explaining the age-related improvement of memory in general and of short-term memory in particular. Short-term memory improvement is commonly captured by the digit span, a measure that triples between ages 2 and 12 from about two to six digits.

Cognitive Speedup
What would account for the increase in working memory capacity between ages 2 and 12? Kail and Park (1994) approached this question by focusing on the rehearsal rate as a function of age. The researchers assumed that information is rapidly lost unless maintained through rehearsal, and further that the amount of information maintained depends on the rehearsal rate the subject can deploy. Kail and Park estimated developmental changes in the rate of rehearsal empirically by having subjects of ages 7 through 14 as well as college students rapidly repeat a set of digits. They found that both the rehearsal rate and various span measures, including the digit span, increased as a function of age. The two researchers interpreted their results in support of the notion that "as processing time declines with age, items can be refreshed more frequently in the articulatory loop, producing more accurate recall" (pp. 289–290). An increase in processing speed is beneficial throughout the memory system—in short-term memory scanning, name retrieval, and problem solving—in addition to phonological processing (Chapter 6).

Kail and colleagues recognized that speed was not the only factor to influence performance because it did not capture all of the variance in the age-related improvement in performance (Kail & Park, 1994). They acknowledged that the growth of content knowledge and the increasing use of strategies contribute to the growing memory proficiency of children. Content knowledge helps even in a task as simple as the digit span. As the child gains facility with numbers from historical and autobiographical dates to telephone numbers, these pieces of knowledge can be used as hooks to memorize digits.

Development of Cognitive Inhibition
The inhibition model of working memory (e.g., Hasher & Zacks, 1988) emerged as an alternative to the capacity model in the context of developmental memory research involving older adults. Hasher and Zacks (1988) criticized the capacity notion for a variety of reasons, among them for its failure to identify the source of the capacity limits and to provide a useful measure of capacity. What matters, then, was not the raw *capacity* but rather the *content* of working memory that could be marshaled in the execution of a given task. Performance was expected to improve to the extent that the processor succeeds in inhibiting irrelevant content and focusing on relevant content.

Harnishfeger and colleagues adapted the inhibition theory to developmental research with children. Harnishfeger and Pope (1996) reasoned that as children learn to inhibit irrelevant information, their memory for target information improves. To the extent that inhibitory processes are still underdeveloped in young children, their working memories are cluttered with irrelevant information, leaving fewer resources for the rehearsal and maintenance of the target information. The researchers examined the development of cognitive inhibition in a directed forgetting task. In this task, a person commits a list of items to memory. When the person has memorized half of the list, he or she is asked to try to forget the items and to remember the remaining items. Following the study phase, a recall test is given for the to-be-remembered half of the list and, unexpectedly, for the to-be-forgotten items. Young adults are very good in discriminating between these two types of items; they succeed in suppressing the to-be-forgotten items in the recall test. Nevertheess, they did not truly forget the items, as their performance on subsequently presented recognition tests reveals (see review by Anderson & Neely, 1996).

Harnishfeger and Pope recruited children from grades 1, 3, and 5 as well as young adults for a directed-forgetting experiment in which subjects were read a list of 20 words. There were three experimental conditions, the remember-all, forget-all, and forget-only conditions. The remember-all group was told to remember and recall every word. The forget-all group was told halfway through the list to forget the first half of the list and remember only the second half, but they were tested on all words anyway. The forget-only group received the same instructions as the forget-all group, except their test was different; these subjects had to recall only the second half of the list.

If cognitive inhibition works and directed forgetting succeeds, subjects in the forget-all and forget-only groups should recall the second half of the list but not the first half relative to the remember-all group. First- and third-graders were not able to suppress the to-be-forgotten words. By the fifth grade, some suppression was evident. The young adults, of course, succeeded very well in suppressing the irrelevant words. The investigators attributed the difficulties of the younger children to inefficient inhibition. Assuming that inhibition is a strategic process under the deliberate control of the learner, they speculated that younger children either cannot activate the process or that it is too imprecise, suppressing both relevant and irrelevant information. Under the inhibition scenario, memory improvement occurs once the ability to repress task-irrelevant information is developed.

As we turn to research on memory in older adults, themes similar to those reviewed in the preceding section (Memory Development during Childhood) will recur in the context of declines in memory performance. Thus, the theory of cognitive speed will appear under the guise of cognitive slowing, and the inhibition theory will be studied in light of a decrease rather than an increase of inhibition.

MEMORY CHANGES DURING OLDER ADULTHOOD

Everybody knows that memory declines with age; researchers have documented it, family members notice it, and the elderly themselves know it. The memory decline occurs in everyday situations, and, as Figure 8.7 illustrates, in a variety of laboratory tasks and psychological tests (Craik & Jennings, 1992; Light, 1996). This section of the chapter reviews the memory changes in older adulthood in memory for facts, for skills, and in working memory. The discussion here is limited to normal aging—that is, in adults typically over 60 years old and not afflicted with diseases. Memory impairments, including Alzheimer's disease, will be treated in Chapter 10.

This section also explores hypotheses for the observed age deficits in memory. None of the proposals is fully satisfactory, in part, because the data are not as clear-cut, as Figure 8.7 suggests. The decline in performance across domains and tasks is not uniform—an observation that some have taken as support for the existence of multiple memory systems (Chapter 11). For example, studies indicate that implicit memory holds up better than explicit memory, that semantic memory holds up better than episodic memory, and that, within episodic memory, the age-related decline is greater for recall than recognition tests. There are also interactions within tasks; for example, in the digit span test, the deficit of elderly subjects increases when they are asked to perform an additional task, and in sentence recall, it increases the more complex the sentences are (Craik & Jennings, 1992).

FIGURE 8.7 Performance on memory tasks in younger and older people.

Memory Declines

Conventional Laboratory Tests
Free recall
Cued recall
Recognition
Sentence and prose memory
Digit span, letter span, word span

Ecological Situations and Neuropsychological Tests
Medicine labels
Activities performed
Names and faces for people
Songs on TV programs they have watched
Layout of museums they have visited
Buildings located on familiar streets
Appearance of common objects such as coins
Fewer flashbulb memories (Schacter, 1996)
Acquisition of new skills (e.g., word processing) (Craik et al., 1995, p. 234)

Contextual Information
Context surrounding significant national events
Memory for whether information was heard or seen
Memory for upper- or lowercase letters
Memory for whether information was read by a man or a woman
Color in which information was presented
Memory for whether they saw a word or generated it themselves
Memory for membership of word in most recent or earlier list

Memory for whether they learned an item recently or knew it before the experiment
Memory for whether an act was already carried out
Memory for which of two orienting tasks they used in encoding
Spatial memory
Temporal memory
Susceptibility to misleading information presented after witnessing an event

Speed Deficits
Rate of rehearsal
Rate of scanning in memory search tasks
Rate of responding in short-term and long-term memory tasks

No Differences
Implicit memory tasks (Craik et al., 1995)
Metamemory (Craik et al., 1995, p. 233)
Maintenance of previously acquired skills (Craik, 1995, p. 234)

Age Advantages
Longer-lasting sensory memory (Craik & Jennings, 1992)
Vocabulary scores (Craik & Jennings, 1992)
Remote memories from childhood (Craik et al., 1995)
Anticipation in expert typists, athletes, and professionals (Krampe & Ericsson, 1996)

The memory decline in older adults has been attributed to neurological, physiological, and endocrinological changes in the aging brain (e.g., Fuster, 1995). As people reach their sixties and seventies, their brain mass declines as much as 10% per decade. In addition, there are decreases in the brain's blood flow, oxygen metabolism, and protein metabolism. There are fewer neurotransmitters and receptors, including fewer acetylcholine and dopamine receptors. Both of these agents are important for memory.

Acetylcholine is instrumental in forming memory connections at the synaptic level and dopamine has been implicated in the operations of working memory, especially when it is being taxed by having the person work on two tasks at the same time (Schacter, 1996).

There is evidence of neuron loss as a result of aging, but the loss is unevenly distributed; there is some loss of neurons in Wernicke's area and in other regions presumably subserving semantic memory, as well as in such subcortical structures as the subiculum and the basal ganglia. However, there is disagreement regarding whether neurons are lost to the hippocampus (see Golomb et al., 1994; Sullivan et al., 1995). The frontal lobes, implicated in working memory functions and executive control, exhibit cell shrinkage and cell loss, as well. Coincidentally, memory tasks that require executive control, organization, and coordination are adversely affected during aging. This includes performance in recall as compared to recognition tests as well as remembering the temporal order of events, the context in which facts were acquired, and the execution of future tasks (e.g., Brandimonte, Einstein, & McDaniel, 1996).

The search for functional factors in age-related memory declines has proceeded in parallel with research on biological factors. Scientists have made advances on functional sources of the decline in memory for facts, for skills, and in working memory. Our discussion will show, however, that no single factor accounts for the decline, and that memory declines may be arrested under certain circumstances.

Memory for Facts

When older people complain about their poor memory, they are referring to the facts they tend to forget, whether it is the name of a television show, the birthday of a grandchild, or a friend's address. Memory declines in the elderly have been observed for semantic memory as well as for episodic memory, where the former refers to generic knowledge people have of the physical and social world and the latter refers to memory for specific episodes the person has experienced.

Episodic Memory

In Chapter 4, we saw that the retention of episodic information depends on an effective encoding of the information coupled with retrieval processes that reinstate the encoding environment. Theoretically, memory deficits in the elderly could result in equal part from difficulties during encoding as well as during retrieval. As for retrieval processes, research indicates that older people appear to be less effective than younger people in the recovery of memorized information. Matters are more difficult to sort out at the stage of encoding. It was once thought that memory deficits in the elderly were due to faulty encoding processes. It turns out, however, that differences in encoding between young adults and the elderly are not as clear-cut as was once thought.

Encoding. According to the levels-of-processing approach, encoding is efficient to the extent that it links the to-be-remembered information with the general knowledge of the learner. In an important study, Hyde and Jenkins (1973) demonstrated that semantic encoding led to better recall than phonological encoding, irrespective of the person's intent to learn. Based on this levels-of-processing effect, researchers advanced the encoding deficit hypothesis. This hypothesis attributes the poorer memory performance of older people to a deficit in processing the target information deeply enough. However, the research evidence on the encoding deficit hypothesis is mixed, with some studies lending support and other studies calling it into question. We consider several studies to illustrate each of the positions.

An early study by Eileen Simon (1979) suggested that elderly subjects did not appear to use contextual information to encode target words, whereas younger people did. In Simon's study, three groups of learners (young, middle-aged, and elderly subjects) memorized a list of 20 words to be tested in a free-recall or a cued-recall test. During study, target words (underlined) were presented as object terms in the final position of brief declarative sentences (e.g., *The farmer drove the truck*). In free recall, the learners recalled the target words in any order they wished without prompts, whereas in cued recall, learners received the sentence frames as prompts.

As Table 8.1 indicates, young and middle-aged subjects used the sentence frame to their advantage in recalling the target words, whereas the older group did not. In agreement with the encoding deficit hypothesis, the older adults apparently did not use the context sentence to encode the target word.

Subsequent research questioned the encoding deficit hypothesis by demonstrating that older adults elaborate target information when it is causally linked with the context sentences. Cherry and colleagues (1993) used 28 adjectives (e.g., *grimacing*) as target words and varied the degree to which the sentences explained the adjective. Thus, the sentence *The grimacing man held the cheese while the mousetrap sprang on his finger* explains why the man is grimacing, whereas the sentence *The grimacing man held the cheese and reached for a cracker* does not. In testing, learners were cued with the base form of the sentences they had studied (e.g., *The ___ man held the cheese*) or with the full sentence without the adjective.

Two aspects of the study by Cherry and colleagues are of interest. First, as Figure 8.8 shows, the recall level in the base condition was poor. When more environmental support in the form of fuller context cues was provided, recall was enhanced significantly for both younger and older learners. The second point is that ex-

FIGURE 8.8 Mean percentage of target words recalled as a function of encoding context (Cherry et al., 1993).

	Condition			
	Nonexplanatory		Explanatory	
	Base	Full	Base	Full
Young (19.1)	22	47	21	76
Old (70.8)	6	20	10	59

Note: Mean ages are given in parentheses.

planatory elaborations increased recall in the older people more than nonexplanatory elaborations did. Thus, encoding and retention in the elderly are successful to the extent that environmental support is given and that elaborations are provided to explain the target information.

If memory deficits in the elderly were the result of not using deep encoding strategies, then those deficits should be reduced by giving older people compensatory training in the deliberate use of effective encoding strategies, such as the method of loci. Furthermore, such training would yield more of a benefit for older than younger learners. However, matters were not that simple (see review by Craik & Jennings, 1992). In some studies, older adults benefited more than young adults from using deeper encoding, as predicted by the hypothesis; in other studies, the effects were equal; and in still other studies, the effects were disproportionally larger for the younger adults. Consider a study by Baltes and Kliegl (1992) in which younger and older adults were taught the use of a mnemonic strategy—the method of loci.

Baltes and Kliegl (1992) had older and younger subjects learn lists of 30 words. Over a series of 38 sessions, they trained the subjects in the use of the methods of loci. In this method, the learner associates to-be-remembered words with well-known geographical landmarks, such

TABLE 8.1 Probability of Recall in Simon's (1979) Experiment on Encoding

	Free	Cued
Young (23.5)	50	70
Middle-aged (42.6)	35	50
Old (65.6)	25	25

Note: Mean ages are given in parentheses.

as monuments, shopping centers, or parks in town. The subjects then retrieve the words by mentally passing by the landmarks and recovering the associated words (Chapter 12). As expected, training in the use of the mnemonic technique produced a substantial improvement in recall in both groups, but, in contradiction to the encoding deficit hypothesis, the advantage of training on the mnemonic strategy was greater for younger than for older people.

Even if there were no age differences in encoding operations, there is evidence that older adults require more time to execute such operations. Treat and Reese (1976) conducted a paired-associate study in which they asked subjects to form images to aid their memory. There were two conditions, allowing young and older learners either 2 seconds or 6 seconds to form an image for each of 10 paired associates (e.g., *seat-book, ship-camp,* and *meat-lake*). In the 2-second condition, the young learners performed better, whereas in the 6-second condition, there was no difference between the groups.

Finally, consider a neuroimaging study in support of the encoding deficit hypothesis. A research team headed by Grady (1995) at the National Institute of Aging conducted a study with 10 people aged about 25 and 10 people aged 70 years. The study involved recognition testing of 32 faces previously not known to the participants. PET scans taken during encoding and testing revealed a contrast between the two groups: During encoding, there was increased activity in the right hippocampus, the left prefrontal cortex, and temporal cortex in younger people, whereas brain activity in the older subjects did not exceed the baseline rate taken as people executed a control task. In recognition testing, the young people achieved a recognition accuracy of 80%, whereas the older people achieved only 66%. The authors speculated that the absence of increased brain activity during encoding in the elderly reflected a "failure to encode the stimuli adequately" (p. 218). However,

the precise nature of the presumed encoding problems remains obscure. Clearly, more research is necessary to clarify this speculation.

To summarize, research evidence both supports and disconfirms the encoding deficit hypothesis. The hypothesis was confirmed in the face recognition study by Grady and colleagues (1995) and in studies where experimenters made the encoding conditions difficult, whether it was by not providing sufficient environmental support (Cherry et al., 1993; Simon, 1979) or by limiting the encoding time (Treat & Reese, 1976). On the other hand, the hypothesis was disconfirmed when environmental support was given (Cherry et al., 1993), when compensatory training aided younger learners more than older learners (Baltes & Kliegl, 1992), and when sufficient time for encoding was provided (Treat & Reese, 1976). Assuming a conservative stance, then, it appears that memory deficits in the elderly cannot be attributed to encoding differences between older and younger people alone.

Retrieval. Failing to retrieve familiar information is a frustrating experience for individuals of any age; the question is whether the elderly have particular retrieval problems that young people do not have. Comparing performance in recall and recognition tests provides a clue: Researchers assume that there is more environmental support in recognition testing than in recall testing. In other words, the burden on the person's retrieval operations is greater in recall than in recognition; more self-initiative and construction are required for recall (Craik et al., 1995). It is for this reason that the performance of young people as well as older people is better in recognition than in recall testing. In older adults, however, the recall deficit is larger, which presumably reflects diminished constructive and retrieval processes.

A specific retrieval deficit was observed in a recall study by Duchek (1984), who combined two encoding and two retrieval conditions—phonological (rhyme) processing and semantic processing—in the factorial design tabulated in Figure 8.9 (see also Figure 4.8). In agreement with the levels-of-processing approach, recall was better for semantic encoding than phonetic encoding, and in agreement with the encoding specificity principle, within each encoding condition, recall was better when there was a match between encoding and retrieval conditions. As for age differences, the deficit of older people occurred in the semantic-semantic condition. As the figure indicates, it was in this condition that the older participants did less well than the younger participants.

Duchek was aware that any performance deficit in the semantic-semantic condition could result from either poorer retrieval or poorer encoding. She ruled out the latter possibility by assessing the encoding effectiveness or capacity usage during learning. In order to do so, she used a secondary task technique: She had subjects monitor and respond to intermittent tones as they were encoding the target information in the phonological and semantic conditions. The subjects were instructed to respond to the tones as fast as they could. Longer reaction times to the tone would indicate that more resources were used in the primary encoding task. However, the latency pattern was the same for older and younger participants, suggesting that both groups devoted comparable encoding efforts to both tasks. Having thus ruled out an encoding effect, Duchek attributed the poorer performance of older people to their deficit "to use a semantic retrieval cue to reinstate the specific semantic context that was encoded earlier" (1984, p. 1179).

In general, older people have greater difficulty than younger people in reinstating the circumstances under which they acquired information. Craik and colleagues (1995) described this phenomenon as *source forgetting,* which is a milder form of source amnesia. They demonstrated source forgetting experimentally by presenting fictitious facts (e.g., *Mozart's sister was a sculptor*) to young volunteers and older volunteers (aged 60 to 84 years). A week later, the researchers queried the subjects on both the fictitious and real facts, asking subjects to recall the information as well as the context in which they had learned the facts (e.g., from a newspaper, TV, book, or the recent experimental session). The older participants exhibited more source forgetting in this test than the younger people. In addition, the scientists demonstrated in a subsequent study that the degree of source forgetting was related to performance measures of frontal-lobe effectiveness such as the Wisconsin Card Sorting Task (Chapters 6 and 10), thus confirming the view that the frontal lobes are implicated in retrieval and that frontal lobe functioning tends to deteriorate with age.

FIGURE 8.9   Mean percentage correct recall as a function of age and of the match between encoding and retrieval (Duchek, 1984).

		Retrieval			
		Young (20.4)		Old (68.3)	
		Rhyme	Semantic	Rhyme	Semantic
Encoding	Rhyme	.17	.07	.17	.10
	Semantic	.21	.41	.23	.36

Note: Mean ages are given in parentheses.

Semantic Memory

Semantic memory is the vast repository of our knowledge of the world and of language, including our knowledge of words and concepts. Consider, for example, the consequences that a decline in linguistic knowledge would have for older individuals. People would have difficulty in all sorts of situations from finding the right word, forming sentences, and generating inferences to comprehending conversations and texts. Fortunately, any differences in linguistic knowledge as a function of age are only slight, if they exist at all (Light, 1996).

Older people tend to complain of the occasional failure to retrieve a sought-after word they usually feel they know. This feeling is known as the *tip-of-the-tongue phenomenon.* Burke and colleagues (1991) induced this phenomenon by having people provide the answers to such questions as *What do you call a formal exercise by a team of marchers?* and *What was the last name of the man who assassinated Robert Kennedy?* The researchers found that older people had greater difficulty in answering these questions than younger people. Their difficulties could not be attributed to educational differences, nor to differences in basic vocabulary knowledge between older and younger people. The poorer performance of older subjects therefore indicates that they had greater difficulty in marshaling the semantic knowledge that they did possess. Burke and colleagues believe that it simply took the older longer to activate the requisite knowledge—a view consistent with the cognitive slowing hypothesis discussed later in this chapter (Salthouse, 1984).

Memory for Skills

Skills comprise perceptual and performance components, many of which have become routine and may not be accessible to awareness. Skills are therefore said to constitute nondeclarative memories. Skilled performance comes into play whenever we perceive an object, a word, or an event; make a motor movement; or solve an arithmetic problem. As we will see, many of these skills remain intact as a person ages, even as the person's declarative memory may exhibit signs of weakening.

Implicit Memory

Implicit memory is demonstrated through the priming effect—the finding that performance is facilitated when a person processes a stimulus that is presented on repeated occasions. Priming in the elderly has been established in a variety of tasks, such as the word-stem completion, lexical decision, and exemplar generation tasks, among others.

Light and colleagues compared the performance of young and older adults in a word-stem completion task and a cued-recall task, where the latter taps explicit rather than implicit memory. In the word completion task, participants initially inspected a series of words without being asked to memorize them. Then they received word stems, such as *riv,* and were asked to report the first word that came to mind. In the cued-recall task, subjects initially memorized the list of words. Then they received the same word stems shown in the word completion test, except with the instruction to recall the words (Light & La Voie, 1993). Young adults outscored their older counterparts in the cued-recall task, but performance in the completion task did not differ between the two groups (Figure 8.10A).

A similar dissociation between implicit and explicit memory measures was observed in the exemplar generation task (Figure 8.10B). In this task, people first read a study list of words, then they were asked to generate exemplars of categories, including some that had occurred during study, and finally they received a cued-recall test. Figure 8.10B indicates that there was no age-related difference in generating previously seen exemplars, but young people enjoyed an advantage in the explicit memory task. These

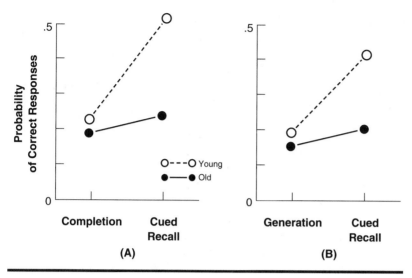

FIGURE 8.10 Dissociation between implicit and explicit memory as a function of age. *(A)* Word-stem completion and cued recall. *(B)* Exemplar generation and cued recall (after Light & La Voie, 1993).

two studies reflect the dissociation commonly found: There are age-related differences for explicit memory measures but only minor differences for implicit memory tasks (Graf, 1990; Light & La Voie, 1993; Mitchell, 1993).

Skill Maintenance and Acquisition

Our review of memory for facts has shown that older people take longer to rehearse and to retrieve words and that they require more time in making a choice in decision tasks. Slowing is the telltale sign of aging in skill execution, as well, whether it involves motor or cognitive tasks. It would be premature, however, to conclude that skilled performance is inferior among older people. On the contrary, there are many instances where older adults compensate for slower responses achieving the same overall level of performance as younger people do.

Professional typists, for example, make relatively fewer typing errors as they get older. They compensate by developing a greater sensitivity to characters beyond the current character and

therefore anticipate upcoming key strokes better. They maintain comparable interresponse times as younger typists, but they do slow down in initiating a typing sequence (Salthouse, 1984). Older athletes certainly exhibit slower motor responses than young athletes, but they compensate by anticipating the trajectories of tennis balls and baseballs more accurately than younger players (Krampe & Ericsson, 1996). Finally, as reflected by their lower insurance premiums, drivers over 60 years old tend to have fewer car accidents than younger drivers (Kausler, 1994).

Not every skill becomes slower with age. Research by Krampe and Ericsson (1996) indicates that speedy execution is preserved for skills that are continuously exercised. In a carefully controlled study involving musicians, the two scientists examined response speed in piano playing among amateurs and experts of different ages. Krampe and Ericsson had four groups of musicians—young amateur pianists, young expert pianists, older amateurs, and older experts—play a set of challenging piano pieces while they took a variety of measures, including the number of errors, the force applied to the keys, and the interkey interval. The important finding was that relative to their younger counterparts, there was a significant slowdown in the interkey interval in older amateurs but not in older elite players.

Were the elite pianists in the Krampe and Ericsson study just smarter or more skillful to begin with? In order to answer this question, the investigators asked the musicians to execute a number of speeded tasks that are standard in studies of aging, including a simple reaction time task, a choice reaction time task, and the digit symbol substitution test. In each of these tasks, the older musicians exhibited the typical slowing down, whether they were experts or amateurs. Thus, it was continued practice on a specific skill (in this case, piano playing) that protected the experts from the age-related decline in speed.

According to Ericsson's theory of skilled practice, experts represent information in long-term memory so as to optimize their working memory capacity, thus facilitating planning and fast retrieval (Ericsson & Kintsch, 1995). These strategies are the result of thousands of hours of practice accumulated over a lifetime devoted to the skill. By the time they are 60 years old, elite musicians are estimated to have accumulated 60,000 hours of practice. It is no wonder that these pianists have reached the pinnacle of their profession.

In contradiction to an adage, everyday experience shows that one *can* teach an old dog new tricks: Older people routinely learn a variety of recreational and professional skills; they can learn to use chopsticks, handle a wheelchair, play mini-golf, and use a word processor, and other skills (Kausler, 1994). However, laboratory research on skill acquisition in the elderly has been surprisingly rare (see Reber, 1997; Russo & Parkin, 1993). Based on research with

memory-impaired individuals, the expectation is that nondeclarative learning would be more robust than declarative learning. The relative immunity of memory for skills in memory-impaired patients has been attributed by some theorists to the developmental primacy of nondeclarative memory systems (Fuster, 1995; Reber, 1993). Whether this hypothesis applies to normal aging as well is not known.

In sum, the majority of studies involving implicit memory or the maintenance of cognitive skills reflect a relatively stable level of retention well into older adulthood. Although theories differ in their conceptual frameworks and processing assumptions, they converge on the notion that implicit memory and automatized skills are less demanding of cognitive resources, whether they are understood in terms of self-initiated actions (Craik et al., 1995) or in terms of working memory operations (Salthouse & Babcock, 1991; Stoltzfus, Hasher, & Zacks, 1996). To the extent that cognitive resources diminish as a person ages, explicit memory decreases and implicit memory remains stable. The final section of this chapter is devoted to the change in working memory resources over time and documents the role played by working memory in the memory performance of the elderly.

Working Memory

Research on the role of working memory in aging reveals a dissociation between the resiliency of such unidimensional measures as the digit span and a deterioration of concurrent task measures that require both storage and processing. In terms of Baddeley's multicomponent model (Baddeley & Hitch, 1974, 1994), this contrast reflects the continued viability of the phonological loop in the face of a weakened executive system as a function of age (Craik et al., 1995). We consider first age-related changes in the digit span and in the computation span, which is a load measure of working memory. Then we revisit the two mechanisms introduced earlier in this chapter: the cognitive speed mechanism and the inhibition mechanism. However, here, the two mechanisms are cast differently—namely, as the cognitive slowing hypothesis (Salthouse & Babcock, 1991; Kliegl, Mayr, & Krampe, 1994) and as the inhibition-deficit hypothesis, respectively (Hasher & Zacks, 1988; Stoltzfus, Hasher, & Zacks, 1996).

As Figure 8.11 indicates, the digit span remains relatively stable through age 70. The information tapped by the digit span is mediated by the phonological loop, assumed to hold up relatively well as the person ages. The small decline is likely to be due to the slower rehearsal rate in older adults than in younger adults. Salthouse (1980) estimated the rehearsal rate for groups of 20-year-old and 70-year-old people, and determined that the rehearsal rate of the older individuals was about 20% less.

Age-related memory declines become apparent when the span task is made more demanding by asking volunteers to manipulate the information—for example, to add numbers and to remember the sums. Salthouse and Babcock

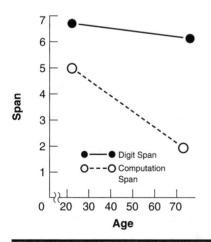

FIGURE 8.11 Digit span and computation spans across the life span (after Salthouse & Babcock, 1991).

(1991) presented to their subjects simple arithmetic problems, such as $3 + 2 = ?; 4 - 1 = ?;$ and $9 - 8 = ?$ The volunteers had to solve the problems and remember the solutions (e.g., 5, 3, 1). This computation-plus-remember task yielded a measure referred to as the *computation span*. Because the computation span taxes both storage and processing functions, it was, as expected, smaller than the digit span across all age groups (Chapter 6; Figure 6.3). Importantly, the decline in the computation span was greater than in the digit span.

The Cognitive Slowing Hypothesis

Salthouse and Babcock (1991) interpreted the age-related decline in the computation span in terms of a three-factor model involving (1) storage capacity, (2) processing efficiency, and (3) coordination effectiveness. If we use a restaurant as a metaphor for working memory here, storage capacity corresponds to the seating capacity of the restaurant, processing efficiency as reflected by response speed corresponds to the number of people that can be fed by the kitchen in a given period of time, and coordination effectiveness corresponds to the maitre d' who supervises operations in the establishment. Using correlational analyses, the two investigators determined that processing efficiency was the most important factor to account for the decline in the computation span (Figure 8.11) and other concurrent memory measures (e.g., the reading span [Chapter 6]) as a function of age. The elderly require more time in rehearsal and other encoding operations and in problem-solving tasks that require the storage of interim results. Their response rate is slower, as well, in short-term memory scanning and in the retrieval of information from long-term memory (Figure 8.7).

Although there are some exceptions to cognitive slowing in the elderly (Kausler, 1994), the empirical support for slowing in memory tasks and other cognitive tasks is not at issue. Where researchers differ is in the explanation for the slowdown, with some theorists favoring a general slowdown factor (Kail & Salthouse, 1994; Salthouse & Babcock, 1991) and others assuming that the slowdown is specific and task dependent (Kliegl, Mayr, & Krampe, 1994).

A General Slowing Factor. Salthouse and Babcock (1991) accounted for cognitive slowing in terms of an activation model where working memory represents the most activated portion of memory (for a related view, see Kail & Salthouse, 1994). Activation for a certain target reaches its maximum at a certain rate; the activation rate is assumed to differ across the age continuum, taking longer in older individuals. The slower activation rate presumably reflects a biological slowing throughout the central nervous system, whether it is caused by greater noise in neural structures, by a weakening or loss in synaptic connections, or even by broken synaptic connections (Birren & Fisher, 1995). Independent evidence for neural slowing in older adults comes from studies involving measurements of event-related potentials, including the P300 response, the peak in an event-related response typically elicited by a surprising event (Chapter 3). Some studies indicate that the P300 response, assumed to reflect an updating of memorial processes, has a longer latency in older subjects (Bashore, 1993).

Slowing Down Depends on Task Complexity. Using visual memory tasks varying in complexity, Kliegl and colleagues (Kliegl et al., 1994; Mayr & Kliegl, 1993) found support for the notion of differential slowdown rates for different tasks depending on task complexity. In order to complete a complex task, whether it is the Tower of Hanoi problem or a visual problem-solving task, continuous switching is necessary between manipulating, storing, and retrieving of information. Interim solutions must be maintained in working memory, facts must be retrieved from long-term memory, and problem-solving steps must be coordinated. As the complexity of the task increases, more processing steps are required. When important information is lost from working memory, the entire process must be started over again—a problem that becomes more difficult as the complexity of the task increases. In agreement with these predictions, Kliegl and colleagues have shown in several experiments that the disadvantage of older people is exaggerated in more complex tasks.

Because cognitive slowing results from task factors rather than a general low-level neural factor (Mayr & Kliegl, 1993, p. 1318), Kliegl's model can readily accommodate Krampe and Ericsson's (1996) finding of preserved speed with continuous practice. Deliberate practice in a certain skill creates mechanisms in memory that enable older experts to circumvent the "processing limitations that inevitably increase with age and constrain other types of unskilled performance in the general population" (Krampe & Ericsson, 1996, p. 353).

In Kliegl's model, information loss from working memory lies at the root of the cognitive slowdown. It still remains to be specified, however, which factors affect information loss and management in working memory. Invoking Hasher and Zacks's (1988) inhibition-deficit hypothesis, Kliegl and colleagues (1994) speculate that older people have diminished control over the contents of working memory with irrelevant information flooding the processor.

The Inhibition-Deficit Hypothesis

The contrast between the digit span and the computation span in Figure 8.11 indicates that memory deficits in older adults cannot be blamed on a decline in the raw capacity of working memory. The performance drop of older adults in concurrent tasks such as the computation task suggests that they are more susceptible to competition from extraneous information. In the computation task, learners must suppress the addends (e.g, 3 + 2) in favor of the sum (e.g., 5);

in divided attention tasks, they must focus on the primary task and ignore the secondary task. According to the inhibition-deficit hypothesis, the difficulty of older adults lies in managing the contents of working memory, in ignoring irrelevant information, and in focusing on the information that is needed to execute the task. In colloquial terms, the memory's working space is swamped with too much material, thus making it difficult to sort relevant from irrelevant information.

Although older adults do not exhibit greater interference in every memory task, there is wide empirical support for the inhibition-deficit hypothesis. Among the effects that the elderly exhibit are the following:

— Greater susceptibility to interference in the Stroop task (more likely to read the color word than to the name color)
— Greater distractibility in flanker tasks where relevant information is flanked by irrelevant information
— Longer reading times when a passage of text contains distracting material
— Longer latency to reject previously relevant information
— Greater breadth of working memory information as reflected in priming effects for partially related information
— Sustained activation of irrelevant material, including greater likelihood of uttering tangential thoughts that come to mind

We can only sample a couple of these effects, selecting the last two for closer examination (see Stoltzfus et al., 1996).

Greater Breadth of Working Memory Information.

In her doctoral thesis at Duke University, Stoltzfus (Stoltzfus et al., 1996) evaluated the idea that older adults have a richer set of concepts in working memory. She employed the lexical decision task using incomplete sentences as primes and sentence-final words as target stimuli. Stoltzfus presented sentence frames with the final word missing (e.g., *The landlord was faced with a strike by the _____*). Before reading on, try to complete this sentence. You are likely to come up with the word *tenants*. A less likely but still acceptable completion would be *residents*. In separate conditions, Stoltzfus presented both of these words along with neutral control words for the lexical decision test. In older subjects, she found a priming effect for *both* of these words, indicating that they were less constrained by the context sentence and activated a wider range of possibilities. The younger subjects exhibited a priming effect only for *tenants,* which is the more appropriate word. The younger people were focusing, however unconsciously, on the most appropriate word, thus activating it alone.

Sustained Activation of Irrelevant Information.

If a person has difficulty eliminating previously relevant information, he or she will likely do poorly on tests such as the directed forgetting task (introduced earlier in this chapter; Harnishfeger & Pope, 1996). In this task, participants study a list of words and are given instructions to remember some of the words and to forget others. In recall testing, they are to produce only the former and not the latter words. Research by Zacks, Radvansky, and Hasher (1996) revealed that older adults, much like children, have greater difficulty than young adults to discriminate between items to be recalled and items to be forgotten. Older adults not only produced to-be-forgotten items from the current list but there were also more intrusions from prior learning lists. Several other effects are consistent with the continued activation of irrelevant material in working memory, among them the finding that the elderly tend to repeat information previously recalled (i.e., tell the same story twice) (Koriat, Ben-Zur, & Sheffer, 1988), and the finding that older people tend to stray from the topic of conversation as they become distracted by tangential details (Arbuckle & Gold, 1993).

All things considered, the inhibition theory of working memory deficit has promise. The appeal of the hypothesis is that it accounts not only for a wide range of data in research on the aged but also on memory development during childhood (Harnishfeger & Pope, 1996), on episodic memory (Chapter 4), and in cognition in general (Stoltzfus et al., 1996).

In summary, in normal aging, memory performance declines in a broad range of situations, from free recall to contextual and temporal memory. In some tasks, such as the recognition and implicit memory paradigms, the deficit is less pronounced. Part of the memory decline in the elderly includes a cognitive slowdown and a greater susceptibility to interference from irrelevant information. However, the age-related memory declines are rarely severe enough to incapacitate the person. Rather, a high performance level can be maintained when the person remains active in a domain, whether it involves declarative memory (Shimamura et al., 1995) or procedural memory (Krampe & Ericsson, 1996). In the case of piano playing, continued practice protects the skill from a decline, thus enabling older pianists to continue to perform as well as young pianists.

CONCLUSION

During the last few decades, developmental research of memory has become an important specialty among the other domains of memory research. The relationship between the developmental approach and the basic research approach to memory has been mutually beneficial. Developmental research has been shaped by formulations from basic research, including the levels-of-processing framework (Craik & Lockhart, 1972; Hyde & Jenkins, 1973), theories of the relation between encoding and retrieval environments (Fisher & Craik, 1977), and the no-

tion of cognitive resources (Baddeley & Hitch, 1974; Navon, 1984). The developmental perspective, in turn, has had an influence on mainstream memory research. Developmental studies of memory have emerged as a fruitful arena to assess theories of memory across domains. Theories of encoding and retrieval, of semantic memory, and of implicit and explicit memory would be very limited if they were only evaluated with the population of college students, the principal source of research participants in memory experiments (e.g., Mitchell, 1993). In developmental research, not only are the ages of research participants different but so are the settings, with studies on children and the elderly often occurring outside the laboratory (e.g., Nelson, 1993b).

Beyond the issue of cross-domain testing, the developmental perspective has had an influence on such substantive topics in mainstream research as metamemory, the relation of explicit versus implicit memory, working memory, and others (see also Keil, 1989; Krampe & Ericsson, 1996; Nelson, 1993a, 1993b). Indeed, taking a global view of cognition, Karmiloff-Smith (1992) believes that an understanding of developmental changes of knowledge has the potential to provide clues to the way in which memory and knowledge are represented in the adult mind.

Metamemory. Research on metamemory came into its own in the context of memory research in children. Flavell and colleagues (1970) and subsequent researchers sought to determine to what extent improving memory performance in children was facilitated by the growing use of strategies and the growing awareness of their memory processes (Ackerman, 1996; Bjorklund & Zeman, 1982). Memory improvement is correlated with a growth of both of these; however, it remains for future research to tease apart the contributions of each of these processes as well as the growth of content knowledge (e.g., Siegler, 1991). Similarly, a deterioration in metamemory has been implicated in the decline of memory in elderly subjects; again, however, many questions remain to be answered (Light, 1996).

Within mainstream research, the concept of metamemory and the monitoring and control processes implied by it has been applied to all stages of memory, acquisition, retention, and retrieval (e.g., Nelson & Narens, 1994). In addition, metamemory issues and metacognition have had an impact on memory retrieval (Reder, 1987), problem solving (Metcalfe, 1996), and the distinction between implicit and explicit memory (Narens, Graf, & Nelson, 1996). Memory monitoring has ecological significance outside the laboratory, as well—for example, when a student prepares for an exam, she determines the study goal and adjusts study practices and study time according to an assessment of her current knowledge of the material. Judgments of the difficulty of the material and of the adequacy of comprehension all reflect the operation of metamemory. When a reader judges a paragraph as difficult, he devotes more time to it, and when he is queried about a piece of information, he will spend the effort of retrieving it only if he believes he knows the information (Metcalfe, 1996; Reder, 1996).

Explicit and Implicit Memory. The distinction between explicit and implicit memory (Chapter 5) dates back to a series of influential papers by Warrington and Weiskrantz (e.g., Warrington & Weiskrantz, 1968; Graf & Schacter, 1985). Explicit memory is assessed in situations where the person studies with the express purpose of recalling it. In implicit memory situations, stimulus materials are presented to people without explicit instructions to learn. Nevertheless, the person's subsequent performance is facilitated as a result of the previous

exposure to the stimulus; for example, the person requires less time to recognize a word. Research with children and older adults has demonstrated a dissociation between explicit and implicit measures of memory. Performance in implicit memory tasks tends to be stable relative to age at both ends of the age continuum, whereas explicit memory performance changes, increasing in children and decreasing in older adults. Dissociations such as these have been cited in support of distinct explicit and implicit memory systems (e.g, Squire, 1995).

Working Memory. Formulations of working memory were enriched by the developmental approach, specifically by research on memory in older adults. The concept of limited capacity has been dominant in early theories of short-term memory and working memory. However, the capacity notion has been plagued by a number of conceptual and empirical problems, one of which is the difficulty of measuring capacity (e.g., Allport, 1993). Should capacity be measured in terms of storage capacity, processing capacity, or the amount of available activation? Investigating working memory processes in older adults, Hasher and Zacks (1988) offered an alternative view of working memory, one that emphasized the contents of working memory and how well the contents fit with the task at hand (Stoltzfus, Hasher, & Zacks, 1996). The Hasher and Zacks (1988) model provides an inhibition mechanism that suppresses irrelevant content and focuses on relevant content. Thus, this model differs both from the capacity model as well as the multicomponent model of working memory (Richardson, 1996). On the other hand, the inhibition view is consistent with inhibition theories that have received increasing attention in memory and cognition research in general (Anderson & Spellman, 1995; Gernsbacher, 1990; Schacter, 1996).

CHAPTER 9

AUTOBIOGRAPHICAL AND EMOTIONAL MEMORIES

In 1973, a national magazine commemorated the tenth anniversary of President Kennedy's assassination with the title "Nobody Forgets." The article carried the recollections of numerous celebrities telling where they were and what they did when they learned that Kennedy had died. Every one of the people interviewed was able to recollect his or her experiences with great vividness and confidence. One person was cooking a gourmet meal, another was on the golf course, and still another remembered the content of a phone conversation he had at the moment when he learned about the assassination. Brown and Kulik (1982) called such vivid lifelike recollections *flashbulb memories.*

Every generation, every community, has its own flashbulb memories. President Lincoln's assassination, Pearl Harbor, Martin Luther King, Jr.'s assassination, the fall of the Berlin Wall, and Princess Diana's death in a car accident—all of these events had an indelible impact on those affected. A severe accident, the death of a loved one, or a catastrophe in one's community has a profound effect on people's emotions, as well. A *flashbulb memory* is the mental trace a person forms of such consequential moments in time. Brown and Kulik (1982) invoked a biological mechanism, the *now print mechanism,* that produces a vivid, although not necessarily accurate, record of the event. The person is struck by the unexpectedness of the event, recognizing its

significance. This experience presumably triggers physiological processes in the brain that consolidate the trace of the experience in memory.

Although less frequent than flashbulb memories, a highly emotional experience (typically a traumatic event) may have the opposite effect and obliterate a person's memory. Schacter (1996) described the case of a young man who had sought assistance from a police officer in downtown Toronto to get him to a hospital for treatment of terrible back pain. The man did not remember his own name, nor did he carry a driver's license or any other form of identification. All he knew was his nickname, Lumberjack. In the course of several days, Schacter managed to uncover bits and pieces of Lumberjack's memory. It turned out that Lumberjack had been abandoned as an infant by his parents and that his grandfather took care of him. His grandfather became Lumberjack's anchor in life. Then his grandfather died unexpectedly; this traumatic event wiped out Lumberjack's memory. Clearly, emotions influence memory.

This chapter treats the many and sometimes opposing effects of emotion on memory as well as autobiographical memories. In flashbulb memories, emotional and autobiographical memories tend to coincide. There is, however, more to autobiographical memories than flashbulb memories. As described in the first section, autobiographical memories combine diverse types of memory, including episodic, semantic, and sensory memories (Conway, 1996a). Going beyond the science of memory, autobiographical recollections make up much of the stories we tell others and ourselves; they are the mental basis for a person's sense of continuity in life.

The second section examines the effects of emotions on memory from the psychodynamic, cognitive, and neuroscience perspectives. Understanding the relation between emotion and memory is interesting for theoretical reasons, and it has become increasingly important for applied reasons. One of the issues, some say *the* issue, of applied memory research is whether some memories are repressed and, if so, whether repressed memories can be recovered or whether they are implanted and therefore false. As we shall see in the third section, it is difficult to disentangle the different strands of this debate. We will review research from child and clinical psychology, discuss research on the suggestibility of memory that bears on the issue, and conclude with a provisional memorandum of the American Psychological Association on the recovered memory versus false memory debate.

AUTOBIOGRAPHICAL MEMORY

Autobiographical memory is not a separate form of memory. Rather, it is integrated with the rest of memory, including contextual information (episodic memory) and components of world knowledge (semantic memory). The recollection of a Wellesley College alumna of an evening with friends in her freshman year illustrates episodic and semantic components of autobiographical memory: "I remember a late night chat with neighboring sophomores shortly after arriving to Wellesley my first year. These older and wiser women were telling me and my roomies that we did not go to a 'girls'' school; we attend a Women's College and be sure to cor-

rect anyone who says otherwise. I also remember that we discussed male/female roles" (Pillemer, Picariello, Law, & Reichman, 1996, p. 329). The temporal and contextual aspect is expressed by the phrase *a late night chat with neighboring sophomores shortly after arriving,* as well as by the woman's recollection that her roommates were also present during the conversation. The discussion of male/female roles reflects semantic memory; it includes stereotypical knowledge of the roles of men and women acquired during childhood and adolescence.

Autobiographical memories also include sensory and perceptual details. The great Argentinean writer Jorge Luis Borges described the sensory quality of the memories of *Funes the Memorious*. Funes had fallen from a horse and become crippled, but his perception and memory were infallible. Looking at three wine glasses on a table, any other person would see the glasses and perhaps remember them, but not Funes.

> *Funes saw all the shoots, clusters, and grapes of the vine. He remembered the shapes of the clouds in the south at dawn on the 30th of April of 1882, and he could compare them in his recollections with marbled grain in the design of a leather-bound book which he had seen only once, and with the lines in the spray which an oar raised in the Rio Negro.... These recollections were not simple; each visual image was linked to muscular sensations, thermal sensations, etc.... He told me: I have more memories in myself alone than all men have had since the world was a world. (Borges, 1967, p. 40)*

Autobiographical memories draw on diverse types of information—sensory, episodic, and semantic—and they include recollections of all sorts of events, both mundane and significant. The events are not intentionally memorized; people remember them simply because they have experienced them. The events are unified by their relation to the experiencing self. Knowledge of the experiences of others is not autobiographical memory, however close the person may be.

Funes's recollections testify to the subjective—indeed, idiosyncratic—character of autobiographical memories. This has not deterred researchers from investigating autobiographical memory systematically and from accumulating a rich body of data. Researchers have learned much about autobiographical memory, including its rate of forgetting, the distribution of autobiographical memories across the life span, and their organization in the mind. This section reviews these research advances as well as the notion of autobiographical memory as a narrative. Case studies of impaired autobiographical memory are also presented.

Studying Autobiographical Memory

For all their immediacy, autobiographical memories do not lend themselves to easy investigation by researchers. There is no clear retention interval, as in episodic memory research, and there are no well-defined concepts against which to check retrieval, as in semantic memory research. The data used in autobiographical memory research are typically self-reports, the kind of source that psychologists have viewed historically with suspicion. Self-reports appeared to be neither replicable, nor reliable, nor subject to verification. Rubin (1986) asked with good justification how one could call the study of autobiographical memories *memory research* when one was not sure of the relation between the verbal reports and the initial events that led to them. Nevertheless, memory researchers have succeeded in developing systematic and replicable procedures to examine autobiographical memory. Next, we will review two of these methods: the diary method and the cue-word method; other methods will be introduced in subsequent subsections, along with such data sources as reflections and personal protocols from individuals, writers, scientists, students, and patients with memory impairments.

Psychologists Study Their Own Memories by Using Diaries

Linton (1986) was among the first to use the diary method of studying autobiographical memories. She described her approach as analogous to that of a population biologist arriving at an island and making an inventory of all the species found on the island. The biologist would study the migratory patterns of the animals, their food sources, their diurnal cycle, the changing patterns of their population, and other aspects. In the same fashion, Linton asked what sort of memories inhabit the human mind. She undertook a study of her own memory over a six-year period. Every day, she would record several items on index cards and date them on the back. For 1972, she recorded 1,345 items, for example. At certain time intervals—weeks, months, or years—she would pick a random sample of cards and try to remember the date of each selected event. In this manner, Linton recorded a forgetting function declining at a rate of 5% per year. She found that she recalled distinctive events best but that events she once thought of as important or as emotional were not necessarily well recalled.

Wagenaar (1986) replicated and expanded Linton's findings in a diary study of his own. He was 37 years old at the beginning of the study, concluding it when he was age 43. Wagenaar, a department head, married, and father of four children, recorded one event per day, sometimes two, totaling 400 events per year, 2,400 over the course of the study. He recorded each event in terms of *who, what, where,* and *when.* For example, one of the events was a visit to see a painting by Leonardo da Vinci in Milano, Italy. Wagenaar gave the event an arbitrary number and recorded the following attributes:

Who: Leonardo da Vinci
What: I went to see his *Last Supper*
Where: In a church in Milano
When: Saturday, September 10, 1983

Wagenaar never looked back at a past record but admitted that it was impossible not to think about some past events since each event has a sequel, a "ripple" that affects other events. He did not include highly personal events so as not to embarrass a colleague who served as his memory file keeper.

At recall, Wagenaar used one, two, or three of these pieces of information to retrieve the full set of facts. Thus, given *Leonardo da Vinci,* he would try to recall the remaining three statements. Wagenaar found recall of these events torturous; he had to limit his retrieval attempts to five per day. As a result, the retrieval period encompassing all of the events took him a full year. Recall decreased as a function of the retention interval in terms of a power function, reaching 20% correct recall after an interval of seven years. Holding other factors equal, Wagenaar found that his recall was better for pleasant than for unpleasant events. Recall depended on the number and types of prompts used. The more cues he used, the better the recall. He found three of the prompts—*who, what,* and *where*—to be equally effective as retrieval cues, whereas *when* was a less effective cue. Wagenaar attributed the difficulty of retrieving *when* to the possibility that dates of events are stored in a very rough form, if at all.

Diary studies have the advantage of depth; the person creates a record of many events categorized in terms of multiple attributes over an extended time span. However, there are disadvantages, as well; only one person's memory is being tapped, which raises the usual questions of generality and replication; the diarist chooses the events he or she personally records, with all the potential problems of such selectivity; and the diary method is very labor intensive, requiring almost the full-time attention of the researcher.

There have been variations on the diary method—for example, using experimenter-provided prompts to record events at certain random times or restricting the domain of remembered events to a small subset of a person's activities, such as visits to a doctor. In subsequent recall tests, researchers noted a tendency for selective recall, where events were omitted or aggregated, but there was little, if any, evidence of fabrication. Thus, repeated visits to the doctor tended to be mixed rather than recalled as individual occasions. Researchers have succeeded to decompose such aggregate memories by using a time line for subjects to recall the most recent visit to a doctor and from there go back year by year to previous years (see review by Baddeley, 1990).

The Cue-Word Method and Temporal Distributions of Autobiographical Memories

It was Sir Francis Galton who pioneered systematic investigations of autobiographical memory in the nineteenth century. He introduced the breakfast questionnaire and the word-cueing method. In his breakfast questionnaire, Galton asked people to describe their most recent breakfast in as much detail as possible. In his word-cueing method, he presented a word to the person and asked him or her to think of any idea that came to mind. Galton's cueing technique was resurrecting by two American memory researchers, Crovitz and Schiffman (1974). Their word-cueing method involves two stages. In the first stage, the experimenter presents a list of words (e.g., *avenue, baby, fire, hospital, paper, plant,* and *window*) to volunteers and asks them to associate autobiographical memories for each word. In the second stage, the set of words for which a person produced autobiographical memories is returned to him or her, with the instruction to tell the interviewer how long ago the event occurred. The Galton-Crovitz cueing method yields a distribution of autobiographical memories across the subjects' lifetimes.

Rubin (1982) used the word-cueing method with college freshmen and found the distribution graphed in Figure 9.1A. This function rep-

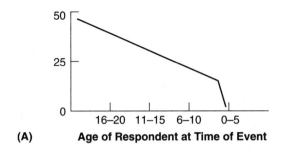

(A)   **Age of Respondent at Time of Event**

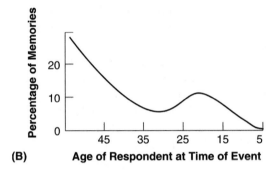

Percentage of Memories

(B)   **Age of Respondent at Time of Event**

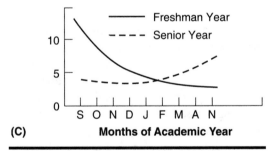

Freshman Year
Senior Year

(C)   **Months of Academic Year**

FIGURE 9.1   Distribution of autobiographical memories for *(A)* first two decades of life, *(B)* five decades, *(C)* the freshman and senior years of college.

resents a retention function if we make the assumption that people experience approximately the same number of events every day of their lives. The curve exhibits a decrease in the number of recollections that is typically found in retention studies. There is a discontinuity at the very right of the curve, indicating a dispropor-

tionally small number of memories from the first three years of life; this drop reflects the phenomenon of childhood amnesia (Chapter 8).

If the use of college-age subjects ever led to a distorted view of a phenomenon, the function in Figure 9.1A represents a good illustration. The function does not represent the distribution of autobiographical memories in older populations. Fortunately, Rubin, Wetzler, and Nebes (1986) were aware of this problem. In a comprehensive study, they had people of various ages fill out the word-cueing forms and they found functions shaped like the one in Figure 9.1B. This function shows a decline as a function of the age of the memories, as the first function does. There is, however, a bump in the function to indicate an increase in recollections from the time period when people were teenagers and young adults. This increase, known as the *reminiscence bump,* has been replicated using different paradigms, different subject populations, and participants from different countries, provided that the respondents were 40 years or older.

What accounts for this mysterious increase in recollections from early adulthood? Could it be that the events during this period are more important than during other periods and that the person more frequently thinks about them? Examining types of events across the life span indicated, however, that important events—moves, jobs, promotions, marriage, birth of children, and so on—occurred in later periods of the person's life, as well. Could it be that encoding processes during this life period are particularly effective so that people remember the events better? Perhaps so, but there is no independent evidence to support this hypothesis, either. Another hypothesis is that during early adulthood, a person forms a concept of self with important goals that define his or her life. The person begins to form the life story, a narrative, to provide a framework for life's events (Conway, 1996b). Plausible as it is, this hypothesis, too, remains unconfirmed, thus leaving the reminiscence bump unexplained.

In sum, the number of memories recalled results from a combination of factors; there is a retention curve for the most recent past; there is an amnesia component for early childhood years; and, if the person is older than age 40, there is, for whatever reason, a reminiscence bump. Memories also differ in their distribution over time spans shorter than the entire life period. In their study of the recollections of college experience, Pillemer and colleagues (1996) found different distributions of recollections depending on the year of college. Recollections from the freshman year peaked in September, the first month of the academic year, whereas recollections from the senior year tended to peak in May, the month of graduation. These functions, shown in Figure 9.1C, indicate that experiences laid down during times of transition, entering and leaving college, are particularly memorable.

Organization of Autobiographical Memory

When a parent asks a teenager about his or her school day, more likely than not the teen will say that the day was *fine* or *awful*. The parent's question taps a small slice of autobiographical memory; the teenager's response is general—no events are provided, let alone details. The teenager produces a response that reflects a mood tone, which is, according to Linton's (1986) view, the most general category of autobiographical memories. Perhaps a day at school is not sufficiently eventful or long to yield a large number of recollections from anyone. Would people provide more events and details if they were asked about a longer time period—for example, last summer's vacation? When you ask friends how they spent their summer vacation, they will tend to respond with general descriptions, such as "We went to the beach," "We took hikes," and "We went to the movies." It is as if people access the most abstract of their autobio-

graphical memories rather than penetrating into lower levels of elaboration and detail.

The notion of autobiographical memory as a structure of levels is embodied in Conway's (1996a, 1996b) model of autobiographical memory. He proposed an organization that included three levels of abstraction: lifetime periods, general events, and event-specific knowledge (Figure 9.2). *Lifetime periods* refer to time spans extended over several years or even decades—for example, "My college years," "My marriage to Jennifer," or "After I became a psychologist" (Linton, 1986). Within lifetime periods, events are classified in terms of relationship themes, work themes, and other themes. Relations include friendships, spouses, and significant others. Work scenarios include the location of the job and one's responsibilities.

General events describe stereotypical situations also known as *scripts* (Chapter 5)—going to the movies, taking a trip, or working in the office. As illustrated in Figure 9.2, general events are related to one another as well as to lifetime periods. Thus, Mary's memory of living with John includes the memory of meeting him first at a dance. Working at XYZ Company includes recollections of working in the human resources office. Although people may not recollect details when they retrieve general events, such as spending a vacation in Hawaii, most people, except for amnesic patients, can be prompted to do so. The patients may be able to recall lifetime periods, but they tend to experience great difficulties in reporting general events and event-specific knowledge.

First-time memories—for example, the first day at college or the first time driving a car on your own—enjoy a privileged status among general events. These events are presumably linked to a person's goals; they are distinctive and they tend to be vivid. Mary's memory of meeting John for the first time, for example, may include such details as returning from the winter break to her university, going to a party at

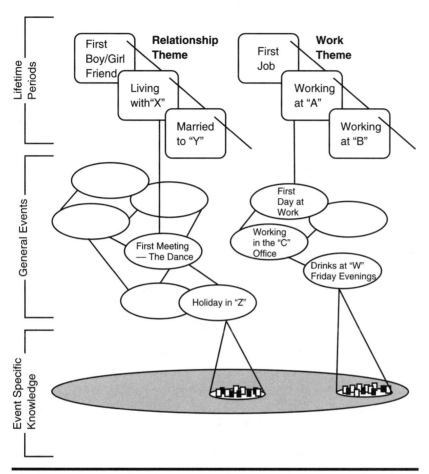

FIGURE 9.2 Hierarchical model of autobiographical memories includes lifetime periods organized according to work and relationship themes, general events, and event specific knowledge (Conway, 1996b).

the Commons, Elly introducing John to her, Mary thinking "John is cute," listening to the music of Jerry Garcia and David Grisman at the party (the song was "Shady Grove"), and Mary and John walking to Mortimer Lake after the party.

Conway and colleagues (Conway, 1996a) wanted to know whether the hierarchical organization of autobiographical memories sketched in Figure 9.2 was psychologically valid. The researchers first undertook a mapping of the auto-biographical memories of the people participating in the study by asking them to report lifetime periods that usually last from several months to one or two years (e.g., primary school) and general events that usually last days or weeks (e.g., a trip to Scotland).

Five months later, the scientists invited the same participants to return to the laboratory for a priming study involving a priming and a neutral condition. In both conditions, subjects were given cue words and phrases and asked to bring to mind a personal memory as quickly and accurately as possible. The dependent variable of interest was the time it took the person to think of the memory. In the priming condition, the cue (e.g., trip to Scotland) was preceded by a prime that represented the lifetime periods (e.g., primary school) the person had told the experimenters about earlier. In the neutral condition, people were simply given the word *ready,* followed by the cue word. There was a large priming effect. When primed with a life period such as primary school or freshman year in college, people recruited their memories almost one second faster (1.8 seconds) than when a neutral prime (2.7 seconds) was used. This effect indicates that autobiographical information is represented in terms of the hierarchical levels envisioned in Conway's model.

In related studies, Conway (1996a) set out to determine how long it took subjects to retrieve autobiographical memories compared to retrieving other memories—for example, semantic information. It took people far longer to retrieve autobiographical information than other information. To verify semantic information took about 1.0 second; to verify personal information, such as one's bank, took 1.2 seconds; and to retrieve autobiographical memories took 3 to 5 seconds. These differences are very large compared to those typically observed in reaction time studies of memory.

Why do autobiographical memories take so much longer to retrieve than semantic memories? Conway believes that autobiographical memories are not reproduced but that they are constructed, much like a solution to a problem (Williams & Hollan, 1981). One only need to ask a 40-year-old person to come up with the names of his or her high school classmates. Doing so presents a palpable problem for most people. They tend to solve it by constructing a scenario of events that remind them of their classmates. One recall protocol ran as follows: "The first thing that comes to mind is [pause] I mean it's almost like images of different snapshots of our high school. You know, I can think of our general science class, and waiting in the lunch line, and halls. Umm, sort of, Jeff Thompson!" The constructive nature of autobiographical memories suggests that the retrieval outcome may differ across different attempts of retrieving the same target memory. Consistent with this expectation, Conway (1996a) found that much of people's autobiographical recollection differed when retrieved on two different occasions only a few days apart.

Autobiographical Memory Viewed as Narrative

In our lives, one thing happens after another; receiving word on college acceptances, making the decision where to go, final exams, graduation, saying good-bye to close friends, working at a new job, and so on. If human memory were like a tape recorder, we would store the events we experience in the sequence they occurred, as speech is recorded on an audiotape. One of the differences between human memory and nonhuman recording systems is that people reflect about the events they experience and they look for meaning in their experiences (Bartlett, 1932). It is the search for meaning that gives autobiographical memories their character as a narrative with goals, with efforts that overcome obstacles and achieve the goals, and with points of closure.

The autobiographical narrative provides a framework for making sense of events and for telling them to someone else (Bruner & Feldman, 1996). As is true of all narratives, the autobiographical narrative is constructed under the aegis of a schema; in this case, the narrative is held together by the person's views of self, the self schema. The narrative does preserve essential events as they were experienced, but it is not a factual report; rather, the account seeks to make a certain point, to unify events, or to justify them.

For lack of access to the original events, it is rare that researchers get an opportunity to document the constructive nature of autobiographical memory in everyday life. The analysis by Neisser (1982b) of John Dean's testimony in the Congressional Watergate Hearings provides a glimpse on the subtle constructions people perform on events. John Dean, counsel to President Nixon, was a key figure in the Watergate affair in the early 1970s. Several staff workers of Nixon's reelection committee were caught burglarizing the Democratic National Committee at the Watergate complex in Washington, DC. One of the key issues for Congress was whether President Nixon knew of the events leading to the burglary and whether there was a cover-up of the break in. Unknown to John Dean, all conversations in the Oval Office were taped, leaving a verbatim record of his Oval Office meetings. The tapes were released in 1973 and provided an excellent opportunity to check Dean's recollections against the recorded conversations. Neisser undertook this analysis, treating the tape-recorded conversations in the Oval Office as the stimulus material and Dean's testimony as the recall protocol.

One of the Oval Office conversations included among Neisser's analyses occurred on September 15, 1972, when it appeared that the worst was over for Nixon. Here is a fragment of Dean's testimony on that conversation given nine months later (cited from Neisser, 1982b):

> The President asked me to sit down.... [He] told me that Bob [Haldeman] [Chief of Staff] had kept him posted on my handling of the Watergate case. The President told me I had done a good job and he appreciated how difficult a task it had been and the President was pleased that the case had stopped with Liddy [one of the staffers]. I responded that I could not take credit because others had done much more difficult things than I had done. As the President discussed the present status of the situation I told him that all I had been able to do was to contain the case and assist in keeping it out of the White House. (p. 147)

The problem with Dean's testimony was that it was inaccurate: According to the taped record

of the meeting, the President did not ask Dean to sit down, nor did he say that Dean had done a good job. Furthermore, Dean did not respond the way he reported it. Had this been a memory experiment, Dean's score of correct recall would have been close to zero. However, Dean did not lie to the Committee, because, although his account of the conversation was inaccurate, his report gave a flavor of the situation in the Oval Office and of the extent of Nixon's knowledge of the Watergate affair. According to Neisser, Dean recalled the conversation as it should have been if Dean could have had his way. In Dean's mind, "Nixon *should* have been glad that the indictments stopped with Liddy, Haldeman *should* have been telling Nixon what a great job Dean was doing; most of all, praising him *should* have been the first order of business" (p. 148). The testimony John Dean gave to the congressional committee is not unusual; it reflects the self-editing property of autobiographical memory to be consistent with one's self-schema, one's wishes, and one's expectations.

Autobiographical memories are similar to narratives in several respects. Both tend to conform to a schema of goals and efforts, successes and retreats; elements of both undergo changes as time passes, with some elements remaining stable and others changing; and, to some extent, both autobiographical memories and narratives are social creations—they are shared with as well as shaped by other people.

Permanence and Change in Personal Recollections

Much like narratives, autobiographical memories include turning points that are particularly defining moments. Bruner (1994, pp. 49–50) cited the case of a former high school football player who was turned off from football and athletics when the coach told him just prior to a game to "get" the opposing end and "get him out of the game," no matter what the cost. The coach's command made the student see the light; the next day, he turned in his uniform and quit the team. He was so offended by the attitude of winning at any price that he decided to turn his back on athletics and become an intellectual instead. Later in his career, the former football player became a Vietnam protester, a graduate student, and a professor. He told Bruner that he will never forget the day of the football game that changed his life forever.

There are, however, many autobiographical memories that do not remain as fixed as this man's memory of the fateful football game. As a result of reflection and new circumstances, many recollections do change as the years go by. In a decade-long study of her autobiographical memory, Linton (1986) noted "remarkable shifts" in the contents of memory. She noticed deletions and revisions in her memory of many events. She wrote that one can see the "internal historian" at work on one's memories and she cited one event appearing in a new light. Meeting a shy scholar years ago was at first not a significant event for her, but then beginning to date him and finally marrying him recast the recollection of that first meeting entirely (see also section on Factors Affecting the Memory Trace after Encoding in Chapter 12).

Social Aspects of Autobiographical Memories

People share their memories with friends and family, colleagues, acquaintances, and even strangers. Much of people's conversations consist of stories relating their past experiences. Researchers have estimated that in family conversations, reminiscences about past events occur as frequently as five to seven times per hour (Fivush, Haden, & Reese, 1996). Children are socialized by their mothers and fathers to share past experiences. Researchers recorded conversations between children of various ages and their mothers and found that mothers seek to elicit recollections of joint experiences from their children, such as a trip to grandma's, going

to the zoo, or taking a vacation. At first, the conversations are one-sided, with the mother prompting her child and providing most of the recollections herself. By age 3, the child increasingly contributes his or her own recollections to the conversation.

It follows from the development of autobiographical memories that a person builds his or her memories in concert with others. In his book *Brothers and Keepers,* novelist John Edgar Wideman (1984) eloquently draws a distinction between his own autobiographical and his brother's memories and describes how his brother's memories gave shape to his own:

> But my heart can break, does break listening to my brother's pain. I just remember differently. Different parts of the incident he's describing come back. Strange thing is my recollections return through the door he opened. My memories needed his. Maybe the fact that we recall different things is crucial. Maybe they are foreground and background, propping each other up. He holds on to this or that scrap of the past and I listen to what he's saved and it's not mine, nor what I saw or heard or felt. The pressure's on me then. If his version of the past is real, then what's mine? Where does it fit? As he stitches his memories together they bridge a vast emptiness. The time lost enveloping us all. . . . My brother's memories are not mine, so I have to break into the silence with my own version of the past. My words. My whistling in the dark. His story freeing me, because it forces me to tell my own. (p. 98)

According to Barclay (1996), autobiographical memories define a person's self relative to others. The *narrative of self* gives continuity and meaning to a person's life. To the extent that people are incapable of sharing their memories, personal stress and psychological disorders may result. Learning to share memories through conversation has been a principle of psychotherapy in helping a person cope with difficult personal experiences, including trauma. Harber and Pennebacker (1992) used writing autobiographical narratives as a means of coping with traumatic memories.

In the Harber and Pennebacker study, students tended to disclose private aspects of their lives in the essays, including intimate and highly emotional events. The death of a loved one was the most frequently chosen topic, followed by conflicts with lovers or friends, family conflict, and academic issues. It appears that people are motivated to reveal such traumatic memories. The students wrote and talked at a faster rate and produced more words when discussing traumatic events than when relating other autobiographical memories, such as their activities since breakfast or some other control topic. According to clinicians, writing about traumatic experiences encourages a person to confront the experience, enhances the person's self-esteem, and gives a feeling of control over one's memory and emotional life (Harber & Pennebacker, 1992).

Impairment of Autobiographical Memory

The impairment of autobiographical memory is a clinical presenting problem for a range of neuropsychological conditions, including closed head injury, Alzheimer's disease, and many cases of amnesia (Rubin, 1996a). To be sure, not all of autobiographical memory is obliterated, nor do all of the patients have problems with autobiographical recollections, and, importantly, implicit memory remains intact. The patients still exhibit priming effects, complete word puzzles correctly, and acquire conditioned responses, much as nonimpaired individuals do. The impairments of autobiographical memories observed by neuropsychologists tend to include the following patterns, sometimes alone, and sometimes in combination:

— There is a temporal gradient of retrograde amnesia such that patients tend to lose access to the most recent events, whereas events in the distant past are spared (Chapter 10).

— The amnesia tends to affect details and specific events to a greater extent than general events or lifetime periods. The difficulty in accessing details suggests a premature stop in executing the retrieval cycles needed to recover specific target information (see the SAM model in Chapter 7; Conway, 1996b). The dependence on autobiographical information on the level of abstractness is consistent with Conway's model of autobiographical memory in Figure 9.2.

— Some patients exhibit selective loss of autobiographical memories. For example, the person may remember events but not the people who participated; other patients may remember people but not the events.

— Certain patients produce confabulations; they mix events from different life periods while insisting on the accuracy of the fabricated memories.

— Researchers have described dissociations between semantic memories and episodic memories, including autobiographical memories (Chapter 4).

— Patients tend to perform poorly on clinical assessments of autobiographical memory, including the Galton-Crovitz cueing test, the famous persons test where the patient attempts to identify photographs of famous people, and the famous events test in which patients are asked to describe a familiar event (e.g., Nixon's resignation, the Oklahoma City bombing).

The case of patient P. Z. (Butters & Cermak, 1986) illustrates some of these problems in a dramatic way. Toward the end of his career, P. Z. began to suffer from Korsakoff's syndrome, a condition resulting from prolonged alcohol abuse (Chapter 10). In his prime, he was a famous scientist who had published extensively in his field and who happened to have completed an autobiography only a few years before his amnesia set in. His memory loss became acute when he was close to 60 years old. By that time, his general memory was very poor, as measured by traditional tests, including paired-associate learning, the famous person test, and the famous scientists test that was fashioned expressly for him.

Researchers were able to determine the loss of P. Z.'s personal memories by using his autobiography as a data base of the events he had experienced and described. Asking P. Z. events from different decades of his life established that his memories were worst for the most recent past; they were poor for back to age 20, when the reminiscence bump typically occurs. His prior memories, however, remained relatively intact. In addition to the losses to his autobiographical memory, P. Z. suffered debilitating losses in his factual memory, including the basic knowledge of his discipline. Unfortunately, there is no ready explanation for P. Z.'s patterns of pervasive memory losses while his adolescent memories were spared. The memory loss could be due to a progressive degrading of encoding operations as a result of 35 years of continued alcohol abuse, to a failure in accessing information from memory, or to a combination of these factors. The sparing of P. Z.'s early memories indicates that these initially episodic memories have assumed the status of semantic knowledge, which tends to be more resistant to impairment than episodic memory (Butters & Cermak, 1986).

The next section is entitled Remembering Emotional Events. Many of these recollections —flashbulb memories, eyewitness accounts of crimes, and the memories of concentration camp survivors—are autobiographical in the sense that the person remembers having experienced the events personally. However, we shift our focus from the self as the interpreter of events to the effect of the emotional content of the events. We examine claims that emotional events (1) inhibit access to memories as stated by Freud's repression hypothesis, (2) preserve memories as proposed by the now print mechanism, and (3) do both, depending on the centrality of the detail (as implied by the notion of tunnel memory to be explained later).

REMEMBERING EMOTIONAL EVENTS

Research on the Repression Hypothesis

The first psychological, and arguably the most enduring, formulation of the forgetting of emotional events is Freud's repression hypothesis. Having analyzed many patients with symptoms of hysteria and neurosis, Freud concluded that recollections of painful and embarrassing events banished to the unconscious were the cause of his patients' problems (Chapter 2). Although Freud later revised the original hypothesis (see Erdelyi, 1985), the repression hypothesis became very popular because of its simplicity. The prediction was clear-cut: Unpleasant events and stimuli are less well remembered than pleasant events and stimuli. Carl Jung, an erstwhile colleague of Freud's, was the first psychologist to report that anxiety-arousing words produced longer response latencies in the free-association task. Levinger and Clark (1961) replicated and validated Jung's observation. Not only did emotionally laden words produce longer response latencies but they also elicited higher galvanic skin responses, an indicator of the person's anxiety. The two investigators interpreted their findings as support of the repression hypothesis.

The repression hypothesis never achieved a firm empirical footing, however. A few years after Levinger and Clark's study was published, a new report appeared that cast doubt on the hypothesis. Researchers had learners memorize paired associates in which nonsense syllables were paired with English words (Kleinsmith & Kaplan, 1964). Some of the words were high-arousal words (e.g., *rape* and *vomit*) with a negative connotation; other words were neutral. The researchers found better recall of the neutral words at short retention intervals (2 and 20 minutes after learning). However, the trend reversed after one week: Here, the recall was better for the high-arousal words.

The reversal in the recall pattern of emotional and neutral items was puzzling to

Kleinsmith and Kaplan. At short intervals, the data supported the repression hypothesis, but at the longer interval, they contradicted it. What mechanism could account for these data? The researchers attributed the reversal to the dynamical effects of arousal on the formation of the memory trace. As the trace is first formed, arousal shields the trace as if placing it in a cocoon, thus momentarily inhibiting access. Thanks to such consolidation, however, the trace becomes more durable for the long term and recall becomes more likely at longer intervals.

Whatever the account for Kaplan and Kleinsmith's cross-over findings, the repression hypothesis was not supported. Among clinical psychologists, too, the repression model gave way to other theories, including the dissociation theory. This theory holds that all people maintain parallel memory processes in the brain; in case of trauma or sustained stress, these processes may become disconnected and thus impede conscious access (e.g., Brewin, Dalgleish, & Joseph, 1996).

Next, we revisit flashbulb memories, the recollections people form of highly surprising and emotionally arousing events. Unlike the presumed inhibiting effect of negative emotions, flashbulb memories are thought to last forever. According to the now print hypothesis introduced earlier, the emotional arousal causes a "permanent registration" of the significant event and of "all recent brain events" (Brown & Kulik, 1982, p. 26).

Are Flashbulb Memories Special?

Flashbulb memories are formed on those rare occasions when a surprising event of national and personal significance occurs. Because the triggering event is surprising, it is difficult to study flashbulb memories in the laboratory. Ingenious researchers have managed to study flashbulb memories and arrive at some important generalizations, nevertheless. When British psychologist Martin Conway (1995) heard on November 22, 1990 (which was coincidentally the 27th anniversary of President Kennedy's assassination), that the then British Prime Minister Margaret Thatcher had suddenly resigned, it occurred to him that "this was one of those rare opportunities to conduct a flashbulb memory study."

Conway and his colleagues contacted researchers in different countries, sent out questionnaires, and interviewed university students willing to participate. They had over 200 volunteers in Great Britain and 150 in the United States and Denmark. The two groups were tested twice for their recollections of the Thatcher resignation, first within the first two weeks after the resignation and again about a year later. Having scores from two tests separated by almost a year enabled the researchers to assess the consistency of the respondents' memories across the time interval. The expectation was that people more affected by the event would remember it better and produce greater consistency in their recollection of what they did, who they were with, and where they were when they heard of the event. This is exactly what Conway found. As reflected by their higher consistency scores, the British respondents remembered Thatcher's resignation better than the American and Danish respondents; the resignation mattered more to them than to the American and Danish students.

The strong level of recall of the British respondents for the resignation contrasts with the memorability of facts memorized in typical episodic memory experiments; those facts are forgotten within hours and days and rarely survive longer than a month. Political events tend to be forgotten very quickly as well. Indeed, many politicians count on the short memory span of the public for budget impasses, ethics violations, and shady deals.

There are several factors that contribute to the longevity of flashbulb memories. The triggering event is, by definition, surprising, distinctive, and emotionally arousing; each of these attributes is known to enhance the memorability of an event (Chapter 4). Memory researchers know that organisms encode unexpected events better than routine events (Rescorla & Wagner, 1972) and that distinctiveness of stimuli strengthens their memory traces (Mäntylä, 1986). To the extent that people are personally involved in the event, it arouses them emotionally. The degree of arousal is greater when one directly experiences the crisis than when one is merely told about it. Neisser (as cited by Conway, 1995) found that people who experienced the California earthquake in 1989 themselves remembered it in greater detail than students in Atlanta 2,500 miles away who learned about it from the media. Finally, because of their national significance, landmark events, such as an assassination or a major disaster, are commemorated by the media and the public in general. These commemorations provide opportunities for rehearsal and make the memory more durable.

Although it may appear frozen in time, the flashbulb event witnessed by a person unfolds in the person's mind, its interpretation changes, and so does the recollection; memories of certain details change, for example, of one's clothing, of one's companions at the time, or of the first thoughts one had when learning of the event. In this respect, flashbulb memories are like other memories. In any case, these changes of flashbulb memories do not support the now print metaphor that implies a durable and veridical record of the event (Christianson & Safer, 1996).

Memories of Witnesses and Victims of Crimes

Eyewitness testimony is one of the most critical pieces of evidence used in establishing guilt or innocence in a court of law. From a research perspective, an eyewitness memory is a personal recollection of an event, albeit an unusual event. Witnessing a crime shares some attributes with flashbulb memories yet differ in others. Like flashbulb events, crimes and accidents elicit powerful emotions—horror, grief, fear, and anger; the cool bystander is rare, except perhaps in traffic accidents. Eyewitness reports differ from flashbulb memories in that they are reports on the event itself, its details, especially the identity of the victim and the perpetrator, whereas the latter describe what the person was doing and where he or she was when learning of an epochal event.

Research on eyewitness testimony has a time-honored history in psychology dating to the beginning of the twentieth century (e.g., Whipple, 1909). In the last three decades, researchers have examined eyewitness memory from the perspective of interference theory, information processing, and memory distortion (e.g., Loftus & Ketchum, 1994; Loftus & Palmer, 1974; Zaragoza & Lane, 1994). Representative experimental research on eyewitness memory will be treated in the context of memory applications in Chapter 12. Here, we consider field studies of eyewitness testimony and the emotionally charged recollections of the survivors of concentration camps during World War II.

Field Studies of Eyewitness Testimony

Field research on memory for crimes is very difficult. One would have to have memory psychologists on hand as police first get to a crime scene or at least shortly thereafter. Yuille and Tollestrup (1992) described one of the rare field studies available. The incident occurred at a gun store and involved a shooting between two men: the owner of the store and a thief who attempted to rob the store. At various times during the incident, 23 different witnesses observed the shooting. The researchers succeeded in getting testimony from 13 of the witnesses within five months after the shooting.

Witnesses' recollections were compared with the police report taken at the scene of the crime. The recollections of the 13 witnesses were not much affected by stress; they were remarkably accurate in their detail, even after several months. Although there were interpretational problems in the Yuille and Tollestrup study—the 13 people who chose to be interviewed may have had accurate recollections and these could have been based on reports in the press—other field studies have replicated the main result of the study.

Results from other field studies have revealed an effect known as *weapon-focus* or *tunnel memory:* Witnesses remember the theme of the crime well, including emotion-provoking details (e.g., blood, the weapon, etc.), but their memories for surrounding context is poor (Christianson & Safer, 1996). As in the crossover effect reported by Kleinsmith and Kaplan (1964), people tend to remember certain core events better after some interval than immediately after the incident. The phenomenon of tunnel memory supports the Easterbrook (1959) hypothesis that emotional arousal focuses attention on the central part of a crime, such as the break-in, the stabbing, or the shooting. Those are the acts that witnesses tend to relive (i.e., rehearse) long after the crime occurred.

Recollections of Concentration Camp Survivors

Concentration camp survivors will never forget the terrible crimes and tortures they experienced and witnessed. Decades later, painful visions return in the form of intrusive flashbacks and nightmares (Brewin et al., 1996). Wagenaar and Groeneweg (1990), two Dutch memory researchers, undertook a systematic study of the recollections of 78 victims who survived several years at camp Erika in the Netherlands. The scientists examined the testimony of the survivors

given to Dutch police on two occasions: immediately after their liberation between 1943 and 1945 and 40 years later, between 1984 and 1987. At issue was the documentation of crimes committed by a certain De Rijke, who, although a prisoner himself, was given the role of supervisor by the German camp authorities.

Analysis of victims' testimonies revealed that they retained their memories over 40 years for the basic facts of their ordeal, the tortures and punishments for cooked-up offenses, and the particularly barbarous treatment of Jewish prisoners. There were, however, errors on other details. Some witnesses forgot the date of their camp entry and particular incidents of torture they suffered, others confused the names of torturers and victims, and others were no longer able to recognize De Rijke on a photograph. Wagenaar and Groeneweg concluded that while almost all witnesses remember the horrible crimes committed at camp Erika, the intervening 40 years also produced forgetting of details typically sought by courts (e.g., faces, names, and clothing).

To the extent that camp survivors have difficulty recounting details, one reason certainly is that the horrors they experienced were singular and indescribable. Barclay (1996) noted that "when some survivors of the Holocaust claim that 'you can't understand,' they speak the truth because the nature of their experiences lacks an explanatory system" (p. 120).

Laboratory Studies of Emotion and Memory

Experimental studies conducted in the quiet of a laboratory cannot match the drama and emotional impact of real-life events. Nevertheless, results from laboratory studies are consistent with the principal findings of field studies: The central aspects of an emotional event are better retained than peripheral details, and there is an improvement in memory on successive tests of retention—a phenomenon known as *hypermne-*

sia (Erdelyi & Kleinbard, 1978). Experimental studies have a number of important advantages compared to field studies. An experimenter can induce and measure the degree of stress rather than having to rely on self-reports of witnesses and victims. Experimenters can introduce a variety of arousing events—such as having subjects watch a series of slides or film clips, or listen to reports of accidents, robberies, and assaults—whereas a field study necessarily involves a single event. Importantly, it is through the systematic control afforded in experiments that investigators can arrive at findings that are generalizable across contexts and situations (Chapter 11; Banaji & Crowder, 1989).

Heuer and Reisberg (1990) presented a series of slides that told a story in two different ways: One version seen by one group of people was boring, the other seen by other subjects was emotional. After two weeks, the participants were given a previously unannounced memory test for the events of the story. Subjects who had seen the emotional story version remembered the story plot better than people who saw the neutral version. The recall pattern was opposite for peripheral events; these were remembered better by subjects who had seen the neutral story version (Heuer & Reisberg, 1990). These results reflect the same sort of tunnel memory that has been observed in field studies: Arousal narrows attention and retention to the central aspects of an event at the expense of peripheral detail. Christianson and Safer (1996) have identified a potential problem for forensic applications resulting from such tunnel memory or weapon focus. When a weapon is used in the crime and witnesses focus on it, their attention and memory for the faces of the perpetrators may be reduced, leading to erroneous judgments in line-up identifications.

Reviewing field studies and laboratory experiments, Christianson and Safer (1996, p. 226) concluded that people tend to remember events well that are negative and highly emotional, whether they are break-ins, shootings, or medical procedures watched on tape. People's memory is best for the central details of the event, whereas surrounding details are less well retained. However, with delayed testing and with appropriate retrieval cues, the disadvantage may be compensated (Chapter 12).

Mood and Memory

Expressions such as *feeling blue, seeing things through rose-colored lenses,* and *black mood* reflect the common knowledge that moods influence feelings, thoughts, and memory. One of the effects of mood on memory was introduced in Chapter 4 in the context of state-dependent memory. This concept refers to the relation between mental or environmental states at encoding and retrieval. The greater the similarity between encoding and retrieval situations, the better the recall. In terms of mood, *state dependency* means that people tend to retrieve all kinds of events—happy, neutral, or sad—better when their mood matches the mood they experienced during the encoding state.

In order to investigate the effects of mood on memory experimentally, researchers induce moods by a variety of means, such as asking the subjects to think happy or sad thoughts, hypnotizing them, or playing different pieces of music. Eich and Metcalfe (1989) had subjects listen to pieces of joyful music (e.g., Mozart's *Eine Kleine Nachtmusik*) or sad music (e.g., Barber's *Adagio pour Cordes*). Every five minutes, listeners gave a rating of their current mood. When people had achieved a criterion level of sadness or happiness, the experimenters presented the information to be remembered. Half of the subjects read a list of words, whereas the other half generated words, such as specific members of a category prompted by the experimenter (e.g., an ice cream flavor beginning with *V*).

During testing, music was played to generate either the same or the opposite mood that prevailed during the study phase. The researchers observed a moderate effect of mood dependency in subjects who had read the words and a very pronounced effect in participants who generated the words (see Table 9.1). The authors attributed the stronger effects in the generate task to the possibility that internal thoughts are more susceptible to moods than are responses externally presented (as in the reading task).

Revising Events When Moods Change. Baddeley (1990) contrasted mood congruency with mood-state dependency based on mood. The latter refers to improved memory when the mood states in encoding and retrieval are matched. *Mood congruency* refers to cases where a given mood tends to evoke memories that are consistent with that mood. In other words, when a person is happy, he or she emphasizes the sunny side in his or her recall; when a person is sad, he or she retrieves the depressing parts, even if the same event is recalled. Baddeley (p. 391) cited the experience of a woman who suffered from periods of depression and who recalled trips to the swimming pool. When she felt depressed, she thought of her excursion as painful and embarrassing; she felt fat and unattractive in her swimsuit. When she was happy, she described the event as wonderful exercise and an outing she would love to do again.

Chronically depressed individuals tend to perceive events in a negative light and they encode their experiences unidimensionally in terms of sadness and boredom. They neither

TABLE 9.1 Probability of Recall as a Function of Orienting Task and Matching of Moods in Encoding and Retrieval (Eich & Metcalfe, 1989)

	Orienting Task	
Encoding/Retrieval Relation	*Generate*	*Read*
Matched moods	.28	.16
Mismatched moods	.19	.13

elaborate nor embellish the events, giving their recall protocols a certain blandness. Even the brain of depressed people is depressed. Brain-imaging studies reveal that during encoding, the metabolic activity in the left frontal lobes of patients is depressed compared to a nonpatient control population (Schacter, 1996).

Emotion, Memory, and the Brain

The saying *Once burned, twice shy* succinctly expresses the idea that pain and fear are powerful means of promoting learning and remembering. Researchers have found that learning through fear is the quickest way of getting animals to learn a response (Chapter 2). Animal researchers introduced the conditioned emotional response (CER) paradigm in which animals are exposed on each trial to a tone immediately followed by an electrical foot shock. After very few trials, sometimes after the first trial, the animal has learned to cease any ongoing activity as soon as the tone appears, whether it is exploring the environment, grooming, or pressing a bar. The tone has become the signal of pain; it induces fear.

The animal remains fearful of the tone, even when the foot shocks are no longer delivered; fear conditioning is resistant to extinction. When the fear response has finally been extinguished after prolonged extinction training, it is easy to reinstate it by presenting incidental cues that may have been present during the original fear training. The same holds true for phobic patients believed cured; patients often regress to their state of fear when a stimulus reminds them of their trauma. The fear has not been forgotten—all that therapy could do was to hold the fear in check (LeDoux, 1992).

On the positive side, ever since Pavlov's and Thorndike's days, psychologists knew of the motivating effects of the stimuli that satisfy hunger, thirst, and the reproductive drive. In the century since, neuroscientists have made great advances in revealing the neural mechanisms of these drives and the powerful emotions that accompany them. Research shows a combination of neural structures and hormones that mediate memory under conditions of arousal. A key structure in the formation of emotional memories is the amygdala, an almond-shaped organ in the limbic system (Figure 3.1).

Amygdala

LeDoux (1994) used fear conditioning as a way of tracing the neural structures involved in learning emotional responses. Using a sound as the warning stimulus, researchers trained rats to avoid electrical foot shock whenever the sound was presented. The scientists reasoned that the animals became fearful of the sound because the electrical shock changed the way in which neurons in critical brain regions interpreted the sound. By lesioning centers in the auditory pathway one at a time, the researchers sought to determine the site of neural change underlying the learned responses. The scientists lesioned the primary auditory cortex, the thalamus, the important relay station along the acoustic pathway, and the amygdala. Surprisingly, animals lesioned in the auditory cortex still acquired the fear response, thus indicating that other centers are implicated in interpreting the significance of the tone as a signal of danger. However, lesions in the thalamus and amygdala blocked learning of the avoidance response.

Understanding the function of the amygdala in emotional processing dates back to the 1930s, when scientists discovered that monkeys lost their fear of snakes and other danger-provoking stimuli when the amygdala was lesioned. Damage to the amygdala impairs fear learning in humans, too. British psychologist Andrew Young (*New York Times,* January 1997), for example, described the case of a patient who underwent neurosurgery to treat epileptic seizures that could not be controlled by medication alone.

The woman's health was restored in all respects except for certain memory deficits resulting from the removal of parts of the amygdala. The woman lost her memory for interpreting the emotional aspects of auditory stimuli, whether they were warning sounds or speech modulated to reflect emotional content ranging from fear to sadness. The woman could recall what it felt like to be afraid, happy, sad, or angry, but she could no longer interpret the tone of voice appropriately.

The amygdala is ideally placed to interpret sensory signals in terms of their emotional significance for the organism. Anatomical studies revealed that the amygdala communicates with such important organs as the neocortex, the thalamus, and the brain stem areas that control muscular, autonomic, and hormonal systems. It was therefore for good reasons that LeDoux (1992) called the amygdala the organism's emotional computer (see also Davis, 1992). According to LeDoux, the amygdala, together with the thalamus, serves as a "quick and dirty" identification system for activating the organism when danger is afoot. Although the stimulus may not be fully analyzed, whatever analysis it receives is sufficient to trigger a defensive reaction, such as the avoidance response. The advantage of the thalamo-amygdala system is that it has fewer synaptic links than the thalamo-cortical-amygdala pathway and is thus capable of faster learning.

It is neural plasticity at the synaptic level that supports the formation of new memories. Several mechanisms of synaptic plasticity have been identified, including the growth of new synapses, increases in the emission of neurotransmitters, and enhancement of the permeability of synaptic membranes (Chapter 3). Each of these processes involves neurochemical processes that are subject to hormones and these, in turn, are triggered by emotionally arousing events.

Hormone Modulation and Sapolsky's Glucocorticoid Cascade Hypothesis

Research has documented that memory traces are modulated by arousal-producing drugs, such as epinephrine, during encoding and immediately afterward (McGaugh, 1995). These drugs are related to natural hormones produced by the body in response to emotionally charged events. McGaugh and colleagues administered epinephrine at various intervals following training; its effect was best when injected immediately after training. Researchers also found that the effect of epinephrine depended on the amygdala; when the amygdala was lesioned, epinephrine no longer improved retention. Other stress-related hormones include vasopressin, ACTH, and the glucocorticoids. When released in small doses right after training, their effect on retention is beneficial. However, the long-term effect of one group of these stress hormones, the glucocorticoids, is damaging to neural structures and possibly to memory (Sapolsky, 1994, 1996).

The glucocorticoids trigger adaptive mechanisms when the organism is in imminent danger, for example, when a zebra sees a lion about to attack (Sapolsky, 1994). The zebra's chance for survival requires a quick activation of all of the body's systems necessary for escape. Blood pressure, heart rate, and oxygen intake suddenly increase; this response provides energy to the muscles, sharpens attention, and reduces susceptibility to pain. Any function, such as digestion or reproduction, that does not speed the animal's escape is temporarily dampened by the glucocorticoids.

When the glucocorticoids are produced for an extended time period, they have a negative effect on neural structures, in particular, on the hippocampus. Critical receptors and neurons in the hippocampus are killed by continuous injections of glucocorticoids; subjecting rats to long periods of stress has the same deleterious effect on hippocampal structures. Atrophy of the hippocampus due to stress has been found in other species, as well, including rhesus monkeys living in their natural habitat. Monkeys low on the social totem pole among their group, those who suffer intimidation and harassment by their stronger peers, have a higher level of stress hormones and a reduced hippocampal mass than monkeys not so stressed (Sapolsky, 1994).

Sustained stress is associated with similar effects on the hippocampus in some human patients (Sapolsky, 1996). Patients suffering from long-term depression and Vietnam veterans have elevated levels of glucocorticoids, and, using fMRI scans, researchers found hippocampal shrinking in these individuals. The shrinkage of the hippocampus was greater the longer the depression lasted and the longer the soldiers were exposed to combat. There are also results at variance with Sapolsky's (1996) data and with the glucocorticoid hypothesis. In a study involving 50 survivors of the Holocaust, Yehuda and colleagues (1995) found *reduced* glucocorticoid levels in those individuals suffering from posttraumatic stress disorder. Survivors not afflicted with the disorder, however, exhibited a normal level of the hormone.

Even if the relation between prolonged stress, glucocorticoid level, and hippocampus size observed by Sapolsky (1996) were to be supported by further observations, the data remain open to interpretation. None of the primate studies cited in support of Sapolsky's hypothesis reveal cause and effect. It could well be that monkeys with a smaller hippocampus tend to be submissive and thus become the target of abuse, and that individuals with a smaller hippocampus are more likely to suffer posttraumatic stress syndrome (Sapolsky, 1996). In order to evaluate the hypothesis, experimental studies are needed. For example, one can record the glucocorticoid level and hippocampus size in high-risk professionals (e.g., police officers, firefighters) before and after experiencing a traumatic event and track these measures longitudinally over a period of months and years. If Sapolsky's hypotheses were right, the glucocorticoid level would be elevated and hippocampus size reduced in individuals who underwent stress.

Other aspects of the relation between stress and memory are not fully understood. On the one hand, there is evidence that patients with posttraumatic stress disorder and individuals who have suffered abuse experience a variety of memory disorders, such as intrusive memories, temporary loss of memory for specific events, short-term memory deficits, and lower scores on the word-cueing test of autobiographic memories. On the other hand, a group of abused women performed as well on explicit memory tests as a control group (Schacter, 1996). Thus, any specific links between abuse, the brain's responses, and memory await further investigation. Research is necessary on these problems, especially in light of the increasing furor among psychologists and in the public at large over the issue of recovered memories.

THE MEMORY WARS

Writers selected the term *memory wars* for the vociferous debate between those who believe that repressed memories of early childhood abuse can be recovered and those who believe that those memories are false (e.g., Schacter, 1996). The debate started with a series of court cases in the 1980s and 1990s that tore communities, congregations, and families apart. Consider three illustrative cases: Case 1 is a schematic case abstracted from cases reported all too frequently in the press, and cases 2 and 3 were reported by Loftus and Ketcham (1994) in their book on repressed memories.

Case 1: Explosive allegations that the coach at Anytown High School sexually abused a young man 21 years ago are based on a "recovered" memory, a controversial therapeutic technique that is legally recognized by nearly two dozen states but is drawing growing skepticism from professionals. M. L. N., age 37, filed a $10 million lawsuit against S. D. T. and another member of the athletic department on March 7, charging that they sexually molested him when he was a 17-year-old high school student in Anytown. But unlike most adults who say they were abused as youngsters, M. L. N. contends he did not deliberately hide his experience for all these years out of shame or fear. Rather, like a growing minority of adults making such claims, he says that he only recalled the abuse a month ago while undergoing therapy.

Case 2: The case of George Franklin, Sr., accused by his daughter Eileen of having murdered 8-year-old Susie Nason, became a landmark case in 1990. The alleged murder took place over two decades years earlier, in September 1969. Eileen's memory did not come back all at once. Rather, she remembered the episodes of abuse in bits and pieces. For example, when playing with her own two children, Eileen seemed to see the face of Susie Nason as she was pleading with George Franklin to leave her alone. Then Eileen remembered riding in a van on the way to school and her father assaulting Susie. Then her father took Susie outside, and she remembers seeing Susie lying on the ground covered with blood. Eileen's report was so sincere and vivid that it was believed by her therapist, by several members of her family, by the District Attorney, and by the jury in the trial against George Franklin. Franklin was convicted, but his conviction was overturned by a federal judge in early 1995 because of certain technical issues.

Case 3: Two adult sisters alleged that their parents, now both in their seventies, forced them to engage in sodomy, torture, and infanticide during their infancy and adolescence. The older sister sought help from a therapist when she was over 40 years old, after her third divorce. She persuaded her younger sister to participate in the therapy sessions. In the course of therapy, the older sister remembered a series of horrible events: her mother killing a rabbit and smearing the blood over the child's body, application of electric shocks to a man who threatened to reveal the deeds of the cult, and the killing of her own baby. The jury found the mother guilty of neglect, and appeals have failed.

Each of these cases depends on the memory of people who claim that they were victims or witnesses of a traumatic crime. The person repressed the experience, but recovered it through the encounter with certain stimuli or through psychotherapy. Many of these claims were persuasive to law enforcement officers and to juries, but are they credible as far as psychological theory is concerned?

The Issues

Cases such as these and the recovered memory versus false memory debate are so intractable because of a clash between two realities: the reality of child abuse and the reality that memories are susceptible to suggestion and thus fallible (Binet, 1900; Loftus & Ketcham, 1994). The reality of child abuse is not in doubt, although objective measures of the incidence of abuse are hard to come by. Many victims are very young and at the mercy of their caregiver(s). The abuse occurs in secrecy and in those rare cases where a child is in a position to complain, caregivers deny any wrongdoing. The public catches a view of abuse either because of chance, or because neighbors, teachers, or law enforcement officers notice problems, or because the crime involves abduction and murder.

Terr (1991) described the case of a 5-year-old girl who had been abused by the caregiver in a day-care home when she was just over 1 year old. The case was discovered by agents of the U.S. Customs Service who happened to came upon pornographic photographs of several victims, including the 5-year-old girl. The girl's parents were horrified and remembered that their daughter would draw pictures of nude adults from the time when she first learned to draw.

The case of the killer Marc Dutroux caused a public uproar in Belgium in 1996. Known as the Monster of Charleroi, Dutroux first admitted to raping and killing two 8-year-old girls whose bodies were found at his house. Later, Dutroux revealed additional murders and led police to bodies of four more victims. Not only were Dutroux's crimes heinous, but the case was mishandled by the judicial authorities. In 1996, Dutroux was out on parole after serving half of a prior 13-year prison sentence for rape. Immediately after his release, he continued and escalated his crimes. The case produced the largest public protest in Belgian history, with 300,000 people demonstrating in Brussels in the fall of 1996 (*Paris Match,* November 14, 1996). Unlike the pornography ring recounted by Terr (1991) and cases like Dutroux's, most cases of child abuse are never reported. Nevertheless, they are traumatic for the victims, scarring them for life. It is certainly understandable that many rape survivors seek support from peers and therapists to alleviate their anguish.

The other side of the recovered memory versus false memory debate includes people unjustly accused of crimes they did not commit. According to their position, memories of alleged crimes may be false, and many recollections are no more than reconstructions from public accounts or confabulations, and, still worse, fabrications implanted by therapists. For instance, Eileen's testimony (Case 2) may have been based on newspaper reports she read about the crime. According to Loftus and Ketcham

(1994), the recollections of the two sisters in Case 3 from infancy are likely to be false, as there was no physical evidence to support the allegation of multiple murders (e.g., human bones). Citing Bass and Davis's (1988) statement, "If you think you were abused and your life shows the symptoms, then you were, " the false memory advocates accuse victims' groups and some therapists of encouraging women to recover memories of abuse, whether they are true or not.

The false memory advocates organized their own advocacy group, the False Memory Syndrome Foundation, intended as a clearinghouse of information on alleged abuses. The foundation reported that many of the alleged abuses are bizarre. For example, there is a report of a claim that young girls were raped, then had to carry their babies to term, who, once born, were killed and eaten (Neisser, 1994). Thousands of other accusations have been brought forward in the United States, according to a survey of the National Center on Child Abuse and Neglect; however, there was no physical evidence in any of them (Hilts, 1996).

Feuding groups of psychologists representing different professional traditions have taken sides in the recovered memory versus false memories debate. Clinical psychologists have tended to support the recovered memory argument, whereas many memory researchers have inclined toward the false memory position. At issue is whether a person remembers painful and traumatic childhood events and, if so, how accurate are those memories. Although no solution to the debate is yet in sight, it is through psychological research on various aspects of the problem—clinical and developmental perspectives of early childhood memories, field research of memory for pain, and research on suggestibility—that one can address the issues in a systematic and dispassionate way. Here, we review each of these research areas in order to get a

fuller understanding of the recovered memory versus false memory debate.

Clinical Views of Early Childhood Memories

Clinical views of memory of abuse have evolved from Freud's repression theory to contemporary dissociation theory. According to these theories, traumatic events become inaccessible, either because they are pushed into the recesses of unconsciousness or because the communication between conscious and traumatic memories is disrupted. It has been difficult to evaluate either theory experimentally, but the notion that memory of traumatic events is lost is at the root of the notion of recovered memories.

As for memories from early childhood, Freud introduced the notion of infantile amnesia, giving the forgetting of early childhood events an aura of pathology. He believed that infantile amnesia was the result of repressing forbidden fantasies. Developmental researchers have attributed the forgetting of early childhood experiences to a qualitative change in the cognitive structure as the child develops (Chapter 8). The forgetting of memories from ages 1 and 2 is real enough, as the distribution of autobiographical memories in Figure 9.1B indicates. Nevertheless, infants at those ages are capable of learning and remembering.

Bauer (1996), for example, has argued that infants have a greater capacity for retention than psychologists have given them credit for. The reason for assuming poor infant memory was that verbal recall, the principal tool of memory research, was not available in infant research. Using nonverbal measures of memory or implicit memory measures gives evidence of memory in children as young as several months (Chapter 8).

Myers and colleagues (1987) used an implicit memory technique to establish long-term retention in children 3 years old. The researchers demonstrated that the children remembered events that had taken place two years before. The children participated in a perceptual experiment between the ages of 6 and 40 weeks. The researchers brought the children back to the same laboratory, and, using the same toys used more than two years ago, compared their behavior with that of a control group who had not participated in the earlier perception study. The retested children behaved differently than the children in the control group; they played more and were more interested in the toys from the earlier study, but when asked whether they remembered having been in the room before, only one child exhibited any explicit recollection.

The Bauer (1996) and Myers (1987) studies indicate that young children have the capacity for remembering events they experienced up to two years ago. Recovered memories are different, however; they are assumed to be recollections of childhood events during adulthood. Which events, if any, do adults remember from early childhood? Two psychologists at Emory University, Usher and Neisser, sought to find an answer to this question by interviewing college freshmen about important events when they were 1 to 5 years old and by having the students' mothers score the accuracy of their recollections (Usher & Neisser, 1993). Controlling for the degree to which the respondents had recourse to family photos and other information sources, the two researchers found that memories for events were available earlier than had been thought previously and that the offset of childhood amnesia depended on the nature of the event itself. Some 60% of the respondents correctly recalled the birth of a younger sibling or their own hospitalization (tonsillectomy) when they were 2 years old. The death of a family member and a family move were recalled from as young as age 3 or 4.

None of these studies addressed memory for painful events from childhood, let alone memory for abuse. Research on memory for abuse is very difficult; most cases of abuse occur in secret and there are no records to validate recall and forgetting, and cases where records do exist may not be representative of other instances of abuse, or the victims may no longer be available. Using hospital records, researchers have taken great efforts to investigate aspects of pain and abuse. We will review two studies. The first study examined recall for pain experienced as a result of a medical procedure to treat urinary tract infection (Goodman, Quas, Batterman-Faunce, Riddlesberger, & Kuhn, 1996), and the second study traced retention of documented sexual abuse that had happened 17 years before (Williams, 1994).

Remembering Pain and Abuse

Goodman and colleagues (1996) investigated the recollections of 48 children regarding a very painful medical procedure that involved contact with the children's genitals. The procedure is a sanctioned medical method to test and treat infections in the urinary tract. It involves insertion of a catheter into the child's bladder; the procedure is painful and embarrassing for the child. The memory test occurred about two weeks after the children underwent the procedure. The test involved free recall, a doll demonstration, and a questionnaire of 61 items. Scores from these measures were combined to yield the composite scores in Table 9.2. The data indicate that correct recall, as measured by Goodman's indexes, improved as a function of age, but did not differ in proportion with the number of times the child received the treatment.

The medical procedure the children underwent has some similarity to sexual abuse. There are, however, important differences. The procedure took place at a hospital; it was undertaken after it had been carefully explained to the child;

TABLE 9.2 Composite Recall Scores from Three Memory Measures as a Function of Age and Number of Treatments (Goodman et al., 1996)

Age	Treatment	
	One	Multiple
3–4 years	9.67	7.00
5–6 years	16.20	18.33
7–10 years	26.86	25.50

and the child was accompanied by his or her parents, who were present until the physician inserted the catheter. Abuse, by contrast, is secretive; indeed, children may be threatened by their abusers not to tell anyone. The retention interval in this preliminary study was only two weeks, not the years typically involved in cases of alleged memory recovery. Nevertheless, the Goodman study provides a baseline for retention when memories are presumably relatively fresh. It provides a model for studies in which hospital records are used as a criterion against which to validate people's recollections.

The Williams (1994) study involves victims of sexual abuse and a retention interval of close to 20 years. Williams interviewed 129 Boston area women to assess their recall of a case of sexual abuse that had taken place more than 17 years ago. Each of the women had suffered acts of rape and sexual abuse between 1973 and 1975 and underwent treatment in an emergency room. For each of the victims, records of the treatment and diagnosis were available. The women were younger than 12 years at the time of their emergency treatments. Williams found that as many as 38% of the women had no recollection of the sexual abuse they had suffered. Table 9.3 reports the proportion of women who recalled the abuse as function of the age at the time of their victimization. These data indicate the trend typical for other developmental memory data: The

younger the child at the time of the abuse, the less likely she or he is to recall the event later.

What is the implication of these data for the repression and recovery hypothesis? Researchers differ in their response to this question. Williams herself regards the forgetting rate of 38% as relatively high, concluding that "if, as these findings suggest, having no recall of sexual abuse is a fairly common event, later recovery of memories of child sexual abuse by some women should not be surprising" (p. 1174). Indeed, she found that 16% of the women who did recall the abuse indicated that there were times in the past when they did not remember the abuse they had suffered.

Loftus and colleagues (1994) interpret the 38% forgetting rate differently. These authors point out that, far from representing repression, Williams's data are comparable to the normal forgetting observed for such other traumatic events as an automobile accident, the death of a family member, or one's hospitalization. Furthermore, Loftus argues that for repression to occur, the event must have been encoded as an incident of abuse. She notes that some of the victims might not have understood the meaning of their experience and that "some of the children never 'knew' that they were traumatized and thus had nothing to repress" (p. 1178). Finally, recall tended to improve with the gravity of the assault, a trend that contradicts the repression hypothesis according to which the reverse should have occurred. Nevertheless, Loftus

TABLE 9.3 Failure of Recall of Sexual Abuse as a Function of Age at Time of Victimization (Williams, 1994)

Age	Percent	N
0–3 years	55	11
4–6 years	62	31
7–10 years	31	36
11–12 years	28	51

does agree that Williams's data disprove the extreme claim that "if you were raped, you'd remember."

Suggestibility of Memory and Implanting False Memories

Based on her research, Williams (1994) suggested that "therapists should be open to the possibility of child sexual abuse among clients who report no memory of such abuse" (p. 1174). It is here that matters tend to become still more complex. According to Loftus (1993), certain styles of therapy may be suggestive and change memories and even implant them. Changes in memories are accommodated by different views of the memory trace, whether it is Bartlett's (1932) notion of reconstructive memory, Loftus's (1993) notion of blending between original information and postevent suggestions, or Estes's (1997) dual-trace theory (see also Schacter, 1995). In his dual-trace theory, Estes postulated the formation of two parallel memory traces as a result of a learning experience: (1) the stimulus trace that encodes multiple attributes of the event and (2) the trace of the response made by the learner to the event. According to the dual-trace model, it is the response trace that undergoes changes when suggestions are made or other postevent information is given.

As for outright fabrication, psychologists have known of such phantom memories at least since the Swiss child psychologist Jean Piaget (1896–1980) described his memory of being kidnapped as an infant. However, there was never any kidnapping; Piaget had just imagined the event and taken it for real. There are many studies that have documented the suggestibility of memories (see also Chapter 12). The general design of the false memory demonstrations involves exposing participants to both true and false events in a sequence of successive interviews. True events are typically contributed by friends and family members, whereas false events are plausible experiences invented by the experimenters. As a result of this manipulation, participants have generated false memories of being lost, visiting hospital emergency rooms, spilling punch bowls at weddings, and getting fingers caught in mousetraps (Hyman & Pentland, 1996). As an illustration of this approach, consider a study from Ceci's laboratory (Ceci, 1995).

Ceci and colleagues succeeded in creating fictitious memories experimentally (Ceci, 1995). Working together with the parents of a group of preschool children, Ceci and colleagues identified for each child real events that they had experienced (e.g., a bike accident) and fictitious but plausible events they had not experienced. One of the fictitious events was the mousetrap accident: The children were asked about an incident where they had "a finger caught in a mousetrap and had to go to the hospital to get the trap off." The procedure was carried out over a 10-week period. Each week the child was shown a set of cards depicting the actual and fictitious events. The child picked a card and the experimenter asked whether the incident had occurred. In the case of the mousetrap incident, for example, the interviewer would instruct the child as follows: "Think real hard, and tell me if this ever happened to you. Can you remember going to the hospital with the mousetrap on your finger?"

At the end of the 10-week period, the researchers changed the context and the nature of the interviews. A different adult interviewed children in a different room and the interview was videotaped. The interview was more detailed than the previous interviews. In addition to asking the questions on each of the situations, as illustrated by the question on the mousetrap, the interviewer prompted the child for details, including: "What did you see or hear? Who was with you? How did it feel?"

The scientists expected some degree of confusion on part of the children between real and fictitious events. However, they were startled by (1) the large number of narratives about the false events, with 58% of the children telling false narratives; and (2) the great detail and the coherence of the narratives. Here is the story involving the mousetrap event told by a child with conviction and sincerity:

> My brother Colin was trying to get Blowtorch [an action figure] from me and I wouldn't let him take it from me, so he pushed me into the wood pile where the mousetrap was. And then my finger got caught in it. And then we went to the hospital, and my mommy, daddy, and Colin drove me there, to the hospital in our van, because it was far away. And the doctor put a bandage on this finger [indicating]. (Ceci, 1995, p. 103)

The children's confusion between actually experienced and merely suggestive events is understandable; they had seen the fictitious events for 10 weeks, had thought about them, and imagined them along with the actual events. As is often the case with source amnesia, people have difficulty in identifying different origins of their memories. Mug-shot studies reveal such source confusion: When experimenters show a witness of a theft a set of mug shots not including the thief, the person is likely to say the thief was not among the pictures. However, after another week has passed, there are more likely to misidentify one of the individuals as the thief (Chapter 12).

Not only were the children inaccurate about the reality of the events but their accounts were so sincere that expert interviewers were fooled by them. Ceci showed the tapes of the interviews to psychologists experienced in interviewing children and asked them to indicate which of the taped narratives were based on true and false events. The experts were not able to tell the true events from the false events; they performed at chance! Schacter (1996) drew the sobering conclusion that Ceci's and similar studies "provide striking evidence that a subjective experience of remembering can be simultaneously compelling and dead wrong" (p. 129).

Can Science Distinguish between True and False Memories?

It is unlikely that scientists will find a means of assessing the truth of such complex memories as childhood abuse years after it occurred. Researchers have, however, developed a technique of telling false from true memories in the context of the memory illusion effect. Memory illusions have been induced by adapting conventional list-learning methods (Chapters 4 and 12). Suppose the experimenter reads a list of related words, including *candy, cake,* and *chocolate,* but not including the word *sweet.* When subjects are later tested and asked whether *sweet* was on the study list, it tends to elicit many more false-alarm responses, false memories, than control words do (Chapter 12).

Schacter and colleagues used PET scans in an effort to distinguish between activity of the brain when it was processing an illusory word like *sweet* or a true word like *candy.* In both cases, there was increased brain activity in a region near the left hippocampus (Hilts, 1996). When the person remembered true words, the left temporal parietal region, a region implicated in the analysis of spoken words, was also active. According to Schacter, this activity reflected the person's memory for the auditory features of the word, the brain's echo. An intruding word, however, had no sensory component, and, as a consequence, there was no echo to detect in the temporal lobe. However promising the detection of memory illusions afforded by brain imaging may be, it is unlikely that scanning methods can reveal the accuracy of memories of abuse. Memories of abuse are far more complex than those of individual words (see Freyd & Gleaves,

1996) and the events they are based on date back much further than the brief retention intervals used in brain-imaging studies.

Where Do We Stand? The American Psychological Association Seeks a Response

Where does this state of scientific knowledge leave victims looking for help and the falsely accused looking for exoneration? Research on childhood sexual abuse remains difficult in the future because of the nature of abuse, the difficulty to document it, and the evolution of a person's interpretation of the abuse as he or she becomes an adult. Laboratory research, the standby of the scientist, cannot duplicate the emotional impact of abuse and its aftermath. Ethical considerations make it impossible for researchers to subject a person to planned and supervised emotional trauma in order to investigate memory of the staged traumatic event. The argument that traumatic memories are special is very hard to assess by experimental studies alone. The legal perspective, however, imposes a more stringent standard: Because false memories can be implanted relatively easily (Ceci, 1995; Hyman & Pentland, 1996; Roediger & McDermott, 1996), corroborative evidence over and above the recovered memory is necessary in order to convict a person of an alleged crime.

The American Psychological Association has sought to issue guidelines for psychologists on the recovered memory versus false memory controversy. After working for several years on the issue, a panel of psychologists, including clinical psychologists as well as memory researchers, published the following memorandum in 1995:

> Can a memory be forgotten and then remembered?
> Can a "memory" be suggested and then remembered as true?

These questions lie at the heart of the memory of childhood abuse issue. Experts in the field of memory and trauma can provide some answers, but clearly more study and research are needed. What we do know is that both memory researchers and clinicians who work with trauma victims agree that both phenomena occur. However, experienced clinical psychologists state that the phenomenon of a recovered memory is rare (e.g., one experienced practitioner reported having a recovered memory arise only once in 20 years of practice). Also, although laboratory studies have shown that memory is often inaccurate and can be influenced by outside factors, memory research usually takes place either in a laboratory or some everyday setting. For ethical and humanitarian reasons, memory researchers do not subject people to a traumatic event in order to test their memory of it. Because the issue has not been directly studied, we can not know whether a memory of a traumatic event is encoded and stored differently from a memory of a nontraumatic event.

What's the bottom line?
First, it's important to state that there is a consensus among memory researchers and clinicians that most people who were sexually abused as children remember all of part of what happened to them although they may not fully understand or disclose it. Concerning the issue of a recovered versus a pseudomemory, like many questions in science, the final answer is yet to be known. But most leaders in the field agree that although it is a rare occurrence, a memory of early childhood abuse that has been forgotten can be remembered later. However, these leaders also agree that it is possible to construct convincing pseudomemories for events that never occurred.

The mechanism(s) by which both of these phenomena happen are not well understood and, at this point it is impossible without further corroborative evidence, to distinguish a true memory from a false one. (American Psychological Association, Office for Public Affairs, August 1995)

In concluding this section, it is worthwhile to consider the point made by psychologists Harvey and Herman (1996) that in many cases, patients may not seek recovery of the horrors or legal action against others but rather are looking for an understanding of their own autobiography. Harvey and Herman described the case of a woman named Carol who was 11 years old when her parents were divorced. Carol's maternal uncle was her male guardian and adult companion. She considered him as her best friend, although he began molesting her immediately. At that time, she did not know what was going on and did not believe that her uncle would ever hurt her. She never told anyone of the abuse, nor did she forget about it. She just did not give much thought to the events, especially since her uncle moved out of town. However, 12 years later, when Carol was aged 25, there was a family reunion, including her uncle as the guest of honor. Carol did not want to see her uncle again nor did she want to reveal her feelings to any member of her family. She sought therapy in order to come to terms with her own feelings and her own past.

CONCLUSION

This chapter has presented an overview of diverse empirical effects of emotion on remembering. Repressed and recovered memories, tunnel memory, mood-dependent memory, autobiographical memory, and flashbulb memories are all manifestations of the multiple influences of affect on the formation and retrieval of memories. Research on this specialty has blossomed since the 1980s and 1990s, as documented in numerous volumes, including Neisser's (1982a) book on remembering in natural contexts, Christianson's (1992) handbook on emotions and memory, and Rubin's (1996b) book on autobiographical memories. In concluding the chapter, let me sketch how the findings on autobiographical and emotional memories might fit with theoretical frameworks used in traditional memory research.

Until the 1980s, the study of affect has been outside the strictly "cognitive" concerns of mainstream memory research, as Mandler (1992) observed. In the tradition of Ebbinghaus, the focus of classical memory research was on the raw information remembered, with little attention paid to the organism and its biological base and emotional context. The agnosticism vis-á-vis affect is reflected in the traditional frameworks of memory, including interference theory (Chapter 4), Atkinson and Shiffrin's memory model (Chapter 6), the levels-of-processing approach (Chapters 4 and 6), and the ACT and SAM models (Chapter 7), none of which accord emotional factors much significance.

In spite of the distance that was traditionally observed between cognitive approaches and research on affect, the latter is compatible with mainstream frameworks of memory, including resource allocation models (Ellis & Ashbrook, 1989), associative models (Chapter 4), schema models (Chapter 4), and neural network models (Chapter 7). According to Bower (e.g., 1992), emotions and autobiographical incidents can be represented as nodes in an associative memory network of the kind shown in Figure 4.10. The emotion and autobiographical nodes are assumed to be governed by the same network principles as any other nodes; they are connected to other nodes and pass spreading activation, as do other nodes. In terms of Bower's (1992) analysis, emotions also work as energizing agents in the memory system when an animal's expectations about the environment are violated (Rescorla & Wagner, 1972). Such surprises tend to be well remembered because they fulfill the function of adapting the organism to changing environmental conditions.

Schema models can readily accommodate autobiographical and emotional memories (but see Hintzman, 1993). Thus, Conway's (1996a, 1996b) model of autobiographical memories in Figure 9.2 was inspired by Schank's (1982) model of memory organization packets, an influential schema model in the field of artificial intelligence. *Memory organization packets* are units of knowledge to represent information of familiar and prototypical scenarios (e.g., holding a job, living with a friend, or taking a trip). Each of the scenarios subsumes smaller units—for instance, attending a sales meeting, buying a car, or planning a long weekend. Conway combined the hierarchical structure of the schema approach with a constructive retrieval process to formulate his framework of autobiographical memory. While Conway (1996a) expected further revisions of his framework, we saw in this chapter that his model has already been successful in accounting for empirical retrieval patterns of autobiographical memories.

Neural network models, such as McClelland's connectionist model (McClelland et al., 1995), are intended to simulate biologically based processes at all levels of neural structure. McClelland's model provides two mechanisms of handling emotional memories: neuromodulators and the basic process of forming associations between patterns. The model includes neuromodulators (e.g., neurotransmitters) much like the living organism (Chapter 3). Certain external stimuli would trigger the release of neuromodulators and thus affect the neural network by influencing the rate of memory formation and retrieval throughout the system.

These sketches served as illustrations of how emotional and autobiographical memories can be integrated into conventional memory frameworks. To be sure, the possibilities of linking affect and memory afforded by the different models have not yet been fully explored. However, in the future, we are likely to witness further theoretical developments of these issues, whether they occur within the frameworks named here or within other formulations. The driving force for the developments will come from applied concerns such as the recovered versus false memory debate as well as from research advances in cognitive psychology, neuroscience, and neuropsychology.

CHAPTER 10

MEMORY
IMPAIRMENTS

In April 1996, the Honolulu Police Department received an anonymous phone call reporting a man found face down and half conscious on a beach. The man had no wallet, no watch, no money, and no memory. Brought to a nearby hospital, the man complained of a headache but there were no external head wounds. However, a swelling of the man's brain indicated that he must have suffered a concussion of some sort.

Interviewed at the hospital, the man thought that the year was 1988, that his name was William Charles D'Souza, and that he was from North Manchester on Long Island. He was wrong on all counts: The year was 1996, his name was not D'Souza, and there is no town by the name of North Manchester on Long Island. So who was this man? Everyone wanted to know, especially the patient himself. Hoping to find an answer, the man agreed to being interviewed on TV. Although hundreds of people called in eager to help, no lead to the man's identity was found.

Several weeks later, the story of the mystery man was carried by *Newsday,* a New York area newspaper, and read by Detective Al Anderson of the Missing Persons Bureau at the Nassau County Police Department, Long Island. Detective Anderson solved part of the mystery by tracing the man's home to North Massapequa on Long Island, by locating the man's mother and brother, and by establishing the man's identity as Philip Charles Cutajar, age 37. Philip Cutajar was a former honors graduate from Columbia University, a former diplomat who had served at U.S. embassies in several countries, and a former advisor to President Bush on issues of military intelligence.

Told of his identity, Cutajar had mixed emotions. He was relieved but also fearful because he did not recognize the voices of his mother and brother, both of whom called him, and because he had no idea how he got to Hawaii, what he was doing there, and what had happened to him.

Cutajar's story was reported by the *New York Times* and other newspapers in July 1996. Readers invariably read such accounts, whether factual or fictional, with a mixture of fright and fascination. One inevitably wonders how so much of memory can disappear; why some functions, such as the use of language, are spared; whether the memories will return; and whether the patient will be the same person or be different, as happened to Henry in the movie *Regarding Henry.*

The radical loss of memory suffered by Philip Cutajar is relatively rare; memory impairments, however, are not. There is great variety among memory disorders, including amnesic disorders and disorders of immediate memory, semantic memory, executive functions, skill learning, implicit memory, and other forms of nondeclarative learning (Mayes, 1996). No single chapter can do justice to all of these impairments. Rather, this chapter discusses highlights of the major disorders—the amnesic syndrome and Alzheimer's disease—and of impairments of specialized memory functions, reviewing for each of the disorders the clinical presentation and psychological explanation.

Amnesic disorders include the loss of memories for past experience and of the ability for new learning; these disorders are attributed, at least in part, to damage to the medial temporal lobe, including the hippocampus, the diencephalon, and the basal forebrain. Special impairments include semantic agnosias, which are deficits in recognizing familiar stimuli, and working memory deficits resulting from injuries to the temporoparietal region or the frontal lobes, respectively. Amnesias, agnosias, and working memory disorders primarily affect memory, leaving other cognitive functions largely intact. Matters are different with Alzheimer's disease; here, the memory impairments are part of a general intellectual and emotional deterioration.

During the last few decades, the study of memory impairments has been a major source of new theoretical developments, typically in the direction of adopting functional divisions of memory in preference over the unitary system assumed by Ebbinghaus and his followers (Baddeley, 1990; Ribot, 1887). Working with her patient, H. M., Milner (1966) discovered the dissociation between short-term retention and long-term learning that was instrumental in advancing the two-store model of memory (Atkinson & Shiffrin, 1968; Cunitz & Glanzer, 1966; Waugh & Norman, 1965).

Subsequently, there were reports of additional dissociations. The dissociation between the occurrence of priming effects in amnesic patients and their inability to learn lists of words for recall and recognition led to the distinction between implicit memory and explicit memory (Warrington & Weiskrantz, 1968). The discovery that procedural memories are spared while declarative memories are affected by amnesia

contributed to the notion of separate procedural and declarative memory systems (Squire, 1987). The interaction of losses for semantic and episodic information promoted the distinction between episodic and semantic memory (Tulving, 1982). Finally, dissociations involving such processors as the phonological loop (Shallice & Warrington, 1970) and the central executive system advanced the multiple component model of working memory (Baddeley & Hitch, 1974, 1994; Becker, 1994).

For all its promise, research on memory disorders faces a number of daunting problems, among which are the following:

— *Taxonomy.* There are problems in classifying, describing, and finding causes for the disorders. Ribot (1887) already observed that a classification of memory impairments is, in many respects, "arbitrary" (1887, p. 70). He thought of two ways of classifying memory dysfunctions: in terms of the brain structures affected and in terms of the deficits observed. Ribot's distinction has survived the passage of a century, for as Baddeley (1990) noted, neurologists today classify patients according to (1) organic origins, such as head trauma, interruption of the blood flow to the brain, neural infection, and toxic effects; and (2) the commonality of symptoms, even if there are different organic origins.

— *Subject variability.* A given memory impairment may result from any one of different etiologies and the deficits may vary widely, with some patients exhibiting pronounced proactive interference, others making errors of intrusion, and still others displaying errors of omission (Schacter & Tulving, 1982). Some patients can be helped by certain strategies of memorization (distributed practice) or retrieval strategies (use of retrieval cues), whereas others cannot. It is difficult to compare different patient groups. Patient numbers are typically small and different research teams frequently examine patients at different stages of a given dysfunction.

— *Interpretation.* It is inherently difficult to interpret the patterns of observed memory loss in amnesia, especially when a researcher fails to establish an effect that is normally found in unimpaired individuals. One such effect is the levels-of-processing effect, where semantic encoding is more effective than phonological encoding (Chapter 4). Two researchers using standard methods and materials failed to find this effect in amnesic patients. The patients learned nothing in the experiment, regardless of whether a semantic or a phonological encoding task was used (Cermak & Reale, 1978). What does this result mean? Are amnesic patients not capable of semantic encoding? Or is it simply an artifact, a floor effect, due to the use of stimulus materials that were too difficult for the patients? A floor effect occurs when retention is as poor as it can be. In other words, the retention measure is no longer sensitive to changes in the independent variable (e.g., the encoding task). It is because of these ambiguities that some theorists question the potential of research on amnesia for basic memory research (Crowder, 1982b; Murdock, 1974; see also Neely, 1989).

— *Application.* Much of the research on memory impairments is motivated by the goal of finding a way to facilitate the daily lives of patients. Although to date, the prospect of rehabilitating memory disorders is modest, research has shown that patients may nevertheless benefit from memory management training. Different research groups have developed techniques to help patients cope with certain aspects of their disabilities by teaching them rudimentary skills, whether it is using computer terminology (Glisky & Schacter, 1987), recalling shopping lists (Wilson, 1996), or remembering to take medication (Raskin & Sohlberg, 1996). The challenge for applied research is to devise means of handling the limits in the amount of information patients can acquire and of generalizing training success from the clinic to everyday situations (Chapter 12).

THE AMNESIC DISORDERS

The term *amnesia* comes from the Greek *amnestia* (as in *amnesty*) or *amnesia,* which means *without memory.* In the psychological literature, the term *amnesia* is usually modified to indicate the pattern of the memory loss, as in *anterograde* and *retrograde amnesia,* or to reflect a presumed cause, as in *psychogenic amnesia,* or to describe the scope of the memory loss, as in *global amnesia.* This section illustrates the diversity of amnesia by reviewing representative cases, discusses patterns of amnesic memory losses, and reviews information processing accounts of the impairments.

Case Studies

Understanding amnesia begins with a description of the memory dysfunction of individual patients. We, too, will begin our discussion of amnesia by considering two cases of amnesia in detail: a patient described by a team of Swiss researchers headed by Armin Schnider (Schnider, Regard, & Landis, 1994) and the case of Clive Wearing, as described by Barbara Wilson and Clive Wearing's wife, Deborah (Wilson & Wearing, 1995).

Schnider's Patient

Schnider's patient (abbreviated S. P.) was a 66-year-old retired mechanic when he suffered the type of stroke technically known as an *embolic infarct.* He had a history of hypertension and heart disease sufficiently severe to necessitate a coronary bypass operation when he was age 60. Magnetic resonance imaging (MRI) revealed that the stroke had affected both of S. P.'s medial temporal lobes, the left hippocampus, and other neighboring areas, except the amygdala.

Shortly after the stroke, S. P. was confused and disoriented in his hospital room. He recovered from the initial confusion but conversations and tests indicated severe anterograde and retrograde amnesia. When he left his room for a couple of moments, he could not find his way back. He could not recall being examined by his physician. He did not recognize any people other than his wife and children. He could talk, read, and write but he had difficulty naming certain objects and experiences. Anterograde memory tests revealed dramatic losses in all tasks but the digit span. His digit span was 5 with a backward span of 3. However, after five minutes, he could not remember any word from a list of 15 words, nor recall a visual design from 10 presented to him, nor reproduce a pantomime from 10 he was shown, although he was able to reproduce each immediately after seeing it. S. P.'s ability to name objects was severely impaired; he was able to name only 1 of 15 drawings of common objects. He suffered from severe retrograde amnesia that affected most of his autobiographical memories: He did not recognize his town and his life-long friends, nor did he have any recollection of major events including World War II and the nuclear accident in Chernobyl in 1986. All he could say about Chernobyl was that it was "bad."

S. P.'s amnesia persisted over several months of observation. He would forget any event, including day trips with his wife. Five minutes after returning from an outing, he would complain of being stuck at his house forever. Although S. P. read the newspaper several times a day, he had no recollection of having done so. The loss of recent and remote autobiographical memories exhibited by S. P. is common among amnesic patients. A patient known as K. C., described by Tulving, had no recollection of events in the decade between the time he left college and the time of his traffic accident in 1980. The patient described the intervening years as blank and his memory as being asleep. When Tulving asked him to describe the state of his mind, the patient responded that his mind was "like being in a room with nothing there" or "like swimming in the middle of a lake" with nothing there to hold one up (Hilts, 1995).

Despite his severe amnesia, S. P. was able to acquire a new procedural skill similar to the mirror drawing task. He successfully learned to draw over geometrical figures without directly looking at the designs. Feedback was provided via a video camera, such that left to right movements of the hand were shown as up to down movements. Over a block of five trials, S. P. improved his performance both in speed and accuracy and he maintained his level of performance over an interval of 24 hours. The level of retention for a perceptual-motor skill is in contrast with his loss of episodic memory. However, such dissociations between declarative and procedural memories are common in other amnesia patients.

Clive Wearing
In the mid-1980s, Clive Wearing was a musician and producer known throughout the United Kingdom. He was famous for his work at the British Broadcasting Corporation, director of a well-known London choir, a conductor, and a highly respected historian of music. He was nationally known as the music director for the wedding of Princess Diana and Prince Charles in 1981 and for singing at services at Westminster Cathedral. Among his colleagues, Wearing had a legendary ability to read the most difficult scores. He worked nonstop seven days a week, consumed by a passion for music. He was in the middle of preparing a concert when illness struck on a weekend in March 1985.

Wearing began to suffer a headache that become nearly intolerable in the next few days. He also exhibited such flu symptoms as feeling cold and a fever of 104 degrees. Wearing received medication to treat the flu and his symptoms apparently improved. However, when Wearing became disoriented, began to confabulate, and got lost in town, it became evident that he suffered from an illness other than the flu. He was admitted to the emergency room of the local hospital. There, his illness was diagnosed as encephalitis, an inflammation of the central nervous system resulting from an infection. He drifted in and out of consciousness and suffered an epileptic seizure within a few days. Over succeeding months, his memory impairment worsened.

Three years later, his wife, Deborah Wearing, described his illness as follows:

> Clive's world now consists of a moment with no past to anchor it and no future to look ahead to. He sees what is right in front of him but as soon as that information hits the brain it fades. Nothing registers. Everything goes in perfectly well.... He perceives his world as you or I do, but as soon as he's perceived it and looked away it's gone for him. So it's a moment to moment consciousness as it were ... a time vacuum. (Wilson & Wearing, 1995, p. 15)

Because of Wearing's fame in Britain and in order to raise the awareness of memory disorders, his wife permitted his case to be presented on national TV and in the press (Wilson & Wearing, 1995). It is for this reason that, unlike other patients, Clive Wearing is referred to by his full name.

Deborah observed problems in Wearing's semantic memory as early as 1985. He could not distinguish between *honey, jam,* and *marmalade*. He ate a lemon, including the peel, apparently mistaking it for another type of fruit, and he confused various bathroom articles, including soap and toothpaste. Six years later, when given a semantic memory test that involved naming words, he scored a low score of only 2 out of a possible score of 30. For Wearing, such a low score was particularly remarkable, considering that he was a crossword puzzle expert before his illness.

Wearing experienced severe losses in his autobiographical memory, both in terms of remembering public events and autobiographical episodes. His amnesia covered his entire adult life and most of his childhood. He had no recollection of where he worked and he believed that he was employed by the hospital. He confabu-

lated memories from actual episodes that came back to him and from imagined events. Having worked as an undergraduate in a hotel during summer vacations, he came to believe that he had been working at a hospital for many years and that his job was to coordinate the work of fellow students during their vacations.

Following the onset of his illness, Wearing lost the capacity for new learning, but in a curious twist, he coined new definitions for words, remaining consistent in their use, thus indicating that he remembered his own word creations. He defined the word *amnesia* as coming from the Latin *anti-amnesia,* meaning *autumn*. Wearing's musical ability appeared intact, at least to untrained observers. He was quite proficient at singing, reading music, and conducting the choir, but there was a noticeable deterioration in his piano playing, as he lost his ability to play difficult contemporary pieces.

As revealed by CT and MRI scans of Wearing's brain, structural changes were seen in both temporal lobes with dilations of certain regions compared to their normal state. Wilson and Wearing (1995) attributed Clive Wearing's semantic memory impairment to the alterations in the temporal lobes. The hippocampus was almost completely destroyed, returning an "abnormal signal," indicating the source of Wearing's lost ability for new learning. There was also damage to the diencephalon, which presumably contributed to Wearing's retrograde amnesia.

Clive Wearing and Schnider's patient are but two of the many cases of amnesia described in the literature. Beginning with Korsakoff's (1996) 1889 report on the memory dysfunction of an alcoholic patient and Ribot's *Diseases of Memory* (1887), this literature spans well over a century. More recent works include Barbizet's (1970) *Human Memory and Its Pathology* and the book *Human Memory and Amnesia* edited by Cermak (1982). The book *Broken Memories* (Campbell & Conway, 1995) contains over 30 case histories, including patients who lost much of their memory following strokes, accidents, or encephalitis. For many of these individuals, neuroimaging records exist in addition to complete batteries of neuropsychological tests (see also O'Connor, Verfaellie, & Cermak, 1995). Hilt's (1995) book, *Memory's Ghost: The Strange Tale of Mr. M and the Nature of Memory,* gives an in-depth account of the case of H. M., beginning with his life as an adolescent prior to his illness and operation in the 1950s and ending with his residence at a Massachusetts nursing home, spanning three decades.

Performance Patterns in Amnesia

Based on a large body of case studies, however diverse in etiology, neuropsychologists have adopted the following features in order to identify the *amnesic syndrome* (Mayes, 1996):

- *Retrograde amnesia* involves impairment in the recollection of facts and episodes experienced before the injury.
- *Anterograde amnesia* involves impairment of remembering new facts and episodes experienced after the injury.
- Relatively spared functions may include memory for skills, implicit memory, semantic memory, and performance on such working memory measures as the digit span.

In brief, the general performance pattern in most amnesics is characterized by adequate retention for the short term with large long-term memory deficits. Whereas memory functions are severely impaired in amnesic patients, they tend to retain a relatively high IQ (Squire, 1995). The dissociation between remembering on the one hand and intellectual functions on the other has been interpreted by Squire as evidence of different brain systems subserving these functions (Chapter 11).

Retrograde Amnesia: Losing Past Memories

When their consciousness returns following an accident or a disease, patients first tend to be disoriented, a condition referred to as *posttraumatic amnesia.* Patients do not know where they are and what happened to them. They have no memory for events preceding the accident, with the duration of the memory loss varying from a few minutes to several years. The difficulty of recollecting past episodes is known as *retrograde amnesia.*

Typically, after some time lag, memories tend to come back, beginning with the most distant memories in accordance with Ribot's law (Chapter 2). In some cases, retrograde amnesia has no temporal pattern and recollections are uniformly lost across preceding decades (Hodges, 1995). In cases of differential retrograde amnesia, some types of information are lost, while others are retained. Following severe encephalitis, patient L. D., for example, had great difficulty recalling autobiographical events that occurred prior to her illness. She was not able to name relatives and friends nor recognize her belongings or her house, but she was able to recognize faces of celebrities and identify public events (Butters, O'Connor, & Verfaellie, 1995).

Retrograde amnesia is assessed by a variety of instruments to measure autobiographical memory, semantic memory, and general event memory (Mayes, 1996). In tests of autobiographical memory, the person tries to recall or is cued about such life periods as childhood, young adulthood, and the recent past, or such themes as schools, friends, marriage, trips, and jobs (Chapter 9). Semantic memory tests assess the patient's knowledge for a set of stimulus items, including both naturally occurring things (e.g., animals) and human-made objects (e.g., furniture). Tests of general memory probe the patient's memory for major events, wars, famous people, the prices of common goods, and

TV programs from the time period 10, 20, 30 or more years prior to the illness. Although there may be islands of recall in retrograde amnesia, there is usually a continuous decline of recollections from remote to recent events and faces in amnesic patients compared to a recall level of up to 80% for all decades tested in control subjects of equal age. In estimating prices, patients tend to understate the prices—the more so, the more severe the amnesia, an effect indicating perseverance of remote memories and memory loss for recent memories.

Anterograde Amnesia: Problems in Acquiring New Information

Amnesic patients may experience difficulties in remembering episodes and acquiring new information after the onset of their disability. This feature is referred to as *anterograde amnesia*. H. M., for example, suffered from anterograde amnesia in addition to retrograde amnesia. Similarly, Clive Wearing and Schnider's patient, S. P., were not able to learn new facts about their environment nor facts presented in list-learning experiments. S. P. did not remember a single word from a list of 15 words presented to him a few minutes ago. If the brain injury is mild, patients tend to recover from anterograde amnesia and regain the ability of new learning. In severe traumatic brain injuries, anterograde amnesia may be severe and persist permanently. Patients commit errors on the content of the information and the context. They tend to confuse between sources of lists (e.g., grocery lists for different days) and fail to recall the context in which they acquired the target information (Goldstein & Levin, 1995).

Anterograde amnesia is assessed by having the patient learn new information (e.g., a list of digits, words, or sentences). The most widely used instrument is the Wechsler Memory Scale, which consists of seven subtests to measure paired-associate learning, story memory, the digit span test, the capacity to reproduce drawings, and other abilities. The Wechsler scale is easy to administer and it has a large normative data base (Wechsler, 1987). The Rivermead Behavioral Memory Test has been designed to evaluate the capacity for learning as well as to assess memory demands patients encounter in their daily lives. The test consists of 12 components, including a recognition test, immediate and delayed recall of a route, remembering a message, and a test of prospective memory. The latter consists of doing a particular task in response to a cue presented after a delay. The Rivermead Test has been standardized on different patient groups and on unimpaired control subjects, it has been validated against memory assessments of therapists and relatives, and it is sensitive to detecting recovery of memory function in patients who suffered severe brain injury.

Although retrograde amnesia and anterograde amnesia were described in separate sections here, it is typically the case that patients—including H. M., S. P., and Clive Wearing—exhibit both of these kinds of memory deficit. Squire (1987) entertained the hypothesis that both deficits are "joined by the fact that the neural system damaged in amnesia prevents new learning from being established and also prevents recently formed memories from becoming fully consolidated" (p. 214). This pattern of dysfunction has been attributed to a faulty mechanism of consolidating the memory trace (Squire, 1995).

Spared Memory Functions

Because of the wide range of etiologies of amnesia, there are no general rules on spared memories in amnesia patients. Some patients retain the capacity, although somewhat reduced, to acquire perceptual skills, motor skills, cognitive skills, and, under very specialized conditions, new declarative knowledge (Hamann & Squire, 1995).

Implicit Memory and Memory for Skills.
Amnesic patients benefit from priming effects, as do nonimpaired control subjects. *Priming* refers to facilitated recognition and identification of a variety of stimuli, whether they are presented visually or aurally and whether they are words or objects (Chapter 5). It was the spared ability of amnesic patients to benefit from priming in the word-stem completion task that prompted Warrington and Weiskrantz (1982) to advocate two different kinds of memory—implicit and explicit memory—assumed to have separate neural bases (Mishkin, Malamut, & Bachevalier, 1984; Chapter 11).

As in normal subjects, reading speed increases as amnesic patients read a passage repeatedly. The rate of improvement in the patients is similar to that of the control subjects, but unlike the latter, the patients do not remember the content of the passages (Squire, 1995). Amnesic subjects can learn artificial grammars, classification tasks, and contingencies between events, such as those that are used in making weather forecasts, for example. In Chapter 5, I mentioned the findings of Squire and colleagues that amnesic patients can learn to predict the weather in the context of a simple computer game. Card patterns were displayed on a computer screen and correlated probabilistically with an icon representing sunshine or rain. For each display, the subjects were asked to predict rain or shine, and then given immediate feedback. Although the amnesic patients felt that they had no understanding of the task, they learned to predict the weather as well as a nonpatient control group did (reported in Squire, 1995). To the extent that patients retain the capacity for procedural learning, they can benefit from occupational and physical therapy, and possibly from training for memory management (Goldstein & Levin, 1995).

There is even one report of an amnesic patient, a highly motivated 47-year-old woman

known as C. S., who succeeded in acquiring rudimentary skills in a second language (Hirst, Phelps, Johnson, & Volpe, 1988). This patient suffered from anterograde amnesia resulting from a cardiopulmonary arrest at age 36. Neuropsychological evaluations revealed that C. S. scored high on the verbal components of the Wechsler Adult Intelligence Scales, but she did disproportionally poorly on the Wechsler Memory Scale and on other memory tests.

Nevertheless, C. S. was able to acquire some Italian and French. Hirst and colleagues determined that her progress after nine hour-long sessions of French tutoring distributed over two weeks was as good as that of her nonamnesic husband, a professor of Spanish. Tutoring expressly emphasized learning by use so that rote memorization was avoided. For example, vocabulary items were learned by pointing to objects. While C. S.'s progress in French was as good as her husband's, she was not able to learn such verbal materials as word lists and sentences from a story. Apparently, C. S.'s language-learning ability was the one domain spared after her illness. Unfortunately, C. S.'s spared language-learning ability is not very common. Patient P. V., an Italian woman who sustained a lesion to the left hemisphere, was not able to learn French or Russian vocabulary (Papagano & Vallar, 1995).

Working Memory. A preserved working memory has traditionally been one of the hallmarks of the amnesias. Baddeley (1990), for example, listed two patients whose performance on the digit span and the Brown-Peterson distractor task exceeded that of many normal comparison subjects. However, in other cases, amnesic patients performed poorly on these and other short-term memory tasks. Parkinson (1982), for example, observed patients with Korsakoff's syndrome who performed less well on repeated administrations of the digit span test and in terms of the recency effect in free-recall testing than a group of control subjects of equal age and background.

Semantic Memory. Typically, amnesic patients have an intact semantic memory (except Clive Wearing); they still understand the meaning of words and can use language correctly. Tulving's patient, K. C., for example, exhibited excellent memory for world knowledge and was able to learn some new general facts, including about new buildings in his hometown, but he had no personal recollection of having acquired the information nor about having seen the buildings in question (Tulving, 1993). He had to learn about his own life the way that we might learn about our parents' lives. In other words, one might have knowledge of the events in one's parents' lives, but no shared experiences.

Acquiring New Declarative Information. Losing the ability to acquire new facts has been a defining feature of amnesia for as long as the disability has been known. It is therefore of great interest that scientists at different hospitals succeeded in training amnesic patients to acquire new declarative knowledge. This achievement was based on special training procedures that minimized errors made by the patient (Chapter 12). Tulving and colleagues at the University of Toronto adapted the word-stem completion task in training patient K. C. to respond correctly to context cues provided by a sentence frame. The key was to restrict the patient's response choices. The researchers presented him with about 80 picture-sentence pairs representing scenarios such as a vacationer surrounded by mosquitos or police shooting an assassin. In testing, phrases such as *Police shot _ss_ss_n* were presented. After 20 training sessions, extending over 20 weeks, K. C. tended to complete the fragments correctly when the two context words were presented.

Tulving's success with K. C. contrasted with failure of the usual training method where the patient saw the sentence frame and had to select a response from all the target words on the training list. The crucial improvement of Tulving's procedure was to minimize errors, and thus interference, produced by those errors (Tulving, Hayman, & MacDonald, 1991). That K. C. was not unique in acquiring new facts was demonstrated by two neuropsychologists at the Veterans Hospital in San Diego, Stephan Hamann and Larry Squire. Using Tulving's procedure, these investigators trained as many as 19 amnesic patients to acquire declarative memories (Hamann & Squire, 1995).

Our review has shown the variety of patterns of impaired and spared memory functions in amnesia, a result that reflects the variety of clinical presentations of amnesia. However different these presentations may be, according to O'Connor and colleagues (1995), they nevertheless share a common feature—*core amnesia*—which is "a core inability to reconstruct past experience from fragments of the initial episode" (p. 77).

Explaining Amnesia

Given the performance patterns of amnesic patients, it is of theoretical and practical interest to identify the functional deficits that underlie the impairment of memory. Knowledge of the processes that are broken may suggest ways of repairing or at least managing the amnesic syndrome. Historically, investigators have tended to attribute amnesia to a malfunction in a single processing mechanism, specifically to greater interference among memory traces in amnesia or to deficits in encoding and retrieval processes. It turned out, however, that the patterns of memory impairments in amnesia were too diverse to implicate a single faulty mechanism. Furthermore, research to evaluate hypotheses of processing deficits in amnesia proved to be difficult because of the problem of establishing appropriate control conditions in nonimpaired individuals to use as a base of comparison. For example, in order to compare forgetting rates in amnesic patients and healthy control subjects, the initial performance level must be equated, a requirement that has been difficult to meet.

In light of these challenges, one should not expect a single mechanism to explain all of the memory deficits observed in amnesia. Rather, the view emerged that there may well be different functional deficits for amnesias of different origin, presentation, and duration. According to recent theoretical views, memory impairments in amnesia are likely to result from a variety of deficits in storage processes (Mayes, 1996; Squire, 1995) and from faulty metamemory processes, such as failures in monitoring and eliminating errors during learning (Baddeley, 1996b).

Difficulties for Interference, Retrieval, and Encoding Hypotheses

Theorists have formulated functional accounts of amnesia in terms of theoretical frameworks that were popular during certain periods. In the 1970s, interference theory, information processing theory, and the levels-of-processing approach provided the conceptual apparatus for hypotheses of the amnesic deficit. These hypotheses attributed the memory impairments to greater interference, to a deficit at retrieval, or to a deficit during encoding, respectively. Although none of the early formulations survived, it is nevertheless worthwhile to sketch the theoretical problems they encountered.

According to the interference hypothesis of amnesia, patients are more susceptible to interference than normal people; they experience a sort of catastrophic interference (Warrington & Weiskrantz, 1970; Chapter 7; McCloskey & Cohen, 1989). The interference hypothesis was called into question when Warrington and

Weiskrantz (1978) tested amnesics and control subjects in an interference design (Chapter 4) demonstrating that the amount of interference in both groups was equivalent. According to retrieval accounts, information, although successfully coded and stored, has become inaccessible as a result of retrieval failure. Baddeley (1982), for example, believed that retrieval involves an automatic component and a strategic recollection component, with the latter being impaired in amnesic patients. But Baddeley changed his view when he discovered an amnesic patient who exhibited excellent recollection of events early in his life (Baddeley, 1990, p. 426).

Encoding deficit hypotheses were framed in terms of the levels-of-processing notion. There is a rich body of evidence from research involving unimpaired people that semantic encoding produces better retention than phonetic or visual encoding (Craik & Tulving, 1975; Chapter 4). Applying the depth-of-processing effect to amnesia, the encoding deficit view suggested that amnesic patients fail to encode information semantically and thus fail to generate a viable trace. Early studies tended to support this hypothesis by demonstrating that Korsakoff patients did not exhibit the typical levels effect (Cermak & Reale, 1978). However, subsequent researchers attributed the failure of the levels effect in amnesics to a floor effect; the retention level of patients was too low to permit a discrimination between degrees of encoding. When highly memorable materials (e.g., cartoons) were used, a levels effect was observed in amnesic patients (Baddeley, 1990).

There are additional reasons that make encoding deficits in amnesics unlikely. Amnesic patients tend to perform remarkably well in intelligence tests, suggesting that they have the ability to encode information effectively. Similarly, at very short retention intervals, amnesics are able to answer questions about pictures just seen. They apparently hold the information in working memory, much as unimpaired people do (Mayes, 1996).

Given the difficulties of the interference, retrieval, and encoding accounts of amnesia, alternative hypotheses gained greater currency. These hypotheses attribute the amnesic memory impairment (1) to deficits in consolidating the memory trace (Squire, 1995), (2) to the failure in fully storing the context of an event (Mayes, 1996), and (3) to the difficulty of amnesic patients to monitor the errors they make (Baddeley, 1996b). Theorists acknowledge that these hypotheses are not mutually exclusive. Indeed, all of the factors envisioned by the models may contribute to the amnesic syndrome.

Consolidation Hypotheses

Consolidation accounts assume that memories undergo a transition from a relatively vulnerable state to a more stable state during the period after learning, where that period is sometimes measured in minutes and sometimes in weeks (Mueller-Pilzecker, 1900; Squire, 1995). There are two compatible and equally plausible versions of the consolidation hypothesis: neurally oriented theories (e.g., Squire, 1995) and functional theories (e.g., Schacter & Tulving, 1982). The former emphasize changes in neural structures, whereas the latter view consolidation in terms of changes in the organization of the target information. Under either version, damage to the memory system would impair recent memories more than remote ones, a prediction consistent with Ribot's law (1887).

Consolidation of Neural Structures.

Squire (e.g., 1995) favored a biologically based consolidation process. According to his model, new information is temporarily held in the hippocampus and subsequently transferred to diverse association areas in the cortex. Consolidation presumably creates networks of neural structures distributed across separate cortical

regions. Any damage to the hippocampus interferes with the transfer or consolidation process. Squire and colleagues examined memory consolidation over a 16-week span in monkeys. As reviewed in Chapter 3, the animals learned to associate different objects with food reward. Learning episodes occurred at different intervals, ranging from 2 to 16 weeks before the hippocampus was lesioned. In testing, retention differed according to the interval between the lesion and the test. When the monkeys learned the association only two weeks before surgery, memory was poor; when 12 weeks elapsed between learning and surgery, retention was far better, thus mirroring the pattern in patients suffering from retrograde amnesia.

Forming an Integrated Memory Trace.

Memory consolidation may also be viewed in functional terms—namely, as forming connections among the aspects of the events a person experiences. Normal people integrate episodes they experience with their personal identity and remember that they have experienced the event. Amnesic patients may learn events—for example, that sometimes pins are hidden in people's hands, as Claparède's amnesic patient learned (Chapter 5)—but they fail to make the connection between the experience and the "I," the experiencer. Schacter and Tulving (1982) suggested that this integration process is impaired in amnesia; thus, the amnesic deficit is a storage deficit of episodic memory. Patients may store facts and episodes, as normal controls do, but this information remains disconnected from the awareness system, from conscious memory. Tulving's (1993) patient, K. C., for example, retained knowledge of facts about the world and about himself following a motorcycle accident, but he did not remember having experienced any of the events he knows. He could learn new facts about his environment; for example, he knew the name of the Sky Dome in Toronto, which was erected following his accident. However, he did not remember ever visiting the Sky Dome, although he had done so many times.

Such disconnections are not necessarily confined to individuals with clinical memory deficits. Nonimpaired people frequently experience dissociations between context and content, referred to as *source amnesia*. For instance, being absorbed in deep thought or conversation, one may arrive at a certain location without remembering how one got there. Everyone puts their shoes on in the morning; however, rarely does anyone remember which shoe he or she put on first. Finally, there is the phenomenon of unconscious plagiarism, committed by the scientist who thinks of a seminal experiment that has already been published (Chapter 5; Marsh & Bower, 1993).

Mayes's Context Memory Deficit Hypothesis

The context memory deficit hypothesis was proposed in distinction to encoding deficit hypotheses of memory impairments in amnesia (Mayes, 1996). According to Mayes (1996), the adequate performance of amnesics on intelligence tests and on short-term memory tests suggests that they encode facts and events normally. Because the difference in performance between patients and nonpatients becomes evident in tests of long-term memory, Mayes attributed the impairment in amnesiacs to a deficit at the stage of storing the information.

Mayes's context memory deficit hypothesis distinguishes between the target information of an event and its context, including the spatial context, the temporal context, and sensory modality information. It is assumed that storage of the latter cues is impaired in amnesia. Mayes assumed further that, whereas retention in the recall paradigm depends largely on associating target items with their background context, performance in recognition tests is primarily based on a familiarity judgment, thus depending less on the context. If the memory deficit of amnesic patients were the result of faulty target-context

associations, as claimed by Mayes's hypothesis, then the rate of forgetting in the context-dependent recall test should be faster than in recognition testing.

Mayes and colleagues conducted several experiments in which they compared the rate of forgetting of amnesic patients and nonamnesic control subjects in the recall and recognition paradigms. In order to ensure an equal rate of initial learning in both groups, the materials were presented repeatedly to the amnesic patients. As predicted by the context memory deficit hypothesis, in amnesic patients the forgetting rate was accelerated in the recall paradigm but comparable to control subjects in the recognition test. Mayes interpreted this result in support of the hypothesis that the patients are deficient in storing the contextual attributes of events, including their spatial and temporal context and their sensory modality.

Baddeley and Wilson's Error Monitoring Hypothesis

We conclude this section by considering Baddeley's hypothesis on the functional deficit in new learning by amnesic patients, the error monitoring hypothesis (Baddeley, 1996b; Baddeley & Wilson, 1994). Baddeley formulated the hypothesis to account for the performance of amnesic patients in a variety of tasks, including the word-stem completion task. Baddeley and Wilson (1994) used the latter to compare the performance of patients in an "errorful," or trial-and-error, condition and in an errorless condition.

In the trial-and-error condition, subjects were shown the first letters of a word (e.g., *br*) and asked to guess the target word (e.g., *bring*). The subject might guess *brain, bread,* and *brown,* but was told that these guesses were wrong. The person was given the correct word (e.g., *bring*) and asked to write it down. In the errorless condition, the experimenter would present the first letters together with the target word, asking people to write down the word.

Thus, people were given the target word in both the guessing and errorless conditions, except they had to guess it in the former condition. In testing, patients were given the initial syllables and asked to write down any word that came to mind. Baddeley and Wilson found that the patients completed the word stems significantly better in the errorless condition, indicating that the errors patients made in the guessing condition interfered with their performance.

According to the error monitoring hypothesis, performance in the word-stem completion task may draw on either explicit or implicit memory. If the explicit memory system is intact, the correct response will occur, thus giving an advantage to unimpaired subjects. If explicit memory is impaired, as it is in amnesic patients, it cannot provide the response, and implicit memory serves as a backup mechanism. Implicit memory, however, provides no mechanism for monitoring and therefore for eliminating errors, and, as a result, the patient tends to repeat the errors. It is for this reason that patients fare better under the errorless study condition.

In concluding this section, recall that, although amnesia research only recently gained visibility in mainstream theories of memory, it has occupied the interest of memory researchers for well over a century (Chapter 2; Ribot, 1887). Research on amnesia was motivated both by the desire of helping patients and by scientists' curiosity about the operations of normal memory. The mix of impaired and spared functions observed in amnesia was thought to allow inferences about memory structures and processes in the intact memory system. These efforts, now aided by neuroimaging and electrophysiological methods, continue and may eventually lead to a fuller understanding of impaired memory as well as normal memory.

The practical concern with helping patients continues to pose a problem because, to date, none of the theoretical accounts of amnesia has sufficiently advanced to furnish the tools to rehabilitate or fully manage amnesic impairments. Nevertheless, as described in Chapter 12, some of these accounts have been instrumental in developing techniques to assist patients in coping with the deficit, even though on a modest scale. Capitalizing on the spared functions of patients, psychologists have trained some patients to learn simple contingencies between events, others to use a rudimentary vocabulary of a second language, and still others to acquire a body of new declarative knowledge.

IMPAIRMENT OF SPECIALIZED MEMORY FUNCTIONS

In contrast to the amnesic syndrome, where new learning and recovery of old memories are severely impaired, there are impairments that affect memory selectively. The patient's performance is hindered in specific tasks, whether it is the ability to recognize specific objects, to express certain words, to keep track of one's responses, or to remember to do things at a future time. Such impairments include the agnosias, which are deficits in recognizing certain classes of objects or specific stimuli. Prosopagnosia, for example, is the failure to recognize faces (*prosopon,* Greek for *face*). Damasio and colleagues (1990) described the case of a woman who suddenly no longer recognized faces, including those of her husband and daughter, as well as her own face reflected in the mirror. However, the woman had not lost the knowledge of her friends and family, because she retained the ability to recognize them by their voices. It was, therefore, the visual access route to memory that was impaired, not the auditory route nor the memory itself (Chapter 3).

Although such deficits occasionally are found in amnesics, they may also occur in isolation. Researchers investigate these dysfunctions in the hope that they may offer an opportunity to uncover relations between brain function and memory performance (see Martin et al., 1996).

This section treats memory impairments of semantic memory and deficits of different working memory components. We will see that the study of these impairments has had implications for the development of models of semantic memory and working memory.

Semantic Memory Deficits

What is an orange? What is a cat? What is a car? These are questions everyone, including toddlers, answer routinely. However, when psychologist Elaine Funnell asked Mrs. P., a retired math teacher, "What is a kitten?" the latter replied, "What on earth is a kitten?" To the question "Does a mouse have a beak?" Mrs. P. replied, "If I knew what a beak was I could tell you" (Funnell, 1995). Mrs. P.'s symptoms are similar to those of patient P. P., who could not define such common animals as dogs and cats (Chapter 4). Both patients had suffered a lesion in the temporal lobe, presumably as the result of encephalitis. The tragic aspect of these cases was that the disability grew progressively worse, so that after several years, patients developed increasing gaps in their knowledge. These are deficits of semantic memory—a person's knowledge of the world remembered independently from specific experiences and episodes (Tulving, 1982). Remarkably, the patients' episodic memory remained largely intact, thus contrasting with the reverse pattern in amnesic patients such as H. M. and K. C.

Warrington and Shallice (1984) reported that the loss of semantic knowledge is not uniform. Examining patients who had suffered from encephalitis, these investigators found that the patients had greater difficulty identifying line drawings of living things than of inanimate objects. The patients also found it more difficult to define living things than nonliving objects. One patient did not know what a parrot was and defined a wasp as a bird that flies. However, the patient still retained the knowledge of a towel as material used to dry people.

Warrington and Shallice interpreted these findings as a clue to the geography of semantic memory. Other researchers, however, were concerned about the possibility of confounds in Warrington and Shallice's stimuli—namely, that the drawings of living things happened to be less discriminable (Gaffan & Heywood, 1993). On the other hand, in a study involving two patients, Hillis and Caramazza (1991) reported a double dissociation that makes confounding from stimulus complexity less likely. Hillis and Caramazza (1991) studied two patients, J. J. and P. S., who exhibited remarkable performance deficits in a category naming task. J. J. was a stroke victim with injuries to the temporal lobe and the basal ganglia. P. S. suffered injury to his temporal lobes from a severe blow to his head. In the naming task, the subject was shown line drawings of objects from different categories and asked to name them. The categories included land animals, water animals, birds, vegetables, fruit, body parts, vehicles, and furniture. Patient J. J. exhibited an advantage of animal identification over such categories as foods, furniture, and body parts. P. S., on the other hand, did much better on the latter categories than on the former.

We may assume, therefore, that the differences in recovering information about different categories are not artifactual. However, there is still the problem of generalizing the results to the population at large. The category-specific effect could be a side effect of the patients' clinical condition and have little relevance for unimpaired individuals. Martin and colleagues (1996) at the National Institutes of Health set out to determine whether there was evidence of the localization of semantic memory functions in nonimpaired individuals. The scientists recruited 16 healthy volunteers and, using PET imaging, recorded changes in blood-flow patterns in specific brain regions as the subjects identified line drawings of animals and of tools. In both tasks, the left and right ventral temporal lobes and Broca's area were activated. There were, however, areas uniquely engaged by each of the tasks: Naming animals activated the left medial occipital lobe, a visual area, whereas naming tools activated a different region, the left premotor area.

What are the implications of category-specific performance patterns in patient and nonpatient populations for general theories of memory? According to Baddeley (1990), such patterns suggest that semantic memory is not a monolithic system; rather, it consists of multiple subsystems. However, it is not clear what those dimensions are: Semantic information could be represented (1) in terms of intrinsic properties of the items, (2) as convergence zones that link different modalities of items, or (3) in terms of the items' sensory and functional properties.

Martin and colleagues (1996) opted for the first of these possibilities. Viewing the findings of their neuroimaging study as consistent with the case studies reviewed here, Martin's team concluded that "the brain regions active during object identification are dependent, in part, on the intrinsic properties of the objects presented" (p. 649). They speculated that semantic knowledge of objects is represented in terms of networks distributed over several brain regions, including the ventral temporal lobe.

Sharing the network view of Martin and colleagues, Schacter (1996) added that information about one entity from such different modalities as acoustic, visual, tactile, and olfactory are connected in *convergence zones* (Damasio, 1990). The medial temporal lobe is a prime candidate for such a convergence zone. It is assumed to link explicit memories for events and objects by pointing to those cortical regions where the separate sensory memories are stored. In other words, the medial temporal lobe contains a set of instructions to assemble the separate memories into an integral explicit recollection (Chapter 3).

Working within the neural network framework (Chapter 6), Farah and McClelland (1991) formulated an alternative model of semantic memory and semantic impairments. These two scientists developed a connectionist network without assuming any category-specific semantic representations; the only distinction provided in the network was between visual and functional features. This contrast was designed to capture the principal contrast between living and nonliving things: Animals typically are distinguished by sensory attributes (e.g., a tiger has stripes) whereas nonliving objects are defined in terms of their uses.

Using the network model, Farah and McClelland successfully simulated category-specific dissociations as they are exhibited by patients. To represent input and output patterns, the network included a set of peripheral units to represent object names and pictures, respectively. The researchers trained the network on 10 living and 10 nonliving things using an error-correcting learning procedure. After 10 learning cycles, the network learned to produce the correct semantic and name pattern when presented with the picture and the correct semantic and picture pattern when presented with the name. Memory deficits were generated by lesioning the network selectively: When a proportion of the visual units was damaged, there were deficits in naming living things; when functional units were lesioned, there were deficits in naming nonliving things. Farah and McClelland concluded that taxonomically based categories of semantic memory are not necessary to account for category-specific memory deficits. Rather, the simple distinction between sensory and functional object features suffices.

Each of the three hypotheses on semantic impairments remains speculative—any one of them or a combination could be correct. Whatever the truth turns out to be, it is evident that neuropsychological research on semantic memory deficits in amnesic and in Alzheimer's patients (discussed later) gave a new lift to semantic memory research—an area once thought to be sterile and moribund (Kintsch, 1980; Patterson & Hodges, 1995).

Neuropsychology of Working Memory Functions

Neuropsychological investigations provided a critical impetus in shaping theories of working memory, beginning with the earliest proposals in the 1950s. Research on short-term memory, the predecessor of working memory, began with Milner's case study of patient H. M., who, following neurosurgery, lost the capacity for new learning. The multicomponent model of working memory authored by Baddeley and Hitch (1974, 1994), the dominant model since the 1970s, owes its existence as much to "natural memory experiments" provided by neurological damage as to traditional laboratory research as (Baddeley, 1992a, 1992b; Baddeley & Hitch, 1974, 1994; Gathercole, 1994). The multicomponent model includes three components: the phonological loop for the maintenance of verbal information, the visuospatial sketchpad to process visual and spatial information, and the central executive to coordinate the activities of working memory (see Figure 6.7; Chapter 6).

Deficits of Phonological Memory

The phonological loop includes two separate components: a phonological short-term store and an articulatory subvocal rehearsal process. The acoustic store holds auditory material for a brief period, after which the information is lost. The rehearsal process is capable of maintaining phonological information beyond the initial period. Because the processor can convert visual information into a phonological format, the former benefits from the rehearsal process. It is for this reason that visually presented materials produce the phonological similarity effect and the word length effect (Chapter 6).

The phonological similarity effect refers to the finding that items that sound similar (e.g., the letters *b, v, d,* and *g*) are more difficult to recall than dissimilar items. This effect is associated with the phonological short-term store. The word length effect is reflected in better recall of short words than of long words. This effect has been attributed to the added time needed to refresh multisyllabic words in the rehearsal process.

Impairments of the phonological system have been observed in patients who have lesions in the posterior left hemisphere, as assessed by CT or MRI scans. Such patients have difficulty to recall spoken names, prices of goods seen on labels, new foreign language vocabulary, and the interim results when doing mental arithmetic. On auditory span tests, patients do poorly; they do not remember more than two digits, letters, or words, and even their visual digit span is reduced to about three. The digit span deficit was neither due to impairments in perception (as patients were able to repeat the stimuli when they were presented individually) nor to problems in the response system (as the span did not improve when the patients were given the option of making a nonspeech response, such as by pointing) (Vallar & Papagano, 1995).

The performance pattern in phonologically impaired patients is as informative as the deficits are in absolute terms. The patients do not exhibit the phonological similarity effect and the word length effect for visual materials that are found in nonpatient populations. Both of these effects reflect the conversion of visual into phonological information, and the conversion depends, of course, on an intact phonological loop. It is for this reason that patients exhibit a reduced visual digit span.

Fortunately, individuals with phonological deficits do not suffer the dramatic symptoms of retrograde and anterograde amnesia observed in H. M., S. P., K. C., and other amnesic patients. The neurological damage in phonologically impaired patients usually is limited, enabling patients to lead almost normal lives. Patient P. V., for example, who had sustained lesions in her left hemisphere as a result of a stroke, sold pottery painted by herself and took care of two children.

Visuospatial Sketchpad
Although there are relatively few case studies documenting isolated impairments of the visuospatial sketchpad, these cases have nevertheless yielded theoretical and practical insights (Gathercole, 1994). The theoretical distinction between visual and spatial sketchpad components has received support from investigations with patient L. H., who had sustained bilateral lesions in the temporo-occipital regions. L. H. underwent a battery of tests probing his spatial processing (e.g., the mental rotation task) and his visual processing (e.g., tests to assess his knowledge for the shape, color, and size of familiar objects). L. H. displayed the dissociation between spatial and visual performance expected on the basis of independent spatial and visual subsystems of the sketchpad. The neuropsychological evidence is consistent with experimental studies on the two subsystems (Smyth & Pendleton, 1989; see Chapter 6) and with neuroanatomical research on separate *what* and *where* systems within the visual modality (Smith & Jonides, 1997; Ungerleider, 1995).

Work with patient E. L. D., who suffered from a lesion in the right parieto-occipital region, revealed the practical utility of the sketchpad in everyday situations. E. L. D. was not able to remember the faces of people she met after her illness, although she retained the ability to recognize faces of famous people familiar to her from before her illness. In laboratory tasks, E. L. D. had difficulty in the span of apprehension task, in which patients try to estimate the number of dots on a display, and in visual tapping tests. Presumably, it is this type of visual memory that supports the acquisition of new visual information, such as memory for faces in everyday situations (Gathercole, 1994).

Impairments of Executive Control: The Role of the Frontal Lobes
According to the multiple component model of working memory, the interconnectedness to other cortical regions makes the frontal lobes a good candidate for housing the central executive system (Baddeley & Hitch, 1994; see also Fuster, 1995; Glisky, 1996; Shimamura, 1995). This system is charged with supervising cognitive and memory functions, including coordinating performance, focusing on the central aspects of a task, initiating responses, and monitoring performance (Glisky, 1996). Damage to the frontal lobes may result in impairments of any of these functions. In addition, frontal lobe patients tend to exhibit amnesia, metamemory deficits, and deficits in cognitive estimation. Following is a partial list of tasks and situations in which patients have been reported to have difficulty:

— Patients have difficulty in tasks that require a focus on relevant information, such as in concept formation tasks (e.g., the Wisconsin Card Sorting Task) (Chapter 6). The patients tend to persevere in previously correct performance patterns; they are susceptible to distraction and to proactive interference (Shimamura, 1995). According to Shimamura's (1995) theory of inhibitory gating, each of these performance deficits is the result of a faulty inhibition mechanism presumably located in the frontal lobes.

— Difficulty is seen in tasks that require the subject to initiate responses, such as recalling words in the free-recall task and clustering the words in terms of semantic categories. Although the patients may know the words when prompted with appropriate cues, they cannot regenerate them or reconstruct their order (Glisky, 1996).

— Certain patients cannot monitor their own accuracy in many tasks. Such deficits of metamemory were observed in a sentence recall task, where patients could not assess the accuracy of their recollections. However patients' recall of target sentences was quite good. This dissociation is consistent with Nelson and Narens's (1994) view that metamemory functions and basic memory functions may be separable.

■ Other patients may find it difficult to estimate quantities, such as the height of the average person or the price of familiar merchandise, in remembering the frequency of occurrence of events in retaining spatial sequences, and in remembering the temporal order of events. Similarly, real-life facts—for example, those that occurred between 1940 and 1985—are recalled by patients but they cannot date the events (for other sources on temporal order, see Glisky, 1996, p. 253). According to Shimamura (1995), all of these difficulties reflect deficits in organizing and manipulating information.

■ Patients have difficulty in monitoring time and initiating retrieval. As a result, prospective memory functions are expected to be impaired in frontal lobe patients (Cockburn, 1995). *Prospective memory* involves remembering to execute a task in response to an external cue or after a certain time has elapsed. This ability is one of the most serviceable assets of memory in everyday situations. When people complain about everyday forgetting, they tend to name failures of prospective memory as one of the most frequent annoyances (Mateer, Sohlberg, & Crinean, 1987; Raskin & Sohlberg, 1996). In Chapter 12, we will learn about an effort to remediate prospective memory deficits.

■ Finally, although not amnesic, frontal lobe patients are susceptible to source amnesia, the dissociation between factual and source memory, as occurs, for example, when one remembers a certain fact (e.g., Whistler Mountain is a great ski resort) but forgets the source of that information (Shimamura, 1995).

In sum, the memory impairments exhibited by frontal lobe patients tend to affect the control functions of memory rather than the recovery of past memories and new learning. Patients are impaired to the extent that a task requires their own initiative, whether it involves self-initiated free recall, the retrieval of specific semantic information, or the monitoring of memory functions.

ALZHEIMER'S DISEASE

Alzheimer's disease is so prevalent that it has been called the disease of the century. Four million people in the United States suffer from Alzheimer's, a number expected to increase in step with people's increasing longevity. It has been estimated that 15% of people over age 65 and 45% of people over age 85 will be afflicted by the disease (Morrison-Bogorad et al., 1997). Unfortunately, there is no cure in sight, despite intensive research programs. The efforts of physicians and health care workers have therefore focused on managing patients and their families, at an estimated cost of $90 billion a year. As observed by Alois Alzheimer, the discoverer of the disease a century ago, a wide range of cognitive functions and the emotional state of the patient are affected.

The disease is progressive; initially, patients exhibit minor memory loss, forget appointments and chores, misplace objects, and frequently experience the tip-of-the-tongue phenomenon (difficulty retrieving familiar words). Subsequently, the disability worsens: The patients develop increasing gaps in their autobiographical and semantic memories, lose track of everyday activities, and fail to recognize friends and family. Along with their memories, the patients lose their pasts and their souls. Emotional and physical problems emerge, including depression, aggression, anxiety, agitation, hallucination, and sleeping and eating disorders. Making matters worse is the fact that many patients retain some awareness of the decline in their mental functions. Personal narratives by victims give testimony of the nightmare they experienced as they literally lose their minds (e.g., McGowin, 1993; Ronch, 1985; Royer, 1991).

In spite of the accelerating advances in medical science, a definite diagnosis of Alzheimer's during a patient's life time is very difficult. Usually, it is through an autopsy that one knows for sure whether a person suffered from Alzheimer's. There are no clearly identifiable infectious, nutritional, vascular, genetic, endocrinological, or toxic causes for the disease, although any of these may aggravate the condition (Lopero et al., 1997; Morrison-Bogorad et al., 1997; Selkoe, 1991). Rather, Alzheimer's disease has been attributed to a general degeneration of the brain and its structures. The condition is associated with anatomical pathology, neurochemical changes, and metabolic abnormalities.

The brains of Alzheimer's patients tend to exhibit both an atrophy of normal structures and a growth of abnormal structures, including plaques. *Plaque* is debris consisting of a compound of neural structures, including diseased glial cells, axons, and dendrites. Among the neurochemical changes observed in Alzheimer's patients is the finding that the level of acetylcholine, the important neurotransmitter implicated in the formation of memories, is significantly reduced in Alzheimer's patients compared to other aging individuals. The reduction in the acetylcholine level is attributed to a pathological deficiency of the enzyme that creates acetylcholine, choline acetyltransferase. It has been speculated that this enzyme is depleted because of cell death of certain neurons in the basal forebrain (La Rue, 1992). Metabolic abnormalities have been revealed by neuroimaging techniques such as PET scanning and Single photon emission computed tomography (SPECT). In normal individuals, metabolic activity tends to be distributed relatively evenly over the brain's gray matter, as well as in the basal ganglia and the thalamus. By contrast, blood flow tends to be reduced in Alzheimer's patients, especially in the temporal and parietal lobes (Holman, 1991).

Behaviorally, Alzheimer's disease differs from the amnesic disorders in important ways: In Alzheimer's, there is a general deterioration of cognitive and emotive functions. It is for these reasons that the condition is referred to as *Alzheimer's dementia*. In Alzheimer's disease, memory deficits are so pronounced that they are considered a signature of the condition. Because linguistic performance, attention, perceptual processing, and motivation are also impaired, it is difficult to disentangle the factors that contribute to specific memory losses (see Karlsson et al., 1989; Tippett & Farah, 1994). A further complication is that the pattern of memory deficits changes as the disease progresses. It is not surprising, then, that researchers have reported different—indeed, contradictory—retention patterns, whether they involve the serial position curve in free recall, the temporal gradient of autobiographical and remote memories, or the extent of deficits of semantic memory and implicit memory. Rather than seeking to identify the factors contributing to the deficits, the strategy adopted here is to describe the patterns of memory deficits as well as spared functions in the principal types of memory, memory for facts, working memory, and memory for skills.

Deficits in Memory for Facts

Loss of memory for facts, whether they involve personally experienced episodes or general world knowledge, is pervasive in the victims of Alzheimer's dementia. The deficits are evident in everyday living, in standardized tests, and in experimental paradigms assessing episodic and semantic memory (La Rue, 1992; Mohs, 1995).

Episodic Memory

Standard Tests. Table 10.1 tabulates the relative loss of mildly demented patients compared to a nonpatient control group for various standard measures of episodic memory. Both groups

TABLE 10.1 Loss in Selected Episodic Memory Tasks (after La Rue, 1992)

	Relative Loss (%)
Paired associates (cued recall)	34.4
Paired associates (recognition)	5.3
Visual retention	62.5
Story memory	80.4

were matched for age (about 72 years) and educational level (12.8 years of education). The table shows loss in each of the tasks as well as the fact that the loss is not uniform across tasks.

When learning of paired associates is assessed in the typical anticipation method, where the person tries to reproduce the response term when shown the stimulus term, patients recall about one-third less than control subjects. When retention for the same targets is assessed in a recognition test, however, the relative deficit amounts to only 5%. The contrast between recall and recognition indicates that one potential bottleneck in performance is the requirement to generate a response.

Patients' memories for pictures, geometric designs, and objects presented to them are very poor. Recognizing faces is severely impaired, whatever testing method is used, whether it is by forced-choice testing or by identifying the most recent face added to a series of faces (Brandt & Rich, 1995).

The scores on story memory in Table 10.1 were based on the Wechsler Memory Scale (see The Amnesic Disorders earlier in this chapter). The low scores do not fully capture the qualitative deficit of patients in stories as simple as story (10.1). Patients do very poorly, failing to recall names, locations, and quantitative details. Using two 450-word stories as stimulus materials, Spilich (1983) found that Alzheimer's patients not only recalled fewer propositions than control subjects but, unlike the latter, the pa-

tients also failed to discriminate between important and tangential text segments. Whether this deficit reflects a problem in comprehending or retrieving the passages has not been resolved. One possibility is that patients, due to deficits in working memory, were not able to form coherent story representations.

(10.1) Anna Thompson of South Boston, employed as a cook in a school cafeteria, was held up on State Street the night before and robbed of $56. She had four small children, the rent was due and they had not eaten for two days. The officers, touched by the woman's story, took up a collection for her.

Free Recall. The free-recall paradigm is among the memory tasks to discriminate most clearly between Alzheimer's patients and control subjects: Patients do less well than the control subjects matched for age and other factors (Brandt & Rich, 1995; Mohs, 1995). In immediate free recall, the shape of the serial position curve differs according to the severity of the disease. In relatively mild cases of Alzheimer's, the serial position curve is shifted downward in equal proportion for all positions, including the

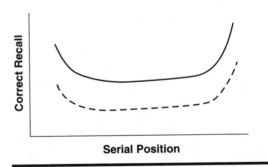

FIGURE 10.1 In mild cases of Alzheimer's disease, the serial position curve in immediate free recall is shifted downward in equal proportion for all positions, including the primacy and recency sections (broken line).

primacy and recency sections (see Figure 10.1). As the disease progresses, however, recall in the primacy section deteriorates most, leaving the recency section spared by comparison (Spinnler et al., 1988). The relative immunity of the recency effect is assumed to reflect the continued operation of the phonological loop, a component similarly resistant to closed-head injury or to such stressors in healthy subjects as distraction by a concurrent task or intoxication (Morris, 1994).

Free-recall performance is particularly vulnerable to a delay following the learning phase. Morris and colleagues used the Word List Memory Test to assess retention in free recall (cited by Brandt & Rich, 1995). The test involves learning a 10-word list on three successive trials. After a delay of as short as five minutes, the effects of these learning trials were wiped out. Intrusion errors, however, revealed that patients tended to retain some aspect of the information that was presented to them. Intrusion errors were based on semantic confusions, such as the word *lion* was recalled in place of the word *tiger*.

Alzheimer's patients fail to benefit from any of the factors known to improve performance in list-learning experiments, whether it is levels of processing, list organization, or self-generation of target items (Chapter 4). Patients fail, as well, to use retrieval cues to their advantage. When control subjects cannot remember a target, prompting with a cue, such as the first syllable of the word, often helps to recover the item. The inability to take advantage of such retrieval aids distinguishes Alzheimer's patients from people who are merely forgetful (Schacter, 1996).

Autobiographical Memory. In tests of autobiographical memory, amnesic patients tend to exhibit a temporal gradient, with more recent memories more vulnerable to loss than remote memories. It is not clear to what extent the memory profile of Alzheimer's patients reflect this *law of regression* (Ribot, 1887). There are stud-

ies reporting that remote memories are spared in Alzheimer's patients (e.g, Sagar, Cohen, Sullivan, Corkin, & Growdon, 1988), as well as studies reporting a flat amnesic function with an equal memory loss for remote and recent information. The reason for these discrepancies remain to be explored—they could be attributable to different testing methods or to testing patients at different stages of the disease (for reviews, see Hodges, 1995; Morris & Kopelman, 1986; Nebes, 1992).

Semantic Memory
Semantic memory refers to people's knowledge of language and of the world remembered independently from particular episodes and contexts (Chapter 4). During the initial stages of Alzheimer's dementia, semantic memory deficits are manifested by the difficulty in recovering familiar terms; they deteriorate as the condition progresses, extending to a variety of situations and tasks, including the following:

— Patients find it difficult to remember objects' names; they tend to substitute words and leave gaps in words, thus producing unclear and occasionally incomprehensible speech.

— Patients do poorly in naming tests where pictures of familiar objects or scenes are presented, where verbal descriptions must be given, and where words must be generated in response to a specific category (Benton & Hamsher, 1983). Patients produce specific errors in naming tasks. For example, when shown a camel, patients are likely to respond with *animal,* and when shown a panther, they might say *tiger*. These errors suggest that the fine distinctions in semantic memory are affected while sparing the more abstract distinctions.

— Patients tend to perform better in visual than in verbal semantic retrieval tasks. Chertkow, Bub, and Caplan (1992) presented pictures or words of common objects (e.g., a saw) and questioned patients about the object (e.g., Is it a tool or clothing? Is the edge made of metal or wood? and Do you cut things with it or lift with it?). The researchers found that patients made fewer errors in response to pictures than to words (see also Hillis, Rapp, & Caramazza, 1995).

— The organization of semantic memory in Alzheimer's patients differs from that of nonpatient controls. Chan and colleagues (1993) used statistical clustering techniques to arrive at a mapping of semantic memory in individual patients. The researchers obtained the mappings from response patterns in the word fluency task, where patients generated animal names. The assumption was that names listed in succession were more closely linked than other names (Chi & Koeske, 1983). Chan and colleagues found that patients' organization of animal names was defined differently from that of the control subjects (see Figure 10.2). According to Chan, the patients tended to represent the animals in terms of concrete dimensions, such as size, rather than in terms of abstract attributes, such as domesticity.

— Deficits in semantic memory affect performance adversely in episodic memory tasks. Unlike certain amnesic patients and older adults, Alzheimer's patients do not benefit from semantic processing when they try to memorize lists of words.

Semantic memory deficits are less pronounced in those tasks where the responses are relatively constrained (e.g., where the person makes a *yes-no* decision, as in the lexical decision task and in the sentence verification paradigm) (Nebes, 1989). In these two tasks, Alzheimer's patients exhibit the same response patterns as nonpatient control subjects, although their response speed is considerably slower. In the lexical decision task, subjects are shown strings of letters (e.g. *door, ride,* and *corfy*) and they must decide whether the string represents an English word. When related words (e.g.,

nurse and *doctor*) are shown in succession, response times to the second word are facilitated as opposed to pairs of unrelated words (e.g., *bread* and *doctor*). In the sentence verification task, subjects verify sentences, such as *Is a canary an animal?* and *Is a bird an animal?* Response times are typically longer to the former than to the latter question, presumably reflecting the greater distance between the concepts (Chapter 4).

Working Memory

We return to the multicomponent model of working memory (Baddeley & Hitch, 1974, 1994) to review working memory deficits in Alzheimer's patients. The model includes the three familiar components—the phonological loop, the visuospatial sketchpad, and the central executive system. Research indicates that phonological functions are relatively well preserved in Alzheimer's patients; they display the recency effect in free recall and they exhibit the phonological similarity and word length effects observed in nonimpaired populations. Although the absolute level of recall is lower in patients than in nonimpaired control subjects, the patterns of immediate recall tend to be similar in both groups (see review by Morris, 1994). Morris credits the absence of neurological damage in language centers in the left hemisphere for the robustness of the phonological loop. Research on the second working memory subsystem, the visuospatial sketchpad, has been less extensive. Some studies revealed deficits in short-term memory for visuospatial information; it is, however, not clear to what extent such deficits are based on impairments in the perceptual system or in the central executive system.

The principal working memory deficits in Alzheimer's patients have been traced to executive dysfunction. The central executive is assumed to provide mechanisms to supervise and to initiate mental operations (Baddeley & Hitch,

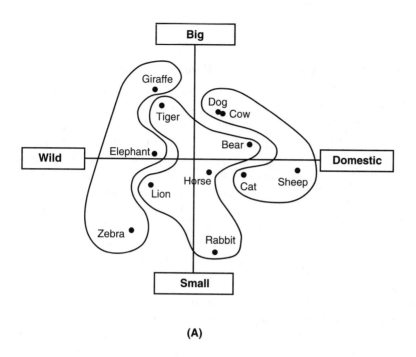

(A)

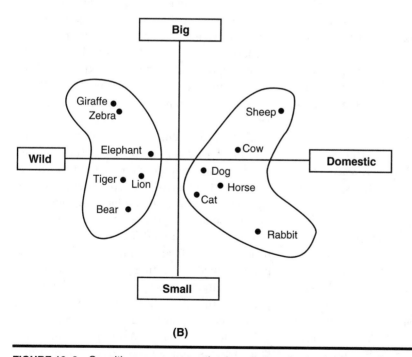

(B)

FIGURE 10. 2 Cognitive map representing knowledge of animals as determined by multidimensional scaling analysis. *(A)* Patients with Alzheimer's disease. *(B)* Elderly control subjects without Alzheimer's disease.

1974, 1994). Because of capacity limits of the executive system, normal individuals tend to exhibit performance decrements when they are required to divide their attention between memorizing nonsense syllables and a difficult distractor task—for example, adding a pair of digits (3 + 8). When the distracting task is easy, such as repeating the word *the* or reversing the pair of digits (38, 83), there is hardly any memory decrement in normal volunteers. Alzheimer's patients, however, are vulnerable to interference from such easy tasks.

Baddeley and colleagues developed a task capable of monitoring the progressive deterioration of the central executive system over a six-month period (Baddeley, Logie, Bressi, Della Salla, & Spinnler, 1986). The investigators had patients and nonpatient control subjects work on a pursuit tracking task and on one of three competing tasks: (1) repeating the digits 1 to 5, (2) activating a foot switch as fast as possible when hearing a tone, or (3) reciting a series of digits in the digit span task. The tracking task required the person to track a moving stimulus with a light pen. The speed of the moving stimulus was calibrated individually for each person so that patients and nonpatients were equated for performance level.

When patients and control subjects were working on individual tasks, the performance of both groups was similar. However, when attention was divided between two tasks, the patients' performance was much poorer and their performance declined over a period of six months, thus indicating an erosion of central executive functions as the dementia worsens. Baddeley and colleagues assessed the performance of patients on the individual tasks over the six-month period and found no performance decrement here. This result is consistent with the view that the deficit in concurrent task performance was due to a deterioration in the executive system (Baddeley et al., 1991).

Deficits in Memory for Skills

Memory for skills includes perceptual skills necessary for word and object recognition, also referred to as *implicit memory,* and the knowledge of cognitive and motor skills, whether they are used in everyday life or acquired in the laboratory. In amnesic patients, there tend to be dissociations between memory for facts and memory for skills, with the latter spared in face of deficits in memory for facts. As the following review shows, this issue is less clear in the case of patients suffering from Alzheimer's disease.

Implicit Memory

Implicit memory is reflected in an improvement in performance without explicit recollection, whether it occurs in stimulus identification, lexical decision making, or word-stem completion tasks. Older adults and amnesic patients exhibit priming effects in identification and completion tasks, even when their explicit memory deteriorates. In Alzheimer's patients, priming results are less well established; priming has been observed in word identification, lexical decision, and category decision tasks (Nebes, 1992), but not in the word completion task (Brandt & Rich, 1995).

Keane, Gabrieli, Fennema, Growdon, and Corkin (1991) examined perceptual priming and word completion priming within a single research study involving 10 patients and 10 age-matched healthy individuals. In both experimental conditions, the target words were presented 0, 1, or 3 times. The researchers established a significant priming effect in the perceptual identification task in both subject groups: Target words that had received prior exposure during the study period were identified more quickly than words not presented. The only difference was an overall speed effect such that patients required word exposure times about twice as long as the healthy volunteers to identify the words (85 vs. 40 milliseconds). In the word completion task, the healthy subjects exhibited a strong priming effect, whereas the patients exhibited a negligible effect. Although it is not clear why the dissociation between perceptual and word completion priming occurs, investigators have speculated that it suggests an impairment in different brain structures that support the two tasks (see also Schacter et al., 1993).

Learning and Remembering Actions
In light of the memory losses in almost all domains—episodic memory, semantic memory, some forms of implicit memory, and autobiographical memory—it is remarkable that many Alzheimer's patients can still carry out certain everyday routines when asked to do so, such as making a telephone call or making tea (Rusted, Ratner, & Sheppard, 1995). Alzheimer's patients also can acquire certain procedural skills, including tracking a moving target in the pursuit rotor task. When groups of nonimpaired volunteers and patients were equated for initial performance on the pursuit rotor task, skill acquisition proceeded at a comparable rate in both groups (for reviews, see Brandt & Rich, 1995; La Rue, 1992).

One of the reasons why memory for actions is relatively spared is that the motor program required to carry out the task makes the memory trace more distinctive and therefore more resistant to forgetting and amnesia (Chapter 4). In addition, histological assessment of the brains of Alzheimer's patients indicates that the principal brain areas affected are the temporoparietal lobes and the hippocampus, whereas the motor areas are impaired to a lesser degree (Karlsson et al., 1989).

Based on the relative sparing of memory for actions, Karlsson and colleagues (1989) sought to find out whether motor encoding might be used to enhance patients' ability to remember a list of manipulable objects such as a cup or glove. The investigators compared acquisition in two conditions: motor encoding and verbal encoding. In the motor encoding condition, the subjects were shown 25 objects one at a time and were asked to use the object for 10 seconds. In the verbal condition, no objects were presented but the objects were listed on cards. Following training, a free-recall phase and a cued-recall phase followed. For all subject groups, including normal 73- and 82-year-olds and three groups of Alzheimer's patients (mild, moderate, severe), recall was better in the motor encoding condition than in the verbal encoding condition. This study is interesting from a theoretical perspective, indicating that motor processing contributes to encoding and thus enhances recall (Chapter 4). Practically, however, this method remains limited, unless a way can be found to have patients encode everyday items and tasks (e.g., taking one's medicine) in terms of a distinct motor code.

Alzheimer's Disease: A Retrospective

Alzheimer's disease is so devastating, not because of deficiencies in one or the other memory functions (e.g., not being able to think of a word or recognize a famous person) but because the losses are so pervasive that they affect almost all manifestations of memory. Furthermore, despite important research advances, there are no treatments to ameliorate, let alone to rehabilitate, the symptoms of the disease. To be sure, hopes for remedies have been raised intermittently, whether they involve vitamins, health foods, herbal medicines, or so-called memory drugs, though none of these have proven effective (Coleman, Fowler, & Williams, 1995). Psychopharmacological researchers have acknowledged the inefficacy of current drugs, but have voiced the opinion that the knowledge base has been sufficiently expanded to offer hope for the development of some candidate drugs (Wein-gartner et al., 1996). The hope is based on recent progress by scientists in determining the complex conditions and parameters of Alzheimer's dementia. There is a better understanding of the multiple factors contributing to the disease, a greater awareness of its different expressions, and a recognition of the need to develop diverse methods to cope with it.

CONCLUSION

Already numbering in the millions, the population of people with memory impairments around the world continues to increase. Patients suffer from accident-related memory disorders and degenerative impairments of memory, including Alzheimer's disease and subcortical dementias brought on by multiple sclerosis, HIV infection, Huntington's disease, or other conditions. Psychologists face a monumental task in developing ways of improving the life of these patients. Patients lose their jobs, many are institutionalized; many have great difficulty in coping even with the simplest daily tasks, and many suffer from depression.

The challenge of helping patients with memory impairments has been taken up by investigators in many labs in different countries and has finally yielded tangible results. However, because knowledge of memory impairments remains limited, the emphasis has been on managing rather than rehabilitating the impairments. Researchers have reported success in helping patients to use spared memory functions—for example, implicit memory and skill learning—in order to perform such tasks as data entry, word processing, and the use of spread sheets. Tulving's (Tulving et al., 1991) training with K. C. and Baddeley and Wilson's (1994) errorless learning technique exemplify this approach. Other investigators have adapted electronic devices as external memory aids to facilitate memory for jobs and errands (Chapter 12).

In all cases, therapists and families must keep in mind the severe constraints under which these patients operate. Therefore, information should always be simplified, presented in small chunks, and repeated as often as, and in as many different contexts as feasible (Wilson, 1996).

Research on memory impairments is driven by practical and humanitarian considerations, but it has had a growing impact on basic memory research, as well. The most visible reflection of this influence has been the breakup of memory from the unitary system assumed in the 1950s to the multiple systems view becoming increasingly popular (Schacter & Tulving, 1994a, 1994b). Thanks to seminal case studies, short-term memory was separated from long-term memory (Milner, 1966), subsystems were identified in working memory (Baddeley & Hitch, 1974, 1994), implicit memory and explicit memory were distinguished (Warrington & Weiskrantz, 1970), and research on semantic memory received a new impetus (Warrington & Shallice, 1984). However, we must keep the caveat in mind that clinical cases tend to be unique and that it is difficult to isolate the cause of a given memory deficit. Generalizing from impaired individuals to the healthy person continues to be controversial among memory researchers (Chapter 3).

Murdock (1974) expressed the resistance toward using memory impairments in the service of basic memory research when he wrote, "It is difficult enough understanding the memory of normal college students; it will be time to consider the abnormal cases after we can cope with the normal cases" (Chapter 11).However, in the decades since Murdock's call for caution, the opposite view has increasingly become accepted. The more inclusive and more contemporary view was articulated by Janet (1901) a century ago when he argued that "disease decomposes and analyzes memory better than psychology" (cited from Schacter & Tulving, 1982).

CHAPTER 11

ISSUES IN
MEMORY RESEARCH

The 10 preceding chapters have shown how large the domain of memory research has become during the last century and a quarter. Empirical memory research began with list-learning studies, paying little attention to biological and neuropsychological considerations. By the 1980s, the considerable momentum of the traditional research—coupled with advances in neuroscience, neuropsychology, and applied memory research—greatly expanded the available paradigms and models as well as the sheer number of memory phenomena under investigation. Theorists have debated theoretical accounts for the memory phenomena, the relation among them, and, in particular, the extent to which all of the different effects represent a single memory or a collection of multiple and separate memory systems, each operating under different mechanisms.

Going beyond such issues of basic research, the relation between basic memory research and memory applications in everyday life has become the focus of an intense debate. Here, the issue is to identify the important questions of memory research (Neisser, 1978). What sort of memory phenomena should researchers investigate? Should they investigate such research questions as the course of forgetting of syllables, the rate of retrieval from working memory, and the effect of semantic encoding on priming? Or should they address such problems as how to improve the retention of foreign language vo-

cabulary, to increase the accuracy of eyewitness testimony, and to help a person remember to take his or her medicine? There has been a growing schism between basic researchers who tend to pursue the former questions and applied memory researchers who are interested in the latter problems. The second part of this chapter reviews these two approaches to memory. In Chapter 12, we leave the debate behind us and discuss applied memory research in several settings from education to memory management in individuals who have memory impairments.

In reviewing these issues, the final chapters of this book both introduce new material and revisit information introduced in prior chapters. In so doing, Chapters 11 and 12 expressly use an important principle of effective remembering: Understanding and retention of information are improved to the extent that the information is repeated in different contexts and presented from different perspectives.

HOW MANY MEMORIES?

Memory research has been progressing rapidly and has become interdisciplinary to a degree that its pioneers hardly could have foreseen. Ebbinghaus, the founding father of the psychology of memory, defined *memory* as the faculty of the mind to bring back past experiences into consciousness. In an effort to study memory uncontaminated by the person's knowledge and attitudes, Ebbinghaus invented the nonsense syllable and introduced such research methods as paired-associate learning, serial learning, and free-recall learning (Chapter 2). Ebbinghaus is the inventor of the laboratory approach to memory that shaped memory research for most of its history.

To be sure, there were alternative approaches to memory, among them Bartlett's and Ribot's. Bartlett studied memory in the context of a person's knowledge of the world, and, based on his study of memory impairments, Ribot proposed different memory systems each with its own fundamental principles (Chapter 2). None of these alternatives, however, had a major impact on memory research. Rather, memory research was concerned with the acquisition and the retention of mostly verbal materials (Crowder, 1976; McGeoch, 1942). Even critical observers (Neisser, 1978; Newell, 1973) concede that the classical approach to human memory was a great success in terms of its productivity and its legacy in the field.

Changes in the field came about because of advances in neuropsychology, computational science, cognitive neuroscience, and traditional experimental psychology itself. The developments have produced a plethora of models, frameworks, and memory systems. Researchers have proposed everything from long-term working memory to prospective memory and phyletic memory. Figure 11.1 includes a list of memory dimensions that have been proposed in the literature. This list is not exhaustive, nor are the dimensions mutually exclusive.

There has been a debate among theorists whether the dimensions listed in Figure 11.1, as well as additional dimensions, should be used as a basis for a taxonomy of distinct memory systems. Some theorists respond to this question in the affirmative; others do not. The first section reviews two influential memory taxonomies and their rationales—Schacter and Tulving's (1994a) taxonomy and Squire's (1995)

FIGURE 11.1   Dimensions of memory.

Declarative–Procedural
Explicit–Implicit
Direct–Indirect
Semantic–Episodic
Primary–Secondary
Short-term–Long-term
Reproductive–Constructive
Phyletic–Individual
Perceptual–Motor
Visual–Auditory
Prospective–Retrospective

taxonomy—and presents the criticisms of the systems view advanced by advocates of a unitary memory.

Before entering into the debate, let us delimit it: The debate is not about a taxonomy of memory *tasks*. Memory researchers agree on differences between tasks such as short-term versus long-term memory tasks, episodic versus semantic memory tasks, and implicit versus explicit memory tasks. Researchers also agree that the distinctions are heuristically useful in order to organize research domains and research questions (e.g., Neely, 1989). The issue where theorists differ is whether there are independent and structurally separate *systems* that support performance in different memory tasks or whether memory is a unitary system.

Advocates of multiple systems seek a memory classification in the hope of organizing the body of findings on human memory, whether from research laboratories, the clinic, or applications. The mass of data keeps growing but it is not clear whether they tell a story or what that story is (Tulving, 1979, 1995). Categorizing the domain of memory in terms of different kinds of memory follows the divide and conquer strategy common in science. It is easier to investigate a limited domain and arrive at empirical generalizations—for example, in the domain of working memory—than it is in the entire field of memory. Developing a classification enables theorists to sharpen the attributes of memory phenomena, as Tulving (1983) illustrated for episodic and semantic memory and as Schacter (1994) did for priming compared to other kinds of memory.

Multiple Memory Systems: Two Taxonomies of Memory

According to Squire (1995), memory systems are based on the "fundamental idea that memory is not a single faculty but consists of different systems that depend on different brain structures and connections" (p. 198). Although the systems are thought to be separate, they presumably interact in fulfilling the common function of acquiring, retaining, and using knowledge. An increasing number of theoretical frameworks characterize the different memory systems, including the proposals authored by Squire (1995), Tulving (1985), Schacter (1994), Fuster (1995), Baddeley (1986), Schacter and Tulving (1994a), and about a dozen additional proposals collected in Schacter and Tulving's volume, *Memory Systems 1994*. Here, we consider two of the taxonomies: Schacter and Tulving's (1994a) and Squire's (1995) frameworks.

Schacter and Tulving's Taxonomy
The Schacter and Tulving (1994a) taxonomy in Table 11.1 draws on the cumulative work of these two authors as well as on the contributions of other scientists. The table draws a distinction between procedural memory, an action system, and four cognitive representation systems: the perceptual representation system, semantic memory, primary memory, and episodic memory. Consider, first, the four representation systems. These systems are believed to produce changes in thought and mental structures (e.g., changing a memory image or a proposition) (Tulving, 1995).

The perceptual representation system (PRS) is closely linked with perceptual and recognition processes. Differing from declarative memory, the PRS is involved in nonconscious expressions of memory for prior experience (Schacter, 1994). According to Schacter (1996), "The PRS allows us to identify objects in our everyday environment and to recognize familiar words on a printed page" (p. 184). The system is implicated in the speeded recognition and performance that results from a previous encounter with a stimulus as occurs—for example, in reading. Researchers create such facilitation experimentally in the priming paradigm. Schacter claims that, although PRS deals with the form and structure of words and objects, "It does not know anything about what words mean or what objects are used for. Meaningful associations and concepts are handled by semantic memory, which cooperates closely with PRS" (p. 184).

The semantic and episodic memory systems were introduced by Tulving as early as 1972 (Tulving, 1972). *Semantic memory* refers to the knowledge individuals have of the physical and symbolic world, including their knowledge of language and word meanings. *Episodic memory* includes people's knowledge of events associated with a specific temporal and spatial context. *Primary memory* corresponds to working memory, formalized in Baddeley's (1986) model. This system holds and processes information temporarily. As described in Chapter 6, *working memory* is assumed to include multiple components, including the central executive as well as subsystems dedicated to processing information from different modalities.

The *procedural memory* system, the first entry in Table 11.1, includes memories not subsumed under any other system. It is nondeclarative and, as a rule, not accessible to consciousness. Unlike declarative knowledge, procedural memory tends to be inflexible, specific to a particular content, and therefore difficult to transfer (Chapters 5, 7, and 12). Another char-

TABLE 11.1   Five Major Memory Systems (Schacter & Tulving, 1994a)

System	Other Terms	Subsystems	Retrieval
Procedural	Nondeclarative	Motor skills Cognitive skills Conditioning	Implicit
PRS	Nondeclarative	Word forms	Implicit
Semantic	Generic factual knowledge	Spatial/Relational	Implicit
Primary	Working memory	Visual + Auditory	Explicit
Episodic	Personal memory Autobiographical memory Event memory		Explicit

acteristic of procedural memory is that its output has no truth value, a feature understood best when compared to declarative memory representations. Declarative representations are said to be propositional; for example, the statement *The table is large* is represented in terms of the proposition *(large, table)*. The proposition is said to reflect an external fact and to have a truth value in that the table is either large or not large. By contrast, procedural information is represented in terms of action routines, also known as production rules (Chapter 7), for which there is no truth value. Finally, procedural memories are acquired gradually in incremental learning; after extended practice, they become automatic.

The rightmost column in Table 11.1 indicates the manner of retrieving the information in terms of implicit or explicit memory measures. In implicit memory tests (e.g., the priming situation), performance improves as a person is repeatedly exposed to a stimulus. It is not necessary, nor even likely, that the person is aware of having encountered the stimuli before (Chapter 5). On the other hand, in explicit memory tests (e.g., recall and recognition testing), the person recalls prior information intentionally and with full awareness (Chapter 4).

According to Schacter and Tulving (1994a), "Explicit and implicit memory are not systems." Rather, these terms refer to expressions of memory, where explicit refers to "intentional or conscious recollection of past episodes" and implicit refers to "unintentional, nonconscious use of previously acquired information" (p. 12).

Squire's Taxonomy

Squire (1995) distinguished between the declarative and nondeclarative memory systems shown in Figure 11.2B and Table 11.2. He defined the two systems in the standard way, where the declarative system includes memory for facts and events and the nondeclarative system governs changes in performance as a result of prior experience. Declarative memory is conscious and intentional, whereas nondeclarative memory is nonconscious. Note that, unlike Schacter and Tulving (1994a), Squire (1995) equated the declarative versus nondeclarative dichotomy with that between explicit and implicit memory. People tend to be conscious of declarative memories, acquire them quickly, and use them flexibly. On the other hand, nondeclarative memories are usually not accessible to conscious inspection; it takes relatively long

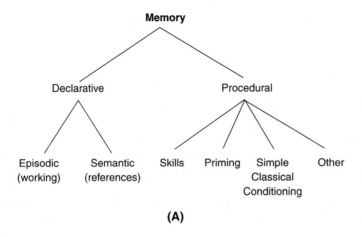

(A)

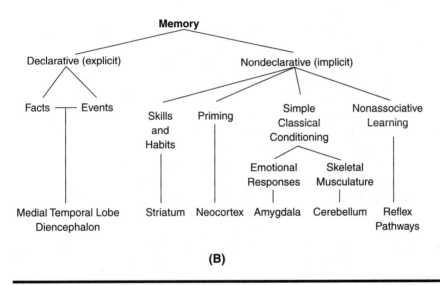

(B)

FIGURE 11.2 *(A & B)* Memory taxonomies proposed by Squire (Squire, 1987, 1995).

TABLE 11.2 Declarative versus Nondeclarative Memory (Squire, 1994)

	Declarative	Nondeclarative
Other terms	Explicit	Implicit
Brain structures	Medial temporal lobe Hippocampus	No single system
Consciousness	Yes	As a rule, no
Acquisition speed	Fast	Slow
Flexibility	Yes	Inflexible and hyperspecific
Development	Late	Early

to acquire a skill or a classically conditioned response; and skills are inflexible and highly specific (see also Anderson, 1993; Chapter 7).

As illustrated in Figures 11.2A and 11.2B, Squire's (1987, 1995) taxonomy of memory has evolved from merely contrasting the two different memory systems to linking them expressly with specific brain structures. The declarative system is subserved by the diencephalon and the medial temporal lobe, including the hippocampal system (Chapters 3 and 10). When these brain structures are damaged, declarative memory is impaired, resulting in amnesia. Nondeclarative memory includes the set of abilities that tend to remain intact in amnesic patients. The acquisition of nondeclarative information is subserved by a variety of brain systems, as indicated in Figure 11.2B.

Squire supported these links by reference to lesion studies involving animals and neuropsychological case studies. The logic of these studies is to link a memory system with a brain structure when lesions to the latter are associated with impairments to the memory system. Thus, the striatum, the region in the basal forebrain implicated in motor control, is assumed to subserve sensorimotor learning because damage to the striatum (as occurs, for example, in Huntington's disease) leads to problems in learning new motor skills. Huntington's disease is a degenerative condition characterized by such symptoms as involuntary irregular movements of whole limbs.

Justifying Systems of Memory

How does one justify classifications such as those in Figure 11.2 and Table 11.1? Theorists have specified several criteria for identifying independent memory systems (e.g., Schacter & Tulving, 1994a; Squire, 1994). This section reviews three such criteria: properties, dissociations, and brain structures assumed to be linked with specific memory systems.

Properties

Schacter and Tulving (1994a) described a memory system in terms of a list of properties to capture the rules of operation, the kind of information, and the uses of the system. The most fully developed property list is available for episodic and semantic memory. Tulving (1983) listed 28 different properties to distinguish these two systems, including the degree to which the information depends on the context, the vulnerability to interference, and the manner in which the two types of information are reported.

Context Dependency of Episodic versus Semantic Memory. The definitions of semantic memory and episodic memory imply that the two types of memory differ in the degree to which they depend on contextualized information. *Semantic memory* refers to general world knowledge whose acquisition context is no longer relevant and therefore not available. On the other hand, *episodic memory* refers to personal events linked with a specific time and place. People tend to forget the context in which they acquired the meaning of such words as *bridge, car,* and *university,* but they remember such occasions as their bar mitzvah, the family dinner at Thanksgiving, or the car accident a couple of weeks ago. Of course, distinguishing between episodic and semantic memory in terms of context dependency is not absolute. It is entirely possible that one remembers the context in which one learned the meaning of a particular word, especially if it is very unusual (e.g., *thermoluminescence*), and that one forgets the time and context of particular episodes.

Vulnerability to Interference. Tulving (1983) suggested that episodic information is more vulnerable to interference than semantic information. Information of episodes is changed, modified, and lost more readily than the knowledge of the world. The greater vulnerability of episodic memory occurs partly because semantic information is overlearned, whereas episodic information tends to be based on individual episodes, and partly because the semantic information is interconnected to a greater degree than episodic information. Tulving noted, however, that the "hypothesis of differential vulnerability to interference of the two systems holds only in a statistical sense" (p. 45). Thus, it is likely that certain individual episodic memories, such as the memory of one's wedding, may well outlast many semantic memories.

Retrieval Report. The English language provides speakers with different verbs to report episodic and semantic information. Episodic memories tend to be reported in terms of the word *remember*, whereas semantic memories tend to be reported in terms of the word *know*. Thus, when referring to episodic information, we say, "The witness *remembers* the suspect wearing an Nike T-shirt," "The subject *remembers* the digits read to her in a memory experiment," and "The professor *remembers* feeling shocked when he learned about the *Challenger* explosion." On the other hand, when we express semantic information, we use such phrases as "I *know* the name of the first president of the United States," "I *know* the square root of 4," and "I *know* that heavy objects drop to the ground." There are, of course, exceptions to the typical uses of *know* and *remember*. These occur when one wishes to convey a special implication. For example, when a person uses the word *remember* to refer to semantic content, as in *I remember that sugar tastes sweet,* the implication is that he or she has not tasted sugar for a very long time but still remembers its taste.

In addition to context dependency, retrieval report, and vulnerability to interference, Tulving (1983) listed many other properties to distinguish between episodic and semantic memory. There are no such extensive lists to characterize the other memory systems listed in Table 11.1. Indeed, one of the systems, procedural memory,

is characterized by the absence of properties in common with the other memory systems.

Schacter and Tulving (1994a) acknowledged that most of the properties advanced to identify different memory systems are based on intuition and speculation rather than on objective rules. Therefore, listing of distinctive properties is not sufficient to identify a memory system. The condition necessary to postulate memory systems is the presence of dissociations. Indeed, the distinction between procedural memory and the other memories has been advocated on the basis of dissociations involving the performance of amnesic patients and nonpatient populations on different memory tasks (Schacter & Tulving, 1994a, 1994b; Squire, 1995; Warrington & Weiskrantz, 1982). Although amnesic patients are impaired in their ability to recall declarative information, they are able learn new procedural skills, such as how to make weather forecasts and how to distinguish rule-based and irregular event patterns (Squire, 1995).

Dissociations

Advocates of multiple memory systems consider dissociations between task outcomes as critical support for the independence of the systems. Tulving (1995) described the logic of using dissociations as follows: "Outcomes of different memory tasks assumed to be differentially weighted by contributions of different memory systems are systematically compared. Dissociations among these outcomes are regarded as providing support for the hypothesis of the separability of systems" (p. 842). Task outcomes are dissociated if performance on a task differs for different groups of subjects, for different brain states, or as a function of an independent variable.

The dissociations that first came to the attention of researchers were observed in amnesic patients described in the previous chapter. We saw that patients are often selectively impaired in executing a specific cognitive function while other functions remained intact. For example, patient K. C. retained an intact semantic memory, but his episodic memory was impaired (Tulving et al., 1991). A similar dissociation between episodic and semantic memory was observed in patients whose episodic memory was defective from early childhood on. Nevertheless, these individuals acquired a body of semantic knowledge that enables them to attend mainstream schools and achieve average scores on IQ tests (Chapter 4; Vargha-Khadem et al., 1997).

Warrington and Weiskrantz (1968) reported a dissociation in amnesic patients between performance on implicit and explicit memory tasks. The patients were able to identify pictures or words when they were recently primed with partial stimuli, but they did not recognize the stimuli in an explicit retention test. By contrast, nonpatient controls do well on both of these types of tasks (Table 11.3A). In general, amnesic patients have specific memory deficits but they have use of other intellectual functions. The interpretation of such dissociations is that diminished performance on one task reflects an impairment of one memory system, whereas the continued performance on the other task reflects the sparing of the other system.

No memory researcher is satisfied when he or she has to depend on such accidents of nature as the case histories of individual patients in order to test hypotheses about the architecture of memory. Researchers have developed a methodology of observing dissociations experimentally. The design to observe dissociations is captured in Table 11.3B. The idea is to use two manipulations in each of two different tasks and to demonstrate a crossover pattern in performance so that manipulation 1 has an effect in Task A, but not in Task B, whereas manipulation 2 has an effect in Task B, but not in A (Table 11.3B and C). Consider a study by Shoben and colleagues as an example of such task comparisons. These researchers interpreted the dissociation they observed in support of the distinction between episodic and semantic memory.

Shoben, Westcourt, and Smith (1978) observed a double dissociation using the task comparison paradigm. The experimenters assessed performance in a semantic memory task and in an episodic memory task. The two tasks—sentence verification and sentence recognition—were crossed factorially with two variables—semantic relatedness and the degree of fanning. Semantic relatedness is known to affect sentence verification latencies, a semantic memory

---

TABLE 11.3 Types of Dissociations

A. Patient versus Nonpatient	Implicit Task	Explicit Task
Patient	Intact	Impaired
Nonpatient	Intact	Intact

B. Experimental Approach	Task A	Task B
Manipulation 1	Yes	No
Manipulation 2	No	Yes

C. Example	Semantic	Episodic
Semantic Relatedness Effect	Yes	No
Fanning Effect	No	Yes

measure, whereas fanning, the number of different facts linked to a concept, affects latencies in the episodic sentence recognition task (see Chapter 7). The stimulus materials were sentences of the format *A subject has/is a predicate,* such as *A canary is yellow* and *A donkey has wings.*

In the sentence verification task, subjects were shown true and false target sentences and instructed to indicate whether the statement was true. In the sentence-recognition task, participants read test sentences during the study phase. In the testing phase, old and new sentences were presented in a mixed sequence and subjects were instructed to respond as quickly and accurately as possible.

In both tasks, semantic relatedness was manipulated by varying the relation between subject and predicate terms. For example, *Tigers have stripes* expressed a close relation, whereas *Tigers have thighs* expressed a distant relation. The degree of fanning was manipulated by combining subject nouns across different sentences with either four or eight predicates (Chapter 7).

Shoben and associates (1978) found a double dissociation such that "semantic relatedness influenced verification latencies but not recognition latencies, whereas fanning influenced recognition latencies but not verification latencies" (p. 304). The researchers sought to interpret this dissociation in terms of unitary memory models. They found that these models could handle the presence of the fanning effect in the episodic task, but not its absence in the semantic memory task. As a result, Shoben and colleagues concluded that their data were "most easily handled by a model that draws a distinction between semantic and episodic representations" (p. 316). For the moment, we will accept this interpretation. There are, however, alternative interpretations, as we shall see when we revisit the Shoben study in the next section (Neely, 1989).

Because of such alternative interpretations, a single dissociation cannot be considered as sufficient evidence for separate memory systems. Indeed, dissociations have been observed within declarative memory—namely, between performance measures in the recognition and recall tasks. Several experimental variables affect performance in these two tasks in different ways. Word occurrence frequency improves performance in recall, but not in recognition. Frequent words, such as *table, tree,* and *light* are better recalled but are recognized less well than infrequent words, such as *cache, merit,* and *fiend.* Similarly, instructing learners to organize materials aids recall performance, but not recognition performance. Finally, recall is affected by interference, whereas recognition is not (Kintsch, 1970). However, no theorist would invoke different memory systems to explain the recognition-recall dissociations.

It is for these considerations that Schacter and Tulving (1994a) called for convergent dissociations in support of separate memory systems. *Converging dissociations* refer to "dissociations of different kinds, observed with different tasks, in different populations, and using different techniques" (p. 18). The failure to look for converging dissociations would strengthen the case of those critics who have pointed out that there are too few constraints on inventing different memory systems.

Brain Structures and Memory Systems

The discovery of different functions of different brain structures is offered by such theorists as Squire as the strongest argument in favor of the existence of multiple memory systems (e.g., Squire & Knowlton, 1995; see also Smith & Jonides, 1997). Knowledge on the relation between brain structures and memory systems has been advanced by a broad range of research paradigms, including lesion studies involving animals as well as behavioral, neuroimaging, and electrophysiological studies involving human participants (Squire, 1994; Squire & Knowlton, 1995). As shown in Figure 11.2B, Squire (1995) relates declarative memory to the medial temporal lobe and the diencephalon, whereas non-declarative memory is heterogeneous, implicating diverse brain structures such as the striatum, the neocortex, the amygdala, and the cerebellum.

Anatomical Base of Declarative and Non-declarative Memory.   The anatomical base of declarative and nondeclarative memory has been investigated in studies of human patients and in animal models. Although patient studies and animal studies each have their own interpretational limits, Squire (1994) considers them as valuable in illuminating the assumed links between memory systems and brain structure. It is necessary, however, to use these types of studies in conjunction with other methods in order to obtain the converging evidence scientists have called for (Chapters 1 and 3).

Patient studies are limited because brain damage is rarely confined to a specific structure, thus making it difficult to link any memory impairments unequivocally with the structure. Using an animal model poses an interpretational problem, because, as Eichenbaum (1994) noted, "unlike humans, animals do not express their memories by verbal declaration" (p. 151). However, it becomes feasible to establish equivalences between human and animal memory when one uses criteria other than verbalization to distinguish declarative and nondeclarative memories. Declarative memory serves, among other functions, as a store for associations, for events and their temporal and spatial contexts. In particular, spatial memories and associations between events have been viewed as expressions of declarative memory in animals. Lesion studies involving rodents and primates indicate that such spatial and associative memories are subserved by the medial temporal lobe, including the hippocampal system (Eichenbaum,

1994; Schacter & Tulving, 1994b; Squire, 1994).

Squire and colleagues lesioned structures in the medial temporal lobe of monkeys and found that the monkeys were no longer able to acquire associations between distinctive objects and the receipt of food reward (Chapter 3). The critical structures included the hippocampus, the entorhinal cortex, and the parahippocampal cortex, but not the amygdala. Squire viewed these results as consistent with neuropsychological case studies involving human patients. Patients, such as H. M., whose hippocampal system was surgically damaged, sustain severe declarative memory impairments but they can learn such skills as mirror drawing, acquire conditioned responses, and exhibit implicit memory (Chapters 3 and 10).

Nondeclarative memory depends on systems other than the hippocampal system. Lesion studies indicate that classical conditioning of skeletal responses is based on the cerebellum, whereas the acquisition of the conditioned emotional response is based on the amygdala (Chapter 9). Damage to the hippocampus does not hinder conditioning and emotional learning. Motor skill learning depends on the striatum, a region in the basal forebrain, implicated in the motor system. Patients suffering from Huntington's disease, for example, tend to exhibit damage to the striatum and, as a result, they acquire sensorimotor skills less well than amnesic patients. On the other hand, they do not exhibit the amnesic syndrome, as amnesic patients do whose medial temporal lobe is damaged (see review by Squire & Knowlton, 1995).

Based on a body of findings such as these, Squire and Knowlton (1995) concluded that hypotheses about links between brain regions and memory systems have become viable. The two authors called for future research in order to broaden the empirical base of the brain-memory links and to identify synaptic mechanisms that presumably support those links. In general,

Squire and Knowlton regard their anatomical research as providing an intermediary level of analysis between the memory research at the molecular level pursued by neuroscientists (Chapter 3) and the research at the functional and behavioral level traditionally carried out by psychologists.

Anatomy of Priming. One line of evidence for the presumed difference between declarative and nondeclarative memory systems comes from neuroimaging and electrophysiological studies involving normal human subjects (Squire, 1994). Squire and colleagues recorded PET images in the word-stem completion paradigm. Test stimuli were presented to the central visual field both during inspection (e.g., *motel*) and the test phases (e.g., *mot--*) of the word-stem completion task. In testing, PET images were compared for old words (*mot--*) and for new words (*wag--*). On trials where subjects were trying to complete old words (*mot--*), there was a reduction in cerebral blood flow in the right hemisphere, specifically in the right extrastriate cortex.

According to Squire, this finding implicates the right hemisphere in priming, a prominent type of nondeclarative memory (Chapter 5; Marsolek et al., 1992). Importantly, the study included a cued-recall test as a control condition for declarative memory. In this condition, the subjects' job was to recall the study words using the word stems as cues. PET scans revealed that brain structures other than the right hemisphere contributed to performance in the declarative memory task. Beyond that, the neuroimaging results illuminate the perceptual attributes of priming effects. The reduced blood-flow activity indicates that less stimulus evidence is required to perceive and recognize a stimulus when it is presented for the second time (Chapter 5; Schacter, 1996).

The notion that different brain systems support declarative and nondeclarative memory is bolstered by evidence from electrophysiological studies (Paller, 1990; Paller & Kutas, 1992). Paller and colleagues found different event-related potential patterns when subjects performed declarative memory tasks (e.g., recall and recognition) than when they performed nondeclarative tasks (e.g., word-stem completion and word identification). ERP responses differed both in terms of latency and in terms of the location in these two tasks. In the declarative memory tasks, ERP peaks occurred after 500 milliseconds, compared to 400 to 500 milliseconds in the priming task. The ERP activity was most pronounced in the left anterior hemisphere in the declarative memory paradigms but in posterior locations for the priming paradigm. Squire (1994) concluded that the ERP findings "demonstrate that declarative and nondeclarative memory are associated with different neural events at different brain foci" (p. 220).

This completes the review of the multiple systems view of memory. As we saw, advocates of the multiple systems position look for a convergence of several criteria in identifying the putative memory systems: properties, dissociations, and brain systems. Properties—for example, those of episodic and semantic memory—include the functions of the system, its rules of operation, and the kind of information the system represents. Dissociations represent a diverging pattern of retention performance on two or more tasks assumed to implicate different memory systems. The distinction between declarative and nondeclarative memory has been supported by dissociations of different kinds, including dissociations involving different population groups (e.g., patients and nonpatients) and functional dissociations observed in experiments (Table 11.3).

Support for the systems view comes as well from neuroscience research, including animal studies, patient studies, neuroanatomical studies, neuroimaging studies, and electrophysiological studies. According to Squire (1994), there is mounting evidence that different memory systems are implemented in different brain systems, with declarative memory based on structures in the medial temporal lobe and nondeclarative memory supported by different structures in the neocortex, brain stem, and cerebellum (Figure 11.2). Although there is a growing body of data cited in support of multiple-memory systems, proponents of the systems view acknowledge that the existing memory classifications are likely to be revised. These theorists view their efforts as a stimulus to critics "to correct their errors and to improve the account" of memory (Schacter & Tulving, 1994a, p. 31).

A Single-Memory System with Different Processes

During the past quarter century, the multiple-systems view of memory has gathered considerable momentum against the view of a unitary memory system held by Ebbinghaus (1885), Melton (1963), Murdock (1974), and Underwood (1972). What has happened to the once dominant view of a unitary memory in light of the broadening of the study of memory, the new paradigms and findings, and the arguments of theorists, including Tulving (1983), Schacter (1994), Squire (1987), Fuster (1995), and Eichenbaum (1994), among others?

The answer is that the unitary view continues to exercise an influence among researchers whose focus is on human memory, specifically on list learning. This section reviews the defense of unitary memory theorists vis-à-vis the challenge of multiple-systems theorists. The traditional theorists have framed their defense in terms of two conceptual arguments (to be reviewed shortly): the mapping argument and the parsimony argument. As for empirical issues, the unitary theorists offer alternative accounts of those results that are typically cited in support of multiple-memory systems, especially of disso-

ciations. The single-memory theorists tend to view some dissociations as a result of confounds (Neely, 1989) and interpret other dissociations in terms of single-memory frameworks, including the neural network models (Farah & McClelland, 1991; Chapter 10) and the transfer-appropriate processing theory (Roediger, 1990).

Mapping Argument

The mapping argument concerns the question of how to carve up the domain of memory. Even if there were multiple systems of memory, it is not clear which of the extant taxonomies best captures those systems. Schacter and Tulving's (1994b) volume, *Memory Systems 1994,* for example, contains about a dozen different memory classifications. Systems theorists differ even on such fundamental dichotomies of memory as the explicit versus implicit memory distinction and the episodic versus semantic memory distinction. Consider the differing positions of prominent systems theorists such as Squire (1994), Schacter and Tulving (1994a, 1994b), and Fuster (1995) on these dimensions of memory.

Explicit versus Implicit Memory. The principal distinction in Squire's (1994) taxonomy is that between the declarative and nondeclarative memory systems illustrated in Figures 11.2A and 11.2B. Squire also called these systems the explicit and implicit memory systems, respectively. He distinguished between explicit and implicit memory systems because of (1) the failure of amnesic patients to retain information in recall and recognition tasks in the presence of spared priming effects and memory for skills, (2) demonstrations of functional dissociations in experiments involving nonpatient populations, and (3) the neuroimaging and electrophysiological studies (reviewed in the previous section).

Schacter and Tulving (1994a; Tulving, 1995), however, were not willing to grant explicit and implicit memory the status of *memory systems.* Is this merely a terminological argument between theorists? Apparently this is not the case, for as Schacter and Tulving argue, although experimenters have found numerous dissociations to distinguish between explicit and implicit memory, one cannot provide an extensive list of properties to distinguish between them. Rather, explicit and implicit memory "refer to two different ways in which memories can be expressed" (p. 19). In other words, explicit and implicit memory tests are two different ways of assessing the same memory representations. The point of the difference between Tulving (1995) and Squire (1995) is that the evidence for a putative memory system that is compelling to one systems theorist may well fail to persuade another theorist.

Episodic versus Semantic Memory. The distinction between episodic and semantic memory systems has been fundamental to Tulving's (1972, 1985) approach for three decades and continues to figure in the taxonomy of Schacter and Tulving (1994a). According to Schacter and Tulving, the two systems are distinct because of (1) dissociations observed in brain-damaged patients who can acquire semantic knowledge but not the source of that knowledge (e.g., K. C., Chapters 10 and 12), and (2) numerous different properties. The two authors believe that there is still insufficient evidence on the neuroanatomical location of the two memory systems, but they conjecture nevertheless that semantic memory depends on the medial-temporal lobe, whereas episodic memory depends on prefrontal-cortical areas.

Fuster (1995) is not persuaded by the evidence that Schacter and Tulving (1994a) list in support of the episodic versus semantic memory distinction. He noted that although the distinction may be "appealing," "the empirical evidence for corresponding neural systems is weak" (p. 17). Rather, Fuster believes that the two types of memory are neurally inseparable as reflected by their phenomenological similarity

and that they blend into one another (but see Vargha-Khadem et al., 1997). Although episodic memory refers more to context than semantic memory, this difference in emphasis is not sufficient "to claim a separate cortical system or process for each" system (p. 17). Fuster's (1995) criticism of the episodic versus semantic memory distinction echoes the criticism by unitary memory theorists (e.g., McKoon, Ratcliff, & Dell, 1986) and computational linguists (Schank, 1976). Schank (1976), for example, argued that Tulving's (1972) "distinction between semantic memory and episodic memory is a false one" (p. 255) because semantic memory is acquired by personal experience and is therefore, by definition, episodic (p. 256).

Proliferation of Systems and Subsystems of Memory. Quite independent of disagreements about the principal dimensions of mapping human memory, the multiple-systems approach entails the possibility of a proliferation of systems and subsystems of memory. Schacter and Tulving's (1994a) memory taxonomy includes both systems and subsystems: Systems are characterized by different rules of operations as they are reflected in their property lists, whereas subsystems operate within systems and are characterized by different kinds of information. The perceptual representation system (PRS), for instance, includes three subsystems depending on the modality, the visual word-form system, the auditory word-form system, and a structural description system to specify the relation among the parts of objects (Schacter, 1994).

Given the notion of systems and subsystems, a theorist could postulate a variety of subsystems, ranging from subsystems for large and small objects to subsystems for animate and humanmade objects. A theorist advocating the latter pair of systems could appeal to a neuroimaging study by Martin and colleagues (1996) where different brain regions were implicated in naming animals and in naming humanmade objects. Roediger (1993) predicted that "the coming years will see the 'discovery' of many more memory systems, unless we agree upon tightened criteria" (p. 520). Failing to do so may yield the memory organization of 32 modules, as proposed tongue-in-cheek by Ed Cutrell, one of Roediger's former undergraduate students (see Figure 11.3).

Parsimony Argument

The temptation to adopt elaborate memory systems, as caricatured in Figure 11.3, has prompted the defenders of the unitary view to invoke the principle of parsimony. It is for good reasons that this principle has appeal among scientists, including memory researchers. The parsimony principle exhorts scientists to describe a body of phenomena in as economical a way as possible without postulating a theoretically insupportable superstructure. Among memory researchers, Melton (1963), Wickelgren (1973), and Underwood (1972) have advanced the parsimony argument. Underwood (1972) was concerned about the proliferation of constructs and dimensions of memory when he asked the pointed question: "Are we overloading memory?"

According to Underwood (1972), memory researchers postulated "iconic, echoic, primary, secondary, and short-, medium, and long-term memories, " and they invoked "addresses, readout rules and holding mechanisms," as well as "T-stacks, implicit associational responses, natural-language mediators, images, multiple traces, tags, kernel sentences, markers, relational rules, verbal loops, and one-buns" (p. 1).

Two decades after Underwood's appeal not to overload memory, Howe and Courage (1993) addressed the multiple- versus single-memory issue. Writing that one cannot distinguish between the systems view and the single-memory view on the basis of data, these authors saw no better solution than to adhere to "the time-honored principle of parsimony, in this case, a single rather than multiple memory system," at least until researchers can conduct crucial tests between these two views (pp. 314–315).

Alternative Accounts of Dissociations

Dissociations have been one of the principal sources of support for the multiple-systems view of memory. The dissociation logic calls for a comparison of performance across tasks presumably supported by different memory systems. Any divergence in performance on these tasks has been considered as evidence for the independence of the memory systems. As shown in Table 11.3, outcomes are dissociated if performance on a task differs for different groups of subjects, for different brain states, or as a function of an independent variable. Critics of the multiple-systems view see two major problems in the dissociation logic: (1) it is difficult to establish equivalence in the different conditions that are used to demonstrate dissociations and (2) even if all necessary control conditions were in place, the empirical dissociations could nevertheless be explained by the unitary memory view without assuming separate memory systems.

Consider, first, the methodological issues. Using the distinction between episodic and semantic memory systems, Neely (1989) examined the rationale of dissociations and the problem of potential confounds. In the case of episodic and semantic memory, a *dissociation* means that a given experimental manipulation produces different patterns of performance in tasks assumed to be supported by the semantic memory system and the episodic memory system, respectively. This was the case in the study by Shoben and colleagues (1978) (reviewed earlier). The degree of fan affected recognition latencies in the episodic memory task, but not in the semantic memory task, whereas semantic relatedness affected verification latencies in the semantic memory task, but not in the episodic memory task. According to multiple-systems

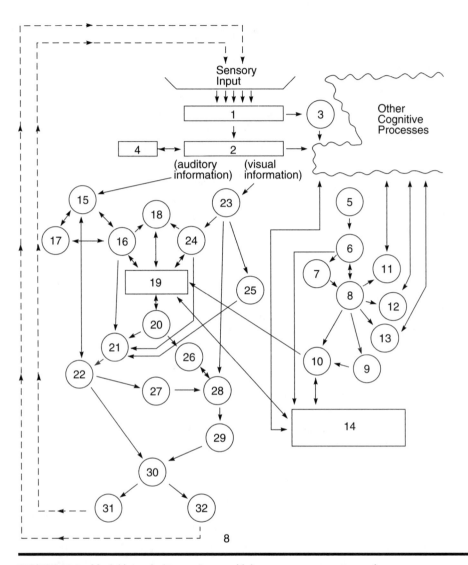

FIGURE 11.3 Model intended to capture multiple memory processes and systems. Roediger (1993) included this figure to characterize the state of affairs when memory systems are being proposed without constraint.

theorists, such interactions result from the operations of different memory systems.

According to Neely's (1989) critical analysis, in order to make the comparison in the Shoben study valid, the two types of memory tests must be equated on all factors other than the instruction. Otherwise, the dissociation could be due to a confound between the experimental variable of interest (e.g., semantic versus episodic memory instructions) and an unspecified variable not under experimenter control. In order to remove potential confounds, Neely (1989) offered the following suggestions, among others:

- Equate the stimulus materials.
- Equate the number of response alternatives.
- Equate the amount of prior study of test items in the episodic and semantic memory tests.

Shoben, Westcourt, and Smith (1978) succeeded in equating the first two of these conditions in that the same stimulus materials and a yes/no choice test were used in both the episodic and semantic memory tasks. However, the third of the criteria, to equate the study period, was not met. As is necessarily the case in episodic memory tests, in the Shoben study, learners studied the target items prior to the memory test, whereas the semantic memory test was given, as is commonly done, without prior study of the test materials. Thus, a comparison was made between *studied* items in the episodic memory test and *nonstudied* items in the semantic memory test. According to Neely, one cannot rule out that the dissociation Shoben and colleagues observed was due to this procedural difference rather than to the operations of two different memory systems

Even if this and other potential confounds were removed and a "clean" dissociation were found, it is not clear that such a dissociation compels the assumption of different memory systems. For two reasons, this is not the case. First, the particular pattern of a dissociation (e.g., the presence of the fan effect in an episodic task and its absence in a semantic task) was not specified in advance by any of the systems theories. In fact, according to the dissociation logic, the opposite pattern (e.g., a fan effect in the semantic task and no fan effect in the episodic task) would have equally counted as support for the multiple systems view (McKoon et al., 1986). Second, as the following section shows, dissociations observed in cognitive studies can

be explained by models based on a unitary memory such as the transfer-appropriate processing theory (Roediger, 1990).

Transfer-Appropriate Processing Theory

Reviewing theories of implicit memory, Roediger (1990) noted that dissociations are not necessarily evidence of different memory systems. Roediger advanced the proposal that the dissociations between implicit and explicit memory tasks reflect the operation of different processes operating *within* a unitary memory system. He noted that performance on explicit memory tests (e.g., the recognition test) and implicit memory tests (e.g., the word identification task) are typically enhanced by different processes during encoding. To the extent that these different processes transfer to the respective test situations, a dissociation is observed. In explicit tasks, conceptual encoding processes—for example, elaboration and generation—are known to improve performance, whereas in implicit tests, performance is enhanced by perceptual processes that take advantage of the similarity of the physical features of the stimuli during encoding and testing.

Roediger cited the study by Jacoby (1983) (reviewed in Chapter 5) to illustrate the role of such transfer-appropriate processing in producing dissociations. Jacoby's (1983) study yielded a dissociation between a recognition test and a word identification test (see Figure 5.1).

Roediger attributed the dissociation in Figure 5.1 to the degree to which encoding processes are appropriate for the retrieval task. Explicit memory performance is improved when learners encode the stimuli via conceptual processes such as elaboration and generation, whereas implicit memory performance is facilitated in proportion with the perceptual similarity of stimuli during the encoding and testing phases (see also Blaxton, 1989). Examining an additional set of dissociations, Roediger (1990) concluded that although these dissociations may implicate different memory systems, they are best "understood by appealing to general principles that apply to both explicit and implicit tests" (p. 1043).

The criticisms of the multiple systems view offered by unitary memory theorists were based on conceptual considerations, the mapping argument, and the parsimony principle, as well as on a critical analysis of empirical dissociations and on an alternative theory to account for such dissociations. According to the mapping argument, assuming that memory did consist of multiple systems, there is no agreement among theorists on the demarcation of these systems. As for dissociations, they may be based on confoundings of variables, and even if there were no confoundings, unitary memory theorists maintain that it is not necessary to assume different memory systems to account for dissociations. The assumption of different processes within a unitary system can handle the patterns of dissociations that have been observed, and it can do so with greater economy than the multiple systems view.

Memory Systems Gain Acceptance

What position should one take in light of the growing popularity of the multiple-systems view of memory and the cogent criticisms offered by the unitary theorists? Are the two views of memory as irreconcilable as the two following positions indicate?

In science, as in chess, a plan or a theory, even a poor one, is better than no plan or theory at all. The confusion that usually prevails in the absence of a theory is likely to breed only more of the same, whereas an incorrect theory can always be corrected. (Tulving, 1995, p. 846)

Premature definitions do nobody good, and hence we should damp the inclination [to advocate] a tidier map of [memory]. Any fool can make a tidy map; the trick is to make an accurate one. (Churchland & Sejnowski, 1992, p. 240)

One could give up all classification efforts, a view implied by Anderson's (1978) stance when he cited the list of failures to support such theoretical dichotomies as short-term versus long-term memory, parallel versus serial processing, semantic versus episodic memory, and analog versus propositional representations (Anderson, 1978). According to Anderson, these distinctions required a precision that was not supported by behavioral data. It could similarly be argued that behavioral data are not sufficiently precise to adjudicate between the multiple systems and unitary approaches to memory.

Another possible position is to look for a convergence between the two approaches. Memory researchers do, after all, agree on many things. They agree on such distinctions as episodic versus semantic memory tasks, implicit versus explicit memory tasks, and so on. They agree that the distinctions are heuristically useful to organize research domains and research questions (e.g., Neely, 1989). Both positions accept the rationale of dissociations and the potential problems of interpreting dissociations (Schacter, 1992). Specifically, theorists from both positions agree that dissociations by themselves are not sufficient to demonstrate multiple memory systems.

Where the two approaches differ is in their emphasis on different aspects of memory research. Using the broad arsenal of cognitive neuroscience methods—brain imaging, electrophysiological recordings, lesioning studies in animals, and neuropsychological case studies—the emphasis of the systems approach is to investigate brain processes with the goal of identifying brain structures and brain processes implicated in specific memory functions. Unitary theorists may be able to account for behavioral data involving priming and recognition, as Roediger (1990) did, but they have difficulty handling data involving brain processes, such as the lesion and neuroimaging data (Squire, 1994).

To be sure, each of the neuroscience methods has its own specific limits. For instance, the use of animal models remains controversial because it is not clear to what extent there is a correspondence among memory systems and among homologous brain structures in animals and humans (Churchland & Sejnowski, 1992). As discussed in Chapter 3, neuroimaging and electrophysiological studies are limited in terms of temporal or spatial resolution. Patient case studies are limited because of the unique conditions of patient histories and the difficulty of generalizing from patients to the normal population (Chapter 3). It is to their credit that neuroscientists have recognized these potential problems and continued to refine the research methods. The strategy has been to use diverse research tools jointly in order to obtain converging evidence on a phenomenon from several paradigms, whether they are psychobiological, behavioral, or computational (Chapter 3).

Thanks to this multiple-prong approach, the neuroscience perspective has gained greater acceptance among memory researchers, and so has the view of multiple memory systems (e.g., Baddeley, 1986; Fuster, 1995; Schacter, 1996; Smith & Jonides, 1997; Squire, 1995; Tulving, 1995). Even Roediger and colleagues (1989) retreated from the strictly unitary approach in noting that "it seems likely that more than one memory system exists in the human brain for comparative and phylogenetic reasons. The human brain is larger and more complex than any other brain and it seems likely that more complicated mechanisms exist than in many creatures with less complex neural structures and relatively simple abilities to learn" (p. 36). In sum, the multiple-systems view becomes more persuasive even to previous critics because of the broadening of the domain of memory research.

If one restricts memory research to the verbal leaning approach dominant from Ebbinghaus's times to the 1960s, the unitary view of memory is plausible. However, once the domain of memory research was broadened to include new topics ranging from perceptual skills to amnesia, the single-system view appeared less tenable. At this stage of memory research, developing memory classifications is a useful exercise; it serves to organize the body of data and to advance it, constrain theories, and invite new research questions (e.g., Tulving, 1985). Of course, classification efforts must be tempered by conceptual and empirical rigor so as to avoid the proliferation of systems and subsystems that Roediger (1993) rightly criticized.

Even though the multiple- versus single-system issue may be moot in light of the putative links between brain structures and memory systems (e.g., Eichenbaum, 1997), it has been widely debated among memory researchers. The issue has implications for topics covered throughout this book, including the relation between implicit and explicit memory (Chapters 5, 8, and 10), between episodic and semantic memory (Chapters 4 and 10), and between the different components of working memory (Chapter 6). Memory researchers, of course, debate many other problems, both specific and global. The specific problems include competing accounts of memory phenomena, whether they are the causes of forgetting (Chapter 4), the factors implicated in the developmental changes of memory (Chapter 8), or the multiple and contradicting effects of affect on memory (Chapter 9). A global issue that has elicited a lively debate in the last two decades concerns the relevance of basic memory research to the real world. Although several early memory researchers, including Binet, Münsterberg, and Whipple, pursued applied research, it was Ebbinghaus's (1885) pure research approach that dominated the field for almost a century. Things began to change in the 1970s and 1980s, in large part because basic researchers failed to address what Neisser (1978) called "the important questions."

MEMORY: WHAT ARE THE IMPORTANT QUESTIONS?

This is the question that Neisser (1978) asked in a provocative address to psychologists who gathered in Cardiff, Wales, to discuss the practical applications of memory research. Neisser's speech elicited a lively debate among applied and basic memory researchers, so much so that one reviewer wondered whether researchers had entered a "holy war or wholly unnecessary war" (Baddeley, 1993b). The debate has pitted researchers working in the basic research tradition inaugurated by Ebbinghaus against researchers who sought to apply memory outside of the laboratory.

The traditional view was articulated by Murdock (1974), a leading member of a group of distinguished memory researchers at the University of Toronto, also known as the Ebbinghaus Empire. The research of this group was devoted to serial learning, paired-associate learning, free recall, and other list learning situations. In the introductory chapter of his book *Human Memory: Theory and Data* Murdock (1974) formulated the attitudes and biases of basic memory researchers, including the bias to study reproductive rather than reconstructive memory and the focus on the behavioral rather than the biological perspective. Although memory is biologically based, the biological perspective does not change the phenomena themselves. Murdock wrote that the serial position curve will still look the same once we know how memories are coded at the molecular level.

Murdock (1974) emphasized:

> No attempt will be made to explain anecdotal evidence. Questions such as how I am able to remember that the people who lived next to us in Missouri ten years ago were named Wilson, or why I can't remember the date of my parents' anniversary, are quite beyond the scope of this book. There will not be any consideration of the unusual or the exotic. I shall not consider the mnemonist, eidetikers, memory under hypnosis, repression, or the like. . . . The reason for

> these exclusions is quite simple. It is difficult enough understanding the memory of normal college students; it will be time to consider the abnormal cases after we can cope with the normal cases. (p. 5)

Murdock is representative of memory research as it existed in the 1970s. The principal journals devoted to memory published almost exclusively studies on such phenomena as interference theory, the comparison of recognition and recall, and various aspects of rehearsal. There were reports on eye movements under different rehearsal strategies, the effects of rehearsal and serial list position on recall, externalized rehearsal, rehearsal of visual and auditory stimuli, forced verbal rehearsal, and rehearsal strategies and spacing effects. Applied concerns played practically no role in the leading memory journals such as *Memory & Cognition, Journal of Experimental Psychology: Human Learning and Memory,* and *Journal of Verbal Learning and Verbal Behavior.*

Neisser's Call to Arms

Neisser (1978) offered his challenge against the background of research devoted to what he considered to be the minutiae of memory. He presented the challenge in his opening remarks at the first conference on Practical Applications of Memory. He denounced the lack of exchange between experimental and applied memory researchers and the triviality of much of basic memory research. He called for a shift in thinking, an orientation toward studying memory in more naturalistic contexts. Neisser continued, "I am often unable to recall the authors of phrases that I would like to quote, and have real difficulties in remembering who told me things. These retrieval failures pose some interesting questions. Why do they occur? Do other people have less trouble recalling sources than I do?"

According to Neisser, these questions were not isolated ones. There were other questions of memory people are interested in: the limits of early childhood memory, the inability to remember appointments, the ease of finding one's way around town after a 30 years' absence, and an aunt's ability to recite poems from memory by the hour. It was discouraging to find that nothing in the extensive literature of the psychology of memory shed much light on these questions, that all psychology offers in response is "thundering silence," and that the omission of these questions from the research agenda is "scandalous." Neisser formulated a principle that he thought governed traditional memory research: "If X is an interesting or socially significant aspect of memory, then psychologists have hardly ever studied X" (pp. 3–4).

Neisser charged that basic memory researchers failed to investigate naturalistic settings because their goal, however elusive, was to develop a scientific theory of memory in general. He contended that memory in general does not exist and that researchers should give up pursuing the notion of a "general memory." Next, Neisser examined a number of popular research paradigms, including the Sternberg short-term retrieval task (Chapter 6). He argued that Sternberg's original discovery that reaction times increase with the number of alternatives was important, but after a decade's worth of research on every aspect of the task, "it has almost become a bore." Neisser said that the results of the first century of memory research are discouraging and he noted that although there are firm empirical generalizations, "most of them are so obvious that every ten-year-old knows them anyway" (p. 12). He concluded his speech with a clarion call to study memory and cognition in all its complexities in the real world.

In the decade following Neisser's call to arms, there was a steady stream of studies and publications addressing memory applications. Books were published, conferences were held, and a new journal *(Applied Cognitive Psychology)* was founded. Applied researchers investigated such topics as eyewitness testimony,

memory for action, memory for faces, memory for places, prospective memory, expert memory, autobiographical memory, and long-term retention of school learning, whether of foreign languages or mathematics. The applied researchers expanded the population of research participants to include children, the elderly, and individuals with disabilities. The basic researchers took note of the new energies released by the everyday memory approach, but, for reasons to be reviewed next, they remained unconvinced of the validity of the approach.

Banaji and Crowder Declare Everyday Memory Bankrupt

Banaji and Crowder (1989) offered the reply of basic researchers to Neisser's criticisms, declaring that the everyday memory approach was "bankrupt" and that it had yielded no new data and insights on memory. The everyday memory movement is doomed to failure, according to these authors, unless ways are found of ensuring that the results observed in everyday settings are generalizable. Banaji and Crowder distinguished between two dimensions of scientific research: ecological validity and generalizability. *Ecological validity* means the methodology of a study is applicable to everyday settings outside the research laboratory. *Generalizability* refers to the extent to which findings obtained in one experiment are replicable in another (Chapter 1). Combining the dimensions of ecological validity and generalizability in a two-by-two array of approaches to memory research, Banaji and Crowder identified the four states shown in Table 11.4.

Of the situations in Table 11.4, the optimal research scenario is the one captured in the first row. This condition combines generalizability and ecological validity. The situation characterized in the bottom row has neither scientific utility nor everyday applicability and therefore is of no interest. According to Banaji and Crowder,

TABLE 11.4 Four Research Situations in Terms of Generalizability and Validity (Banaji & Crowder, 1989)

Generalizability of Results	Ecological Validity of Method
High	High
High	Low
Low	High
Low	Low

the situations in rows 2 and 3 of Table 11.4 mirror the status of most studies published in the literature. These two scenarios represent the focus of the debate between basic and applied memory researchers. Banaji and Crowder (1989) examined the two conditions in detail, coming down solidly in favor of "accepting contrived methods as long as the payoff in generality of conclusions is great enough" (p. 1188).

High Ecological Validity of Method but Low Generalizability of Results. Banaji and Crowder cited a study by Diges (1988) to illustrate the combination of high ecological validity of method and low generalizability of results. The Diges study investigated the relation between witness recall of a car accident and the stereotypes witnesses held of drivers (e.g., that women were poor drivers). He examined the testimony of witnesses and assessed their opinion of drivers after the accident occurred. Banaji and Crowder's analysis of this study revealed several confounding variables that were not examined, including the stereotypes the witnesses had *prior* to the accident. Indeed, Diges (1988) analyzed only 13 out of 500 cases. Thus, this study could not illuminate the relation between driver stereotypes and eyewitness memory. It failed in the most important goal of a real-life study—namely, to generalize to the real world.

Low Ecological Validity but High Generalizability of Results. In order to illustrate the case of low ecological validity but high generalizability of results, Banaji and Crowder selected a paired-associate study by Landauer and Bjork (1978) on the learning of proper names. Subjects memorized pairs of first and last names during the study phase according to different schedules of distributed practice. In one of the conditions, the lags between repetitions of the study pairs expanded (e.g., 1, 4, 10 intervening items between repetitions), whereas in the other condition, the lags contracted (e.g., 10, 4, 1 intervening items). The researchers found that expanded lags improved recall significantly relative to the contracting condition. The advantage was comparable to the benefits gained from mnemonic techniques.

The important point of the Landauer and Bjork study is that the careful scheduling of spaced trials required the kind of experimental control that cannot be achieved in everyday memory situations. Yet, the result has proven replicable in other experiments (Dempster, 1996). Furthermore, the expanded rehearsal effect has implications for applied contexts, such as for the learning of foreign language vocabulary, multiplication facts, and word spellings (Baddeley, 1990; Dempster, 1996). The lesson of the Landauer and Bjork study of rehearsal practice is to refresh a memory trace just as it is on the verge of being forgotten. This lesson is generalizable, but the study was conducted in an artificial setting using contrived conditions.

Clearly, laboratory studies are more powerful than naturalistic studies precisely when the issues are complex and when the goal is to generalize. Generalization is possible only when one controls and isolates factors that influence the dependent variable, much as in physics and chemistry research. On the other hand, naturalistic studies that use retrospective analyses of events observed by people (e.g., classroom lectures, summer vacations, or eyewitness reports) lack the analytical control of experiments. In general, it does not matter much when an individual laboratory study yields no information about everyday memory. The important point, according to basic researchers, is that the study confirms or disconfirms a theory. It is the theory that has implications for everyday memory phenomena (also see Anderson, Reder, & Lebiere, 1996; Hintzman, 1993).

Rebuttals to Banaji and Crowder

Banaji and Crowder's (1989) bankruptcy verdict had a speedy response when, two years later, a dozen memory researchers weighed in on both sides of the issue. Here, we consider two rebuttals from applied researchers to Banaji and Crowder's criticism that (1) the latter had failed to acknowledge field data that do permit generalization and (2) contrary to Banaji and Crowder's position, the everyday memory approach has, in fact, produced new data.

Findings from Field Studies
Are Generalizable

In defense of field research, Conway (1991) criticized Banaji and Crowder for selecting admittedly "weak" sample studies rather than "strong" studies that would weather the challenge of methodological scrutiny. Conway (1991) cited studies on the dating and retrieval of autobiographical memories that are replicable and generalizable, among them Linton's (1986) long-term study of her own autobiographical memory. Using a diary, Linton daily recorded several events on index cards and dated them on the back. She accumulated well over 1,000 items of varying significance over a six-year period. She tested her memory by selecting a small set of cards at random and trying to remember each event and its date. Linton found a forgetting rate of 5% a year.

Examining the dating of autobiographical events over the entire life span, Rubin and colleagues (e.g., Rubin, 1986) observed a general decline of memory except for the reminiscence bump at around 20 years (see Figure 9.1B). Conway (e.g., 1996a, 1996b) himself proposed an organization of autobiographical memory, including different levels of abstraction from detailed events to lifetime periods, and reported that autobiographical memories are more accessible the more global they are (Chapter 9). According to Conway (1991), all of these findings are replicable and generalizable, the criticism of Banaji and Crowder notwithstanding.

Loftus (1991) made a similar point in referring to a study by Bahrick and Phelps (1987) on the long-term benefits of spaced practice (Chapters 4 and 12). Students learned Spanish vocabulary in massed or distributed training. The students were tested both immediately after training and after an eight-year interval. Although there were no differences in retention in immediate testing, the advantages of distributed learning were evident eight years later. Retention of words learned in the distributed condition was 2.5 times better than in the massed condition. In other studies, Bahrick examined retention at intervals of up to 50 years following learning. These results have been proven replicable and they are certainly not obtainable in laboratory studies.

Neisser (1991) cited several lines of research in support of the everyday memory approach, among them Nelson's (reviewed in Nelson, 1993b) research on memory development in children. In the Nelson studies, everyday events were used as targets of the studies (Chapter 8). Frequently occurring events, such as baking cookies or going to the babysitter's, are assumed to be represented in generic knowledge structures known as scripts. Children retained routine events, beginning at age 3, in relatively abstract terms without remembering details. It is only when they are 4 years or older that children tend to elaborate events more fully. Hudson (1988) discovered that children, much like adults, tend to remember unusual incidents that occur within familiar routines particularly well. Subsequent researchers have built on these discoveries, thus demonstrating their generalizability (Chapter 8).

Everyday Memory Research Has Produced New Findings

Clock Monitoring Differences between the Laboratory and the Home.   Several authors defended the everyday memory approach against Banaji and Crowder's claim that the applied research had not yielded any information that was not already known from laboratory studies. As an example of such new data, Ceci and Bronfenbrenner (1991) cited their own study on prospective memory in children. Children were asked to participate in one of two realistic time-keeping activities: baking cupcakes or charging motorcycle batteries for 30 minutes. They were allowed to play a video game during the interval until the 30 minutes had elapsed. One group of children fulfilled these tasks in the laboratory, whereas another group performed the tasks in their own homes. The researchers recorded the frequency with which the children checked the clock to see if the 30-minute interval had elapsed. Ceci and Bronfenbrenner (1991) found a striking difference between the children's clock monitoring activity at home and in the laboratory. When at home, the children produced a U-shaped curve of clock checking, as shown in the schematic in Figure 11.4. However, when performing the tasks in the laboratory, their clock monitoring behavior was captured by a monotonously increasing function.

According to Ceci and Bronfenbrenner, the U-shaped time checking pattern observed at the children's home is the better strategy. When at home, the children presumably used the first few minutes to calibrate their internal clocks. Having done so, they let their internal clocks "run on autopilot" until the last few minutes and conse-

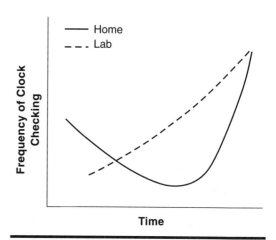

FIGURE 11.4   Differences between lab results and everyday results. Children's clock checking behavior differs between the home and the laboratory. When tested at home, the children check the clock initially and toward the end of the target interval. When tested in the laboratory, the children check the clock with increasing frequency throughout the interval (Ceci & Bronfenbrenner, 1991).

quently gained more time to play the video game. In the unfamiliar environment of the laboratory, however, the children were relatively anxious and felt compelled to be increasingly vigilant as the interval elapsed, thus producing the linear increase in time monitoring shown in the figure. Whatever the explanation for the contrast in Figure 11.4, the point is that prospective memory performance may differ between the laboratory and the real-world environments.

Recall Superiority versus Recognition Superiority.   Neisser (1988) found that the recognition superiority typically found in laboratory studies (Chapters 1 and 4) did not occur in a memory study conducted in a setting outside the typical laboratory. The setting was a seminar course at Emory University entitled "Theories of Attention" and taught by Professor Neisser himself. It was taken by 15 seniors majoring in psychology. The seminar involved lectures, paper presentations by the students, and discussions. As in the typical psychology seminar, there were demonstrations (e.g., selective listening), interruptions (e.g., the instructor was called out of the room), and surprises that elicited the instructor's wrath (e.g., one time a student who was to present a paper skipped class). All of these activities and events were tape recorded by an assistant. At the end of the semester, the taped record was used as a base against which students' recollections of the seminar were compared.

The students were tested in one of two ways about their recollection of the events in the seminar. The first test was an open-ended cued-recall test and the other was a multiple-choice recognition test. It turned out that accuracy was much better in the recall test than in the recognition test, thus contradicting the recognition versus recall superiority effect that is typically found in basic research studies (Chapters 1 and 4). Neisser attributed the recall superiority to a methodological difference between the recall and recognition test. The difference was that the cued-recall test was open ended, giving the students the choice of whether they wanted to respond at all, whereas the recognition test forced them to respond even if they were not sure of their answers. In the cued-recall test, students apparently took advantage of the opportunity of screening their responses in order to boost the accuracy of the answers.

Not all of the responses to the Banaji and Crowder (1989) paper expressed a spirit of contentiousness. Several psychologists saw similarities between the laboratory and the real-world approaches. Klatzky (1991) entitled her paper "Let's Be Friends" and called for a rapprochement between the two camps. There are good reasons for doing so because of the common ground that exists between them. No applied researcher would deny the principal points Banaji and Crowder (1991) made in support of scientific control in empirical research

and of the generalizability of results. Similarly, basic researchers would not deny that important basic research has been inspired by applied concerns and by observations made in the real world (Baddeley, 1976; Klatzky, 1991; Morton, 1991). In concluding this section, consider a couple of examples of the influence of practical issues on basic research. The first example dates back to Ebbinghaus and the second example involves insights gained from working with amnesic patients.

Even Ebbinghaus, supposedly the shining model of a basic researcher, had practical considerations in mind in his investigations of memory (Ebbinghaus, 1885, 1905). He was fully aware that retention in applied contexts— for example, in classroom learning—is substantially improved by making the content as meaningful as possible and by repeating the materials, preferably in sessions of distributed practice (Chapters 2, 4, and 12). Ebbinghaus (1905) demonstrated the advantage of distributed practice relative to massed practice in a series of experiments and acknowledged that "thanks to the intuition of [educational] practitioners the benefit of distributed learning has long been established" (p. 660). Contemporary researchers have documented the remarkable benefits of distributed practice in a wide range of settings, from second-language learning to the acquisition of motor skills (e.g., Bahrick, Bahrick, Bahrick, & Bahrick, 1993; Bahrick & Phelps, 1987; Dempster, 1996; Schmidt & Bjork, 1992).

The other instance of the influence of practical concerns on basic memory research comes from the insights gained from work with patients with memory impairments. Warrington and Weiskrantz (1968) were able to demonstrate that amnesic patients, even in the absence of forming new declarative memories, continued to exhibit the ability to improve their performance in perceptual identification and other tasks (Chapters 5, 10, and 12). Warrington and Weiskrantz's discovery, together with subsequent findings on the dissociation between priming and declarative memories, have provided the key impetus for theories of multiple memories (reviewed earlier). This theoretical development, in turn, led to a practical application—namely, the use of teaching amnesic patients new content knowledge by training methods based on the priming technique (see Chapter 12; Intons-Peterson, 1997).

The final section of this chapter reviews Koriat and Goldsmith's (1996) correspondence metaphor, a conception of memory that was expressly motivated by the challenge of everyday memory. According to these two authors, the debate between everyday memory and basic memory research is based on the clash between the correspondence metaphor and the storehouse metaphor of memory (Chapter 1). A researcher's choice among these metaphors influences the topics he or she chooses to investigate and the methods of doing so. Researchers working under the umbrella of the storehouse metaphor tend to favor traditional memory research based in the laboratory (Murdock, 1974), whereas researchers working under the correspondence metaphor emphasize research that has implications for applications in the real world.

The Correspondence Metaphor of Memory

The correspondence metaphor of memory was introduced by Koriat and Goldsmith (1996) as an alternative to the storehouse metaphor that has dominated traditional memory research. According to the storehouse metaphor, memory is viewed as a storehouse of information that receives, stores, and discharges items to be learned. The storehouse metaphor provided the rationale and methodology for experimental research that emphasized a strict quantification of memory. The list-learning technique exemplifies this approach in that a list of *n* words is placed into storage during the study phase and

retrieved during the recall test. Performance is assessed by counting the number of items correctly reproduced and comparing them to the number of items in the input list. As far as the storehouse metaphor is concerned, the items' content is irrelevant to the count and the items are completely interchangeable. Whether a person remembers *gun* or *glasses* in a recall experiment makes no difference to the storehouse metaphor.

The correspondence metaphor reflects a different conception of memory and of how memory should be measured. This metaphor is inspired by the everyday memory approach. Theorists working under this metaphor prefer situations typically found outside the laboratory as models for their research rather than list-learning experiments. For example, a courtroom witness may try to describe a crime he witnessed or a person may attempt to relate an event, whether it was experienced recently or long ago. According to Koriat and Goldsmith (1996), these situations invite a different emphasis from that used by the storehouse metaphor. The criterion is not the *number* of list items the person can recover from the store, but rather the *goodness of fit*, the *correspondence,* between the person's report and the actual event. Emphasis is on memory for events actually experienced rather than on "material that has no reference beyond itself" (Neisser, 1982b, p. 142).

The correspondence-based approach to memory seeks to emulate the attributes of real-world uses of memory in its research methodology and consequently offers a different approach to the nature of forgetting, and to the stimuli and methods of memory assessment employed in research.

■ Forgetting is not considered as a loss of items but rather as a qualitative change in the memory representation, a loss of correspondence. Under this view, researchers investigate changes of memory such as simplification, confabulation, and fabrication (Bartlett, 1932; Bower, Black, & Turner, 1979; Loftus & Palmer, 1974; Schacter, 1995).

— The stimuli favored by proponents of the correspondence metaphor—discourses, pictures, and films—are more complex than the lists of syllables or words used in conventional experiments.

— The focus of memory assessment is on the person's accuracy in reproducing the stimulus in all of its complexity. Here, content does matter and items are not simply interchangeable. For example, in eyewitness testimony, there is a vital difference in whether a witness remembers that the suspect was handling a *gun* but forgot that he was wearing *glasses* rather than vice versa (Koriat & Goldsmith, 1996).

— Whereas the storehouse metaphor emphasizes the stimulus input (e.g., a list of words) and records how many items the learner reproduced, memory assessment under the correspondence metaphor emphasizes the person's output (e.g., an eyewitness report) and assesses the degree to which the person's report corresponds to the perceived event. Thus, accuracy is measured relative to what the person reports, not counting what the person omitted. This approach yields an accuracy measure computed in terms of the total of the information the person reports rather than in terms of the stimulus input

Response Options in Reporting Recollections

In order to implement the accuracy measure of memory, Koriat and Goldsmith introduced *report option*—free reporting versus forced reporting—as a factor in their research. In everyday situations, people typically have the choice of what information to report and how to do so. In traditional laboratory research, however, matters are more complex; there exists a confounding between the report option and the test format. Recognition testing involves the forced report option. Here, the experimenter presents a list of items requiring the person to respond to each and every one of them with a *yes/no* response (Chapters 1, 4, and 7). By contrast, in free-recall testing, the experimenter gives the person a choice of responding. Nevertheless, even in free recall, performance is usually assessed by calculating the number of items recalled correctly relative to all items in the input list.

One of the standard results of traditional memory research is the superiority of recognition memory relative to recall memory. Koriat and Goldsmith believe that this effect is difficult to interpret because of the confounding between test format (recognition versus recall) and report option (free responding versus forced responding). The two investigators succeeded in separating these two factors in a series of studies using a 2 × 2 factorial design where test format and report option were covaried. Koriat and Goldsmith used two measures of assessing performance: (1) the traditional quantity assessment and (2) a new accuracy score.

Here is how the quantity measure and the accuracy score are calculated: Assume an experimenter uses a question-answering technique to assess memory and presents 100 questions. Further assume that a respondent gives 60 correct answers. According to a quantity measure, the person's performance is expressed as the ratio of the number of correct responses relative to the number of input questions. In the case of our example, this ratio is 60/100 = .60. To obtain the accuracy score, assume that the same question-answering test is given in a free-report test where the respondent has a choice whether to respond to each question. Say the person chooses to respond to 80 questions and achieves 60 correct answers. The accuracy score is computed as the number of correct responses relative to the number of attempted questions, which, is in this case, comes to 60/80 = .75.

In one of their studies, a semantic memory experiment, Koriat and Goldsmith used 60 general knowledge questions, each requiring a one-word answer—for example, *What was the name of the composer who wrote "The Moonlight Sonata"?* (Alternatives: Beethoven, Bach, Tchaikovsky, Schuman, Brahms). Retention was measured in a recall test and in a recognition test, varying the report option in each case. Recall was assessed in two ways: (1) in the free-report option, typical for the recall paradigm, and (2) in the novel-forced report option, where the subject was forced to produce a response, any response, for each question. Recognition was assessed in the usual forced-choice format and in the novel-free report option where the subject was given the choice of not responding to a question.

When Koriat and Goldsmith used the quantity measure and made the standard comparison between forced recognition and free recall, they found the typical recognition superiority over recall (.67 vs. .48). Using the accuracy measure that they introduced and comparing free recall and forced recognition, however, the opposite was found: Recall was more accurate than recognition (.77 vs. .67). When subjects were given a free-report option in the recall and recognition tests, the performance was equal in terms of the accuracy score (.77 vs. .77). In every case, accuracy was improved when people were given the free-response option. The two scientists attributed the improvement to the possibility that subjects were screening their answers before making a response.

In sum, in their semantic memory experiment, Koriat and Goldsmith found that performance in terms of quantity was better for forced recognition than free recall, whereas accuracy performance was better for free recall than forced recognition. In a follow-up study, the two researchers observed the same dissociation in an episodic memory study that involved the standard list-learning paradigm. The results from both of these studies confirm the findings of Neisser's (1988) seminar study where the stu-

dents achieved greater accuracy in the recall test than in the recognition test, provided that the free-report option was used. The point of all of these results is that memory assessed in terms of quantity was dependent on the test format (recall vs. recognition), but memory assessment in terms of accuracy depended on the report option (free response vs. forced response).

Koriat and Goldsmith's results have important implications for eyewitness memory, where there is a premium on accuracy. Given the Koriat and Goldsmith findings, the accuracy of eyewitnesses increases to the extent that the free-response option is used. Witnesses will report what they know to be correct and not report what they screen out as inaccurate. The price paid for greater accuracy, however, is a smaller number of responses. If the goal is to increase the number of responses, one can introduce the forced-choice option but one should do so only after employing the free-response option (Chapter 12).

In general, the work by Koriat and Goldsmith (1996) illuminates the regulation of memory exercised by people in everyday situations. Under normal circumstances, people pursue goals other than simply reproducing as much information as possible. They may elect to report certain aspects of events and ignore others, and they may vary the level of generality of their accounts. Koriat and Goldsmith challenged memory researchers to introduce these features of everyday memory into the research laboratory. Doing so will entail problems—for example, the problem of maintaining experimental rigor as researchers yield more control to the subject. The gain, however, will be a fuller understanding of the dynamics of memory, both in the laboratory and in real life.

CONCLUSION

In Chapter 11, we have reviewed two sets of issues: (1) the debate between advocates of multiple-memory systems and proponents of a unitary memory system and (2) the debate between basic and applied memory researchers. As for the dispute over the architecture of memory, we noted the ascendancy of the multiple-systems view even among some erstwhile critics. Undoubtedly, the increasing acceptance of memory classifications stems from the expanding domain of memory research and the increasing contribution of brain research to theories of memory. This is not to suggest that the mapping of memory has been achieved—far from it. Theorists have yet to decide what the systems of memory are and how to guard against inventing systems without sufficient justification.

As for the debate between applied and basic memory researchers, new directions have been offered by several theorists who sought to apply their theoretical work beyond the laboratory. The neural network models and the ACT model described in Chapter 7 are representative of this orientation. Neural network models lend themselves well to applications involving memory impairments. When lesioned, the models exhibit a selective decline in performance, also known as *graceful degradation*. There is no total memory breakdown; rather, the model, much like a patient, continues to exhibit performance that is partially adequate. Using a neural network, McClelland and Rumelhart (1986), for example, have accounted for memory deficits in amnesic patients. Similarly, Farah and McCelland (1991) succeeded in simulating impairments of semantic memory by lesioning a relatively simple neural network (see Chapter 10).

The ACT model has been used to construct computer-based tutors to train students in diverse cognitive skills, such as programming computers, solving geometry problems, and navigating through complex neighborhoods. A mathematics tutoring system based on ACT was selected by Pittsburgh area educators for the Pittsburgh Urban Mathematics Project to train over 2,000 students in diverse quantitative skills. According to the developers of ACT, models such as ACT serve as a vehicle to apply laboratory findings to everyday situations (Chapter 7).

Of course, not every model lends itself readily to applications in the real world (e.g., the SAM model introduced in Chapter 7). However, this should not be held against the model, let alone against the modeling approach, in general. The history of science shows that many models and discoveries of basic researchers offered no immediate practical payoff. When physicists first introduced models of the atom, for example, there were no apparent applications. When oxygen was first discovered in the eighteenth century, scientists did not know what it was good for (Banaji & Crowder, 1989). The same was true when electricity was first discovered; nobody thought that it was applicable to anything other than parlor games.

Nevertheless, although the debate between applied and basic researchers may have lost some of its earlier rancor, there has been little substantive change in the respective positions. According to Koriat and Goldsmith (1996), the rift between the two camps reflects the complex nature of memory itself. The two authors consider the competition between the two approaches, as represented by the correspondence and storehouse metaphors, as salutary. In their view, each of the two approaches can make distinctive contributions to advancing our knowledge of memory. Koriat and Goldsmith (1996) concluded that precisely because memory is heterogenous, no single approach or metaphor will do justice to it. Sharing this view, Tulving (1991) called for tolerance among the camps when he noted, "As in other fields of science, there is room for many different kinds of facts and ideas about memory and for many approaches. So let us stop squabbling and go back to more creative work" (p. 42).

CHAPTER 12

MEMORY IN EVERYDAY LIFE

The goals of basic memory researchers and applied memory researchers are substantially different. Whereas basic researchers seek to understand memory processes in general, applied researchers seek to improve the performance of memory in a specific domain (Neisser, 1978). Basic researchers want to discover the laws that govern encoding and retrieval of information in many different situations, ranging from the acquisition of nonsense syllables to performance in an implicit memory task. Applied researchers want to find out how to improve memory in specific applications in the real world. They want to help readers remember passages of text, improve the accuracy of eyewitness accounts, and train amnesic patients in managing their memory disorder. As noted in Chapter 11, both approaches share the commitment to the empirical method, to the control of factors thought to influence retention, and to the prediction of performance in some future experiment or application.

Taking the perspective of applied memory research, this chapter considers four classes of memory application: remembering and forgetting in everyday life, memory and education, memory and the law, and coping with memory disorders. Each use differs in terms of setting, principles supporting the application, and the issue of generalization discussed in Chapter 11. In many everyday and educational situations, people seek to learn facts and skills deliberately. In these situations, success in remembering facts depends on the ability to encode materials in terms of familiar content and to create effective cues to permit access to the memorized information. In the area of skills, extended, deliberate, and distributed practice, ideally supported by feedback from a teacher, is the key to mastering a skill.

Issues of memory use in law-enforcement settings differ from those in educational and everyday settings. Here, people are called on to report events that they have not memorized deliberately. The witness happened to pass by an accident or crime and he or she is asked to recall the event, frequently after an extended interval. In the context of such eyewitness testimony, the goal is to recover the information after it has been encoded. It is no longer possible to influence the perception of the event. In eyewitness testimony, then, the issue is one of achieving effective retrieval of event information, while minimizing the many opportunities for memory distortion.

Coping with memory impairments poses other challenges altogether. Here, the goal is to restore an impaired memory function or, failing that, to find another function that would compensate for the impaired function. Scientists and practitioners face multiple issues in meeting these goals, foremost among them is the limit in our knowledge of the dynamics of memory disorders. Scientists still do not know enough about the organization of memory and the relation among the functions of memory for the development of programs that would rehabilitate impaired functions. In addition, impairments that are apparently similar may be the result of different underlying conditions, and therefore require different strategies of coping. Perhaps worst, certain memory disorders occur as part of degenerative diseases, thus erecting additional barriers to helping patients manage the impairment. Nevertheless, as the final section of this chapter shows, neuropsychologists have mounted research efforts that hold the promise of helping patients to cope with their memory impairment.

Judging by the increasing stream of publications and conferences, research in each of these applications—everyday memory, educational settings, eyewitness testimony, and neuropsychological work—is progressing by leaps and bounds. Applied researchers tackle more applications than they used to and they do so with improved research methods (Conway, 1991; Intons-Peterson, 1997). Importantly, in the wake of the debate on research goals and methods reviewed in Chapter 11, applied researchers have become fully mindful of the issue of generalizability. To reiterate, *generalizability of results* refers to the extent to which an effect found in one context is replicable in another context, including an application outside the research laboratory (Banaji & Crowder, 1989).

The mandate of generalizability appears in a different guise in each of these four applied research domains. In everyday and in educational situations, it means, among other things, to what extent does knowledge transfer from the learning episode to the application (Schmidt & Bjork, 1993), and to what extent is there transfer from one skill to another. In the case of eyewitness testimony, generalizability from the research context to the applied context poses a particular problem. When a researcher examines eyewitness memory in a laboratory setting, it is very

difficult to duplicate the emotional impact that an accident or crime has in real life. Yet, researchers are confident that this problem can be handled, if not overcome (Chapter 9; Christianson & Safer, 1996; Heuer & Reisberg, 1990). In clinical applications, the task is to develop for each patient a technique that helps the person cope in everyday settings as well as in the clinic. Despite the efforts to address the issue of generalizability and other issues, practitioners are still likely to use their intuitions as they seek to meet an applied goal. It is for this reason that memory applications in the real world retain much of what Yates (1996) once called *The Art of Memory*.

REMEMBERING AND FORGETTING IN EVERYDAY LIFE

Mnemonic Techniques

When we remember well, we usually do not worry much about memory. It is forgetting—in particular, forgetting of details—that prompts our concern with memory. We forget last week's baseball scores, personal identification numbers (PINs), passwords, locker combinations, and telephone numbers. We forget that there was a downpour the last Sunday in August. We forget most of the names of our classmates in first grade (30 years from now you will have forgotten most of the names of your college friends and acquaintances). We forget what we had for breakfast a week ago and possibly even yesterday (Linton, 1982). We forget the names of rarely used concepts (e.g., try to recall the name of a navigational instrument used in measuring angular distances) (Brown & NcNeill, 1966). We forget these items because many of them are relatively unimportant; forgetting fulfills a selective function by uncluttering our memories and thereby increasing the chance of recalling important information (Ribot, 1887).

Forgetting can be painful if the information is important. Forgetting a PIN number can be a nuisance, especially if it is needed to get cash from an ATM machine. Forgetting the name of an important customer is an embarrassment. Forgetting the answers to exam questions is likely to cost valuable points and lower the grade. Mnemonic techniques were designed to improve memory in just such situations.

Mnemonic techniques are named for the Greek goddess of memory, Mnemosyne, and have a time honored history as internal memory aids. According to legend, it was the poet Simonides who invented the mnemonic techniques. Frances Yates (1966) recounts the invention of the art of memory as follows:

At a banquet given by a nobleman of Thessaly named Scopas, the poet Simonides of Ceos chanted a lyric poem in honor of his host but including a passage in praise of Castor and Pollux. Scopas meanly told the poet that he would only pay him half the sum agreed upon for the panegyric (Greek for poem*) and that he must obtain the balance from the twin gods to whom he had devoted half the poem. A little later, a message was brought in to Simonides that two young men were waiting outside who wished to see him. He rose from the banquet and went out but could find no one. During his absence the roof of the banqueting hall fell in, crushing Scopas and all the guests to death beneath the ruins; the corpses were so mangled that the relatives who came to take them away for burial were unable to identify them. But Simonides remembered the places at which they had been sitting at the table and was therefore able to indicate to the relatives which were their dead. The invisible callers, Castor and Pollux, had handsomely paid for their share in the panegyric by drawing Simonides away from the banquet just before the crash. And this experience suggested to the poet the principles of the art of memory of which he is said to have been the inventor. Noting that it was through his memory of the places at which the guests had been sitting that he had been able to identify the bodies, he realized that orderly arrangement is essential for good memory. (pp. 1–2)*

As described in the fable, the poet mentally organized information in terms of discrete locations within a building. According to the method of loci (see the Preface), he recalled the information by visualizing each location and by retrieving the name stored there. Expressed in contemporary terminology, the learner associates information with a familiar scheme, such as a set of places, and retrieves the information by mentally revisiting the places.

Suppose a person wants to memorize a list of names. One way of doing this is to transform the list into a cast of characters and make a story involving the characters. When it comes to recalling the names, the learner does so by retrieving the story and its characters. Another method is to associate the new names with TV shows familiar to the learner. Each name is linked with a show, and at recall, the show titles and the associated names are retrieved. The only difference between such informal strategies and mnemonic techniques is that the latter use a schematic as a hook for the to-be-remembered information.

The peg method illustrates the use of such hooks. In this method, the learner forms a rhyme of a number and a noun according to the following system:

> One is a bun,
>
> two is a shoe,
>
> three is a tree,
>
> four is a door,
>
> five is a hive,
>
> six is sticks,
>
> seven is heaven,
>
> eight is a gate,
>
> nine is wine,
>
> ten is hen.

An ordered list of items, whether it is a shopping list or a list of names, is learned by associating the target items in vivid images with each of the peg nouns, *bun, shoe*, and so on. At retrieval, the pegs are used to recover the associated target items (Lorayne & Lucas, 1974).

Another mnemonic system uses the first letters of target words as hooks for retrieval by creating a memorable phrase of familiar words beginning with the same first letters. Medical students memorize the 12 cranial nerves olfactory, optic, oculomotor, trochlear, trigeminal, abducens, facial, auditory, glossopharyngeal, vagus, spinal, and hypoglossal by the phrase "On Old Olympus' towering top a Finn and German viewed some hops." The first-letter formula used here illustrates a limit of the mnemonic techniques. Their use does not obviate the need of memorizing the individual items themselves. Thus, this particular mnemonic works only when students remember the names of individual nerves. Murdock (1974) referred to such memory as *item memory* to distinguish it from *serial-order memory.* Item memory is required to remember individual stimuli whether they are names, pictures, or tastes. Serial-order memory is the memory for such sequences as the seasons of the year or the spellings of words.

Mnemonic formulae of great sophistication have been used by preliterate societies to remember the fables and tales of the culture. Neisser's (1982a) volume, *Memory Observed: Remembering in Natural Contexts,* contains several accounts of story memory in the oral traditions of different cultures, the Tswana in South Africa, the Iatmul in New Guinea, and Serbocroatians in the Balkans. Common to most of these is the use of stereotypical formulas, certain recurrent themes, rhymes, and melodies. It is through stories and ballads that many cultures have carried on their cultural tradition.

Although less widely used than in the past, mnemonic techniques continue to be used today (Wilding & Valentine, 1996). Indeed, these techniques are based on the principles of skilled memory as documented by basic memory researchers.

Skilled Memory

Figure 12.1 lists some of the principal factors researchers have identified as instrumental in the successful encoding and retrieval of facts (Chapters 4, 5, 6, and 8; Bäckman, Mäntylä, & Herlitz,1990; Kihlstrom, 1996). These factors are neither mutually exclusive nor equally effective for every application. Rather, the idea is to use them flexibly to aid retention and to realize

FIGURE 12.1   Factors that improve retention.

Encoding
Increased study time (Ebbinghaus, 1885)
Increased number of learning episodes (Ebbinghaus, 1885)
Spacing of learning episodes (Madigan, 1969; Schmidt & Bjork, 1993)
Organization, imagery (Bower et al., 1969)
Use of distinctive cues, including motor enactment (Glenberg, 1997)
Self-generation (Slamecka & Graf, 1978)

Retrieval
Category cues (Tulving & Psotka, 1971)
Distinctive cues (Mäntylä, 1986)
Reinstate encoding environment (Fisher & Craik, 1977)
Use of different retrieval schemes (Whitten & Leonard, 1981)
Retrieval practice (Dempster, 1996)

Materials
Interest level of the material
Organization of materials, conceptual, spatial (Bower, Clark, Lesgold, & Winzenz, 1969)
Richness and distinctiveness of features (Bower, 1970)
Causal relations (van den Broek, 1990)

Learner Activities and Attributes
Deep processing (Craik & Tulving, 1975)
Construct retrieval structure (Chase & Ericsson, 1981)
Practice retrieval (Carrier & Pashler, 1992)
Self-generation (Healy & Sinclair, 1996)

that, as the goals of remembering differ, so do the optimal methods of memorization.

In general, memory improvement is based on the principles of elaborative processing during encoding, the use of an effective retrieval structure, and the reinstatement of the encoding environment during retrieval. Elaboration in encoding means to process information deeply by assimilating it to the learner's prior knowledge through mnemonics, imagery, or organizational schemes and by forming causal links between facts to be learned. If the information is important, one can overcome the limits of memory by overlearning the materials. This means people should encode the information in different contexts, thus giving it sufficient resistance against forgetting and retrieval failure.

Next, we illustrate effective encoding and retrieval by reviewing several principles in greater detail. We consider the distinctiveness of cues, the elaboration principle illustrated by the story method, the encoding specificity principle, and the use of a retrieval structure. The emphasis is on how each of these strategies specifically enhances memory performance.

Distinctiveness of Cues

We tend to remember anything that is distinctive, even when the number of items is large. A study by Mäntylä (1986) demonstrates that learners can retain over 500 items, provided they make the items distinctive. Mäntylä presented lists of 600 words to eight subjects. Un-

der the usual free-recall conditions, people would recall 40 of the 600 words. In Mäntylä's study, however, the usual free-recall procedure was changed and subjects were asked to generate one or three associations for each word shown to them. For the target *table,* the following associations illustrate the one- and three-association conditions, respectively: *table*-chair, and *table*-dinner, chair, cloth. The subjects were asked to write their associations in a booklet; they were not told there would be a subsequent recall test. After the association phase, a surprise recall test was given. People were shown the associations they had generated and asked to recall the corresponding target words. The results are shown in Table 12.1 (from Mäntylä, 1986).

Table 12.1 shows a spectacular result. When they developed three associates to each of 600 target words, subjects remembered 90% of the targets. This represents 550 words compared to the 40 words one would typically remember. Recall was so much better than usual because, as a result of generating the associates, people processed the materials more thoroughly and because the associates served as individualized and distinctive retrieval cues.

Other methods of making items distinctive include embedding them in vivid images, generating unique verbal labels, or encoding them in terms of a motor act. For example, people remember a list of items—such as cup, book, pencil, and so on—better when they perform an ac-

TABLE 12.1   Probability of Recall as a Function of Number of Properties (Mäntylä, 1986)

	Subject				
Condition	1	2	3	4	M
3 properties	.932	.872	.900	.915	.905
1 property	.635	.692	.623	.515	.616

tion, even if only imagined, on each item (i.e., the learner would imagine drinking from the cup, opening the book, and sharpening the pencil) (Glenberg, 1997).

Elaboration: The Story Method

As Figure 12.1 indicates, there are diverse ways of embellishing study materials. Learners can form images, organize items in terms of categories, or use spatial layouts. In each case, the material to be remembered is connected to some prior knowledge. The story method illustrates the principle of elaboration. It builds on people's natural interests and skills in telling stories. The success of the story method was demonstrated by Bower and Clark (1969). These investigators presented lists of 10 nouns by one of two methods: the typical rote learning method and a novel story method. In one list, the nouns were the following: *lumberjack, dart, skate, hedge, colony, ducks, furniture, stocking, pillow,* and *mistress.*

In the story condition, learners were told that a good way to learn a list of items is to make up a story relating the items to one another. Each person in the story condition was allowed as much time as needed to compose a story, which took from 40 to 200 seconds. Matched control subjects in the rote learning group were given the same amount of time to commit the 10 nouns to memory. The story method was vastly superior. Recall in the story condition was six times that in the rote learning condition (95% vs. 15%). This is easy to understand if one looks at one of the stories composed by a person in the story condition. Using the preceding list, the person created this story: "A LUMBERJACK DARTed out of a forest, SKATEd around a HEDGE past a COLONY of DUCKs. He tripped on some FURNITURE, tearing his STOCKING while hastening toward the PILLOW where his MISTRESS lay." These results accord well with principles of elaborative encoding and distinctiveness as established in basic memory research (Chapter 4).

Creating a Retrieval Structure

Mnemonic techniques work because they make use of a structure that serves as a mental scaffold during learning and retrieval. Almost anyone can be trained to create a retrieval structure and thus improve retention, provided he or she is willing to put in the effort of doing so. Chase and Ericsson (1981) reported the experience of one person, S. F., an undergraduate at Carnegie-Mellon University who had no particular distinction other than being a long-distance runner. He was average in all other respects, including his SAT and digit span scores when the study began. Over a two-year span, S. F. participated in the experiment for about 250 sessions, being paid each time. During the course of the training sessions, his digit span increased tenfold!

As described in Chapter 5, S. F. achieved this feat by developing a coding scheme of converting the test digits into a sequence of numbers (e.g., running times for various events) that were meaningful to him. The point of the Chase study is this: Learners can strengthen retention by mapping the to-be-remembered information in terms of something that is familiar and sensible. This is the principle that the inventors of mnemonic techniques have used unwittingly since ancient times.

The Encoding Specificity Principle

Assume a learner has taken all the steps recommended in Figure 12.1 to acquire a body of facts. She or he devoted sufficient time to studying the materials, distributed the study periods well, and elaborated the information. All these efforts would be of little value if there were no way to recover the information when needed. Pioneers of memory research, such as William James and Richard Semon, understood this issue well: In order to achieve successful recall, there must be an effective way of accessing the underlying memory records.

However, researchers did not evaluate the notion of memory access experimentally until the 1970s. The critical demonstration was to show that information temporarily unavailable could be made accessible by providing additional retrieval cues, preferably cues that were present during learning. Based on findings such as these, Tulving (1974) formulated the encoding specificity principle that memory is best when the retrieval environment matches the environment present during encoding.

The encoding specificity principle has the following practical implication: Learners can improve retention by memorizing the target information in a context, whether it is external or internal, that is as similar as possible to the test situation. Considering the context dependence of memory in a different light, learners should understand that the encoding specificity principle reveals a limit of performance. Because retention depends on the context, it is also limited by the context. Knowing this principle suggests a way to overcome its limitations. To improve memory, one should study the information several times under different occasions so that it is associated with different contexts rather than one specific context.

Verbatim Memory versus Giving Plausible Answers

In this section, two rather different ways of recalling information from long discourses are selected: verbatim recall and giving plausible answers. When asked questions about a lengthy conversation, a person can respond adequately for most everyday purposes; he or she does so by coming up with plausible answers. People do this naturally and efficiently. Verbatim recall, however, is neither natural nor efficient, as students of eyewitness memory know: People tend to recall the gist of conversations but not the exact words and phrases. Nevertheless, the human memory is adaptable and quite capable of verbatim recall when the need arises.

Repertory Memory Is Aided by Remembering Causal Paths

Take a moment to think of your favorite comedy show on TV. The show is a success because of its witty dialogue and the natural give and take between the actors. Have you ever wondered how the actors, both on the screen and on stage, manage to perform as well as they do? One very important part of an actor's job is to memorize the play's lines verbatim, however long they are. Consider the lengthy statement of Willy Lohman, the principal character in Arthur Miller's play *Death of a Salesman* in Act Two:

> *Oh yeah, my father lived many years in Alaska. He was adventurous man. We've got quite a little streak of self-reliance in our family. I thought I'd go out with my older brother and try to locate him, and maybe settle in the North with the old man. And I was almost decided to go, when I met a salesman in the Parker House. His name was Dave Singleman. And he was eighty-four years old. (1976, p. 81)*

Try to memorize this piece plus the 500 additional words spoken by Willy in just one of several exchanges during a lengthy dialogue with his boss Howard Wagner, and you can begin to appreciate just how many words an actor must memorize.

Intons-Peterson and Smyth (1987) investigated such repertory memory by comparing verbatim recall of actors and novices; they recruited theater students and psychology majors of comparable age and intelligence. The drama students had at least four years' experience in theater and repertory groups and thus were relative experts. Subjects were asked to memorize two 200-word passages, rehearsing the passages aloud. In recall testing, verbatim recall was very good for the experts. It was also surprisingly good for most of the novices, even after a three-day interval. The experts did have, however, an important advantage over the novices; they managed to retrieve the words faster than the novices. On the first recital, an expert took 0.8 second to retrieve a word, whereas a novice required 1.1 seconds. The faster retrieval of experts stems from the extended practice they have in their drama and repertory experience.

Research by Noice and Noice (1994) indicates that professional actors outdo nonprofessionals when the texts are longer and that actors use causal structures focused on the character's goals to aid their recall. The actors pay attention to the motivation and intentions of the play's characters and use those internal states to help them memorize the conversations. The actors' learning activities are thus consistent with the lessons of memory research that causal links enhance retention (Chapter 4; van den Broek, 1990).

Giving Plausible Answers

How does one retrieve facts learned from a conversation, an article, or a talk? Does one search memory for the factual information or for the gist of the passage? Does one make an inference to produce a response, or does one use some combination of these techniques? Research indicates that people first make an implicit guess as to how likely it is that the information exists in memory. If it does, people use one of two basic strategies to answer questions, depending on the retention interval. When a question is posed immediately after one has read or heard a discourse, one tends to make a time-consuming search of memory for the stored information. On the other hand, after a couple of days, the strategy changes and people decide how plausible the question is. It turns out that people become faster at making plausibility judgments as the retention interval increases, indicating that plausibility judgments and trace retrieval are different memory operations (Reder, 1987).

The studies on repertory memory and giving plausible answers illustrate the adaptive nature of memory. When necessary, we can remember verbatim information, but for most other purposes, memory for the gist of a conversation is sufficient.

EDUCATION

One of the stated goals of education is to impart skills for a lifetime. Teachers want their students to remember quantitative skills, to remain fluent in foreign languages, to retain problem-solving skills, and, if possible, to transfer knowledge across domains. Research indicates that the factors that exert the greatest influence on competence are those over which learners have considerable control, including the length of study and the type and the distribution of practice. Grades received in school and the person's gender may have small effects on skilled performance, but they are negligible compared to those factors that people can control themselves.

Practicing Skills

Memory researchers have practical advice for those who want to remember a skill for the long haul, whether it is a quantitative skill such as arithmetic, a foreign language such as Spanish, or playing a musical instrument such as the violin or the piano (e.g., Bahrick, 1984; Bahrick & Hall, 1991; Conway, Cohen, & Stanhope, 1991; Ericsson & Charness, 1994). According to several research studies, retention of a skill improves when learners devote extended initial practice to it, distribute practice sessions, and take advantage of relearning opportunities. Given these conditions, one can maintain the skill for 10, 30, or even 50 years.

The typical approach of studying skill acquisition has been to train a people on a skill in a laboratory setting and record their learning and retention curves. This approach has the advantage of experimental control over the acquisition variables (Banaji & Crowder, 1989), but it does not afford an opportunity to study skill retention over longer time intervals. Ericsson, Krampe, and Tesch-Römer (1993) sought to investigate skilled performance during an expert's entire professional career. They examined this issue by contrasting the performance of experts and novices in such fields as athletics, chess, and music, discovering results with important implications. Perhaps the most significant implication of Ericsson's research is that, in principle, anyone can become an expert in a domain.

Accumulating Hours of Deliberate Practice

Ericsson and colleagues (1993) examined expert performance in the domain of music by comparing the amount of practice for groups of young violinists ranked by independent criteria. Such rankings exist, for example, for chess players: grand master, master, class A player, and beginner (Chase & Simon, 1973). In their study of musical expertise, Ericsson and colleagues (1993) ranked two groups of violinists studying to become performers according to the nominations of their professors. The "best" violinists were those students nominated as having the potential to become international soloists, whereas "good" violinists were judged likely to become good performers. As a control group, the researchers recruited a group of violinists who were students preparing to become music teachers rather than concert violinists.

Using diary studies, the researchers estimated the amount of practice of these three groups of musicians and found substantial differences similar to those illustrated in Figure 8.3. This body of data offers two significant lessons for anyone aspiring to become an elite performer. The first lesson is that the level of expertise is a function of the accumulated hours of practice. The second lesson is that, as professionals grow older, the difference in accumulated practice time widens between groups, thus giving the most highly ranked group an increasing advantage.

Ericsson and colleagues also explored what kind of practice is required to promote outstanding performance in a domain. Through extensive interviews with experts in different domains, the researchers determined that it is not mere repetition that leads to superior achievement. Rather, the experts followed a regimen of deliberate practice characterized by the following features:

— *Feedback.* The student must receive feedback and supervision from a tutor or coach who observes the performance, correcting any errors on specific components of the skill. This schedule differs from working, playing, or observing someone else, in that no feedback is given in these activities.

— *Motivation.* Unlike play, deliberate practice is hardly enjoyable. During training, one rarely gets to play a piece to completion. Rather, interruption, criticism, and effort at improving are the constant features of practice sessions. Nobody would endure extended training under these circumstances without an interest in the domain and the motivation to succeed at it. In the case of many experts, the initial interest was awakened by their parents, who gave them the opportunity to discover and enjoy the activity when they were children. Mozart, for example, was raised in the supportive environment of a family of musicians who listened to music, talked about music, and played music, and involved the young Mozart when he was as young as age 3.

— *Head start.* Begin early in life to accumulate the hours of practice necessary for success in the long run. The earlier one starts, the greater is the opportunity for getting the best balance between a large absolute amount of practice and the best pacing of the practice sessions.

From the perspective of theories of memory, there are several effects of practice, all of which result in the development of long-term memory structures that enable the expert to overcome the limits of working memory. The representation of the cognitive and motor components that support the skill becomes more compact and more accessible. The execution of the skill becomes faster, less prone to errors, and more robust vis-à-vis distraction; in short, the skill becomes automatized (Chapters 5 and 7). As far as retention is concerned, extended training makes the skill durable and resistant to forgetting; however, learners pay a price in that the skill is highly specific and not readily transferable to other domains (Ericsson & Charness, 1994; Healy & Bourne, 1995).

The Benefits of Distributed Practice

Most people have relatively little control over educational opportunities during childhood. However, the basic principles of optimizing practice are valid for skill acquisition in general. In addition to accumulating practice time, a key to successful skill acquisition is captured in the principle of distributed learning. According to this principle, spaced practice is more effective than massed practice. This generalization has been known for well over a century, but it is not one that novices tend to use. Rather, most undergraduate students tend to cram for exams in a small number of lengthy study sessions just preceding the examination. Research, however, has demonstrated that several learning sessions spaced apart are superior to a marathon session.

Spacing of study sessions yields both quantitative and qualitative benefits. Students can double the amount of learned information and achieve a fuller understanding of the study materials when they use two separate sessions rather than a single session of equal length (Bahrick, Bahrick, Bahrick, & Bahrick, 1993; Dempster, 1996; Chapter 4). Even the elite musicians studied by Ericsson took daily naps and other breaks to liven up the rigor of their practice sessions.

An important consideration from a real-world perspective is that trainees retain information well after termination of the training period. Schmidt and Bjork (1993) found that spaced practice not only produced better initial learning results but also better long-term retention. Going beyond the initial training period, these researchers found that under certain conditions, there exists a conflict between factors that promote initial acquisition and those that enhance long-term retention. Thus, frequent feedback may help initial acquisition but diminish long-term retention. If the goal is to enhance long-term retention, trainers should provide intermittent rather than continuous feedback during initial acquisition—a principle long familiar to behavioral psychologists (e.g., Hull, 1943). Introducing variations in the scheduling of practice sessions is also beneficial for long-term retention. Variable training periods resemble the cluttered environment and spontaneous changes in the workplace more closely than the quiet and controlled conditions of the classroom.

Remembering Skills for the Long Haul

Remembering Math for a Life Time

Consider a study by Bahrick and Hall (1991) on the retention of algebra and geometry over a lifetime. These researchers tested 1,700 individuals ranging in age from 19 to 84 years on their knowledge in mathematics. They used two tests consisting of 100 problems taken from high school math courses. Sample problems are shown in Figure 12.2. The investigators scored the test results and correlated them with a number of variables, such as the time elapsed since

FIGURE 12.2 Sample math problems.

1. Find the difference between 42.78 and −41.67 degrees Celsius, the extreme temperatures for North Dakota one year.
2. Multiply $(-1)(2x^2 - x + 3)$.
3. A box contains 30 coins—pennies, nickels, dimes, and quarters—with a total value of $2.37. There are twice as many pennies as nickels and two more dimes than quarters. How many of each kind of coin are there?

Note: The answer to problem 3 is 12 pennies, 6 nickels, 7 dimes, and 5 quarters.

the respondents took their last math course, the number and the level of math courses in mathematics taken in college, the grades received in the courses, the amount of time devoted to mathematical activities since graduation, the person's gender, and others.

For each participant, Bahrick and Hall estimated hours per week devoted to mathematical activities, ranging from balancing a checkbook to tutoring students in math and helping children with math homework. The researchers found that the retention interval was the variable that predicted memory for mathematics best. The large effect of retention interval was to be expected because the study involved intervals of as long as several decades. The other two important variables that improved the level of retention were practice related, the number of courses taken in college, and the extent to which people engaged in activities involving mathematical operations since college (e.g., helping their children with homework). Note that neither course grade nor gender made much of a difference in retaining mathematical knowledge. The data of Bahrick's group are consistent with Ericsson's theory of skilled memory. However, unlike Ericsson, who studied the performance of a small group of elite performers, the Bahrick study included hundreds of participants from all walks of life.

Foreign Languages

Bahrick (1984) contacted almost 800 individuals who had taken high school Spanish up to 50 years ago. He gave the volunteers a Spanish test assessing their reading comprehension, vocabulary, knowledge of grammar, and idioms. As in the study on math retention, he obtained information about a wide range of predictor variables, including the retention interval, the number and level of Spanish courses taken, the mean grade in the courses, and rehearsal opportunities (e.g., travel to a Spanish speaking country). Bahrick found that, after the retention interval,

the factor that most influenced retention was, once again, the amount of original training.

Retention of Spanish declined for the first six years after learning; after that, retention barely declined for 30 years. Bahrick calls this the *permastore*—a bedrock of knowledge that is apparently unaffected by interference or the passage of time. According to Bahrick's results, therefore, one of the goals of education should be to get information into this permastore. This is best done during original learning in high school or college, but subsequent repetition would certainly help.

The beneficial effects of distributed practice were demonstrated in a series of studies by Bahrick and colleagues (Chapter 4). A long-term study by Bahrick, Bahrick, Bahrick, and Bahrick (1993) involved 300 pairs of English and foreign words acquired by learners in either 13 or 26 learning sessions. Under each condition, there were intervals of 14, 28, or 56 intervening days, with 50 words studied under each condition. The retention intervals were one, two, three, or five years after the end of training. Including training and retention phases, this project spanned a period of nine years.

As Ebbinghaus found a century earlier, it was difficult to find subjects who would endure a nine-year commitment to participate in such a study. The design of the experiment required a demanding acquisition schedule, self-monitoring of testing procedures, and avoiding extra experimental exposure to the foreign language for nine years. Bahrick recruited his family to serve as participants; their reward was joint authorship on the paper—and knowledge of 300 words in French or German!

Per session, the students learned 50 word pairs in a self-paced method using index cards that contained the English word on one side and its foreign equivalent on the other. The acquisition rate depended on the distribution of practice; it was somewhat slower, the more spaced the training sessions. However, as Table 12.2 in-

TABLE 12.2   Retention as a Function of Intersession Interval and Session Number (mean percentage recall) (Bahrick, Bahrick, Bahrick, & Bahrick, 1993)

Interval	13 Sessions	26 Sessions
14 days	43	56
28 days	50	68
56 days	57	76

dicates, this deficit was made up by a significantly higher level of retention. Thus, 13 sessions with a 56-day interval were as effective as 26 sessions with a 14-day interval.

The Bahricks call on educators to take the lesson of distributed practice to heart by instituting a curriculum that would allow for repeated rehearsal opportunities stretched out over several weeks. Some creativity and willingness to use innovative academic calendars are required to translate this discovery into practice. Fortunately, individual learners can benefit from the discovery by the Bahricks without awaiting global curricular changes.

In addition to the distribution of practice trials, there are other means of enhancing vocabulary learning, including use of the keyword method of vocabulary learning. Atkinson and Raugh (1975) used this method in training students to learn Russian words by forming images to connect them with English words. Learners were presented with an English-Russian word pair together with a keyword to represent a memorable concept. For example, the Russian equivalent for the English word *battleship* is *linkor*. The keyword given to students was *Lincoln*. Students memorized the chain *link or* → *Lincoln* → *battleship* and found an advantage over the standard paired associate method where the Russian and English words were linked without intermediary (e.g., *linkor* → *battleship*).

Ellis and Beaton (1993) extended the keyword technique to training words in the order English → foreign word. The keyword method has been used for a variety of different languages, including French, German, Russian, and Spanish, and has proven advantageous to teach such features of language as the gender of a word or its pronunciation. As with mnemonic techniques, in general, initial training of vocabulary by the keyword method may take longer than the standard method. This is offset, however, by faster access in recall testing (Higbee, 1994).

However important vocabulary is, acquiring word meanings represents only one of the aspects of language learning. There are syntactic, phonological, semantic, and pragmatic components learners must acquire to achieve competence in a foreign language. Undoubtedly, diverse teaching and learning strategies are necessary to help acquire these aspects of language.

Study Skills in Reading

The often predicted demise of written texts in preference of visual images has been exaggerated. The printed word is alive and well, as demonstrated by the increasing number of books being published every year, the superbookstores, and the many text passages disseminated on the Internet. Reading assignments in college courses are as common today as they were decades ago, and reading comprehension remains one of the most important skills employers look for in job candidates. There is no doubt that reading, comprehending, and remembering texts continue to be vital skills.

In light of the accelerating publication rate of printed materials, there has been great interest among the public for finding ways of increasing the efficiency of reading comprehension. Various speed-reading methods were introduced to meet this need. The speed-reading movement culminated in the 1960s with the Evelyn Wood reading courses. Readers were trained to concentrate better, skip unimportant words and sections, and try to extract information from peripheral vision. Claims of a reading rate of 2,000 to 3,000 words per minute were made, but speed-readers paid a price, in that their comprehension and retention suffered compared to the usual reading rates of 200 to 300 words per minute.

Deep Processing in Reading

Psychologically informed reading methods are based on the principle that retention depends on the depth of processing (Chapter 4). Deep processing in the case of reading, as in other applications, involves elaborating the information and establishing links between new and familiar content. One of the strategies of improving comprehension is Robinson's (e.g., 1970) SQR3 method. This method includes five steps to improve the understanding and remembering of texts: Survey, Question, Read, Recite, and Review. Each of these activities may be executed at different levels of the text, whether it is a paragraph, a subsection, a section, or the entire passage.

— *Survey.* Survey the text, identify the text segments, and scan the titles, subtitles, and other organizational devices included by the author.

— *Question.* Based on the initial survey, formulate a set of questions you expect to answer by reading the text.

— *Read.* Read the text, sentence by sentence. Try to determine answers to your questions, and pay attention to information that is new to you.

— *Recite.* Examine your questions again and answer them. Reread those segments that you did not understand. Relate the content of the passage to information that is familiar to you. Jot down important ideas.

— *Review.* Take additional notes and reread certain sections of the text, answering your questions fully. Devote particular attention to important sections and those that contain surprising information.

Applying the SQR3 method to this chapter, you would select titles, subtitles, and other terms, write them out, and think of ways in which to link them. Research has shown that these strategies, as opposed to merely reading the text once or twice, result in better retention (e.g., Just & Carpenter, 1987).

Material Appropriate Processing

Reading strategies such as the SQR3 method are general reading aids independent of the type of text, whether it is a story, a journal article, or a textbook chapter. According to the theory of material appropriate processing, comprehension of different types of texts is aided best by different types of reader processes (McDaniel, Waddill, & Shakesby, 1996). Specifically, the theory predicts that an encoding activity helps when it does not duplicate the type of processing that the text genre elicits on its own. Narratives are assumed to trigger a reader's relational processing in that the reader establishes connections between the goal of the character, the attempts of achieving the goal, and so on. In contrast, expository texts are assumed to engender a type of processing that is oriented toward definitions of individual items and propositions.

The optimal study strategy for a reader is to compensate for the type of processing that is automatically elicited by the passage. In the case of narratives, this means that readers would benefit from a strategy that orients them toward details, whereas in expositions, readers would benefit from a strategy that orients them toward making connections across different sections of the text. A major assumption of the material appropriate processing account is that factual questions reflect propositional processing, whereas outlining of a text reflects relational processing. Given this assumption, the prediction is that asking questions should aid the comprehension of narratives, and outlining should aid expository comprehension. This is what the researchers found in an experiment manipulating text type and adjunct strategy, as Table 12.3 indicates.

There were three conditions in the experiment: a baseline condition, where readers simply read the passage; a questions condition, where they answered questions after each of four paragraphs; and an outline condition. Factual questions were stated at the bottom of each paragraph probing information that was explicitly stated in the paragraph, such as the identity of a person doing a particular action. Outline subjects were asked to determine the most important statements in the text and to write them down for each of the four paragraphs or in any other organization that they found useful.

The results in Table 12.3 are relative to the baseline condition. They indicate an improvement for all cells, which one would expect from the SQR3 strategy, that any additional activity improves recall. But more interestingly, as predicted, adjunct questions helped fairytales more than outlines did, whereas outlines helped recall of expositions more than questions did.

In another study, Hines and McDaniel wanted to determine whether the content of college textbooks could be made more memorable by presenting the information in a narrative format (see McDaniel, Waddell, & Shakesby, 1996). They rewrote a chapter of a social psychology textbook as a narrative and found that students' free recall improved relative to the standard expository version. However, there

was a tradeoff in that inferences on technical information were less accurate in the narrative version than in the textbook version. Next, the investigators assessed the benefit of outlining for the original textbook and the narrative version. They found that outlining produced significant gains in recall for the original version but not for the narrative version. Note, however, that outlining requires additional time: Outliners required three times as much time as the read-only volunteers!

The lesson of the Hines and McDaniel study is this: If the goal is to retain information from an expository text, then generate an outline of the material. If the goal is to improve recall of a narrative passage, then use adjunct questions that probe for item-specific details. In each case, the idea is to use a strategy that complements the kind of processing that the text engenders on its own.

Is There Transfer of Training?

It would be convenient for learners and teachers alike if training in one skill would help students achieve competence in other skills. This was the credo of formal discipline—that the study of rigorous subjects, such as Latin and logic, would strengthen mental faculties, in general. The formal discipline approach was shaken by empirical research that demonstrated the limits of transfer (e.g., Thorndike & Woodworth, 1901). Thorndike formulated an alternative theory of transfer, the theory of identical elements. According to this view, transfer occurs only to the extent that the skills involve the same response routines, or, in terms of Anderson's ACT model, the same production rules (Chapters 5 and 7).

Contemporary research has confirmed Thorndike's (Thorndike & Woodworth, 1901) finding of the domain-specificity of training. In order to perform well in a domain, practice in that domain is necessary. Lack of transfer be-

TABLE 12.3 Percentage Increase in Recall as Function of Text Type and Type of Adjunct Strategy (see McDaniel et al., 1996)

Text Type	Strategy	
	Questions	*Outline*
Fairytale	31	13
Expositions	28	64

tween skills has been demonstrated in many instances, even when the skills are apparently related. Consider the following set of findings, all making the same point. Chase and Ericsson's (1981) volunteer, S. F., succeeded in expanding his digit span tenfold, but there was only a minimal improvement in his letter span. Gick and Holyoak (1983) failed to find transfer between problems that were phrased in different contexts but were analogous in all other respects. Anderson and Fincham (1994) trained students in a simple mathematical operation and found that students had difficulty in inverting the operation (Chapter 7). Finally, Carraher, Carraher, and Schlieman (1985) failed to find transfer between the real world and the classroom when the same skill was tested. These investigators did research with Brazilian children who were street vendors. The youngsters executed complex calculations flawlessly when selling their merchandise on the street, but they were stumped when they were brought from the street into classroom and given the same problems.

The formal discipline notion experienced a small revival with the introduction of the computer language LOGO. Seymour Papert (1980), inventor of the LOGO language, claimed that there is transfer of training between computer languages and nonprogramming skills. Klahr and Carver (1988) put Papert's transfer thesis to the test and found that there was, in fact, transfer between debugging of LOGO programs and debugging in novel test tasks that the students had not been trained in, including the arrangement of furniture in a limited space and finding a map route. However, the transfer observed in the LOGO study is more consistent with the theory of identical elements than the theory of formal discipline. According to the identical elements model, there is transfer between skills to the degree that the skills are based on the same response routines. If debugging in one domain involves the same routines of checking steps as in the other domain, then there is transfer. By con-

trast, according to the theory of formal discipline, training in a rigorous skill, whether it is logic or LOGO programming, strengthens the memory faculty for all contents.

The conclusion, then, remains that domain-specific training is necessary to attain competence in a field. The best predictors of long-term retention in a field are related to the amount of exposure to the field, the distribution of practice, and the opportunities of relearning one has taken advantage of. If you want to excel at a skill later in life, take several courses in the discipline and seek out occasions to practice the skill as frequently as possible.

MEMORY AND THE LAW

Memory serves us well for most of the demands of everyday life. We tend to remember locations, routines, errands, and frequently used skills without problems. Memory for one-time occurrences and for details such as someone's hair color, the make of a certain car, or the exact time of a phone call is usually not required. Yet, this is the kind of information that is sought in criminal and civil investigations of the legal justice system. The following questions are commonplace in such proceedings:

> Did the defendant wear a gray or a blue hat?
>
> Was it a Ford Taurus or a Mercury Sable that came down Allston Boulevard?
>
> Did Mr. Jones carry a hammer?
>
> Did Mr. Watson use the words *I'll pay for the stuff myself*?
>
> Did Ms. Smith leave the office before 8:30 P.M.?

In most cases, these questions are posed well after the witness observed the incident, thus providing an opportunity for forgetting and for changes of the memory trace from extraneous sources. It is not surprising, then, that contradictions among witnesses are more the rule than the exception, as the following well-publicized cases demonstrate:

▬ *The confirmation hearings of Supreme Court Justice Clarence Thomas.* In October 1991, Thomas was accused by Professor Anita Hill, a former colleague, of sexually harassing her a decade earlier when she used to work for him. In her testimony to the U.S. Senate Judiciary Committee, Professor Hill charged, among other things, that Judge Thomas repeatedly spoke to her about movies depicting sexual scenes in graphic detail. She supported her allegations with specific episodes and details, all of which were denied by Judge Thomas in his testimony (Christianson & Safer, 1996).

▬ *Where was O. J. Simpson's white Bronco?* Many conflicting statements were presented to the court in the O. J. Simpson criminal case in 1995. Among the most striking of these was the issue of the location of Simpson's white Bronco on the night of the murder of Simpson's wife, Nicole, on June 12, 1994. The housekeeper, Rosa Lopez, remembered with certainty that the Bronco was located in its usual place on the street outside Simpson's house, whereas Simpson's driver, Allan Park, and neighbor, Charles Cale, claimed that the car was not parked there that night (*Los Angeles Times,* August 25, 1995, p. B9).

▬ *The Oklahoma City bombing.* How many people emerged from the Ryder truck that was used in the Oklahoma City bombing on the morning of April 19, 1995? In pretrial interviews in 1996, Daina Bradley, a survivor of the bombing of the Alfred Murrah federal building and a key defense witness, told defense lawyer, Cheryl Ramsey, that she had seen one man, an olive-skinned man with curly hair, who bore no resemblance to McVeigh, the defendant in the Oklahoma City bombing. In May 1997, the witness changed her testimony and said that she remembered two men stepping from the truck, the olive-skinned man and a light-skinned man who

could have been McVeigh (*Boston Globe,* May 24, 1997, p. A1).

Which of these recollections is correct? We do not know without corroborating evidence. In these examples, there were contradictions among different accounts, whether they were offered by different witnesses or by the same witness.

Eyewitness testimony is no less problematic when there is agreement among different witnesses. Consider the case of Father Pagano, a Catholic priest accused of several armed robberies in Delaware in August 1979 (Loftus, 1980). Pagano, age 53, tall and almost bald, had been positively identified by all of seven different witnesses as the Gentleman Bandit, a criminal who robbed his victims in the most polite and deferential manner possible. As the eyewitness testimony indicting Father Pagano continued during the court proceedings, the trial came to a sudden halt, when a 40-year old man, a certain Ronald Clouser, stood up and confessed that he had committed the robberies. Police questioned Clouser and became convinced that he was the real bandit when they determined that he knew certain previously unpublished facts that could be known only to the perpetrator. Charges against Father Pagano were immediately dropped and the State Attorney General extended "a sincere apology to Father Pagano." The physical differences between Clouser and Pagano could not have been greater, yet the seven witnesses were mistaken. The priest was free, but troubling questions for memory researchers and for the legal profession remain.

Memory Distortions

Partial recall, memory confusions, and common errors of memory are known to all of us, and researchers have documented such distortions for well over a century. Bartlett (1932) viewed memory distortions as the reflection of the normal functioning of memory; in his view, the distortions simply reflected the blending of facts a person reads with his or her prior knowledge. The interest in memory errors was fueled in the 1990s by a convergence of several influences, including the false versus repressed memory controversy (Chapter 9), the phenomenon of source amnesia, the forgetting of the context of a remembered event (Chapter 8), and the growing body of research evidence of the suggestibility of eyewitness testimony.

Books and journal volumes have been devoted to memory distortions, including such special issues as *The Journal of Memory and Language* in April 1996 and the books *Memory Distortions* edited by Daniel Schacter (1995) and *The Recovered / False Memory Debated* edited by Kathy Pezdek and William Banks (1996). Among the most widely investigated instances of memory distortions are the schema effect, memory illusions, and confusions between imagined and actual events.

— *The schema effect.* People falsely remember statements that are implied by sentences but that were never actually presented. Bransford, Barclay, and Franks (1972) had participants study sentences, including *Three turtles rested on a floating log, and a fish swam beneath them.* In recognition testing, people saw distractor sentences, such as *Three turtles rested on a floating log, and a fish swam beneath it,* believing that it had been part of the passage.

— *Memory illusion.* People assert with confidence having encountered a word in a list when the word was related to a set of target words but never presented to the subjects (Chapter 9; Payne, Elie, Blackwill, & Neuschatz, 1996; Roediger & McDermott, 1995). For example, learners might see a list of words such as *hill, valley, climb, summit,* and *top.* In subsequent testing, subjects falsely believed that the word *mountain,* a word closely related to the studied words, had been presented as part of the list.

(See the exchange between Freyd and Gleaves, 1996, and Roediger and McDermott, 1996, for the issue of generalizing such memory illusions beyond the laboratory.)

— *Confusing real and imagined events.* Imagined events often take on the reality of actual events. One of Piaget's most vivid childhood memories was that of a kidnapping. Interestingly, the kidnapping never took place; Piaget simply imagined it and remembered it. Marcia Johnson (e.g., 1996) reported several such confusions, among them the following: The more often people imagined seeing a picture, the more likely they were to believe that they had actually seen it.

Problems in Eyewitness Testimony

Eyewitness memory has been a fruitful arena for the study of memory distortions. In fact, the first systematic studies of memory distortions were done in the context of examining eyewitness testimony (e.g., Whipple, 1909). The issue of eyewitness testimony and identification is very important in light of the wrongful conviction of innocent people. Although the frequency of wrongful convictions is low in percentage terms, the absolute number of wrongful convictions is high. Analysis of more than 1,000 wrongful convictions indicates that eyewitness error was responsible (Wells, 1993). There are many opportunities for memory distortions in eyewitness testimony, beginning with the moment when the person witnesses the event to the time when he or she is called on to report the event or identify a witness.

Encoding Problems

The effects of stress on encoding are complex; certain aspects of an event may be encoded and remembered well, whereas other, often vital, information is neither perceived nor encoded (Chapter 9). A field study of eyewitness testimony involving over 200 students by Peters

(1988) illustrates this problem. Peters found in a real-life setting that people's memory for faces depended on the degree of their emotional arousal. As part of a training program, the students were required to be inoculated against measles at an immunization clinic. The researchers measured the students' pulse rates during the inoculation and two minutes later as an indicator of their average level of stress. The mean rates were 88 versus 71 beats per minute, indicating a higher level of arousal when people were inoculated.

The students encountered two individuals during their clinic visit who served as targets in the experiment: the nurse who inoculated them and a researcher who scheduled a second clinic visit for each participant. During their second visit, the students had to take a surprise memory test. They were given a face recognition test of the two target individuals who, according to an independent control study, did not differ in terms of their distinctiveness or memorability. Face recognition and memory of certain attributes of the researcher were better than that of the nurse, indicating that stress had a deleterious effect on encoding. This result is consistent with the weapon focus effect and the tunnel memory effect, where witnesses of crimes tend to focus on the weapon(s) used during the crime at the expense of other aspects of the scene, including the features of the perpetrator and other individuals (Chapter 9).

Factors Affecting the Memory Trace after Encoding

Once the memory of an event has been encoded in whatever form, the stored information remains subject to change. This section identifies different sources of memory distortion affecting memory records in the time period following the original event: the suggestibility effect, source confusion, and verbal overshadowing. The *suggestibility effect* refers to errors in testimony produced by misleading information, including leading questions, presented to the witness subsequent to an event. *Source confusion* describes the failure of an eyewitness to remember the source of misleading suggestions and, therefore, include those suggestions in their account of an event (Reyna & Titcomb, 1997). The *overshadowing effect* refers to the phenomenon that giving a verbal report of a face may reduce the accuracy of recognizing the face in a subsequent recognition test.

Suggestibility Effect. Elizabeth Loftus and her colleagues have amassed a rich body of data on the effects of leading questions on retention (Loftus & Ketcham, 1994). Leading questions are a staple of courtroom drama; attorneys use them all the time. In an early study, Loftus and Palmer (1974) examined the influence of leading questions on people's judgments of the speed of cars involved in a traffic accident shown on film. The film showed one car driving into another. After viewing the clip, the subjects were asked to describe the accident; then they were asked a series of questions that included a target question about the speed of the cars. The critical variable was the choice of the verb in the question—for example, *About how fast were the cars going when they contacted each other?* versus *About how fast were the cars going when they smashed into each other?*

Subjects' speed estimates differed depending on the verb used in the question, with the verb *smash* yielding the fastest estimate. When subjects were asked a week later whether there was any broken glass in the scene, people who had heard the verb *smash* reported having seen broken glass; the other subjects did so, too, but to a smaller extent.

Loftus, Miller, and Burns (1978) had subjects view a series of slides of a red car making a right turn and knocking down a pedestrian. The experimenters varied two variables: the type of traffic sign that initiated the series and the type of target question asked after the subjects had seen the slides. At the beginning of the set of slides, half of the subjects saw a Stop sign; the other half saw a Yield sign. After having seen the slides, subjects were asked a set of 20 questions, including a target question, such as *Did another car pass the red car while it was stopped at the Stop sign?* For half the subjects, the target question named the sign they had actually seen; for the other half, the question mentioned the sign they had not seen. Of interest is the memory performance of the latter group on a subsequent recognition test. Up to 80% of the subjects who had been misled tended to remember having seen the incorrect sign.

What happened to the memory trace of the original event in these experiments? Was it obliterated and no longer accessible? Or was it simply overlaid by the postevent information and potentially recoverable? Even if these issues continue to be debated, the upshot of the studies is that, while the original information can be recovered under certain circumstances, memory errors and source confusion are unavoidable (e.g., Belli & Loftus, 1996; McCloskey & Zaragoza, 1985; Zaragoza & Lane, 1994). Studies demonstrated the misinformation effect, even when subjects were offered $25 for remembering the correct information and when they were warned about the suggestive nature of postevent information (Belli & Loftus, 1996).

A debate between Loftus and McCloskey on the effect of postevent information on the trace of the original event offers an interesting perspective for those who believe that the basic research tradition has not raised important issues (e.g., Neisser, 1978; Chapter 11). The Loftus versus McCloskey argument mirrors a debate among basic researchers on the fate of memory traces in the 1950s and 1960s (Roediger, 1991). That debate arose in the context of seeking to understand the nature of forgetting in the retroactive interference design (Chapter 4). In the retroactive interference design, there are two suc-

cessive learning phases: original learning and new learning. The disagreement among theorists concerned the effect of the new learning on the retention of the original material. Does new learning lead to unlearning of the originally acquired information (which corresponds to Loftus's position) or does it continue to exist and compete with the more recently acquired associations (which corresponds to McCloskey's position)? Interestingly, the memory researchers of the 1950s and 1960s never fully resolved this issue!

Source Confusion. In everyday situations, people often confuse context and content of a particular event, especially after the passage of time. This happens, for example, when someone hears some unsavory gossip about a public figure that, at first, is dismissed as a rumor but later turns out to be a fact. Memory researchers have documented such source confusions using different techniques, including the false-fame paradigm and the implanted-memory paradigm.

In the false-fame paradigm, subjects are given a list of names and asked to judge each name for its fame. The list would include names of moderately famous people—such as Robert DeNiro, Chelsea Clinton, and Christie Whitman—as well as fictitious individuals who are, by definition, nonfamous—such as James Milton, Mary Houten, and Sebastian Weisdorf. When subjects judge the names immediately after reading the list, they readily discriminate famous and nonfamous people, but as soon as one day later, they tend to confuse names, rating nonfamous people as famous (Chapter 5).

In the implanted-memory paradigm, information extraneous to an actual event is repeatedly presented to people. After a time interval ranging from days to weeks, people tend to blend the fictitious events with their actual memories. Ceci and colleagues generated implanted memories in preschool children by having them repeatedly talk about real events, such as a bike accident they suffered, and about ficti- tious events such as having their finger caught in a mousetrap (Ceci, 1995). After a period of 10 weeks, the children were prompted to tell a story about the events they had been discussing with the researchers. Based on the narratives the chil- dren told, it was evident that they took the ficti- tious events to be real. Their descriptions were sincere and vivid, so much so that independent observers, asked to judge whether the events de- scribed were real or false, could not tell the dif- ference (Chapter 9).

In the context of eyewitness memory, re- searchers have demonstrated source confusion, as well. In a typical study, subjects were shown a staged crime and then inspected a series of mug shots (Brown, Deffenbacher, & Sturgill, 1977). A few days later, participants viewed a line-up of targets to identify any individuals involved in the crime. Subjects tended to pick out persons actually involved in the crime, but they also se- lected innocent people whom they had seen in the mug shots. It appears, then, that witnesses tend to remember faces quite well, but they tend to forget the circumstances under which they had encountered the face.

Verbal Overshadowing in Memory for Faces. When police question witnesses about a crime, their interest focuses on the identity of the sus- pect as they ask the witnesses to describe the suspect's features, including the color of the eyes, the shape of nose and mouth, the hairstyle, and so on. Such descriptions are undoubtedly valuable; however, the act of describing a face can interfere with the memory of the face. Re- searchers had two groups of volunteers watch a movie of a crime—for example, of a bank rob- bery. One group, the verbalization group, was asked to give a detailed report of the robber's ap- pearance, whereas the control group performed an unrelated activity after seeing the movie. Af- ter a delay of 20 minutes, both groups took a rec-

ognition test. Unexpectedly, the verbalization subjects did poorer than the control subjects (Schooler & Engstler-Schooler, 1990). The ver- bal report apparently overshadowed the trace supporting the recognition performance.

The overshadowing was unexpected because recognition performance should have improved if one assumes that the verbal report serves as an opportunity for rehearsal, thus strengthening the memory trace. Clearly, however, not all mem- ory records are strengthened by verbal re- hearsal. Schooler and colleagues therefore dis- tinguished between memory components that can be aided by subsequent rehearsal from those that are disrupted. The study indicated that ver- balization improves recognition of such verbal materials as word lists, sentences, and passages, but disrupts recognition of such sensory stimu- lus aspects as colors, forms, musical tunes, tastes, and affective judgments, as well as map memory (Schooler, Ryan, & Reder, 1996). As for face memory, Schooler found several factors that interacted with verbalization to affect face recognition: the number of trials, the number of faces involved, and the expertise of the ob- server.

The studies reviewed here illustrate how eas- ily memories can be altered by subsequent infor- mation. A witnesses' account of a crime or an accident is easily influenced by subsequent questions, and, while witnesses may remember faces, their memories for the faces may be re- duced by talking about them, and they tend to confuse the occasions when they encountered particular faces. Findings such as these present a challenge to cognitive and forensic psycholo- gists alike (e.g., Loftus & Ketcham, 1994; Reyna & Titcomb, 1997; Wells, 1993). Given that we cannot do without eyewitness testi- mony, psychologists ask quite pragmatically: How can reporting accuracy be improved, given that memory is so susceptible to suggestions and changes?

Improving Eyewitness Testimony

Even if flawed, eyewitness testimony remains a vital part of the judicial process. The goal, then, is to improve eyewitness testimony and the conditions under which it is given. From the perspective of memory research, improving eyewitness memory means to protect the memory trace from potential contamination, to minimize response bias on the part of the witness, and to enhance the retrieval of the trace. Memory researchers have sought to aid in these efforts for almost a century. The first 15 volumes of *Psychological Bulletin* contain a wealth of research articles dedicated to improving testimony, including papers on the power of leading questions, the types of errors frequently committed by witnesses, and how to avoid such errors (e.g., Whipple, 1909). With the advances of memory theories and research methodologies in the 1980s and 1990s, added techniques of improving eyewitness testimony have been developed. Here, we consider a small sample of the recommendations of memory researchers: the use of open-ended questions, techniques of reducing bias in line-ups, and the use of retrieval mnemonics in the cognitive interview. These methods are not mutually exclusive; rather, they are complementary and depend on the goal of the investigation.

Open-Ended Questions
Given the body of evidence documenting the influence of leading questions on testimony, an important lesson is to constrain the witness as little as possible by using open-ended questions, such as *Describe what happened* or *Tell me what you have witnessed* (Geiselman & Fisher, 1997; Koriat & Goldsmith, 1996; Loftus, 1980). Asking neutral questions soon after the event was witnessed can protect the information and "inoculate" it against subsequent misleading questions (Reyna & Titcomb, 1997). Using open-ended questions is consistent with the accuracy approach to memory, as compared to the quantity approach sketched in Chapter 11. Comparing the accuracy in traditional forced-choice recognition tests and an innovative free-choice recognition test, Koriat and Goldsmith found improved accuracy in the free-choice test. However, the investigators observed a trade-off in that the free reporting option yielded less complete responses than the forced reporting option (Chapter 11). In order to obtain more complete data, the open-ended question period could be followed up by the more structured cognitive interview (described later).

Bias in Line-Ups
In recognition and recall tests, people frequently believe that a stimulus was presented when, in fact, it was not presented at all. This type of error, known as a false alarm (Chapters 1, 4, and 7), is more likely the less distinctive the event and the less certain the observer is—two conditions characteristic of most eyewitness situations. Whether due to stress or to a narrowing of attention, witnesses often perceive such critical aspects as the suspect's face rather poorly.

In line-ups, a false alarm is not merely an experimental error; it can send an innocent person to jail or worse (Loftus & Ketcham, 1994; Wells, 1993). In order to help address this problem, memory researchers have developed estimates of two different types of bias that affect identification in line-ups: observer bias and external bias. *Observer bias* refers to the tendency of the witness to make a false alarm, whereas *external bias* refers to the bias that results from receiving external information about the suspect (e.g., from the media). In order to get an estimate of observer bias, researchers use the recognition paradigm as a model (Chapter 1). Using the idea of blank trials, researchers have introduced the blank line-up, a line-up of people that does not contain the suspect. This type of line-up gives investigators an estimate of the bias of a witness to falsely identify a person, even though it is known that the person is innocent.

The extent of external bias can be assessed by using mock witnesses. These are individuals who have not been at the scene of the crime and not seen the suspect. However, they are told about the crime and given a description of the suspect as it might be published by the media. If the mock witnesses can identify the suspect, the police know that identification was possible on the basis of general information without actually having seen the suspect.

As for selecting foils for the line-up, researchers distinguish between two selection strategies: the culprit description strategy and the suspect similarity strategy (Wells, 1993). In the culprit description strategy, police officers select foils on the basis of a verbal description of the suspect (e.g., *He was male, white, about 5 feet 8 inches, dark hair, and . . .*). In the suspect similarity strategy, an officer compares photos of the suspect with other photos in a mug-shot album and selects those that appear to be most similar. Wells argued in favor of using the former strategy, noting that the suspect similarity strategy may confuse witnesses. Here, the similar foils may actually serve as "clones" of the suspect and make the job of discriminating the target unnecessarily difficult.

Not only are false identifications by witnesses a problem but so is the certainty with which the false identifications are often made (Wells, 1993). The confidence of an eyewitness matters because it tends to influence his or her credibility: The more confident the witness, the more credible he or she appears to a jury. Research, however, indicates that the relation between confidence and accuracy is low, at best (Metcalfe, 1996). There is no easy solution to this dilemma. According to a technical analysis by Juslin and colleagues (1996), the correlation between confidence and accuracy of eyewitness testimony can be improved if a calibration procedure is introduced in addition to the typical binary yes/no identification. In the calibration procedure, a witness judges suspects on a subjective probability scale—for instance, involving 11 alternative categories from 0% to 100% (there is a probability of 1.0 that the person is the culprit). Using the calibration procedure, Juslin and colleagues reported an increase in the confidence-accuracy correlation in a situation that faithfully mimicked realistic police investigations (for details, see Juslin, Olsson, & Winman, 1996).

The Cognitive Interview

The cognitive interview differs from the interview techniques commonly used by police departments in that it is based on principles experimentally documented to enhance retrieval processes. This approach is consistent with the strategy of initially asking open-ended questions in order to minimize observer bias, as discussed earlier (see also Chapter 11). The cognitive interview uses such retrieval mnemonics as the encoding specificity principle and the strategy of multiple retrieval paths to access records assumed to exist in the memory of the witness (Fisher & Geiselman, 1988; Geiselman & Fisher, 1997).

■ *Encoding specificity principle.* Recall accuracy is improved to the extent that the encoding and retrieval contexts are similar (Chapter 4). Accordingly, interviewers should encourage the witness to think of the context at the scene of the crime and bring that context back to mind.

■ *Multiple retrieval paths.* If memories are stored in terms of networks, as many models assume (Chapters 4 and 7), memory records must be accessible via different paths. Accordingly, witnesses are encouraged to report everything that comes to mind, even if the information appears to be unimportant. They are asked not to edit anything, because even apparently insignificant details may become important when they are pieced together (Tulving, 1974; Whitten & Leonard, 1981).

Geiselman and his colleagues demonstrated memory enhancement using the cognitive interview in a variety of studies. In one experiment, the researchers compared three retrieval conditions: the cognitive interview condition, a hypnosis condition, and a standard condition. Subjects in all three conditions saw four films borrowed from the Los Angeles Police Department depicting a crime: a bank robbery, a liquor store robbery, a family fight, and a warehouse break-in. Each film was realistic enough to trigger measurable physiological reactions that were comparable to those police officers often exhibit in a real-life crime scene. Subjects viewed one of the films per condition, and two days later were interviewed by professional law-enforcement officers. In the cognitive interview condition, subjects were prompted by retrieval mnemonics, as illustrated earlier; in the hypnotic condition, officers experienced in hypnotic techniques interviewed the subjects; and in the standard condition, the interview normally given in police departments was administered.

Recall was better in the cognitive interview condition than in the hypnosis condition and the standard interview condition. Incidentally, the finding that the hypnosis condition was not any better may surprise readers, but it accords well with results from research labs. Any beneficial effects attributed to hypnosis are better explained in terms of other variables, including the opportunity for repeated testing (Erdelyi, 1996; Erdelyi & Kleinbard, 1978). In any case, based on over 40 laboratory studies and field studies in several countries, Geiselman and Fisher (1997) concluded that the cognitive interview elicited between 25 and 35% more correct information than did a standard police interview, without generating more incorrect information. There are, however, limits to the technique: It works less well at longer retention intervals, in face recognition, and for subjects who are not willing to cooperate. The interview takes longer to conduct than the standard interview and requires trained personnel.

In conclusion, we have seen that eyewitness testimony is subject to a variety of distortions depending on the level of stress of the witness, the nature of postevent information, and the types of questions posed to the witness. Memory researchers have made progress in identifying the conditions that enhance or impede valid eyewitness testimony (Wells, 1993). Conditions that improve the validity of testimony include the use of open-ended questions early in an investigation, the use of appropriate control procedures to assess witness bias in line-ups, and the use of retrieval techniques that reinstate the encoding context and use multiple retrieval paths to access event traces. Of course, the methods of collecting eyewitness testimony should be used flexibly, keeping in mind the trade-off between accuracy and quantity (introduced in Chapter 11) (Koriat & Goldsmith, 1996).

COPING WITH MEMORY IMPAIRMENTS

Coping with memory impairment depends on the severity of the condition. When the impairment is relatively minor, affecting a limited memory function such as the rehearsal loop or a subset of semantic memory, individuals are able to resume their occupation as patients P. V. and P. S. did (Chapter 10). P. V., a 26-year-old woman, sustained a lesion in the left temporal lobe and an impairment of the rehearsal system that did not interfere with running her business, a small pottery shop. P. S., a 45-year-old owner of a small contracting business, suffered brain injury and subsequent problems in semantic retrieval as a result of a blow to his head. P. V. was able to continue working several months later

(Hillis & Caramazza, 1991). In relatively severe cases of amnesia, whether they result from encephalitis, as in the case of the musician Clive Wearing, or from accidents, as in the case of Tulving's patient K. C. (Chapter 10), major life changes occur. Both of these patients lost the ability to maintain their jobs and to care for themselves. Memory loss in dementias, such as Alzheimer's, are the most difficult to cope with because the condition deteriorates progressively.

Although neuroscientists and neuropsychologists have made major strides in seeking to uncover the physical roots of memory dysfunction, to date there is no generally accepted theory of the functional causes of memory impairment and, as a result, there is no blueprint of how to treat such disorders. Nevertheless, psychologists have developed intuitions of how to help patients and have devised techniques to improve patient lives. The general goal is to find for each individual a balance between challenge and realism: Try to get the patient to use the remaining memory functions to the extent possible without frustrating the person so that he or she gives up the effort of memory rehabilitation and management.

Neuropsychologists use general guidelines as they seek to help patients with memory impairments (Wilson, 1996). The guidelines are consistent with principles known to enhance encoding and retrieval in nonpatient populations, as well (see Figure 12.1). Here are some of these principles:

- Simplify the information to be remembered.
- Reduce the amount of information during any learning episode.
- Associate the information with material familiar to the learner.
- Repeat learning episodes as frequently as is practically feasible.
- Repeat learning episodes in different contexts so as to facilitate generalization.

Beyond these guidelines, neuropsychologists have introduced behavioral and cognitive approaches to coping with memory disorders, including the use of internal and external memory aids, methods of capitalizing on spared memory functions, and strategies of improving prospective memory.

Internal and External Memory Aids

Memory aids for patients with memory impairments are scaled-back versions of the aids used by everyone else, including mnemonic techniques and external aids. These aids are used in the assumption that recovery and restoration of the impaired memory functions are no longer possible. Their goal is to alleviate patients' memory dysfunctions.

Mnemonic Techniques

Mnemonic techniques are ways of improving memory by using internal strategies. They are intended to teach patients new information such as the names of their caregivers, lists of items, and the locations of personal belongings. Neuropsychologists have adapted almost all of these techniques to memory rehabilitation, including imagery, organization, and elaboration (Figure 12.1).

One of the most effective mnemonic methods is Crovitz's (1979) story method. This method is based on Bower and Clark's finding of dramatically increased list recall when subjects used the words of the list to make up a story. A story might start as follows: "The first word is *airplane* and you can remember that anyway you like. The second word is *giraffes* because the airplane was full of giraffes. The third word is *bologna* because the giraffes were all eating bologna sausages." Wilson (1966) found that the story method was more effective than other mnemonic techniques both for individuals with and without brain injury. She noted, however, that the method is not readily applicable in everyday situations.

In general, the use of mnemonic techniques—already a challenge to normal individuals—is limited in patients with memory impairments. Only patients with relatively mild disorders can understand the techniques, and even these patients do not employ the techniques spontaneously; rather, they must be trained to use them. As in nonimpaired individuals, the usefulness of these techniques is restricted to the specific information memorized; they do not improve memory performance in general. Finally, the mnemonic techniques are used less frequently because external memory aids are easier to use and widely available.

External Memory Aids

External memory aids are popular among nonimpaired individuals. People use them spontaneously. They place their watches on the opposite wrists, put a pebble in their pockets, and write notes and memos (Searleman & Herrmann, 1994). External memory aids specifically developed for patients with memory impairments include wall charts, calendars (Kapur, 1995), a memory log book (Raskin & Mateer, 1994), a memory wallet (Bourgeois, 1993), and electronic memory aids. As illustrations, consider the use of the memory wallet as a retrieval aid in Alzheimer's patients and the use of electronic memory aids.

The Memory Wallet.
Michelle Bourgeois used the memory wallet in the context of training four Alzheimer's patients aged over 70 years to carry out conversations. The memory wallet is a portfolio of those autobiographical facts that Alzheimer's patients find difficult to remember, including birthdays, holidays, family gatherings, and the names of caregivers and family members. Facts such as these were written on index cards and included in the memory wallet, along with photographs of friends and family members.

The patient was trained to use the memory wallet in conversations with other people, both with nonpatients and with other patients. In the first stage of training, the use of the wallet helped to improve the patient's accuracy of memory and his or her ability to carry on a conversation with staff and family members. In the second stage, conversation partners were the other Alzheimer's patients. Pairs of patients met three times a week for an encounter of five minutes. Using the memory wallets, the patients were told that the wallets might aid them in remembering things and help them in chatting with their friends. The therapist then prompted the patient with the following request: "I'd like you to talk about your family, what your life was like when you were younger, and what you do now during the day." During the course of a dozen conversations, patients continued meetings with and without use of the wallets. The researchers found that in three of the four patients, the quality of the conversation was superior in the aided condition than in the unaided condition. Although this is a relatively limited use, it illustrates a manner by which the quality of the social lives of Alzheimer's patients can be improved.

Electronic Memory Aids.
The introduction of electronic devices spawned a variety of aids, ranging from electronic organizers to "prosthetic" memory tools, such as NeuroPage, that combine recordings customized for each patient with a radio and paging system (Glisky, 1995; Kapur, 1995). Electronic organizers can be set to chime at different times on different days and play prerecorded reminders of appointments and chores to do. They are compact, relatively inexpensive, and readily usable by patients with mild impairments. In order to use the organizers, the patients need to learn three operations: enter information into the organizer, remember to review the entries, and delete entries that are no longer relevant.

NeuroPage is a portable paging system that was originally designed by an engineer for his son who was brain injured and was later adapted for other patients (Wilson, 1996). NeuroPage combines the use of a computer, a telephone, a radio transmitter, and a paging system. Reminders for each patient are stored in individual files in the computer. At the scheduled time, the information for an individual is sent automatically via modem to the transmitter and from there to the specific patient. Advantages of the NeuroPage system include its ease of use; the fact that, after initial programming, no further human intervention is necessary; and that patients prefer the system as well as other electronic memory aids to mnemonic strategies (Kapur, 1995).

The use of electronic aids has revived the hope that computers might be placed in service for patients, whether in everyday living or for vocational tasks. In the 1980s, efforts were made to train patients to use computers, but only individuals with relatively intact cognitive functions could be trained. As the next section illustrates, Schacter, Glisky, and McGlynn (1990) succeeded where previous computer-based methods fell short—namely, in the training of patients with severe amnesia. The key was to capitalize on memory functions that were not affected by the amnesia.

Capitalizing on Spared Functions

The goal of capitalizing on spared functions is to identify a mechanism to serve as a substitute for the impaired function, even if only to a partial extent. Different teams of researchers have reported success in using an unimpaired function such as implicit learning to train patients on a specific target task. Here, we consider two techniques illustrating this approach: the vanishing cue technique (Schacter, Glisky, & McGlynn, 1990) and the procedure of minimizing errors (Baddeley & Wilson, 1994; Tulving, Hayman, & MacDonald, 1991).

Vanishing Cue Technique

Schacter and colleagues (1990) used the vanishing cue procedure with patient H. D., who, at age 32, began to show symptoms of amnesia resulting from encephalitis. After her recuperation from the infection, H. D. returned to work as a clerk but was unable to perform her duties because she could not remember her assignments. A neuropsychological diagnosis confirmed the memory deficits, but indicated that H. D. had some residual learning and attentional abilities.

In cooperation with H. D.'s employer, the neuropsychologists undertook a training program with H. D., who was highly motivated and eager to return to work. The goal of training was to develop data-entry skills. The job was a mapping task that involved entering data from "meter cards" (e.g., from a water meter) into a computer file. The operator had to enter data from the meter card into nine designated positions on the screen. The correspondence between cards and display was not always clear, however. There was irrelevant information on the cards, and some of the fields appeared in one order on the cards and in a different order on the computer display.

H. D. had to learn the general terminology of her data-entry tasks, the meaning of the codes on the meter cards and the display, their different locations, the mapping between cards and display, and some editing functions. Training was based on the technique of vanishing cues. It was implemented in the context of an interactive dialog between H. D. and the computer. For example, the sentence *Information from one document is entered into a single row and is called a ???* was presented and H. D. was to supply the answer *record*. If she was not able to produce the response, she was given incremental recall cues, such as *r, re, rec,* until she gave the correct answer. After additional training, fewer cues were given, hence the term *vanishing cue.* Training continued until H. D. was able to provide the correct answers for all test sentences while requiring fewer hints and responding faster. Eventually, H. D. was able to return to part-time employment.

The vanishing cue procedure has been customized for individual patients and used successfully for other individuals with relatively mild memory impairments. One patient was able to learn the names of business forms and the manipulation of spreadsheets; another acquired simple word-processing skills and the knowledge of her daily schedule; and a third person managed to acquire knowledge on introductory sociology.

However successful the vanishing cue technique proved with a small number of patients, it is not a panacea: Only a small amount of information can be conveyed, and training is very time consuming and does not generalize to other tasks (Glisky, 1995). Indeed, Schacter and colleagues pointed out that they have used the technique on only a small number of patients "so we cannot be certain of the generalizability of our findings" (Schacter et al., 1990, p. 252). Schacter and colleagues suggest, however, that success of the vanishing cue technique and other forms of memory management is more likely when the job is broken down into small steps and the laboratory task simulates the work task closely. The lack of transfer from one domain to others is harder to come by, if at all. This problem stems from the property of skills to be domain specific rather than general (Chapters 5 and 7). People may retain skills they have practiced but they cannot generalize them (Healy & Bourne, 1995).

Minimizing Errors in Learning

The idea of minimizing errors in learning is based on Baddeley's error monitoring hypothesis (Chapter 10). According to this hypothesis, the function of explicit memory in learning is to monitor and therefore avoid errors. To the extent that explicit memory is impaired in patients, they have lost the ability to track errors and thus

have difficulties acquiring new information. Training would succeed if one could reduce and, indeed, eliminate errors (Baddeley & Wilson, 1994). Consider two illustrative studies: one by Baddeley and Wilson (1994) and the other by Tulving involving K. C., a densely amnesic patient who was the victim of a traffic accident.

Baddeley and Wilson (1994) reduced errors in learning by adapting Terrace's (1964) errorless learning procedure from animal discrimination learning (Chapter 2). In discrimination learning, pigeons are presented with two stimuli, such as a vertical bar and a horizontal bar, or a green light and a red light, one of which is reinforced while the other is not. Such discriminations are difficult in the standard procedure where the two stimuli are introduced simultaneously at the beginning of training. The pigeons tend to respond both to the reinforced and nonreinforced stimuli, presumably because they cannot tell the difference between the stimuli. In his errorless procedure, Terrace minimized subject errors by initially presenting only the reinforced stimulus. After the reinforced stimulus elicited a stable response, the nonreinforced stimulus was gradually faded in by increasing its exposure duration. Terrace found this to be a highly effective way of training pigeons to discriminate between different colors that were otherwise easily confused.

Baddeley and Wilson (1994) introduced the errorless learning procedure in the context of the word-stem completion task (Chapter 10). This task involves a study phase in which participants see a sequence of words and a performance phase where fragments of previously presented words and of new words are shown. Baddeley and Wilson used this paradigm to compare the performance of patients in an "errorful" condition and in an errorless condition. In the former condition, the patients were shown the first letters of a word (e.g., *br*) and asked to guess the target word (e.g., *bring*). The person might guess *brain, bread*, and *brown,* but was told that these guesses were wrong. The person was given the correct word, *bring,* and asked to write it down. In the errorless condition, guessing and making errors were avoided by presenting the first letters together with the target word and by asking people to write down the correct word. In testing, patients were given the initial syllables of the target words and asked to write down any word that came to mind. The patients performed much better in the errorless condition, indicating that the errors patients made in the guessing condition interfered with their performance.

Tulving, Hayman, and MacDonald (1991) used a procedure similar to Baddeley and Wilson's error minimizing technique to train patient K. C. to acquire new declarative knowledge. The researchers adapted the word-stem completion task in training K. C. to respond correctly to context cues provided by a sentence frame. The patient's response choices were restricted by providing cues that constrained the response. K. C. was shown 80 picture-sentence pairs representing scenarios, such as medicine curing a hiccup. In testing, phrases such as *Medicine cured _i_c_ p* were presented. After 20 training sessions extending over 20 weeks, K. C. tended to complete the fragments correctly when the two context words were presented.

The success of Tulving's research group and of other groups (e.g., Hamman & Squire, 1995) contrasts with the failure of the standard training method where patients are required to provide a response chosen from the entire target set of 80 items when given the sentence frame. The crucial improvement of Tulving's procedure was to minimize errors and thus interference, as it was in Baddeley and Wilson's (1994) procedure. The practical lesson is that learning in amnesic patients improves when guesses and errors are eliminated. The procedure has been applied to train patients with various memory disabilities in different skills: An agnosic patient learned to recognize pictures, a stroke patient learned to remember names of the medical staff, and a Korsakoff patient learned to program an electronic apparatus (Wilson, 1996).

Prospective Memory Training

Prospective memory refers to memory for tasks to be performed in the future, whether the task is to mail a letter, run an errand, or keep an appointment. Prospective memory is attracting growing interest among memory researchers because it involves practical and theoretical issues (Einstein & McDaniel, 1996). It represents a real-world application, a topic that has come into its own since Neisser's (1978) challenge to take memory out of the laboratory (Chapter 11). Prospective memory is also of interest for theoretical reasons. It is triggered spontaneously without conscious intervention. It is thus similar to implicit memory, a domain that has commanded growing attention (Chapter 5). Prospective memory is equally of interest to memory researchers who investigate memory changes in older people and in memory-impaired patients. It involves self-initiated retrieval, a process that has been said to deteriorate with aging and in memory-impaired individuals (Craik et al., 1995; Glisky, 1995).

Time-Based and Event-Based Prospective Memory

Theorists have distinguished between time-based and event-based prospective memory (e.g., Einstein & McDaniel, 1996). Self-initiated prospective memory is required for tasks to be executed at a certain time, such as taking the cookies out of the oven in 20 minutes. Event-based prospective memory is required for acts triggered by a designated event, such as taking the cookies out when a timer rings. Einstein and McDaniel (1996) found that these two types of prospective memory behave differently as a function of aging: Event-based prospective memory holds up as the person ages, whereas time-based prospective memory diminishes.

The two researchers devised a simple technique to measure event-based prospective memory. They had old and young volunteers participate in a free-recall experiment, which is a retrospective memory task. The experimenters presented lists of nine words in the recall test. Included in the list were certain target items. Whenever a target occurred, the person was to press a key on a computer keyboard. There were no age differences in this task, indicating that event-based prospective memory was equally effective in old and young participants.

Time-based prospective memory was assessed in a continuous recall experiment where the subjects were presented with long lists of words and intermittently prompted to recall the last 10 words. As they were working on the retrospective recall task, the participants had to remember a prospective memory task, as well: They were to press a key every 10 (or 20) minutes. A clock was located behind the subjects to give them the opportunity to monitor the time. In this task, there was an age-related decrement. Apparently, older people have difficulties in keeping track of time or in estimating time. One possibility is that aging slows down a person's biological clock. Although this task was rather difficult, it reflects the nature of prospective memory tasks in everyday life in that people must remember errands while they perform many other activities.

Improved Prospective Memory in Patients with Traumatic Brain Injury

As other memory functions are impaired in traumatic brain injuries, so is prospective memory. Particularly patients with frontal lobe injuries exhibit prospective memory problems; they fail to remember assignments, appointments, and errands. In fact, in many cases, the failure to remember errands is a telltale sign of other memory impairments. Raskin and Sohlberg (1996) developed a program to train two frontal lobe patients to improve their prospective memories. The two investigators describe two patients,

both males in their mid-twenties, who were injured in different accidents. One of the patients, J. M., was riding his motor bike when he was struck by a car. The other patient, M. G., was injured at work, a railroad company, when a metal bar sprung loose and hit him in the face. He lost consciousness, sustained facial fractures, and lost several teeth. Both patients suffered from learning and memory impairments, including prospective memory deficits. The investigators devised a treatment regimen to help these patients to recall doing errands and chores in the future.

Prior to treatment, both patients were tested on a variety of cognitive measures—including attention, working memory, and problem solving—and a baseline of prospective memory performance was established. Treatment included 60 one-hour sessions of prospective memory training and retrospective memory training distributed over a period of six months. In prospective memory training patients were required to perform a specific task—for example, clapping their hands after intermittent time intervals. On some trials, the patient had to monitor the time on his own while on others the experimenter would provide an agreed upon cue, such as standing up. During the intervening interval, patients worked on a distractor task, such as doing some simple math problems.

In retrospective memory training, the two men were asked to recount a series of experimenter-prompted activities they had just completed—for example, standing up or clapping their hands. The criterion variable was performance on a prospective memory test that required patients to perform specific tasks at certain intervals ranging from 1 minute to 24 hours in the future. The patient received points for performing the target task at the correct time.

With the generalization issue in mind, Raskin and Sohlberg assessed whether the training in the clinic would generalize to everyday settings. They evaluated such transfer by having the patients call the laboratory at specified times and by having them remember errands (e.g., getting specific items in the grocery store, filling the car with gas, or taking medication). Prior to training, neither patient fulfilled any of these tasks, but, according to the evaluation of patients' relatives, training resulted in a measurable improvement. However, problems persisted; for example, one of the patients remembered to initiate telephone calls, but he made them at the wrong time. In order to illuminate the dissociation between remembering the action and the failure to remember its correct timing observed in this patient, the authors called for additional basic research on prospective memory—for example, on the involvement of working memory in monitoring time and estimating intervals.

Even with the progress on memory management using cognitive and behavioral models reported in this section, much work remains to be done in this domain. Among other tasks, future research must determine the optimal size of learning units in the various memory management techniques, expand the range of skills and contents used in different procedures of memory management, and adapt the techniques proven successful with amnesic patients to individuals suffering from degenerative diseases such as Alzheimer's. In their quest to advance clinical applications, neuropsychologists are likely to benefit from the expanding horizons of neuroscience, including new discoveries from research on the plasticity of the brain (Bach-Y-Rita, 1990; Kolb, 1989) and on the uses of neuroimaging techniques to monitor brain processes as rehabilitation training is undertaken (Posner & Raichle, 1994).

CONCLUSION

You are about to complete this course in memory. How much do you think you will remember after the final examination, in the next semester, in 1 year or 10 years from now? Based on re-search results, chances are that you will remember more than you might expect. Researchers have found that students who take a course in cognitive psychology remember research methods, concepts, and names, in that order, for many years after taking the course. Conway and colleagues (1991) tested hundreds of their former students at retention intervals ranging from 3 months to 12 years. Using recognition, sentence verification, and recall tests, the scientists assessed retention of five topic areas: memory, perception, language, problem solving, and research methods.

In the recognition test, retention of names and concepts was evaluated. Proper names of cognitive psychologists—such as *Baddeley, Bower, Farah, Kintsch,* and *Shiffrin*—were mixed with names selected at random from a telephone book. Concepts included such terms as *context cues, preattentive processing,* and *spreading activation,* all introduced in the course. Foil concepts were written to be stylistically similar to the targets—for example, *chronometric cycle* and *quadratic activation effect.* The sentence verification test was modeled after the semantic memory task introduced by Collins and Quillian (Chapter 4). The test involved the presentation of true sentences, such as *The behaviorists considered learning to be a passive process,* and distractors, such as *The British empiricists were the first researchers to examine mental processes in experiments.*

According to the different memory measures used in the study, long-term retention was best for research methods, followed by concepts and names in cognitive psychology. These results reflect several principles discovered in basic memory research, including the principle of learning facts in different contexts and the principle of elaboration. Research methods were better retained because students were exposed to them in courses other than cognitive psychology. Concepts were remembered better than names because students were able to form schemas to help them remember the concepts. Names were more difficult to retain because they are not inherently linked with any substantive information. Nevertheless, people's memories for names was consistently better than chance level at all retention intervals, including the 12-year interval.

In conclusion, then, your memory is better than you thought. Even if you fail to remember a set of facts explicitly, this does not mean that you have forgotten. Should the need arise to revisit the materials, you will have an easier time relearning them than if you had never studied them before. This is the lesson of Ebbinghaus's savings method and the principle underlying implicit memory. Repeated exposure to materials facilitates processing on the next occasion they are encountered. Remember this when you ask yourself why you should learn mathematics, foreign languages, and other subjects in the face of such rapid "forgetting" and give your memory the credit it deserves!

Abel, T., Alberini, C., Ghirardi, M., Huang, Y., Nguyen, P., & Kandel, E. (1995). Steps toward a molecular definition of memory consolidation. In D. L. Schacter (Ed.), *Memory distortion: How minds, brains, and societies reconstruct the past* (pp. 298–325). Cambridge, MA: Harvard University Press.

Ackerman, B. (1996). Induction of a memory retrieval strategy by young children. *Journal of Experimental Child Psychology, 62,* 243–271.

Adler, T. (1991, July). Memory researcher wins Troland award. *APA Monitor,* pp. 12–13.

Allport, A. (1993). Attention and control: Have we been asking the wrong questions? A critical review of twenty-five years. In D. E. Meyer & S. Kornblum (Eds.), *Attention and performance XIV* (pp. 183–218). Cambridge, MA: Bradford/MIT.

American Psychological Association. (1995, August). *Can a memory be forgotten and then remembered?* (Office for Public Affairs). Washington, DC: Author.

Anders, T. R., Fozard, J. L., & Lillyquist, T. D. (1972). Effects of age upon retrieval from short-term memory. *Developmental Psychology, 6,* 214–217.

Anderson, J. A. (1995). *An introduction to neural networks.* Cambridge, MA: MIT Press.

Anderson, J. A., & Hinton, G. E. (1981). *Parallel models of associative memory.* Hillsdale, NJ: Erlbaum.

Anderson, J. R. (1974). Retrieval of propositional information from long-term memory. *Cognitive Psychology, 6,* 451–474.

Anderson, J. R. (1976). *Language, memory, and thought.* Hillsdale, NJ: Erlbaum.

Anderson, J. R. (1978). Arguments concerning representations for mental imagery. *Psychological Review, 85,* 249–277.

Anderson, J. R. (1981). *Cognitive skills and their acquisition.* Hillsdale, NJ: Erlbaum.

Anderson, J. R. (1983a). *The architecture of cognition.* Cambridge, MA: Harvard University Press.

Anderson, J. R. (1983b). Retrieval of information from long-term memory. *Science, 220,* 25–30.

Anderson, J. R. (1985). Ebbinghaus's century. *Journal of Experimental Psychology: Learning, Memory, and Cognition, 11,* 436–438.

Anderson, J. R. (1990). *Cognitive psychology and its implications* (3rd ed.). New York: Freeman.

Anderson, J. R. (1993). *Rules of the mind.* Hillsdale, NJ: Erlbaum.

Anderson, J. R. (1995a). *Learning and memory.* New York: Wiley.

Anderson, J. R. (1995b). *Cognitive psychology and its implications* (4th ed.). San Francisco: Freeman.

Anderson, J. R., & Bower, G. H. (1972). Recognition and retrieval processes in free recall. *Psychological Review, 79,* 97–123.

Anderson, J. R., & Bower, G. H. (1973). *Human associative memory.* Washington, DC: Winston.

Anderson, J. R., Conrad, F. G., & Corbett, A. T. (1989). Skill acquisition and the LISP tutor. *Cognitive Science, 13,* 467–505.

Anderson, J. R., & Fincham, J. (1994). Acquisition of a procedural skill from examples. *Journal of Experimental Psychology: Learning, Memory, and Cognition, 20,* 1322–1340.

Anderson, J. R., & Reder, L. M. (1979). An elaborative processing explanation of depth of processing. In L. S. Cermak & F. I. M. Craik (Eds.), *Levels of processing in human memory* (pp. 385–403). Hillsdale, NJ: Erlbaum.

Anderson, J. R., Reder, L. M., & Lebiere, C. (1996). Working memory: Activation limitations on retrieval. *Cognitive Psychology, 30,* 221–256.

Anderson, J. R., & Schooler, L. J. (1991). Reflections of the environment in memory. *Psychological Science, 2,* 396–408.

Anderson, M. C., Bjork, R. A., & Bjork, E. L. (1994). Mechanisms of inhibition in long-term memory: A new taxonomy. *Journal of Experimental Psychology: Learning, Memory, and Cognition, 20,* 1063–1087.

Anderson, M. C., & Neely, J. H. (1996). Interference and inhibition in memory retrieval. In E. L. Bjork & R. A. Bjork (Eds.), *Memory* (pp. 237–313). San Diego, CA: Academic Press.

Anderson, M. C., & Spellman, B. A. (1995). On the status of inhibitory mechanisms in cognition: Memory retrieval as a model case. *Psychological Review, 102,* 68–100.

Arbuckle, T. Y., & Gold, D. P. (1993). Aging, inhibition, and verbosity. *Journal of Gerontology: Psychological Sciences, 48,* 225–232.

Atkinson, R. C., & Crothers, E. J. (1964). A comparison of paired-associate learning models having different acquisition and retention axioms. *Journal of Mathematical Psychology, 1,* 285–315.

Atkinson, R. C., & Raugh, M. R. (1975). An application of the mnemonic keyword method to the acquisition of a Russian vocabulary. *Journal of Experimental Psychology: Human Learning and Memory, 104,* 126–133.

Atkinson, R. C., & Shiffrin, R. M. (1968). Human memory: A proposed system and its control processes. In K. W. Spence & J. T. Spence (Eds.), *The psychology of learning and motivation: Advances in research and theory* (pp. 89–195). New York: Academic Press.

Bachevalier, J. (1992). Cortical vs. limbic immaturity: Relationship to infantile amnesia. In M. R. Gunnar & C. A. Nelson (Eds.), *Developmental behavioral neuroscience* (pp. 129–153). Hillsdale, NJ: Erlbaum.

Bach-Y-Rita, P. (1990). Brain plasticity as a basis for recovery of function in humans. *Neuropsychologia, 28,* 547–554.

Bäckman, L., Mäntylä, T., & Herlitz, A. (1990). Optimization of episodic remembering in old age. In P. B. Baltes & M. M. Baltes (Eds.), *Successful aging: Perspectives from the behavioral sciences* (pp. 118–163). New York: Cambridge University Press.

Baddeley, A. D. (1976). *The psychology of memory.* New York: Basic Books.

Baddeley, A. D. (1982). Domains of recollection. *Psychological Review, 89,* 708–729.

Baddeley, A. D. (1986). *Working memory.* Oxford: Oxford University Press.

Baddeley, A. D. (1990). *Human memory: Theory and practice.* Boston: Allyn and Bacon.

Baddeley, A. D. (1992a). Is working memory working? The fifteenth Bartlett lecture. *Quarterly Journal of Experimental Psychology, 44A,* 1–31.

Baddeley, A. D. (1992b). Working memory. *Science, 255,* 556–559.

Baddeley, A. D. (1993a). Working memory and conscious awareness. In A. F. Collins, S. E. Gathercole, M. A. Conway, & P. E. Morris (Eds.), *Theories of memory* (pp. 11–28). Hillsdale, NJ: Erlbaum.

Baddeley, A. D. (1993b). Holy war or wholly unnecessary? Some thoughts on the "conflict" between laboratory studies and everyday memory. In G. M. Davies & R. H. Logie (Eds.), *Memory in everyday life* (pp. 532–536). Amsterdam: North-Holland.

Baddeley, A. D. (1996a). Exploring the central executive. *Quarterly Journal of Experimental Psychology, 49A,* 5–28.

Baddeley, A. D. (1996b). Applying the psychology of memory to clinical problems. In D. J. Herrman, C. McEvoy, C. Hertzog, P. Hertel, & M. K. Johnson (Eds.), *Basic and applied memory research: Practical applications* (Vol. 1, pp. 195–220). Mahwah, NJ: Erlbaum.

Baddeley, A. D., Bressi, S., Della Salla, S., Logie, R., & Spinnler, H. (1991). The decline of working memory in Alzheimer's disease: A longitudinal study. *Brain, 114,* 2521–2542.

Baddeley, A. D., & Hitch, G. (1974). Working memory. In G. H. Bower (Ed.), *The psychology of learning and motivation: Advances in research and theory* (Vol. 8, pp. 47–89). New York: Academic Press.

Baddeley, A. D., & Hitch, G. (1994). Developments in the concept of working memory. *Neuropsychology, 8,* 485–493.

Baddeley, A. D., Logie, R., Bressi, S., Della Salla, S., & Spinnler, H. (1986). Dementia and working memory. *Quarterly Journal of Experimental Psychology, 38A,* 603–618.

Baddeley, A. D., & Wilson, B. A. (1994). When implicit memory fails: Amnesia and the problem of error elimination. *Neuropsychologia, 32,* 53–68.

Baddeley, B. A., Wilson, B. A., & Watts, F. N. (1995). *Handbook of memory disorders.* New York: Wiley.

Bahrick, H. P. (1984). Semantic memory content in permastore: Fifty years of memory for Spanish learned in school. *Journal of Experimental Psychology: General, 113,* 1–29.

Bahrick, H. P., Bahrick, L. E., Bahrick, A. S., & Bahrick, P. E. (1993). Maintenance of foreign language vocabulary and the spacing effect. *Psychological Science, 4,* 316–321.

Bahrick, H. P., & Hall, L. K. (1991). Lifetime maintenance of high school mathematics content. *Journal of Experimental Psychology: General, 120,* 20–33.

Bahrick, H. P., & Phelps, E. (1987). Retention of Spanish vocabulary over eight years. *Journal of Experimental Psychology: Learning, Memory, and Cognition, 13,* 344–349.

Baltes, P. B., & Kliegl, R. (1992). Further testing of limits of cognitive plasticity: Negative age differences in a mnemonic skill. *Developmental Psychology, 28,* 121–125.

Banaji, M. R., & Crowder, R. G. (1989). The bankruptcy of everyday memory. *American Psychologist, 44,* 1185–1193.

Barbizet, J. (1970). *Human memory and its pathology.* San Francisco: Freeman.

Barclay, C. R. (1996). Autobiographical remembering:

Narrative constraints on objectified selves. In D. C. Rubin (Ed.), *Remembering our past* (pp. 94–125). New York: Cambridge University Press.

Barnes, J. M., & Underwood, B. J. (1959). "Fate" of first-list associations in transfer theory. *Journal of Experimental Psychology, 58,* 97–105.

Barsalou, L. W. (1992). *Cognitive psychology: An overview for cognitive scientists.* Hillsdale, NJ: Erlbaum.

Barsalou, L. W. (1995). ACT-R: Cognitive theory's simple, elegant tool. *American Scientist, 83,* 185–186.

Bartlett, F. C. (1932). *Remembering: A study in experimental and social psychology.* Cambridge, UK: Cambridge University Press.

Bartus, R. T. (1990). Drugs to treat age-related neurogenerative problems. *Journal of American Geriatric Society, 38,* 680–695.

Bashore, T. R. (1993). Differential effects of aging on the neurocognitive functions subserving speeded mental processing. In J. Cerella, I. Rybash, W. Hoyer, & M. Commons (Eds.), *Adult information processing: Limits on loss* (pp. 37–76). San Diego, CA: Academic Press.

Bashore, T. R., & Rapp, P. E. (1993). Are there alternatives to traditional polygraph procedures. *Psychological Bulletin, 113,* 3–22.

Bass, E., & Davis, L. (1988). *The courage to heal.* New York: Harper and Row.

Bauer, P. (1996). What do infants recall of their lives? *American Psychologist, 51,* 29–41.

Bear, M. F., Connors, B. W., & Paradiso, M. A. (1996). *Neuroscience: Exploring the brain.* Baltimore, MD: Williams and Williams.

Bechtel, W., & Abrahamson, A. (1991). *Connectionism and the mind.* Oxford, UK: Blackwell.

Becker, J. T. (1994). Introduction to the special section: Working memory and neuropsychology—interdependence of clinical and experimental research. *Neuropsychology, 8,* 483–484.

Bekerian, D. A., & Baddeley, A. D. (1980). Saturation advertising and the repetition effect. *Journal of Verbal Learning and Verbal Behavior, 19,* 17–25.

Belli, R. F., & Loftus, E. F. (1996). The pliability of autobiographical memory: Misinformation and the false memory problem. In D. C. Rubin (Ed.), *Remembering our past* (pp. 157–179). New York: Cambridge University Press.

Benton, A. L., & Hamsher, K. DeS. (1983). *Multilingual aphasia examination [Manual].* Iowa City, IA: University of Iowa.

Biederman, I., & Cooper, E. E. (1991). Priming contour-deleted images: Evidence for intermediate representations in visual object recognition. *Cognitive Psychology, 23,* 393–419.

Binet, A. (1900). *La suggestibilité.* Paris: Schleicher Freres.

Binet, A., & Henri, V. (1894). La mémoire des phrases. *L'Année Psychologique, 1,* 24–59.

Birren, J. E., & Fisher, L. M. (1995). Aging and speed of behavior: Possible consequences for psychological functioning. *Annual Review of Psychology, 46,* 329–353.

Bjork, E. L., & Bjork, R. A. (1996). *Memory.* San Diego, CA: Academic Press.

Bjork, R. A. (1988). Retrieval practice and the maintenance of knowledge. In M. M. Gruneberg, P. E. Morris, & R. N. Sykes (Eds.), *Practical aspects of memory: Current research and issues* (Vol. 1, pp. 398–401). Chichester, UK: Wiley.

Bjork, R. A., & Whitten, W. B. (1974). Recency-sensitive retrieval processes in long-term free recall. *Cognitive Psychology, 6,* 173–189.

Bjorklund, D. F., & Schneider, W. (1996). The interaction of knowledge, aptitude, and strategies in children's memory performance. In H. W. Reese (Ed.), *Advances in child development and behavior* (Vol. 26, pp. 59–89). San Diego, CA: Academic Press.

Bjorklund, D. F., & Zeman, B. R. (1982). Children's organization and metamemory awareness in their recall of familiar information. *Child Development, 53,* 799–810.

Black, J. B. (1982). Psycholinguistic processes in writing. In S. Rosenberg (Ed.), *Handbook of applied psycholinguistics* (pp. 199–216). Hillsdale, NJ: Erlbaum.

Blaxton, T. A. (1989). Investigating dissociations among memory measures: Support for a transfer-appropriate processing framework. *Journal of Experimental Psychology: Learning, Memory, and Cognition, 15,* 657–668.

Bliss, T. V. P., & Lomo, T. (1973). Long-lasting potentiation of synaptic transmission in the dentate area of the anaesthetized rabbit following stimulation of the perforant path. *Journal of Physiology, 232,* 331–356.

Borges, J. L. (1967). *A personal anthology* (A. Kerrigan, Ed. and Trans.). New York: Grove.

Bourgeois, M. S. (1993). Effects of memory aids on the dyadic conversations of individuals with dementia. *Journal of Applied Behavior Analysis, 26,* 77–87.

Bovair, S., & Kieras, D. E. (1985). A guide to propositional analysis for research on technical prose. In B. K. Britton & J. B. Black (Eds.), *Understanding expository text: A theoretical and practical handbook for analyzing explanatory text* (pp. 315–362). Hillsdale, NJ: Erlbaum.

Bower, G. H. (1970). Analysis of a mnemonic device. *American Scientist, 58,* 496–510.

Bower, G. H. (1992). How might emotions affect learning? In S. A. Christianson (Ed.), *The handbook of emotion and memory: Research and theory* (pp. 3–31). Hillsdale, NJ: Erlbaum.

Bower, G. H., Black, J. B., & Turner, T. J. (1979). Scripts in memory for text. *Cognitive Psychology, 11,* 177–220.

Bower, G. H., & Clark, M. (1969). Narrative stories as mediators for serial learning. *Psychonomic Science, 14,* 181–182.

Bower, G. H., Clark, M., Lesgold, A. M., & Winzenz, D. (1969). Hierarchical retrieval schemes in recall of categorized word lists. *Journal of Verbal Learning and Verbal Behavior, 8,* 323–343.

Bradley, B. P., & Baddeley, A. D. (1990). Emotional factors in forgetting. *Psychological Medicine, 20,* 351–355.

Bradshaw, G. L., & Anderson, J. R. (1982). Elaborative encoding as an explanation of levels of processing. *Journal of Verbal Learning and Verbal Behavior, 21,* 165–174.

Brandimonte, M., Einstein, G. O., & McDaniel, M. A. (1996). *Prospective memory: Theory and applications.* Mahwah, NJ: Erlbaum.

Brandt, J., & Rich, J. B. (1995). Memory disorders in the dementias. In A. D. Baddeley, B. A. Wilson, & F. N. Watts (Eds.), *Handbook of memory disorders* (pp. 243–270). New York: Wiley.

Bransford, J. D., Barclay, J. R., & Franks, J. J. (1972). Sentence memory: A constructive versus interpretive approach. *Cognitive Psychology, 3,* 193–209.

Bransford, J. D., & Johnson, M. K. (1973). Considerations of some problems of comprehension. In W. G. Chase (Ed.), *Visual information processing* (pp. 383–438). New York: Academic Press.

Breuer, J., & Freud, S. (1955). Studies on hysteria. In J. Strachey (Ed. and Trans.), *The standard edition of the complete psychological works of Sigmund Freud* (Vol. 2, pp. 3–47). London: Hogarth. (Original work published 1895).

Brewin, C. R., Dalgleish, T., & Joseph, S. (1996). A dual representation theory of post-traumatic stress disorder. *Psychological Review, 103,* 670–686.

Briggs, G. E. (1954). Acquisition, extinction, and recovery functions in retroactive inhibition. *Journal of Experimental Psychology, 47,* 285–293.

Broadbent, D. E. (1958). *Perception and communication.* London: Pergamon.

Brooks, L. R. (1968). Spatial and verbal components of the act of recall. *Canadian Journal of Psychology, 22,* 349–368.

Brooks, L. R., Norman, G. R., & Allen, S. W. (1991). Role of specific similarity in a medical diagnostic task. *Journal of Experimental Psychology: General, 120,* 278–287.

Brown, E. L., Deffenbacher, K. A., & Sturgill, W. (1977). Memory for faces and the circumstances of encounter. *Journal of Applied Psychology, 62,* 311–318.

Brown, J. (1958). Some tests of the decay theory of immediate memory. *Quarterly Journal of Experimental Psychology, 10,* 12–21.

Brown, J. (1968). Reciprocal facilitation and impairment in free recall. *Psychonomic Science, 10,* 41–42.

Brown, R., & Kulik, J. (1982). Flashbulb memories. In U. Neisser (Ed.), *Memory observed: Remembering in natural contexts* (pp. 23–40). San Francisco: Freeman.

Brown, R., & McNeill, D. (1966). The "tip of the tongue" phenomenon. *Journal of Verbal Learning and Verbal Behavior, 5,* 325–337.

Brown, W. (1923). To what extent is memory measured by a single recall trial? *Journal of Experimental Psychology, 6,* 377–382.

Bruner, J. (1994). The "remembered" self. In U. Neisser & R. Fivush (Eds.), *The remembering self: Construction and accuracy in the self-narrative* (pp. 41–54). New York: Cambridge University Press.

Bruner, J., & Feldman, C. F. (1996). Group narrative as a cultural context of autobiography. In D. C. Rubin (Ed.), *Remembering our past* (pp. 291–317). New York: Cambridge University Press.

Bruner, J. S., Goodnow, J., & Austin, G. A. (1956). *A study of thinking.* New York: Wiley.

Buchner, A. (1994). Indirect effects of synthetic grammar learning in an identification task. *Journal of Experimental Psychology: Learning, Memory, and Cognition, 20,* 550–566.

Buckner, R. L. (1996). Beyond HERA: Contributions of specific prefrontal brain areas to long-term memory retrieval. *Psychonomic Bulletin & Review, 3,* 149–158.

Bugelski, B. R. (1962). Presentation time, total time, and mediation in paired-associate learning. *Journal of Experimental Psychology, 63,* 409–412.

Burke, D. M., MacKay, D. G., Worthley, J. S., & Wade, E. (1991). On the tip of the tongue: What causes word finding failures in young and older adults? *Journal of Memory and Language, 30,* 542–579.

Burke, D. M., & Yee, P. L. (1984). Semantic priming during sentence processing by young and older adults. *Developmental Psychology, 20,* 903–910.

Burtt, H. E. (1941). An experimental study of early childhood memory: Final report. *The Journal of Genetic Psychology, 58,* 435–439.

Butters, N., & Cermak, L. S. (1986). A case study of the forgetting of autobiographical knowledge: Implications for the study of retrograde amnesia. In D. C. Rubin (Ed.), *Autobiographical memory* (pp. 253–272). New York: Cambridge University Press.

Butters, N., O'Connor, M. G., & Verfaellie, M. (1995). My own remembered past: Insights into the structure and processes of retrograde amnesia from a patient with visual access problems subsequent to encephalitis. In R. Campbell & M. A. Conway (Eds.), *Broken memories: Case studies in memory impairment* (pp. 160–169). Cambridge, MA: Blackwell.

Campbell, R., & Conway, M. A. (Eds.). (1995). *Broken memories: Case studies in memory impairment.* Cambridge, MA: Blackwell.

Canli, T., & Donegan, N. H. (1995). Conditioned diminution of the unconditioned response in rabbit eyelid conditioning: Identifying neural substrates in the cerebellum and brainstem. *Behavioral Neuroscience, 109,* 874–892.

Cantor, J., & Engle, R. W. (1993). Working-memory capacity as long-term memory activation: An individual differences approach. *Journal of Experimental Psychology: Learning, Memory, and Cognition, 19,* 1101–1114.

Carlson, N. R. (1991). *Physiology of behavior* (4th ed.). Boston: Allyn and Bacon.

Carlson, N. R. (1994). *Physiology of behavior* (5th ed.). Boston: Allyn and Bacon.

Carpenter, P. A., & Just, M. A. (1989). The role of working memory in language comprehension. In D.

Klahr & K. Kotovsky (Eds.), *Complex information processing: The impact of Herbert A. Simon* (pp. 31–68). Hillsdale, NJ: Erlbaum.

Carpenter, P. A., Miyake, A., & Just, M. A. (1995). Language comprehension: Sentence and discourse processing. *Annual Review of Psychology, 46,* 91–120.

Carraher, T. N., Carraher, D. W., & Schliemann, A. D. (1985). Mathematics in the streets and in the schools. *British Journal of Developmental Psychology, 3,* 21–29.

Carrier, M., & Pashler, H. (1992). The influence of retrieval on retention. *Memory & Cognition, 20,* 633–642.

Carrol, M., & Nelson, T. O. (1993). Failure to obtain a generation effect during naturalistic learning. *Memory & Cognition, 21,* 361–366.

Case, R. (1972). Validation of a neo-Piagetian mental capacity construct. *Journal of Experimental Child Psychology, 14,* 287–302.

Castellucci, V. F., & Kandel, E. R. (1976). Presynaptic facilitation as a mechanism for behavioral sensitization in Aplysia. *Science, 194,* 1176–1178.

Ceci, S. J. (1995). False beliefs: Some developmental and clinical considerations. In D. L. Schacter (Ed.), *Memory distortions* (pp. 91–125). Cambridge, MA: Harvard University Press.

Ceci, S. J., & Bronfenbrenner, U. (1991). On the demise of everyday memory: "Rumors of my death are much exaggerated" (Mark Twain). *American Psychologist, 46,* 27–31.

Cermak, L. S., & Reale, L. (1978). Depth of processing and retention of words by alcoholic Korsakoff patients. *Journal of Experimental Psychology: Learning, Memory, and Cognition, 4,* 165–174.

Chan, A. S., Butters, N., Paulsen, J. S., Salmon, D. P., Swenson, M. R., & Maloney, L. T. (1993). An assessment of the semantic network in patients with Alzheimer's disease. *Journal of Cognitive Neuroscience, 5,* 254–261.

Chappell, M., & Humphreys, M. S. (1994). An autoassociative neural network for sparse representations: Analysis and application to models of recognition and cued recall. *Psychological Review, 101,* 103–128.

Chase, W. G., & Ericsson, K. A. (1981). Skilled memory. In J. R. Anderson (Ed.), *Cognitive skills and their acquisition* (pp. 141–189). Hillsdale, NJ: Erlbaum.

Chase, W. G., & Simon, H. A. (1973). The mind's eye in chess. In W. G. Chase (Ed.), *Visual information processing* (pp. 215–281). New York: Academic Press.

Cherry, K. E., Park, D. C., Frieske, D. A., & Rowley, R. L. (1993). The effect of verbal elaborations on memory in young and older adults. *Memory & Cognition, 21,* 725–738.

Chertkow, H., Bub, D., & Caplan, D. (1992). Constraining theories of semantic memory processing: Evidence from dementia. *Cognitive Neuropsychology, 9,* 327–365.

Chi, M. T. H., & Koeske, R. D. (1983). Network representation of a child's dinosaur knowledge. *Developmental Psychology, 19,* 29–39.

Chomsky, N. (1957). *Syntactic structures.* Paris: Mouton.

Chomsky, N. (1965). *Aspects of the theory of syntax.* Cambridge, MA: MIT Press.

Christianson, S. A. (1992). *Handbook of emotion and memory.* Hillsdale, NJ: Erlbaum.

Christianson, S. A., & Safer, M. A. (1996). Emotional events and emotions in autobiographical memories. In. D. C. Rubin (Ed.), *Remembering our past* (pp. 218–243). New York: Cambridge University Press.

Churchland, P. S., & Sejnowski, T. J. (1992). *The computational brain.* Cambridge, MA: MIT Press.

Claparede, E. (1911). Recognition et moité [Recognition and me-ness]. *Archives de psychologie, 11,* 79–90.

Cockburn, J. (1995). Task interruption and prospective memory: A frontal lobe function. *Cortex, 31,* 87–97.

Cohen, G. (1993). *Memory for proper names.* Hove, UK: Erlbaum.

Cohen, J. D., Forman, S. D., Braver, T. S., Casey, B. J., Servan-Schreiber, D., & Noll, D. C. (1994). Activation of prefrontal cortex in a non-spatial working memory task with functional MRI. *Human Brain Mapping, 1,* 293–304.

Cohen, J. D., & O'Reilly, R. C. (1996). A preliminary theory of the interactions between prefrontal cortex and hippocampus that contribute to planning and prospective memory. In M. Brandimonte, G. O. Einstein, & M. A. McDaniel (Eds.), *Prospective memory: Theory and applications* (pp. 267–295). Mahwah, NJ: Erlbaum.

Cohen, R. L. (1981). On the generality of some memory laws. *Scandinavian Journal of Psychology, 22,* 267–281.

Coleman, L. M., Fowler, L. L., & Williams, M. E. (1995). Use of unproven therapies by people with Alzheimer's disease. *Journal of the American Geriatrics Society, 43,* 747–750.

Collins, A. M., & Quillian, M. R. (1969). Retrieval time from semantic memory. *Journal of Verbal Learning and Verbal Behavior, 8,* 240–247.

Conrad, R. (1964). Acoustic confusions in immediate memory. *British Journal of Psychology, 55,* 75–84.

Conway, M. A. (1991). In defense of everyday memory. *American Psychologist, 46,* 19–26.

Conway, M. A. (1995). *Flashbulb memories.* Hillsdale, NJ: Erlbaum.

Conway, M. A. (1996a). Autobiographical memories. In E. L. Bjork & R. A. Bjork (Eds.), *Memory* (pp. 165–194). San Diego, CA: Academic Press.

Conway, M. A. (1996b). Autobiographical knowledge and autobiographical memories. In. D. C. Rubin (Ed.), *Remembering our past* (pp. 67–93). New York: Cambridge University Press.

Conway, M. A. (1997). *Recovered memories and false memories.* New York: Oxford University Press.

Conway, M. A., Cohen, G., & Stanhope, N. (1991). On the very long-term retention of knowledge acquired through formal education: Twelve years of cognitive psychology. *Journal of Experimental Psychology: General, 120,* 395–409.

Craik, F. I. M., Anderson, N. D., Kerr, S. A., & Li, K. Z. H. (1995). Memory changes in normal aging. In A. D. Baddeley, B. A. Wilson, & F. N. Watts (Eds.), *Handbook of memory disorders* (pp. 211–241). New York: Wiley.

Craik, F. I. M., & Jennings, J. M. (1992). Human memory. In F. I. M. Craik & T. A. Salthouse (Eds.), *The handbook of aging and cognition* (pp. 51–110). Hillsdale, NJ: Erlbaum.

Craik, F. I. M., & Lockhart, R. S. (1972). Levels of processing: A framework for memory research. *Journal of Verbal Learning and Verbal Behavior, 11,* 671–684.

Craik, F. I. M., & Tulving, E. (1975). Depth of processing and the retention of words in episodic memory. *Journal of Experimental Psychology: General, 104,* 268–294.

Craik, F. I. M., & Watkins, M. J. (1973). The role of rehearsal in short-term memory. *Journal of Verbal Learning and Learning Behavior, 12,* 599–607.

Crovitz, H. F. (1979). Memory training in brain-damaged patients: The airplane list. *Cortex, 15,* 131–134.

Crovitz, H. F., & Schiffman, H. (1974). Frequency of episodic memories as a function of their age. *Bulletin of the Psychonomic Society, 4,* 517–518.

Crowder, R. (1976). *Principles of learning and memory.* Hillsdale, NJ: Erlbaum.

Crowder, R. (1982a). The demise of short-term memory. *Acta Psychologica, 50,* 291–323.

Crowder, R. (1982b). General forgetting theory and the locus of amnesia. In L. S. Cermak (Ed.), *Human memory and amnesia* (pp. 33–42). Hillsdale, NJ: Erlbaum.

Crowder, R. (1989). Modularity and dissociations in memory systems. In H. L. Roediger & F. I. M. Craik (Eds.), *Varieties of memory and consciousness: Essays in honour of Endel Tulving* (pp. 271–294). Hillsdale, NJ: Erlbaum.

Crowder, R. (1993). Short-term memory: Where do we stand? *Memory & Cognition, 21,* 142–145.

Dale, H. C. A., & Gregory, M. (1966). Evidence of semantic encoding in short-term memory. *Psychonomic Science, 5,* 153–154.

Damasio, A. R. (1990). Synchronous activation in multiple cortical regions: A mechanism for recall. *Seminars in the Neurosciences, 2,* 287–296.

Damasio, A. R., Tranel, D., & Damasio, H. (1990). Face agnosia and the neural substances of memory. *Annual Review of Neuroscience, 13,* 89–109.

Daneman, M., & Carpenter, P. A. (1980). Individual differences in working memory and reading. *Journal of Verbal Learning and Verbal Behavior, 19,* 450–466.

Daneman, M., & Merikle, P. M. (1996). Working memory and language comprehension: A meta-analysis. *Psychonomic Bulletin & Review, 3,* 422–433.

Danserau, D. F. (1983). *Learning strategy research.* Fort Worth, TX: Texas Christian University.

Davidson, D. (1994). Recognition and recall of irrelevant and interruptive atypical actions in script-based stories. *Journal of Memory and Language, 33,* 757–775.

Davis, M. (1992). The role of the amygdala in conditioned fear. In J. Aggleton (Ed.), *The amygdala* (pp. 255–306). New York: Wiley-Liss.

Demb, J. B., Desmond, J. E., Wagner, A. D., Vaidya, C. J., Glover, G. H., & Garbrieli, J. D. (1995). Semantic encoding and retrieval in the left inferior prefrontal cortex: A functional MRI study of task difficulty and process specificity. *Journal of Neuroscience, 15,* 5870–5878.

Dempster, F. N. (1981). Memory span: Sources of individual and developmental differences. *Psychological Bulletin, 89,* 63–100.

Dempster, F. N. (1996). Distributing and managing the conditions of encoding and practice. In E. L. Bjork & R. A. Bjork (Eds.), *Memory* (pp. 318–344). San Diego, CA: Academic Press.

Desimone, R., & Ungerleider, L. G. (1989). Neural mechanisms of visual processing in monkeys. In F. Boller & J. Grafman (Eds.), *Handbook of neuropsychology* (pp. 267–299). New York: Elsevier Science Publishers.

Diamond, A. (1991). Neuropsychological insights into the meaning of object concept development. In S. Carey & R. Gelman (Eds.), *The epigenesis of mind: Essays on biology and cognition* (pp. 67–110). Hillsdale, NJ: Erlbaum.

Diges, M. (1988). Stereotypes and memory of real traffic accidents. In M. M. Gruneberg, P. E. Morris, & R. N. Sykes (Eds.), *Practical aspects of memory: Current research and issues* (pp. 59–65). Chichester, UK: Wiley.

Dijkstra, T., & de Smedt, K. (1996). *Computational psycholinguistics: AI and connectionist models of human language processing.* London: Taylor and Francis.

Dooling, D. J., & Christiaansen, R. E. (1977). Episodic and semantic aspects of memory for prose. *Journal of Experimental Psychology: Human Learning and Memory, 3,* 428–436.

Duchek, J. M. (1984). Encoding and retrieval differences between young and old: The impact of attentional capacity usage. *Developmental Psychology, 20,* 1173–1180.

Easterbrook, J. A. (1959). The effect of emotion on cue utilization and the organization of behavior. *Psychological Review, 66,* 183–201.

Ebbinghaus, H. (1885). *Über das gedächtnis* [On memory]. Leipzig, Germany: Duncker and Humblot.

Ebbinghaus, H. (1905). *Grundzüge der psychologie* (Vol. 1). Leipzig, Germany: Veit.

Ebbinghaus, H. (1913). *Grundzüge der psychologie* (Vol. 2). Leipzig, Germany: Veit.

Eich, E., & Metcalfe, J. (1989). Mood dependent memory for internal versus external events. *Journal of Experimental Psychology: Learning, Memory, and Cognition, 15,* 443–455.

Eich, J. E., Weingartner, H., Stillman, R. C., & Gillin, J. C. (1975). State dependent accessibility of retrieval cues in the retention of a categorized list.

Journal of Verbal Learning and Verbal Behavior, 14, 408–417.

Eich, J. M. (1982). A composite holographic associative recall model. *Psychological Review, 89,* 627–661.

Eichenbaum, H. (1997). How does the brain organize memories? *Science, 277,* 330–332.

Eichenbaum, H. (1994). The hippocampal system and declarative memory in humans and animals: Experimental analysis and historical origins. In D. L. Schacter & E. Tulving (Ed.), *Memory systems 1994* (pp. 147–201). Cambridge, MA: MIT Press.

Eimer, M., Goschke, T., Schlaghecken, F., & Stuermer, B. (1996). Explicit and implicit learning of event sequences: Evidence from event-related brain potentials. *Journal of Experimental Psychology: Learning, Memory, and Cognition, 22,* 970–987.

Einstein, G. O., & McDaniel, M. A. (1996). Remembering to do things: Remembering a forgotten topic. In D. J. Herrman, C. McEvoy, C. Hertzog, P. Hertel, & M. K. Johnson (Eds.), *Basic and applied memory research: Practical applications* (Vol. 2, pp. 79–94). Mahwah, NJ: Erlbaum.

Elkind, D. (1961). The development of quantitative thinking: A systematic replication of Piaget's studies. *Journal of Genetic Psychology, 98,* 37–46.

Ellis, H. C., & Ashbrook, P. W. (1989). The state of mood and memory research: A selective review. *Journal of Social Behavior and Personality, 4,* 1–22.

Ellis, N., & Beaton, A. (1993). Factors affecting the learning of foreign language vocabulary: Imagery keyword mediators and phonological short-term memory. *Quarterly Journal of Experimental Psychology, 46A,* 533–558.

Erdelyi, M. H. (1985). *Psychoanalysis: Freud's cognitive psychology.* New York: Freeman.

Erdelyi, M. H. (1996). *The recovery of unconscious memories: Hypermnesia and reminiscence.* Chicago: University of Chicago Press.

Erdelyi, M. H., & Kleinbard, J. (1978). Has Ebbinghaus decayed with time? The growth of recall (hypermnesia) over days. *Journal of Experimental Psychology: Human Learning and Memory, 4,* 275–289.

Ericsson, K. A., & Charness, N. (1994). Expert performance. *American Psychologist, 49,* 725–747.

Ericsson, K. A., & Kintsch, W. (1995). Long-term working memory. *Psychological Review, 102,* 211–245.

Ericsson, K. A., Krampe, R. T., & Tesch-Römer, C. (1993). The role of deliberate practice in the acquisition of expert performance. *Psychological Review, 100,* 363–406.

Ericsson, K. A., & Polson, P. G. (1988). A cognitive analysis of exceptional memory for restaurant orders. In M. T. H. Chi, R. Glaser, & J. J. Farr (Eds.), *The nature of expertise* (pp. 23–70). Hillsdale, NJ: Erlbaum.

Eslinger, P. J., & Damasio, A. R. (1985). Severe disturbance of higher cognition after bilateral frontal lobe ablation: Patient EVR. *Neurology, 35,* 1721–1741.

Estes, W. K. (1955). Statistical theory of distributional phenomena in learning. *Psychological Review, 62,* 369–377.

Estes, W. K. (1985). Levels of association theory. *Journal of Experimental Psychology: Learning, Memory, and Cognition, 11,* 450–454.

Estes, W. K. (1994). *Classification and cognition.* Oxford: Oxford University Press.

Estes, W. K. (1997). Processes of memory loss, recovery, and distortion. *Psychological Review, 104,* 148–169.

Eysenck, M. W. (1986). Ebbinghaus: An evaluation. In F. Klix & H. Hagendorf (Eds.), *Human memory and cognitive capabilities: Mechanisms and performances.* (Vol. A, pp. 53–62). Amsterdam: North-Holland.

Fabiani, M., & Donchin, E. (1995). Encoding processes and memory organization: A model of the von Restorff effect. *Journal of Experimental Psychology: Learning, Memory, and Cognition, 21,* 224–240.

Farah, M. J., & McClelland, J. L. (1991). A computational model of semantic memory impairment: Modality specificity and emergent category specificity. *Journal of Experimental Psychology: General, 120,* 339–357.

Feigenbaum, E. A. (1963). The simulation of verbal learning behavior. In E. A. Feigenbaum & J. Feldman (Eds.), *Computers and thought* (pp. 297–309). New York: McGraw-Hill.

Feltovich, P. J., Johnson, P. E., Moller, J. H., & Swanson, D. B. (1984). LCS: The role and development of medical knowledge in diagnostic expertise. In W. J. Clancey & E. H. Shortliffe (Eds.), *Readings in medical artificial intelligence* (pp. 275–319). Reading, MA: Addison-Wesley.

Fisher, R. P., & Craik, F. I. M. (1977). Interaction between encoding and retrieval operation in cued recall. *Journal of Experimental Psychology: Human Learning and Memory, 3,* 701–711.

Fisher, R. P., & Geiselman, R. E. (1988). Enhancing eyewitness memory with the cognitive interview. In

M. M. Gruneberg, P. E. Morris, & R. N. Sykes (Eds.), *Practical aspects of memory: Current research and issues* (pp. 34–39). Chichester, UK: Wiley.

Fitts, P. M. (1964). Perceptual-motor skill learning. In A. W. Melton (Ed.), *Categories of human learning* (pp.164–182). New York: Academic Press.

Fivush, R., Haden, C., & Reese, E. (1996). In D. C. Rubin (Ed.), *Remembering our past* (pp. 341–359). New York: Cambridge University Press.

Flavell, J. H. (1971). Stage-related properties of cognitive development. *Cognitive Psychology, 2,* 421–453.

Flavell, J. H., Friederichs, A. G., & Hoyt, J. D. (1970). Developmental changes in memorization processes. *Cognitive Psychology, 1,* 324–340.

Freud, S. (1964). New introductory lectures on psychoanalysis. In J. Strachey (Ed. and Trans.), *The standard edition of the complete psychological works of Sigmund Freud* (Vol. 22, pp. 5–182). London: Hogarth. (Original work published 1933).

Freyd, J. J., & Gleaves, D. H. (1996). "Remembering" words not presented in lists: Relevance to the current/false memory controversy. *Journal of Experimental Psychology: Learning, Memory and Cognition, 22,* 811–813.

Friedman, H. R., & Goldman-Rakic, P. S. (1994). Coactivation of prefrontal cortex and inferior parietal cortex in working memory tasks revealed by 2DG functional mapping in the rhesus monkey. *Journal of Neuroscience, 14*(5, Pt. 1), 2775–2788.

Funahashi, S., Bruce, C. J., & Goldman-Rakic, P. S. (1989). Mnemonic coding of visual space in the monkey's dorsolateral prefrontal cortex. *Journal of Neurophysiology, 61,* 331–349.

Funnell, E. (1995). A case of forgotten knowledge. In R. Campbell & M. A. Conway (Eds.), *Broken memories: Case studies in memory impairment* (pp. 224–236). Cambridge, MA: Blackwell.

Fuster, J. M. (1995). *Memory in the cerebral cortex.* Cambridge, MA: MIT Press.

Fuster, J. M., & Jervey, J. P. (1981). Inferotemporal neurons distinguish and retain behaviorally relevant features of visual stimuli. *Science, 212,* 952–955.

Gaffan, D., & Heywood, C. A. (1993). A spurious category-specific visual agnosia for living things in human and nonhuman primates. *Journal of Cognitive Neuroscience, 5,* 118–128.

Gathercole, S. E. (1994). Neuropsychology and working memory: A review. *Neuropsychology, 8,* 494–505.

Gaultney, J. F., Bjorklund, D. F., & Goldstein, D. (1996). To be young, gifted, and strategic: Advantages for memory performance. *Journal of Experimental Child Psychology, 61,* 43–66.

Geiselman, R. E., & Fisher, R. P. (1997). Ten years of cognitive interviewing. In D. G. Payne & F. G. Conrad (Eds.), *Intersections in basic and applied memory research* (pp. 291–310). Mahwah, NJ: Erlbaum.

Gentner, D., & Grudin, J. (1985). The evolution of mental metaphors in psychology: A 90-year retrospective. *American Psychologist, 40,* 181–192.

Gernsbacher, M. A. (1990). *Language comprehension as structure building.* Hillsdale, NJ: Erlbaum.

Gick, M. L., & Holyoak, K. J. (1983). Schema induction and analogical transfer. *Cognitive Psychology, 15,* 1–38.

Gillund, G., & Shiffrin, R. M. (1984). A retrieval model for both recognition and recall. *Psychological Review, 91,* 1–67.

Glanzer, M., & Cunitz, A. R. (1966). Two storage mechanisms in free recall. *Journal of Verbal Learning and Verbal Behavior, 5,* 351–360.

Glenberg, A. M. (1976). Monotonic and nonmonotonic lag effects in paired-associate and recognition memory paradigms. *Journal of Verbal Learning and Verbal Behavior, 15,* 1–16.

Glenberg, A. M. (1987). Temporal context and recency. In D. S. Gorfein & R. R. Hoffman (Eds.), *Memory and learning: The Ebbinghaus Centennial Conference* (pp. 173–190). Hillsdale, NJ: Erlbaum.

Glenberg, A. M. (1997). What memory is for. *Behavioral and Brain Sciences, 20,* 1–55.

Glisky, E. L. (1995). Computers in memory rehabilitation. In A. D. Baddeley, B. A. Wilson, & F. N. Watts (Eds.), *Handbook of memory disorders* (pp. 557–575). New York: Wiley.

Glisky, E. L. (1996). Prospective memory and the frontal lobes. In M. Brandimonte, G. O. Einstein, & M. A. McDaniel (Eds.), *Prospective memory: Theory and applications* (pp. 249–266). Mahwah, NJ: Erlbaum.

Glisky, E. L., & Schacter, D. L. (1987). Acquisition of domain-specific knowledge in organic amnesia: Training for computer-related work. *Neuropsychologia, 25,* 893–906.

Gluck, M. A., & Bower, G. H. (1988). From conditioning to category learning: An adaptive network model. *Journal of Experimental Psychology: General, 117,* 227–247.

Godden, D., & Baddeley, A. D. (1975). Context-dependent memory in two natural environments: On land and under water. *British Journal of Psychology, 66,* 325–331.

Goldman-Rakic, P. S. (1988). Topography of cognition: Parallel distributed networks in primate association cortex. *Annual Review of Neuroscience, 11,* 137–156.

Goldman-Rakic, P. S. (1990). Cortical localization of working memory. In J. L. McGaugh, N. M. Weinberger, & G. Lynch (Eds.), *Brain organization and memory: Cells, systems, and circuits* (pp. 285–298). New York: Oxford University Press.

Goldman-Rakic, P. S. (1994a). Specification of higher cortical functions. In S. H. Broman & S. Grafman (Eds.), *Atypical cognitive deficits in developmental disorders* (pp. 3–17). Hillsdale, NJ: Erlbaum.

Goldman-Rakic, P. S. (1994b). Cerebral cortical mechanisms in schizophrenia. *Neuropsychopharmacology, 10,* 22S-27S.

Goldstein, F. C., & Levin, H. S. (1995). Post-traumatic and anterograde amnesia following closed head injury. In A. D. Baddeley, B. A. Wilson, & F. N. Watts (Eds.), *Handbook of memory disorders* (pp. 187–209). New York: Wiley.

Goldstone, R. L. (1996). Alignment-based nonmonotonicities in similarity. *Journal of Experimental Psychology: Learning, Memory, and Cognition, 22,* 988–1001.

Golomb, J., et al. (1994). Hippocampal formation size in normal human aging: A correlate of delayed secondary memory performance. *Learning & Memory, 1,* 45–54.

Goodman, G. S., Quas, J. A., Batterman-Faunce, J. M., Riddlesberger, M. M., & Kuhn, J. (1996). Predictors of accurate and inaccurate memories of traumatic events experienced in childhood. In K. Pezdek & W. P. Banks (Eds.), *The recovered/false memory debate* (pp. 3–28). San Diego, CA: Academic Press.

Gopher, D. (1993). The skill of attention control: Acquisition execution of attention strategies. In D. E. Meyer & S. Kornblum (Eds.), *Attention and performance XIV* (pp. 299–322). Cambridge, MA: Bradford/MIT.

Grady , C. L., et al. (1995). Age-related reductions in human recognition memory due to impaired encoding. *Science, 269,* 218–221.

Graesser, A. C., Gordon, S. E., & Sawyer, J. D. (1979). Recognition memory for typical and atypical actions in scripted activities: Tests of a script pointer + tag hypothesis. *Journal of Verbal Learning and Verbal Behavior, 19,* 319–332.

Graf, P. (1990). Life-span changes in implicit and explicit memory. *Bulletin of the Psychonomic Society, 28,* 353–358.

Graf, P., & Schacter, D. L. (1985). Implicit and explicit memory for new associations in normal and amnesic patients. *Journal of Experimental Psychology: Learning, Memory, and Cognition, 11,* 501–518.

Graf, P., Squire, L. R., & Mandler, G. (1984). The information that amnesic patients do not forget. *Journal of Experimental Psychology: Learning, Memory, and Cognition, 10,* 164–178.

Greco, C., Rovee-Collier, C., Hayne, H., Griesler, P., & Earley, L. (1986). Ontogeny of early event memory: I. Forgetting and retrieval by 2- and 3-month olds. *Infant Behavior and Development, 9,* 441–460.

Greeno, J. G. (1973). The structure of memory and the process of solving problems. In R. L. Solso (Ed.), *Contemporary issues in cognitive psychology: The Loyola symposium* (pp. 103–133). Washington, DC: Winston.

Greenwald, A. G., & Banaji, M. R. (1995). Implicit social cognition: Attitudes, self-esteem, and stereotypes. *Psychological Review, 102,* 4–27.

Grossberg, S. (1987). Competitive learning: From interactive activation to adaptive resonance. *Cognitive Science, 11,* 23–63.

Haberlandt, K., & Graesser, A. C. (1985). Components of sentence and word reading times. *Journal of Experimental Psychology: General, 114,* 357–374.

Hall, S. (1998, February 15). Our memories, our selves. *The New York Times Magazine,* p. 26.

Hamann, S. B., & Squire, L. R. (1995). On the acquisition of new declarative knowledge in amnesia. *Behavioral Neuroscience, 109,* 1027–1044.

Harber, K. D., & Pennebaker, J. W. (1992). Overcoming traumatic memories. In S. A. Christianson (Ed.), *The handbook of emotion and memory: Research and theory* (pp. 359–387). Hillsdale, NJ: Erlbaum.

Harnishfeger, K. K., & Pope, R. S. (1996). Intending to forget: The development of cognitive inhibition in directed forgetting. *Journal of Experimental Child Psychology, 62,* 292–315.

Hart, J. T. (1967). Memory and the memory-monitoring process. *Journal of Verbal Learning and Verbal Behavior, 6,* 685–691.

Harvey, M. R., & Herman, J. L. (1996). Amnesia, partial amnesia, and delayed recall among adult survivors of childhood trauma. In K. Pezdek & W. P. Banks (Eds.), *The recovered/false memory debate* (pp. 29–40). San Diego, CA: Academic Press.

Hasher, L., & Zacks, R. T. (1988). Working memory, comprehension, and aging: A review and a new view. In G. H. Bower (Ed.), *The psychology of learning and motivation: Advances in research and theory* (Vol. 22, pp. 193–225). San Diego, CA: Academic Press.

Hawkins, R. D., & Bower, G. H. (1989). *Computational models of learning in simple neural systems.* San Diego, CA: Academic Press.

Hayes, B. K., & Hennessy, R. (1996). The nature and development of nonverbal implicit memory. *Journal of Experimental Child Psychology, 63,* 22–43.

Healy, A. F., & Bourne, L. E. (1995). Preface: Durability and specificity of knowledge and skills. In A. F. Healy & L. E. Bourne (Eds.), *Learning and memory of knowledge of skills* (pp. ix–xiv). Thousand Oaks, CA: Sage.

Healy, A. F., & Sinclair, G. P. (1996). The long-term retention of training and instruction. In E. L. Bjork & R. A. Bjork (Eds.), *Memory* (pp. 525–564). San Diego, CA: Academic Press.

Hebb, D. O. (1949). *The organization of behavior.* New York: Wiley.

Heuer, F., & Reisberg, D. (1990). Vivid memories of emotional events: The accuracy of remembering minutiae. *Memory & Cognition, 18,* 496–506.

Hickey, T. L., & Peduzzi, J. D. (1987). Structure and development of the visual system. In P. Salapatek & L. Cohen (Eds.), *Handbook of infant perception* (Vol. 1, pp. 1–42). San Diego, CA: Academic Press.

Higbee, K. L. (1994). More motivational aspects of an imagery mnemonic. *Applied Cognitive Psychology, 8,* 1–12.

Hillis, A. E., & Caramazza, A. (1991). Category-specific naming and comprehension impairment: A double dissociation. *Brain, 114,* 2081–2094.

Hillis, A. E., Rapp, B., & Caramazza, A. (1995). Constraining claims about theories of semantic memory: More on unitary versus multiple semantics. *Cognitive Neuropsychology, 12,* 175–186.

Hilts, P. J. (1995). *Memory's ghost: The strange tale of Mr. M. and the nature of memory.* New York: Simon and Schuster.

Hilts, P. J. (1996, July 2). In research scans, telltale signs sort false memories from true. *New York Times,* p. C3.

Hintzman, D. L. (1984). MINERVA 2: A simulation model of human memory. *Behavior Research Methods, Instruments, and Computers, 16,* 96–101.

Hintzman, D. L. (1991). Why are formal models useful in psychology? In W. E. Hockley & S. Lewandowsky (Eds.), *Relating theory and data: Essays on human memory in honor of Bennet B. Murdock* (pp. 39–56). Hillsdale, NJ: Erlbaum.

Hintzman, D. L. (1993). Twenty-five years of learning and memory: Was the cognitive revolution a mistake? In D. E. Meyer & S. Kornblum (Eds.), *Attention and performance XIV* (pp. 359–391). Cambridge, MA: Bradford/MIT.

Hirst, W., Phelps, E. A., Johnson, M. K., & Volpe, B. T. (1988). Amnesia and second language learning. *Brain and Cognition, 8,* 105–116.

Hodges, J. R. (1995). Retrograde amnesia. In A. D. Baddeley, B. A. Wilson, & F. N. Watts (Eds.), *Handbook of memory disorders* (pp. 81–107). New York: Wiley.

Holman, B. L., Nagel, J. S., Johnson, K. A., & Hill, T. C. (1991). Imaging dementia with SPECT. *Annals of the New York Academy of Sciences, 620,* 165–174.

Hoosain, R., & Salili, F. (1988). Language differences, working memory, and mathematical ability. In M. M. Gruneberg, P. E. Morris, & R. N. Sykes (Eds.), *Practical aspects of memory: Current research and issues* (pp. 512–517). Chichester, UK: Wiley.

Houston, J. P. (1991). *Learning and memory.* San Diego, CA: Harcourt.

Howe, M. L., & Courage, M. L. (1993). On resolving the enigma of infantile amnesia. *Psychological Bulletin, 113,* 205–326.

Hudson, J. A. (1988). Children's memory for atypical actions in script-based stories: Evidence for a disruption effect. *Journal of Experimental Child Psychology, 46,* 159–173.

Hudson, J. A., & Nelson, K. (1986). Repeated encounters of a similar kind: Effects of familiarity on children's autobiographical memory. *Cognitive Development, 1,* 253–271.

Hull, C. L. (1943). *Principles of behavior.* New York: Appleton-Century-Crofts.

Hunt, E., & Love, T. (1972). How good can memory be? In A. Melton & E. Martin (Eds.), *Coding processes in human memory* (pp. 237–260). Washington, DC: Wiley.

Hunter, I. M. (1977). Mental calculation. In P. N. Johnson-Laird & P. C. Wason (Eds.), *Thinking:*

Readings in cognitive science (pp. 35–45). Cambridge, UK: Cambridge University Press.

Hyman, I. E., & Pentland, J. (1996). The role of mental imagery in the creation of false childhood memories. *Journal of Memory and Language, 35,* 101–117.

Hyde, T. S., & Jenkins, J. J. (1973). Recall of words as a function of semantic, graphic, and syntactic orienting tasks. *Journal of Verbal Learning and Verbal Behavior, 12,* 471–480.

Intons-Peterson, M. J. (1997). How basic and applied research inform each other. In D. G. Payne & F. G. Conrad (Eds.), *Intersections in basic and applied memory research* (pp. 3–23). Mahwah, NJ: Erlbaum.

Intons-Peterson, M. J., & Smyth, M. M. (1987). The anatomy of repertory memory. *Journal of Experimental Psychology: Learning, Memory, and Cognition, 13,* 490–500.

Jacoby, L. L. (1983). Remembering the data: Analyzing interactive processes in reading. *Journal of Verbal Learning and Verbal Behavior, 22,* 485–508.

Jacoby, L. L., Woloshyn, V., & Kelley, C. (1989). Becoming famous without being recognized: Unconscious influences of memory produced by dividing attention. *Journal of Experimental Psychology: General, 118,* 115–125.

James, W. (1890). *The principles of psychology.* New York: Holt, Rinehart and Winston.

James, W. (1892). *Psychology: Briefer course.* New York: Holt and Company.

Janet, P. (1901). *The mental state of hystericals.* New York: Putnam.

Janet, P. (1904). L'amnésie et la dissociation des souvenirs par l'émotion. *Journal de Psychologie Normale et Pathologique, 1,* 417–453.

Jarvella, R. J. (1979). Immediate memory and discourse processing. In G. H. Bower (Ed.), *The psychology of learning and motivation: Advances in research and theory* (pp. 379–421). New York: Academic Press.

Johnson, M. (1996). Fact, fantasy, and public policy. In D. J. Herrman, C. McEvoy, C. Hertzog, P. Hertel, & M. K. Johnson (Eds.), *Basic and applied memory research: Practical applications* (Vol. 1, pp. 83–103). Mahwah, NJ: Erlbaum.

Jonides, J. (1995). Working memory and thinking. In E. E. Smith & D. N. Osherson (Eds.), *An invitation to cognitive science: Thinking* (Vol. 3, pp. 215–265). Cambridge, MA: MIT Press.

Jost, A. (1897). Die assoziationsfestigkeit in ihrer abhängigkeit von der verteilung der wiederholungen [Association strength as a function of distributed practice]. *Zeitschrift für Psychologie, 14,* 436–472.

Juslin, P., Olsson, N., & Winman, A. (1996). Calibration and diagnosticity of confidence in eyewitness identification: Comments on what can be inferred from the low confidence-accuracy correlation. *Journal of Experimental Psychology: Learning, Memory, and Cognition, 22,* 1304–1316.

Just, M. A., & Carpenter, P. A. (1980). A theory of reading: From eye fixations to comprehension. *Psychological Review, 87,* 329–354.

Just, M. A., & Carpenter, P. A. (1987). *The psychology of reading and language comprehension.* Boston: Allyn and Bacon.

Just, M. A., & Carpenter, P. A. (1992). A capacity theory of comprehension: Individual differences in working memory. *Psychological Review, 99,* 122–149.

Kail, R. (1986). Sources of age differences in speed of processing. *Child Development, 57,* 339–364.

Kail, R. (1997). Processing time, imagery, and spatial memory. *Journal of Experimental Child Psychology, 64,* 67–78.

Kail, R., & Park, Y. (1994). Processing time, articulation time, and memory span. *Journal of Experimental Child Psychology, 57,* 281–291.

Kail, R. & Salthouse, T. A. (1994). Processing speed as a mental capacity. *Acta Psychologica, 86,* 199–225.

Kalat, J. W. (1995). *Biological psychology* (5th ed.). Pacific Grove, CA: Brooks/Cole.

Kandel, E. R. (1991). Cellular mechanisms of learning and the biological basis of individuality. In E. R. Kandel, J. H. Schwartz, & T. M. Jessell (Eds.), *Principles of neuroscience* (pp.1009–1031). New York: Elsevier.

Kapur, N. (1995). Memory aids in the rehabilitation of memory disordered patients. In A. D. Baddeley, B. A. Wilson, & F. N. Watts (Eds.), *Handbook of memory disorders* (pp. 533–556). New York: Wiley.

Kapur, S., Craik, F. I. M., Tulving, E., Wilson, A. A., Houle, S., & Brown, G. M. (1994). Neuroanatomical correlates of encoding in episodic memory: Levels of processing effect. *Proceedings of the National Academy of Sciences (USA), 91,* 2008–2011.

Karlsson, T., Bäckman, L., Herlitz, A., Nilsson, L. G., Winblad, B., & Österlind, P. O. (1989). Memory improvement at different stages of Alzheimer's disease. *Neuropsychologia, 27,* 737–742.

Karmiloff-Smith, A. (1992). *Beyond modularity: A*

developmental perspective on cognitive science. Cambridge, MA: MIT Press.

Karni, A., Meyer, G., Jezzard, P., Adams, M., Turner, R., & Ungerleider, L. (1995). Functional MRI evidence for adult motor cortex plasticity during motor skill learning. *Nature, 377,* 155–158.

Kausler, D. H. (1994). *Learning and memory in normal aging.* San Diego, CA: Academic Press.

Keane, M. M., Gabrieli, J. D., Fennema, A. C., Growdon, J. H., & Corkin, S. (1991). Evidence for a dissociation between perceptual and conceptual priming in Alzheimer's disease. *Behavioral Neuroscience, 105,* 326–342.

Keil, F. (1989). *Concepts, kinds, and cognitive development.* Cambridge, MA: MIT Press.

Keppel, G., & Underwood, B. J. (1962). Proactive inhibition in short-term retention of single items. *Journal of Verbal Learning and Verbal Behavior, 1,* 153–161.

Kihlstrom, J. F. (1996). Memory research: The convergence of theory and practice. In D. J. Herrman, C. McEvoy, C. Hertzog, P. Hertel, & M. K. Johnson (Eds.), *Basic and applied memory research: Practical applications* (Vol. 1, pp. 5–26). Mahwah, NJ: Erlbaum.

Kimberg, D. Y., & Farah, M. J. (1993). A unified account of cognitive impairments following frontal lobe damage: The role of working memory in complex, organized behavior. *Journal of Experimental Psychology: General, 122,* 411–428.

Kintsch, W. (1970). *Learning, memory, and conceptual processes.* New York: Wiley.

Kintsch, W. (1972). Notes on the structure of semantic memory. In E. Tulving & W. Donaldson (Eds.), *Organization of memory* (pp. 240–308). New York: Academic Press.

Kintsch, W. (1977). *Memory and cognition.* New York: Wiley.

Kintsch, W. (1980). Semantic memory: A tutorial. In R. Nickerson (Ed.), *Attention and performance VIII* (pp. 595–620). Hillsdale, NJ: Erlbaum.

Kintsch, W. (1985). Reflections on Ebbinghaus. *Journal of Experimental Psychology: Learning, Memory, and Cognition, 11,* 461–463.

Kintsch, W., & Buschke, H. (1969). Homophones and synonyms in short-term memory. *Journal of Experimental Psychology, 80,* 403–407.

Kintsch, W., Kozminsky, E., Streby, W. J., McKoon, G., & Keenan, J. M. (1975). Comprehension and recall of text as a function of content variables. *Journal of Verbal Learning and Verbal Behavior, 14,* 196–214.

Kintsch, W., & van Dijk, T. A. (1978). Toward a model of text comprehension and reproduction. *Psychological Review, 85,* 363–394.

Klahr, D., & Carver, S. M. (1988). Cognitive objectives in a LOGO debugging curriculum: Instruction, learning, and transfer. *Cognitive Psychology, 20,* 362–404.

Klapp, S. T., Marshburn, E. A., & Lester, P. T. (1983). Short-term memory does not involve the "working memory" of information processing: The demise of a common assumption. *Journal of Experimental Psychology: General, 112,* 240–264.

Klatzky, R. L. (1991). Let's be friends. *American Psychologist, 46,* 43–45.

Kleinsmith, L. J., & Kaplan, S. (1964). Interaction of arousal and recall interval in nonsense syllable paired-associate learning. *Journal of Experimental Psychology, 67,* 124–126.

Kliegl, R., Mayr, U., & Krampe, R. T. (1994). Time-accuracy functions for determining process and person differences: An application to cognitive aging. *Cognitive Psychology, 26,* 134–164.

Knowlton, B. J., Ramus, S. J., & Squire, L. R. (1992). Intact artificial grammar learning in amnesia: Dissociation of classification learning and explicit memory for specific instances. *Psychological Science, 3,* 172–179.

Knowlton, B. J., & Squire, L. R. (1992). Intact prototype learning by amnesic patients: Evidence for parallel learning of item-specific and general information. *Society for Neuroscience Abstracts, 18,* 168.

Knowlton, B. J., & Squire, L. R. (1996). Artificial grammar learning depends on implicit acquisition of both abstract and exemplar-specific information. *Journal of Experimental Psychology: Learning, Memory, and Cognition, 22,* 169–181.

Kobasigawa, A. (1974). Utilization of retrieval cues by children in recall. *Child Development, 45,* 127–134.

Kolb, B. (1989). Brain development, plasticity, and behavior. *American Psychologist, 44,* 1203–1212.

Kolb, B., & Whishaw, I. Q. (1990). *Fundamentals of human neuropsychology* (3rd ed.) New York: Freeman.

Kolers, P. A. (1975). Memorial consequences of automatized encoding. *Journal of Experimental*

Psychology: Human Learning and Memory, 1, 689–701.

Koriat, A., Ben-Zur, H., & Sheffer, D. (1988). Telling the same story twice: Output monitoring and age. *Journal of Memory and Language, 27,* 23–39.

Koriat, A., & Goldsmith, M. (1996). Memory metaphors and the real-life/laboratory controversy: Correspondence versus storehouse conceptions of memory. *Behavioral and Brain Sciences, 19,* 167–228.

Korsakoff, S. S. (1996). Medico-psychological study of a memory disorder. *Consciousness and Cognition, 5,* 2–21. (Original work published in 1889).

Kounios, J. (1996). On the continuity of thought and the representation of knowledge: Electrophysiological and behavioral time-course measures reveal levels of structure in semantic memory. *Psychonomic Bulletin and Review, 3,* 265–286.

Krampe, R. T., & Ericsson, K. A. (1996). Maintaining excellence: Deliberate practice and elite performance in young and older pianists. *Journal of Experimental Psychology: General, 125,* 331–359.

Kutas, M., & Hillyard, S. A. (1980). Reading senseless sentences: Brain potentials reflect semantic incongruity. *Science, 207,* 203–205.

Kyllonen, P. C., & Christal, R. E. (1990). Reasoning ability is (little more than) working memory capacity! *Intelligence, 14,* 389–433.

Landauer, T., & Dumais, S. (1997). A solution to Plato's problem: The latent semantic analysis theory of acquisition, induction, and representation of knowledge. *Psychological Review, 2,* 211–240.

Landauer, T. K., & Bjork, R. A. (1978). Optimum rehearsal patterns and name learning. In M. M. Gruneberg, P. E. Morris, & R. N. Sykes (Eds.), *Practical aspects of memory* (pp. 625–632). New York: Academic Press.

La Pointe, L. B., & Engle, R. W. (1990). Simple and complex word spans as measures of working memory capacity. *Journal of Experimental Psychology: Learning, Memory, and Cognition, 16,* 1118–1133.

Large, E. W., Palmer, C., & Pollack, J. B. (1995). Reduced memory representations for music. *Cognitive Science, 19,* 53–96.

La Rue, A. (1992). *Aging and neuropsychological assessment.* New York: Plenum.

Lashley, K. (1917). The effects of strychnine and caffeine upon the rate of learning. *Psychobiology, 1,* 141–170.

Lashley, K. (1950). In search of the engram. *Symposia of the Society for Experimental Biology: Physiological*

mechanisms of animal behavior (Vol. 4). New York: Academic Press.

Lasnik, H. (1990). Syntax. In D. N. Osherson & H. Lasnik (Eds.), *Language: An invitation to cognitive science* (pp. 5–21). Cambridge, MA: MIT Press.

LeDoux, J. (1992). Emotion and memory: Anatomical systems underlying indelible neural traces. In S. A. Christianson (Ed.), *The handbook of emotion and memory: Research and theory* (pp. 269–288). Hillsdale, NJ: Erlbaum.

LeDoux, J. (1994). Emotion, memory, and the brain. *Scientific American, 270,* 50–57.

Levinger, G., & Clark, J. (1961). Emotional factors in the forgetting of word associations. *Journal of Abnormal and Social Psychology, 62,* 99–105.

Lewicki, P. (1986). Processing information about covariations that cannot be articulated. *Journal of Experimental Psychology: Learning, Memory, and Cognition, 12,* 135–146.

Light, L. L. (1991). Memory and aging: Four hypotheses in search of data. *Annual Review of Psychology, 42,* 333–376.

Light, L. L. (1996). Memory and aging. In E. L. Bjork & R. A. Bjork (Eds.), *Memory.* (pp. 443–490). San Diego, CA: Academic Press.

Light, L. L., & LaVoie, D. (1993). Direct and indirect measures of memory in old age. In P. Graf & M. E. J. Masson (Eds.), *Implicit memory: New directions in cognition, development, and neuropsychology* (pp. 207–230). Hillsdale, NJ: Erlbaum.

Linton, M. (1982). Transformations of memory in everyday life. In U. Neisser (Ed.), *Memory observed: Remembering in natural contexts* (pp. 77–91). San Francisco: Freeman.

Linton, M. (1986). Ways of searching and the contents of memory. In D. C. Rubin (Ed.), *Autobiographical memory* (pp. 50–67). New York: Cambridge University Press.

Loftus, E. F. (1980). *Memory.* Reading, MA: Addison-Wesley.

Loftus, E. F. (1991). The glitter of everyday memory . . . and the gold. *American Psychologist, 46,* 16–18.

Loftus, E. F. (1993). The reality of repressed memories. *American Psychologist, 48,* 518–537.

Loftus, E. F., Feldman, J., & Dashiell, R. (1995). The reality of memory illusions. In D. L. Schacter (Ed.), *Memory distortion: How minds, brains, and societies reconstruct the past* (pp. 47–68). Cambridge, MA: Harvard University Press.

Loftus, E. F., Garry, M., & Feldman, J. (1994). Forgetting sexual trauma: What does it mean when 38% forget? *Journal of Consulting and Clinical Psychology, 62,* 1171–1181.

Loftus, E. F., & Ketcham, K. (1994). *The myth of repressed memory.* New York: St. Martin's.

Loftus, E. F., & Loftus, G. R. (1980). On the permanence of stored information in the human brain. *American Psychologist, 35,* 409–420.

Loftus, E. F., Miller, D. G., & Burns, H. J. (1978). Semantic integration of verbal information into a visual memory. *Journal of Experimental Psychology: Human Learning and Memory, 4,* 19–31.

Loftus, E. F., & Palmer, J. C. (1974). Reconstruction of automobile destruction: An example of the interaction between language and memory. *Journal of Verbal Learning and Verbal Behavior, 4,* 19–31.

Logie, R. H. (1995). *Visuo-spatial working memory.* Mahwah, NJ: Erlbaum.

Logie, R. H. (1996). The seven ages of working memory. In J. T. E. Richardson, R. W. Engle, L. Hasher, R. H. Logie, E. R. Stoltzfus, & R. T. Zacks (Eds.), *Working memory and human cognition* (pp. 31–65). New York: Oxford University Press.

Logie, R. H., Gilhooly, K. J., & Wynn, V. (1994). Counting on working memory in mental arithmetic. *Memory & Cognition, 22,* 395–410.

Longoni, A. M., Richardson, J. T., & Aiello, A. (1993). Articulatory rehearsal and phonological storage in working memory. *Memory & Cognition, 21,* 11–22.

Lopero, F., et al. (1997). Clinical features of early-onset Alzheimer disease in a large kindred with an E289A presenilin-1 mutation. *JAMA, 277,* 793–799.

Lorayne, H., & Lucas, J. (1974). *The memory book.* New York: Stein and Day.

Lovett, M. C., & Anderson, J. R. (1996). History of success and current context in problem-solving: Combined influences on operator selection. *Cognitive Psychology, 31,* 168–217.

Luria, A. R. (1976). *The mind of a mnemonist: A little book about a vast memory.* Chicago: Henry Regnery.

Mackintosh, N. J. (1994). *Animal learning and cognition.* San Diego, CA: Academic Press.

Madigan, S. A. (1969). Intraserial repetition and coding processes in free recall. *Journal of Verbal Learning and Verbal Behavior, 8,* 828–835.

Malt, B. C., & Smith, E. E. (1984). Correlated properties in natural categories. *Journal of Verbal Learning and Verbal Behavior, 23,* 250–269.

Mandler, G. (1992). Memory, arousal, and mood: A theoretical integration. In S. A. Christianson (Ed.), *The handbook of emotion and memory: Research and theory* (pp. 93–110). Hillsdale, NJ: Erlbaum.

Mandler, J. M., & Johnson, N. S. (1977). Remembrance of things parsed: Story structure and recall. *Cognitive Psychology, 9,* 111–151.

Mäntylä, T. (1986). Optimizing cue effectiveness: Recall of 500 and 600 incidentally learned words. *Journal of Experimental Psychology: Learning, Memory, and Cognition, 12,* 66–71.

Markowitsch, H. J. (1995). Anatomical basis of memory disorders. In M. S. Gazzaniga (Ed.), *The cognitive neurosciences* (pp. 765–779). Cambridge, MA: MIT Press.

Marsh, R. L., & Bower, G. H. (1993). Eliciting cryptomnesia: Unconscious plagiarism in a puzzle task. *Journal of Experimental Psychology: Learning, Memory, and Cognition, 19,* 673–688.

Marsolek, C. J., Kosslyn, S. M., & Squire, L. R. (1992). Form specific visual priming in the right cerebral hemisphere. *Journal of Experimental Psychology: Learning, Memory, and Cognition, 18,* 492–508.

Martin, A., Haxby, J. V., Lalonde, F. M., Wiggs, C. L., & Ungerleider, L. G. (1995). Discrete cortical regions associated with knowledge of color and knowledge of action. *Science, 270,* 102–105.

Martin, A., Wiggs, C. L., Ungerleider, L. G., & Haxby, J. V. (1996). Neural correlates of category-specific knowledge. *Nature, 379,* 649–652.

Martin, R. C., & Romani, C. (1994). Verbal working memory and sentence comprehension: A multiple-components view. *Neuropsychology, 8,* 506–523.

Massaro, D. W. (1988). Some criticisms of connectionist models of human performance. *Journal of Memory and Language, 27,* 213–234.

Massaro, D. W., & Loftus, G. R. (1996). Sensory and perceptual storage: Data and theory. In E. L. Bjork & R. A. Bjork (Eds.), *Memory* (pp. 68–99). San Diego, CA: Academic Press.

Masson, M. E. J. (1995). A distributed memory model of semantic priming. *Journal of Experimental Psychology: Learning, Memory, and Cognition, 21,* 3–23.

Mateer, C., Sohlberg, M., & Crinean, J. (1987). Perceptions of memory functions in individuals with closed head injury. *Journal of Head Trauma Rehabilitation, 2,* 74–84.

Matlin, M. (1994). *Cognition* (3rd ed.). Orlando, FL: Harcourt Brace.

Mayes, A. R. (1996). The functional deficits that underlie amnesia: Evidence from amnesic forgetting rate and item-specific implicit memory. In D. J. Herrman, C. McEvoy, C. Hertzog, P. Hertel, & M. K. Johnson (Eds.), *Basic and applied memory research: Practical applications* (Vol. 2, pp. 391–405). Mahwah, NJ: Erlbaum.

Mayr, U., & Kliegl, R. (1993). Sequential and coordinative complexity: Age-based processing limitations in figural transformation. *Journal of Experimental Psychology: Learning, Memory, and Cognition, 19,* 1297–1320.

McCarthy, G., Blamire, A., Rothman, D. L., Gruetter, R., & Shulman, R. G. (1993). Echo-planar magnetic resonance imaging studies of frontal cortex activation during word generation in humans. *Proceedings of the National Academy of Sciences (USA), 90,* 4952–4956.

McCarthy, R. A., & Hodges, J. R. (1995). Trapped in time: Profound autobiographical memory loss following a thalamic stroke. In R. Campbell & M. A. Conway (Eds.), *Broken memories: Case studies in memory impairment* (pp. 31–44). Cambridge, MA: Blackwell.

McClelland, J. L. (1981). Retrieving general and specific knowledge from stored knowledge of specifics. *Proceedings of the Third Annual Conference of the Cognitive Science Society* (pp. 170–172). Hillsdale, NJ: Erlbaum.

McClelland, J. L., McNaughton, B. L., & O'Reilly, R. C. (1995). Why there are complementary learning systems in the hippocampus and neocortex: Insights from the successes and failures of connectionist models of learning and memory. *Psychological Review, 102,* 419–457.

McClelland, J. L., & Rumelhart, D. E. (1981). An interactive activation model of context effects in letter perception: Part I. An account of basic findings. *Psychological Review, 102,* 375–407.

McClelland, J. L., & Rumelhart, D. E. (1986). Amnesia and distributed memory. In J. L. McClelland, D. E. Rumelhart, & The PDP Group (Eds.), *Parallel distributed processing: Explorations in the microstructure of cognition* (pp. 503–527). Cambridge, MA: MIT Press.

McClelland, J. L., Rumelhart, D. E., & Hinton, G. E. (1986). The appeal of parallel distributed processing. In D. E. Rumelhart, J. L. McClelland, & The PDP Group (Eds.), *Parallel distributed processing: Explorations in the microstructure of cognition* (pp. 3–44). Cambridge, MA: MIT Press.

McCloskey, M., & Cohen, N. J. (1989). Catastrophic interference in connectionist networks: The sequential learning problem. In G. H. Bower (Ed.), *The psychology of learning and motivation* (Vol. 24, pp. 109–165). San Diego, CA: Academic Press.

McCloskey, M., & Zaragoza, M. (1985). Misleading postevent information and memory for events: Arguments and evidence against memory impairment hypotheses. *Journal of Experimental Psychology: General, 114,* 1–16.

McDaniel, M. A., Waddill, P. J., & Shakesby, P. S. (1996). Study strategies, interest, and learning from text: The application of material appropriate processing. In D. J. Herrman, C. McEvoy, C. Hertzog, P. Hertel, & M. K. Johnson (Eds.), *Basic and applied memory research: Practical applications* (Vol. 1, pp. 385–397). Mahwah, NJ: Erlbaum.

McElree, B., & Dosher, B. A. (1993). Serial retrieval processes in the recovery of order information. *Journal of Experimental Psychology: General, 122,* 291–315.

McGaugh, J. L. (1995). Emotional activation, neuromodulatory systems, and memory. In D. L. Schacter (Ed.), *Memory distortions* (pp. 255–273). Cambridge, MA: Harvard University Press.

McGaugh, J. L., Weinberger, N. M., & Lynch, G. (1995). *Brain and memory: Modulation and mediation of neuroplasticity.* New York: Oxford University Press.

McGeoch, J. A. (1942). *The psychology of human learning.* New York: Longmans.

McGowin, D. F. (1993). *Living in the labyrinth: A personal journey through the maze of Alzheimer's.* San Francisco: Elder Books.

McKoon, G., Ratcliff, R., & Dell, G. S. (1986). A critical evaluation of the semantic-episodic distinction. *Journal of Experimental Psychology: Learning, Memory, and Cognition, 12,* 295–306.

Medin, D. L., & Ross, B. H. (1992). *Cognitive psychology.* Orlando, FL: Harcourt.

Medin, D. L., & Shaffer, M. M. (1978). Context theory of classification learning. *Psychological Review, 85,* 207–238.

Melton, A. W. (1963). Implications of short-term memory for a general theory of memory. *Journal of Verbal Learning and Verbal Behavior, 2,* 1–21.

Melton, A. W., & Irwin, J. M. (1940). The influence of degree of interpolated learning on retroactive inhibition and the overt transfer of specific responses. *American Journal of Psychology, 53,* 173–203.

Meltzer, H. (1930). Individual differences in forgetting

pleasant and unpleasant experiences. *Journal of Educational Psychology, 21,* 399–409.

Metcalfe, J. (1991). Recognition failure and the composite memory trace in CHARM. *Psychological Review, 98,* 529–553.

Metcalfe, J. (1996). Metacognitive processes. In E. L. Bjork & R. A. Bjork (Eds.), *Memory* (pp. 383–407). San Diego, CA: Academic Press.

Miller, A. (1949). *Death of a salesman.* New York: Penguin.

Miller, G. A. (1956). The magic number seven plus or minus two: Some limits on our capacity for processing information. *Psychological Review, 63,* 81–97.

Miller, G. A., Galanter, E., & Pribram, K. H. (1960). *Plans and the structure of behavior.* New York: Holt, Rinehart and Winston.

Milner, B. (1963). Effects of different brain lesions on card sorting. *Archives for Neurology, 9,* 90–100.

Milner, B. (1966). Amnesia following operation on the temporal lobes. In C. W. M. Whitty & O. L. Zangwill (Eds.), *Amnesia* (pp. 109–133). London: Butterworths.

Mishkin, M., & Appenzeller, T. (1987). The anatomy of memory. *Scientific American, 256,* 80–136.

Mishkin, M., Malamut, B., & Bachevalier, J. (1984). Memories and habits: Two neural systems. In G. Lynch, J. L. McGaugh, & N. M. Weinberger (Eds.), *Neurobiology of learning and memory* (pp. 65–77). New York: Guilford.

Mitchell, D. B. (1993). Implicit and explicit memory for pictures: Multiple views across the life span. In P. Graf & M. E. J. Masson (Eds.), *Implicit memory: New directions in cognition, development, and neuropsychology* (pp. 171–190). Hillsdale, NJ: Erlbaum.

Mohs, R. (1995). Neuropsychological assessment of patients with Alzheimer's disease. In F. E. Bloom & D. J. Kupfer (Eds.), *Psychopharmacology: The fourth generation of projects* (pp. 1377–1388). New York: Raven.

Morris, C. D., Bransford, J. D., & Franks, J. J. (1977). Levels of processing versus transfer appropriate processing. *Journal of Verbal Learning and Verbal Behavior, 16,* 519–533.

Morris, R. G. (1994). Working memory in Alzheimer-type dementia. *Neuropsychology, 8,* 544–554.

Morris, R. G., & Kopelman, M. D. (1986). The memory deficits in Alzheimer-type dementia: A review. *Quarterly Journal of Experimental Psychology, 38A,* 575–602.

Morrison-Bogorad, M., Phelps, C., & Buckholtz, N.

(1997). Alzheimer disease research comes of age: The pace accelerates. *JAMA, 277,* 837–840.

Morton, J. (1991). The bankruptcy of everyday thinking. *American Psychologist, 46,* 32–33.

Moscovich, M. (1994). Memory and working with memory: Evaluation of a component process model and comparison with other models. In E. Tulving & D. L. Schacter (Eds.), *Memory systems 1994* (pp. 269–310). Cambridge, MA: MIT Press.

Mueller, G. E., & Pilzecker, A. (1900). Experimentelle beitraege zur lehre vom gedaechtnis. *Zeitschrift fuer Psychologie, 1,* 1–288.

Murdock, B. B., Jr. (1974). *Human memory: Theory and data.* Potomac, MD: Erlbaum.

Murdock, B. B., Jr. (1982). A theory for the storage and retrieval of items and associative information. *Psychological Review, 89,* 609–626.

Murdock, B. B., Jr. (1985). The contributions of Hermann Ebbinghaus. *Journal of Experimental Psychology: Learning, Memory, and Cognition, 11,* 469–471.

Myers, N. A., Clifton, R. K., & Clarkson, M. C. (1987). When they were young: Almost-threes remember two years ago. *Infant Behavior and Development, 10,* 123–132.

Nairne, J. S. (1996). Short-term/Working memory. In E. L. Bjork & R. A. Bjork (Eds.), *Memory* (pp. 102–126). San Diego, CA: Academic Press.

Naito, M. (1990). Repetition priming in children and adults: Age-related dissociation between implicit and explicit memory. *Journal of Experimental Child Psychology, 50,* 462–484.

Narens, L., Graf, A., & Nelson, T. O. (1996). Metacognitive aspects of implicit/explicit memory. In L. M. Reder (Ed.), *Implicit memory and metacognition.* Mahwah, NJ: Erlbaum.

Navon, D. (1984). Resources—A theoretical soup stone? *Psychological Review, 91,* 216–234.

Nebes, R. D. (1989). Semantic memory in Alzheimer's disease. *Psychological Bulletin, 106,* 377–394.

Nebes, R. D. (1992). Cognitive dysfunction in Alzheimer's disease. In F. I. M. Craik & T. A. Salthouse (Eds.), *The handbook of aging and cognition* (pp. 373–446). Hillsdale, NJ: Erlbaum.

Neely, J. H. (1989). Experimental dissociations and the episodic/semantic memory distinction. In H. L. Roediger & F. I. M. Craik (Eds.), *Varieties of memory and consciousness: Essays in honour of Endel Tulving* (pp. 229–270). Hillsdale, NJ: Erlbaum.

Neisser, U. (1967). *Cognitive psychology.* New York: Appleton-Century Crofts.

Neisser, U. (1978). Memory: What are the important questions? In M. M. Gruneberg, P. Morris, & R. N. Sykes (Eds.), *Practical aspects of memory* (pp. 3–24). London: Academic Press.

Neisser, U. (1982a). *Memory observed: Remembering in natural contexts.* San Francisco: Freeman.

Neisser, U. (1982b). John Dean's memory: A case study. In U. Neisser (Ed.), *Memory observed: Remembering in natural contexts* (pp. 139–159). San Francisco: Freeman.

Neisser, U. (1988). Time present and time past. In M. M. Gruneberg, P. E. Morris, & R. N. Sykes (Eds.), *Practical aspects of memory: Current research and issues* (Vol. 2, pp. 545–560). Chichester, UK: Wiley.

Neisser, U. (1991). A case of misplaced nostalgia. *American Psychologist, 46,* 34–36.

Neisser, U. (1994). Self-narratives: True and false. In U. Neisser & R. Fivush (Eds.), *The remembering self: Construction and accuracy in the self-narrative* (pp. 1–18). New York: Cambridge University Press.

Nelson, K. (1993a). The psychological and social origins of autobiographical memory. *Psychological Science, 4,* 7–14.

Nelson, K. (1993b). What develops? In C. A. Nelson (Ed.), *Memory and affect in development: The Minnesota symposia on child psychology* (Vol. 26, pp. 1–24). Hillsdale, NJ: Erlbaum.

Nelson, K., & Gruendel, J. (1981). Generalized event representations: Basic building blocks of cognitive development. In M. E. Lamb & A. L. Brown (Eds.), *Advances in developmental psychology* (Vol. 1, pp. 131–158). Hillsdale, NJ: Erlbaum.

Nelson, K., & Ross, G. (1980). The generalities and specifics of long-term memory in infants and young children. In M. Perlmutter (Ed.), *Children's memory: New directions for child development* (Vol. 10, pp. 87–101). San Francisco: Jossey-Bass.

Nelson, T. O. (1977). Repetition and depth of processing. *Journal of Verbal Learning and Verbal Behavior, 16,* 151–171.

Nelson, T. O. (1985). Ebbinghaus' contribution to the measurement of retention: Savings during relearning. *Journal of Experimental Psychology: Learning, Memory, and Cognition, 11,* 472–479.

Nelson, T. O., & Narens, L. (1994). Why investigate metacognition? In J. Metcalfe & A. P. Shimamura (Eds.), *Metacognition: Knowing about knowing* (pp. 1–26). Cambridge, MA: MIT Press.

Newell, A. (1973). You can't play twenty questions with nature and win. In W. Chase (Ed.), *Visual information processing* (pp. 283–308). New York: Academic Press.

Newell, A., & Rosenbloom, P. S. (1981). Mechanisms of skill acquisition and the law of practice. In J. R. Anderson (Ed.), *Cognitive skills and their acquisition* (pp. 1–56). Hillsdale, NJ: Erlbaum.

Newell, A., Rosenbloom, P. S., & Laird, J. E. (1989). Symbolic architectures for cognition. In M. Posner (Ed.), *Foundations in cognitive science* (pp. 93–131). Cambridge, MA: MIT Press.

Newell, A., & Simon, H. A. (1972). *Human problem solving.* Englewood Cliffs, NJ: Prentice-Hall.

Noice, H., & Noice, T. (1994). An example of role preparation by a professional actor: A think-aloud protocol. *Discourse Processes 1994, 18,* 345–369.

Norman, D. (1970). *Models of human memory.* New York: Academic Press.

Norman, D. A. (1982). *Learning and memory.* San Fransisco, CA: Freeman.

Norman, D. A. (1988). *The psychology of everyday things.* Dunmore, PA: Basic Books.

Norman, D. A., & Shallice, T. (1986). Attention to action: Willed and automatic control of behavior. In R. J. Davidson, G. E. Schwarts, & D. Shapiro (Eds.), *Consciousness and self-regulation. Advances in research and theory* (Vol. 4, pp. 1–18). New York: Plenum.

Nottebohm, F. (1985). Neuronal replacement in adulthood. *Annals of the New York Academy of Science, 457,* 143–161.

Nyberg, L., Cabeza, R., & Tulving, E. (1996). PET studies of encoding and retrieval: The HERA model. *Psychonomic Bulletin & Review, 3,* 135–148.

O'Connor, M., Verfaellie, M., & Cermak, L. S. (1995). Clinical differentiation of amnesic subtypes. In A. D. Baddeley, B. A. Wilson, & F. N. Watts (Eds.), *Handbook of memory disorders* (pp. 53–80). New York: Wiley.

Ohlsson, S. (1992). The learning curve for writing books: Evidence from Professor Asimov. *Psychological Science, 3,* 380–382.

Ojeman, G. A. (1991). Cortical organization of language. *The Journal of Neuroscience, 11,* 2281–2287.

O'Keefe, J., & Dostoyevsky, T. (1971). The hippocampus as a spatial map: Preliminary evidence from unit activity in the freely moving rat. *Brain Research, 34,* 171–175.

Olton, D. S., Collison, C., & Werz, M. A. (1977). Spatial memory and radial arm maze performance in rats. *Learning and Motivation, 8,* 289–314.

O'Sullivan, J. T. (1996). Children's metamemory about the influence of conceptual relations on recall. *Journal of Experimental Child Psychology, 62,* 1–29.

Paller, K. A. (1990). Recall and stem-completion priming have different electrophysiological correlates and are modified differently by directed forgetting. *Journal of Experimental Psychology: Learning, Memory, and Cognition, 16,* 1021–1032.

Paller, K. A., & Kutas, M. (1992). Brain potentials during memory retrieval provide neurophysiological support for the distinction between conscious recollection and priming. *Journal of Cognitive Neuroscience, 4,* 375–391.

Paller, K. A., Kutas, M., & McIsaac, H. K. (1995). Monitoring conscious recollection via the electrical activity of the brain. *Psychological Science, 6,* 107–111.

Papagano, C., & Vallar, G. (1995). To learn or not to learn: Vocabulary in foreign languages and the problem with phonological memory. In R. Campbell & M. A. Conway (Eds.), *Broken memories: Case studies in memory impairment* (pp. 334–343). Cambridge, MA: Blackwell.

Papert, S. (1980). *Mindstorms: Children, computers, and powerful ideas.* New York: Basic Books.

Pardo, P. J., Pardo, K. W., Janer, W., & Raichle, M. E. (1990). The anterior cingulate cortex mediates processing selection in the Stroop attentional conflict paradigm. *Proceedings of the National Academy of Sciences (USA), 87,* 256–259.

Paris, S. C., & Lindauer, B. K. (1976). The role of inference in children's comprehension and memory for sentences. *Cognitive Psychology, 8,* 217–227.

Parkin, A. J., & Stampfer, H. G. (1995). Keeping out the past: A study of temporary memory loss. In R. Campbell & M. A. Conway (Eds.), *Broken memories: Case studies in memory impairment* (pp. 80–92). Cambridge, MA: Blackwell.

Parkinson, S. R. (1982). Performance deficits in short-term memory tasks: A comparison of amnesic Korsakoff patients and the aged. In L. S. Cermak (Ed.), *Human memory and amnesia* (pp. 77–96). Hillsdale, NJ: Erlbaum.

Pashler, H., & Carrier, M. (1996). Structures, processes, and the flow of information. In E. L. Bjork & R. A. Bjork (Eds.), *Memory* (pp. 3–29). San Diego, CA: Academic Press.

Patel, V. L., Arocha, J. F., & Kaufman, D. R. (1994). Diagnostic reasoning and medical expertise. In D. L. Medin (Ed.), *The psychology of learning and motivation* (Vol. 31, pp. 187–252). San Diego, CA: Academic Press.

Patterson, K., & Hodges, J. R. (1995). Disorders of semantic memory. In A. D. Baddeley, B. A. Wilson, & F. N. Watts (Eds.), *Handbook of memory disorders* (pp. 167–186). New York: Wiley.

Payne, D. G., Elie, C. J., Blackwill, J. M., & Neuschatz, J. S. (1996). Memory illusions: Recalling, recognizing and recollecting events that never occurred. *Journal of Memory and Language, 35,* 261–285.

Penfield, W. (1951). Memory mechanisms. *Transactions of the American Neurological Association, 76,* 15–31.

Peters, D. P. (1988). Eyewitness memory and arousal in a natural setting. In M. M. Gruneberg, P. E. Morris, & R. N. Sykes (Eds.), *Practical aspects of memory: Current research and issues* (Vol. 1, pp. 89–94). Chichester, UK: Wiley.

Peterson, L. R., & Peterson, M. J. (1959). Short-term retention of individual verbal items. *Journal of Experimental Psychology, 58,* 193–198.

Petrides, M. E., Alivisatos, B., Meyer, E., & Evans, A. G. (1993). Functional activation of the human frontal cortex during the performance of verbal working memory tasks. *Proceedings of the National Academy of Sciences (USA) 90,* 878–882.

Pezdek, K., & Banks, W. P. (1996). *The recovered/false memory debate.* San Diego, CA: Academic Press.

Pillemer, D. B., Picariello, M. L., Law, A. B., & Reichman, J. S. (1996). In. D. C. Rubin (Ed.), *Remembering our past* (pp. 318–337). New York: Cambridge University Press.

Pinel, J. P. (1993). *Biopsychology.* Boston: Allyn and Bacon.

Pinker, S. (1990). Language acquisition. In D. N. Osherson & H. Lasnik (Eds.), *Language: An invitation to cognitive science* (pp. 199–241). Cambridge, MA: MIT Press.

Pinker, S. (1994). *The language instinct.* New York: Morrow.

Pinker, S., & Mehler, J. (1988). *Connections and symbols.* Cambridge, MA: MIT Press.

Pirolli, P. L., & Anderson, J. R. (1985). The role of practice in fact retrieval. *Journal of Experimental Psychology: Learning, Memory, and Cognition, 11,* 136–153.

Polster, M. R. (1993). Drug-induced amnesia: Implications for cognitive neuropsychological investigations of memory. *Psychological Bulletin, 114,* 477–493.

Posner, M. I. (1969). Abstraction and the process of recognition. In G. H. Bower & J. T. Spence (Eds.), *The psychology of learning and motivation* (Vol. 3, pp. 44–96). New York: Academic Press.

Posner, M. I., Peterson, S. E., Fox, P. T., & Raichle, M. E. (1988). Localization of cognitive operations in the human brain. *Science, 240,* 1627–1631.

Posner, M. I., & Raichle, M. E. (1994). *Images of mind.* New York: Freeman.

Posner, M. I., & Rossman, E. (1965). Effect of size and location of informational transforms upon short-term retention. *Journal of Experimental Psychology, 70,* 496–505.

Potter, M. C. (1993). Very short-term conceptual memory. *Memory & Cognition, 21,* 156–161.

Proust, M. (1988). A la recherche du temps perdu. Paris: Gallimard.

Quillian, M. R. (1968). Semantic memory. In M. Minsky (Ed.), *Semantic information processing* (pp. 227–270). Cambridge, MA: MIT Press.

Raaijmakers, J. G. (1993). The story of the two-store model of memory: Past criticisms, current status and future directions. In D. E. Meyer & S. Kornblum (Eds.), *Attention and performance XIV* (pp. 467–488). Cambridge, MA: Bradford/MIT.

Raaijmakers, J. G., & Shiffrin, R. M. (1981). SAM: Search of associative memory. *Psychological Review, 88,* 93–134.

Racine, R. J., & de Jonge, M. (1988). Short-term and long-term potentiation in projection pathways and local circuits. In P. Landfield & S. Deadwyler (Eds.), *Long-term potentiations: From biophysics to behavior* (pp. 167–197). New York: Liss.

Raichle, M. E. (1994). Visualizing the mind. *Scientific American, 270,* 58–64.

Rajaram, S. (1993). Remembering and knowing: Two means of access to the personal past. *Memory & Cognition, 21,* 89–102.

Raskin, S., & Mateer, C. (1994). Rehabilitation of cognitive impairments. In D. C. Good & J. R. Couch, Jr. (Eds.), *Handbook of neurorehabilitation* (pp. 243–259). New York: Marcel-Dekker.

Raskin, S. A., & Sohlberg, M. M. (1996). An investigation of prospective memory training in two adults with brain injury. *Journal of Head Trauma Rehabilitation, 11,* 32–51.

Ratcliff, R., & McKoon, G. (1978). Priming in item recognition: Evidence for the propositional structure of sentences. *Journal of Verbal Learning and Verbal Behavior, 17,* 403–417.

Ratcliff, R., & McKoon, G. (1988). A retrieval theory of priming in memory. *Psychological Review, 95,* 385–408.

Reber, A. S. (1967). Implicit learning of artificial grammars. *Journal of Verbal Learning and Verbal Behavior, 6,* 855–863.

Reber, A. S. (1969). Transfer of syntactic structure in synthetic languages. *Journal of Experimental Psychology, 81,* 115–119.

Reber, A. S. (1989). Implicit learning and tacit knowledge. *Journal of Experimental Psychology: General, 118,* 219–235.

Reber, A. S. (1993). *Implicit learning and tacit knowledge: An essay on the cognitive unconscious.* New York: Oxford University Press.

Reber, A. S. (1997). Implicit ruminations. *Psychonomic Bulletin & Review, 4,* 49–55.

Reder, L. M. (1982). Plausibility judgments vs. fact retrieval: Alternative strategies for sentence verification. *Psychological Review, 89,* 250–280.

Reder, L. M. (1987). Strategy selection in question answering. *Cognitive Psychology, 19,* 90–138.

Reder, L. M. (1996) *Implicit memory and metacognition.* Mahwah, NJ: Erlbaum.

Redington, M., & Chater, N. (1996). Transfer in artificial grammar learning: A reevaluation. *Journal of Experimental Psychology: General, 125,* 123–138.

Reisberg, D., & Schwartz, B. (1991). *Learning and memory.* New York: Norton.

Rescorla, R. A., & Wagner, A. R. (1972). A theory of Pavlovian conditioning: Variations in the effectiveness of reinforcement and non-reinforcement. In A. H. Black & W. F. Prokasky (Eds.), *Classical conditioning 2* (pp. 64–99). New York: Appleton-Century-Crofts.

Reyna, V. F., & Titcomb, A. L. (1997). Constraints on the suggestibility of eyewitness testimony: A fuzzy-trace theory analysis. In D. G. Payne & F. G. Conrad (Eds.), *A synthesis of basic and applied approaches to human memory* (pp. 157–174). Hillsdale, NJ: Erlbaum.

Ribot, T. (1887). *Diseases of memory.* New York: Appleton-Century-Crofts.

Richardson, J. T. E. (1996). Evolving concepts of working memory. In J. T. E. Richardson, R. W. Engle, L. Hasher, R. H. Logie, E. R. Stoltzfus, & R. T. Zacks

(Eds.), *Working memory and human cognition* (pp. 3–30). New York: Oxford University Press.

Richman, H. B., Staszewski, J. J., & Simon, H. A. (1995). Simulation of expert memory using EPAM IV. *Psychological Review, 102,* 305–330.

Rips, L. J., Shoben, E. J., & Smith, E. E. (1973). Semantic distance and the verification of semantic relations. *Journal of Verbal Learning and Verbal Behavior, 12,* 1–20.

Roberts, K. (1988). Retrieval of a basic-level category in prelinguistic infants. *Developmental Psychology, 24,* 21–27.

Robinson, F. P. (1970). *Effective study.* New York: Harper and Row.

Roediger, H. L., III (1980). Memory metaphors in cognitive psychology. *Memory & Cognition, 8,* 231–246.

Roediger, H. L., III (1990). Implicit memory: Retention without remembering. *American Psychologist, 45,* 1043–1056.

Roediger, H. L., III (1991). They read an article? A commentary on the everyday controversy. *American Psychologist, 46,* 37–40.

Roediger, H. L., III (1993). Learning and memory: Progress and challenge. In D. E. Meyer & S. Kornblum (Eds.), *Attention and performance XIV* (pp. 509–528). Cambridge, MA: Bradford/MIT.

Roediger, H. L., III, & Guynn, M. J. (1996). Retrieval processes. In E. L. Bjork & R. A. Bjork (Eds.), *Memory* (pp. 197–236). San Diego, CA: Academic Press.

Roediger, H. L., III, & McDermott, K. B. (1995). Creating false memories: Remembering words not presented in lists. *Journal of Experimental Psychology: Learning, Memory and Cognition, 21,* 803–814.

Roediger, H. L., III, & McDermott, K. B. (1996). False perceptions of false memories. *Journal of Experimental Psychology: Learning, Memory, and Cognition, 22,* 814–816.

Roediger, H. L., III, Stadler, M. L., Weldon, M. S., & Riegler, G. L. (1992). *Journal of Experimental Psychology: Learning, Memory, and Cognition, 18,* 1251–1269.

Roediger, H. L., III, Weldon, M. S., & Challis, B. H. (1989). Explaining dissociations between implicit and explicit measures of retention: A processing account. In H. L. Roediger & F. I. M. Craik (Eds.), *Varieties of memory and consciousness: Essays in honour of Endel Tulving* (pp. 3–41). Hillsdale, NJ: Erlbaum.

Roland, P. E. (1985). Cortical organization of voluntary behavior in man. *Human Neurobiology, 4,* 115–167.

Roland, P. E., Kawashima, R., Gulyas, B., & O'Sullivan, B. (1995). Positron emission tomography in cognitive neuroscience: Methodological constraints, strategies, and examples from learning and memory. In M. S. Gazzaniga (Ed.), *The cognitive neurosciences* (pp. 781–788). Cambridge, MA: MIT Press.

Rolls, E. T., Baylis, G. C., Hasselmo, M. E., & Nalwa, V. (1989). The effect of learning on the face selective responses of neurons in the cortex in the superior temporal cortex of the monkey. *Experimental Brain Research, 76,* 153–164.

Ronch, M. (1985). *Another name for madness.* Boston: Houghton Mifflin.

Rosenzweig, M. R. (1979). Responsiveness of brain size to individual experience: Behavioral and evolutionary implications. In M. E. Hahn, C. Jensen, & B. Dudek (Eds.) *Development and evolution of brain size: Behavioral implications* (pp. 263–294). New York: Academic Press.

Rovee-Collier, C. (1997). Dissociations in infant memory: rethinking the development of explicit and implicit memory. *Psychology Review, 104,* 467–498.

Royer, S. R. (1991). *Sarah R. Royer—A young Alzheimer's patient: My memory of her.* New York: Vantage.

Rubin, D. C. (1982). On the retention function for autobiographical memory. *Journal of Verbal Learning and Verbal Behavior, 21,* 21–38.

Rubin, D. C. (1996a). Introduction. In D. C. Rubin (Ed.), *Remembering our past* (pp. 1–15). New York: Cambridge University Press.

Rubin, D. C. (1996b). *Remembering our past.* New York: Cambridge University Press.

Rubin, D. C., & Wenzel, A. E. (1996). One hundred years of forgetting: A quantitative description of retention. *Psychological Review, 103,* 734–760.

Rubin, D. C., Wetzler, S. E., & Nebes, R. D. (1986). Autobiographical memory across the adult lifespan. In D. C. Rubin (Ed.), *Autobiographical memory* (pp. 202–221). New York: Cambridge University Press.

Rugg, M. D. (1995). Event-related potential studies of human memory. In M. S. Gazzaniga (Ed.), *The cognitive neurosciences* (pp. 789–801). Cambridge, MA: MIT Press.

Rumelhart, D. E., & McClelland, J. L. (1987). Learning the past tenses of English verbs: Implicit rules or parallel distributed processing? In B. MacWhinney (Ed.), *Mechanisms of language acquisition* (pp. 195–248). Hillsdale, NJ: Erlbaum.

Rumelhart, D. E., & Ortony, A. (1977). The representation of knowledge in memory. In R. Anderson, R. Spiro, & W. Montague (Eds.), *Schooling and the acquisition of knowledge* (pp. 99–135). Hillsdale, NJ: Erlbaum.

Rumelhart, D. E., & Todd, P. M. (1993). Learning and connectionist representations. In D. E. Meyer & S. Kornblum (Eds.), *Attention and performance XIV: Synergies in experimental psychology, artificial intelligence, and cognitive neuroscience* (pp. 3–30). Cambridge, MA: MIT Press.

Rundus, D. (1971). Analysis of rehearsal processes in free recall. *Journal of Experimental Psychology, 89,* 63–77.

Russo, R., & Parkin, A. J. (1993). Age differences in implicit memory: More apparent than real. *Memory & Cognition, 21,* 73–80.

Rusted, J., Ratner, H., & Sheppard, L. (1995). When all else fails, we can still make tea: A longitudinal look at activities of daily living in an Alzheimer patient. In R. Campbell & M. A. Conway (Eds.), *Broken memories: Case studies in memory impairment* (pp. 397–410). Cambridge, MA: Blackwell.

Rymer, R. (1993). *Genie: A scientific tragedy.* New York: Harper Collins.

Sachs, J. S. (1967). Recognition memory for syntactic and semantic aspects of connected discourse. *Perception & Psychophysics, 2,* 437–442.

Sagar, H. J., Cohen, N. J., Sullivan, E. V., Corkin, S., & Growdon, J. H. (1988). Remote memory function in Alzheimer's disease and Parkinson's disease. *Brain, 111,* 185–206.

Salthouse, T. A. (1980). Age and memory: Strategies for localizing the loss. In L. W. Poon, J. L. Fozard, L. S. Cermak, D. Arenberg, & L. W. Thompson (Eds.), *New directions in memory and aging: Proceedings of the George A. Talland Memorial Conference* (pp. 47–65). Hillsdale, NJ: Erlbaum.

Salthouse, T. A. (1984). Effects of age and skill in typing. *Journal of Experimental Psychology: General, 113,* 345–371.

Salthouse, T. A., & Babcock, R. L. (1991). Decomposing adult age differences in working memory. *Developmental Psychology, 27,* 763–776.

Sapolsky, R. (1994). *Why zebras don't get ulcers: A guide to stress, stress related distress, and coping.* New York: Freeman.

Sapolsky, R. M. (1996). Why stress is bad for your brain. *Science, 273,* 749–750.

Schacter, D. L. (1992). Understanding implicit memory: A cognitive neuroscience approach. *American Psychologist, 47,* 359–369.

Schacter, D. L. (1994). Priming and multiple memory systems: Perceptual mechanisms of implicit memory. In D. L. Schacter & E. Tulving (Eds.), *Memory systems 1994* (pp. 233–269). Cambridge, MA: MIT Press.

Schacter, D. L. (1995). *Memory distortions.* Cambridge, MA: Harvard University Press.

Schacter, D. L. (1996). *Searching for memory.* New York: Basic Books.

Schacter, D. L., Alpert, N. M., Savage, C. R., Rauch, S. L., & Albert, M. S. (1996). Conscious recollection and the human hippocampal formation: Evidence for positron emission tomography. *Proceedings of the National Academy of Sciences (USA), 93,* 321–325.

Schacter, D. L., Chiu, C., & Ochsner, K. N. (1993). Implicit memory: A selective review. *Annual Review of Neuroscience, 16,* 159–182.

Schacter, D. L., Glisky, E. L., & McGlynn, S. M. (1990). Impact of memory disorder on everyday life: Awareness of deficits and return to work. In D. E. Tupper & K. D. Cicerone (Eds.), *The neuropsychology of everyday life: Assessment and basic competencies* (pp. 231–257). Boston: Kluwer Academic.

Schacter, D. L., & Tulving, E. (1982). Amnesia and memory research. In L. S. Cermak (Ed.), *Human memory and amnesia* (pp. 1–32). Hillsdale, NJ: Erlbaum.

Schacter, D. L., & Tulving, E. (1994a). What are the memory systems of 1994? In D. L. Schacter (Ed.), *Memory distortions* (pp. 1–38). Cambridge, MA: Harvard University Press.

Schacter, D. L., & Tulving, E. (1994b). *Memory systems 1994.* Cambridge, MA: MIT Press.

Schank, R. C. (1973). Identification of conceptualizations underlying natural language. In R. C. Schank & K. M. Colby (Eds.), *Computer models of thought and language* (pp. 187–247). San Francisco: Freeman.

Schank, R. C. (1976). The structure of episodes in memory. In D. G. Bobrow & A. Collins (Eds.), *Representation and understanding: Studies in cognitive science* (pp. 237–272). New York: Academic Press.

Schank, R. C. (1982). *Dynamic memory.* New York: Cambridge University Press.

Schank, R. C., & Abelson, R. P. (1977). *Scripts, plans, goals, and understanding.* Hillsdale, NJ: Erlbaum.

Schmajuk, N. A., & DiCarlo, J. J. (1992). Stimulus configuration, classical conditioning, and hippocampal function. *Psychological Review, 99,* 268–305.

Schmidt, R. A., & Bjork, R. A. (1992). New conceptualizations of practice: Common principles in three paradigms suggest new concepts for training. *Psychological Science, 3,* 207–217.

Schnider, A., Regard, M., & Landis, T. (1994). Anterograde and retrograde amnesia following bitemporal infarction. *Behavioral Neurology, 7,* 87–92.

Schooler, J. W., & Engstler-Schooler, T. Y. (1990). Verbal overshadowing of visual memories: Some things are better left unsaid. *Cognitive Psychology, 22,* 36–71.

Schooler, J. W., Ryan, R. S., & Reder, L. (1996). The costs and benefits of verbally rehearsing memory for faces. In D. J. Herrman, C. McEvoy, C. Hertzog, P. Hertel, & M. K. Johnson (Eds.), *Basic and applied memory research: Practical applications* (Vol. 2, pp. 51–66). Mahwah, NJ: Erlbaum.

Schwartz, B., & Reisberg, D. (1991). *Learning and memory.* New York: Norton.

Searlemann, A., & Herrmann, D. (1994). *Memory from a broader perspective.* New York: McGraw-Hill.

Seger, C. A. (1994). Implicit learning. *Psychological Bulletin, 115,* 163–196.

Seidenberg, M. (1992). Connectionism without tears. In S. Davis (Ed.), *Connectionism: Theory and practice* (pp. 84–137). New York: Oxford University Press.

Sejnowski, T. J., & Churchland, P. S. (1989). Brain and cognition. In M. I. Posner (Ed.), *Foundations of cognitive science* (pp. 301–356). Cambridge, MA: MIT Press.

Sejnowski, T. J., & Rosenberg, C. R. (1986). *NETtalk: A parallel network that learns to read aloud* (Report No. JHU/EECS-86/01). Baltimore, MD: Johns Hopkins University.

Selkoe, D. J. (1991). Amyloid protein and Alzheimer's disease. *Scientific American, 265,* 68–78.

Semon, R. (1921). *The mneme.* New York: Macmillan.

Servan-Schreiber, E., & Anderson, J. R. (1990). Learning artificial grammars with competitive chunking. *Journal of Experimental Psychology: Learning, Memory, and Cognition, 16,* 592–608.

Shadmehr, R., & Holcomb, H. H. (1997). Neural correlates of motor memory consolidation. *Science, 277,* 821–825.

Shallice, T., & Warrington, E. K. (1970). Independent functioning of verbal memory stores: A neuropsychological study. *Quarterly Journal of Experimental Psychology, 22,* 261–273.

Shaw, J. S., Bjork, R. A., & Handal, A. (1995). Retrieval-induced forgetting in an eyewitness-memory paradigm. *Psychonomic Bulletin and Review, 2,* 249–253.

Shiffrin, R. M. (1993). Short-term memory: A brief commentary. *Memory & Cognition, 21,* 193–197.

Shimamura, A. (1986). Priming effects in amnesia: Evidence for a dissociable memory function. *Quarterly Journal of Experimental Psychology, 38A,* 619–644.

Shimamura, A. P. (1995). Memory and frontal lobe function. In M. S. Gazzaniga (Ed.), *The cognitive neurosciences* (pp. 803–813). Cambridge, MA: MIT Press.

Shimamura, A. P., Berry, J. M., Mangles, J. A., Rusting, C. L., & Jurica, P. J. (1995). Memory and cognitive abilities in university professors: Evidence for successful aging. *Psychological Science, 6,* 271–277.

Shoben, E. J., Westcourt, K. T., & Smith, E. E. (1978). Sentence verification, sentence recognition, and the semantic-episodic distinction. *Journal of Experimental Psychology: Human Learning and Memory, 4,* 304–317.

Shors, T. J., & Matzel, L. D. (in press). Long-term potentiation: What's learning got to do with it? *Behavioral and Brain Sciences.*

Shulman, H. G. (1972). Semantic confusion errors in short-term memory. *Journal of Verbal Learning and Verbal Behavior, 11,* 221–227.

Siegel, S., & Allan, L. G. (1996). The widespread influence of the Rescorla-Wagner model. *Psychonomic Bulletin & Review, 3,* 314–321.

Siegler, R. (1991). *Children's thinking.* Englewood Cliffs, NJ: Prentice-Hall.

Siegler, R. (1996). *Emerging minds: The process of change in children's thinking.* New York: Oxford University Press.

Simon, E. (1979). Depth and elaboration of processing in relation to age. *Journal of Experimental Psychology: Human Learning and Memory, 5,* 115–124.

Simon, H. A. (1974). How big is a chunk? *Science, 183,* 482–488.

Simon, H. A. (1975). The functional equivalence of problem solving skills. *Cognitive Psychology, 7,* 268–288.

Siqueland, E. R., & Lipsitt, L. P. (1966). Conditioned head turning in human newborns. *Journal of Experimental Child Psychology, 3,* 356–376.

Slamecka, N. J. (1985). Ebbinghaus: Some associations. *Journal of Experimental Psychology: Learning, Memory, and Cognition, 11,* 414–435.

Slamecka, N. J., & Graf, P. (1978). The generation effect: Delineation of a phenomenon. *Journal of Experimental Psychology: Human Learning and Memory, 4,* 592–604.

Sloman, S. A., Hayman, C. A., Ohta, N., Law, J., & Tulving, E. (1988). Forgetting in primed fragment completion. *Journal of Experimental Psychology: Learning, Memory, and Cognition, 14,* 223–239.

Smith, E. E. (1988). Concepts and thought. In R. J. Sternberg & E. E. Smith (Eds.), *The psychology of human thought* (pp. 19–49). Cambridge, UK: Cambridge University Press.

Smith, E. E., & Jonides, J. (1997). Working memory: A view from neuroimaging. *Cognitive Psychology, 33,* 5–42.

Smith, E. E., & Medin, D. L. (1981). *Categories and concepts.* Cambridge, MA: Harvard University Press.

Smyth, M. M., & Pendelton, L. R. (1989). Working memory for movements. *Quarterly Journal of Experimental Psychology, 41A,* 235–250.

Smyth, M. M., & Scholey, K. A. (1994). Interference in immediate spatial memory. *Memory & Cognition, 22,* 1–13.

Sperling, G. (1960). The information available in brief visual presentations. *Psychological Monographs, 74,* (No. 11).

Spilich, G. J. (1983). Life-span components of text processing: Structural and procedural differences. *Journal of Verbal Learning and Verbal Behavior, 22,* 231–244.

Spinnler, H., Della Salla, S., Bandera, R., & Baddeley, A. D. (1988). Dementia, aging and the structure of human memory. *Cognitive Neuropsychology, 5,* 193–211.

Squire, L. R. (1987). *Memory and brain.* New York: Oxford University Press.

Squire, L. R. (1993). Neuroanatomy of memory. *Annual Review of Neuroscience, 16,* 547–563.

Squire, L. R. (1994). Declarative and nondeclarative memory: Multiple brain systems supporting learning and memory. In D. L. Schacter & E. Tulving (Eds.), *Memory systems 1994* (pp. 203–231). Cambridge, MA: MIT Press.

Squire, L. R. (1995). Biological foundations of accuracy and inaccuracy of memory. In D. L. Schacter (Ed.), *Memory distortions* (pp. 197–225). Cambridge, MA: Harvard University Press.

Squire, L. R., & Knowlton, B. J. (1995). Memory, hippocampus, and brain systems. In M. S. Gazzaniga (Ed.), *The cognitive neurosciences* (pp. 825–837). Cambridge, MA: MIT Press.

Squire, L. R., Zola-Morgan, S., Cave, C. B., Haist, F., Musen, G., & Suzuki, W. A. (1993). Memory: Organization of brain systems and cognition. In D. E. Meyer & S. Kornblum (Eds.), *Attention and performance XIV* (pp. 393–423). Cambridge, MA: MIT Press.

Srivinas, K. (1993). Perceptual specificity in nonverbal priming. *Journal of Experimental Psychology: Learning, Memory, and Cognition, 19,* 582–602.

Stern, Y., Gurlan, B., Tatemichi, T. K., Tang, M. X., Wilder, D., & Mayeux, R. (1994). Influence of education and occupation on the incidence of Alzheimer's disease. *JAMA, 271,* 1004–1010.

Sternberg, S. (1966). High speed scanning in human memory. *Science, 153,* 652–654.

Stevens, C. F. (1996). Spatial learning and memory: The beginning of a dream. *Cell, 87,* 1147–1148.

Stoltzfus, E. R., Hasher, L., & Zacks, R. T. (1996). Working memory and aging: Current status of the inhibitory view. In J. T. E. Richardson, R. W. Engle, L. Hasher, R. H. Logie, E. R. Stoltzfus, & R. T. Zacks (Eds.), *Working memory and human cognition* (pp. 66–88). New York: Oxford University Press.

Stuss, D., & Gow, C. (1992). "Frontal dysfunction" after traumatic brain injury. *Neuropsychiatry, Neuropsychology, and Behavioral Neurology, 5,* 272–282.

Sullivan, E. V., Marsh, L., & Pfefferbaum, A. (1995). Age-related decline in MRI volumes of temporal lobe gray matter but not hippocampus. *Neurobiology of Aging, 16,* 591–606.

Swain, R. A., Armstrong, K. E., Comery, T. A., Humphreys, A. G., Jones, T. A., Kleim, J. A., & Greenough, W. T. (1995). Speculations on the fidelity of memories stored in synaptic connections. In D. L. Schacter (Ed.), *Memory distortions* (pp. 274–297). Cambridge, MA: Harvard University Press.

Swets, J. A., Tanner, W. P., & Birdsall, T. G. (1961). Decision processes in perception. *Psychological Review, 68,* 301–340.

Terr, L. (1991). Childhood traumas: An outline and overview. *American Journal of Psychiatry, 148,* 10–20.

Terrace, H. S. (1964). Wavelength generalization after discrimination learning with and without errors. *Science, 144,* 78–80.

Thapar, A., & Greene, R. (1993). Evidence against a short-term store account of long-term recency effect. *Memory & Cognition, 21,* 329–337.

Thibadeau, R., Just, M. A., & Carpenter, P. A. (1982). A model of the time course and content of reading. *Cognitive Science, 6,* 101–155.

Thieman, T. J., & Brewer, W. F. (1978). *Genetic Psychology Monographs, 97,* 243–264.

Thompson, C. P., Cowan, T. M., & Frieman, J. (1993). *Memory search by a memorist.* Hillsdale, NJ: Erlbaum.

Thompson, R. F. (1989). *Learning and memory.* Boston, MA: Birkhaeuser.

Thorndike, E. L. (1911). *Animal intelligence.* New York: MacMillan.

Thorndike, E. L., & Woodworth, R. S. (1901). The influence of improvement in one mental function upon the efficiency of other functions. *Psychological Review, 9,* 374–382.

Tippett, L. J., & Farah, M. J. (1994). A computational model of naming in Alzheimer's disease: Unitary or multiple impairments. *Neuropsychology, 8,* 3–13.

Toppino, T. C., & Gracen, T. F. (1985). The lag effect and differential organization theory: Nine failures to replicate. *Journal of Experimental Psychology: Learning, Memory, and Cognition, 11,* 185–191.

Tranel, D., & Damasio, A. R. (1995). Neurobiological foundations of human memory. In A. D. Baddeley, B. A. Wilson, & F. N. Watts (Eds.), *Handbook of memory disorders* (pp. 27–50). New York: Wiley.

Treat, N. J., & Reese, H. W. (1976). Age, pacing, and imagery in paired-associate learning. *Developmental Psychology, 12,* 119–124.

Tsien, J. Z., Huerta, P. T., & Tonegawa, S. (1996). The essential role of hippocampal CA1 NMDA receptor-dependent synaptic plasticity in spatial memory. *Cell, 87,* 1327–1338.

Tulving, E. (1972). Episodic and semantic memory. In E. Tulving & W. Donaldson (Eds.), *Organization of memory* (pp. 382–403). New York: Academic Press.

Tulving, E. (1974). Cue-dependent forgetting. *American Scientist, 62,* 74–82.

Tulving, E. (1979). Memory research: What kind of progress? In L. G. Nillson (Ed.), *Perspectives on memory research* (pp. 19–34). Hillsdale, NJ: Erlbaum.

Tulving, E. (1983). *Elements of episodic memory.* New York: Oxford University Press.

Tulving, E. (1985). How many memory systems are there? *American Psychologist, 40,* 385–398.

Tulving, E. (1989). Remembering and knowing the past. *American Scientist, 77,* 361–367.

Tulving, E. (1991). Memory research is not a zero-sum game. *American Psychologist, 46,* 41–42.

Tulving, E. (1993). What is episodic memory? *Current Directions in Psychological Science, 2,* 67–70.

Tulving, E. (1995). Organization of memory: Quo vadis? In M. S. Gazzaniga (Ed.), *The cognitive neurosciences* (pp. 839–847). Cambridge, MA: MIT Press.

Tulving, E., & Arbuckle, T. Y. (1963). Sources of intra-trial interference in paired-associate learning. *Journal of Verbal Learning and Verbal Behavior, 1,* 321–334.

Tulving, E., & Hastie, R. (1972). Inhibition effects of intralist repetition in free recall. *Journal of Experimental Psychology, 92,* 297–304.

Tulving, E., Hayman, C. A., & MacDonald, C. A. (1991). Long-lasting perceptual priming and semantic learning in amnesia: A case experiment. *Journal of Experimental Psychology: Learning, Memory, and Cognition, 17,* 595–617.

Tulving, E., & Psotka, J. (1971). Retroactive inhibition in free recall: Inaccessibility of information available in the memory store. *Journal of Experimental Psychology, 87,* 1–8.

Tulving, E., & Schacter, D. L. (1990). Priming and human memory systems. *Science, 247,* 301–306.

Tulving, E., & Thomson, D. M. (1973). Encoding specificity and retrieval processes in episodic memory. *Psychological Review, 80,* 352–373.

Tulving, E., & Watkins, M. J. (1973). Continuity between recall and recognition. *American Journal of Psychology, 86,* 739–748.

Turner, A. M., & Greenough, W. T. (1985). Differential rearing effects on rat visual cortex synapses. *Brain Research, 329,* 195–203.

Underwood, B. J. (1972). Are we overloading memory? In A. W. Melton & E. Martin (Eds.), *Coding processes in memory* (pp. 1–23). New York: Wiley.

Underwood, B. J. (1983). *Attributes of memory.* Glenview, IL: Scott, Foresman.

Ungerleider, L. G. (1995). Functional brain imaging studies of cortical mechanisms for memory. *Science, 270,* 769–775.

Usher, J. A., & Neisser, U. (1993). Childhood amnesia and the beginnings of memory for four early life events. *Journal of Experimental Psychology: General, 122,* 155–165.

Vallar, G., & Papagano, C. (1995). Neuropsychological impairments of short-term memory. In A. D. Baddeley, B. A. Wilson, & F. N. Watts (Eds.), *Handbook of memory disorders* (pp. 135–165). New York: Wiley.

van den Broek, P. (1990). Causal inferences and the comprehension of narrative texts. In A. C. Graesser & G. H. Bower (Eds.), *The psychology of learning and motivation: Inferences and text comprehension* (Vol. 25, pp. 175–196). San Diego, CA: Academic Press.

VanLehn, K. (1990). *Mind bugs: The origins of procedural misconceptions.* Cambridge, MA: MIT Press.

VanLehn, K. (1996). Cognitive skill acquisition. *Annual Review of Psychology, 47,* 513–539.

Vargha-Khadem, F., Gadian, D. G., Watkins, K. E., Connelly, A., Van Paesschen, W., & Mishkin, M. (1997). Differential effects of early hippocampal pathology on episodic and semantic memory. *Science, 277,* 376–380.

Vokey, J. R., & Brooks, L. R. (1992). Salience of item knowledge in learning artificial grammars. *Journal of Experimental Psychology: Learning, Memory, and Cognition, 18,* 328–344.

von Restorff, H. (1933). Über die wirkung von bereichsbildungen im spurenfeld. *Psychologische Forschung, 18,* 299–342.

Wagenaar, W. A. (1986). My memory: A study of autobiographical memory over six years. *Cognitive Psychology, 18,* 225–252.

Wagenaar, W. A., & Groeneweg, J. (1990). The memory of concentration camp survivors. *Applied Cognitive Psychology, 4,* 77–87.

Warrington, E. K., & Shallice, T. (1969). The selective impairment of auditory verbal short-term memory. *Brain, 92,* 885–896.

Warrington, E. K., & Shallice, T. (1984). Category specific semantic impairments. *Brain, 107,* 829–854.

Warrington, E. K., & Weiskrantz, L. (1968). A new method of testing long-term retention with special reference to amnesic patients. *Nature, 217,* 972–974.

Warrington, E. K., & Weiskrantz, L. (1970). Amnesic syndrome: Consolidation or retrieval? *Nature, 228,* 629–630.

Warrington, E. K., & Weiskrantz, L. (1978). Further analysis of the prior learning effect in amnesic patients. *Neuropsychologia, 16,* 169–177.

Warrington, E. K., & Weiskrantz, L. (1982). Amnesia: A disconnection syndrome? *Neuropsychologia, 20,* 233–248.

Watkins, M. J. (1979). Engrams as cuegrams and forgetting as cue overload: A cueing approach to the structure of memory. In C. R. Puff (Ed.), *Memory organization and structure* (pp. 347–372). New York: Academic Press.

Waugh, N. C. (1970). Retrieval time in short-term memory. *British Journal of Psychology, 61,* 1–12.

Waugh, N. C., & Norman, D. A. (1965). Primary memory. *Psychological Review, 72,* 89–104.

Wechsler, D. (1987). *Wechsler Memory Scale—Revised [Manual].* New York: Psychological Corporation.

Weingartner, H. J., Hommer, D., Molchan, S., Raskin, A., Robinson, J. K., & Sunderland, T. (1996). Conceptual and practical issues in the development and assessment of drugs that would enhance cognition. In D. J. Herrman, C. McEvoy, C. Hertzog, P. Hertel, & M. K. Johnson (Eds.), *Basic and applied memory research: Practical applications* (Vol. 2, pp. 439–454). Mahwah, NJ: Erlbaum.

Wells, G. L. (1993). What do we know about eyewitness identification? *American Psychologist, 48,* 553–571.

Wertheimer, M. (1986). The annals of the house that Ebbinghaus built. In F. Klix & H. Hagendorf (Eds.), *Human memory and cognitive capabilities: Mechanisms and performances* (Vol. A, pp. 35–44). Amsterdam: North-Holland.

Whipple, G. M. (1909). The observer as reporter: A survey of the "psychology of testimony." *Psychological Bulletin, 6,* 153–170.

Whitten, W., & Leonard, J. (1981). Directed search through autobiographical memory. *Memory & Cognition, 9,* 566–579.

Wickelgren, W. A. (1973). The long and short of memory. *Psychological Bulletin, 80,* 425–438.

Wideman, J. E. (1984). *Brothers and keepers.* New York: Vintage.

Wilding, J., & Valentine, E. (1996). Memory expertise. In D. J. Herrman, C. McEvoy, C. Hertzog, P. Hertel, & M. K. Johnson (Eds.), *Basic and applied memory research: Practical applications* (Vol. 1, pp. 399–420). Mahwah, NJ: Erlbaum.

Williams, D. M., & Hollan, J. D. (1981). The process of retrieval from very long-term memory. *Cognitive Science, 5,* 87–119.

Williams, L. M. (1994). Recall of childhood trauma: A prospective study of women's memories of childhood abuse. *Journal of Consulting and Clinical Psychology, 62,* 1167–1176.

Wilson, B. A. (1996). Management and rehabilitation of memory problems. In D. J. Herrman, C. McEvoy, C. Hertzog, P. Hertel, & M. K. Johnson (Eds.), *Basic and applied memory research: Practical applications* (Vol. 1, pp. 277–293). Mahwah, NJ: Erlbaum.

Wilson, B. A., & Wearing, D. (1995). Prisoner of consciousness: A state of just awakening following herpes simplex encephalitis. In R. Campbell & M. A. Conway (Eds.), *Broken memories: Case studies in memory impairment* (pp. 14–30). Cambridge, MA: Blackwell.

Wilson, F. A. W., O'Scalaidhe, S. P., & Goldman-Rakic, P. S. (1993). Dissociation of object and spatial processing domains in primate prefrontal cortex. *Science, 260,* 1955–1957.

Wilson, T. D., & Brekke, N. (1994). Mental contamination and mental correction: Unwanted influences on judgments and evaluations. *Psychological Bulletin, 116,* 117–142.

Wittgenstein, L. (1953). *Philosophical investigations.* New York: Academic Press.

Wixted, J. T., & Ebbesen, E. B. (1991). On the form of forgetting. *Psychological Science, 2,* 409–415.

Wixted, J. T., & Ebbeson, E. B. (1997). Genuine power curves in forgetting: A quantitative analysis of individual subject forgetting functions. *Memory & Cognition, 25,* 731–739.

Wixted, J. T., Ghadisha, H., & Vera, R. (1997). Recall latency following pure- and mixed-strength lists: A direct test of the relative strength model of free recall. *Journal of Experimental Psychology: Learning, Memory, and Cognition, 23,* 523–538.

Woodruf-Pak, D. S., & Li, Y. T. (1994). Nefiracetam (DM-9384): Effect on eyeblink classical conditioning in older rabbits. *Psychopharmacology, 114,* 200–208.

Wyer, R. S., & Srull, T. K. (1989). *Memory in its social context.* Hillsdale, NJ: Erlbaum.

Yates, F. A. (1966). *The art of memory.* Chicago: University of Chicago Press.

Yehuda, R., et al. (1995). Low urinary cortisol excretion in holocaust survivors with post-traumatic stress disorder. *American Journal of Psychiatry, 152,* 982–986.

Yuille, J. C., & Tollestrup, P. A. (1992). A model of diverse effects of emotion on eyewitness memory. In S. A. Christianson (Ed.), *The handbook of emotion and memory: Research and theory* (pp. 201–215). Hillsdale, NJ: Erlbaum.

Zacks, R. T., Radvansky, G. A., & Hasher, L. (1996). Studies of directed forgetting in older adults. *Journal of Experimental Psychology: Human Learning and Memory, 22,* 143–156.

Zajonc, R. B. (1980). Feeling and thinking: Preferences need no inferences. *American Psychologist, 35,* 151–175.

Zangwill, O. L. (1937). An investigation of the relation between the processes of reproducing and recognizing simple figures, with special reference to Koffka's trace theory. *British Journal of Psychology, 27,* 250–276.

Zangwill, O. L. (1972). Remembering revisited. *Quarterly Journal of Experimental Psychology, 24,* 123–138.

Zaragoza, M., & Lane, S. (1994). Source misattributions and the suggestibility of eyewitness memory. *Journal of Experimental Psychology: Learning, Memory, and Cognition, 20,* 934–945.

Zeller, A. F. (1950). An experimental analogue of repression: I. Historical summary. *Psychological Bulletin, 47,* 39–51.

Zwaan, R. A. (1994). Effects of generic expectations on text comprehension. *Journal of Experimental Psychology: Learning, Memory, and Cognition, 20,* 920–933.

A

Abstract ideas, learning, 113–114
Abuse, memories of, 238–246
Acetylcholine (ACh), 54
Acoustic-code hypothesis, 131
Acquisition phase of learning, 37–38
ACT model, 117, 149, 153, 178–187
    memory and rational analysis, 182–183
    research applications, 183–186
Activation levels in neural network, 167–171
Activation rule, 169
Adaptive strategy choice model (ASCM), 195–196
Aging and memory, 204–216
    memory for facts, 206–210
    memory for skills, 210–216
Agnosias, definition of, 33, 261
Aitken, A. C., 121
Alzheimer's disease, 51, 100, 229–230, 266–274
Amnesia, 229–230, 251–261
    case studies, 251–254
    childhood, 190–191
    performance patterns, 254–257
    and priming effects, 108–109
    taxonomy of, 31–33
Amnesic patients learning artificial grammar,
    112–113
Animal learning research, 35–38
Anterograde amnesia, 254, 255
Articulation length, 144, 146
Artificial grammars, 111–113
Association (Ebbinghaus), 22–24
Associative stage of skill acquisition, 118
Asymmetry in use of skills, 184–185
Atkinson and Shiffrin's model of memory,
    132–134
Attention and memory, 12–13
Attention control model, 149
Attentional effects hypothesis, 75
Attributes of memory, 3–4
Autobiographical memory, 220–230
    and Alzheimer's disease, 269
    definition of, 197
    as narrative, 226–229
    organization of, 224–226
Autonomous stage of skill acquisition, 118

B

Backpropagation learning, 173, 175–177
Bartlett, Sir Frederic, 4, 27–30
Bias in line-ups, 323–324
Binet, Alfred, 24–26
Brain activity revealed by PET scan, 140, 142
Brain anatomy, 41, 42
Brain and memory, 41–68
    frontal lobes, 65–68
    hippocampus, 62–65
    location of memories, 58–62
    neuroscience research, 43–52
    plasticity in the brain, 52–58
Brain scanning, 8
Brain structures and memory systems, 283–286
Brain-imaging methods, 43–47
Broca, Paul, 30–31, 50, 59–60
Brown-Peterson distractor task, 127, 129

C

Case studies, 50–52, 99–101, 103, 131–132, 227,
    230, 251–254, 264–265, 328
Category learning in infants, 192
Category size effect, 90–91
Causal chains, 97
Causal relations and propositions, 95–97
Cell activity, recording, 49–50
Central executive, 142, 149–154
Cerebral blood flow, 43–45
Chess masters and memory, 124
Childhood amnesia, 190–191
Childhood memory development, 190–204
    clinical views of, 240–241
    memory for facts, 197–202
    memory for skills, 194–196
    working memory, 202–204
Chunking, 20, 123, 128
    letters, 113
    numbers, 122
Classical conditioning (Pavlov), 36
    in *Aplysia,* 57
    definition of, 56
Cognitive functions, 12–15
Cognitive inhibition, development of in children,
    203–204

Cognitive resource, definition of, 190
Cognitive skills:
    of children, 195–196
    learning and remembering, 115–125
    production rules, 117
    skill acquisition, 117–120
    supermemory, 120–125
Cognitive slowing hypothesis, 213–214
Cognitive speedup, 203
Cognitive stage of skill acquisition, 118
Computation span, definition of, 213
Computed tomography (CT) scans, 43
Computer programming, 185
    as a skill, 116
Concealed memories, detection of, 48–49
Concentration camp survivors, memories of, 233
Concrete-operational period of childhood skill
    development, 195
Concurrent task paradigm, 150–151
Conditioning (Pavlov), 36
Conflicting demands, 151
Confusing real and imagined events, 319
Conjugate reinforcement paradigm and childhood
    memory, 192–193
Consciousness:
    amnesia, 249, 252, 259
    attention, 12
    dissociation, 259
    Ebbinghaus, H., 3, 18, 275
    event-related potentials, 48
    Freud, S., 33, 128
    implicit learning, 111–113
    implicit memory, 103–104
    James, W., 3, 128
    memory systems, 31, 277–279
    physiological correlate, 48
    repression, 230–231, 240
    working memory, 128
Consolidation hypothesis, 75
    and amnesia, 259
Consolidation of memories, 62–63
Construction and schema, 28–29
Constructive memory, 99
Constructivism (Bartlett), 27–30
Content knowledge, definition of, 189
Context memory deficit hypothesis of
    amnesia, 260
Continued practice of a skill, 118

Continuous paired-associate task, 74
Convergence of evidence, definition of, 49
Convergence zones linking different modalities of
    items, 263
Converging dissociations, definition of, 283
Conversion hysteria, definition of, 33–34
Coping with memory impairment, 325–332
Core amnesia, definition of, 257
Correspondence metaphor of memory, 299–301
Cross-category interference, 89
Cross-modality priming, 107, 111
Cue overload, 81
Cues:
    and autobiographical memories, 222–224
    distinctiveness of, 307–308
    for retrieval, 82–83

D

d' measure, 70
Decay theory (forgetting), 81, 129, 130
Declarative knowledge, 181–182
Declarative memory, 3, 179
    definition of, 62
    and nondeclarative memory, anatomical base
        of, 284–285
Deep encoding condition, 67
Deficits in organizing and manipulating
    information, 266
Delta learning, 173–174
Depth of processing approach, 75, 77
Developmental changes in memory, 189–217
    childhood, 190–204
    older adulthood, 204–216
Diary writing and memory study, 221–222
Digit span (Ebbinghaus), 19, 144, 146
Digit span test, 123–124, 128
Diseases of memory, 32, 249–274
Dissociation, 35
    in amnesic patients, 282
    between episodic and semantic memory, 100
    between explicit and implicit memory, 105
    definition of, 288
    and memory, 89
    in performance, 32
Distinctiveness of cues and memory improvement,
    307–308
Distinctiveness hypothesis, 77
Distortions of memory, 4

Distraction, definition of, 152
Distractor items, 6
Distractor paradigm, 127
Distractor strength of words, 161
Distributed memories, 32, 59, 167–169
Distributed practice (Ebbinghaus), 20
    benefits of, 312
    of a skill, 118–119
Distributed representations, 167–169
    and retrieval of two patterns from one network,
        171–172
Disuse theory (forgetting), 79
Dot-location task, 144
Dysexecutive syndrome, 151–152
    definition of, 66

E

Ebbinghaus, Hermann, 3, 4, 18–24
Ecological validity, definition of, 294
Ecphory, definition of, 26
Educational setting and memory, 310–317
Elaborative rehearsal, 135
Elaborative talk, definition of, 201
Elderly, memory in, 189, 204–216
    memory for facts, 206–210
    memory for skills, 210–216
Electroencephalogram (EEG), 47
Electronic memory aids, 327–328
Emotion and memory laboratory studies, 233–235
Emotional events, remembering, 230–238
Encoding:
    definition of, 2
    hypothesis of amnesia, 258–259
    and older adults, 206–208
    and problems with eyewitness testimony,
        319–320
    processes of children, 200–201
    and retrieval environments, 84–85
Encoding specificity principle, 5, 84, 165
    and cognitive interview, 324
    and improving memory, 308–309
Encoding variability hypothesis, 75
Engram, 38
    definition of, 26
Engraphy, definition of, 26
Environmental conditions and recall, 84
Episode schema, 97
Episodic memory, 69, 70–89

acquiring facts, 71–78
and Alzheimer's disease, 267
of children, 200–202
definition of, 6, 197, 277, 280
forgetting, theories of, 78–82
of older adults, 206–209
retrieval of information, 82–89
vs. semantic memory, 280, 287
Error monitoring hypothesis of amnesia, 260–261
Errors in immediate recall, 25
Event memory:
    in children, 200–201
    in preverbal infants, 191–194
Event-based prospective memory, 330–331
Event-related potentials (ERPs), 47–49
    patterns and priming, 110
Executive attention network, 149, 152
Executive control, impairments of, 265–266
Executive function, 66–67
Exemplar hypothesis, 113
Exemplar models, 93–94
Experiences:
    and memory, 18, 29
    and performance, 107
Experts in memory, 120–123
Explicit memory, 3
    definition of, 22
    and implicit memory, 217, 286–287
External bias, definition of, 323
Extinction phase of learning, 37–38
Eyewitness testimony, 82, 232–233, 317–325

F

Facts:
    acquiring, 71–78
    memory for, 69–101, 179
    memory for episodes, 70–89
    memory for forgetting, theories of, 78–82
    memory for semantics, 90–101
    retrieving from semantic networks, 90–91
False alarm, 6, 70, 160–161, 323
False memories, 238–246, 319–320
False Memory Syndrome Foundation, 240
False-frame effect, 106–107, 321
Familiarity check in recognition tests, 164
Familiarity value of words, 160
Fan effect, 183–184, 290
Fictitious memories, 243

First-time memories, 224–225
Flashbulb memories, 231–232
    definition of, 219
Flourens, Pierre, 59
Forgetfulness, 31, 35, 129–130, 304–310
    and priming, 107–108
    rate of, 5
    theories of, 78–82
Forgetting curve (Ebbinghaus), 19
Formal-operational period of childhood skill
        development, 195
Forming an integrated memory trace, 259–260
Free recall:
    Alzheimer's patients, 268–269
    compared to recognition, 6, 166, 297–298, 301
    paradigm, 5, 6
    retrieval in recall, 164–165
    two-store model of memory, 129–130
Free recall test, 24
Frequency of exposure effect, 106
Freud, Sigmund, 31, 33–35
Frisch, Gustav, 60
Frontal lobe syndrome, 151–152, 265–266
Frontal lobes, 65–68, 144, 149, 330
Functional magnetic resonance imaging (fMRI),
        46–47
Functional map of the brain, 60

G

Gall, Franz, 59
Generalizability, definition of, 294
Generalizability of results, definition of, 304
Generalization, definition of, 5
Generation effect, 76
Glucocorticoid cascade hypothesis, 237–238
Glucocorticoids, 55

H

Habitual responses, suppressing, 67
Habituation:
    in *Aplysia,* 57
    definition of, 56
    in infants, 191–192
HAM model, 149
Hebbian learning, 173
Hemispheric encoding retrieval asymmetry
        (HERA), 67

High-arousal words, 230
Hippocampus, 62–65, 131, 259, 278–280
Hit response, definition of, 70
Hitzig, Eduard, 60
Hormone modulation, 237–238
Hughlings-Jackson, John, 31
Hypermnesia, 233–234
    definition of, 33, 79

I

Imitation paradigm and childhood memory,
        193–194
Immediate memory, definition of, 19
Impairments of memory (*see* Memory
        impairments)
Implanted-memory paradigm, 321–322
Implicit learning, 111–115
Implicit memory, 7, 103–115
    and Alzheimer's disease, 272–273
    of children, 194–195
    definition of, 22
    vs. explicit memory, 286–287
    memory for skills, 256
    of older adults, 210–211
    priming, 104–111
Implicit social cognition, 105
Importance effect in sentence and passage recall,
        25–26, 96–97
Improving retention, 20, 71–76, 77–78, 84–86,
        123–125, 306–309
Improving reading comprehension, 315
Infancy and childhood, memory in, 189,
        190–204
Infantile amnesia, 191, 197, 223, 240–241
Inferotemporal cortex, 61–62, 148
Inhibition-deficit hypothesis, 214–215
Inhibition and retrieval practice, 85–89
Inhibitory gating, theory of, 265
Instrumental conditioning (Thorndike),
        36–37
Interference:
    in memory, 129–130
    and neural networks, 176–177
    and priming, 108
Interference hypothesis of amnesia, 258
Interference theory (forgetting), 35, 79–82
Item cue, strength of, 161

J

James, William, 3, 4, 12–13, 128, 132

K

Knowledge and memory, 29, 89, 96–99, 124–125, 197–199, 210
Korsakoff's syndrome, 229

L

Lag effect, 73
Language comprehension:
    as a skill, 116
    and working memory, 136–138
Language rules, 174–175
Lashley, Karl, 38
Law of regression, and Alzheimer's patients, 269
Law-enforcement setting and memory, 317–325
Learning:
    definition of, 4
    implicit, 111–115
    and memory, 4
    in neural networks, 173–174
    rules, 111–113
    rules and exceptions in language, 174
    in the sea hare *Aplysia,* 56–58
Letter recall confusions, 131
Levels of processing, 75–78, 134, 206
Lexical decision task, 105
Lifetime periods, definition of, 224
Line-ups, bias in, 323–324
LISP computer language, 185–186
List-length effects (Ebbinghaus), 19–20, 24
Localization theory of memory, 59–60
Location in brain of memories, 58–62
LOGO language, 317
Long-term depression (LTD), 58
Long-term memory:
    definition of, 10–11
    encoding and retrieval, 67–68
Long-term potentiation (LTP), 56, 58, 64
Losing past memories, 254–255

M

Maintaining information in memory, 65
Maintenance rehearsal, 135
Mapping:
    motor centers in the brain, 60

and single-memory system, 286
Mathematical models, 159
Means-end strategy, 180–181
Memorizing lists of items, 69, 70
Memory *(see also specific types of memory)*
    ACT model, 178–187
    aids for patients, 326–328
    consolidation, 62–63
    decline in older adults, 204–216
    definition of, 4, 18, 275
    dimensions of, 276
    dissociations, 31–32
    distortions, 318–319
    drugs, 54–55, 274
    and experiences, 18
    and face cells in the inferotemporal cortex, 61–62
    for faces, 322
    for facts, deficits in, 267–270
    and the law, 317–325
    models of, 157–188
    neural network models, 166–178
    representations, 3
    SAM model, 159–166
    search, 138, 164–165
    for skills, 31, 120–125
    for skills, deficits in, 272–273
Memory illusion, 238–246, 319
Memory impairments, 249–274
    amnesia, 229–230, 251–261
    coping with, 325–332
    selective functions, 261–266
Memory organization packets, definition of, 246
Memory research, history of, 4–12, 17–39
    Bartlett, Sir Frederic, 27–30
    Binet, Alfred, 24–26
    Ebbinghaus, Hermann, 18–24
    Freud, Sigmund, 33–35
    Lashley, Karl, 38
    Pavlov, Ivan, 36–38
    Ribot, Theodule, 31–33
    Semon, Richard, 26–27
Memory retention and practice, 71–78
Memory skill theory, 125
Memory strength of words, 160, 161
Memory trace in the brain, 38
Memory wallet, 327

Memory wars, 238–246
Memory-enhancing drugs, 54–55
Mental activity in working memory, 135–142
    language comprehension, 136–138
    problem solving, 135–136
    searching, 138
    storage vs. computation, 136
    tracking mental work, 139–142
Mental and mood states of learners and recall, 84
Metamemory:
    and basic memory functions, 266
    definition of, 189–190, 200
    research, 216–217
Metaphors of memory, 2–3, 299–300
Minimizing errors in learning, 329–330
Mnemonic techniques for improving memory,
    304–306, 326–327
Modality effect of priming, 107
Mood congruency, definition of, 235
Mood and memory, 234–235
Motor sequencing, 151
Motor skill, tracking the learning of, 46
Multiple memory systems, 277–280
Multiple retrieval paths and cognitive interview,
    324–325
Multiple-components model of working memory,
    142–154
Musical performance, as a skill, 116–117, 121

N

NETtalk, 176
Network model of semantic memory, 263
Neural network models, 11–12, 166–178
    distributed memories, 167–169
    learning, 173–174
    retrieval, 169–173
    and retroactive interference, 176–177
Neural structure, size of, 55–56
Neuroimaging study, 8–9, 143–144, 146, 208
    on executive processes, 152
Neurons, 52–53
Neuroscience research methods, 43–52, 109,
    139–142
    event-related potentials, 47–49
    imaging methods, 43–47
Neurotransmitters and the formation of memories,
    53–54

New information:
    acquiring, 257
    problems in acquiring, 255
Nondeclarative memory, 3
    anatomical base of, 284–285
    definition of, 65
    implicit memory, 103–115
    multiple memory systems, 275–280
Nonsense syllables (Ebbinghaus), 18–24, 71
    features of, 23
Nootropics, 54–55
Now print mechanism, 219

O

Observer bias, definition of, 323
Old/new effect in recognition testing, 48
Older adulthood memory changes, 204–216
    memory for facts, 206–210
    memory for skills, 210–216
Organic memories, 31
Overshadowing effect, definition of, 320

P

Painful memories, 33–34
Paired-associate learning, 22–24, 70
Parsimony principle, 288
Part-list cueing effect, 87, 165–166
Pattern recognition, 13–14
    routines of, 117
Pavlov, Ivan P., 36–38
Penfield, Wilder, 60
Perceptual representation system (PRS),
    277
Performance patterns:
    in amnesia, 254–257
    in phonologically impaired patients, 264
Periodic amnesia, definition of, 33
Permanence of memories, 34
Permastore, definition of, 313
Perseveration, definition of, 152
Phantom memories, 243
Phonological loop, 142, 144, 146–147
Phonological memory, deficits of, 264–265
Phonological similarity, 146
Phonological store versus rehearsal
    buffer, 146
Phonological suppression, 144

Phrenology, 59
Physostigmine, 54
Piaget, Jean, 195, 243
Picture priming studies, 105
Picture writing and memory, 28
Place cells in the hippocampus, 63
Plaque, definition of, 267
Plasticity in the brain, 52–58
Plausible answers and memory, 310
Population studies, 50–52
Positron emission tomography (PET) scan, 8–9,
    43–45, 109, 143–144, 146
Posttraumatic amnesia, 254
Power law of forgetting, 79
Power law of practice, 5, 8, 72–73, 118
Practice:
    in improving memory, 71–78, 123
    and performance, 5, 311–312
    and skill acquisition, 310–312
Pragmatic talk, definition of, 201
Preoperational period of childhood skill
    development, 195
Presynaptic membrane/postsynaptic membrane,
    52
Primary memory, 3, 132
    definition of, 277
Priming, 7
    anatomy of, 285–286
    definition of, 64, 256
Priming effect, 103, 104–111
Proactive interference, 80
    definition of, 23, 130
Probe digit task, 132
Problem solving, as a skill, 14–15, 106, 115–116,
    135–136, 180–181
Procedural knowledge, 181–182
Procedural memory, 3, 31, 179–181
    definition of, 277
Procedural skills, 20–21
Processing capacity, definition of, 13
Production rules, 117, 179–180
Progressive amnesia, definition of, 33
Propositions and causal relations, 95–97
Prose memory, 24–26, 96–97, 315–316
Prosopagnosia, 61
    definition of, 261
Prospective memory:
    definition of, 153, 266, 330

in patients with traumatic brain injury, 331
Prototype model, 92–93
Psychological memory, 31

R

Rajan (famous memorist), 121–123
Random generation task, 150
Rapid serial visual presentation (RSVP), 149
Rate of acquiring language and knowledge, 190
Rational analysis and memory, 182–183
Reaction time, 94–95, 115
Reading, study skills in, 314–316
Reading span test, 137
Recall errors, 25
Recall performance, 166
Recall vs. recognition performance, 6, 166,
    297–298, 301
Recency effect, 6, 134, 165
Recognition:
    by infants, 193
    latencies, 72–73
Recognition testing, 5–6
    in SAM model, 160
Recollections, 31
Reconstructive memory, 4, 243
Recovered memory, 238–246
Rehearsal buffer versus phonological store, 146
Rehearsal processes, 133–134
Relearning information, 19
Remembering:
    in everyday life, 304–310
    for a lifetime, 312–313
Reminiscence bump, definition of, 223
Repeated reproductions to assess remembering,
    27–28
Repertory memory, 309–310
Repressed memories of early childhood, 238–246
Repression, definition of, 35
Repression hypothesis (Freud), 34–35, 230–231
Reproduction and consciousness (Ebbinghaus), 20
Research issues, 275–302
    multiple memory systems, 277–280
    Rescorla-Wagner rule, 174
    single memory system, 286–291
Retention intervals, 73–75, 129, 165
    of infants, 193
Retrieval:
    definition of, 2

in episodic memory, 281
of facts, improving, 306–309
failure, 82, 257
of information, 82–89, 208–209
in list learning, 163–165
of memories, 26
from neural nets, 169–173
practice and inhibition, 85–89
in recall, 164–165
SAM model, structure of, 161–163
strategies of children, 201–202
of words, 25
Retrieval hypothesis of amnesia, 258
Retroactive interference, 79–80
definition of, 23
by infants, 193
and neural networks, 176–177
Retrograde amnesia, 254–255
Ribot, Theodule, 31–33
Ribot's law, 33
Rule-learning hypothesis, 113

S

SAM model, 159–166
memory experiments, 165–166
retrieval in list learning, 163–165
Savings method (Ebbinghaus), 3, 7, 19, 71
Schacter and Tulving's taxonomy of memory, 277–278
Schemas, 97–99, 319
definition of, 29
Scripts, 98–99, 224
definition of, 98, 199
Searching in working memory, 138
Secondary memory, 3, 132
Self-generation of skill acquisition, 119
Self-reports of autobiographical memories, 221
Semantic dementia, 100
Semantic information in working memory, 148–149
Semantic memory, 4, 6, 69–70, 90–101, 197–199
and Alzheimer's disease, 269
and amnesia, 257
deficits, 262–263
definition of, 197, 277, 280
of older adults, 210
Semantic network models, 90–91
Semantic processing and retention, 75–76
Semantic versus episodic memory, 287

context dependency of, 280
Semon, Richard, 26–27
Sensitization in *Aplysia,* 57
Sensitization, definition of, 56
Sensorimotor period of childhood skill development, 195
Sensory memory, definition of, 13
Sensory trace of visual information, 132–134
Sentence verification task, 6–7
Sequence-learning paradigm, 114–115
Serial position curve of Alzheimer's disease, 268
Serial position effect, 5, 6
definition of, 24
in free recall, 165
Sexual abuse, remembering, 241–243
Short-term memory:
capacity limit of, 13
definition of, 10
vs. long-term memory, 128–132
Single-cell brain activity, 139–140, 141
Single-memory system, 286–291
Skill acquisition, 31, 117
Skill learning, measurement of, 7–8
Skill maintenance and acquisition of older adults, 211–212
Skills, memory for, 103–126, 179–181
cognitive skills, 115–125
implicit memory, 103–115
Slowing throughout the central nervous system, 214
Social aspects of autobiographical memories, 228–229
Social cognition, 106–107
Source amnesia, 260
Source confusion, 321–322
definition of, 320
Space cells in the hippocampus, 63–64
Spacing of practice, 73–75
Spacing training session of infants, 193
Spared memory function, amnesia, 254, 255–257
Spatial learning, 64
Spatial pattern of brain activity and PET scans, 49
Spatial vs. visual processes, 147–148
Speed of making responses, 7
Spontaneous recovery, 37, 80–81
SQR3 method, 315
Squire's taxonomy of memory, 278–280
Sternberg, S., 138–139
Stimulus-response associations, definition of, 22

Storage, definition of, 2
Storage capacity, definition of, 13
Story method of improving memory, 308
Story schema, 97
Strength theory of recognition memory, 164
Stroop test, 67, 151
Study skills:
    and memory, 310–317
    in reading, 314–316
Study time and memory, 73–74
Subsequent memory effect and ERP patterns, 48
Suggestibility effect in eyewitness testimony,
        320–321
Supermemory, 120–125
Supervisory activating system (SAS), 149
Synaptic changes, 55–56

T

Task complexity and slowing down of older
        adults, 214
Technology and neural processes of the brain,
        42–43
Temporal memory, 149
Temporal pattern of brain activity and ERPs, 49
Temporary amnesia, definition of, 32
Thorndike, Edward L., 35, 37
Time-based prospective memory, 330–331
Tip-of-the-tongue phenomenon, 210, 266
Toscanini, Arturo, 121
Total time hypothesis, 73
Tower of Hanoi puzzle, 116, 135–136
Tracking mental work on-line, 139–142
Transfer of training, 316–317
Transfer-appropriate processing hypothesis, 78,
        290–291
Traumatic brain injury patients, 331–332
Tulving, Endel, 69–70, 82
Tunnel memory, 233
Two-back task, 144, 145, 146
Two-store model of memory, 127–135
    Atkinson and Shiffrin, 132–134
    critics of, 134–135
    short-term vs. long-term memory, 128–132
    Waugh and Norman, 132

U

Unlearning hypothesis (forgetting), 80–81

V

Vanishing cue technique, 328–329
Verbal fluency task, 151
Verbal materials and recall, 84
Verbal reports and memory, 191
Verbatim recall, 309
Victims of crimes, memories of, 232–233
Visual icon, 132–134
Visual learning:
    and fMRI, 46
    and PET imaging, 44
Visual memory, 28
Visuospatial sketchpad, 142, 147–148, 265
Vocabulary development, 196, 197–199
Vulnerability of episodic memory to interference,
        280–281

W

Watergate affair, John Dean's recollections of, 227
Waugh and Norman's two-store model, 132
Wernicke, Carl, 30–31, 50
Wideman, John E., 228
Wisconsin card sorting task, 151
    and executive function, 66–67
Witnesses, memories of, 232–233
Word association and ERP patterns, 49
Word completion task, 105
Word length and working memory, 144, 146
Word recognition, 11
Word-cueing and autobiographical memories,
        222–224
Word-stem completion task, 7
Working memory, 127–155, 217
    of ACT, 182
    and Alzheimer's disease, 270, 272
    and amnesia, 256–257
    of children, 202–204
    definition of, 277
    functions, neuropsychology of, 264–266
    mental activities in, 135–142
    multiple-components model, 142–154
    of older adults, 212–216
    two-store model of memory, 127–135

X

XOR-type patterns, 172–173

This page constitutes a continuation of the copyright page.

Figure 7.9, page 185   From "Skill Acquisition and the LISP Tutor" by J. R. Anderson, F. G. Conrad, and A. T. Corbett, 1989, *Cognitive Science, 13*, p. 479. Copyright 1989 by Ablex Publishing Corporation. Reprinted by permission.

Figure 8.1, page 191   From "Evolution of Cognitive Processes for Solving Simple Additions during the First Three School Years" by O. Svenson and K. Sjoberg, 1983, *Scandinavian Journal of Psychology, 24*, p. 121. Copyright 1983 by Scandinavian University Press. Reprinted by permission.

Figure 8.3, page 197   From "The Role of Deliberate Practice in the Acquisition of Expert Performance" by K. A. Ericsson, R. T. Krampe, and C. Römer-Tesch, 1993, *Psychological Review, 100*, p. 384. Copyright © 1993 by the American Psychological Association. Reprinted with permission.

Figure 8.4, page 198   From "Network Representation of a Child's Dinosaur Knowledge" by M. T. H. Chi and R. D. Koeske, 1983, *Developmental Psychology, 19*, p. 33. Copyright © 1983 by the American Psychological Association. Reprinted with permission.

Figure 9.2, page 225   From "Autobiographical Knowledge and Autobiographical Memories" by M. A. Conway in *Remembering Our Past* (p. 68) by D. C. Rubin (Ed.), 1996, New York: Cambridge University Press. Copyright 1996 Cambridge University Press. Reprinted by permission.

Figures 10.2A and 10.2B, page 271   From "An Assessment of the Semantic Network in Patients with Alzheimer's Disease" by A. S. Chan, N. Butters, J. S. Paulsen, D. P. Salmon, M. R. Swenson, and L. T. Maloney, 1993, *Journal of Cognitive Neuroscience, 5* (2), pp. 254–261. Copyright © 1993 by the Massachusetts Institute of Technology. Reprinted by permission.

Table 11.1, page 278   From "What Are the Memory Systems of 1994?" by D. L. Schacter and E. Tulving in *Memory Distortions* (p. 26) by D. L. Schacter (Ed.), 1994, Cambridge, MA: MIT Press. Copyright © 1994 The MIT Press. Reprinted by permission.

Figure 11.2A, page 279   From *Memory and Brain* by Larry R. Squire (p. 170). Copyright © 1987 by Oxford University Press, Inc. Used by permission of Oxford University Press, Inc.

Figure 11.2B, page 279   From "Memory, Hippocampus, and Brain Systems" by L. R. Squire and B. J. Knowlton in *The Cognitive Neurosciences* (p. 834) by M. S. Gazzaniga (Ed.), 1995, Cambridge, MA: MIT Press. Copyright © 1995 The MIT Press. Reprinted by permission.

Figure 11.3, page 289   From "Learning and Memory: Progress and Challenge" by H. L. Roediger in *Attention and Performance, XIV* (p. 523) by D. E. Meyer and S. Kornblum (Eds.), 1993, Cambridge, MA: MIT Press. Copyright © 1993 The MIT Press. Reprinted by permission.